THE GRIFFONI POLYPTYCH REBORN IN BOLOGNA

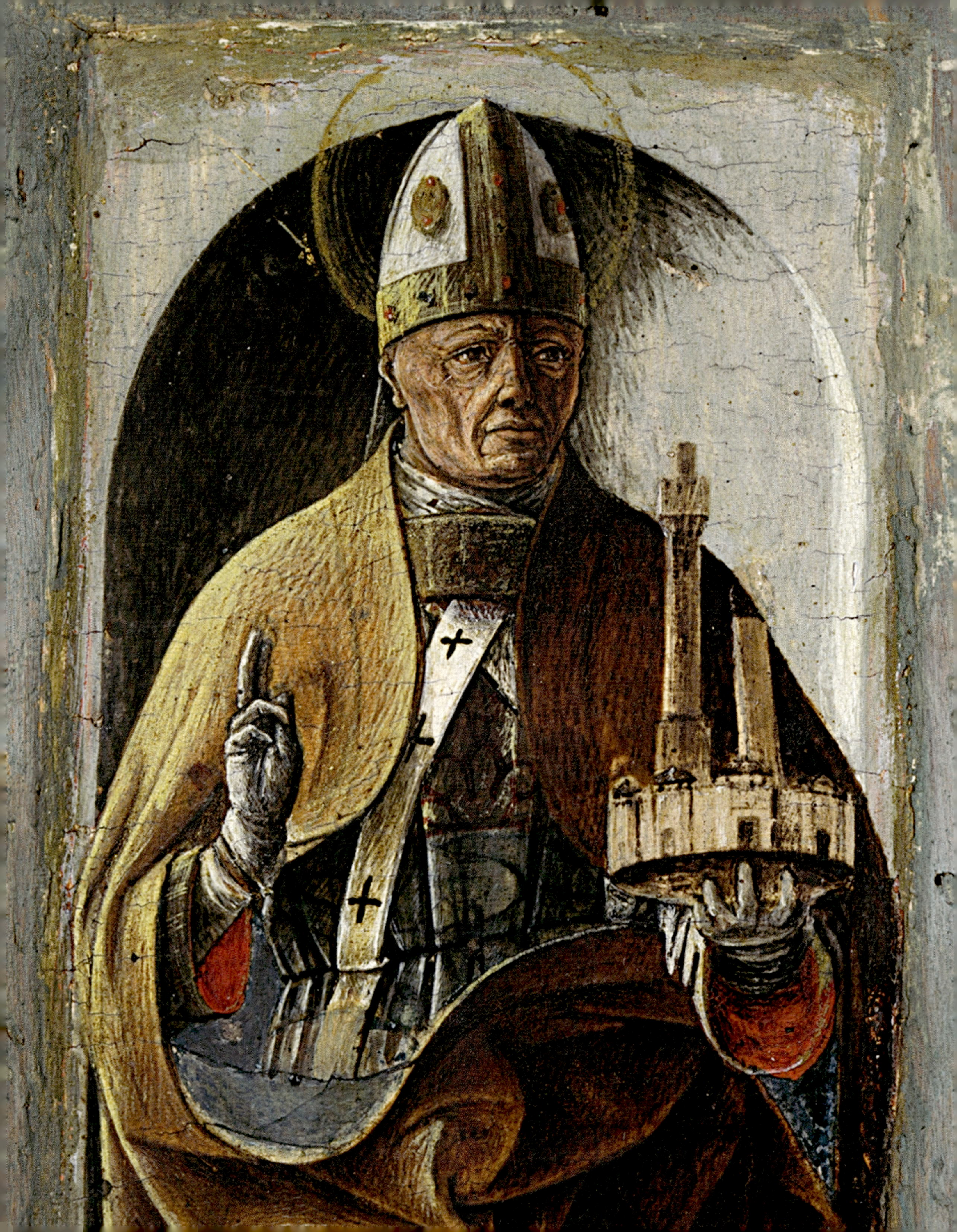

THE GRIFFONI POLYPTYCH REBORN IN BOLOGNA

THE REDISCOVERY OF A MASTERPIECE

edited by
Mauro Natale
Cecilia Cavalca

THE GRIFFONI POLYPTYCH REBORN IN BOLOGNA
THE REDISCOVERY OF A MASTERPIECE

March 12, 2020 – January 10, 2021
Palazzo delle Esposizioni, Palazzo Fava, Bologna

A project by

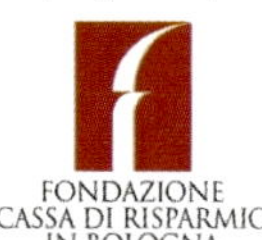

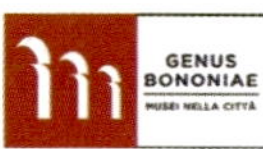

In collaboration with

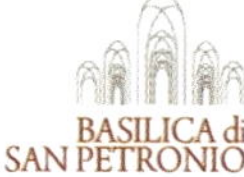

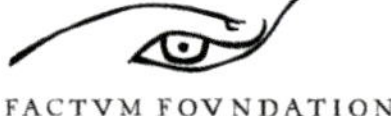

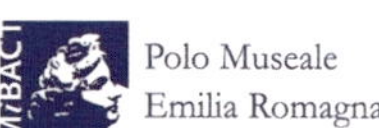

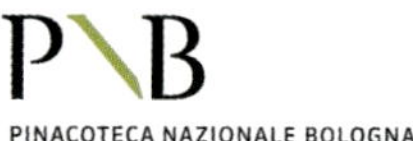

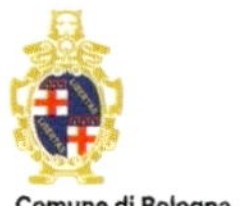

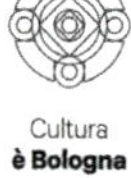

Under the patronage of

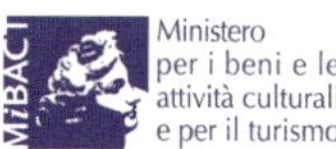

Pontificio Consiglio della Cultura

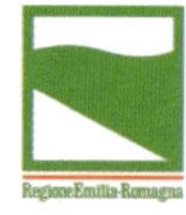

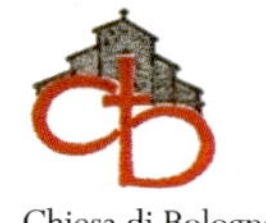
Chiesa di Bologna

With the contribution of

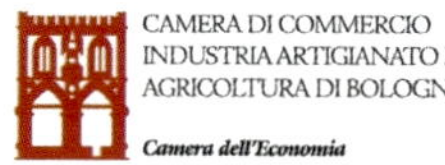

Main sponsor

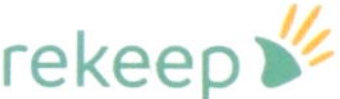

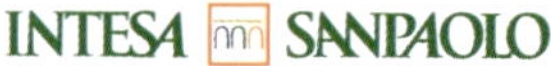

Special partner

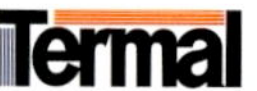

Sponsors

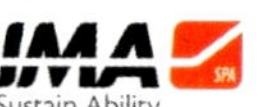

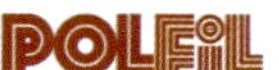

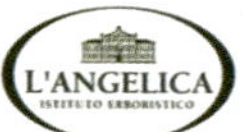

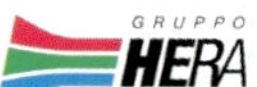

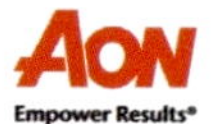

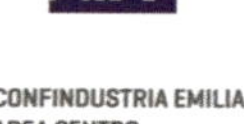

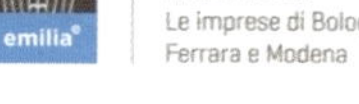

Technical sponsor

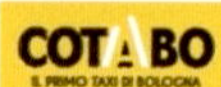

Project conceived by
Fabio Roversi-Monaco

Project manager
Roberto Terra

Honor committee

Dario Franceschini
Minister of Cultural Heritage and Activities and Tourism

Gianfranco Ravasi
Chairman of Pontifical Council for Culture

Matteo Maria Zuppi
Metropolitan Archbishop of Bologna

Francesco Ubertini
Rector of Alma Mater Studiorum, University of Bologna

Patrizia Impresa
Prefect of Bologna

Gianfranco Bernabei
Police commissioner of Bologna

Virginio Merola
Mayor of Bologna

Stefano Bonaccini
Governor of Emilia-Romagna

Carlo Monti
Chairman of Fondazione Cassa di Risparmio in Bologna

Organizing committee

Fabio Roversi-Monaco
Chairman of Genus Bononiae. Musei nella Città

Oreste Leonardi
Senior official of Basilica of San Petronio, Bologna

Adam Lowe
Chairman of Factum Foundation, Madrid

Mario Scalini
Director of Polo Museale della Regione Emilia-Romagna

Gabriele Finaldi
Chairman of The National Gallery, London

Barbara Jatta
Director general of Vatican Museums, Vatican City

James Bradburne
Director general of Pinacoteca di Brera, Milan

Luca Massimo Barbero
Director of the Institute of Art History, Giorgio Cini Foundation, Venice

Monsignor Eros Monti
Director of Museo di Villa Cagnola, Gazzada (Varese)

Martina Bagnoli
Director of Gallerie Estensi, Modena

Sjarel Ex
Director of Museum Boijmans Van Beuningen, Rotterdam

Cristina Ambrosini
Superintendent of Archaeology, Fine Arts, and Landscape for the city of Bologna and the provinces of Modena, Reggio Emilia, and Ferrara

Mina Gregori
President of Fondazione Roberto Longhi, Florence

Massimo Giansante
Acting director of Archivio di Stato di Bologna

Executive scientific committee

Mauro Natale, Cecilia Cavalca
Exhibition curators for the section "The Griffoni Polyptych Reborn in Bologna"

Adam Lowe, Guendalina Damone
Exhibition curators for the section "The Aura in the Age of Digital Materiality"

Sébastien Allard
Musée du Louvre, Paris

Maria Cristina Bandera
Scientific director of Fondazione Roberto Longhi, Florence

Andrea Bardelli
Museo di Villa Cagnola, Gazzada (Varese)

Thomas Bhol
Musée du Louvre, Paris

Elisabetta Bianchi
Pinacoteca di Brera, Milan

Francesca Boris
Archivio di Stato di Bologna

David Alan Brown
National Gallery of Art, Washington, DC

Antonio Buitoni
Museum of the Basilica of San Petronio, Bologna

Caroline Campbell
The National Gallery, London

Guido Cornini
Vatican Museums, Vatican City

Emanuela Daffra
Polo Museale della Regione Lombardia

Angela De Benedictis
Alma Mater Studiorum, University of Bologna

Lisanne den Besten
Museum Boijmans Van Beuningen, Rotterdam

Rosanna Di Pinto
Vatican Museums, Vatican City

Jill Dunkerton
The National Gallery, London

Mario Fanti
Archivio della Fabbriceria e della Basilica di San Petronio, Bologna

Silvia Gaiba
Gallerie Estensi – Pinacoteca Nazionale di Ferrara

Gretchen A. Hirschauer
National Gallery of Art, Washington, DC

Letizia Lodi
Pinacoteca di Brera, Milan

Alessandro Martoni
Institute of Art History, Giorgio Cini Foundation, Venice

Angelo Mazza
Fondazione Cassa di Risparmio in Bologna

Marta Monopoli
Vatican Museums, Vatican City

Elena Rossoni
Pinacoteca Nazionale di Bologna

Maria Teresa Sambin De Norcen
IUAV, Venice

Roberto Terra
Exhibition architect and project manager

Marcello Toffanello
Gallerie Estensi – Pinacoteca Nazionale di Ferrara

THE GRIFFONI POLYPTYCH REBORN IN BOLOGNA

Exhibition curators and catalogue editors
Mauro Natale
Cecilia Cavalca

Catalogue texts
Cecilia Cavalca, Angela De Benedictis,
Jill Dunkerton, Mario Fanti, Letizia Lodi,
Angelo Mazza, Mauro Natale,
Maria Teresa Sambin De Norcen,
Marcello Toffanello

Lenders
The National Gallery, London
National Gallery of Art, Washington, DC
Vatican Museums, Vatican City
Pinacoteca di Brera, Milan
Musée du Louvre, Paris
Institute of Art History, Giorgio Cini Foundation, Venice
Museo di Villa Cagnola, Gazzada (Varese)
Gallerie Estensi – Pinacoteca Nazionale di Ferrara
Museum Boijmans Van Beuningen, Rotterdam
Fabbriceria di San Petronio, Bologna
Archivio di Stato di Bologna
Fondazione Roberto Longhi, Florence
Fondazione Cassa di Risparmio in Bologna
Polo Museale regionale dell'Emilia-Romagna
Soprintendenza Archeologia, Belle Arti e Paesaggio per la Città Metropolitana di Bologna e le Province di Modena, Reggio Emilia e Ferrara
Reale Collegio di Spagna, Bologna

Restorers
Lucia Laita, Varese
Valerio Garofalo, Milan

Insurance
Axa – Aon, Bologna
Blackwall Green, London
Ciaccio Art Broker, Milan
Kuhn & Bülow, Rome
NGA's Insurance, Washington, DC
Willis Towers Watson, Amsterdam

Shipping
Arterìa S.r.l.
Artifigurative, Crespellano (Bologna)

Condition report of exhibited works
Beatrice Miserocchi

Installation design
Roberto Terra and Alice Cocco,
Cavina Terra Architetti

Lighting design
Claudio Fiorini

Graphic concept
Mauro Luccarini

Installation
Tosetto, Jesolo (Venice)

Didactic equipment
Benedetta Basevi, Cecilia Cavalca,
Adam Lowe, Angelo Mazza, Mauro Natale,
Maria Teresa Sambin De Norcen

Technological equipment
SONEPAR Italia, Milan
R.I.B.O. S.r.l., Bologna
ADCOM S.r.l., Bologna

Panel translations
Anna Merlini

Video installations
"The Griffoni Polyptych.
The Rediscovery of a Masterpiece"
Special Artbox realized by
3D Produzioni for Sky Arte
curated by Arianna Marelli
directed by Claudio Poli
scientific consultant Paolo Cova

Social media videos
"La riscoperta di un capolavoro"
curated by Luis Sal

Exhibited photographs
Carlo Vannini

Photo prints and mounts
Sabrina Borsetti
Mimmo di Todaro

Audioguides
Gestione Multiservizi, Florence
Audio tours for children:
Simona Pinelli with Anthea Danaro
and Carmelina Ivone

Reception and security
Nazareno Work, Carpi (Modena)

Acknowledgments
Giovanni Bazoli, President Emeritus of Intesa Sanpaolo
Andrea Bacchi, Director of Fondazione Federico Zeri, University of Bologna
Kaywin Feldman, Director of the National Gallery of Art, Washington, DC
Matteo Lepore, Councillor for Culture, Tourism, and City promotion, Municipality of Bologna
Anna Manfron, Director of Istituzione Biblioteche, Municipality of Bologna
Jean-Luc Martinez, Chairman and Director of Musée du Louvre, Paris
Gioia Martini, Galleria Cavour, Bologna

Federico Angelini, Pierangelo Bellettini, Paolo Benassai, Andrei Bliznukov, Graziano Campanini, Veronica Ceruti, Enrica Coser, Marcella Culatti, Vincent Delieuvin, Patrizia Farinelli, Sebastian Felmann, Helmy Frank, Valentina Gabusi, Franco Gatti, Tanisha Ghanshyam, Alessandra Giannotti, Peter Huestis, Polly Jones, Olivier Laville, Lisa MacDougall, Elena Marconi, Alessandro Martoni, Roberto Martorelli, Antonella Mampieri, Ilaria Negretti, Gianluigi Pagani, Osvaldo Panaro, Sergio Pasquesi, Gianluca Poldi, Elisabetta Polidori, Marco Pradelli, Cristina Quattrini, Davide Ravaioli, Giovanni Sassu, Daniela Schiavina, Elisa Tosi Brandi

Bologna Welcome S.r.l.
IGERSBologna

The Griffoni Polyptych, one of the most important Renaissance artworks, was crafted by Francesco del Cossa and Ercole de' Roberti for the Griffoni family chapel in the Basilica of San Petronio in Bologna. Between 1725 and 1731, the altarpiece was dismembered at the behest of new owner Pompeo Aldrovandi, who had acquired the chapel from the last surviving Griffoni heir and was keen to modernize its furnishings. Trimmed down to painting size, the painted panels were taken to Aldrovandi's country villa at Mirabello di Ferrara to subsequently appear on the antiques market.
Of that magnificent altarpiece, numerous panels have been preserved at nine different locations: The National Gallery, London; National Gallery of Art, Washington, DC; Musée du Louvre, Paris; Museum Boijmans Van Beuningen, Rotterdam; Pinacoteca di Brera, Milan; Vatican Museums, Vatican City; Cini Foundation, Venice; Pinacoteca Nazionale, Ferrara; and Villa Cagnola, Gazzada (Varese).
This exhibition brings this extraordinary story back to life. For the first time in three hundred years, all known panels from the Griffoni Polyptych have returned to the site for which they were created. But that's not all: it is also a precious opportunity to showcase significant scholarly progress, since research and direct study of the materials on this exceptional occasion have made it possible to update information about the original appearance of this masterpiece.
Committed to the project from the very beginning, many public and private institutions have worked with us to create this unique, unrepeatable exhibition and its catalogue. First of all, the Fondazione Cassa di Risparmio in Bologna, without whose support this idea could never have taken shape; the Fabbriceria di San Petronio, Factum Foundation, the Municipality of Bologna, the Emilia-Romagna Region, the Polo Museale dell'Emilia-Romagna; in addition, the Bologna Chamber of Commerce, Intesa Sanpaolo, Rekeep, Termal and many other partners listed in full in the book's colophon, because the space here is insufficient to do so.
To conclude, we wish to acknowledge the concerted involvement of many of the world's top museums, persuaded to become part of this initiative as a result of the scholarly authority and decisive enthusiasm of curator Mauro Natale, supported by Cecilia Cavalca and the committee of scholars and researchers who wrote this book.
With this exhibition, which is the culmination of a truly remarkable organizational effort, we have striven to stage an event of huge cultural value that, based on serious and rigorous research, is able to connect this city, its artworks, and its history with the wider national and international context, while at the same time generating a virtuous circuit of collaboration.

Fabio Roversi-Monaco
Chairman, Genus Bononiae Musei nella Città

Contents

INTRODUCTION

Mauro Natale

This exhibition is the result of an idea so simple and ambitious that it seems to be almost out of date in our times: to restore to its city of origin, at least for the short duration of a show, one of the masterpieces of its Renaissance artistic culture that, two hundred and fifty years after its creation, was dismembered because at that time it must have seemed not just inadequate for the tastes of the day, but also unsuitable for the new functions of the space for which it was intended.

The story of how the Griffoni Polyptych was dismembered, which the exhibition and the catalogue retrace with the addition of new details,[1] is common to many artworks today in the collections of museums or cultural institutions in Italy and around the world. Reassembly in Bologna of all known elements of this great altarpiece has, however, long been one of the city's art history priorities, not just because the retable was created by two of the best and most original masters of fifteenth-century Italy, but because the figurative void left by this dismembered and dispersed masterpiece has long weighed upon the understanding of the role Bologna played artistically at one of the most vibrant and delicate times in Italian history.

Based on these premises, the exhibition has been made possible by a historiographical recovery of the role the city once played as a center of convergence and as an interface between different figurative expressions in the latter part of the fifteenth century.[2] This critical awareness, which studies have slowly brought into focus since World War II, had yet to be backed up through the necessary verification provided by an exhibition. The chance to bring together all of the hitherto known elements of the great altarpiece that the Griffoni family commissioned to be erected on the altar of their chapel in the Basilica of San Petronio is therefore an exceptional and very likely unrepeatable event, both for its precious material delicacy and the extremely high quality of the works that have been brought here, many of which leave the museums where they are usually conserved for the first time; not to mention the huge efforts this undertaking has required in terms of handling and preserving the paintings.

Credit is due to the belief and determination of Fabio Roversi-Monaco, Chairman of Genus Bononiae Musei nella Città, for what may have seemed like a utopian exhibition to come to fruition. Credit is also due to the directors at institutions where the works are preserved, who responded to this idea and to the project with rare willingness. To find all this back in Bologna once more, against the backdrop of an evocative museum layout that

---

1 See Mazza's narration in this volume.

2 Volpe 1958 ed. 1993; Volpe 1961 ed. 1993; Volpe 1979 ed. 1993; Volpe 1980 ed. 1993; Benati 1982; Benati 1984; D. Benati in *Le Muse e il principe* 1991, I, pp. 300–7; Benati 2012a; Benati 2012b; Bacchi 1984; Bacchi 1991; Bacchi in *Le Muse e il principe* 1991, pp. 211–14; Lucco 1987; Cavalca 2004–5 (2005); Cavalca 2013; Cavalca 2018a; Cavalca 2018b; Medica 2007; Ferretti 2011; Calogero 2012; Calogero 2016 (2018).

conveys the incredible story of a work that, over the passage of more than five centuries, was dismembered and then reassembled,[3] will (and this is our greatest wish) be an unforgettable, mind-altering visual experience for visitors, one that only coming face-to-face with the live works, their individual faults, fragile materiality, different paths, and varying notoriety may bring into being. Thanks to the stunning facsimile reproductions created by Factum Foundation, visitors may also enjoy the large mosaic in which the various tiles have come together to compose the overall original design.

No archival document or contemporary chronicle attests to the commissioning of the great polyptych, whose placement in the Griffoni family chapel in San Petronio (the sixth on the left, dedicated to Saint Vincent Ferrer) is recorded in a single paper relating to a relatively incidental part of the whole: the *capsa*, that is to say the wooden structure intended to protect the retable from dust and other external accidents, for which the officers of the Fabbrica of San Petronio paid master woodcarver Agostino de' Marchi of Crema on July 19, 1473. Located by Francesco Filippini and published by Igino Benvenuto Supino in 1938,[4] this document contains crucial information about the correct location of the monument and has repeatedly been cited by scholars who, ever since, have delved into this matter.[5]

First of all, it records the name of the craftsman commissioned to complete the wooden portions of the polyptych and who, before creating the protective structure, had without doubt worked on the frame around the whole. At the date of the archive document (1473), the name and work of Agostino de' Marchi were well-known in the city and on the Collegiate Basilica worksite. Long esteemed for his carving and marquetry work, since 1458 the artist from Crema (although his activity is recorded exclusively in Bologna) had been working for the Fabbrica of San Petronio where, on November 8, he was commissioned to build half of the choir at the chapel dedicated to Saint Bridget, which in that period was the busiest and most ground-breaking construction site within the Basilica.[6] The name of Marco Zoppo also appears in documents relating to that chapel. As Romano[7] suggested, it is likely that at that time, the painter (who originally hailed from Cento, not far from Ferrara) supplied the woodcarver with cartoons for the inlays to be executed on the backrests. The choir of Santa Brigida has long since been lost, but another splendid example of the two artists' consolidated collaboration remains intact: it's the polyptych for the church of San Clemente inside the monumental complex of the Royal College of Spain in Bologna.[8]

A series of fortunate discoveries have made it possible to ascertain the paternity of the wooden structure at San Clemente, for which payment was made to Agostino de' Marchi in 1459,[9] and the name of the client, Luis de Fuente Encalada,[10] who chose for the altar at this prestigious institution two artists from apparently different cultural

3 Roberto Terra, assisted by Alice Cocco, designed the installation layout.

4 Supino 1938, pp. 196, 231 note 42; Cavalca 2013, pp. 380–81, doc. XI.6; and Fanti's contribution in this book.

5 An extensive bibliography is provided in Cavalca 2013, pp. 334–36, no. 19 for consultation.

6 Volpe 1983, pp. 271–72, 280–84; Benati 1984, pp. 144–49; Romano 1984, pp. 268, 274 note; Biagi Maino 1993, p. 65; Guarino 1990; Calogero 2012, pp. 83–87; Calogero 2019, pp. 58–59; Cavalca 2013, pp. 50–52; Cavalca 2018b, p. 325.

7 Romano 1984, p. 269.

8 Crowe and Cavalcaselle 1871 ed. 1912, p. 51; Ruhmer 1966, pp. 784–85; Armstrong 1976, pp. 29–46; Volpe 1979 ed. 1993, pp. 141–51; Bacchi 1984, pp. 288–90; Lucco 1987, pp. 241–42; Biagi Maino 1993, pp. 61–70; Humfrey 1993, pp. 171–74; Biagi Maino 2007, pp. 29–35; Medica 2007, p. 17; De Marchi 2012, p. 201; Calogero 2016 (2018), pp. 28–49; and above all, Cavalca 2013, pp. 107–19, 322–23; Cavalca 2018b.

9 Biagi Maino 1993, pp. 65–67; Biagi Maino 2007, pp. 23–27.

10 Cavalca 2013, pp. 115–16, 322–23 ; Cavalca 2018b, pp. 319–43.

backgrounds. In the perfectly-mastered decorative lexicon of its pinnacles, twisted columns, and polylobed arches Agostino's shaped and carved frame, rich in fretwork, exhibits the most highly-esteemed repertoire of altarpieces Gentile da Fabriano had produced some thirty years earlier: a comparison between the cornice of the Bolognese polyptych and that of Gentile's *Adoration of the Magi* (1423) in Florence[11] effectively shows that the carver from Crema fully subscribed to the late-Gothic ornamental tradition. But if in the Florentine specimen the precious gilded frame encloses the broad figurative narration as if in a treasure chest, in the polyptych at San Clemente the tripartite structure segmenting the painted figuration, the compact quality of the carvings, and the simplified design of the pillars delimiting the sides of the altar dialogue so closely with the painted areas that there can be no doubt about the master woodcarver and the painter working on this together.[12] Marco Zoppo inscribed his name on the cartouche painted at the foot of the Virgin's throne at the center of a space unified in terms of perspective, in which, mindful of Donatello's altar in Padua (c. 1444–50) and Andrea Mantegna's altarpiece in San Zeno in Verona (c. 1456–59), the figures of the saints are firmly placed. The painter failed to write the year in which the polyptych was completed, but such is the osmosis between the painting and the carving that the delivery date of the completed altar cannot have differed much from the date on which the carpentry was paid for.

This deduction is heavy with implications, because the marked similarities to Piero della Francesca's style, which Zoppo reveals above all in the figures housed inside the cusped niches of the pillars and in the hemispherical niches from which the busts of the Blessing Redeemer, the Archangel Gabriel, and the Announced Virgin emerge, confirm how quickly Piero's luminous and rigorous painting spread through the Emilia region. Carlo Volpe[13] was among the first to recognize traces of the approach espoused by the painter from Borgo Sansepolcro in Zoppo's Bolognese work, and indeed there is a chance that the Maestro sojourned in Bologna, although this hypothesis is based exclusively on a brief mention by Luca Pacioli.[14] According to Vasari,[15] Piero was invited to Ferrara by Borso d'Este in 1450 (or slightly later) to work in the Ducal Palace and at the now destroyed church of Sant'Agostino;[16] it is, however, beyond doubt that his modern approach to perspective was widely taken up in Rimini, Ferrara, Bologna, and Modena thanks to widespread circulation of cartoons used by inlayers (first and foremost, the brothers Cristoforo and Lorenzo da Lendinara).[17]

Agostino de' Marchi and Marco Zoppo began working together against this backdrop of influences. Bolognese documents paint the picture of an extremely lively working environment, in which professional relationships, kinship, and simple friendship all intertwined—something that must have facilitated an exchange of opinions

---

11 This comparison was advanced in Cavalca 2013, p. 115. Gentile da Fabriano's retable, formerly in the Palla Strozzi Chapel at Santa Trinita in Florence, is now in the Uffizi.

12 Cavalca insists on this osmosis: see Cavalca 2013, pp. 107–19 and Cavalca 2018b, p. 324.

13 Volpe focuses on this: Volpe 1958 ed. 1993 and Volpe 1979 ed. 1993, as does Benati 1988, pp. 35–67; it also appears in subsequent literature, up to the recent Calogero 2016 (2018).

14 Pacioli 1509, f. 33r: "*el monarca a li dì nostri della pictura e architectura, Maestro Piero de li franceschi con suo penello mentre pote come apare in urbino, bologna, ferara arimini ancora e in la terra nostra in muro e taula a ogli e guaççο maxime in la cita dareççο.*"

15 Vasari 1550, 1568 ed. 1971, p. 259. The core information on painters plying their trade in Bologna must have been collected by Giorgio Vasari in 1539–40, during work decorating the refectory for the Augustinians at San Michele in Bosco (Agosti 2013, pp. 38–43).

16 This information is reprised in Benati 1987, p. 256.

17 For more on this, see the essay by Massimo Ferretti (1982), which to this day remains crucial.

and experiences among artists whose training and area of specialty may have differed a great deal. Relations between Tommaso Garelli, who was also involved in the decoration of the chapel dedicated to Saint Bridget and, from 1465 on, was the official Municipality painter,[18] and Marco Zoppo are well known: Zoppo became godfather to Elena, Garelli's daughter, in 1461; returning the favor, in 1463 Garelli baptized Lucrezia, Marco's daughter; finally, in 1468 Agostino de' Marchi was named godfather to another of Tommaso Garelli's sons.[19] All this is evidence of solid and long-lasting interwoven ties that, because of our predilection for a more idealistic view of art, have long been neglected. It is common knowledge that such exchanges of expertise also involved leading figures such as Francesco del Cossa: he was rewarded in 1473 by the Fabbrica of San Petronio for supplying two half-bust figure cartoons of *Saint Petronius* and *Saint Ambrose*, which Agostino de' Marchi converted into marquetry for the choir at the main chapel of the Basilica.[20]

The accounting slip dated July 19, 1473 also informs us of the client who commissioned our polyptych, Floriano Griffoni, member of one of Bologna's oligarchic families that, until the fifteenth century, had belonged to the Guelph faction: this choice, "after initial hesitation, would push them to openly support the Bentivoglio, other Guelphs, in their ascent to the seigniory of Bologna."[21] Between the fourteenth and fifteenth centuries, some members of the Griffoni family were notaries, Giacomo was made *Gonfaloniere* several times between 1376 and 1379,[22] while Matteo was enrolled in the Council of the Elders for the first time in 1389, was chosen in 1408 and then in 1412 as a member the Private Council of Cardinal Baldassarre Cossa (later anti-pope John XXIII), and authored the famous *Memoriale* on Bologna's history.[23]

Against the backdrop of the city's conflictual mid-fifteenth century history, for a long time the Griffoni family faithfully supported the faction of Giovanni II Bentivoglio (see De Benedictis's contribution in this catalogue). The kinship between Girolamo Griffoni, who was a good friend of Giovanni II's and was murdered in Ferrara in the summer of 1471, and his cousin Floriano is worthy of further investigation, even if we can have no doubt that the two shared the same family interests. Another important member of the Griffoni lineage was Giovanni di Giacomo, who held various public offices in Bologna in the first half of the fifteenth century[24] and in 1429, as Mario Fanti notes in the essay published here, was appointed *camerario* (i.e. cashier) for life at the Fabbrica of San Petronio. Giovanni Griffoni's long-term work undertaking administrative management of the Basilica's gigantic building site ensured that his family group won the patronage of one of the most sought-after chapels; work on the chapel began in 1437 and its structure was probably completed the following year.[25] Despite his clash with Nicolò Sanuti, Giovanni held on to the post of *camerario* until his death in 1471. A careful reading of the accounting entry for the year 1473 advanced here by Fanti makes us realize how truly significant this document is: it attests that the cost of

18 Calogero 2012; Calogero 2019.

19 Filippini and Zucchini 1968, pp. 116, 159, and 160.

20 Gatti 1914, p. 76; Filippini and Zucchini 1968, p. 55; Ferretti 1982, p. 502; Romano 1984, p. 276 note 14.

21 Torella (1985–87) 1988, p. 44.

22 Angiolini 2002b.

23 Zabbia 2002.

24 Regarding this figure, in addition to important research by Torella (1985–87) 1988, pp. 44–45, see De Benedictis's contribution in this catalogue.

25 Torella (1988–89) 1991, pp. 39–40.

the polyptych's *capsa* (we cannot know whether the fee extended to other elements of the chapel's furnishings) was taken on by the Basilica administration (a truly exceptional fact), most probably as a result of a financial and moral debt toward the deceased *fabbriciere*.

On Floriano Griffoni, the man who commissioned the polyptych and who appears elegantly dressed in the upper register of the retable in the guise of the saint whose name he shares, we have but scarce, fragmentary information, mostly deduced from legal deeds and family chronicles.[26] A friend and protectee of Giovanni II Bentivoglio's, he accompanied him when he traveled to Milan to pay his respects to Francesco Sforza (1464), and between 1459 and 1481 he was on several occasions named an Elder. In his biography, which appears to be devoid of significant events, his marriage to Lucia Battaglia in 1457 was of particular importance; the young woman, "daughter of Messer Andrea Bataglia Fiamengo, an immensely rich man,"[27] must have substantially contributed to increasing her husband's wealth. As Cecilia Cavalca has made clear in her series of contributions here,[28] Floriano's father-in-law Andrea Battaglia had made his fortune in Flanders, whence he returned with great wealth and five daughters, all of whom were destined to contract socially-prestigious marriages with the scions of Bolognese leading families (Bolognini, Malvezzi, Magnani, and Griffoni). Andrea Battaglia owned a large palazzo overlooking Via Santo Stefano, a building long-since demolished. The inventory drawn up after his death in October 1455 chronicles the furnishings of a richly decorated residence, with "a great variety of luxury furniture," five domestic altarpieces, a collection of arms and armor, and "a great array of fabrics."[29] Lucia's contribution to the Griffoni household must therefore have been important: Floriano Griffoni's will (August 6, 1483), only partially published[30] and reinterpreted by Fanti for our purposes, reveals a patrimony consisting of movable and immovable property, both in the city and countryside.

The polyptych with which Floriano Griffoni endowed the chapel was therefore a reflection of this accumulated wealth, in a certain sense preserving its history; the crypto-portraits of the owner and his bride, whose faces were portrayed as the saints in the upper register on a date that must be closer to 1469 (when Lucia was still alive) than 1472 (in January of that year, Floriano remarried Ludovica Lambertini),[31] enshrined the matrimonial arrangements of one of the city's leading families.

The Fabbrica's statutes required patrons of the chapels to make adequate investments for their furnishings,[32] and commissioning Francesco del Cossa (assisted by Ercole de' Roberti), who between 1469 and 1472 was at the height of his artistic career, to undertake pictorial execution of the retable perfectly corresponded to this imperative. Calling on the services of Agostino de' Marchi, the most highly-rated *marangone* (carpenter) working in Bologna at that time, confirms the client's ambition for an artistic work of the highest order, both in its monumental architectural structure (de rigeur, given

26 Torella (1985–87) 1988, p. 45, along with the key clarifications Fanti makes in this volume.
27 Torella (1985–87) 1988, p. 45.
28 Cavalca 2013, pp. 31–33, 44; Cavalca 2018 b, pp. 26–31; Cavalca and Negretti 2018.
29 Cavalca 2018a, p. 29.
30 Cavalca 2013, p. 381, doc. XI.11 (transcription by Ilaria Negretti).
31 Cavalca 2018a, p. 34 note 81.
32 Fanti 1980, pp. 57–79; Cavalca 2013, pp. 48, 76 note 6. See also Fanti's contribution in this volume.

the dizzying elevation of San Petronio's side chapels)[33] and its use of high-quality materials to ensure pictorial results of the finest caliber. The decision to dedicate the altar to Saint Vincent Ferrer, whose figure dominates the central panel, holding the sacred book[34] in his left hand, his right indicating "the heavenly hierarchies waiting in Judgment," was hardly a standard approach at that time. The Dominican saint had recently been canonized (1455) and a quick comparison between the austere figure painted by Cossa here and the more rustic and massive version of Tommaso Garelli (1467) on one of the pillars of the Basilica of San Petronio,[35] or even more famous examples by Giovanni Bellini (c. 1465),[36] Angelo and Bartolomeo degli Erri (1467–80),[37] and Colantonio (c. 1456–57)[38] would be sufficient to see that, despite common references to the Dominican order of which the saint wears the habit, his poses, in some cases attributes, and especially the physiognomic definitions all differ. Such variations are even more evident in the illustration of the apocalyptic Valencian preacher's miracles. For the choice of narrative scenes on the predella, where the hagiographic cycle of the saint's extraordinary deeds is presented, Floriano Griffoni must have relied on an expert adviser whose name we are yet to identify: fifteenth- and early sixteenth-century literature on the life and miracles of Vincenzo Ferrer spans a number of narrative versions that Laura Ackerman Smoller[39] has examined

33 Maria Teresa Sambin De Norcen covers this topic here. The scholar unearthed a document published by Angelo Gatti (1914, p. 90, no. 258) certifying a February 6, 1481 payment to master glassmaker Vincenzo Cabrini "for four glass windows to be made for the Griffoni Chapel." The document does not specify whether these windows featured figures, but significantly the name Cabrini (in 1467, to a Cossa cartoon, Jacopo and Domenico Cabrini made a stained-glass window with *Madonna enthroned and Angels* for San Giovanni in Monte) appears once again at a building site where Francesco del Cossa played a major role; for more on the Cabrinis and Cossa, see Varignana 1985 and Bacchi 1991, p. 42.

34 Interpreted as the apocalyptic text of Saint John by Gentili 1982.

35 Cavalca 2013, p. 128; Calogero 2019, pp. 63–64.

36 Church of Santi Giovanni e Paolo, Venice.

37 Seminario Arcivescovile, Modena, from the town church of San Domenico: Benati 1988, pp. 135–43.

38 Pinacoteca Nazionale di Capodimonte, Naples; P. Leone de Castris summarizes these Mediterranean events in *Rinascimento visto da Sud* 2019, pp. 296–97.

39 Ackerman Smoller 2014; see also Kaftal 1978, cols. 1065–84.

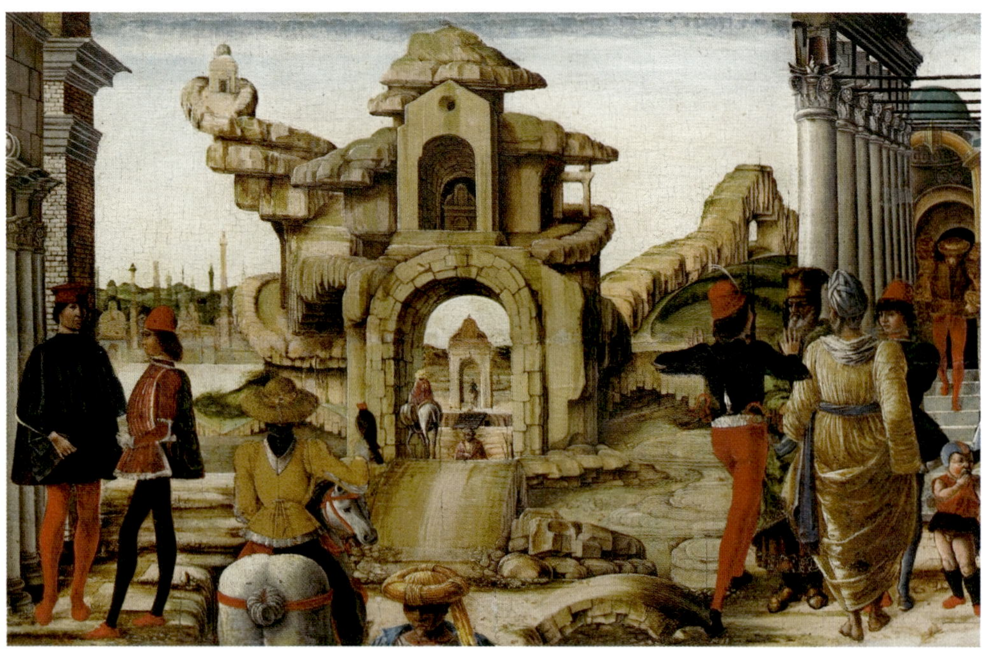

1

Ercole de' Roberti, *Miracles of Saint Vincent Ferrer*, detail. Vatican Museums, Vatican City

and compared with surviving figurative translations. It has in the past been assumed[40] that Bolognese polygraphist Giovanni Garzoni, a humanist and intellectual closely associated with the Dominican order who may well have authored a life of Saint Vincent Ferrer, perhaps collaborated in this enterprise.

For the unified space of the polyptych predella (Vatican Museums, Vatican City) Ercole de' Roberti chose a continuous and perhaps somewhat extended narrative in which one miraculous act follows another without cease, creating a space that becomes unitary through perspective in a factitious alternation of ruined classically-inspired buildings, Renaissance constructions, and a visionary rocky landscape with a jagged profile that runs the entire length of the painting's background. It is the figures, some impassive, others in dialogue, still others participating in the dramatic events that are taking place that constitute the figurative interface between the scenes depicted, which in this chronological period are usually confined within ad hoc boxes.[41] In order to make this new spatial invention credible, the painter undertook a sort of hierarchical inversion between the subjects depicted: the saint, who acts across the entire width of the panel, is represented as a full-length figure only once, and in an offset position, while exorcising a woman invaded by the devil.[42] Other effects of his miraculous acts are narrated in the adjacent spaces: from left to right, an expectant mother healed after risking the loss of her baby following a fall; the healing of an obsessed woman; a man who miraculously recovers from gout sitting in a classic "*spinario*" pose; the rescue of a young man who fell asleep during the saint's preachings and nearly fell from a roof; a miraculously tamed fire; the macabre drama of a mad woman who shreds and cooks her own child, put back together and brought back to life after the father laid the child's limbs onto

40 Torella (1985–87) 1988, pp. 46–47.

41 Among the various examples, Giovanni Bellini's altarpiece in Pesaro with the *Coronation of the Virgin*, contemporaneous to the Griffoni Polyptych.

42 Gentili 1982, p. 570; Torella (1985–87) 1988, pp. 47–48.

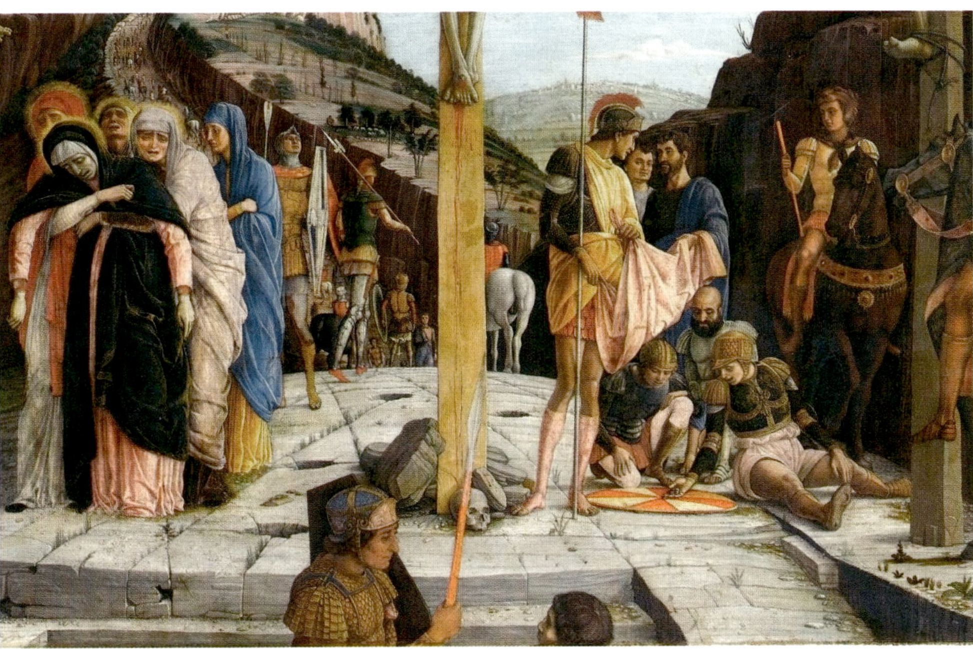

2

Andrea Mantegna, *Crucifixion*, detail. Musée du Louvre, Paris

the saint's tomb. These terrifying events take place in a fanciful "borderland" populated by wealthy citizens and courtiers, characters in Oriental dress, and a variety of workers and laborers. Devotees are invited to observe this inaccessible world by looking through the deep space from which a knight and an exotic beturbaned traveler emerge into the foreground, like in Andrea Mantegna's *Crucifixion* predella from the San Zeno polyptych in Verona[43] (figs. 1 and 2).

At the center of the main register, above the predella, the titular saint is flanked and hierarchically supported by two "pillars" of the Church. On the left the apostle Peter, who in one hand holds the huge pontifical keys and in the other, an open liturgical book with strips of paper marking passages for quick reference. The saint is portrayed in an upright position, his feet resting on rough, sharp, rocky ground in front of a deserted but not uninhabited landscape (a bridge, small buildings, and a circular temple stand out in the middle distance and background). A fish-hunting bird (a cormorant, according to Augusto Gentili) is depicted on the shore of a lake,[44] alluding to Peter's apostolic vocation as a "Fisher of Men." This figure is in front of a powerful, highly-sculpted pillar, its elegant finesse contrasting with the desolate surrounding landscape. In addition to the figures' dimensional identity and proportional ratios, this is an important element of formal connection with the corresponding panel to the right of the main section. Here, Saint John the Baptist, recognizable from his hermit's garb and customary attributes (a prophet's reed crowned by a circular sign, made out of gold and precious stones, within which the Eucharistic lamb symbol is depicted), is also presented in an erect position on a rocky pedestal, in front of an arid and impervious landscape pockmarked by caves, deep furrows, and ravines. In the background, it is possible to make out a fortified city above this natural architecture. The middle-ground features a temple devoid of religious symbols, its layout nevertheless freely evoking well-known devotional buildings in the Venice area. This *ante legem* landscape is vividly animated by small figures going about their business who seem totally indifferent to the saint's call; only a monk and a layman, represented on the left, on the edge of a cave, seem to be engaged in debate on spiritual themes. Contrary to a correct interpretation of John's Gospel text ("I am the voice of one crying out in the wilderness," I, 23), the plural version of the statement is reproduced on the crumpled scroll the saint is holding in one hand ("EG[O SUM] VOC[ES] C[LAMAN]TES IN DESERTO"), which seems to associate the holy Dominican orator with Saint John's preaching as a hermit. Peter and John are, in this context, conceived as authoritative backers of the Spanish saint's militant preaching, sacralized not just by his glittering and foreshortened halo but also by being placed on a platform that, more than a standing place, is reminiscent of an altar-table. The fruits of Vincent Ferrer's apostolate are plain to see: Christian symbols abound at the top of the buildings, while the landscape is at least partially animated by bushes the pale green of a meadow among the parched rocks (fig. 3).

Francesco del Cossa was able to translate the immanent apocalypse foretold by the saint with a plastic strength both yielding and incisive at the same time (his association with the naturalism of Niccolò dell'Arca's clay figures is evident and well-known). Saints Florian and Lucy appear with a worldly, almost irreverent grace above this lucid, fear-inspiring foreshadowing of the future. Their faces and clothes are those

43 Musée du Louvre, Paris, inv. 368.

44 Gentili 1982, p. 572.

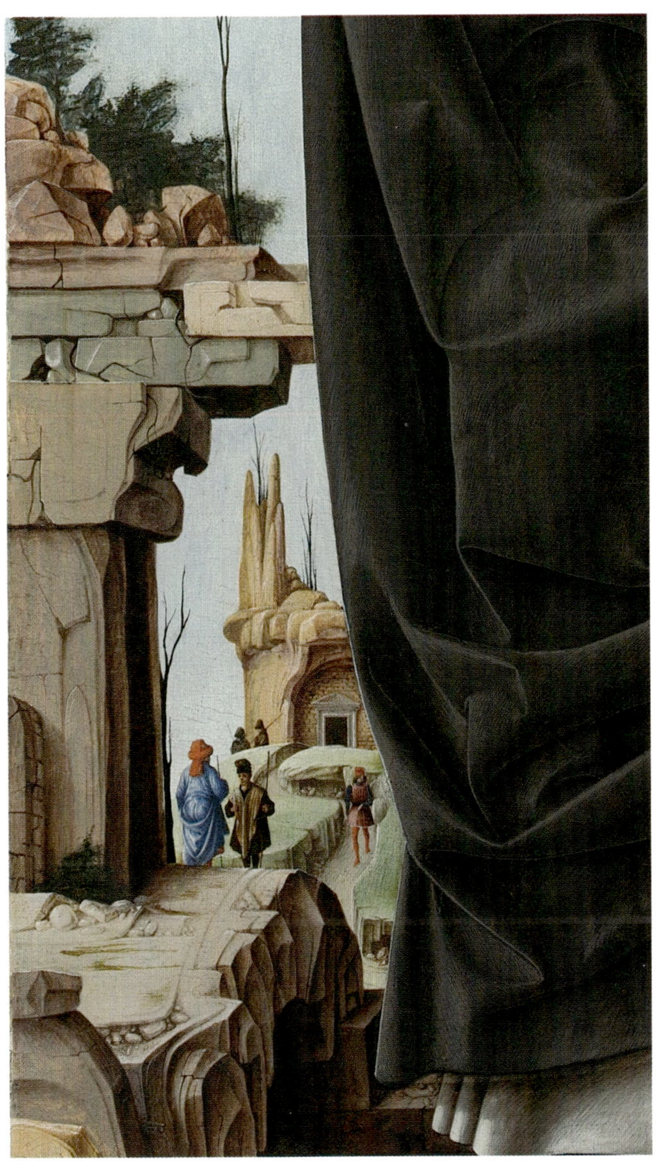

3

Francesco del Cossa,
Saint Vincent Ferrer, detail.
The National Gallery, London

of the commissioning family, privileged spectators at the sacred representation, softened through the poetic fantasy with which the painter has endowed them and their respective attributes: "What could be more life-like than an iconography extracted instantly, on the spot, from an apparent etymology? Cossa chose to depict Florian with a flower in his hand (indeed, a beautiful popular consonance); not just any old flower but a rose, the flower par excellence."[45] Lucy is instead distinguished by her "eyes miraculously blooming on the stem"[46] that she holds in her left hand. Depictions in which the people who commissioned and financed a sacred work have such prominence are especially rare in Northern Italy early Renaissance history. The exceptional integration of their portraits, albeit concealed under the garb of the patron saints, at first glance evokes the Flemish painting tradition, in which, unlike had long been the case in the Italian custom, donors were not subject to a hierarchical relationship with the sacred figures but occupied the same space, the dimensions of all players being equal. Cossa was not without Flemish influence: indeed, something "in his air or technical treatment recalls Roger van der Weyden."[47] Jill Dunkerton's comments on the preparatory drawings for the panels further confirm the painter's familiarity with artistic techniques from the North, given that, in the days of Leonello and Borso d'Este, Ferrara was one of the earliest places in Italy where their works became known. Florian and Lucy's faces, however, were not portrayed with the same lens-like, detailed rendering of a Flemish portrait, which would immortalize the expression and skin tones of the person portrayed; here, light slips off the faces' smooth surface without any roughness, albeit still retaining the subjects' somatic features.

It has quite rightly been noted that this volumetric simplification brought about by the light and the forced perspective with which the two figures face one another from the edge of the upper floor are a sign of Piero della Francesca's influence over the eastern side of the Po Valley by the 1450s.[48] The figurative traces of his masterly skill gained renown over a wide area, even if all that remains, according to historical sources, of the only direct witness of his teachings in the province of Ferrara, a certain Galasso di Matteo Piva of Consandolo, is hidden in ancient memories and in a few historical descriptions of the *Funerals of the Virgin* that Cardinal Bessarione commissioned in 1455 for the Chapel of the Assumption at Santa Maria del Monte in Bologna.[49]

45 Longhi 1940 ed. 1956, p. 131.
46 Benati 1984, p. 169.
47 Crowe and Cavalcaselle 1871 ed. 1912, II, p. 232.
48 Ibid. See also note 13.
49 For an introductory historical background of this elusive personality, see Rebecchini 1998.

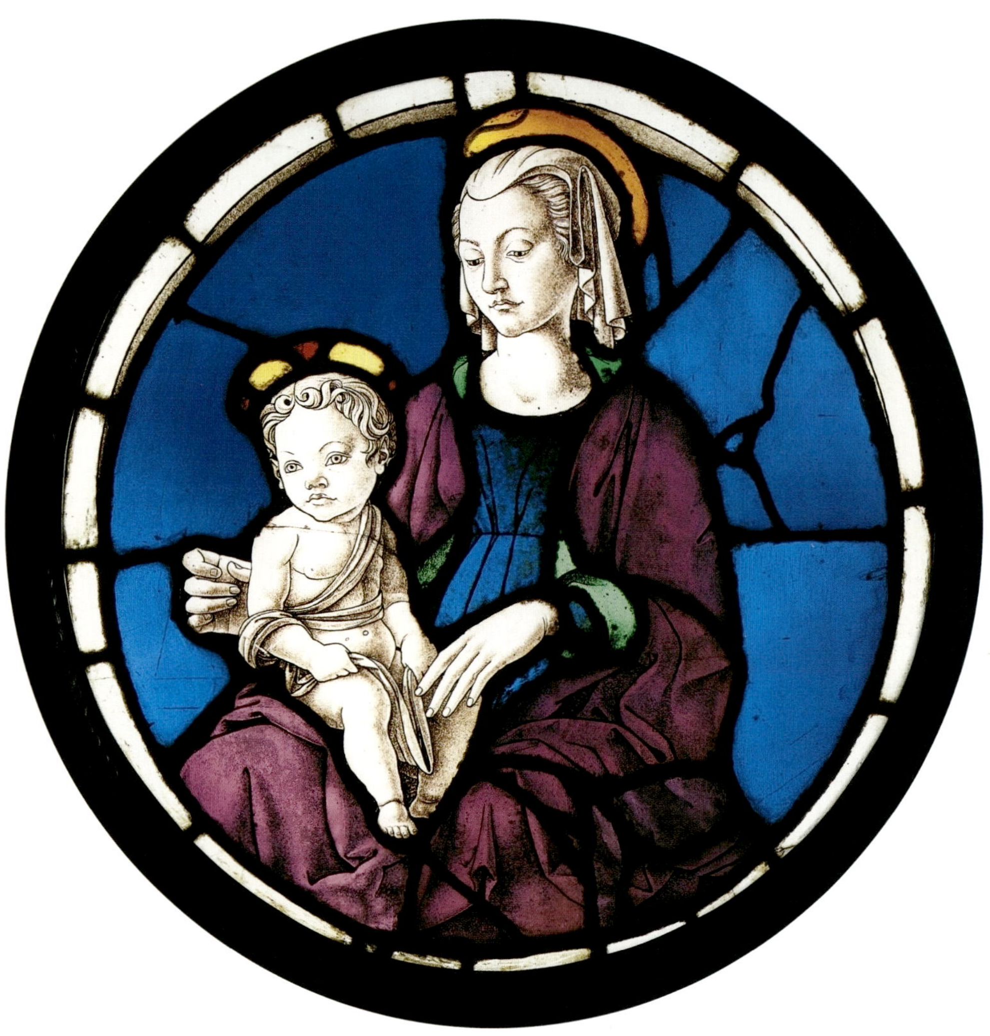

4

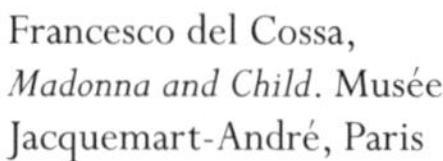
Francesco del Cossa, *Madonna and Child*. Musée Jacquemart-André, Paris

Unlike in the main register, where the landscape runs continuously through all three frames, here the figures of the saints and the *Crucifixion*, originally at the top of the central section (where the use of perspective insistently follows Tuscan models),[50] are painted against a golden background that, as with Piero della Francesca's *Polyptych of the Misericordia* in Borgo Sansepolcro (c. 1445–58),[51] serves as a chromatic screen that reflects light onto the figures. In Cossa, however, the outline of the surrounding drawing has a formal and expressive function completely foreign to Piero della Francesca's works. His meticulously confident and fluid graphic representation refers rather to a Squarcione- or Mantegna-like approach, adopting effects singularly similar to those found in Carlo Crivelli's works in the Marches: compare for example one of the Venetian painter's best-known images, *Saint Mary Magdalene* in the polyptych of Montefiore dell'Aso, with the *Madonna and Child* stained glass window at the Musée Jacquemart-André in Paris (fig. 4),[52] or with Lucy's face: all these works were executed during the same few years.

50 Significantly, the panel was previously attributed by Bode to Andrea del Castagno; see Cavalca's documentary sheet in this volume.

51 Betti, Fronsini, and Refice 2010.

52 C. Cavalca in *Cosmè Tura e Francesco del Cossa* 2007, pp. 394–95, no. 105.

Despite the stylistic coherence of the various elements, the considerable difference between the proportions of the figures and the narrative tone of the two registers long stood in the way of acknowledging that all of these different elements belonged to a single whole. This is one of the reasons why the fundamental reassembly proposed by Roberto Longhi in 1934 ("one of the main strivings in my *Officina ferrarese* book," the scholar would write a few years later),[53] on which Marcello Toffanello contributed an essay to this book, was at first met with bewilderment in some quarters: first of all, Ellis Waterhouse,[54] who in the *Officina*'s subsequent enlarged edition was the object of Longhi's contemptuous "comradely" derision. The reconstruction proposed by the Italian scholar called for placement of the six main paintings on two registers, after they had been recognized as belonging to the same ensemble on the basis of style and material data: *Saint Vincent Ferrer* flanked by *Saint Peter* and *Saint John the Baptist* in the main strip, and above them the *Crucifixion*, with *Saint Florian* and *Saint Lucy* placed alongside and slightly below. Longhi envisaged the predella of the Vatican Museums (which Gustavo Frizzoni had already linked with the London and Milan panels)[55] and six smaller panels with figures of saints in semicircular niches that would be placed along the altarpiece's side pillars. Later discoveries prompted Longhi to enhance his reconstruction a few years later (1940)[56] by including a seventh saint figure (all in all, the side pillars would have included eight elements, one of which was either lost or as yet unidentified) and the two roundels with the *Archangel Gabriel* and the *Virgin annunciate* from Guido Cagnola's Lombard collection.

Roberto Longhi's ingenious hypothesis, one that was almost clairvoyant given the fragmentation and dispersion of these elements, was confirmed by the discovery (by Francesca Montefusco, published by Daniele Benati in 1984)[57] of a pen drawing jotted down by Stefano Orlandi when the polyptych was removed from the chapel which, until then (1725), had belonged to the Griffoni family.[58] The drawing validated Longhi's reconstruction as a whole: it recorded the correct positioning of the painted parts and indicated the presence of twelve panels (rather than the eight theorized by the scholar) in the side pillars. Cecilia Cavalca subjected this valuable new information to rigorous study and realized that, "ideally inserting the panels into the frame designed by an eighteenth-century artist by respecting the proportional ratios imposed by the actual dimensions of the surviving pieces, one may immediately see that for many of the panels the measurements envisaged in the sketch are completely different, so much so that the painted parts float embarrassingly in the woodcarved tracery."[59]

Working with Chiara Tarana, Cavalca reviewed the layout of the ensemble, recalculating the correct proportional ratios for the panels and their possible insertion into the large ornate frame (taking into account the mixtilinear profile of Orlandi's drawing, the most reliable model appears to be the frame for Marco Zoppo's polyptych at the Royal

---

53 Longhi 1940 ed. 1956, p. 128.

54 Waterhouse 1936, pp. 150–51.

55 Frizzoni 1888, p. 300.

56 Longhi 1940 ed. 1956, pp. 128–31.

57 Benati 1984, pp. 166–70; subsequently, De Marchi 2012, pp. 201–2.

58 The bloodline, which ran out in the later part of the eighteenth century (Dolfi 1670, p. 404: "The Griffoni family ... seems inclined to extinction;" quoted by Torella [1988–89] 1991, pp. 44–45 note 18), ended with Giovanni Riniero Griffoni, who appointed Monsignor Pompeo Aldrovandi as his sole heir. On the history of this dispersion, see Mazza's informative essay in this volume.

59 Cavalca 2013, p. 139.

College of Spain, which had been sculpted by the same carver some ten years earlier). As visitors may see for themselves when looking at the simulation of the altarpiece, "the impression is that of looking at some kind of clever modern transcription of the layout of some major late-Gothic polyptychs,"[60] with a monumental *serliana* in the lower register and a loggia in the upper one from which Florian and Lucy look out. The vertical development of the construction would imply an increase in the number of figurines of saints on the two side pillars, from the twelve recorded in Orlandi's drawing to fourteen, which would in turn raise the number of tablets still to be found to seven (or nine).

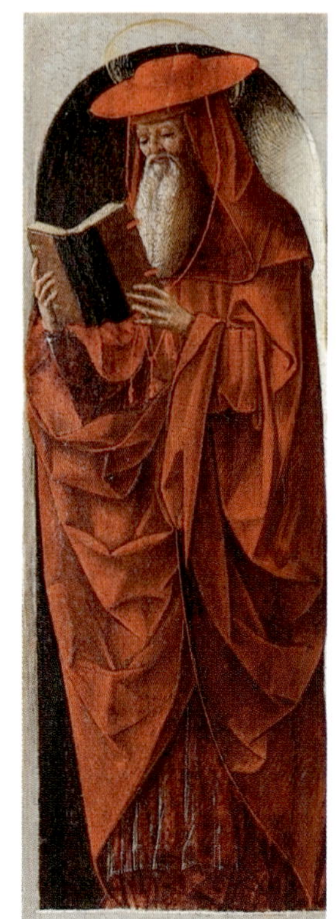

5

Ercole de' Roberti, *Saint Jerome*. Giorgio Cini Foundation, Venice

Ideally embedded in this mighty structure, the surviving panels regain an organic spatial coherence that had been lost, offering an opportunity for new reflections. Next to one another, the pillar panels with their diminutive figures of saints reveal that they cannot all come from the same whole, contrary to what until now has been believed. The panels with *Saint Catherine* and *Saint Jerome* (Giorgio Cini Foundation, Venice) are in fact considerably larger than the other elements in the series, even if their style, the setting of the figures, and the painted architectural frame in which they are placed are perfectly consistent with the whole. This simple observation, made possible thanks to reassembly of various elements from the polyptych, confirms how important direct comparative examination of works can be, even though these days it is conducted less frequently, with the preference for virtual images and reconstructions. It is not possible to rule out that in the future the two Cini saints may find their place within the polyptych—a place that, in the short space of time available for study prior to the exhibition, we were unable to recognize. These two splendid figures, caressed by light just a little brighter than the light illuminating the other saints on the pillars, are probably the two inventions in the series most closely associated with Francesco del Cossa: it is probable that the Ferrara master conceived the design, of which an anonymous follower from Romagna must have been well aware, since he reproduced the same figure of Saint Jerome in a small altarpiece with the *Madonna and Child between Saints Dominic and Jerome*[61] (figs. 5 and 6).

As Luca Siracusano has had occasion to note,[62] back in 1933 Nino Barbantini presented the two Cini panels at the exhibition on Ferrara's Renaissance painting next to *Saint Michael* and *Saint Apollonia* from the Louvre (also on display here), although suggesting that they came from two distinct ensembles.[63] Despite minimal fluctuations in form, the style of the entire series of small-sized saints is fairly homogeneous and, as has long been unanimously acknowledged by scholars, references the art of a young Ercole de' Roberti, who was also responsible for the beautiful predella with the *Miracles of Saint Vincent Ferrer*. A variation of this approach is represented instead by the two roundels with the *Annunciation*, charcaterized by a more rarefied range of colors and a formal perfection that comes close to mannerism: the Archangel Gabriel's wings cast a very light shadow on his pleated gown, while the dalmatic absorbs the warm light reflected from the gold of the frame enclosing the painted disc and from the pink marble of the building in which the Virgin prays.

60 Ibid., p. 141

61 Private collection: Bacchi and De Marchi 2016, p. 416, fig. 60 (as "Pittore cossesco," formerly Venice, Vittorio Cini collection). The painting was presented in 1933 at the *Esposizione della pittura ferrarese del Rinascimento* (p. 112, no. 134) as the work of a "Follower of Roberti" belonging to the collection of a Commander Mario Calderara in Rome, who had bought it from the Lovatelli of Ravenna.

62 L. Siracusano in *La Galleria di Palazzo Cini* 2016, p. 179.

63 *Esposizione della pittura ferrarese del Rinascimento* 1933, pp. 94–95, nos. 109–10, 111–12.

6

Follower of Francesco del Cossa, *Madonna and Child between Saints Dominic and Jerome*. Private collection

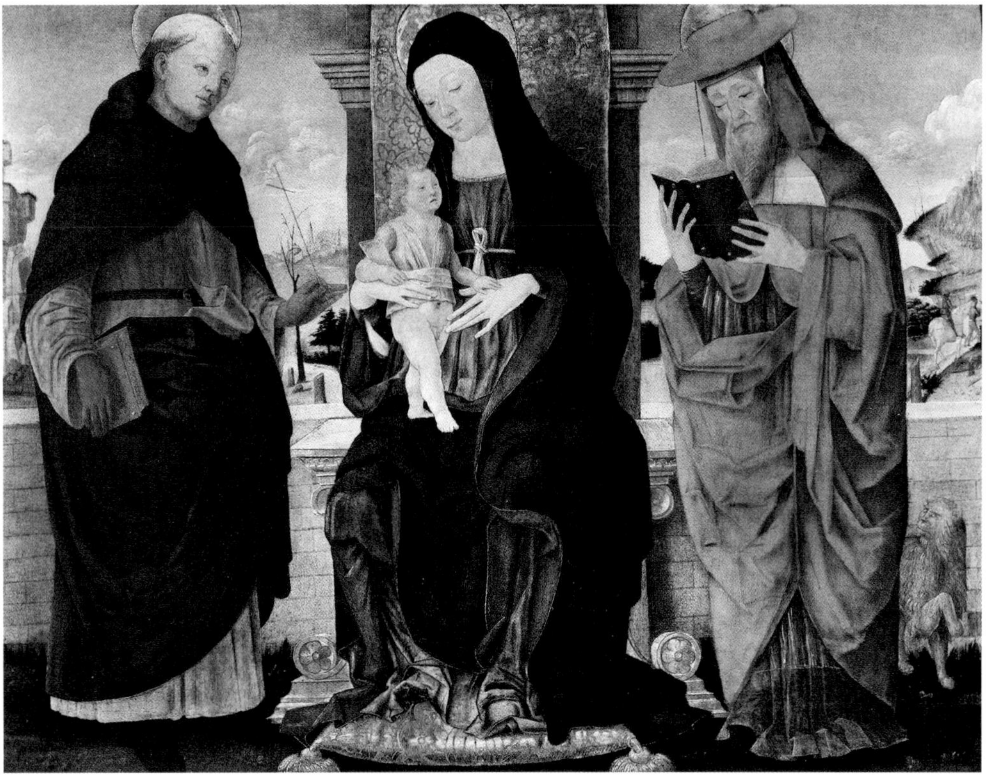

In the Griffoni Polyptych, we come to a rather radical division of work: Cossa for the main frames, de' Roberti for the side frames and the predella. It is likely that this choice was envisaged right from the start, even if the boundaries between the two artists are not always so certain, as Longhi suggested in the many editions of his *Officina* and as will undoubtedly be confirmed by our examination of the various fragments that, for the first time, this exhibition in Bologna allows us to study side by side.

To take our investigation further still, we would have liked to have reflectographic images for all panels, but in order for comparisons to be reliable and to some degree conclusive, such analyses would have had to be carried out using the same piece of equipment, and preferably by the same operator; it does not take a flight of imagination to understand how difficult such an investigation would be for works conserved in locations so far apart. Jill Dunkerton therefore had to work with uneven documentation that, thanks to her long experience, she was able to calibrate adequately. She has, in the process, highlighted the extraordinary graphic qualities of both painters, particularly of Francesco del Cossa in the panels at the Brera in Milan.

Given this new examination of documentary data, to all intents and purposes the execution of the Griffoni Polyptych coincides with Francesco del Cossa and Ercole de' Roberti's work at the Hall of the Months in Palazzo di Schifanoia, Ferrara (before March 1470), where the destiny of the two artists was truly played out. We do not have the scope here to reopen the debate on that famous cycle of wall paintings, which in recent years has benefited from Giovanni Sassu's[64] and Vincenzo Farinella's[65] elucidatory work, but in this volume you will find Cecilia Cavalca's brief account of the story behind this

64 Sassu 2007.

65 Farinella 2007.

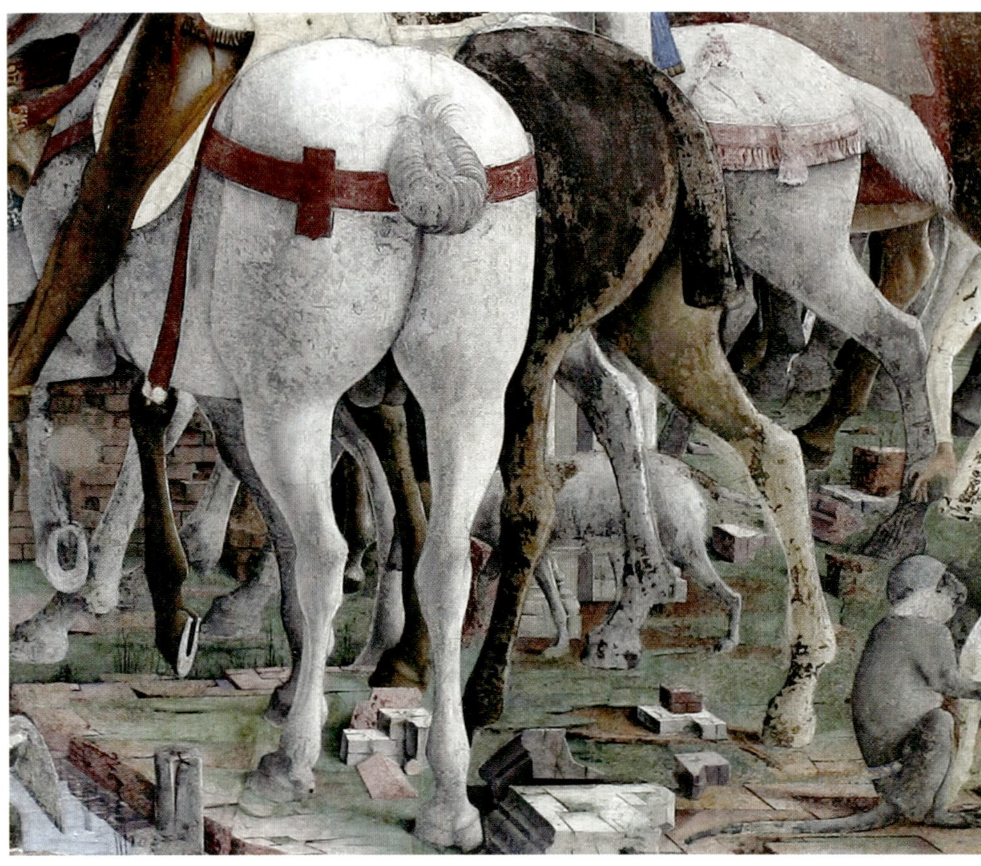

7

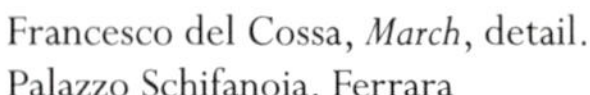
Francesco del Cossa, *March*, detail. Palazzo Schifanoia, Ferrara

famous hall's decoration, which archival information known to us today narrows down to just a few months—a time span that, in my opinion, is too short—between the second half of 1469 and March 1470. It is commonly known that Cossa was given responsibility for decorating the eastern wall of the hall with a representation of allegories, constellations, doyens, and the activities of Borso d'Este and his court during the months of March, April, and May. Fresh from an initial work session in Bologna and a probable stay in Florence,[66] once in Ferrara the painter found a new mode of expression capable of fitting with the eccentric refinement required by the Este court and Cosmè Tura's precious style. However, these luminous narratives, touched with a naturalism not extraneous to local tradition, also convey recollections of his experience in Tuscany: the fluted, cabled pilasters crowned with a Corinthian capital that vertically separate the representations of this and the western wall (very patchy indeed) reproduce almost to the letter the decorative structure of the chapel apse painted by Benozzo Gozzoli (1459–62/63) at Palazzo Medici in Florence.[67] Furthermore, it is not impossible that Cossa recalled the Medici procession of the Magi when he arranged the figures of the wise men and the philosophers to the left of the chariot on which Minerva triumphs, in the upper register of the month of March. It is also interesting to compare a detail from Borso's cavalcade in the lower part of the same month with a detail from *The Counterattack of Micheletto Attendolo da Cotignola* (Louvre, Paris), one of the three panels that made up *The Battle of San Romano*

66 Cavalca 2004–5 (2005), with preceding bibliography.
67 Acidini Luchinat 1993; Ahl 1996, pp. 81–112, 219–20.

8

Paolo Uccello, *The Counterattack of Micheletto Attendolo da Cotignola*, detail. Musée du Louvre, Paris

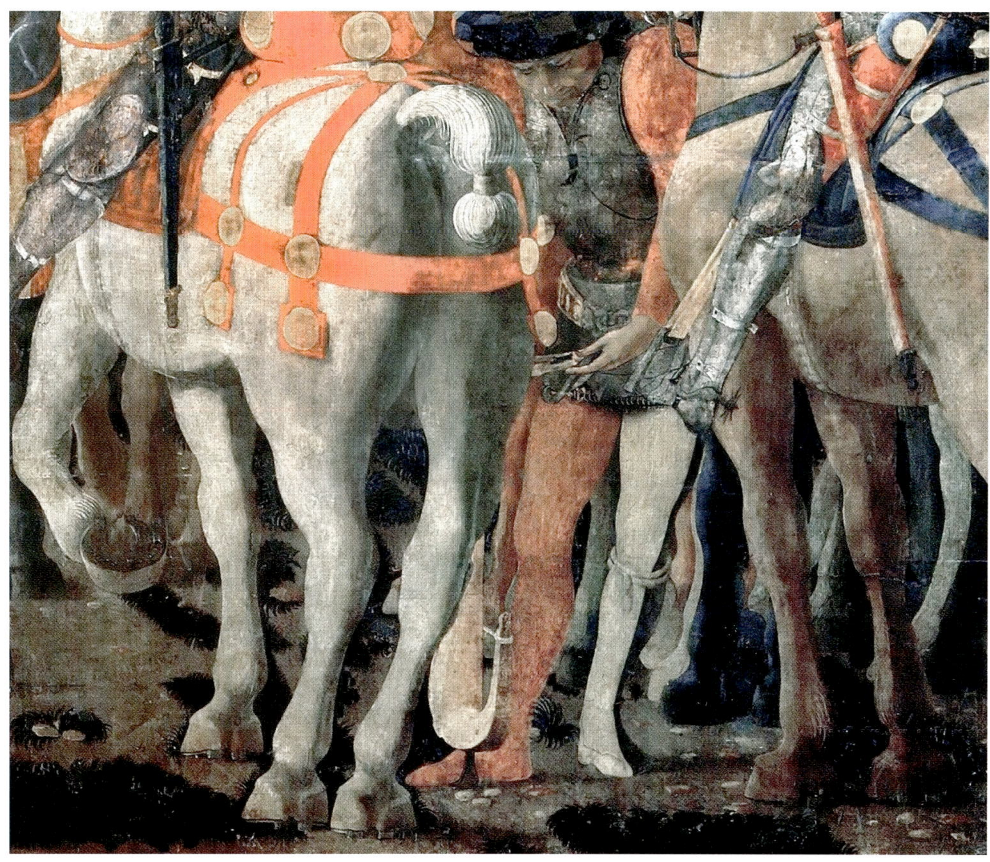

painted by Paolo Uccello (as Francesco Caglioti[68] discovered) around 1438 for the Sala Grande in Leonardo Bartolini Salimbeni's palazzo in Florence[69] (figs. 7 and 8).

The beautiful fragment frescoed with the *Adoration of the Child* that emerged during restoration of San Martino Maggiore in Bologna in 1978–79, which Carlo Volpe[70] attributed to the Florentine master, was just a little earlier than the famous battles. This offers one clue among many of how important the Florentine and Tuscan artists Domenico Veneziano, Alesso Baldovinetti, Giovanni di Piamonte and the team of perspective-based inlayers who laid out the furnishings in the Sacristy of Masses at Santa Maria del Fiore were for artists working in Bologna.[71]

Alongside these new insights, we touch upon the still-open question of Francesco del Cossa's training, of how and where he and his younger fellow-townsman Ercole de' Roberti began working together. It is our hope that this exhibition may reopen this debate and perhaps help clarify these and other issues of importance to Bolognese Renaissance figurative culture.

---

68 Caglioti 2000, pp. 265–81.

69 Lorenzo de' Medici appropriated the *Battle* a little prior to 1497, placing it in his own palazzo in Via Larga (Caglioti 2000, p. 265).

70 Volpe 1980 ed. 1993, pp. 102–23.

71 This direction of research, one that Carlo Volpe initiated in 1958, was later pursued by Andrea Bacchi (1984, pp. 287–88), Daniele Benati in various works (1984, 1987, 2012a, and 2012b), and more in detail by Cecilia Cavalca (2004–5 [2005], 2013). A recent hypothesis regarding the impact of Tuscany on young Cossa is in De Marchi 2018, pp. 439–40.

BOLOGNA IN THE RENAISSANCE POLICY OF THE FIFTEENTH CENTURY AND THE ROLE OF THE GRIFFONI FAMILY

Angela De Benedictis

"Bologna dicta con tuttol' bolognese
Ispechio e luce di tutto luniverso"

"With all its territory, Bologna is called a mirror and light of the whole universe."The city was indeed a cultural crossroads at European level, a place of reference for many intellectuals, especially thanks to the presence of the ancient *Studium generale*, the university. A civic society structured in corporations of arts and crafts and religious confraternities. An economy characterized by peaks of excellence, such as the silk trade. A city able to negotiate its relationships with the State of the Church, in spite of the tensions between the aristocratic government and the people's government. A well-established civic religion, the focus of which was the Basilica of San Petronio. A palace for the ruler of the city, the beauty of which even exceeded that of the Medici family's palace in Florence. For some thirty years now, the most recent historiography, with the crucial contribution of the American scholars,[1] has confirmed, on the one hand, some past acquisitions, but most of all, on the other hand, has uncovered aspects and dynamics of the history of Bologna in the fifteenth century that, for a long time, were regarded as incomparable to those of other, better known Italian Renaissance cities such as Florence and Venice. As far as historiography is concerned, Bologna is now no longer a periphery, but has become a center—just like it was in the eyes of the majority of contemporary observers. And, just like any other city, in the fifteenth century it was involved in a number of recurring frictions, being located as it was in the Italian peninsula, then dominated by continuous conflicts and open wars, along with the corresponding attempts at reaching agreements and restoring the peace.[2]

At the current state of research, as far as the role played by the Griffoni family in that general background is concerned, we are unable to go much further than what we

1 Basile 1984; *Bologna e l'umanesimo* 1988; *Sapere e/è potere* 1990;Terpstra 1999; *L'architettura a Bologna* 2002; Robertson 2002; *Lorenzo Valla* 2009; *Crocevia e capitale* 2010; Lantschner 2012; *Bologna. Cultural Crossroads* 2013; Terpstra 2013; Lantschner 2014; Severi 2015; Sambin De Norcen and Schofield 2018. Lastly, Rubin Blanshei 2018a, and in it, Anselmi and Scioli 2018; Cuvini 2018; De Benedictis 2018; De Silva 2018; Drogin 2018; Duranti 2018; Gardi 2018; Giusberti and Roversi-Monaco 2018; Lines 2018; Milani 2018; Rubin Blanshei 2018b; Rubin Blanshei and Cucini 2018; Tamba 2018;Terpstra 2018; Zarri 2018.

2 Gamberini and Lazzarini 2014.

already know of the position they held at the Fabbriceria of the Basilica of San Petronio.[3] A few pieces of information not specifically emphasized to date can be drawn from the histories and chronicles of the fifteenth and the sixteenth century,[4] as well as from some valuable products of the Renaissance culture dating back to the same period as the design and execution of the Griffoni Polyptych. As sketchy as this information may be, it clearly emerges that the different members of the various branches of the family mentioned therein were involved both in that scenario of continuous conflicts and open wars referred to above, and in the rise and supremacy of the then lord *de facto* of the city, Giovanni II Bentivoglio.

Bologna, a city of the State of the Church, and the Bentivoglio family

As is known, the State of the Church—one of the many states in the northern-central Italian peninsula—had a lord, the Pope, who exercised both the temporal power over the territory of the state and the spiritual power over the entire Christianity at the same time.[5] Likewise, it is well known that the popes that sat in the chair of Saint Peter in the fifteenth century were very much interested in the temporal power; and that in order to protect and increase it, they entered into and broke alliances and went to war just like all the other Italian states' lords.

Bologna had been part of the State of the Church since 1278. During the fourteenth century, the papal government—which was exercised on a local basis by a vicar who represented the Pope—alternated, on several occasions, with that of local *signorie* (lordships), as well as with a number of longer or shorter experiences of restoration of the original communal liberty of the city government. Between 1311 and 1392, Bologna "removed itself" (in the words of early sixteenth-century chronicler Fileno dalla Tuata) from the State of the Church four times, always going back to it after a while. Two of the five occasions of leaving and returning were especially relevant in the fifteenth-century political history of the city. The first event was the uprising against the bad government of vicar Guillaume Noellet, followed by the restoration of the institutions of the Commune's ancient autonomy, the Council of the Elders and Consuls, and the establishment of the so-called *Signoria del Popolo e delle Arti*, a lordship of the people and of the arts that lasted two years (1376–78). Later, Bologna went back to the Church through the crucial contribution of renowned jurist and professor John of Legnano[6]—thanks to whom, in 1382, Pope Urban VI granted to the people of Bologna the "state of liberty," appointing John of Legnano as the city's vicar until 1383. The second event was the transfer of the powers of the government offices of the *Signoria del Popolo e delle Arti* (comprised of *Massari delle Arti* and *Gonfalonieri del Popolo* or *Tribuni della Plebe*, as well as the Elders and Consuls) to a smaller body, in charge of reforming the *Signoria del Popolo e delle Arti* itself. The Reformers of the Status of Liberty were a collegial body established for the

3 In relation to which I refer, of course, to Fanti 1980 and to the essay by the same author in this volume.

4 Research in the Archivio di Stato di Bologna, Archivio Aldrovandi Marescotti, and the Fondo Griffoni has so far proved useless to add anything new to the information we already have on Giacomo (c. fourteenth century–1399), Giovanni (c. 1380–1446), and Floriano Griffoni (1404–1434) drafted by Angiolini 2002a, 2002b, and 2002c, as well as on the more famous chronicler Matteo (1351–1426), drafted by Zabbia 2002.

5 On which Prodi 1982 remains essential.

6 See Pio 2018.

first time between 1393 and 1394; from then on, they acted as the office that represented the "government of the optimates," while the previous offices constituted the "people's government" of Bologna.[7]

From these transformations, which were much more complex than one could ever describe, stemmed all the political and social dynamics that led to the rise of the Bentivoglio family in the fifteenth-century city government—from the short rule of Giovanni I (1401–2) to the dominance of Antongaleazzo (1416–20), to the years of Annibale (1438–45), to the period of Sante (1446–63), and finally to that of Giovanni II (1464–1506).[8] These governments were all inextricably interrelated with—and the direct expression of—the fights involving, from time to time and among fleeting alliances, the Canetoli, Zambeccari, Malvezzi, and Marescotti factions. Furthermore, they were heavily affected by the conflicts between Milan, Florence, and Venice, by the role that the State of the Church played in them, and by the establishment and cancellation of alliances and covenants among these powers. One should also bear in mind that the reports, debates, and positions around the Council of Constance (1414–18) first and the Council of Basel later (1431–49), both regarded as the continuation of those of Ferrara and Florence, contributed directly to that scenario in the first half of the century; another relevant aspect, in the second half of the century, was the "Turkish" issue, that is to say, the Italian states having to deal with and confront the consequences of the fall of the thousand-year-old Byzantine Empire (1453).

Although in the thirty-five years between the beginning of the Council of Constance (1414) and the end of the Council of Basel (1449) Bologna had left and joined the Church again five times, in the last of these occasions the relationships between the city government and the papacy were established in such a way that the city would then refrain from "removing itself" from the Church (again in the words of Fileno dalla Tuata) for the thirteenth time in the second half of the fifteenth century.[9] Even before the conflicts arising from the Councils and the subsequent submissions to popes and anti-popes finally led to recognize Pope Nicholas V (1449), in August 1447, under the rule of Sante Bentivoglio, the city of Bologna and the Pope had signed the so-called "capitula of Nicholas V," which put an end to the long and complex negotiations involving the government of the city and its countryside, based on the claims made by the people of Bologna. In brief, the role of the collegial offices forming the people's government (*Massari delle Arti* and *Gonfalonieri del Popolo*), as well as that of the Elders and Consuls, was finally recognized. It was established that they would rule together with the papal legate and none of them could resolve without the legate's consent—and vice versa. The participation of the Sixteen Reformers in the government of the city was also foreseen; however, as to the claims regarding the

---

7 De Benedictis 2007; De Benedictis 2018 (with past bibliographical references). For similar vicissitudes in the other Italian states, see Shaw 2006.

8 Recent studies in Duranti 2007 and Tamba 2018.

9 The calculation was made back in the early sixteenth century by chronicler Fileno dalla Tuata. See dalla Tuata ed. 2005, I: 1311, p. 48: "*Bologna tolta ala Ghiexia la prima volta*"; 1327, p. 55: "*Bologna dela Ghiexia la segonda volta*"; 1337, p. 69: "*Bologna tolta ala Ghiexia la terça volta*"; 1360, p. 91 "*Bologna dela Ghiexia la 4ª volta*"; 1378, p. 126: "*Bologna dela Ghiexia la quinta volta d'acordo*"; 1392, p. 156: "*Bologna dela Ghiexia con pati la 6 volta*"; 1401, p. 167: "*Bologna de Zoane Bentivogli tolta ala Ghiexia la 6 volta*"; 1403, p. 189: "*Bologna dela Ghiexia la 7ª volta*"; 1411, p. 207: "*Bologna tolta ala Ghiexia la 7ª volta*"; 1412, p. 214: "*Bologna dela Ghiexia la 8ª volta*"; 1416, p. 219: "*Bologna tolta ala Ghiexia la 8ª volta*"; 1420, p. 229: "*Bologna dela Ghiexia la 9ª volta*"; 1428, p. 233: "*Bologna tolta ala Ghiexia la 9ª volta*"; 1429, p. 241: "*Bologna dela Ghiexia la 10ª volta*"; 1430, p. 243: "*Bologna tolta ala Ghiexia la 10ª volta*"; 1431, p. 250: "*Bologna del papa la XIª volta*"; 1434, p. 251: "*Bologna tolta ala Ghiexia la XIª volta*"; 1435, p. 258: "*Bologna dela Ghiexia la dodeçima volta*"; 1438, p. 265: "*Bologna tolta ala Ghiexia la dodeçima volta*"; 1447, p. 296: "*Bologna dela Ghiexia la terdeçima volta.*"

election of successors and their role in the choice of the legate, the Pope had serious reservations. In any case, the city government was comprised of the Reformers (government of the optimates) and the *Gonfalonieri del Popolo* with the *Massari delle Arti* (people's government), which could only resolve with the consent of the legate as the representative of the papal monarchy (monarchical government). The government of the optimates and the monarchical government were granted predominance over the people's government—the Sixteen Reformers and the legate were in charge of electing the Elders, the *Gonfaloniere di Giustizia*, the *Gonfalonieri del Popolo*, and the *Massari delle Arti*.[10]

It should be noted that, at first, the newly elected (on March 6, 1447) Pope Nicholas V aimed at free dominion ("*libero dominio*") over Bologna, that is, the city's unconditional obedience. In that, he followed in the footsteps of Martin V (1417) and Eugene IV (1431–47) at the beginning of their papacy—a "tradition" for Bologna, so to speak, which humanist Lorenzo Valla clearly identified when reporting the consequences of the temporal power of the popes in the way it was exercised based on Constantine's donation.[11] In his *De falsa et ementita Constantini donatione* (1440), Valla pointed out that the Pope was a threat to the liberty of peoples. Six years earlier, when it had had the chance, even Rome had turned against the slavery imposed by the popes based on the prescription on which the Church relied to continue to own the land "donated" by Emperor Constantine.[12] Other peoples and cities were doing the same, whenever it was possible, to restore their own liberty and laws. Nonetheless, the cities that had voluntarily submitted to papal rule had never accepted to become slaves. They had never accepted to be unable to escape the yoke of slavery forever. That would have been too unjust. Those who had given themselves to the popes in order to be governed by them had done so by their own will. However, the popes had wanted to rule against that will. Along with their officials, they had offended those they governed. Then, those who were governed in that way called God to witness and acknowledge that those very offences led them to rise up, just like Israel had risen up against Rehoboam. According to Valla, the uprisings against the Pope in the cities of the Church were as legitimate as that of Israel against their ujust ruler. According to the humanist scholar, Bologna was a prime example of that as well: "*ad Bononiam modo respice*."[13]

The popes' desire to exercise free dominion over Bologna, that is, to rule it directly through their representatives from the upper ecclesiastical hierarchy, certainly did not end with the papacy of Nicholas V. After him, in the second half of the century, the same intention emerged initially in Callixtus III (1455–58), Pius II, humanist Enea Silvio Piccolomini (1458–64), Paul II (1464–71),[14] and Sixtus IV (1471–78)—just to mention those that fall within the scope of this study. And it continued, albeit in a different way, during the following papacies of Innocent VIII (1484–92) and Alexander VI (1492–1503), and peaked with Julius II's "war" against Bologna (1506),[15] as it was also referred to by humanist Erasmus of Rotterdam.[16]

10 Specifically on the matter, see De Benedictis 2007 and Duranti 2009.

11 See De Benedictis 2009.

12 During the Councils conflicts in 1434, Eugene IV had to seek refuge in Florence after he was effectively forced to flee Rome, were a markedly anti-papist government of Roman citizens had been created.

13 Valla ed. 2001, XXVIII.92, p. 238.

14 Specifically on the relationships with Bologna, see Robertson 2002.

15 De Benedictis 2004.

16 Erasmus of Rotterdam ed. 2014, pp. 22–23, 28–29, 36–39, 102–3.

As chronicler Girolamo Borselli noted for the first decades of the fifteenth century, the claims of the popes to exercise free dominion over Bologna took the form of actual wars against the city, also using those spiritual weapons that only popes could wield (interdicts).[17] Under the Bentivoglio rule, this was also painfully noted by well-known humanist Giovanni Sabadino degli Arienti in his *De Civica Salute*, a biography of praise of Ludovico Bentivoglio, which also offered a thorough portrait of the city in the early fifteenth century.[18] I shall refer only to a small, yet significant excerpt concerning the capitulations of Nicholas V.

In 1438, after Bologna had left the Church for the twelfth time (according to Fileno dalla Tuata's calculation), the cry "long live civic liberty" resonated across the city.[19] In Sabadino's opinion, civic liberty could only be sustained by civic virtue—which was missing from those citizens who would later lead Nicholas V to erroneously think that the "Bentivoglio State" of Bologna was misgoverned, therefore urging the Pope to freely acquire dominion over the city ("*liberamente el dominio de Bologna nele sue mane*").[20] According to Sabadino, Ludovico Bentivoglio would be the one to take Nicholas V's mind off the idea of "having Bologna." In a message, the noble knight addressed the Pope and uncovered the deceit of those who advised him to conquer the city with their help ("*havere Bologna liberamente offerendosi de fargliela acquistare*").[21] These thoughts, he wrote, were disrespectful for the Pope because they stemmed not from love but from envy ("*queste persuasione e pensieri sono vani che questi tali fano ala vostra Beatitudine non procedono da perfecto amore che ad essa portino ma per invidia che gli affligge dentro al pecto d'essere magiori degli altri*").[22] And, later on in his speech, he added that those citizens were deprived of civic virtues ("*vivono ingrati al mondo e sença virtu civile*")[23] and did not fail to highlight the past faults of the papal representatives ("*la iniquità de multi Recturi de sancta Chiesa stati a Bologna: che non humane ma inhumanissime et iniuste sono state verso noi le loro operationi*").[24]

The Griffoni family in the policy and literature of fifteenth-century Bologna

Among those who had tried to persuade Nicholas V to have free dominion over Bologna even after signing the capitulations in 1447, there was perhaps a member of the Griffoni family too—at least according to Fileno dalla Tuata's chronicle. The latter reports that, at the beginning of 1448, Ludovico Griffoni and Giacomo Zambeccari had a bitter argument while they were in Acquapendente (currently in the province of Viterbo), both traveling back from Rome, where the two "Bolognese rebels" had been to find an agreement with the Pope against their city ("*per tratare contra el stado de Bologna con papa Nichola*"). The fact that a number of factions conspired against the rule of Sante Bentivoglio at that time is widely testified by the Canetoli family's repeated attempts to overthrow the government

17 Borselli 1912–29, LX: 1420, p. 75; 1428, p. 77; 1429, p. 77–78; 1429, p. 78.
18 Quaquarelli 2004, p. 24.
19 Here I shall use the transcription of Sabadino degli Arienti: Arienti ed. 1983–84, f. 31r.
20 Ibid., f. 103r.
21 Ibid., f. 105v.
22 Ibid., f. 105v.
23 Ibid., f. 114v.
24 Ibid., f. 107v. A reading of Borselli and degli Arienti is in De Benedictis 2009.

of their Bentivoglio enemies.[25] The most important aspect, as far as the Griffoni family is concerned, is that this altercation led to Ludovico Griffoni's attempt to kill Zambeccari. Incidentally, not only did he fail, but the opposite actually occurred—indeed, Griffoni was assassinated by Zambeccari. According to the chronicles, Zambeccari was jailed for this murder but later the public prosecutor acquitted and freed him, because it had emerged that Griffoni wanted to betray Zambeccari.[26]

An actual feud stemmed from this episode: the same chronicler reports that in July–August 1464, that is to say sixteen years later, the Griffoni family finally took their revenge, clearly believing that Giacomo Zambeccari's acquittal had been unfair. And so it was that Ludovico Griffoni's son Andalò murdered Cambio, the son of Giacomo Zambeccari, to vindicate his father's assassination at Acquapendente while he was traveling back from Rome with Giacomo (*"perché Jachomo avea morto Lodovico Grifon vegnendo da Roma [a] Aquapendente l'ano 1448"*).[27]

This narration, also according to the chronicles, as confused as they may be, confirms that in the 1420s and '30s the Griffoni and the Canetoli, Zambeccari, and Bentivoglio families were sometimes friends, sometimes foes. It is undisputed that in 1432 Giovanni Griffoni was trying to reconcile Battista Canetoli and Abbot Zambeccari, who was suspected of supporting the Bentivoglio faction. We know this from humanist Giovanni Garzoni's *Historie*, the third book of which, concerning the years 1420–35, is aptly titled *Historia belli civilis*.[28] Garzoni pointed out what we have already noted through the comments of Lorenzo Valla and Sabadino degli Arienti: at the beginning of chapter 3 he raises the issue of whether, and to what extent, the situation in those years could be referred to only as internal wars, since the citizens fought each other, or as an external war against Bologna and its citizens, considering that the popes repeatedly laid siege on the city.[29]

The name of Giovanni Griffoni[30] appears rather frequently between 1420 and 1450, and always in a somehow significant role. According to Fileno dalla Tuata's chronicle, in February 1420 Giovanni was one of the Sixteen Reformers and remained in office for six months, with the aim of negotiating the conditions of the city's obedience to the Church and Pope Martin V, who aimed instead at exercising free dominion over Bologna.[31]

Then, in 1431, Floriano Griffoni (the father of another Floriano, who commissioned the polyptych) was appointed ambassador and traveled to Rome to sign the peace with Pope Eugene IV, when Bologna went back to the Church for the eleventh time.[32]

Between 1437 and 1446, Giovanni's name appears four times and his role in the political life of the city is always rather relevant. In 1437, he was appointed a knight and went to Florence as a captain;[33] in 1439, then a knight, he served as ambassador to con-

25 As dalla Tuata himself (ed. 2005) reports for the same year, I, ff. 175r–v, p. 299. See also Robertson 2002, p. 172.

26 dalla Tuata ed. 2005, I, f. 175r, p. 298: "*Vegnando Jachomo Zanbecharo e Lodovigo Grifon tuti due ribelli de Bologna da Roma per tratare contra el stado de Bologna con papa Nichola, quando funo a Aquapendente aveno alcune parole insieme, e Lodovigo volse amaçare Jachomo per posere tornare a Bologna e Jachomo amaço lui, di che fu preso Jachomo, e visto e chonosuto che Lodovigo lo volea tradire fu liçençiato Jachomo de presone e absoluto delo homicidio.*"

27 Ibid., I, f. 191v, p. 328.

28 Garzoni ed. 2010. This important work, only a manuscript until a few years ago, was then properly published by Alessandra Mantovani, with a preface by the same scholar and an updated biography of Giovanni Garzoni. See also Mantovani 2012. For 1432, Garzoni ed. 2010, p. 425.

29 Garzoni ed. 2010, p. 411.

30 Information on Giovanni Griffoni's role in Duranti 2007, p. 53, no. 125, and especially *ad vocem* in Angiolini 2002a.

31 dalla Tuata ed. 2005, I, f. 134r, p. 227.

32 Ibid., I, f. 146v, p. 250, dated May 14, 1431.

33 Ibid., I, f. 155r, p. 263, dated October 27, 1437.

dottiere Niccolò Piccinino;[34] in 1443, after Bologna was taken away from Piccinino, he was one of the Reformers of the State, elected for one year by the *Consiglio dei Seicento*.[35] Giovanni's role was especially important in 1446. When Sante Bentivoglio, arriving in Bologna in November of that year, went to visit the Elders and Consuls, he was appointed a knight by the *podestà* of Bologna, Giacomo Lavagno da Verona, by the Florentine ambassador Francesco Corbini, by Niccolò Sanuti, Count and knight of Bologna, and by knight Giovanni Griffoni.[36] Fileno dalla Tuata reports at this point that the noble and ancient Griffoni family ended with Giovanni (as far as we know, in 1450), although others—originally from Sant'Agata—remained and took the family name.[37]

In the second half of the century, with the exception of the 1464 episode of revenge mentioned above, and besides the role of the Griffoni family in the Fabbriceria of San Petronio,[38] Girolamo Griffoni rose to fame thanks to Bologna's diplomatic relations with the Sforza in Milan, based on his documented friendship with Giovanni II Bentivoglio. We know this especially from someone directly involved, Galeazzo Maria Sforza's secretary Gerardo Cerruti, who sent messages to his *princeps* almost on a daily basis between 1470 and 1474[39]—that is to say, in the same years when the polyptych commissioned by Floriano Griffoni was being executed. Between the end of December 1470 and July 6, 1471 Cerruti's letters to Sforza mention a dozen missions that involved Girolamo: to Pieve di Cento, Castelfranco, Rome, to Sforza himself, to the House of Este in Ferrara,[40] and finally record the murder of Girolamo in a letter dated July 4, 1471.[41]

Griffoni was on a mission to Ferrara to talk to Borso d'Este, who, however, did not receive him. Conversely, he was honorably welcomed by Ercole d'Este in Castelnuovo. Shortly after leaving, he was approached by a man who pretended to want to talk to him; instead, he stabbed him to death in the chest, although four of five men that were with him tried to stop the assassin. According to Cerruti, the reason behind Girolamo's murder was the "huge hatred" between the Griffoni and the Zambeccari ("*era stato tra la case de' Griffoni et alcuni Zambechari per la morte d'homini, l'ultimo di quali morti era di Zambechari, et fu mo fa circa cinque anni*").[42] This means that Girolamo's murder in 1471 was a consequence of the killing of Cambio Zambeccari by Andalò Griffoni in 1464, which in turn had been the consequence of Ludovico Griffoni's homicide by Giacomo Zambeccari in 1448. The people of Ferrara who condoled with Giovanni II Bentivoglio were sure, according to Cerruti, that the instigators of the crime were the *diamanteschi*, i.e. the members of the faction of Ercole d'Este. Cerruti goes on: "Whoever he may be, messer Giovanni was with great sorrow deprived of a very cordial friend, for whom he had great esteem for so many things, and whom he trusted as he trusted himself; this friend was taken from him, with no regard for

34 Ibid., I, f. 158r, p. 268, dated January 29, 1439.
35 Ibid., I, f. 163r, p. 277, dated June 8, 1443.
36 Ibid., I, f. 173v, p. 296, dated November 13, 1446. See also Garzoni ed. 2010, p. 478.
37 dalla Tuata ed. 2005, I, f. 173v, p. 296.
38 In this connection I refer, of course, to Fanti 1980 and to his contribution in this volume. Pini 1994 is key too, as it also covers, as well as the chapel in San Petronio, the other Griffoni patronages in different churches of the city. See also De Silva 2013, pp. 178–82.
39 We have known this for a few years now thanks to the careful research and publication of the correspondence by Duranti 2007, the importance of which was also noted by Cavalca 2013, p. 171 notes 55 and 56.
40 Duranti 2007: letter 96, December 30, 1470, p. 124; letter 97, December 31, 1470, p. 124; letter 99, January 4, 1471, pp. 125–27; letter 119, January 25, 1471, pp. 144–45; letter 216, June 27, 1471, p. 223; letter 219, June 30, 1471, pp. 231–32; letter 223, July 4, 1471, pp. 233–35.
41 Ibid., letter 223, pp. 234.
42 Ibid.

the fact that Giovanni himself had sent him as an envoy. Apart from being an insult, this state of affairs was in various ways an offence to his honor: I believe that if he could do as he wished, he would have shown how hurt he was."[43] Borso d'Este later expressed his sorrow and bitterness to Giovanni II and ensured that he had placed a bounty on the murderer's head. On the other hand, Ercole d'Este sent one of his men to Giovanni II to express his condolences and let him know that, in his opinion, the instigator of Girolamo Griffoni's homicide was his brother, Rinaldo d'Este.[44]

Another direct testimony of Giovanni II's friendship with Girolamo Griffoni is found in a completely different source—a product of the courtly literature of the same time just as the episode it narrated and celebrated, that is, the great tournament held by Giovanni II on the occasion of the feast of Saint Petronius, on October 4, 1470. Two different works were composed as products of this literary genre, one by Giovanni Sabadino degli Arienti, and a short poem by Francesco Cieco of Florence, using the *ottava rima*.[45]

Two teams, the white (Bentivoglio) and the red (Bolognesi), faced each other at the tournament. The captain of the former was Giovanni II Bentivoglio, while the latter was led by Antonio Trotto of Alessandria. Each captain had fifty-four men divided into six ranks and equipped with non-deadly weapons (after all, it was a game), i.e. blunt short lances and wooden clubs. The prize was a silver embroidered tapestry. Within Bentivoglio's team, the first rank was led by Teseo Marescotti, the second by Pier Giorgio da Nor, commissioner of Parma for Duke Galeazzo Sforza, the third one by Antonio Bentivoglio, the fourth one by Giovanni Francesco Poeti, the fifth one by Giulio and Carlo, sons of Virgilio Malvezzi, the sixth and last one by Giovanni II himself. In Cherubino Ghiradacci's late-sixteenth-century history of Bologna, which resumed previous narratives, a portion of the rank was described as follows, "Before him [Giovanni II] four buglers and sixteen horses richly decorated with a gold and silver surcoat and pearl embroidery, each of them with a squire and pages, all wearing a drape and carrying a white lance, two of whom also carried the helmet with a golden lion between fire flames on the crest, and the motto *Non vole amore forza*. The helmet was also decorated with pure white veils and silverwork, with skillfully made ostrich feather works. They were followed by six buglers and four fifers. Behind them, Jeronimo Griffoni with the white silk banner and, after him, captain Giovanni with many of his honorable knights, all dressed in white with gold embroidery."[46] Hence, Girolamo Griffoni occupied a leading position in Giovanni II Bentivoglio's rank.

I

Francesco Cieco of Florence, *Description of the tournament made in Bologna on October 4, 1470 by the order of Giovanni Bentivoglio* (Bologna: Scipione Malpigli, after October 4, 1470), f. 1r

---

43 Ibid.: "*Chi se sia, messer Zohanne ne sta con affanno inestimabile privato de amico cordialissimo, del qual poteva in molte cose farsi grande estima et pigliarne fede como di se medesimo, toltoli per questa via et non havuto respecto che da lui fusse mandato. Che oltre l'iniuria, in più e più modi non è senza denigratione del suo onore: fate conto che s'el potesse quel che vorria, dimostrarene haverne avuto a male.*"

44 Ibid., letter 225, pp. 235–36.

45 On these two works, see Pezzarossa 1984, pp. 45–49, who partially reads them in the framework of other types of celebratory literature such as wedding poems. The writing by Sabadino degli Arienti, *Torneo*, is mostly known in its 1888 transcription from a manuscript (Arienti ed. 1888). The incunables of Cieco's short poems were already mentioned by Sorbelli ed. 2003, p. 9 (and p. 12 on printer Scipione Malpigli, Doctor of Medicine and Philosophy); however, he did not take into consideration the precious document that I shall use now, Cieco of Florence 1470, a digital copy of which is currently available for free via open access (see entry in Reference literature).

46 Ghirardacci ed. 1933, p. 205: "*Davanti a lui quattro trombetti e sedici corsieri riccamente ornati con sopraveste d'oro e d'argento e con ricami di perle con scudiero per ciascuno e paggi tutti vestiti di drappo con una lancia bianca in mano, due dei quali portavano l'elmo con il cimiero di un leone d'oro nel mezzo delle fiamme di fuoco, con il motto 'Non vole amore forza'. L'elmo era poi ornato di veli candidissimi con lavori d'argento, con certe pelli di penne di struzzo fatte con bellissimo magistero. Seguivano sei trombetti e quattro pifferi. Dietro di loro Jeronimo Griffoni con lo stendardo di seta bianca e dopo di lui Giovanni capitano con molti dei suoi degni cavalieri vestiti tutti di bianco con ricami d'oro.*"

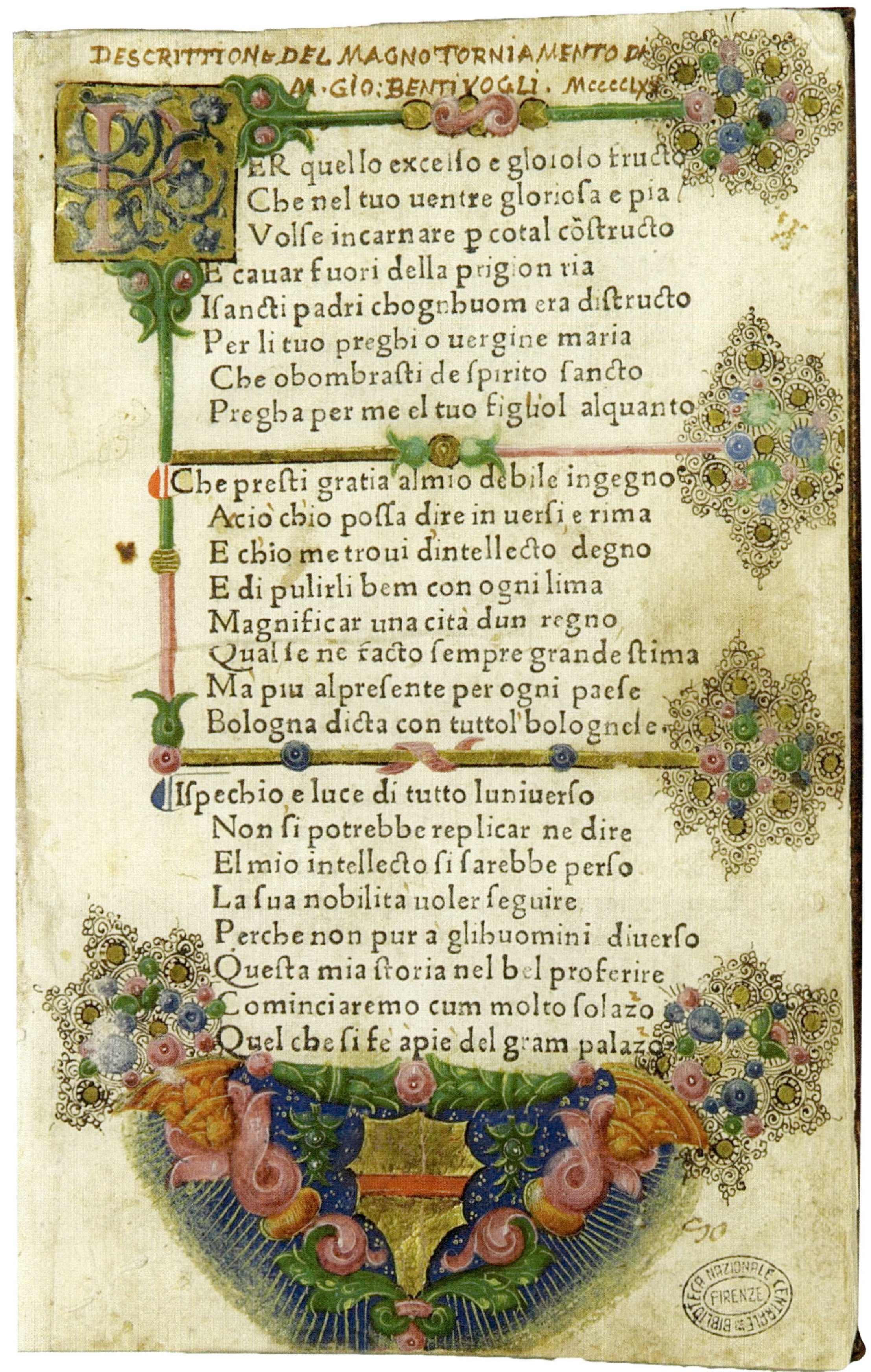
DESCRITTIONE DEL MAGNO TORNIAMENTO DI M. GIO: BENTIVOGLI. Mcccclxx

PER quello excelſo e glorioſo fructo
Che nel tuo uentre glorioſa e pia
Volſe incarnare p coſtal cōſtructo
E cauar fuori della prigion ria
Iſancti padri chognhuom era diſtructo
Per li tuo preghi o uergine maria
Che obombraſti de ſpirito ſancto
Pregha per me el tuo figliol alquanto

Che preſti gratia almio debile ingegno
Acio chio poſſa dire in uerſi e rima
E chio me troui dintellecto degno
E di pulirli bem con ogni lima
Magnificar una cità dun regno
Qual ſe ne facto ſempre grande ſtima
Ma piu alpreſente per ogni paeſe
Bologna dicta con tuttol bologneſe.

Iſpechio e luce di tutto luniuerſo
Non ſi potrebbe replicar ne dire
El mio intellecto ſi ſarebbe perſo
La ſua nobilita uoler ſeguire
Perche non pur a glihuomini diuerſo
Queſta mia ſtoria nel bel proferire
Cominciaremo cum molto ſolazo
Quel che ſi fe apie del gram palazo

241

Simil insegna in la giornea portoe
Questo signor e capitan gentile
Messer zoan per nome si chiamoe
Che exercito di marte el grande stile
E sempre suo figliuol se appelloe
Nel bellicoso gioco si uirile
Che se disse di lui in ogni parte
Come piu oltre sera nelle carte.

Sendo lui gionto apie dello stechato
Cum la sua compagnia adorna e bella
E quel che la bandier hauea portato
Anchora lui si era armato in sella
Gironimo grifon si fu chiamato
Messer giouanni si gli disse in quella
Entra di drento e girerai dintorno
E in questo luogho poi farai ritorno.

Gironimo ubidi al suo comando
Cum lo stendardo splendido e sereno
Intorno al campo lo uenne portando
Cum buona uolõta che nõ uien meno
Messer giouanni landa seguitando
Sopral supbo che sotto il terreno
Tremaua p gram furia a quel destrieri
Ognhuõ guardaua el signor el corsieri

2

Francesco Cieco of Florence, *Description of the tournament made in Bologna on October 4, 1470 by the order of Giovanni Bentivoglio* (Bologna: Scipione Malpigli, after October 4, 1470), f. 29r

And the same leading role is referred to in the two works by Sabadino degli Arienti and Francesco Cieco, written just after the tournament.

In degli Arienti's *Torneo*, we learn that Girolamo Griffoni, a "dashing man," carried a white silk banner "with great honor and grand style," and rode a horse covered in white silk. His feet were partly decorated with diamonds and fine gold. His helmet had three braids of white silk and a "rich golden griffin" as emblem.[47]

In Francesco Cieco's *Descrittione del magno torniamento di M. Gio. Bentivogli*, the place of Griffoni in the sixth rank is described as follows, using the *ottava rima*: "When he [Giovanni II] arrived near the fence/ with his beautifully adorned, handsome company of soldiers/ one of whom carried the flag/ also armed, astride his steed/ he had Gironimo Grifone summoned/ and then messer Giovanni said to him/ "Go inside, take a look round/ and then come back here."/ Gironimo obeyed his order/ and took the banner splendid and serene/ around the field/ without ever losing his good will/ messer Giovanni went after him,/ on his superb steed, while beneath him the ground/ trembled with the great fury of that horse,/ and everyone stared at the lord and the horse."[48] Griffoni himself is described, just after that, as a proud and steady man ("*Gironimo Grifon fier e constante*").[49]

Hence, the Renaissance literature of the celebration shows the reason why the murder of Girolamo Griffoni deprived Giovanni II, in Gerardo Cerruti's words, of a dear and trustworthy friend ("*amico cordialissimo, del qual poteva in molte cose farsi grande estima et pigliarne fede como di se medesimo*").[50]

At the beginning of his short poem, using the typical style of that literary genre, Francesco Cieco announces that he wants to praise a city that has always been held in great esteem, but especially so at the present time: "To glorify the city of a kingdom/ which has always benefitted from great esteem/ but more than ever today, for every nation/ with all its territory, Bologna is called/ a mirror and light of the whole universe."[51] In this complex Renaissance universe made of internal wars, external wars, civic religion, and artistic patronage, the Griffoni family played an important role.

At the beginning of the year 1500, Fileno dalla Tuata still included the Griffoni in the list of the one hundred most influential families of Bologna, beside the twenty-one of the Reformers of the Status of Liberty[52].

47 Arienti ed. 1888, pp. 33–34.

48 Cieco of Florence 1470, f. 29r. Here I am quoting the original text without making any changes, as you can see in fig. 2: "*Sendo lui gionto apie dello stechato/ Cum la sua compagnia adorna e bella/ E quel che la bandier havea portato/ Anchora lui si era armato in sella/ Gironimo grifon gli fu chiamato/ Messer giovanni gli si disse in quella/ Entra di drento e girerai dintorno/ E in questo luogho poi farai ritorno./ Gironimo ubidi al suo comando/ Cum lo stendado splendido e sereno/ Intorno al campo lo venne portando/ Cum buona volonta che non vien meno/ Messere giovanni landa seguitando/ Sopral superbo che sotto il terreno/ Tremava per gram furia a quel destrieri/ Ognhuom guardava el signor el corsieri.*"

49 Cieco of Florence 1470, f. 62v.

50 Duranti 2007, letter 223, p. 234: "*Magnificar una cità dun regno/ Qual se ne facto sempre grande stima/ Ma piu al presente per ogni paese/ Bologna dicta con tuttol' bolognese/ Ispechio e luce di tutto luniverso.*"

51 Cieco of Florence 1470, f. 1r (fig. 1).

52 dalla Tuata ed. 2005, II, f. 245r, p. 414.

BUILDING SAN PETRONIO: THE FIRST CENTURY

Maria Teresa Sambin De Norcen

"La più magna e bella de crestianitade"

At the time when Floriano Griffoni undertook the decoration of the family chapel, in around 1470,[1] the Basilica of San Petronio, "the greatest and most beautiful in all Christendom," was significantly different from the church we see today (fig. 1). The central nave was covered with a roof on wooden trusses, set at a lower height than the current ogival vaults; the altar overlooked the nave at the end of the fourth bay. Indeed, a payment dated December 31, 1469 for paving the main nave provides us with information about its length: "from the great altar to the base of the large door of San Petronio ... *perteghe* 19 *piè* 8:"[2] the equivalent, in fact, of four bays, the two-foot difference evidently occupied by the area reserved for the altar, which stretched forward from the main chapel behind it, and in those years underwent a great deal of furnishing.
Begun in 1392, the Basilica was going through yet another phase of "provisional completion," something that due to the overall volume of the church would not be achieved until the mid-seventeenth century, or if we take the arrangement of the side chapels into account, no earlier than last century.

Faced with the complexity of the building site and divergent historiographical positions, in an attempt to shed some light on the reason for these repeated additions and the site's condition in 1470, it is necessary to reconsider, at least briefly, how work progressed from the start.[3]

---

1 Supino 1938, pp. 196–98; Giacomelli 1994, p. 123; Cavalca 2013, pp. 136–38.

2 Gatti 1913, p. 71, dates the document to December 31, 1470, failing to consider that at that time in Bologna the Nativity-style calendar was in use; Supino 1913, p. 135; Lorenzoni 1983, p. 61.

3 A great many monographic studies exist on San Petronio. Bibliography until the final decade of the nineteenth century is in Bacchi della Lega 1892–93. After Guidicini's writings on the Basilica in his monumental work (Guidicini 1870, pp. 359–71), a fundamental contribution to research into San Petronio was made by Angelo Gatti (Gatti 1887, 1889, 1913, 1914). Indeed, we owe to him publication of an exceptional amount of documents, albeit in a disorderly and sometimes inaccurate manner, accompanied by errors of interpretation. Igino Benvenuto Supino challenged him on this (Supino 1909, 1913, 1914a, 1932, pp. 315–46, 1938, pp. 155–232). A bitter row broke out between the two of them about the Basilica's various building phases and the initial blueprint. Bibliography updated to the mid-twentieth century is in Zucchini 1953. Interest in San Petronio increased significantly after the publication of Fanti 1980 (from which, on p. 117, we take the quotation opening this essay), which reconstructed the site's institutional history and contextualized it within the Italian panorama of the day, as well as bringing new documents to critics' attention. This was followed by the two books *La Basilica di San Petronio* (Fanti, Lorenzoni, Matteucci, Roli, and Volpe 1983 and 1984, both reprinted in 2003), containing important contributions, among which we cite for now just Lorenzoni 1983, which tackles the same issues as we are interested in. Then, chronologically, *Il tramonto del Medioevo* 1987, D'Amico 1990, and *Una basilica per una città* 1994. On the other hand, Supino 1914b, Matteucci 1966, Beck 1970, and Emiliani 1981 deal specifically with Jacopo della Quercia's work on the *Porta magna* and sixteenth-century projects for completion, which we do not cover here as they go beyond the scope of this research. The many essays published in journals or in miscellaneous volumes will be cited as necessary in the following notes; we only recall that Anna Maria Matteucci's many contributions on San Petronio and its architect were published in updated form in Matteucci 2008, pp. 39–119.

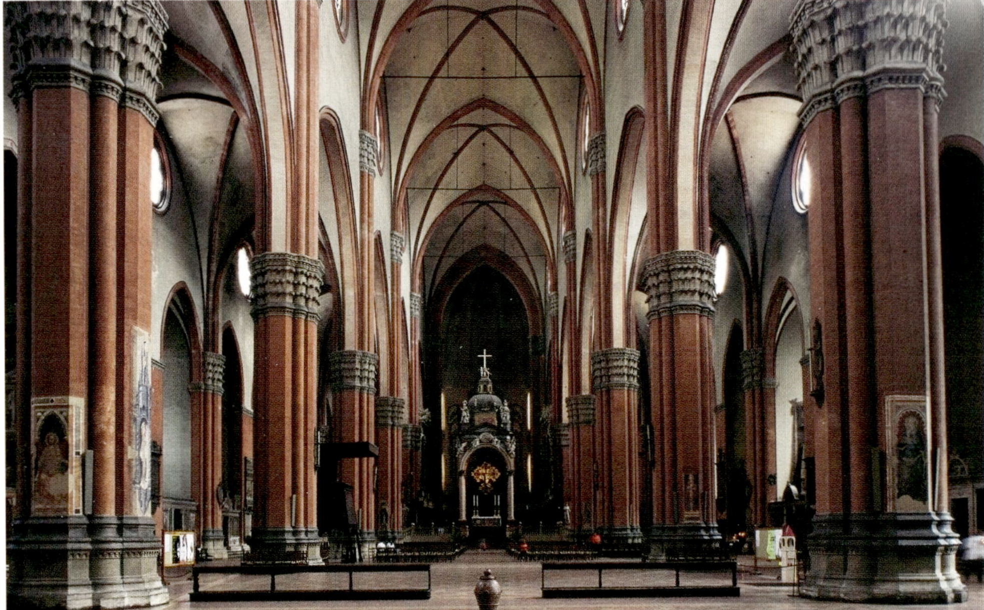

1

Basilica of San Petronio, Bologna, interior view

Foundation

The year is 1388. In Florence's Cathedral, all that was missing were the finishing touches to the great aisles, the construction having been completed eight years earlier to Francesco Talenti's expansion project, approved in 1367.[4] In Milan, construction of the new Cathedral had been underway for two years.[5] And in Venice, construction of a new, large, Gothic Basilica (the lost Santa Maria dei Servi) had begun in the early decades of the century, along with reconstruction in expanded and updated form of the old churches of the beggars, the Dominican Basilica of San Giovanni e Paolo and the Basilica of the Frari.[6]

No strangers to the wave of proud renewal sweeping across Italy, the people of Bologna made an unconventional choice: they decided to build a civic church from scratch, freed from the bishop's authority and any monastic order, dedicated to a saint elected as an incarnation of democratic freedom.[7] Government by the people and by the guilds—which had been in power once more for over a decade—was determined to show faith in its own means and resources, as well as to ensure the protection of Petronius, with whom Bolognese patriotic feelings were now firmly intertwined. As Richard Tuttle writes, the Basilica constituted a veritable "sacred vow to communal freedom and political autonomy."[8] The site selected for the building was the main city square, which the church would overlook from the south end: this results in the unusual orientation of the Basilica, with its apse to the south, and in the works starting from the facade (fig. 2); such an unconventional choice would cause the altar and the bell tower to be relocated many times over the centuries.[9]

4 *La Cattedrale di Santa Maria del Fiore* 1994–95.
5 On Milan Cathedral, lastly, see Ceriani Sebregondi, Gritti, Repishti, and Schofield 2019, above all pp. 15–87, covering the period we are dealing with.
6 Concina 2003, pp. 77–85; Dellwing 2010, pp. 89–110.
7 Fanti 1980, pp. 1–35 on the cult of the saint, pp. 37–39 on the decision to build the Basilica.
8 Tuttle 1998, p. 258.
9 We will deal with the altar later. On the provisional bell towers, see Gatti 1914, *ad indicem*; Supino 1932, pp. 324–25.

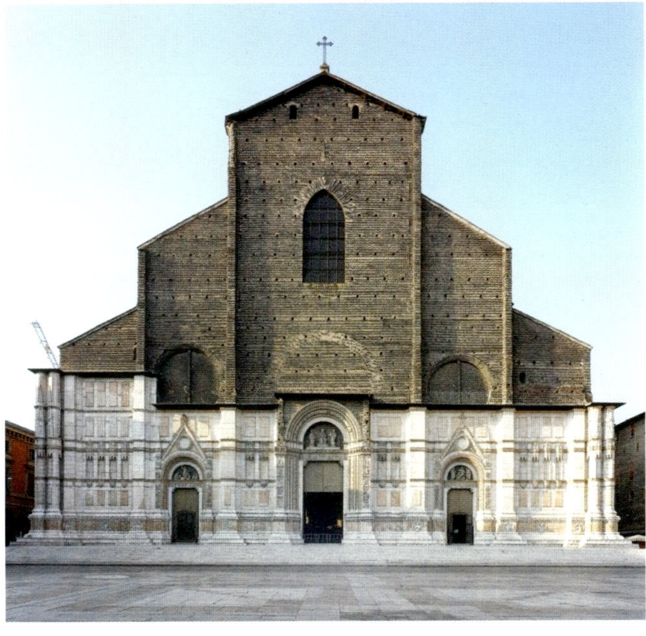

The area where the church would be constructed was highly built-up. In consequence, expropriation and clearance was required, eating up a not-insignificant proportion of the finances available.[10]

Master Antonio di Vincenzo was put in charge of the project. Despite his qualification as a "mason," he was an established military engineer, having served the Municipality on documented works since 1382. In 1384, together with Lorenzo di Bagnomarino, he worked as architect on the Palazzo della Mercanzia and a portion of the Palazzo dei Notai (he was responsible for the windows), as well as, two years later, the Chamber of Acts at the Palazzo Re Enzo.[11]

On February 26, 1390 Antonio was commissioned to build a 1:12 scale model of the Basilica (so that one inch of the model corresponded to one foot of the building),[12] based on drawings he already completed with the aid of the learned friar Andrea Manfredi of Faenza, an architect who had drafted the project for Santa Maria dei Servi, the Bolognese church of the order of which he was in charge.[13] Historiographers tend to diminish the clergyman's role in the project, but his input could not have been entirely

2

Basilica of San Petronio, Bologna, facade

3

Egidio Maria Bordoni, *Plan of San Petronio in its current state, with sundial path*, 1695, engraving. Biblioteca dell'Archiginnasio, Bologna, Collezione Antolini, 119

10 Guidicini 1870, pp. 361–63; Fanti 1980, p. 47 note 12; Trombetti Budriesi 1994, p. 52.

11 Gatti 1891, pp. 199–201; Orioli 1892, pp. 394-395. On the major renovations of the Palazzo dei Notai e della Mercanzia, see Zucchini 1959, pp. 16–18, 89–94.

12 Guidicini 1870, p. 360; Gatti 1889, pp. 68–69; Supino 1909, p. 124; Gatti 1913, pp. 295–96; Lorenzoni 1983, p. 54. On Bolognese units of length, see Martini 1883, p. 92.

13 Gatti 1913, pp. 293–94; Fanti 1983, pp. 17–19; Matteucci 2008, pp. 25–26. The friar's sepulchral inscription at Santa Maria dei Servi reads: "*Mores et muros ubique instauravit / hocque amplissimum structurae templum porticumque peramplum / generosa animi magnitudine excitavit*" (Branchesi 1992, pp. 44–45).

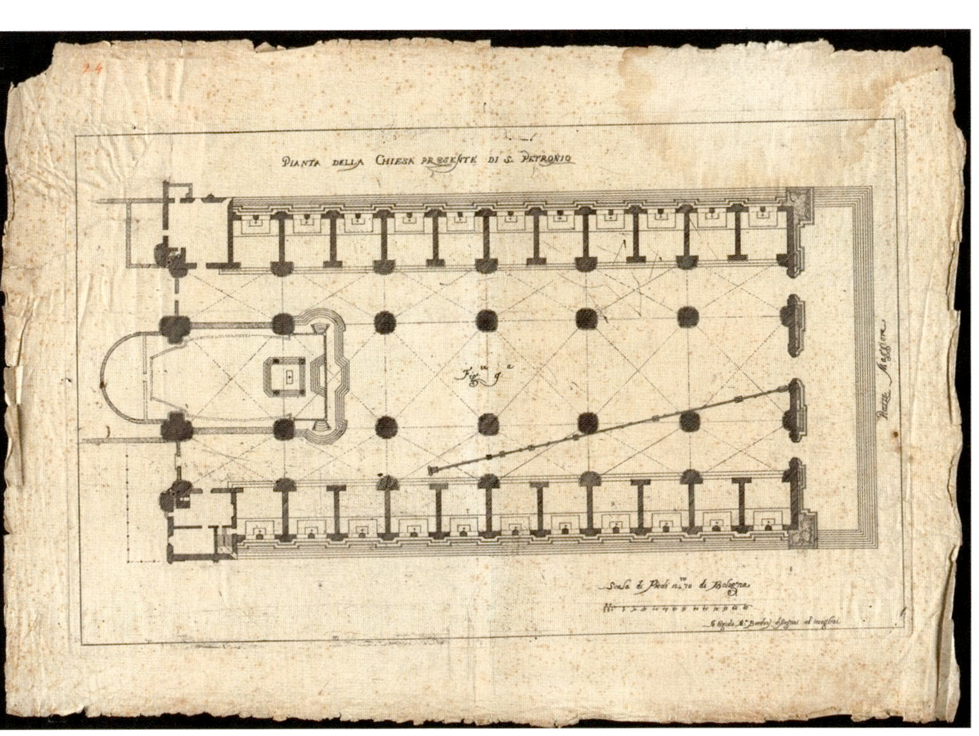

secondary, given that in June 1390 the *fabbricieri* (administrators) stated that Antonio designed San Petronio, "his industry, art, and genius being one with those of Reverend Father Andrea, General of Santa Maria dei Servi."[14]

Despite repeated attempts to reconstruct the events that took place over the span of more than a century, we remain in the dark about Antonio's design. Given that the first two bays were erected while the architect was still alive, there is no uncertainty about the planimetric layout of each single transverse unit of the longitudinal arm, consisting of the juxtaposition of three squares (side 50 Bolognese feet), the central one of which was occupied by the main nave and the side ones divided in half between smaller rectangular naves and paired chapels (fig. 3). On the other hand, the design for the head of the apse, for which the documentation is lacking, remains wholly unknown to us.

The only overall data about the building is its total size, foreseen in the first design that Antonio drafted on *bombicina* paper; it may be obtained from the dimensions of the scale model, which evidently featured a long transept. The masonry model commissioned from the architect was supposed to measure 40 feet by 30 "*et ultra secundum cuncurentem cursum*," i.e. 15.2 × 11.4 meters or more, constituting a veritable walk-through sacellum, erected in a room specially built in the palace "that had belonged to Jacopo de' Pepoli" on Via Castiglione.[15] In addition to making detailed design possible, models of this type were a sort of "rehearsal," a small-scale verification before clients of how the structure would work. A brick model was built as early as 1367 for the dome of Santa Maria del Fiore, while in 1418–19, under Filippo Brunelleschi's direction, the Opera del Duomo of Florence paid a team of workers for a new prototype.[16]

San Petronio was therefore conceived to measure at least 480 × 360 feet, i.e. 182.4 × 136.8 meters. From the model testing stage, on August 8, 1392, we learn that Antonio made it "*ultra ordinamentum et propositum ipsius generalis in augmento laborerii ipsius Ecclesie sive capelle tam in magnitudine ipsius quam in ciborriis et aliis factis per eum in ecclesia*:"[17] that is, the architect created an outline of furnishings, which had not been provided for in the contract, and built a model of greater "magnitude," larger than the 30 × 40 feet specified in the contract. It is likely that, rather than a change of design, which should have been submitted in advance to the church *fabbricieri* and Andrea Manfredi, it was a "*secundum cuncurentem cursum*" increase, i.e. due to the pitch of the bays, which in the drawings had evidently only been calculated approximately. Assuming that Antonio had drawn the entire plan according to the fifty-foot square module indicated above, it seems likely that his project envisaged a building with ten bays along the longitudinal body and seven in the transept.[18] As for the roofing over the crossing, as Supino has pointed out, there was never any mention of a dome. Rather, the contract for building the model specified that it had to be built "*cum quibuscumque portis, fenestris, voltis, capellis, pillastris, turribus et aliis opportunis*."[19] These elements were reiterated in a 1402 document commissioning the painter Jacopo di Paolo to reproduce Antonio's model on a smaller scale, given that it was due for demolition. The new model was supposed to faithfully follow the prototype "*cum tot capellis illic*

14 Gatti 1913, p. 295; Fanti 1983, pp. 17–19; Matteucci 2008, pp. 25–26, 46.

15 Trombetti Budriesi 1994, pp. 67–68 note 29; Gatti 1913, pp. 293–94, 297.

16 Millon 1994, p. 21; documents on the Brunelleschi phase are published in Guasti 1857, pp. 17–26.

17 Trombetti Budriesi 1994, p. 67 note 28. The document was published earlier, albeit with transcription errors, by Gatti 1913, p. 294.

18 Gatti 1913, fig. 1 on pp. 16–17, fig. 4 on pp. 24–25, figs. 7 and 8 on pp. 24–25; Giovannoni 1933, p. 167; Lorenzoni 1983, p. 110.

19 Gatti 1913, pp. 293, 311–12.

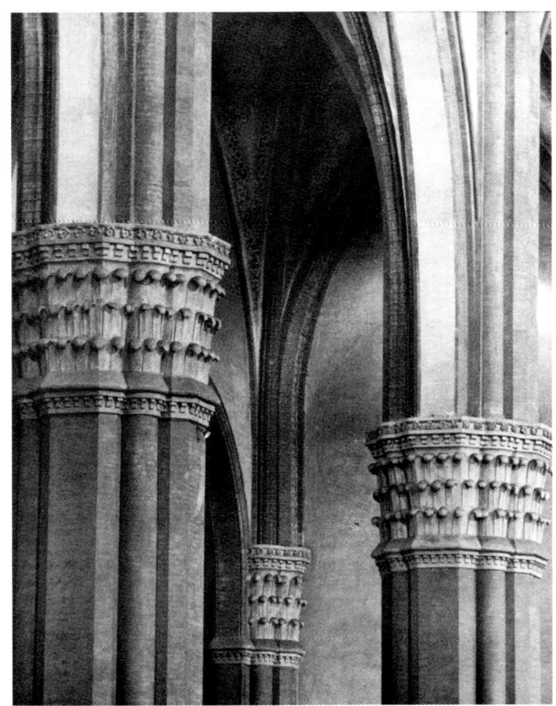

4

Basilica of San Petronio, Bologna, capitals of the central nave pillars

que sunt in dicto hedificio devastando … cum similitudine eorundem intagliorum mediorum fenestrarum et crucis ac campanillorum pro ut sunt in hedificio predicto."[20] So, the crossing was referred to simply as "*crux*," without specifying how it would be roofed.

We are not aware of any other churches designed by Antonio, which could be useful for purposes of comparison and to foster new research. According to surviving documents, it seems that apart from the great Basilica to which he owes his renown, the artist was only marginally involved in sacred architecture: in the now-lost cloisters at Santa Maria dei Servi, where his name was mentioned in 1389, under Andrea da Faenza's supervision, and in the bell tower and sacristy of San Francesco, where building work began in 1397.[21] It has also been suggested that his participation in the design for the Chiesa dei Servi was supported by Andrea Manfredi, given that he worked with him on the plan for San Petronio, but as yet no documents have emerged to confirm this hypothesis.[22]

According to Giuseppe Guidicini, on September 3, 1390 Antonio was sent on a mission to Florence.[23] Although at that time the general drawings for San Petronio had already been drafted, it seems highly unlikely that the architect had never previously visited the Tuscan capital, which is not far from Bologna. The similarities between San Petronio and Santa Maria del Fiore have been highlighted many times: Antonio borrowed the cadence of the aisles in square-based bays, flanked by smaller rectangular naves half their width, from the Florentine Cathedral.[24] Even the multi-styled pillars bear some resemblance, both in their section and the large capitals with three rings of leaves—acanthus in Florence, waterleaf in Bologna—crowned by moldings held up by corbels, which in San Petronio are dotted around in every type of shaped profile[25] (fig. 4).

The real new development that Antonio and Andrea da Faenza ushered in is the design of a large three-nave church with two rows of side chapels, rationally arranged along the aisles from the very beginning rather than the result of disorderly later additions, as was common in north-eastern Italy (fig. 5). This distribution scheme became the most widespread from the fifteenth century onwards, but it was not so at the time. In Bologna in particular, radial chapels were common in the apse, following the early (for Italy) example of San Francesco.

In 1400, engineers Bartolino da Novara and Bernardo da Venezia proposed chapels lining the aisles during Milan Cathedral's tortuous design process. Although not directly pertinent to San Petronio, the document helps us understand the reasons that may have prompted this choice, which are of a static order: "There was a need to eternally fortify this addition … Because the church body buttresses are not as large as would be necessary, considering the width and height of the church, it was decided to reduce the first

20 Ibid., pp. 311–12.

21 For Santa Maria dei Servi, see Branchesi 1992, p. 44; for San Francesco, Gatti 1891, p. 201; Ghidiglia Quintavalle 1961. On the drawings for San Francesco bell tower, once believed to be the work of Antonio di Vincenzo, see now Ceriani Sebregondi, Gritti, Repishti, and Schofield 2019, pp. 68–69.

22 Branchesi 1992, p. 44; Matteucci 2008, pp. 60–61.

23 Guidicini 1870, pp. 360–61.

24 Supino 1909, p. 126; Tuttle 1994.

25 Lorenzoni 1983, p. 60; Matteucci 1987, pp. 30–31.

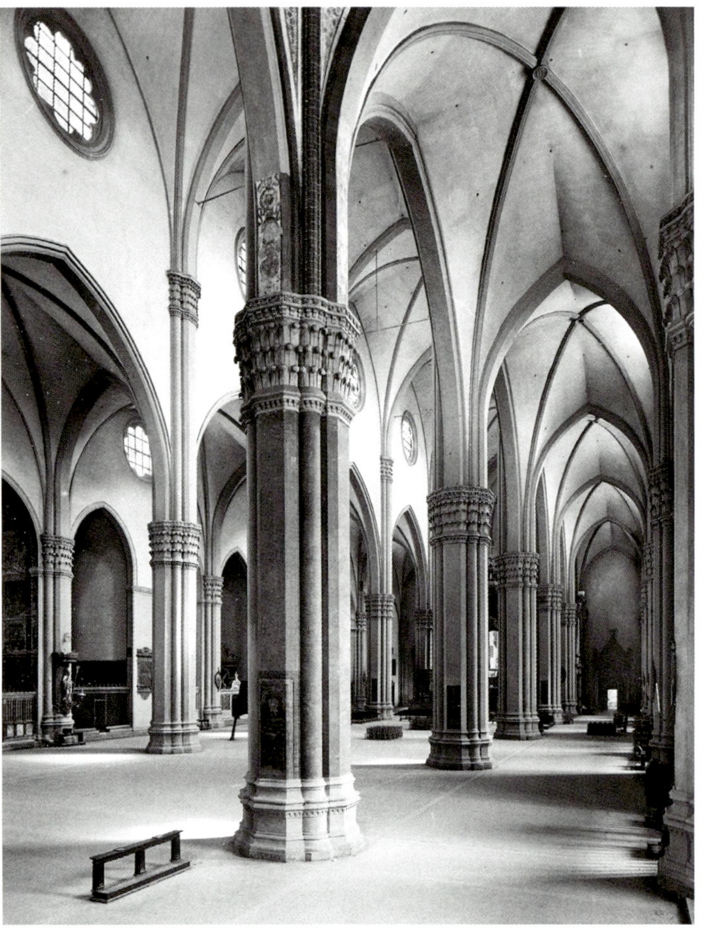

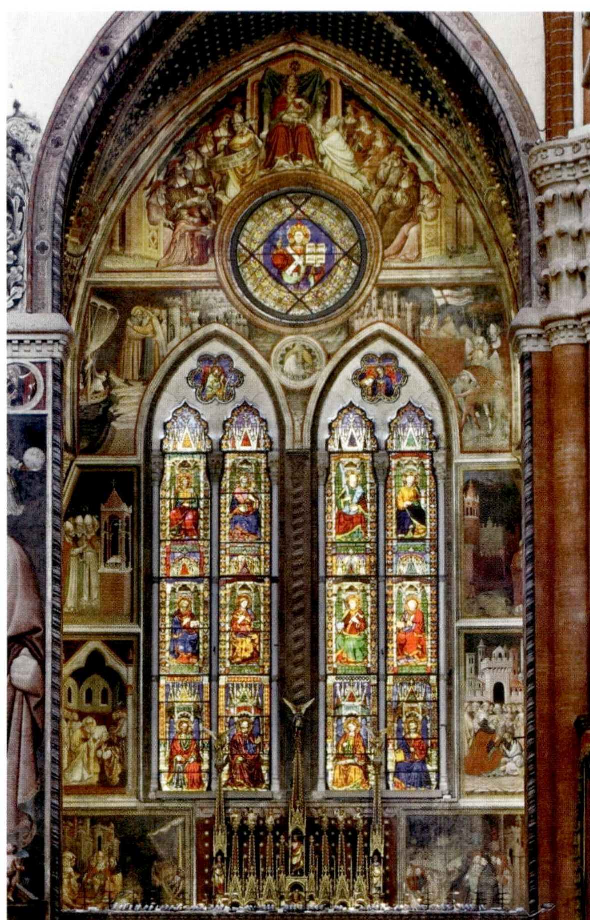

5

Basilica of San Petronio, Bologna, view of the side aisles and the arches leading to the chapels

6

Basilica of San Petronio, Bologna, Bolognini Chapel

nave into the form of chapels with dividing walls between one chapel and the next ... by so doing, great strength shall be added to the other three naves."[26]

So, structural reasons are likely to have played a significant role in the choice made by Antonio di Vincenzo and Andrea da Faenza, who were engaged in designing a church of uncommon size.[27]

But the chapels were also viewed as a source of funding for the work. In a social context in which self-promotion through art and architecture was becoming more and more important every day, chapels inside the city's largest church were highly desirable. In 1395, the church administrators drew up a charter that set out the rates for granting options on chapels. The sums were far from modest: 200 or more liras for the concession to place a sepulcher with one's own painted coat of arms, increasing to a minimum of 300 if the coat of arms was sculpted "*in pariete*," on the wall; at least 500 liras, in addition to an endowment allowing for the celebration of one mass per day, for the concession of rightful ownership, with the obligation to raise an altar with "*tabula seu ancona pulcra*" and provide adequate sacred vestments.[28] Naturally, all works would have to be carried out by concession-holders at their own expense.

26 *Annali* 1877, p. 213. See Romanini 1964, p. 363.
27 Matteucci 1987, p. 30.
28 Fanti 1980, p. 67; Fanti 1983, p. 22.

We do not know whether the church administrators already had in mind buyers to whom they would assign the chapels, but it is significant that the first chapel assigned was given to an important public magistracy, the Dieci di Balia, who back in 1393 obtained rightful ownership of the first chapel on the left, dedicated to Saint George and equipped at the Fabbriceria's expense: an altar would be added the following year and their coats of arms sculpted there in 1397.[29] In 1396, the next chapel was purchased by the Cospi brothers, the sons of a member of the Dieci di Balia; in 1399, the church administrators assigned the third chapel on the left to Francesco Foscherari, paying off a debt of 100 liras to him and awaiting the balance.[30] This was followed, in 1400, by the purchase of patronage of the fourth chapel by Bartolomeo Bolognini, who appeared several times among the church administration officials; soon work began on the polyptych, which was entrusted to Jacopo di Paolo (who had already worked for the *fabbricieri*), and in 1408 Bolognini completed the famous iconographic program for the frescoes later painted by Giovanni da Modena[31] (fig. 6). The Griffoni would only acquire rightful ownership several decades later, after additional lots of chapels were built.[32]

Thanks to the presence of the chapels, by 1419 it was possible without let or hindrance to legally take over the income of the churches demolished or due to be demolished to make way for the new Basilica, including their lay patronage and care of souls,[33] transferring all of their deeds. It is no coincidence that the first four chapels on the left side were originally dedicated to the city temples cleared to allow the first phase of the Basilica construction: Santa Maria dei Rustegani, Santa Tecla dei Lambertazzi, Sant'Ambrogio, and Santa Croce.[34] In 1437–38, as a new set of works began, San Cristoforo and San Geminiano were demolished, while Santa Maria dei Bulgari, destined to be razed to the ground to make way for the long transept, was only demolished around the middle of the sixteenth century, making way for the new Schools premises.[35] Another church scheduled for demolition was Santa Maria Rotonda dei Galluzzi.[36]

The building site

With retroactive effect from March 1, on June 3, 1390 Antonio di Vincenzo was appointed "*Principale caput et magister totius fabrice et constructionis laborerii Ecclesie.*" The architect was indicated as *"vir probus, expertus, praticus, famoxus et subtili ministerio edotatus … hiis omnibus supra enaratis et aliis … plenissime eruditus;*"[37] although the appointment was temporary, it would be reconfirmed over the following years.[38]

29 Gatti 1889, p. 76; Supino 1938, pp. 176–78; Fanti 1980, p. 50; Pini 1994, pp. 87–88; Giacomelli 1994, p. 119.

30 On the Cospi Chapel, see Pini 1994, p. 89 Giacomelli 1994, p. 119; on the Foscherari Chapel, see Pini 1994, pp. 89–92; Giacomelli 1994, p. 122.

31 Supino 1938, pp. 180–90; Pini 1969; Kloten 1987, p. 266; Cavalca 2013, pp. 48–49.

32 See below for more on the construction work.

33 Supino 1932, pp. 321–22; Fanti 1980, pp. 132–34.

34 Guidicini 1870, pp. 362–63, 367–68; Supino 1932, pp. 321–22; Fanti 1980, pp. 132–34; Fanti 1983, pp. 19–20; Pini 1994; Giacomelli 1994. The registry entry for the agreement regarding Santa Tecla dei Lambertazzi (December 23, 1400) appears in Guidicini 1870, p. 365.

35 Lorenzoni 1983, p. 61. On San Geminiano, see Guidicini 1870, pp. 368–69; on Santa Maria dei Bulgari, Guidicini 1872, pp. 57–58.

36 Guidicini 1870, p. 366; Fanti 1980, p. 132.

37 Guidicini 1870, p. 361; Gatti 1913, pp. 295–96, with publication of the document from which the quotes were excertpted; Trombetti Budriesi 1994, pp. 54, 68 note 30.

38 Gatti 1889, p. 73; Gatti 1913, pp. 303–6; Trombetti Budriesi 1994, pp. 54–56.

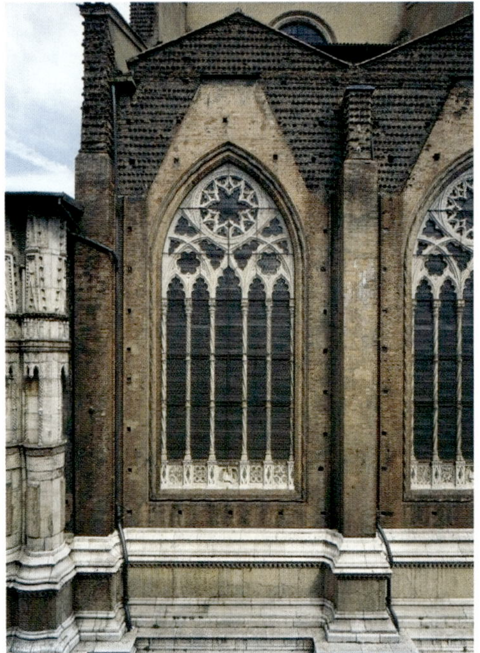

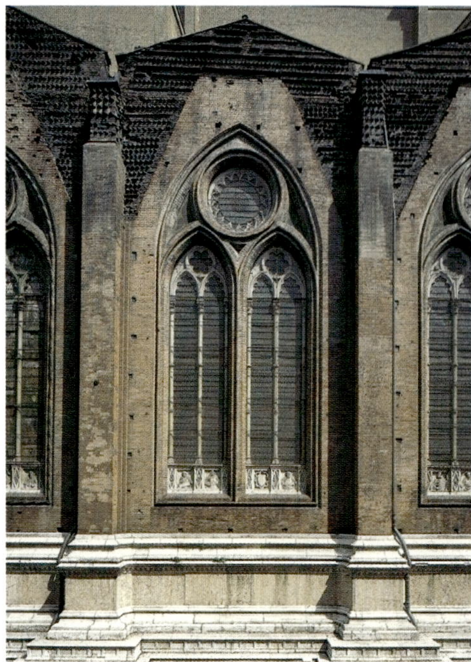

7

Basilica of San Petronio, Bologna, pentaphor

8

Basilica of San Petronio, Bologna, double-mullioned window

Attended by all of the most important civil and religious authorities, the solemn foundation stone-laying ceremony took place four days later.[39]

Work proceeded rapidly after the demolition of buildings that occupied the first site plot. The first span was completed in 1393 under Antonio's very close supervision[40] and the church was immediately officiated. Guidicini dates the first mass celebrated in the Basilica, on a chapel altar,[41] to October 4 (the saint's feast day) 1392. On April 25 the following year, the Municipality stipulated a contract with Brother Bartolomeo, former Bishop of Dragonara, committing him to hold three masses per week at San Petronio in exchange for a reasonable fee.[42] That same year, 1393, the church administrators commissioned Lippo di Dalmasio and Giovanni di Ottonello "*unam tabulam magnam Sanctorum cum multis figuris … positam et deputatam ad altare dicte ecclesie Sancti Petronii*,"[43] leading us to imagine a high altar set up in a church that, at the time, did not appear to have a roof or an apse, although the chapels and naves were cross-vaulted as pillars were raised, as we learn from a later document; each span of the side aisles was covered externally by a single gabled roof according to a document from 1625, as confirmed by marks on the walls found during restoration.[44]

Stonework proceeded all the while. By 1391, stone was being supplied from Istria and Verona for the external pedestal, contracted to the Venetian Girolamo Barozzi (or Baresso) who was later joined by Francesco Dardi, in charge of both supplying the materials and processing them, "*sicut latius evidenter apparet in picturis et dessignatis iam factis et pictis in facie anteriori muri palacii ressidentie Dominorum Antianorum*," with the exception

39 Pietro di Mattiolo ed. 1885, pp. 22–23; Guidicini 1870, p. 363; Gatti 1913, p. 296.

40 Trombetti Budriesi 1994.

41 Guidicini 1870, p. 363. We do not know on what basis the scholar identified the chapel as the one that would later be assigned to the Bolognini (the fourth on the left); however, this would indicate very rapid progress in masonry work.

42 Ibid., p. 364; Fanti 1980, pp. 51–52, 164–65; Trombetti Budriesi 1994, p. 59.

43 Guidicini 1870, p. 363; Volpe 1983, pp. 218–19 for information on the paintings made in San Petronio during those years.

44 Gatti 1889, p. 127; Gatti 1913, p. 314; Piconi 1994, pp. 331–33.

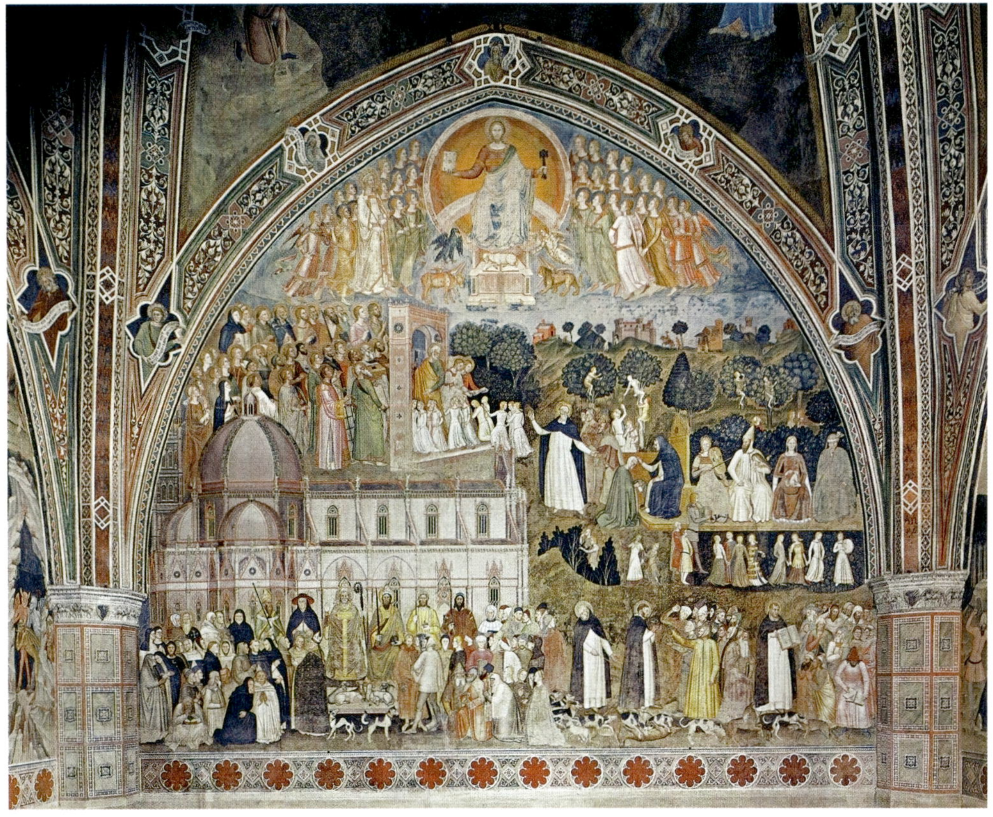

9

Andrea di Bonaiuto, *Militant, Triumphant Church*, fourteenth century. Basilica of Santa Maria Novella, Florence, Cappella degli Spagnoli

of medallion portraits.[45] This contract was renewed in later years (1392, 1393, 1396, 1400).[46] Istrian stone was also supplied for the chapel windows: the contract for the first four windows was signed in December 1393 and two years later, the balance was settled after the supplies duly arrived;[47] in 1397, stone was supplied for the next two windows. The design of the frames—less complex than previously—would appear to have been modified by Antonio di Vincenzo:[48] the elaborate, Nordic-influenced inlay of the pentaphors (fig. 7) was abandoned in favor of an ogive hosting pairs of mullioned windows surmounted by an oculus with a much broader profile, which meant they were less expensive and easier to make (fig. 8).

Despite this simplification, stained-glass windows still played an undisputed lead role on the exterior of the chapels in exposed brickwork (a well-rooted tradition in the Po Valley), most likely ending with a stone cornice on the slopes of the Gothic pediments, interspersed with pinnacles. This was an unprecedented choice: neither the windows below the tympanums planned originally around the triconch at Florence Cathedral (as we see in the famous fresco of the Cappella degli Spagnoli at Santa Maria Novella, fig. 9) nor those on the side of Mantua Cathedral (where stonemasons Jacobello and Pierpaolo dalle Masegne built side chapels from 1395 onwards, in all likelihood inspired by San Petronio, where the latter worked in 1391), managed to take on comparable importance.[49]

45 Gatti 1913, pp. 298–301; Grandi 1983, pp. 125–32.
46 Gatti 1889, pp. 69–74, 77; Gatti 1913, pp. 306–12.
47 Gatti 1889, p. 77; Supino 1910, pp. 31–34; Gatti 1913, pp. 308–10; Trombetti Budriesi 1994, pp. 63, 75 note 91.
48 Gatti 1889, p. 77; Gatti 1913, pp. 310–11; Trombetti Budriesi 1994, p. 63.
49 Supino 1910, p. 10. On Venetians' work on Mantua Cathedral, see Marani 1960.

More stone was purchased for the chapel windows by the Bologna church administrators: in 1398 from Pierpaolo dalle Masegne and then in 1400 once more from Girolamo Barozzi.[50]

Back in February 1393, the painter Jacopo di Paolo had designed six figures for the base of the facade to be sculpted by stonemason Paolo da Venezia[51] (fig. 10). The following month, Antonio traveled to Milan for ten days and then (in April) to Florence for six days to recruit new stonecutters:[52] there was a shortage of skilled stone workers in Bologna, given that there were no quarries nearby from which to extract the valuable building material. After these trips and many others, with messengers being sent specially to the Lombard capital,[53] stonecutters continued to flock to Bologna over the following years, and work proceeded apace on the figures of saints for the four-lobed medallions on the pediment and, later, on the windows (fig. 11).[54]

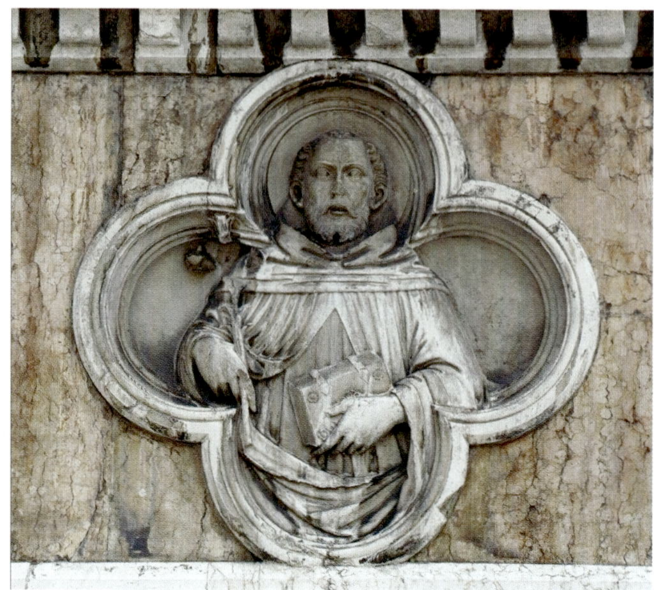

10

Paolo da Venezia, after a drawing by Jacopo di Paolo, *Saint Dominic*. Basilica of San Petronio, Bologna, base of the facade

Finally, in 1401, the first two bays were completed and it was decided that the work accomplished thus far would require a proper closure. Contemporary chronicler Pietro di Mattiolo wrote:

> MCCCCI, taking several days and months of the said year, roofing was constructed for the middle body of the new church of San Petronio, which lies on the edge of the square of the municipality of Bologna, on the top side; this roofing is made of a wooden structure held together by nails and iron rods, and above it is covered by tiles. So long is the roof that it covers eight chapels in length, i.e. four on each side. And above these four chapels, in the middle of the body of the church, a beautiful and large chapel was created with a large altar… enameled with plaster. And before this altar, between two large pillars, a walled parapet of stone and limestone was made as wide as the chapel, with a small door to get in and out, covered inside in baked stone. After the altar, on the right, is a small door from which to access the sacristy and rooms reserved for the church guardian.[55]

San Petronio was therefore covered in trusses and equipped—"in the middle of the body"—with a main chapel, surrounded by a brick parapet, paved in terracotta, and crowned by lathwork. On either side were two gates, which were walled up in 1402 during Gian Galeazzo Visconti's brief rule and then promptly reopened when he died in 1403.[56]

---

50 Gatti 1889, p. 77; Gatti 1913, p. 311; Trombetti Budriesi 1994, pp. 62–63.

51 Gatti 1889, pp. 74–75; Grandi 1983, pp. 125–32.

52 Gatti 1889, p. 75; Trombetti Budriesi 1994, pp. 61, 73 notes 70 and 71. The documents have recently been published in Ceriani Sebregondi, Gritti, Repishti, and Schofield 2019, p. 283.

53 Gatti 1889, pp. 75–77.

54 Ibid., pp. 75–76; Grandi 1983.

55 Pietro di Mattiolo ed. 1885, pp. 92–93. A blank space was left in line with the number of feet for how high the main chapel parapet was. On this chronicler and his work, see Quaquarelli 1993, pp. 146–52.

56 Pietro di Mattiolo ed. 1885, pp. 130–31.

11

Basilica of San Petronio, Bologna, stone base of the facade

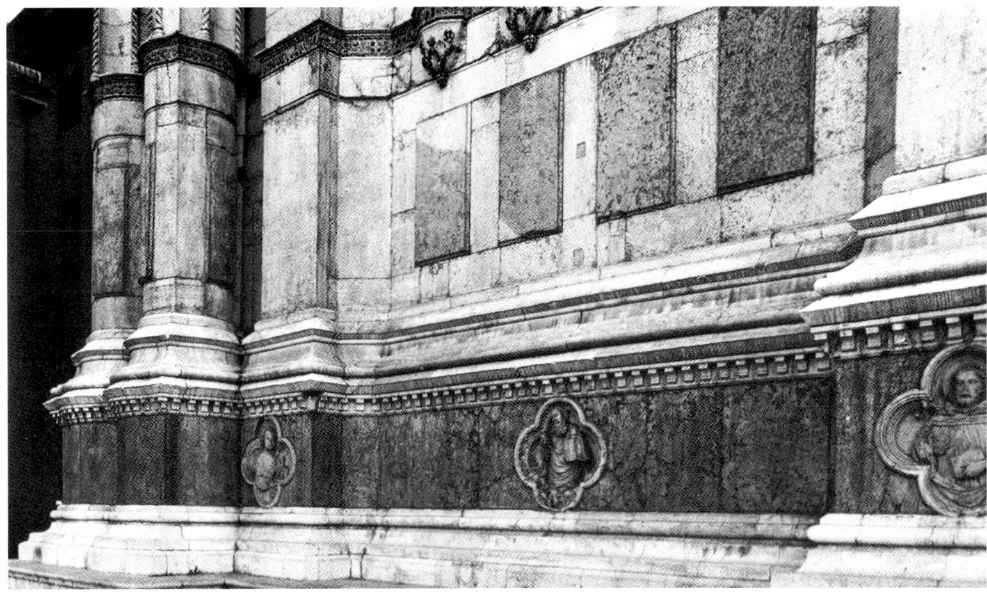

Antonio remained alive just long enough to see completion of this reduced version of the church he designed; then he died some time between October 1401 and the summer of the following year.[57]

On September 21, 1402 the church administrators commissioned painter Jacopo di Paolo to make a model of the church on *bombicina* paper glued onto the wood, erected on planking of about 10 × 10 feet: a smaller-scale version of the one Antonio built in masonry, which was destined for demolition probably because it was too cumbersome.[58] The practice of gluing paper onto wood to show details drawn in ink that would have cost too much and taken too long to be carved became rather widespread over the centuries, including for models of great importance, such as Antonio da Sangallo's famous one for Saint Peter's (1539–64), where the coffers in the intrados of the transept and nave barrel vaults were fashioned using this technique.[59] We do not know exactly when this model of San Petronio was lost: however, an attachment to the "concept" shown in the primitive design for the Basilica continued to remain alive in the Bolognese community, even if we cannot know for how long true knowledge of it actually endured.[60] By way of reference, later contracts always indicated the portions that had already been built and the model was no longer mentioned, while new models were repeatedly prepared for the facade, none of which were ever built.

After the architect's death, in part as a consequence of a political upheaval that brought about the end of the Government of the People and the Guilds, all work was suspended. To make matters worse, probably a little after 1403, the papal legate and then anti-pope Baldassarre Cossa stepped in and took over all of the Fabbriceria's

57 Matteucci 1987, pp. 50–51 note 1.

58 Guidicini 1870, p. 366; Gatti 1889, pp. 77–78; Gatti 1913, pp. 311–12. See above.

59 Millon 1994, p. 40. Another example is the model for Como Cathedral: see Repishti 2018, pp. 143–47.

60 See the memorial addressed to Cardinal Legate Capranica in 1463—a crucial moment for the works—by one Achille Angelelli, who rails against those keen to distance themselves from the church's "*desegno vechio*," the old design (Fanti 1980, pp. 116–17; see also Matteucci 1994); this phrase, however, should be referred to the original proposal for a Basilica of giant dimensions, rather than any one specific design.

assets, in particular the materials prepared for the construction and the annual income supporting the work: "*et opus omnino cessari fecit*."[61]

After John XXIII was deposed, work resumed in 1418, albeit without the momentum of the initial construction phase.[62] On March 25, 1425 Jacopo della Quercia was commissioned to build the *Porta magna*, which at this time captured the church administrators' attention.[63]

Meanwhile, work continued apace on the decoration of the chapels. The chapel dedicated to Saint George was frescoed beginning in 1420 by Giovanni da Modena with scenes from the Old and New Testament;[64] later on, Eugene IV donated the "Table of Saints" for the altar.[65] In 1438, Raffaello Foscherari obtained that a share of municipal taxes be destined for embellishment and worship in his chapel, which was dedicated to Saint Bridget.[66] The following year, the *fabbricieri* ordered that the chapel, "*que est immediate iuxta capellam illorum de Bologninis versus plateam Communis Bononiae ornetur picturis, fenestris vitreis, tabulis*."[67] In 1451, Cardinal Bessarione stripped the Foscherari of their privileges and transferred the dedication to Saint Bridget to the second chapel on the right, together with Saint Thecla.[68] After prerogatives over the old chapel had been rescinded, ornamentation work began immediately: glass was ordered in, the choir was commissioned from Tommasino da Baiso in 1457, and a contract was signed for frescoes in 1459, which was passed on from hand to hand without ever being executed.[69]

In the meantime, work began on raising a new span. In 1437, while the capital for the third pillar on the left was in the making,[70] the churches of San Geminiano and San Cristoforo were being demolished to free up the space needed for enlargement.[71] On January 26, 1441 it was decreed that four new chapels would be completed within two years.[72] On May 21 the following year, a contract was signed with the masons Paolo di Tebaldo Liazzari and his partners; the document states that by that date, the central supports for the third span had already been erected, but the side walls, their pillars, and the access arches to the four chapels had not yet been completely raised. The contract provided for construction of the missing parts and vaults for the side aisles, as well as roofing the nave with trusses. Once these works had been completed, "the walls that hold the naves together on all sides" were to be demolished, and subsequently rebuilt "at the end of new work."[73]

---

61 Guidicini 1870, p. 366; Gatti 1889, pp. 78–79; Fanti 1980, pp. 128–29. On Baldassarre Cossa, in brief see Uginet 2001.

62 Gatti 1889, p. 79.

63 Gatti 1913, pp. 312–14. At the very least, Bellosi 1983 and Beck 1991 should be added to the bibliography cited in note 4.

64 Supino 1938, p. 177.

65 Ibid., p. 176.

66 Ibid., pp. 190–91.

67 Supino 1909, p. 32; Lorenzoni 1983, p. 61. Nevertheless, they both misconstrued the location of the chapel, identifying it as the fifth, which at that time had not yet been built.

68 Pini 1994, pp. 89–92; Cavalca 2013, pp. 49–50.

69 Supino 1938, pp. 190–95; Cavalca 2103, p. 50.

70 Supino 1913, p. 132; Supino 1938, p. 165; Lorenzoni 1983, p. 68.

71 Guidicini 1870, p. 369.

72 Ibid.

73 Gatti 1913, p. 314. See Supino 1913, p. 132; Lorenzoni 1983, p. 68.

However, progress was slow due to a snowfall that caused the roof to collapse the following year, requiring a rebuild in 1444.[74] In 1445, a new model was commissioned for the facade: evidently, there was a desire to complete the church, albeit temporarily.[75]

In February the following year, outstanding amounts owed to Paolo di Tebaldo's company were finally paid.[76] It is clear from both the contract and the balance payment that in 1446 only the third span had been completed, not the fourth, as Gatti claimed in his dispute with Supino.[77] Arbitrators who assessed the works ruled that they should be enhanced: the vaults and the east side wall reinforced, along with the addition of iron rods ("*coregie de fero*") in the trusses above the new vaults. Then followed payment "for the expense of demolishing and rebuilding from scratch the arch across the church of San Petronio and the wall below and above it, and for the flat wall to go above said arch ... for the expense of dismantling and rebuilding and all things necessary for the two wall elements that contain and enclose the church in the middle..."[78]

The two walls dismantled and rebuilt coincide with "the walls that keep the naves closed on all sides" mentioned in the 1441 contract: the term used for walls, "*sponde*," indicates that they were not full-height walls but parapets that had to keep the naves "closed on all sides." Consequently, they cannot be the church's end walls, as assumed until now, but rather low walls enclosing the space of the final span, used to create room for the main chapel as indicated in the 1401 plan. It is no coincidence, therefore, that in the months immediately following the choir was roofed over, once again with lath-work.[79] The southern closing wall was, on the other hand, indicated as "the arch across the church ... and the wall below and above it," which was indeed dismantled in the previous position to be rebuilt to the south. Clearly the temporary wall was reinforced by an arch to stiffen the structure.[80]

Over the following years, work continued apace on foundations for pillars and chapels, still "*vigliando la sira*," that is, working late into the night; then structures began to be raised above ground.[81] In 1454, payments were recorded for fitting out the main chapel, which had been built in 1446: work was underway to "arrange and redo the monsignor's seat in the choir" and to "paint and decorate the ceiling of the main altar at San Petronio;" in 1454, the painter Antonio da Venezia was paid "for a figure of Saint Petronius to be placed before the altar and an antependium."[82] Meanwhile, works for raising the pillars, walls, vaults, and windows continued uninterruptedly until 1460,[83] and in 1457–58, activity was in full swing on the new bell tower.[84]

In November 1459, the stonecutters Albertino Rusconi of Mantua and Domenico di Antonio of Milan were commissioned to make the pediments for four chapels "*jam*

---

74 Guidicini 1870, p. 370; Supino 1909, pp. 106–7; Lorenzoni 1983, p. 68.

75 Gatti 1914, pp. 25, 83–84.

76 Ibid, pp. 25–26.

77 Gatti 1913, p. 315; Supino 1913; Sighinolfi 1913; Gatti 1914, pp. 28–39; Supino 1932, p. 324; Lorenzoni 1983, p. 74.

78 Gatti 1914, pp. 25–26.

79 Ibid, pp. 27–28.

80 A temporary wall consisting of an arch closed by a partition made partly of bricks and partly of wooden planking would at a later date enclose the nave of Sant'Andrea in Mantua while work was underway on the transept. The image has come down to us in a drawing from 1580: see F. Cerchiari in *Leon Battista Alberti* 2006, pp. 512–13. In Alberti's church, however, the arch corresponds to the projection of the nave barrel vault.

81 Gatti 1914, pp. 28–34 (quote on p. 31).

82 Ibid., p. 35.

83 Ibid., pp. 36–51.

84 Ibid., pp. 40–43.

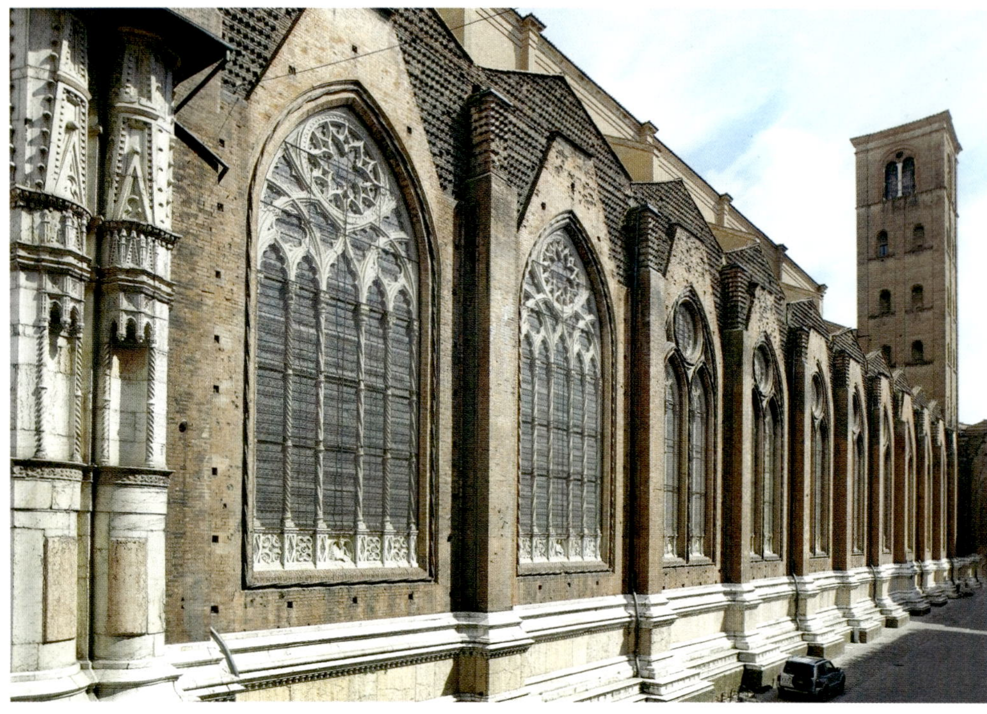

12

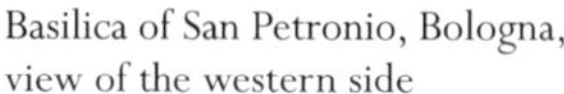
Basilica of San Petronio, Bologna, view of the western side

inceptarum et nondum finitarum, positarum versus sero [west], *iuxta sex capellas jam constructas et finitas*." The following year, they were commissioned to undertake the same work in the chapels opposite, "*versus mane*," toward the east;[85] we may therefore be certain that in the early 1480s, the church had been extended to include ten chapels on each side (fig. 12).

Indeed, in May 1455 expenses were recorded for decorating the altar dedicated to Saint Anthony, which was placed in its location in 1458: if it corresponds with the current one, that means the ninth chapel on the right had already been built and roofed by then.[86]

Work almost reached the intensity of the initial phase, given that in a little over a decade the structure of two bays was built, bringing the church to a total depth of five. Beginning in 1451, funding of the works received a boost from Pope Nicholas V, who had formerly been Bishop of Bologna and was well aware of the problems of the large construction site. Reiterating his will in three successive bulls, he declared privileges and exemptions to be forfeited and abolished all useless church administration offices, which were the source of unnecessary salary disbursements.[87]

Building work continued on aisles and chapels until 1463,[88] but the regular arrival of windows for the oculi in the side aisle walls, above the chapels, shows that by now the work was really focused on the finishing touches.[89]

New patronage was issued. Some chapels were granted to important corporations: the first was to the Guild of Notaries, which in 1459 bought the chapel of the Holy Cross (the fourth on the right); four years later, the Butchers, the closest guild to the

85 Guidicini 1870, p. 370; Supino 1932, p. 323.
86 Gatti 1914, p. 38.
87 Fanti 1980, pp. 148–49.
88 Gatti 1914, pp. 45–57.
89 Ibid., pp. 51, 54, 56.

Bentivoglio family, who were then firmly in power, took possession of the tenth chapel on the same side, dedicated to Saint Peter the martyr.[90]

Another chapel—the tenth on the left, dedicated to Saint Barbara—was reserved for the Magistracy of the Sixteen, granted the benefit in 1463, and equipped with stained glass windows in 1473 and with a grille sculpted by Antonio da Firenze in 1476; finally, the following year Tommaso Garelli was paid in full for the altarpiece and Giovanni da Ravenna for painting its encasement.[91]

A surviving inscription at the Basilica reveals that in 1460, the four chapels on the right were completed at the behest of Cardinal Legate Angelo Capranica—a key figure in subsequent progress on site—and thanks to input from Nicolò Sanuti, Giovanni Guidotti, Giovanni Bianchetti, and Bartolomeo Cospi.[92] Sanuti's chapel is identified with the eighth, dedicated to Saint Christopher, for which a glass oculus was purchased in 1476.[93]

On several occasions the chapels were plastered, whitewashed, paved, and fitted with altars to ensure overall decorum even where they had not been assigned and, in consequence, fitted and furnished.[94]

When these masonry works were completed, thoughts turned again to a facade worthy of the church. In January 1463, Agostino di Duccio, who had already worked on the interior decoration of the Malatesta Temple in Rimini, and had recently completed the stone facade for the Oratory of San Bernardino in Perugia, was commissioned to make a model.[95] The following year, a limited reorganization of the existing elevation was carried out, as we may see from a payment receipt made out to "master Antonio d'Agostino, who repaired the facade of San Petronio and walled up the windows and closed up all holes." In 1469, "one key was added to the wall toward the piazza to attach the marble when the facade is constructed" and a glass oculus for the opening above the *Porta magna*.[96] But that is as far as works went.

Again, once construction finished, preparation work began on the main chapel.[97] Since, as we mentioned, by 1470, the flooring of the main nave extended for 198 feet (75.2 meters) from the facade to the altar, occupying the space of four 50-foot bays, it is clear that the presbytery was placed in the fifth bay, in consonance with the choice made in 1401 and 1446. Now, however, the layout was far more challenging, due to the presence of a veritable faux architecture within the church's walled enclosure.

According to documents relating to the first two versions of the presbytery, it was located in the final span of the nave, which was separated from the side aisles by walled parapets: this central area, which probably had a straight end that formed part of the southern wall enclosing the entire church, housed the Bishop's seat and the altar, covered by lathwork.

Work undertaken in 1464, on the other hand, included construction inside the wall envelope of a large "*nicchia storata*," that is, made out of wattle and then painted

90 Giacomelli 1994, respectively pp. 111–12 and 117; Pini 1994, p. 97.

91 Gatti 1914, p. 83; Supino 1938, pp. 195–96. See also Cavalca 2013, pp. 323–24. For more on the benefit, Giacomelli 1994, p. 127.

92 Fanti 1980, p. 159.

93 Gatti 1914, p. 82.

94 Ibid, pp. 64–70, 75.

95 Gatti 1889, pp. 14–15, 90. See Belli Barsali 1960; Matteucci 1994, p. 207.

96 Gatti 1914, pp. 65–66, 67–68.

97 Ibid., pp. 58–81.

"*in calzina*" (with lime) by Zanobi of Florence[98] with fake tapestries on the walls and God the Father and the Virgin annunciate painted on the vault.[99] Probably this structure is to be identified with the one that stood above the fifth span, which indeed was made with lathwork. From now on, the main chapel would be known as the "*truna*" (tribune) and the vault as the "*chupola*" (dome), a word used frequently in the fifteenth and sixteenth centuries to refer to the quarter-sphere calottes of niches and chapels.[100]

Unfortunately, documents available to date fail to reveal much about the construction of this particular small-windowed structure. Above all, it is unclear whether the wall behind it was rectilinear or followed its curved shape, making it protrude from the bottom of the building. Very common for false ceilings but much less so for vertical structures, this procedure—which required a large number of master craftsmen at San Petronio—was related to techniques developed for complex ephemeral architecture erected for countless public events, held on a regular basis and actually transfiguring entire cities. The span of the nave was instead separated from the side aisles by a "*murello*" (low wall).[101]

It's interesting to note that the advancement of works went hand in hand with reorganization of officiating at the Basilica. Given that the church was "*a pauco tempo mirifice adaucta ... et admirable opere constructa*," in October 1463 the Sixteen donated a share of municipal taxes to pay for the salaries of clergy and furnishings; authorized by the Pope, Cardinal Capranica converted funds from a pious legacy intended for various uses to cover the appointment of canons, chaplains, and clerics.[102]

Not long afterwards, San Petronio would become a collegiate church. Given that building work had finally reached an advanced stage, the time came for a stable organization of worship, and this made furnishings a matter of some urgency. On January 20, 1467 a contract was drawn up for the canons' stalls, as shown in a sketch of the seating, subsequently modified during execution, which has survived to this day.[103] Work was begun immediately by marquetry artist Agostino de' Marchi from Crema, a follower of the Canozi master carvers and himself a "master of soft art woodwork," who began working at the Basilica in 1458 on half of the choir in Saint Bridget's chapel, taking over from Tommasino da Baiso after his death.[104] It was during construction of the main furnishings, on June 19, 1473 that Agostino received the balance for the *capsa* of the Griffoni Polyptych.[105] His relationship with Francesco del Cossa was well established, given that the Ferrarese painter also provided some drawings for the backs of the choir stalls.[106]

From the very beginning, the choir was laid out in "Roman style," that is, with the officiant facing the faithful so that the latter had an unimpeded view of the altar, in accordance with the innovations implemented by Pope Nicholas V in the Lateran and

98 Ibid., pp. 60–61.

99 Ibid., pp. 59–60.

100 Ibid., p. 62. For use of the term "*truina*" to indicate the apse—in this case at the Cathedral of Ferrara between the fourteenth and sixteenth century—see *Chronicon Estense* ed. 1937, p. 111; Cittadella 1868, pp. 53, 57.

101 Ibid., p. 73 (payment "for eight windows in glass—four in the chapel for the choir and four in the chapel for the organ toward east") and p. 77. See Gatti 1914, p. 75.

102 Fanti 1980, p. 168.

103 Zucchini 1942, p. 162; D'Amico 1990, pp. 62–63; Romano and Ferretti 1984.

104 Gatti 1914, pp. 63, 65, 69, 74,75, 79. See Romano and Ferretti 1984, pp. 269–76. For Saint Bridget's choir, Romano and Ferretti 1984, p. 269.

105 Supino 1938, p. 196 and, more recently, Cecilia Cavalca's contribution on the Griffoni Polyptych in this book.

106 Gatti 1914, p. 76; Supino 1938, p. 199; Romano and Ferretti 1984, pp. 270–72.

13

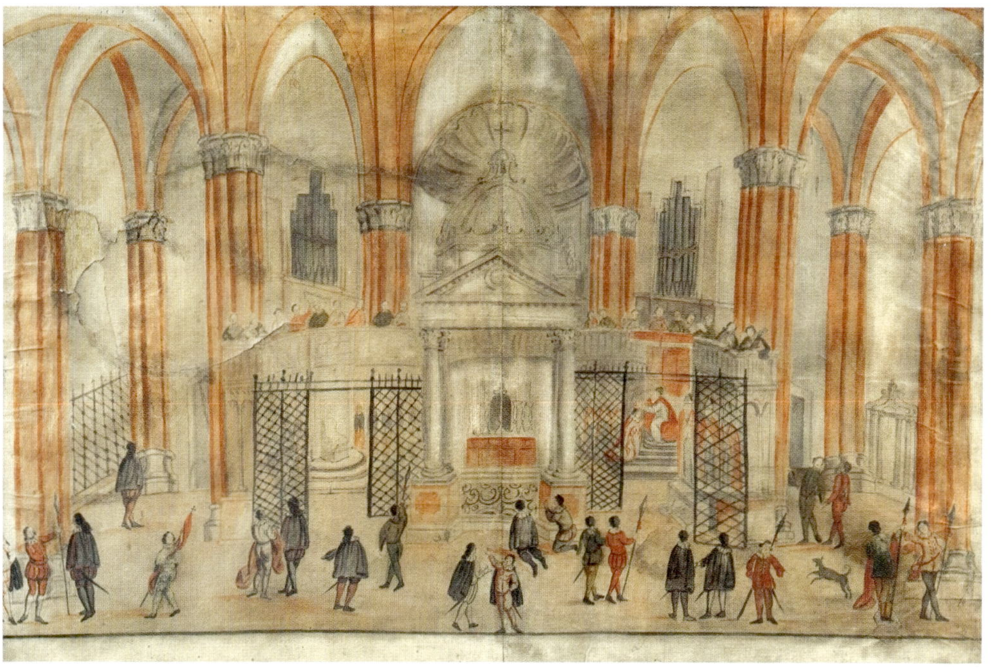

Coronation of Charles V at San Petronio, watercolor drawing. Archivio di Stato di Bologna

Vatican.[107] Indeed, at Saint Peter's the Pope had commissioned Bernardo Rossellino to build a new apse far larger than Constantine's in order to place the papal throne and the curia stalls facing the altar-table and nave.[108] If such a configuration was still rather uncommon when it was chosen for San Petronio, over the following decades it would become popular across Central and Northern Italy, in particular in Emilia and Veneto, far in advance of Council of Trent prescriptions.[109]

In June 1474, by which time the stalls for the canons had essentially been completed, Agostino was commissioned to manufacture seating reserved for the *Gonfaloniere di Giustizia*, the Elders, and the Judges, which were completed five years later.[110] At the same time, he helped in building the organ, for which Lorenzo da Prato was commissioned in 1470.[111] In 1474, the organ's supporting structure was erected to the east of the presbytery; it was painted by Tommaso Garelli, along with the instrument's shutters and choir pulpit.[112]

To confirm that the layout of the tribune was finally being completed, soon afterwards payment was made for the design of the iron gate, which would be erected over the next two years.[113]

An image of the main chapel—at least its fundamental features—may be found in pictorial representations that date back to the late sixteenth century, made to record major events inside the Basilica during the Cinquecento, notably the coronation

107 See the documents dated to around 1660 that describe the old choir prior to construction of the new apse (Gatti 1913, pp. 333–36).

108 de Blaauw 2006, pp. 43–49; Frommel 1995–97.

109 Sambin De Norcen 2018, p. 54; Ceccarelli, Marchesi, and Sambin De Norcen 2019, p. 142.

110 Guarino 1990.

111 Gatti 1914, pp. 70, 74, 75. On the work carried out by master Agostino, see Romano and Ferretti 1984, p. 273.

112 Gatti 1914, pp. 74, 76, 78, 81. On Tommaso Garelli and his activities at San Petronio, see Benati 1984, pp. 143–51; Cavalca 2013, pp. 64, 127–33, 323–24, no. 8.

113 Gatti 1914, pp. 78, 79.

of Charles V and Clement VIII's visits to Bologna.[114] The space in fact did not seem to have undergone substantial changes from its late fifteenth-century architectural configuration until the mid-seventeenth century, when the tribune was demolished and rebuilt after the new sixth span, in the form that we see today; what changed, albeit only in part, are the furnishings.[115]

Obviously, we cannot consider these images as objective surveys: they are, on the contrary, rather sketchy backgrounds, and we must not forget the purpose for which they were made, which was to convey the setting in a recognizable way. According to these pictures, the iron grating had two symmetrical openings and—in the middle and across it—a ciborium, most likely the one designed by Vignola in 1547 to overlook the altar. The *Coronation of Charles V* (fig. 13) highlights the location of the main chapel, set between the side aisles and the chapels sketched in rapid perspective: the pillars, the cross vaults and the gates are all clearly visible. The *Visit of Clement VIII* (fig. 14), which frames a far more restricted space, underlines the elevation of the presbyterial area, accessible via steps, the curve of the choir stalls (which may be made out, albeit in a deformed perspective), and the bare walls that close the aisles, including the doors to access from the outside and the windows above, whose existence is chronicled in documents. There were two organs now (the second was added in 1596–97) facing one another above the choir, the position of the original one having been modified.[116] One element that we are unable to date with certainty is the large shell in the apse calotte (which was probably made of stucco), since the documents published by Gatti do not mention it at all. Shells became a widespread motif in the early part of the century, including in the niches designed by Donatello; in architecture, it is found in the blind tribunes of Brunelleschi's dome and would not be adopted in an apse until the building of Faenza Cathedral (1492–93).

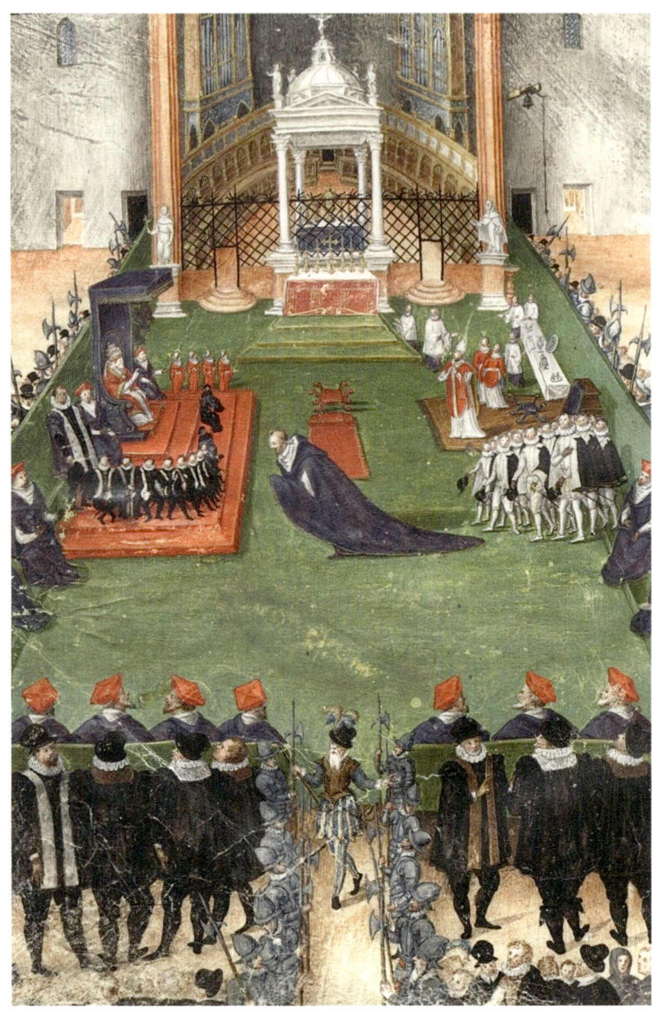

14

Pope Clement VIII Receives Tributes from the Senate at San Petronio, miniature. Archivio di Stato di Bologna, Consiglio degli Anziani, *Insignia*, vol. II, f. 203b

In the 1480s, the eleventh chapels were built on both sides beyond the church's southern wall (at that time used as service rooms by church administrators), along with part of the roof and the bell tower we see today.[117] A payment was made to Vincenzo Cabrini on February 6, 1481 "for four glass windows for the Griffoni Chapel:" this proves

114 Archivio di Stato di Bologna, respectively, watercolor, XVI–XVII century; Consiglio degli Anziani, *Insignia*, vol. II, f. 203b. The *Coronation of Charles V* was published in Prodi 1944, pp. 154–55; *Clemente VIII's visit to Bologna* was published in Gatti 1913, fig. 57 on pp. 244–45. Both appear in Fanti 2008, pp. 252–53.

115 Gatti 1913, pp. 326–36; Romano and Ferretti 1984, p. 274.

116 On the windows, see Gatti 1914, p. 57. On the new sixteenth-century furnishings, see Fanti 2008, pp. 252–54. Lorenzo da Prato's organ was originally located in a chapel: see Gatti 1914, pp. 73, 76 and note 101 above. On the two instruments, see Mischiati and Tagliavini 1984. On the subsequent iconography of the main chapel at San Petronio, see Fanti 2008, pp. 250–51. I thank the author for pointing this out.

117 Fanti 2008, pp. 84–102.

15

Attributed to Arduino Arriguzzi, wooden model for the completion of San Petronio, c. 1514. Museo di San Petronio, Bologna

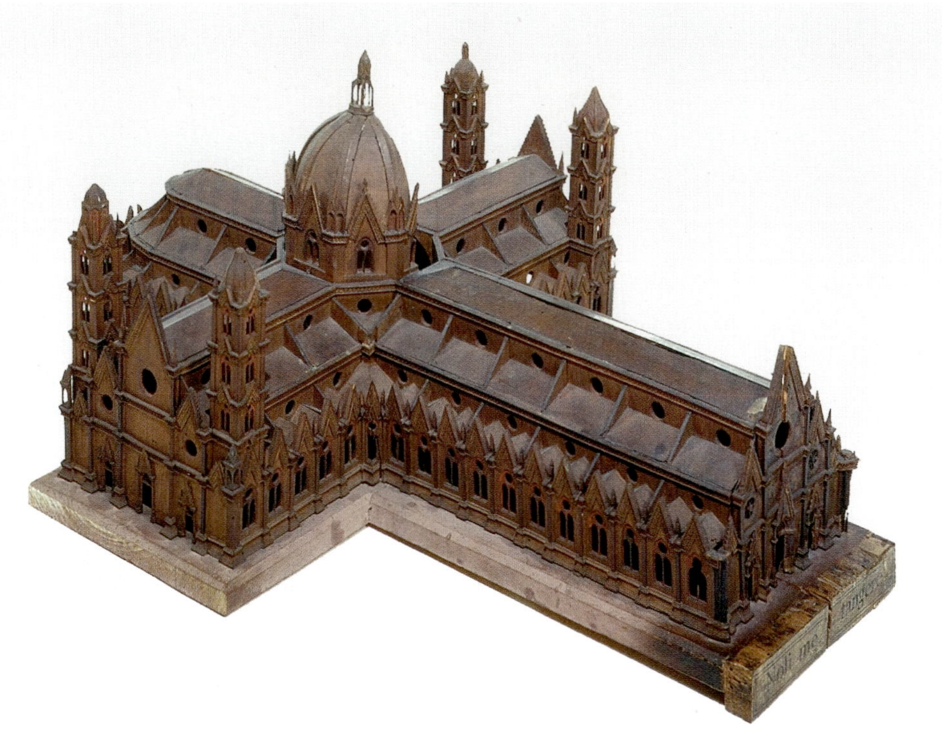

that work on furnishing the sacellum continued over the entire decade.[118] As the centuries passed, like the ones in the other chapels, these windows were walled up, and then reopened and fitted with colorless glass some time between the late nineteenth century and the 1930s (1896 for the Griffoni Chapel).[119]

Throughout the sixteenth century, the projects for the completion of the Basilica became increasingly ambitious, which led to design buildings even larger than the one conceived by Antonio di Vincenzo and, in consequence, destined to inevitable failure: a model attributed to Arduino Arriguzzi is tangible evidence of this (fig. 15).[120]

Only in the mid-seventeenth century did the pragmatic spirit that had characterized construction in the late fifteenth century reappear. At the end of interminable debate, the high vaults of the nave and the new, permanent, main chapel were built.[121] Later developments did not regard the architectural structure, but rearrangements and decorative alterations.[122]

Such was the fate of the Griffoni Chapel, whose polyptych—which survived the changes made to church structures—was dismantled between 1725 and 1731 "to make a modern ornament" in its stead.[123]

118 Fanti 2008, p. 90. See also Zucchini 1917, p. 89.

119 Cavazza 1905; Zucchini 1959, pp. 54–58.

120 Lorenzoni 1983, pp. 90–96.

121 Gatti 1913, pp. 320–36; Lorenzoni 1983, pp. 96–118.

122 On refurbishment of the chapels, see Giacomelli 1994.

123 Cavalca 2013, pp. 138–41 and p. 383 with the document from which the quote is taken. See also Cavalca's contribtion in this book.

THE GRIFFONI FAMILY AND THE FABBRICA OF SAN PETRONIO: FAMILY AND POLITICAL REASONS BEHIND THE COMMISSION FOR THE GRIFFONI POLYPTYCH

Mario Fanti

The only document in the Fabbriceria of San Petronio archives in Bologna that refers directly to the so-called "Griffoni Polyptych" is an accounting entry dated July 9, 1473 regarding the payment of 6 liras by the officials of the Fabbrica to Agostino de' Marchi of Crema, the master woodworker who had built the *capsa* (frame or container) for the *tabula* of Floriano Griffoni's altar, located in a chapel of the Basilica: "Furthermore, the officials promised to give master woodworker Messer Agostino de Marchis of Crema six liras for the frame he made around Floriano Griffoni's altarpiece."[1]

The document was discovered by scholar Francesco Filippini, who informed the renowned art historian Igino Benvenuto Supino. The latter mentioned it in a paper,[2] where he did not fail to grasp the significance of the information it contained—the name of the altar's patron (Floriano Griffoni) and a *terminus ante quem* for the paintings contained therein, for which Agostino de' Marchi[3] had already built the *capsa*, which the administrators of the Fabbrica (so-called *fabbricieri*) had promised as a gift to Floriano and for which, on July 19, 1473 they paid an amount of 6 liras. As a consequence, the painted parts of the Griffoni Polyptych had most certainly already been completed before July 1473. This allowed correcting a prior hypothesis of Supino, who, based on Floriano's will dated August 6, 1483, had speculated that the polyptych could not date before then. However, Supino had to correct himself later on, since the will makes no reference to the acquisition of the chapel at San Petronio, which is mentioned instead only in connection with the appointment of an officiating priest, who had to be designated, on Griffoni's proposal, by the Bologna Archiepiscopal Curia.[4] Hence, Antonio

1 "*Item magistro Augustino de Marchis de Crema magistro lignaminis libras sex quatrinorum pro capsa quam fecit circa tabulam altaris Floriani de Griffonibus quam promiserunt officiales ei donare.*" Archivio della Fabbriceria di San Petronio, Bologna (hereafter ASP), folder 558, no. 3, Quaderno di cassa 1473–1479, f. 13v; it bears a seventeenth-century title ("Vacchetta de mandati della Fabrica 1473 1479"), thus the book has sometimes been referred to as "Mandati." At f. 14r, under August 2, 1473, another payment of 5 liras to Agostino de' Marchi is recorded: although the reason is not specified, it was probably a second instalment for the Griffoni altar's *capsa* (figs. 1 and 2).

2 Supino 1938, p. 196, in which the text of the document omits "*quam*" after the words "*de Griffonibus*." We share the opinion of of Torella ([1985–87] 1988, p. 51 note 4), who remarked that the meaning of the document changes without the "*quam*." Later, that document was mentioned by many scholars, including Benati 1984, pp. 168–69, in which, due to a clear transcription error, the date is July 14 instead of July 19.

3 Agostino de' Marchi of Crema is known for other woodworks at San Petronio, including the choir in the apse and the chairs of the Chapel of San Sebastiano, carved between 1467 and 1495.

4 Floriano Griffoni's will dated August 6, 1483 is referred to by Supino (1938, p. 196) without identifying the location of the document. This can be read in Archivio di Stato di Bologna (hereafter ASBo), Archivio Fantuzzi Ceretoli, b. 8, no. 43, certified copy by Filippo Sacchi aka Avenante (active between 1543–83) from the deeds of Giacomo Boccaferri; an uncertified paper copy from the late seventeenth century or early eighteenth is attached to this parchment copy. It was partially published by I. Negretti in Cavalca 2013, p. 381. Three more copies of the will, from the eighteenth century,

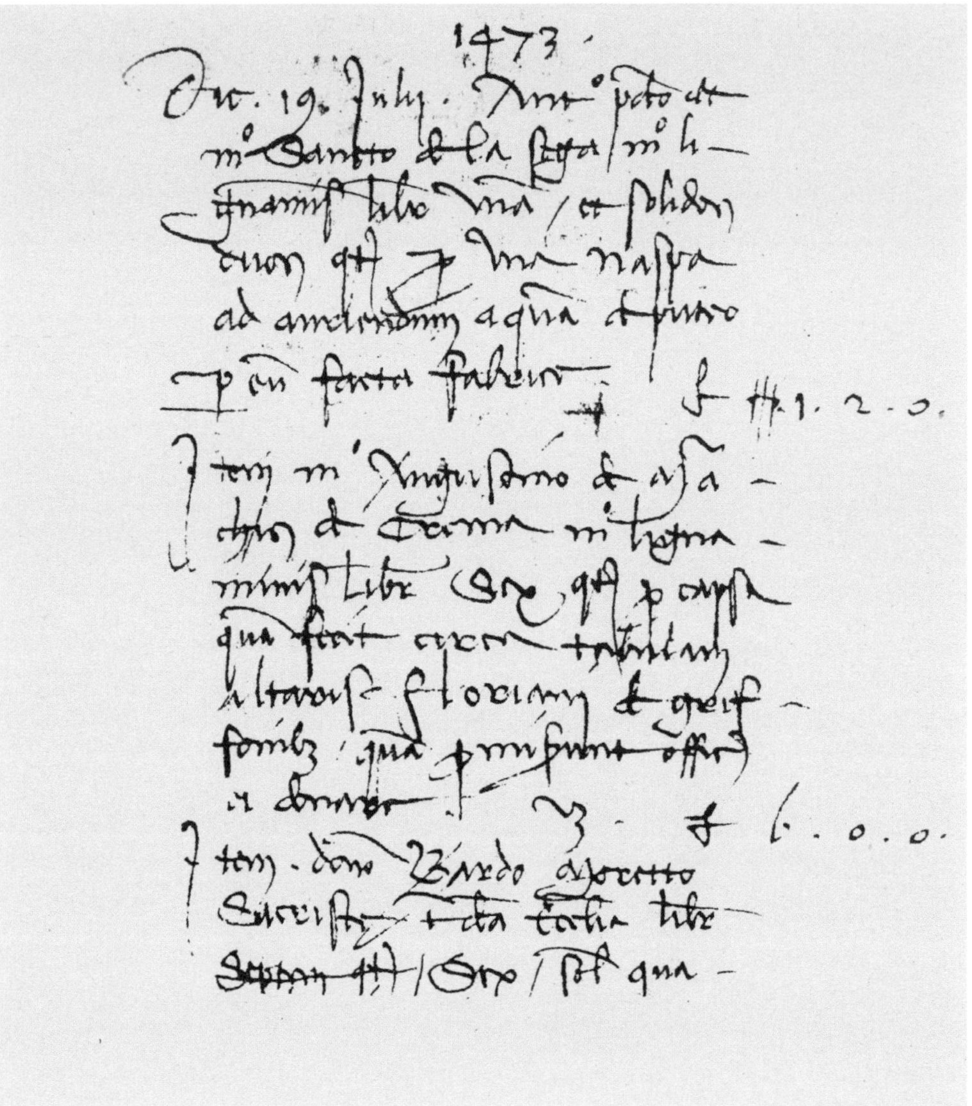

1

July 19, 1473: payment of 6 liras by the officials of the Fabbrica of San Petronio to Agostino de' Marchi of Crema who had built the *capsa* for the paintings of Floriano Griffoni's altar

Ivan Pini was right in claiming that the first patron of the chapel devoted to Saint Vincent Ferrer at San Petronio was Floriano Griffoni and not Matteo, the well-known chronicler, as Sorbelli had erroneously maintained.[5]

However, the accounting entry of July 19, 1473 contains another significant element, which has been disregarded to date: that is, the *fabbricieri*'s payment for the *capsa* must have had a special reason, if they promised it as a gift to Floriano Griffoni. Indeed, it was extremely uncommon for the Fabbrica of San Petronio to contribute toward the costs that the patrons of the chapels were to bear: the 1395 statutes of the Fabbrica required that any individual, family, or corporation that intended to acquire the patronage of a chapel pay at least 500 liras, establish an endowment to ensure the daily celebration of a mass, and equip the chapel, at their expense, with an altar, a "*tabula seu ancona pulcra*," and appropriate liturgical garments.[6]

---

are in ASBo, Aldrovandi Marescotti, b. 842, document marked Lib. III, no. III. All these late copies could help providing a more accurate transcription of the text.

5 Pini 1994, pp. 94–96.

6 ASP, vol. 1 (Statutes of 1395), f.26r: "*Et si voluerit aliquis ius Patronatus in una ex dictis capellis habere, solvere teneatur ad minus quingentas libras bononinorum, et ultra teneantur doctare ipsam capellam ita quod unus sacerdos possit pro illa dote stare in dicta*

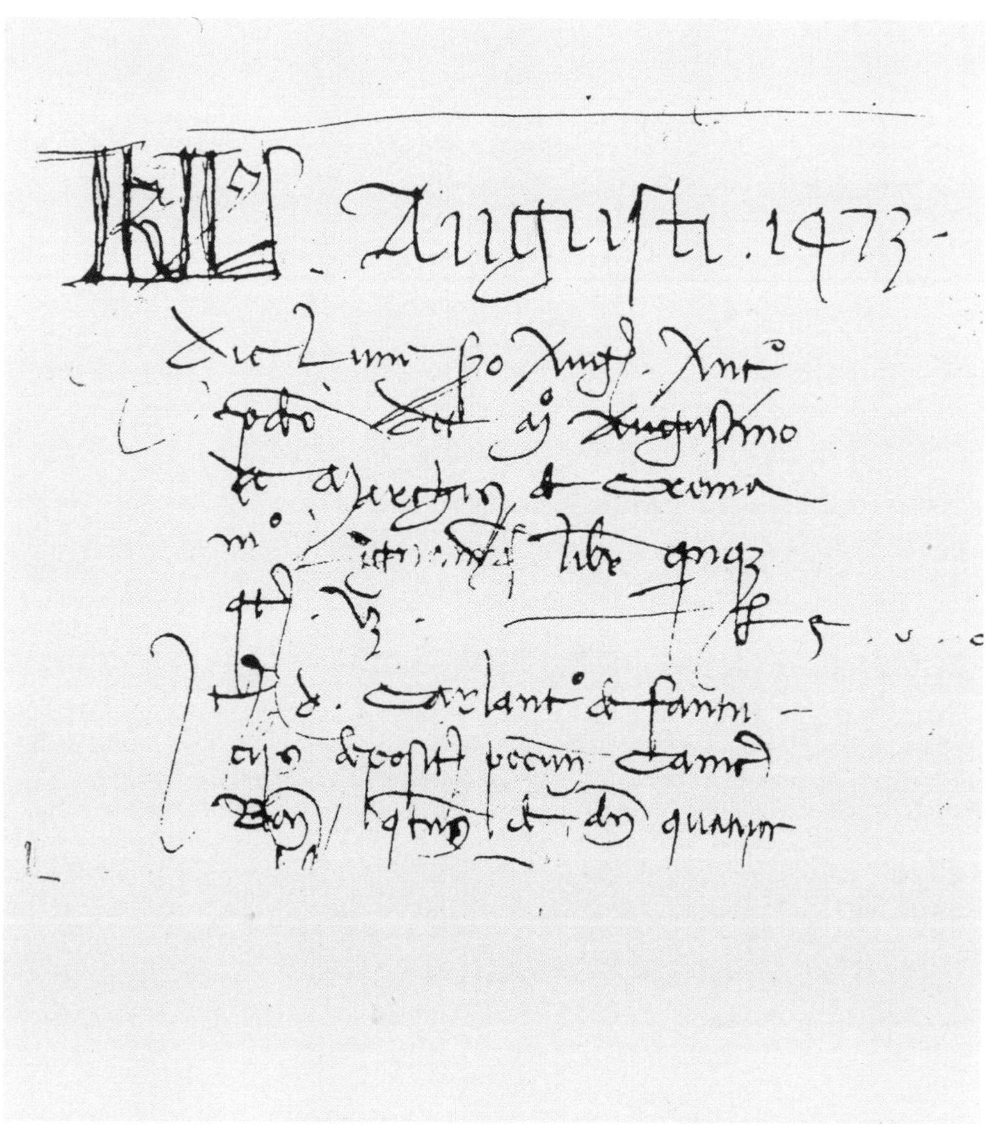

Augusti. 1473

2

August 2, 1473: another payment of 5 liras to Agostino de' Marchi, certainly for the *capsa* of the Griffoni Polyptych

Then, why did the *fabbricieri* commit to donate to Floriano Griffoni the *capsa* or frame for the altarpiece that he had commissioned for his own altar or chapel? The reason lies in the special relation between the Griffoni family and the Fabbrica of San Petronio, which started in 1429, when Giovanni Griffoni was appointed as administrator, an office he held until his death in 1471—that is to say, for over forty years.

Who was Giovanni Griffoni? The son of Giacomo, who died in 1399,[7] he belonged to a different branch of the Griffoni family from that of his better-known relative, chronicler Matteo (1351–1426).[8] Giovanni held a number of public offices throughout the complex political vicissitudes of Bologna in the first half of the fifteenth century.[9]

---

ecclesia sancti Petronii horis congruis et missam omni die in ipsa capella celebrare arbitrio dictorum procuratorum [i.e. the *fabbricieri*] *et tenatur etiam fulcire altare ipsius capelle tabula seu ancona pulcra et pulcris et decentibus paramentis necessariis pro celebrando in dicta capella arbitrio predictorum procuratorum*."

7 See the Griffoni genealogy sketch drafted by A. Sorbelli in *Matthaei de Griffonibus* 1902, p. 122 (RIS[2], tom. XVIII, part II).

8 On him, see the *Memoriale Historicum* mentioned in the note above, and also *Matteo Griffoni* 2004.

9 See Ghirardacci ed. 1933, p. 638 of the index.

Being an experienced and diligent man, as well as already a member of the *Consiglio dei Soprastanti* at the Fabbrica of San Petronio, on September 2, 1429, the Sixteen Reformers of the Status of Liberty of Bologna appointed him as *camerario* (that is, treasurer) of the Fabbrica for life. The instrument of appointment reveals that the Sixteen, having to choose "*unum honorabilem virum laicum civitatis Bononie origine propria, paterna et avita... attesa circumspetione, diligentia, conditione et probitate nobilis viri Joannis quondam Jacobi de Griffonibus civis bononiensis origine propria, paterna et avita, aetateque provecti et nunc de numero superstitum dicte Fabrice existentis, nullique exercitio alteri occupato*," appointed him as "*camerarium dicte Fabrice ecclesie sancti Petronii per totum tempus eiusdem Joannis utilis naturalis vitae... cum salario mense quolibet librarum duodecim bononinorum*" and vested him with very broad management powers.[10]

3

November 26, 1453: order issued by the *fabbricieri* of San Petronio to refund Giovanni Griffoni for the expenses he incurred when traveling to Rome to obtain from the Pope confirmation of the economic privileges for the Fabbrica of San Petronio

An uninterrupted series of documents allows us to follow the vicissitudes of Giovanni Griffoni as *camerario* of the Fabbrica of San Petronio until his death, in 1471. On June 20, 1433, Pope Eugene IV confirmed Griffoni's election in the office of *camerario* or perpetual camerlengo,[11] and later, on October 13, the Bishop of Avignon, governor of Bologna, issued the decree enforcing the papal brief.[12]

On December 24, 1446, the *Gonfaloniere* and the Elders of the Municipality of Bologna appointed Giovanni Griffoni as one of the officials of the Fabbrica for a two-year period.[13] At the same time, however, on December 15, 1445, Nicolò Sanuti was also appointed as an official for two years;[14] on January 1, 1449, Sanuti, who was a distinguished figure in Bologna at the time, joined, on an extraordinary basis, the *Soprastanti* already in office,[15] and therefore an antagonism must have arisen between him and Griffoni. Griffoni reacted by obtaining Pope Nicholas V's confirmation of his office as perpetual *camerario* of the Fabbrica, with a monthly salary of 6 gold florins, on March 7, 1449;[16] the papal brief was addressed for enforcement to Cardinal Bessarione, the papal legate of Bologna, who issued the corresponding decree on March 21, 1450.[17] Later, on November 16, 1452,[18] Griffoni was confirmed again by the same Pope.

Giovanni Griffoni was committed to make sure that the Pope confirmed the economic privileges of the Fabbrica,[19] and he traveled to Rome for such purpose. On that occasion, he incurred many expenses, for which he was refunded by the Fabbrica on November 26, 1453.[20] Moreover, in recognition for his efforts, he was confirmed once again as camerlengo for life of the Fabbrica by Pope Callixtus III on April 22, 1455.[21]

10 ASP, folder 217, no. 1 (Libro + 1° n. 2), p. 53 (seventeenth-century copy); Fanti 1980, p. 135.

11 ASP, folder 217, no. 1 (Libro + 1° n. 2), p. 77 (seventeenth-century copy); Fanti 1980, p. 136.

12 ASP, folder 107, no. 48 (sixteenth-century copy) and also folder 217, no. 1 (Libro + 1° n. 2), p. 78 (seventeenth-century copy); Fanti 1980, p. 136.

13 ASP, folder 110, no. 22 (sixteenth-century copy); Fanti 1980, p. 154.

14 ASP, vol. 8 (Atti della Fabbrica, 1439-1454), f. 182r; Fanti 1980, p. 154.

15 ASP, folder 217, no. 1 (Libro + 1° n. 2), p. 25; Fanti 1980, p. 154.

16 ASP, folder 110, no. 39; Fanti 1980, p. 154.

17 ASP, folder 231 (Processi, lib. C), no. 34, file D, f. 40r (sixteenth-century copy).

18 ASP, folder 111, no. 19 (sixteenth-century copy); Fanti 1980, p. 154.

19 Namely, the restoration of the tithe on pious bequests and of the tax known as *dazio di piazza e frutti*; on these sources of income of the Fabbrica, see Fanti 1980, pp. 70 and 143.

20 ASP, folder 111, no. 31: the *fabbricieri* instruct Bartolomeo Zenzifabri, their depository, to refund the costs incurred by Giovanni Griffoni in Rome to obtain the Pope's apostolic concessions in favor of the Fabbrica (fig. 3). In the journal of the Fabbrica (ASP, vol. 481, f. 61v), a payment of 144 liras was recorded on November 26, 1453 to "*meser Zoane de Grifoni per spexe fe in andare stare e tornare da Roma per dì 60 stette fuora... per fatti de S. Petronio, che partì dotobre a dì 6 1452 e tornò de Dezembre adì 6.*"

21 ASP, folder 112, no. 4 (sixteenth-century copy); Fanti 1980, p. 155.

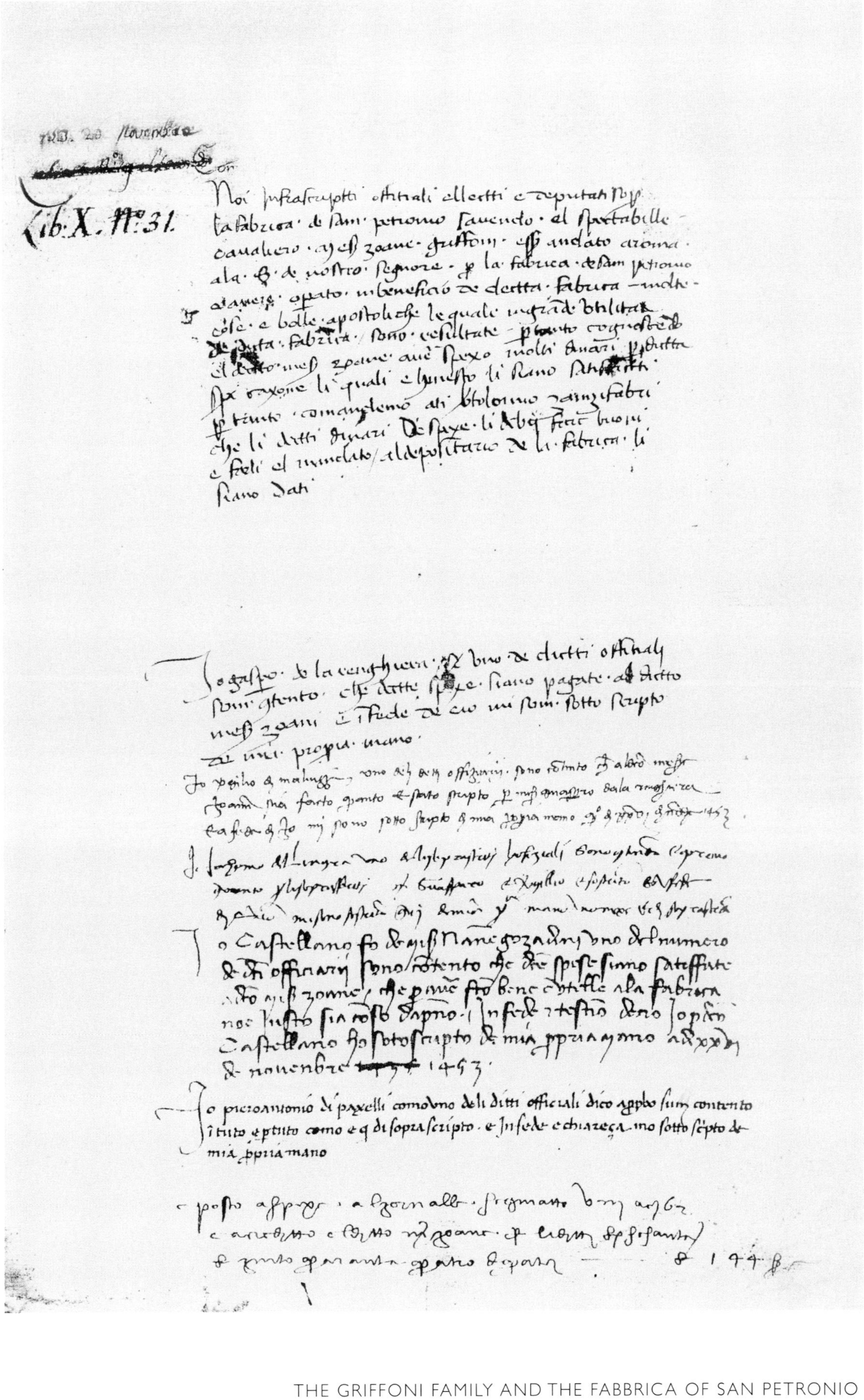

1453. 20 novembre

Lib. X. N°. 31.

Noi infrascripti offitiali elletti e deputati sopra la fabrica de San petronio sauendo el spectabille cavaliero messer zoane griffoni esser andato a roma ala S. de nostro signore per la fabrica de San petronio e operato in beneficio de detta fabrica molte cose e bolle apostoliche le quale in grande utilitate de detta fabrica sono resultate [illegible] el detto messer zoane avere spexo molti denari per detta casone li quali e honesto li siano satisfatti per tanto comandemo a ti Bartolomeo [illegible] che li detti denari de spexe li debi fare buoni [illegible] al depositario de la fabrica li siano dati

Io [illegible] de la [illegible] uno de detti offitiali [illegible] che dette spexe siano pagate al detto messer zoane e in fede de cio mi sono sotto scripto de mia propria mano.

Io [illegible] uno deli detti offiziali sono contento [illegible] quanto e sopto scripto [illegible] e in fede de zo mi sono sotto scripto de mia propria mano [illegible] 1453

[illegible]

Io Castellano [illegible] de messer Nane gozadini uno del numero de detti officiarii sono contento che dette spexe siano satisfatte al detto messer zoane, che pure fo bene e utille ala fabrica [illegible] e in fede e testimonio de cio io sopraditto Castellano ho sotoscripto de mia propria mano a di xx de novembre 1453

Io pieroantonio di paxelli como uno deli ditti officiali dico apperho sum contento in tuto e per tuto como e q(ui) di sopra scripto e in fede e chiareza mo sotto scripto de mia propria mano

posto [illegible] a zornalle [illegible] e [illegible] messer zoane [illegible] 144

By then, however, there were two different factions in the city government—one supporting Griffoni, the other Sanuti. The latter prevailed on March 24, 1456 when the legate of Bologna, Giovanni Lodovico Milani of Valencia, Bishop of Segovia, appointed Nicolò Sanuti as official and camerlengo for life of the Fabbrica, albeit without the monthly emolument of 6 florins which Griffoni had always enjoyed.[22] The gratuitous office, however, did not remain such for long: a year later, on April 7, 1457 the same legate confirmed Sanuti's appointment with the same powers and salary previously granted to Giovanni Griffoni.[23] And, on September 9, 1458 Pope Pius II confirmed Sanuti's position as official and camerlengo for life.[24]

At that point, Griffoni had been removed from the office for good; however, he was still a member of the Council of the Fabbrica,[25] and it would even appear that he later resumed his previous role, since, on September 14, 1471, when Sixtus IV appointed Galeazzo Marescotti as perpetual president of the Fabbrica, he pointed out that he did so following the death of Giovanni Griffoni.[26] With the passing of Griffoni, the vicissitudes that had linked his family to the Fabbrica of San Petronio for 42 years also came to an end, and it is odd that none of the authors who have mentioned him in their works make reference to the role he played there—that office being far from negligible, but instead greatly relevant in the politics of the city and in the public life of Bologna at the time.

The memory of Giovanni Griffoni and of his long term of office was still alive at the Fabbrica at the time of Galeazzo Marescotti, perpetual president since 1471, and we understand why, in 1473, the *fabbricieri* undertook to pay for the *capsa* of the polyptych that Floriano Griffoni had commissioned for his family chapel at San Petronio: it was a promise they had made to him, as we read in the accounting entry of 1473, and they would keep it as a homage to the memory of Giovanni Griffoni and to his family.

Floriano Griffoni was the son of another Floriano, in turn the son of chronicler Matteo, and therefore his grandson. It has been reported that, in 1450, Floriano married Ludovica Lambertini;[27] however, this date is certainly wrong, as we shall see. What is undisputed instead is that Floriano served as one of the Elders of the city government for seven times between 1459 and 1481.[28]

Floriano's choice to decorate the family chapel at the Basilica of San Petronio with a high-quality painting work by Francesco del Cossa and Ercole de' Roberti met the requirements that the statutes of the Fabbrica imposed on the patrons of the chapels. Furthermore, it emphasized the Griffoni family's contribution to and significance in the political, religious, and cultural context of the city, both as a family and as individuals.

From this perspective, it should be pointed out that, besides the saint to whom the chapel is dedicated (Vincent Ferrer), the polyptych commissioned by Floriano Griffoni also portrays other popular saints and the patron saint of Bologna Saint Petronius, as

---

22 ASP, vol. 219 (Sommario dei documenti), p. 204, document quoted from the now lost Libro + 1° n. 3, f. 13; Fanti 1980, p. 155.

23 ASP, vol. 219 (Sommario dei documenti), p. 206, document quoted from the now lost Libro + 1° n. 3, f. 12v; Fanti 1980, p. 155.

24 ASP, vol. 219 (Sommario dei documenti), p. 213, document quoted from the now lost Libro + 1° n. 3, f. 12v.

25 On January 12, 1459 Griffoni was one of the officials who signed an agreement with painters Giacomo and Bartolomeo Maineri for the Chapel of Santa Brigida (ASP, folder 115, no. 36; the agreement is mentioned in another document dated December 18, 1470); Fanti 1980, p. 155.

26 ASP, folder 115, no. 42 (sixteenth-century copy of the now lost Libro + 1° n. 3, f. 49).

27 A. Sorbelli, introduction to *Matthaei de Griffonibus* 1902, p. XVIII note 7.

28 See Pasquali Alidosi 1670, pp. 4, 5, 9, 12, 14, 25, and 26; he was one of the Elders in the years 1459, 1460, 1462, 1467, 1469, 1480, and 1481.

well as two figures of saints who certainly represented a direct and current reference to individual members of the family, as it has been noted.[29] These are Saint Florian, the secondary patron saint of Bologna,[30] whose features would resemble those of the client (the panel is now at the National Gallery in Washington, DC). The other character that could be a portrait is Saint Lucy (kept at the same gallery in the United States), which is probably to be identified with Lucia of Andrea Battaglia, the first wife of Floriano Griffoni.

As far as the marriages of Floriano are concerned, the information on which the various scholars have relied to date is taken from *Memorie antiche della casa Griffoni*, of which three versions exist (A, B, and C), all written by the same author in the sixteenth century, yet often diverging, in ASBo, Archivio Fantuzzi Ceretoli (sometimes wrongly referred to as Fantuzzi Canetoli), b. 167.[31]

Finally, as to the contribution of the Fabbrica of San Petronio toward the expenses for the *capsa* of the polyptych as a personal gift to Floriano Griffoni, it is worth noting that, at least in another case, the *fabbricieri* also cooperated with the patron of a chapel and took on themselves some of the costs for the decoration works. The reference is to *God the Father* painted by Guido Reni, for which the Fabbrica paid 16 liras on October 17, 1595.[32] The work was intended for the top of the altarpiece of the Chapel of Santa Brigida, the patrons of which were the Pepoli family. Having been removed from that location in the nineteenth century, in 1907 it was sold to a private collector, with the permission of the local authorities; today, after a sale at Christie's in Rome on March

29 Torella (1985–87) 1988, p. 49; Cavalca 2013, pp. 137–38: Cavalca 2018a, p. 31.

30 See Pini 2007, which, at p. 231, refers to Saint Florian in the Griffoni Polyptych.

31 Versions A and C report that Floriano "married twice": the first time with Lucia, daughter of Andrea Battaglia, in 1457, and the second with Ludovica Lambertini in 1472. Version B mentions that Floriano, after Lucia's passing, married the second time in 1463 with a certain Polissena of Giovanni Felicini, and again (which would be the third time) in 1472 with Lambertini. As far as we know, there is no documentary evidence of Floriano's marriage with Felicini in 1463, therefore we regard this as an unreliable information, also because, in 1469, Lucia was still alive. Thus, it is worth mentioning here some of the documents regarding his first wife, Lucia Battaglia. There is a "will" in her name, dated June 3, 1457 (ASBo, Aldrovandi Marescotti, b. 841, document marked Libro II, no. XVI). However, this does not contain her last will, as the name of the document would seem to imply; it is a rather different instrument indeed. Lucia declares that she is in good health—"*mente, sensu, corpore et intellectu*"—and that she merely intends to give instructions regarding her personal assets, consisting of paraphernalia (i.e. assets not included in her dowry, which already belonged to her before marrying Floriano); she had received such assets from her father Andrea, and Lucia left them to her and Floriano's (future) children for a half and to Floriano himself for the other half. Andrea Battaglia was a wealthy gentleman, who lived in the Flanders before permanently moving to Bologna. In his will dated October 6, 1455 (ASBo, Aldrovandi Marescotti, b. 841, document marked Lib. II, no. XIV, notary Domenico Amorini; quoted by C. Cavalca in Cavalca and Negretti 2018, p. 10), he left a dowry of 3,000 liras in *bolognini* coins to each of his five daughters (including Lucia). Many significant news on Andrea Battaglia and his daughters can be found in Cavalca and Negretti 2018, pp. 3–30. In another document, dated December 30, 1461, Lucia, in acknowledging her husband Floriano Griffoni's good faith ("*bonam fidem agnoscere*"), frees him from any obligations in connection with the use he had made, for charity purposes, of an amount that Lucia had received following her brother Girolamo's death (ASBo, Aldrovandi Marescotti, b. 841, document marked Lib. II, no. XX, notary Bartolomeo Formaglini). A third document, dated August 1, 1469 is referred to in brief by Torella ([1985–87] 1988, p. 52 note 24) as "a sale by Giacomo Bolognetti on August 1 to '*Luciam uxorem Floriani de Griffonibus*.'" More specifically, from the document we learn that Giacoma (and not Giacomo) Bolognini (and not Bolognetti), the second wife and widow of Andrea Battaglia and his heir, ordered that, after her death, her assets be assigned to Lucia, wife of Floriano Griffoni, to Elena, wife of Pirro Malvezzi, to Lucrezia, wife of Matteo Bolognini, to Margherita, wife of Giacomo Magnani, and to Elisabetta, wife of Ippolito Malvezzi: that is to say, to the five daughters of Andrea Battaglia from his first marriage, for a fifth each. Giacoma continued to hold all of the assets in usufruct, yet she transferred immediately their bare ownership to the five sisters, who undertook to leave to their stepmother Giacoma the furniture, furnishings, and objects of a long list (ASBo, Archivio Fantuzzi Ceretoli, b. 7, document marked Tom. 7, no. 27, notary Matteo Curialti, who, being unable to do so, had the notary Paganello Paganelli draft the instrument). For the purposes of our research, the document certifies that, on August 1, 1469 Lucia was still alive. Therefore, the news of an alleged marriage between Floriano and Polissena Felicini in 1463, contained in the *Memorie antiche* of the Griffoni family, is totally groundless.

32 The document was found by Oscar Mischiati: see Winkelmann 1987, pp. 28–29; *Guido Reni* 1988, pp. 14–15 and 195; Pepper 1988, p. 327.

23, 1988, it is part of a private collection. What is worth noting here is that, also in that case, the (albeit partial) contribution of the Fabbrica toward the decoration of a chapel regarded that of Santa Brigida, the patrons of which were, as we mentioned, the Pepoli who, in the sixteenth century, had two of their members in a row serving as perpetual presidents of the Fabbrica itself: Count Filippo Pepoli (1513–53) and his son, Count Giovanni (1555–85).[33] Once again, as it is the case with the Griffoni, it should be noted that the administrators of the Fabbrica showed special consideration for the families that had close ties with the Fabbrica itself. It should be borne in mind that the Fabbrica was directly dependent on the city government and was managed by the same political and noble class that formed the government itself. For the families of that oligarchy, having played a role in the administration of the Fabbrica of the city's great church and having their own chapel at the Basilica was an enduring sign of social and political distinction.

The choice of the artists for the Griffoni Polyptych should also be considered from this perspective, as the extraordinary artistic quality of the work would guarantee the meaning that the painting was to acquire as a visible proof of the social, economic, and political standing of the family. Floriano Griffoni most certainly took this into account when he selected Francesco del Cossa and Ercole de' Roberti to paint the *tabula* for his chapel at San Petronio.

It is however worth noting that it was only ten years after 1473, when the polyptych was placed in the chapel together with its *capsa*, that Floriano managed to fully comply with what he was required to do in connection with the endowment of the chapel. Indeed, in his will dated August 6, 1483 he appointed two commissioners or executors of the will (Giovanni q. Francesco Bolognini and Giovanni of Musotto Malvezzi) to establish an endowment for his chapel at the Basilica of San Petronio; such endowment was necessary to designate a priest who would celebrate a mass there every day (in accordance with the statutes of the Fabbrica governing the granting of chapels to privates) for the soul of the patron, whose heirs and successors would forever maintain the patronage of the chapel.[34] The priest was appointed on June 15, 1485 by Floriano's sons and heirs Luigi Maria and Marco Antonio, who chose Martino di Simone Scardovi of Castel Bolognese, canon of Faenza, who was then confirmed on the following June 25 by the general vicar of the Bologna Episcopal Curia.[35]

One would wonder about the reasons for such a delay in establishing the beginning of a regular celebration of the mass at the chapel, since the polyptych, which was its main decoration, had been already there for almost ten years. The reasons were probably of financial nature, which led—or forced—Floriano to postpone the operation.

His financial conditions, in accordance with the legal inventory of the movable and immovable assets forming his inheritance, drafted on October 20, 1483 (i.e. approximately three months after his will and his death)[36] appear substantial. They comprise a long list of movables (furniture, furnishings, linen, jewelry, and sundry objects) kept at his home in Bologna in the parish of San Barbaziano, which also included a stable and three horses worth

---

33 Fanti 1980, pp. 175–79.

34 Floriano Griffoni's will referred to in note 4.

35 ASBo, Aldrovandi Marescotti, b. 840, file no. I, tom. I of Griffoni's businesses, including the altar at San Petronio, doc. 2, notary Francesco Formaglini, certified copy of the seventeenth century.

36 ASBo, Aldrovandi Marescotti, b. 842, document marked Lib. III, no. IIII, notary Giacomo Boccaferri. There are three copies: an uncertified copy from the first half of the sixteenth century, another uncertified copy of the eighteenth century, and a certified copy, also of the eighteenth century.

of 14, 8, and 5 ducats respectively. His rural properties were located in the countryside of Bologna: in the plain, in the municipalities of Budrio, San Martino in Argine, Vedrana, and Castelfranco; and in the mountains, in the municipalities of Barbiano, Ancognano, Paderno, Mongardino, and Pizzocalvo. All these estates (comprising rural houses, stables with animals, and warehouses with cereals and wine) amounted, in aggregate, to 2,005 *tornature*,[37] that is to say 417.12 hectares, partly cultivated and partly wild or woodland.

In Bologna, besides his home, Floriano also owned another house in the parish of Santissimo Salvatore and had outstanding claims with a number of public institutions (the Crescimonie, Moliture, and Sale pawnshops), totalling 385 liras. The actual value of his assets is impossible to quantify, as the inventory provides a list of goods without giving an estimate. It is undisputed that, after the initial, certainly large expenditure to pay the artists involved in the polyptych, as many as ten years would pass before Floriano Griffoni could complete the family chapel at San Petronio with the endowment for celebrating the mass. He only took care of the matter upon his death, in his will, and passed on to his heirs and successors the duty and burden of doing what he could not or did not want to do when he was alive. However, it is certainly significant that the Fabbrica of San Petronio tolerated Floriano's considerable delay in complying with one of the main duties imposed on those who had been granted the patronage of a chapel at the Basilica. The presence, inside the Griffoni Chapel, of a remarkable work of art like the polyptych that Floriano had already supplied and the consideration that the Fabbrica had always shown for his family probably played a crucial role in that situation as well.

One last interesting information can be found in the above-mentioned inventory of Floriano Griffoni's inheritance. Among the objects found in his house, there were some accounting books of Floriano himself—a register of approximately 300 pages and its journal of approximately 200 pages, marked B, started in 1469; another register of approximately 200 pages and its journal of approximately 150 pages, marked C, started in 1478. This is a clear instance of "double-entry bookkeeping"—that is, two books kept at the same time, the ledger and the journal, according to the accounting practice of merchants at the time. Given that these books kept track of Floriano's administration since 1469, and at least until his death in 1483, they probably also recorded the costs incurred for the famous polyptych. Unfortunately, however, no trace of those registers has been found to date.

37 A Bolognese *tornatura* equals 2080.44 square meters.

FRANCESCO DEL COSSA AND ERCOLE DE' ROBERTI: IN FERRARA AND BOLOGNA

Cecilia Cavalca

When at the end of the eighteenth century Luigi Lanzi set about describing the lineage of the Ferrara school of painting, favored, in his opinion, by the "convenience of its location"—near Venice, Parma, and Bologna, not too distant from Florence, and not very far from Rome, it offered "students the possibility to choose among the schools in Italy the one most in keeping with everyone's genius"—Francesco del Cossa came last, along with Baldassarre d'Este. Before him, and not only for reasons of chronology, Lanzi mentioned Galasso Galassi and Cosimo "Cosmè" Tura, his "disciple" who grew up in an artistic environment "modernized" by the example of "two foreigners"—Piero della Francesca and Squarcione, with a school in Padua and "innumerable followers throughout Italy." There was also Lorenzo Costa, famous in his local area before being commissioned by Giovanni II Bentivoglio to make paintings for his palazzo. Such was the fame of the Ferrara school if compared to the situation in Bologna: "toward the end of the century, the city suffered a shortage of good craftsmen." Lanzi may only suspect that Francesco del Cossa was among them. The guilty party for this situation was Giorgio Vasari, who led Lanzi to confuse Cossa with Costa; writing on what he knew of as by Cossa with certainty, because it was signed and dated, that is to say the so-called "Pala dei Mercanti" (1474, Pinacoteca Nazionale, Bologna), this seemed to him to be "coarse in its features and mediocre in coloring." Cosmè was instead court painter to Borso d'Este, and once celebrated in verse by Tito Strozzi. His style was "dry and humble" as was customary in that age, but "muscles [were] clearly delineated; architecture drawn up with the utmost care; bas-reliefs highly ornamented and finely labored, with a taste for extreme minuteness and exactness." The frescoes in Palazzo Schifanoia, highly praised by Girolamo Baruffaldi, are attributed to him. And if Tura was the star of a school that some say surpassed any other "after the five Italian primaries," Cossa was most certainly not favored by his expatriation to Bologna.[1]

This introductory digression is of help in bringing into focus the core argument of a critical judgment that continued to be relevant throughout the nineteenth century and featured in the most distinguished critical contributions of the early twentieth. To this day, little is known about Francesco del Cossa.[2] What little we do know is part of an artistic realm considered to be second-tier. What progressively re-emerged has been observed with ill-concealed detachment for its excessive scruple to stick to real life: "rustic and graceless," as Jacob Burckhardt put in his *The Cicerone* (1855), while still appreciating it.[3] In Roberto Longhi's *Officina ferrarese* (1934), a text that had an enormous influence

1 Lanzi 1795–96 ed. 1968–74, III, 1974, pp. 145–51.
2 See Ciammitti 2007.
3 Burckhardt 1855 ed. 1952, II, p. 891.

on our understanding of Ferrara artists from this period, Cossa's pictorial genius is established among the greatest of the school to which he belonged. The naturalistic trait of his painting,[4] contrasted positively with Tura's excessively artificial approach (which passed "from exact and minute diligence," as in Lanzi's words, to the "creation of a stalagmitic nature, a humanity of enamel and ivory, with crystal joints"[5]), remains a double-edged sword, as implied in Adolfo Venturi's pages.[6] The housewifely lineage ("*stirpe casalinga*") of Cossa's Madonnas and the roughness ("*rudezza acciliata*") of his saints indeed retain a realistic/popular quality in their utmost attention to details of real life, something that according to Longhi would be fully redeemed only in the supra-regional language of Ercole de' Roberti. Ercole is the one artist who emerges redefined from the pages of *Officina* as the noblest of Ferrara's artists, endowed with a singular, distinctive greatness that makes him the equal of the best masters of the period.[7]

When, between the 1950s and 1980s, research fostered by Carlo Volpe and continued by his closest pupils recentered the role Bologna played in relation to Ferrara, in contrast with Lanzi's established approach, Cossa's verism—traced in the wake of Longhi in clear opposition to Tura's intellectualism[8]—was redrawn as a hallmark feature of the spirit of place, a catalyst of its deepest and most medieval, Romanesque dimension. Volpe thought that Cossa's "powerful expressiveness" was the result of contact with Bologna. So, if Longhi could rhetorically wonder why the "Bolognese" Marco Zoppo (who around the middle of the fifteenth century was influenced by both Squarcione and Piero della Francesca) managed to achieve no real advancement to his city's art,[9] Volpe insisted on Zoppo's Piero-inspired transformation while he was in Bologna, and beginning here he started to reconstruct the path of the great Ferrarese.[10]

Ever played out against the backdrop of insidious opposition between different artistic milieus, the personality of Francesco del Cossa and the role he played in this delicate situation are not easy to define. The way we understand him inevitably conditions our judgment about the work of Ercole de' Roberti, his pupil according to Vasari, who worked with him in Bologna (before 1473) on the polyptych that Floriano Griffoni commissioned.

Two important written chronicles recorded Cossa's personality and artistic qualities as perceived by his contemporaries. The first was a small autograph sent in the spring of 1470 to Borso d'Este, in which he claims his role as author of the frescoes on the east wall of Palazzo Schifanoia.[11] The second is a funereal commendation in prose and verse dedicated to him by two friends from Bologna, humanists Angelo Michele Salimbeni and Sebastiano Aldrovandi, who fled the city to escape the plague that in 1478 took the artist's

4 Longhi 1934 ed. 1956, p. 29.

5 Ibid., p. 24.

6 Venturi (1901–40, VII/3, 1914, pp. 586–650) ended up judging Cossa to be a "simple, good-hearted man of the people, who lavished the best of his rustic upbringing and his most tenacious work on altars" (p. 650).

7 Longhi 1940 ed. 1956, p. 133: "Ercole's greatness stands apart from that of his greatest peers, Leonardo and Botticelli, or from elders like Melozzo and Mantegna." For more on Longhi's *Officina*, see Toffanello's contribution in this volume.

8 Volpe 1958 ed. 1993, p. 156, with reference to the "Pala dei Mercanti": "The rough, peasant lineage of Saints Petronius and John is the opposite of the cultured and hypocritical humanity of Borso's courtiers. Nothing could be further from the cracked, drugged smiles at Schifanoia, and yet it is the very same painter, in the gruff and awkward manner of these giant saints, father and son from the same peasant family, next to the dark idol of Our Lady."

9 Longhi 1935 ed. 1973, pp. 194–95.

10 Volpe 1958 ed. 1993, p. 155. For Volpe's idea of the Renaissance in Bologna and how it relates to Longhi's view, *Officina ferrarese*, see Raimondi 2010, pp. 113–20 and Benati 2012a.

11 Known since 1885 through Adolfo Venturi; transcribed several times in full, now available to read in Franceschini 1993, doc. 1204; for a commentary, Rosenberg 1975–76.

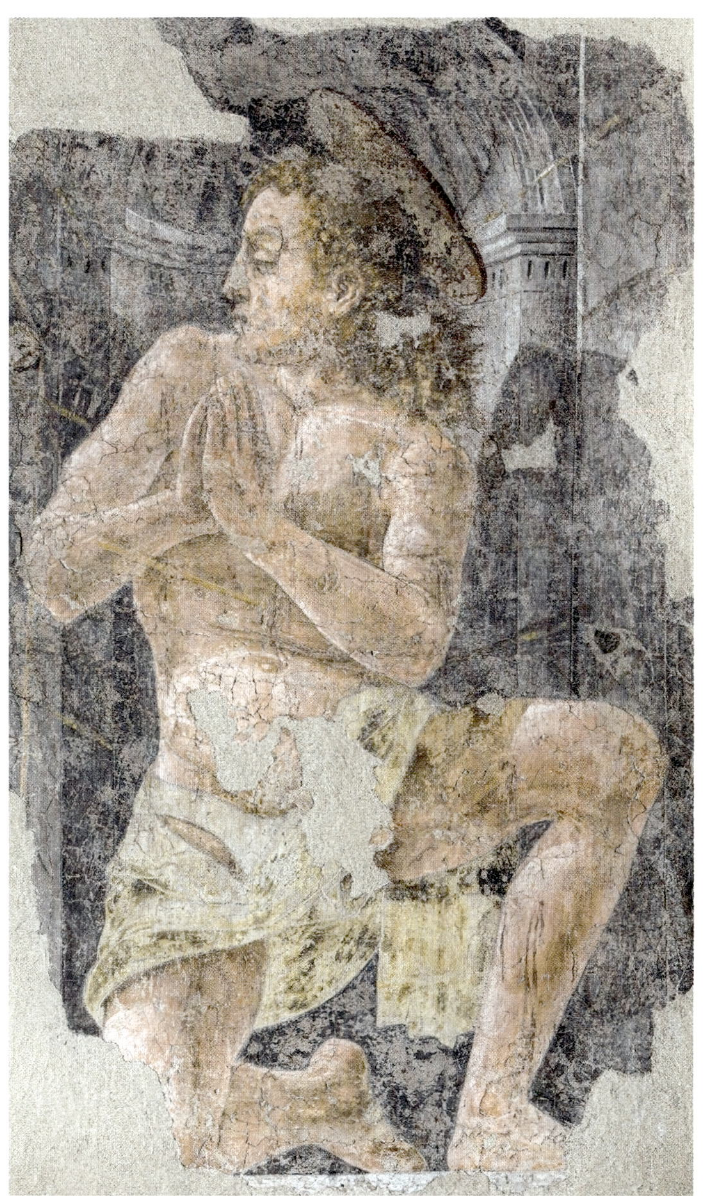

1

Ferrarese artist, *Saint Sebastian*. Pinacoteca Nazionale, Ferrara

life at just forty-two years of age.[12] These scraps of text are as well-known as they are elusive. Both are undoubted evidence of the artist's most excellent mastery of the tools of the trade, but they leave us the challenging task of reconciling against the correct historical backdrop the austere and somewhat grudging traits of a man who, at the age of thirty-one, began to earn a little name ("*ad avere uno pocho di nome*") and was unwilling to be cheated and treated as the most inept ("*il più tristo*") of the laborers by the Duke of Ferrara,[13] with the man whose passing just eight years later in Bentivoglio's Bologna was lamented by the intellectual elite as that of a creator endowed with a universal and matchless talent and yet eager to reduce himself to the religious state, a mortal enemy of pomp and riches, in contemplation of the celestial glory ("*nimico mortale de pompe et di richeze, sitibondo della celestial gloria*").[14]

With only a handful of documents to draw on, the historical chronicles attest that Francesco was born around 1436, the son of a master bricklayer and heir to an important dynasty started by his grandfather Giovanni di Ranieri (1391–1428) who, in the first half of the fifteenth century, joining with other workers, had won important contracts in Ferrara.[15] Early works procured by Giovanni included in 1414–15 the foundations of the Cathedral bell tower, in partnership with Giacomo di Lorenzo. Cristoforo Cossa, son of Giovanni and father of Francesco, was back on this site forty years later, between 1454 and 1458, supervising construction of the first dado with Pietro di Benvenuto dagli Ordini[16] (see fig. 9 on p. 114). A few years later, a cousin of Cristoforo's, Andrea di Antonio Cossa, according to payments that date back to January 1462, helped with the construction of the cells and new dormitory at the old church of Sant'Andrea, a favorite place of worship for the Este lords.[17]

No time-honored document throws light on when and from which master Francesco learned the rudiments of the painterly arts, thereby becoming able to free himself from his father's and his family's craft. The first mention of him as a painter is associated with a very important building site the Cossa family had frequented at the turn of the century: the Cathedral. Here, on September 11, 1456 Cristoforo's son was

12 *Philomathia* [1478], made known by Frati 1900, cited here in Ruhmer's transcription (Ruhmer 1959, p. 49).
13 See Franceschini 1993, doc. 1204.
14 See *Philomathia* [1478]; Ruhmer 1959, p. 49.
15 Chiappini 1955; see Toffanello 2010, pp. 40–41, 127, 133–38.
16 Cittadella 1864, p. 97; Chiappini 1982, p. 436.
17 Franceschini 1993, doc. 986.

paid to decorate the body of the high altar with "three half-figures of piety" on the front and faux marble squares on the remaining sides.[18] In 1460, Francesco worked on another building site where his family had worked before him, Sant'Andrea, where he stood as a witness to a deed relating to the erection of the Alberico Manfredi Chapel; again, alongside a former work contact of his father's, Pietro di Benvenuto dagli Ordini, in 1467 he witnessed a notarial concession for Nicolò Savonarola's *fontico.*[19] The skill with which this Ferrara-born artist arranged the spatial layout in his mature paintings and his meticulous visual rendering of the materials suggest that we should not underestimate his youthful exploits in the building trade. Equally, we should not neglect the traces left by major decorative works at building sites where the Cossa family worked before Francesco emancipated himself from his father on November 29, 1460.

As has been noted,[20] completion of the first dado for the Cathedral bell tower with the inclusion of the internal chapel for relics was one of the most striking manifestations of Borso's new ducal rank in the architectural field, the body of this "marble-encrusted chapel" projecting toward the square with dynastic monuments. In 1455, while Cristoforo Cossa was busy working on ashlar masonry, young Meo del Caprina from Settignano was entrusted with directly receiving from the Venetian quarries "'live prey' of different colors: white, red, black or gray and yellow, in some cases already hewn into a round shape."[21] An important Tuscan stonecutter trained in the workshop of Nicolò Baroncelli, Meo also worked on site, specifically on the high altar,[22] where Baroncelli (d. 1453) and Domenico di Paris were creating a superb iconostasis with five bronze statues depicting the *Crucifixion* between patron saints George and Maurelio (1451–54/56). Against this backdrop, it is easy to imagine Francesco's dedication executing the sequence of faux marble squares credibly assigned to him through his father and conceived, as everything leads us to believe, with conscious reference to models of classicism as conveyed by Leon Battista Alberti's aesthetics. The latter perhaps also conditioned the expressive register of the *Imago Pietatis* painted by the young Ferrara artist on the front of the altar (perhaps in the guise of an antependium, with a horizontal setting). So, even though we are unable to trace the relationships that linked Francesco, his cousin, Andrea, and Alberico Manfredi with the Hermit Friars of the church of Sant'Andrea, we know that the ruined church later provided detached frescoes of *Saint Christopher* and *Saint Sebastian*, today in the Pinacoteca Nazionale of Ferrara (1455–60), as early and particularly resonant evidence of the examples left by Piero della Francesca in town at the dawn of the 1450s[23] (fig. 1).

If, as we should believe, the young painter who did the rounds of these building sites and with his father frequented the home of Prisciano Prisciani[24] and his son

18 See Chiappini 1955, p. 109. Toffanello 2010, pp. 243–44.

19 See Franceschini 1993, doc. 934 (June 18, 1460); doc. 1104 (February 11, 1467).

20 Ceccarelli 2009, p. 320, cit. in the same passage. Sambin De Norcen (2015) 2017.

21 Ibid., p. 317.

22 Ibid., pp. 316, 314–15: after his Ferrara commission, in the 1460s Meo traveled to Rome, where under the pontificates of Paul II and Sixtus IV he was a leading figure in religious architectural renewal.

23 Pinacoteca Nazionale, Ferrara, inv. 31–33; see Natale 1991, pp. 30–31, 44; A. Mazza in *La Pinacoteca Nazionale* 1992, pp. 56–59, nos. 61–62. Piero's stay during the time of Borso d'Este was recalled and became widely known through Giorgio Vasari (eds. 1550 and 1568). It was discussed by critics, especially with regard to dating, which many prefer to circumscribe to the government of Borso's brother, Leonello (Bertelli 2007, pp. 34–39), even if it was more likely shortly after his death; at this juncture, of particular importance is the close relationship with inlayers Lorenzo and Cristoforo da Lendinara, employed in the Studiolo that was commissioned by Leonello and continued by Borso between 1449 and 1453 (Bagatin 2004, pp. 67–135; see Toffanello 2010, pp. 103–7).

24 Franceschini 1993, doc. 928. *La città come spettacolo* in press.

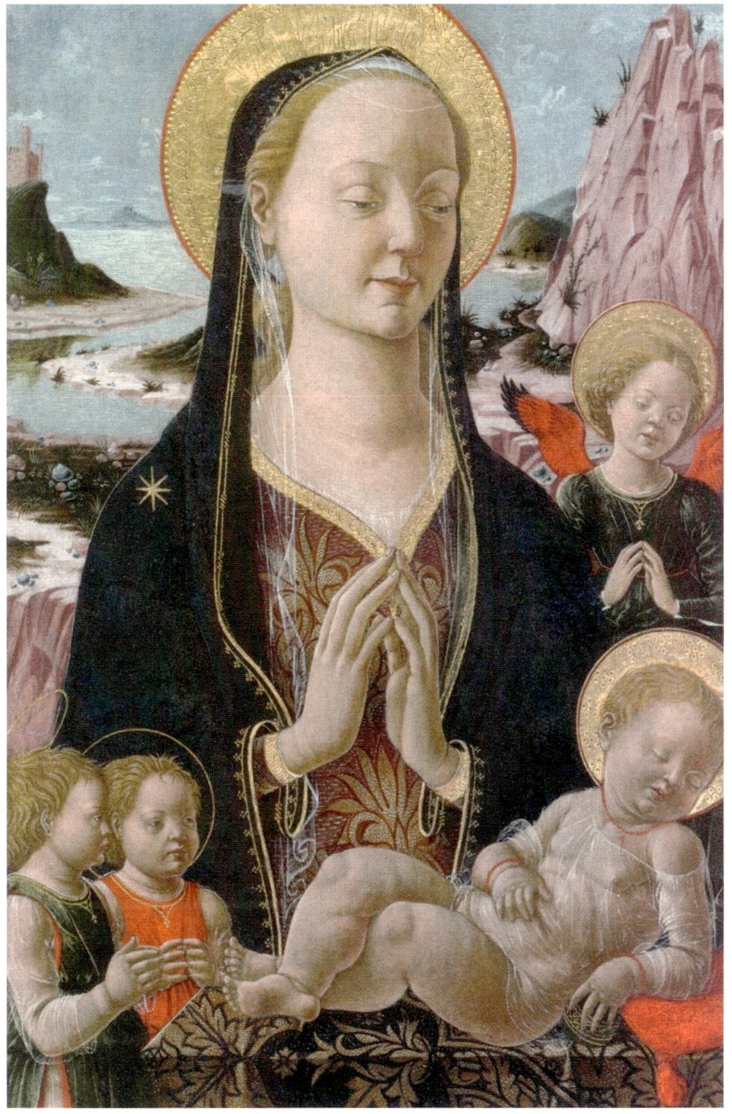

2

Francesco del Cossa, *Madonna and Child with Angels*. National Gallery of Art, Washington, DC

Pellegrino—one of the greatest scholars of the period—was the artist who created the *Madonna and Child with Angels* at the National Gallery of Art in Washington, DC[25] (fig. 2), his beginnings are those of a man who, with great sensitivity, was involved in some of the highest moments of figurative renewal underway at the Este court. The panel is a little jewel destined for personal devotion, following Tuscan models widespread in Ferrara and clearly appreciated in the selected circles among which Cossa moved, as demonstrated by the Ferrara mold of the similar Cambó *Madonna* (Museo Nacional d'Art de Catalunya, Barcelona) and the group of works associated with it.[26] The variant conceived by Francesco has the characteristics of a style that may effortlessly be understood by looking at the wide, carved profiles of the figures in Baroncelli's and Domenico di Paris's Donatello-like iconostasis—in those years a point of reference for many other painters, including Tura[27]—and is ideally reminiscent of the powerful layout of the heads in Piero della Francesca's lost frescoes for the Ducal Palace and the church of the Hermit Friars. Other accents coexist in this ambitious if not fully-resolved composition: among the most interesting, a highly-refined taste for the preciousness of materials; the luminous reflections in the shaded portions that remind many of Domenico Veneziano's approach;[28] and above all, Francesco's uncommon descriptive skill of background landscape. This very deep view is crossed by a light-flecked river, its mirror-like waters crystal clear and steep, meandering banks stretching wide, where every pebble and blade of grass receives the utmost attention. This is the cipher that marks out the huge collective decorative enterprises Borso sponsored, linking the Tuscan *Madonna* from Washington to Ferrara via a double thread.[29]

We must therefore assume that Cossa held the most impressive credentials when in December 1462 we find him in Bologna to become godfather to Ludovico Garganelli, son of Bartolomeo and Margherita.[30] It should also come as no surprise that, having

25 Venturi 1930; C. Cavalca in *Cosmè Tura e Francesco del Cossa* 2007, p. 376, no. 94 (with bibliography).

26 D. Benati in *Le Muse e il principe* 1991, I, pp. 300–7, no. 77.

27 M. Ferretti in ibid., I, p. 370.

28 The closest correlation, previously in Nicolson (1950, pp. 12, 19), is with the *Madonna and Child* in the Berenson collection, Villa I Tatti, Settignano.

29 Work included among Cossa's youthful output, among others by Berenson 1936, p. 134; Nicolson 1950, pp. 12, 19; Ruhmer 1959, p. 67; Volpe 1958 ed. 1993, p. 154; it was anticipated in the early 1960s by Bacchi (1984, pp. 294–95); see note 25 above. It is appropriate to consider the date as closest to the first of these chronological end-points, around 1460–62.

30 Filippini 1913, p. 315.

abandoned his paternal guardianship, he was immediately in familiar relations with leading figures in the Bentivoglio court and circle, such as the Garganelli family, who were his confidants in the years to come and sponsors of one of the most important commissions in his artistic career.

Bologna was a city marked by a strong persistence of late-Gothic tradition and accustomed to the sumptuousness of the Vivarinis' workshop, even though new tastes expressed in the Washington *Madonna* had long since started to attract attention. A Tuscan-influenced central Italian trend had, since the 1430s, relied on the presence of major artists active in the city (Paolo Uccello's *Nativity* in the church of San Martino Maggiore is dated to c. 1437),[31] strengthened over time by a possible stopover by Piero della Francesca. Mid-century, this trend mixed in to the more pervasive and punctilious northern substratum, resulting in remarkable and original artworks such as the triptych with *Saint Francis between Saint Ludovic of Toulouse, Saint Bernardino of Siena and the Clients* (1455–60) today in the Collezioni Comunali d'Arte[32] (fig. 3). The arrival in Bologna of Marco Zoppo, fresh from a stormy apprenticeship at Squarcione's workshop and a period in Venice,[33] during these same years helped to forge a living link, a kind of triangulation, between the city ruled by the Bentivoglio and the Ferrara art world which, at the time of Donatello's altar and the Ovetari Chapel, had strengthened ties with Padua through an early invitation to Mantegna (1449) and Bono da Ferrara commuting between the two towns (1449–51).

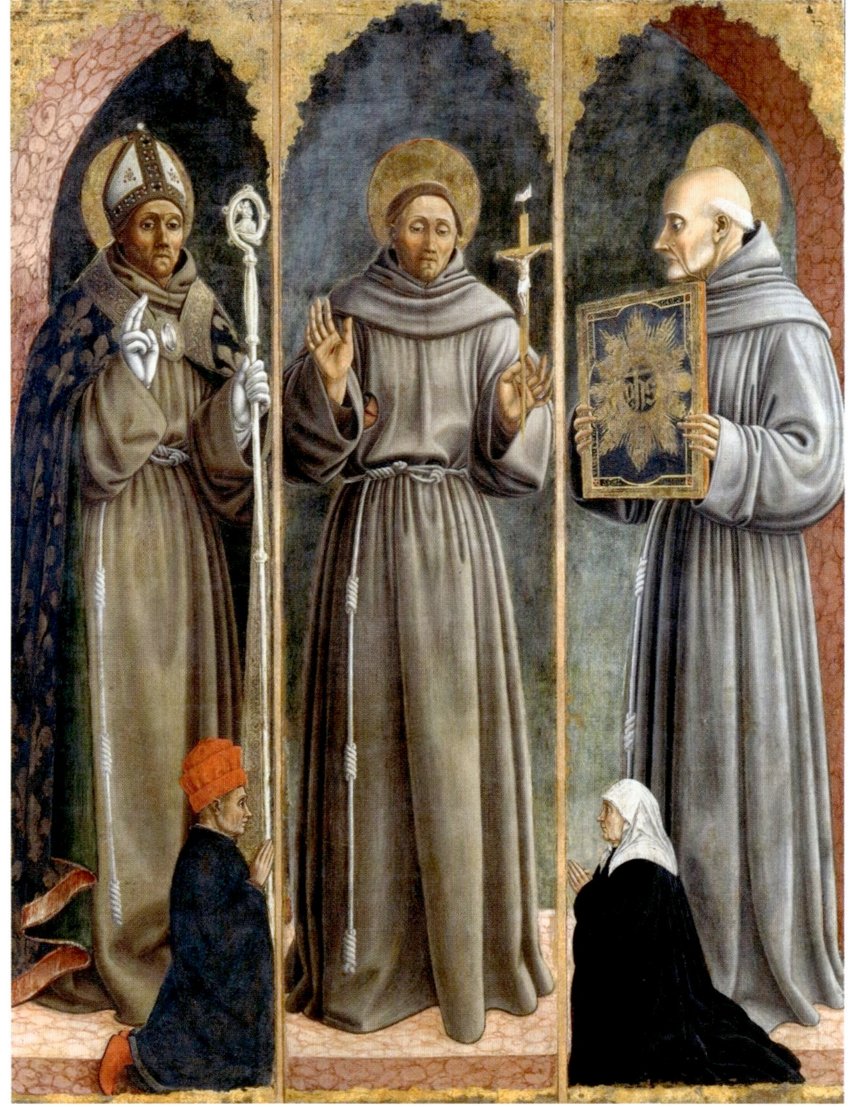

3

Bolognese artist, *Saint Francis between Saint Ludovic of Toulouse, Saint Bernardino of Siena and the Clients*. Collezioni Comunali d'Arte, Bologna

The interest of Bolognese patrons in young Francesco's art must have been triggered by the exceptional success, around 1455, of the now lost *Funeral of the Virgin*,[34] frescoed by his fellow townsman Galasso di Matteo Piva da Consandolo[35] at the Madonna

31 Volpe 1980 ed. 1993, pp. 102–23.

32 See Medica 2007, esp. pp. 14–16; Cavalca 2013, p. 321, no. 5 (with bibliography).

33 In October 1455 he was still in Venice: Lazzarini 1908, pp. 279–81; Armstrong 1976, pp. 326–27, no. II; see note 46 below.

34 Resonance without weakness from Borselli *ante* 1497 ed. 1912–29, p. 92, to Oretti c. 1760–80, ms. 123, f. 237; for a more detailed account of the sources, Cammarota 2002, pp. 31–32.

35 Giorgio Vasari (1550 ed. 1986, I, pp. 409–10) writes of an early talent, who cut his teeth on a work left in Ferrara by Piero della Francesca and ready, after the departure of the master from central Italy, to move to Venice in order to learn the

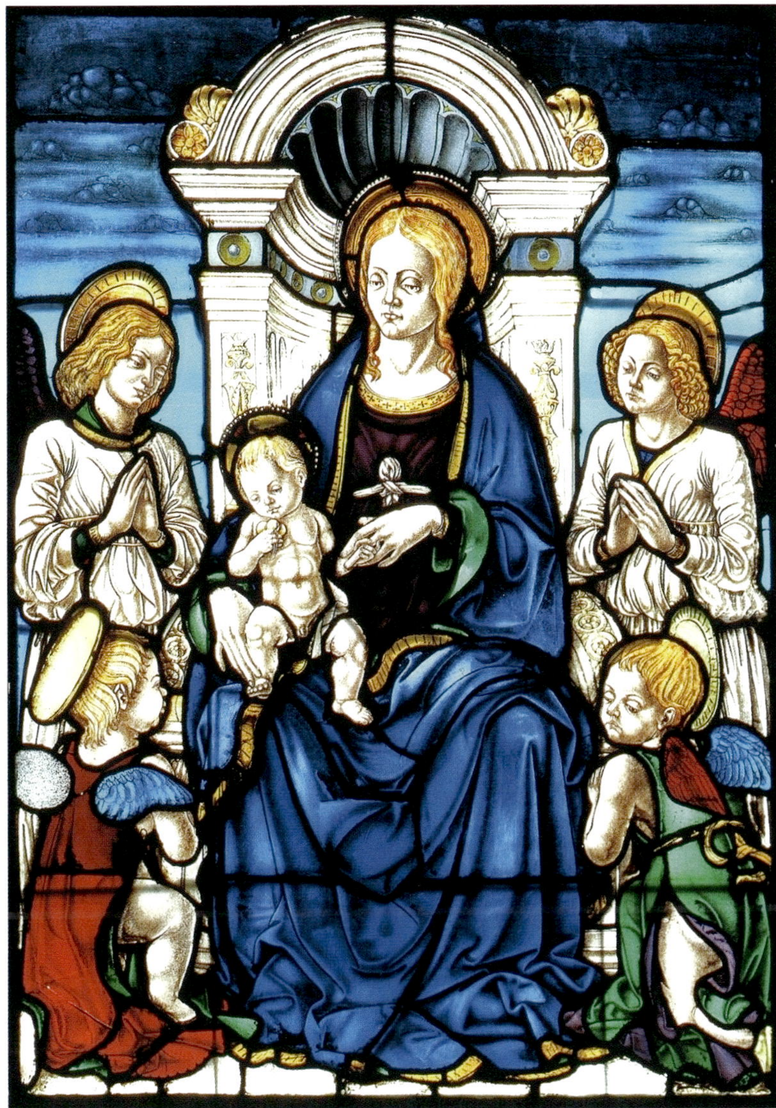

4

Giacomo and Domenico Cabrini to a cartoon by Francesco del Cossa, *Madonna and Child enthroned and four angels*. Church of San Giovanni in Monte, Bologna

del Monte, commissioned by Bessarione. In the mid-fifteenth century, this commemorative scene updated sacred themes in Bologna through the inclusion of a number of "natural" portraits, arousing wonder among observers for the stunning urban settings: a street overlooked by palaces of uncommon beauty, where everything is depicted with the utmost care (including bystanders' clothes down to tiny shimmering gold garments, according to the chronicles). A number of times in years gone by, historiography has attempted to add tangibility to Galasso's work; however, none of the proposals advanced, not even ones that in the past have dared to associate paintings of considerable stature with his name, such as the Berlin *Polymnia* and the Budapest *Muses*, would seem to coincide fully with the complex artistic qualities traced in source chronicles.[36] Given the extreme paucity of surviving testimony as regards the global climate of those years, the loss of Galasso's frescoes results in an incalculable damage,[37] preventing us from knowing how much concrete demand there actually was for realism in Bentivoglio's capital in that crucial period.

From the mid-1460s onwards, that is, only five years after the first documented contact with the Garganelli family, three works, certainly made by Cossa, were carried out in Bologna credibly one after another. This sequence marked a fundamental step forward, both in the figurative environment we just described and in the artist's stylistic research, which entered a new phase. These works are: the stained-glass window with the *Madonna and Child enthroned and four angels*, made in 1467 by master glassmakers Giacomo and Domenico Cabrini[38] after his cartoon for the facade of the church of San Giovanni in Monte (fig. 4); the altarpiece with the *Annunciation*

---

new technique of oil-tempered colors. On this latter skill, see also Lamo 1550 ed. 1996, pp. 66–67. Certainly, in 1449 the artist collaborated with Nicolò Panizzato's workshop, engaged in various decorative enterprises for the Este court, and was still in Ferrara in 1452. For documentary evidence of activity in Ferrara, see Toffanello 2010, pp. 241–42; for his arrival in Bologna in 1455, Borselli *ante* 1497 ed. 1912–29, p. 92; Vasari 1550 ed. 1986, I, p. 409.

36 For the attribution to Galasso of the Berlin *Polymnia* and the Budapest *Muses*, see Venturi 1901–40, VII/3, 1914, p. 498; Longhi 1934 ed. 1956, p. 104; in discontinuity, Boskovits 1978, p. 377 note 24; see A. Bacchi in *Le Muse e il principe* 1991, I, pp. 408–16, no. 97 (as Anonymous Ferrara artist); D. Benati in *Le Muse e il principe* 1991, I, pp. 428–30. On the reprise of the traditional attribution to Galasso of the *Deposition* from the Este Corpus Christi Monastery in Ferrara, now in the Pinacoteca Nazionale, and another group consistent with it formed by five *Madonnas with Child*: D. Benati in *La Pinacoteca Ala Ponzone* 2004, pp. 188–89, no. 58.

37 Formerly in Volpe 1958 ed. 1993, pp. 154 (cit.), 164–65 note 9: this evokes the critical weight of the loss of Galasso's frescoes, which "were perhaps his fundamental monuments."

38 Oretti 1767, f. 265; see Varignana 1985.

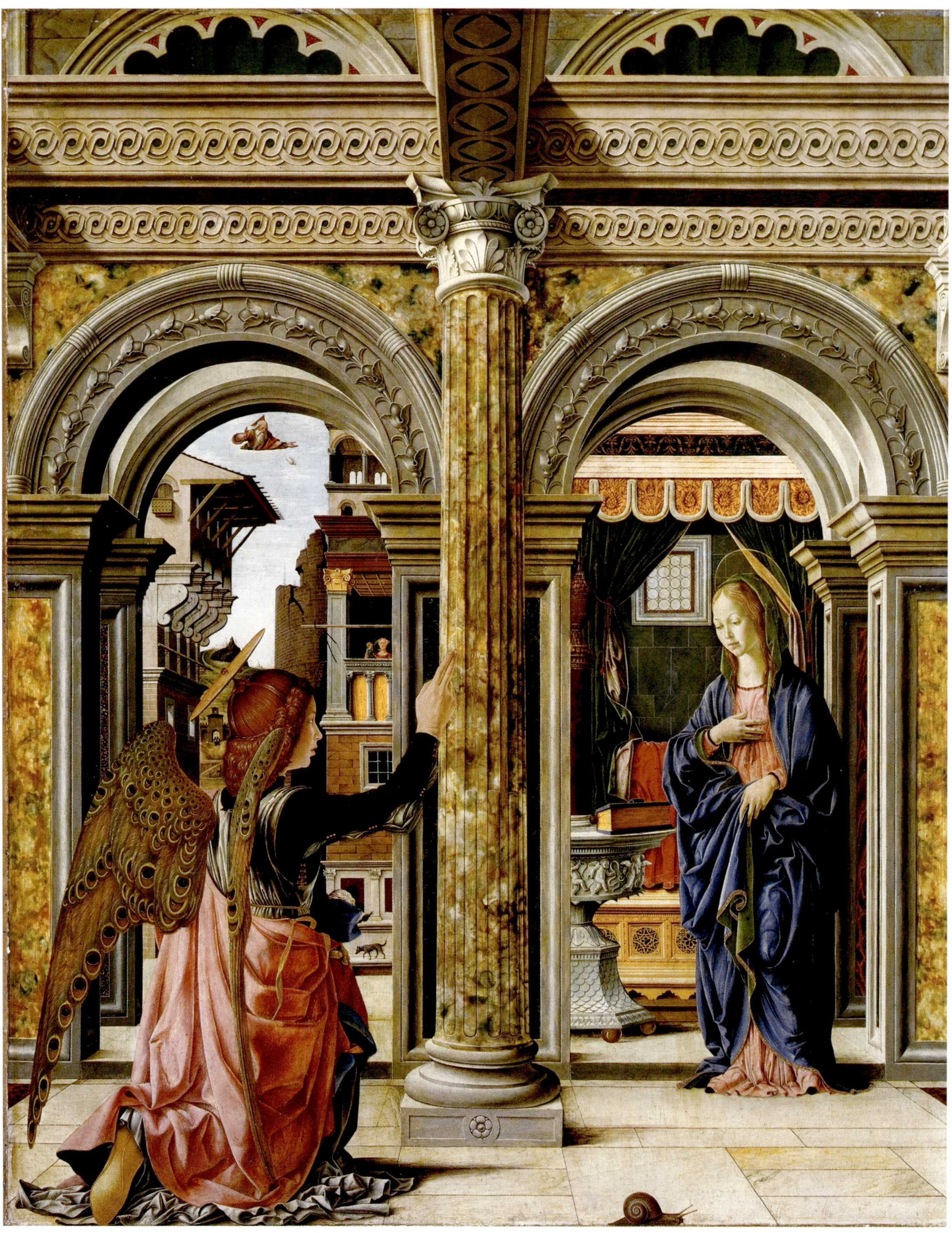

5

Francesco del Cossa, *Annunciation*. Gemäldegalerie Alte Meister, Dresden

6

Francesco del Cossa, *Annunciation*, detail. Gemäldegalerie Alte Meister, Dresden

7

Giuliano da Maino, Maso Finiguerra, and Alesso Baldovinetti, *Annunciation*, detail. Cathedral of Santa Maria del Fiore, Florence, Sagrestia delle Messe

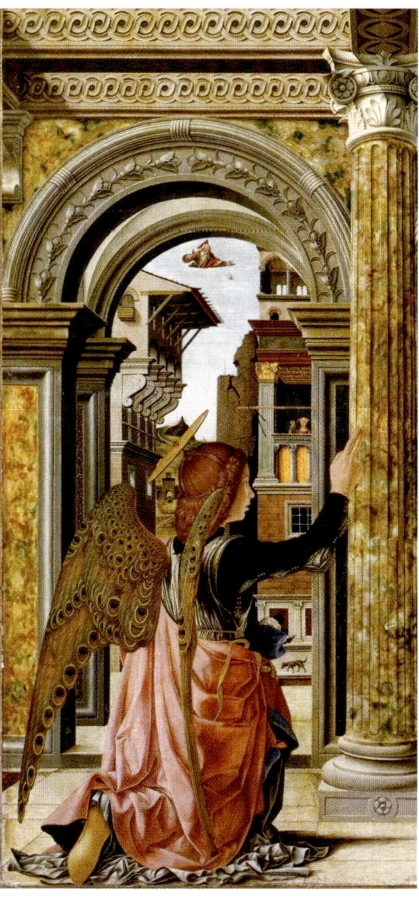

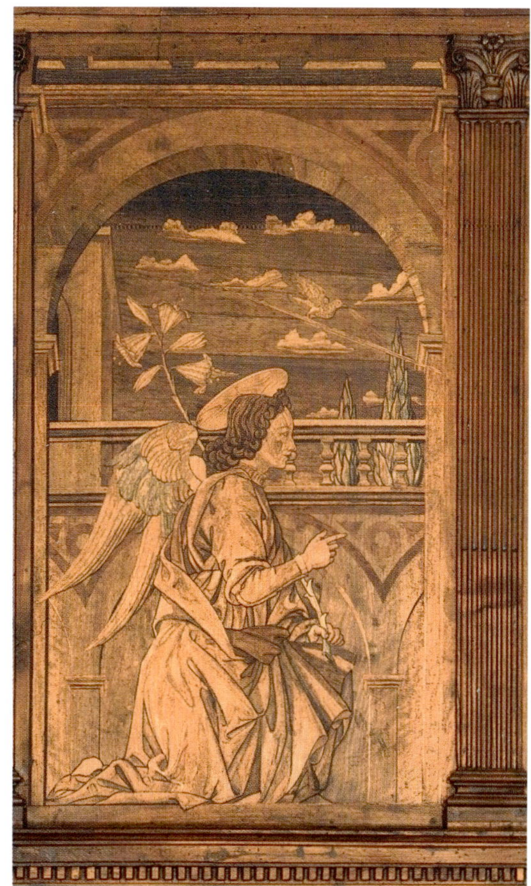

of 1467–68 (fig. 5), today at the Gemäldegalerie in Dresden (dismembered: it originally included the predella with the *Nativity* preserved in the same museum, *Saint Catherine of Alexandria* and *Saint Clare* of the Museo Nacional Thyssen-Bornemisza in Madrid and, in all likelihood, the *Franciscan Friar in prayer* at Scuola Grande di San Rocco;[39] see fig. 10 on p. 115); and another stained-glass window, also after one of his cartoons (1468–69), today at the Musée Jacquemart-André in Paris[40] (see fig. 4 on p. 22).

The solid formal framework of the stained-glass window at San Giovanni in Monte, the complexity of the spatial articulation in the Dresden *Annunciation* altarpiece (an innovative masterpiece modeled without hesitation on the squared altarpiece type of old-Florentine style), and the charming grace of the figures in the Paris stained-glass window,

---

39 Dating of the Dresden altarpiece is still a matter of debate. Starting with Longhi (1934 ed. 1956, p. 31), who recomposes the whole (the addition of the Franciscan saint was a later proposal by Carlo Volpe, circulated by D. Benati in Volpe 1993, p. 194), for the majority of critics the chronology runs from immediately after Cossa's signing up for the Schifanoia, around 1470–71. The first perceptive reading of the *Annunciation* as a youthful work, distinguished from the sections of the Griffoni Polyptych in Brera and London, is ascribed to Crowe and Cavalcaselle 1871 ed. 1912, II, pp. 237–38 note 1. In modern times, it has been put forward by Bacchi (1984, pp. 295–97 and 1991, pp. 46–50, no. 4), supported by Lucco (1987, pp. 241–42); Benati 1993; Ciammitti 1995, pp. 32–33; Benati 2012a, pp. 46, 53 note 26; Cavalca 2005; Cavalca 2013, pp. 151–60, 331–32, no. 17.

40 Dating of the Paris stained glass window is debatable as well, either from before or after the 1469 Schifanoia frescoes. Considering it to be posterior to the Ferrara undertaking, as part of a chronological series that ranges from 1470–73 to 1474, among others: Volpe 1958 ed. 1993, p. 168 note 22; Ruhmer 1959, p. 79; Bacchi 1991, p. 52; the following, among others, consider it to be prior: Neppi 1958, p. 35; Salmi 1958, p. 3; Varignana 1985, p. 50; Lucco 1987, p. 242; M. Medica in *Gli Este a Ferrara* 2004, p. 298; and C. Cavalca in *Cosmè Tura e Francesco del Cossa* 2007, p. 394, no. 105 (with bibliography).

enclosed within an oculus defined by the well-calculated perspective of the framing, allow us to make comparisons with the highest expressions of Ferrara and Bologna figurative art that came before them, noting the differences and perceiving the affinities.

Cossa certainly knew the *Muses* in the Studiolo at Palazzo Belfiore, made between 1455 and 1463: Michele Pannonio's *Talia* now in Budapest, Tura's *Calliope* now in London, from which he studied the elegant handling, the abandonment of the wrists and the inflection of the holding out gesture (one that would feature in the Griffoni Polyptych saints), and above all the Berlin *Polymnia*, serving as inspiration for the angels populating the *Madonna* at San Giovanni in Monte.[41] He studied Tura's canvas altarpiece with the *Madonna enthroned with Child between Saints Jerome and Apollonia* (c. 1455) today at the Musée Fesch in Ajaccio,[42] delving deeply to discover the secrets of the architecture turned toward the viewer, and observed Marco Zoppo's polyptych of San Clemente (1458–61), in which he found an alternative way to draw on the new compositional formulas under development at that time in Padua.[43] Nonetheless, Cossa's works preserve their own precise identity, distinguished by his special mastery of constructing the figures and his consistent organization of space. What he brought was not just an impeccable discipline in defining the planes of depth with respect to the foreshortened figures, but also meticulous attention to the treatment of outlines, which enclose and define the luminous transparency of the materials. It is as if everything that was in seed form in the Washington *Madonna* had moved in the wake of Domenico Veneziano, in parallel with figurative approaches spawned in Florence during the early 1460s as a result of the latter's most ingenious inventions.[44] The importance of the most frankly Florentine component of Cossa's stylistic approach has always been remarked upon in critical literature, albeit at a background level. This was due to a certain ill-concealed prejudice toward Vasari (who had the Ferrarese artist—Costa, *sic*!—stay in the Tuscan capital for many months, studying the works of leading artists of the day),[45] as well as to a distancing of Italian Longhi-inspired historiography from the critical line led by Bernard Berenson, who was the first to dwell on this issue.[46] Fostering this reticence, progressively weaker though it became,[47]

41 On the *Muses* of Belfiore's Studiolo, see *Le Muse e il principe* 1991.

42 Boskovits 1978, p. 387; G. Galansino in *Mantegna* 2008, pp. 96–98 (with bibliography).

43 With particular reference to comparisons that may be made between the oculi with the *Annunciation* and the Jacquemart-André stained-glass window: Lucco 1987, p. 242; C. Cavalca in *Cosmè Tura e Francesco del Cossa* 2007, p. 394; reprised in Calogero 2018, p. 38. Commissioning of the polyptych for the College of Spain took place after May 1, 1458 when the rector Luis de Fuente Encalada took office, and lasted until at least 1461: Cavalca 2013, pp. 110–11; see p. 371, docs. I.2–I.3. Calogero (2018, p. 43 note 18) tried to invalidate the significance of the documentary sequence by questioning the content of the note included in a document of September 25, 1461, concerning funds necessary to complete the work. But his attempt failed: indeed, the use of the imperfect tense, which is a durational past, indicates undoubtedly an action not yet completed.

44 Definition of this current of painting, evolving from the altarpiece at Santa Lucia dei Magnoli, spanning the years 1460–65, is due, as we know, to Bellosi (1990 and 1992, esp. p. 23); for the scholar, besides Domenico Veneziano, it includes "totally or partially" Paolo Uccello, Angelico in his late phase, Andrea del Castagno, Giovanni di Francesco, Alesso Baldovinetti, and the so-called Maestro di Pratovecchio. This was a losing line for Florence, to whom the scholar conceived a continuation, in the wake of Donatello and Piero della Francesca, in the painters of Ferrara and the period of Squarcione, including with specific reference to Cossa (Bellosi 1990, p. 45).

45 Vasari 1568 ed. 1878–81, III, pp. 131–32: "Being by nature much disposed towards the art of painting, and hearing how greatly Fra Filippo, Benozzo Gozzoli, and others, were renowned and extolled in Tuscany, repaired to Florence to see their works, and finding when he arrived, that their manner pleased him greatly, he remained in that city many months" (translation from Vasari 1898, vol. 2, p. 147).

46 Berenson 1907 ed. 1952, p. 162; Berenson 1968, p. 93: "Strongly influenced by Domenico Veneziano, Castagno and Baldovinetti; and to some extent by Benozzo Gozzoli." Many well-written pages in Garboli 1993 focus on the relationship between Berenson's and Longhi's vision of the Renaissance.

47 Bacchi 1991, p. 20.

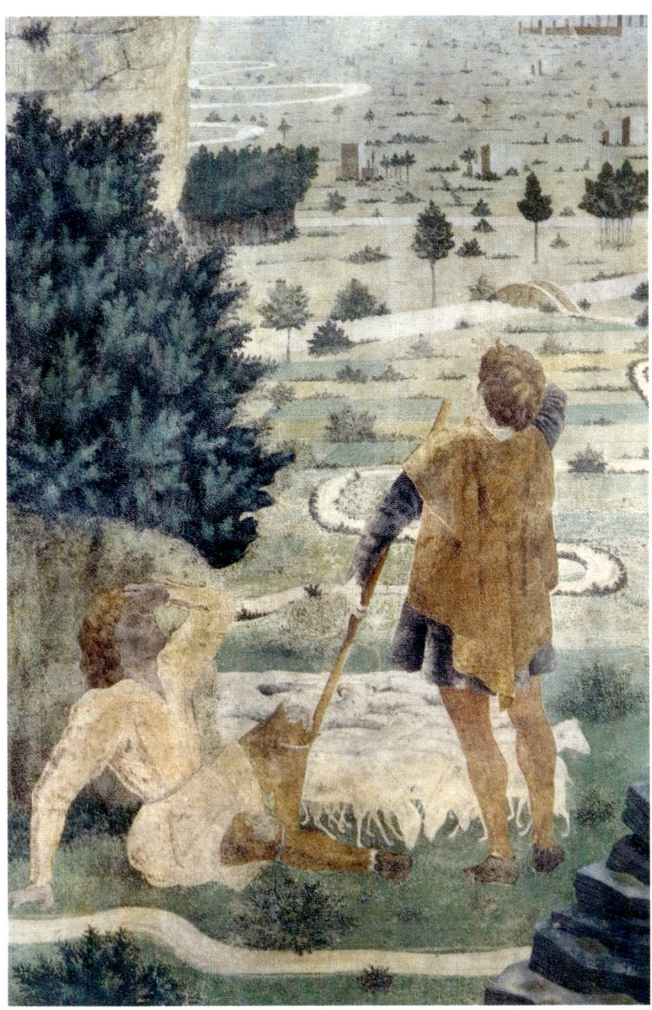

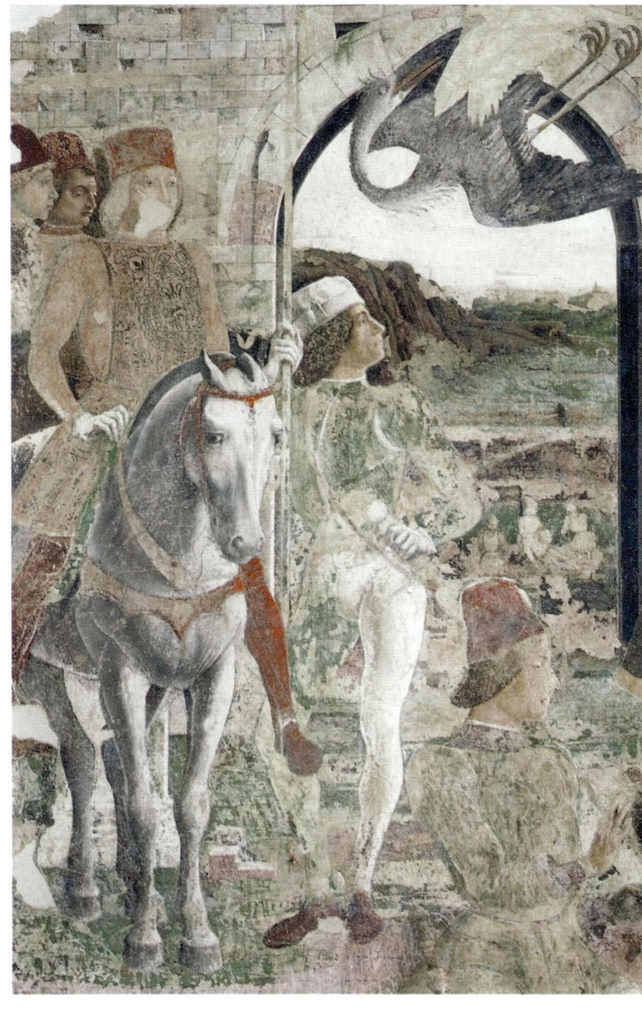

8

Alesso Baldovinetti, *Nativity*, detail. Church of Santissima Annunziata, Florence

9

Francesco del Cossa, *April*, detail. Palazzo Schifanoia, Ferrara, Hall of the Months

was the difficulty in detailing times and modes of this learning experience without any concrete evidence.[48] But today, it is possible to put this experience into focus by relying on a series of clues that immediately insist on Cossa's skills as a "great master" in the arts of drawing,[49] as a designer of projects destined to be translated into a variety of media, and often of intrinsic value. This was the case of his drawings for a series of important embroidered panels conserved in the Florentine church of San Francesco dei Vanchetoni, in which the model of *Saint Catherine of Alexandria* from the Thyssen-Bornemisza collection, originally on the side pillars of the altarpiece with the Dresden *Annunciation*, returns.[50] Through these activities, we know—notwithstanding the silence of chronicling documents—that in the period 1462–67 Cossa was at the center of an extraordinary hub of relationships that put him in touch with the "figure masters" who worked on the fine Sacristy for Mass at the Cathedral of Florence (Maso Finiguerra and Alesso Baldovinetti, especially) and allowed him to study, thanks to an eye trained since his very childhood, the architectural language of some of the most prestigious monuments of

48 See the major new developments in Ginzburg 1994, p. 121, establishing a relationship between Cossa's *Pietà* at the Musée Jacquemart-André in Paris (inv. MJAP-OA 1928) and the fresco of a similar subject by Giovanni di Piamonte in the small Rucellai temple.

49 As noted by Sebastiano Aldrovandi: *Philomathia* [1478]; see Ruhmer 1959, p. 94.

50 Cavalca 2005; on embroidery, previously Garzelli 1973, pp. 16–17.

Medici Florence: those sponsored by the Rucellai and the complex of the Chapel of the Crucifix in San Miniato al Monte, commissioned around that time by Piero de' Medici.

Without venturing into complex questions, on the painting front it is sufficient to cite the influence Alesso Baldovinetti's *Nativity* frescoed in the Cloister of the Vows of the Santissima Annunziata (figs. 8–9) exerted on Cossa'art. From that masterpiece, congenial to him for the optical precision of its luminous, perspective-based painting, he picked up a new way of tackling Flemish art, as well as of interpreting the lessons imparted by Piero della Francesca. The landscape, figures, and portraits in the oculars of the frame left a deep impression on him not only in terms of composition but also and above all with regard to the selection of natural data (figs. 10–11).

We know not whether Cossa traveled to Florence from Ferrara or from Bologna. However, neither in Tura's Ferrara nor in Galasso's and Zoppo's Bologna would that Tuscan experience have earned him the "name" he so proudly proclaims in his letter to Borso, if he had not been able to skillfully harmonize it with the memory of the illusionary devices that Mantegna had very early on revealed to artists in his hometown—in other words, if he had not at that time combined the expressive content with a scenographic conception of painting. The Dresden *Annunciation* is a veritable manifesto in this sense. Here Cossa manages to elevate figuration in a unified field to a new level of descriptive richness. He has sufficient authority to overturn the point of view of the works taken as a model in Florence—the *Annunciation* in the inlay of the Cathedral Sacristy (figs. 6–7), the sacred family in Baldovinetti's fresco at the Annunziata—so that the observer, placing himself behind the angel, finds himself directly involved in the holy event. The main effect of this powerful dramatization of sacred subjects is the creation of an open perspective view, based on a striking projection out of the plane of the painted panel of some of the details and a hyperbolic distancing of others. The effect must have been increased by the frame—credibly, a monumental structure of Renaissance type, no less important than the painted area, which, as is the case with Mantegna's San Zeno altarpiece, by invading the physical space of the beholder helps complete the perspective, exalting the affective impact of the images (see fig. 10 on p. 115).

The exceptional illusionistic effort he experimented in the Dresden *Annunciation* was developed on a larger scale at Palazzo Schifanoia where, to our knowledge, no other wall has the unity, precision, and creative impetus of Cossa's. We know that the decoration of the Hall of the Months, in which the Ferrara-born artist was involved in 1469, was a collective enterprise completed to a tight deadline, probably in the second half of that year, with several masters working on the final band cheek by jowl.[51] In order to conclude the work in the most effective manner, Borso likely commissioned an iconographic consultant to provide the various artists with reference drawings (but not specific cartoons),[52] calling back to Ferrara the famous portraitist Baldassarre d'Este and commissioning him to prepare models for the images of Borso himself and some courtiers replicated, with minor variations, in the lower register.[53] Certainly, Cossa's claim for a salary, which remained unpaid by the client, makes it clear, as others have noted, that the creative control and the executive

51 Varese 1989a, p. 186; Lippincott 1989, p. 133; on the decorative cycle, Settis and Cupperi 2007.

52 On this shared opinion, Syson 2002, p. 55 and Toffanello 2010, p. 74.

53 On the hypothesis that Baldassarre provided the model for Borso's portraits in the lower register at Schifanoia, see Toffanello 2004–5, pp. 88–90; Farinella 2007, pp. 106–13; Sassu 2007, pp. 417–19; Toffanello 2010, pp. 75 ff.

10

Alesso Baldovinetti, *Portrait of a Man*. J. Paul Getty Museum, Los Angeles

11

Francesco del Cossa, *Portrait of a Man*, detail. Museo Nacional Thyssen-Bornemisza, Madrid

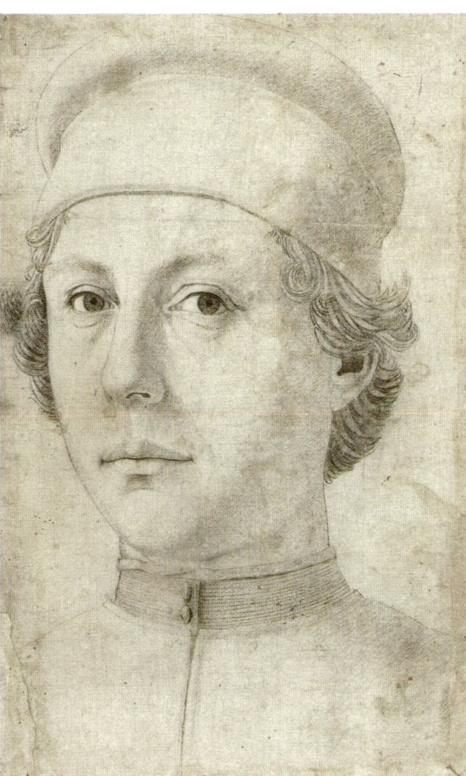

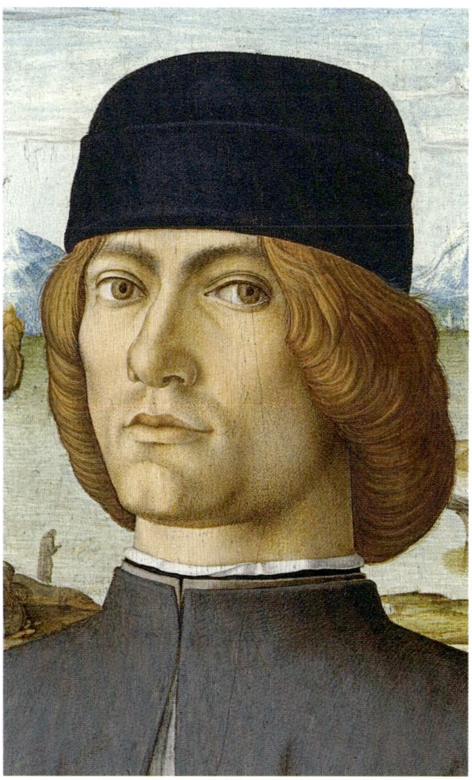

accuracy he exercised in the sectors for which he was responsible were not qualities sought of the masters engaged in the rest of the decoration. It should also be borne in mind that the work on sections of wall entrusted to Cossa began with *May* and proceeded on toward *March*.[54] Cossa's cartoons were without doubt used in the *May* portion of the wall painting, yet we struggle to recognize the hand of the artist,[55] given a number of rather distinguishable ruptures to the overall formal consistency. The fact that many hands worked on this section is indicated by the somewhat lax work in the left-hand portion, by the heavy formal nuisance that, notwithstanding the more sustained tone, affects the group of twins and the band with the deans, and by the rather crude—if meticulous—execution that distinguishes the lower strip of figuration (fig. 13).

Given that the scaffolding moved from top to bottom, we may conjecture that when Cossa agreed to work for Borso, from the very beginning and throughout the process he availed himself of assistants who ended up executing almost a third of the total. Providing them with graphic models and checking their pictorial transposition was a matter that for the Ferrara master coincided with full executive responsibility, since in his letter to the client he declares that he undertook "those three fields toward

---

54 Gheroldi 2007.

55 The use of help for the month of *May* is discussed by Harck (1884 ed. 1886) and accepted, to varying degrees, by the majority of scholars, split between those who deny the use of Cossa's cartoons (Ortolani 1941, pp. 118–19); those who exclude direct intervention and propose the identification of a collaborator (Lippincott 1989, p. 126: de' Roberti as a young man; Bacchi 1991, p. 72: the author of the *Madonna and Eight Saints*, published by Longhi 1940 ed. 1956, p. 180, figs. 408–9; see Toffanello in Settis and Cupperi 2007, pp. 269–70); those who believe he was active in the zodiacal band (Volpe 1977 ed. 1988, p. 17; G. Sassu in *Cosmè Tura e Francesco del Cossa* 2007, p. 438, which relates the lower portion of the fresco on the left of the predella of the altarpiece with the Dresden *Annunciation*). There has been no lack of opinions put forward in support of restoring complete Cossa authography (Ferretti 2011, pp. 280–81).

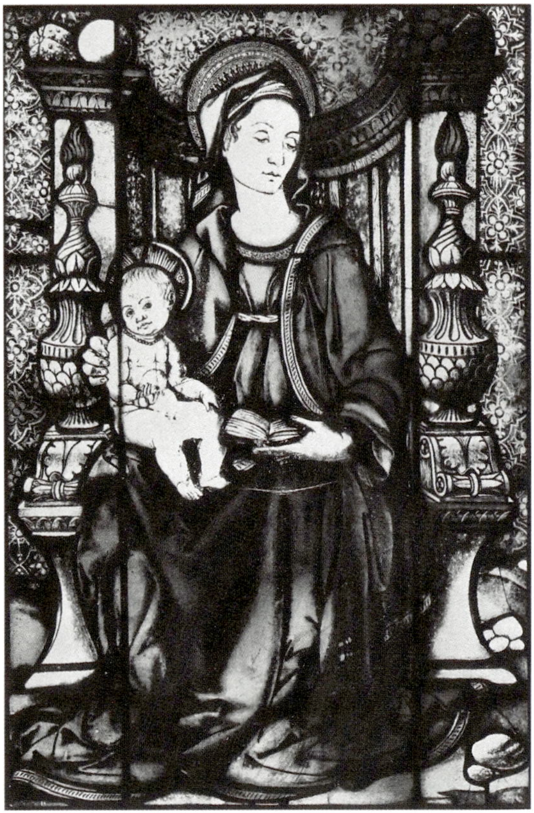

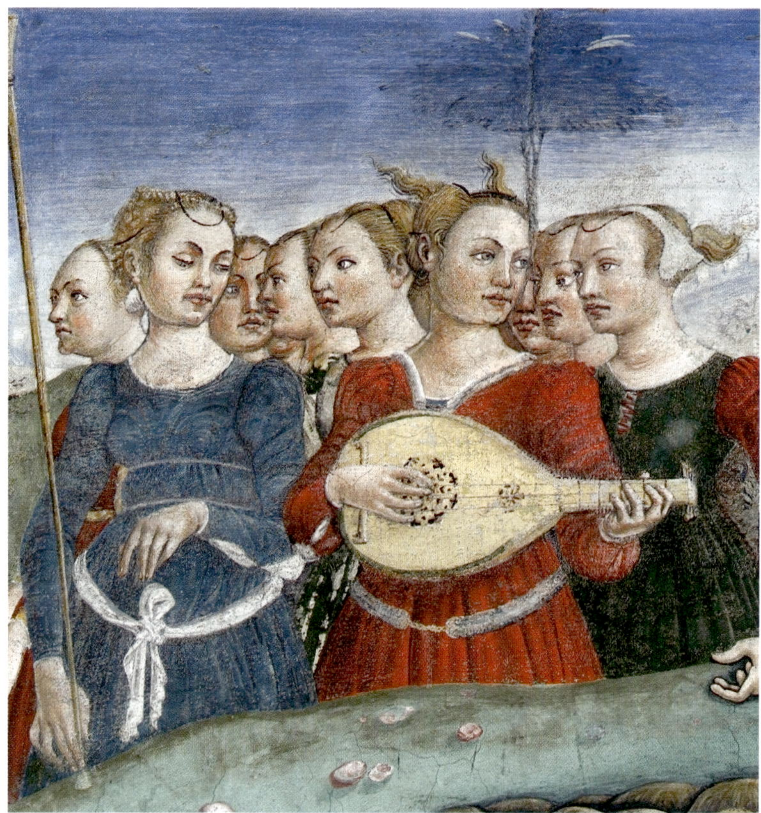

the antechamber."[56] The identification of these figures allows us to suppose that by around 1466–67, after his journey to Florence, Cossa had his own workshop. Without wishing to imagine a coercive production line of sorts, it is certain that the "hand" of some of the painters who collaborated with him on the famous Ferrara fresco cycle is easy to pick out in the weaker parts of the works created at the end of the 1470s in Bentivoglio's Bologna: in the cherubim with eagle and goblet that complete the stained-glass window of San Giovanni in Monte, for example, or in certain parts of the Dresden predella or in the lost stained-glass window with the *Madonna enthroned*, formerly in Berlin at the Kunstgewerbemuseum (fig. 12). At the risk of going too far, the presence of as many as three windows in the rather sparse catalogue from those years—manufactured articles of high quality, adopting inventions that would later meet with a certain success—leads us to believe that Cossa had already set up shop in Bologna, in fruitful partnership with the Cabrinis, a major family of local master glassmakers who signed and dated the *Madonna enthroned with four angels* on the Lateran church facade.

12

Giacomo and Domenico Cabrini (?) to a cartoon by an assistant of Francesco del Cossa's, *Madonna and Child*, detail. Formerly Kunstgewerbemuseum, Berlin

13

Francesco del Cossa and assistant, *May*, detail. Palazzo Schifanoia, Ferrara, Hall of the Months

14

Francesco del Cossa, *March*, detail. Palazzo Schifanoia, Ferrara, Hall of the Months

He did not obtain any response from Borso, but his work at Schifanoia was, in fact, unparalleled: it was there that Francesco del Cossa fully became the master of his own unmistakable style.

The sculptural conception of figures grouped inside architectural structures of classical inspiration is fully integrated into a spatial partition that connects the

56 See Franceschini 1993, doc. 1204.

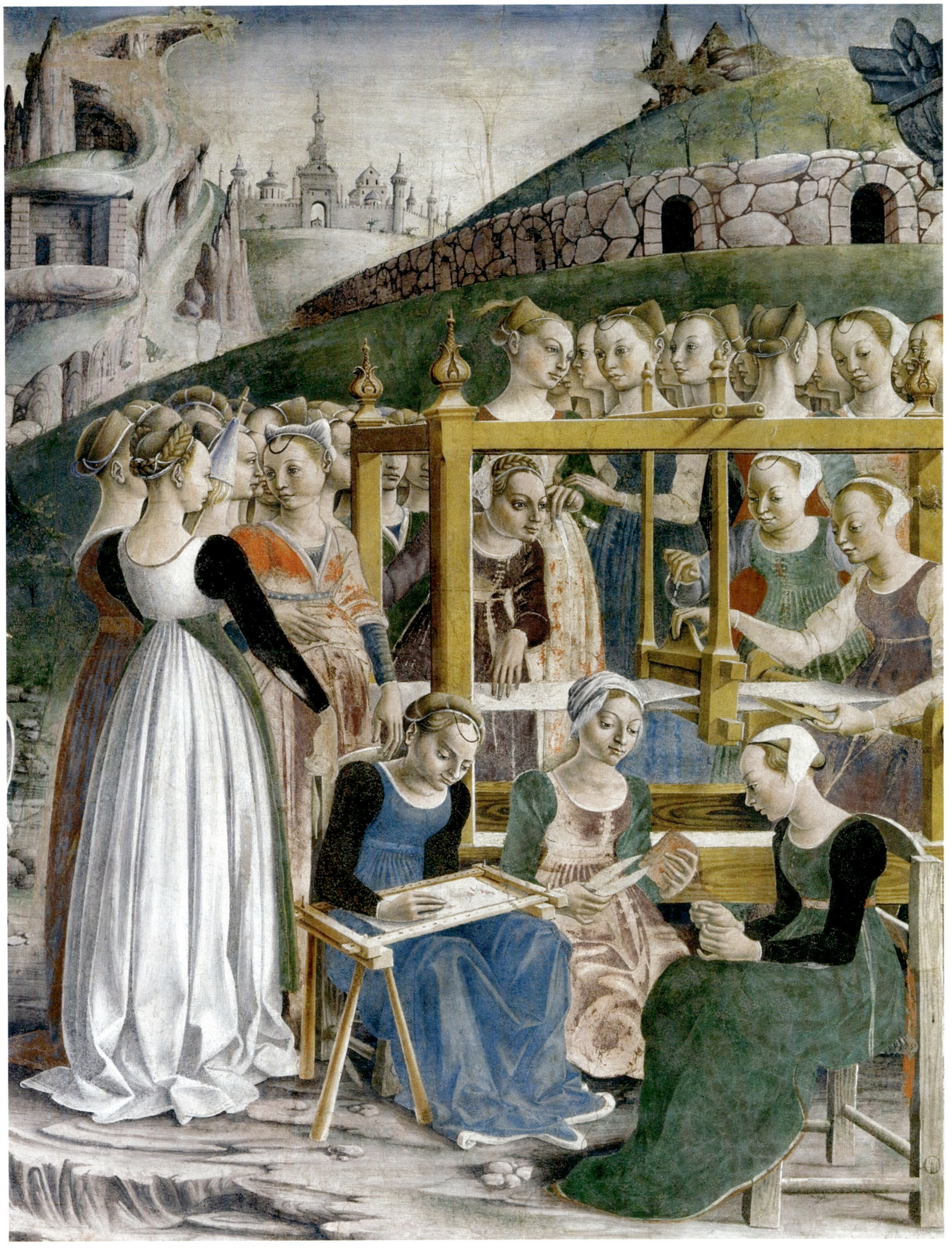

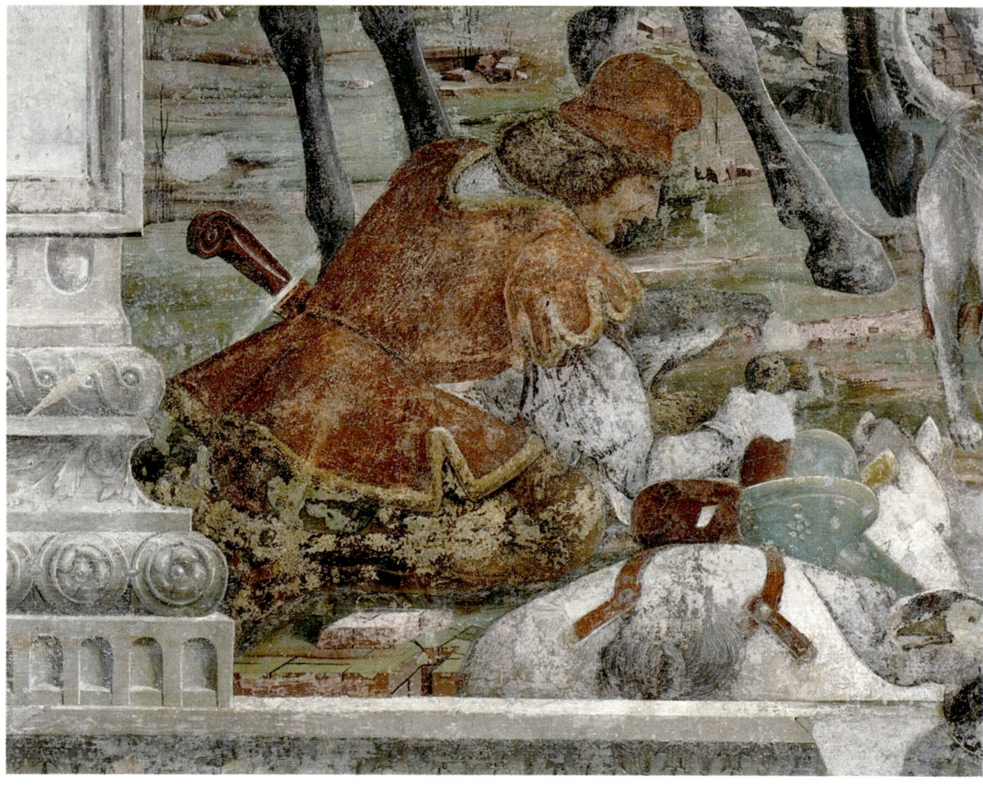

15

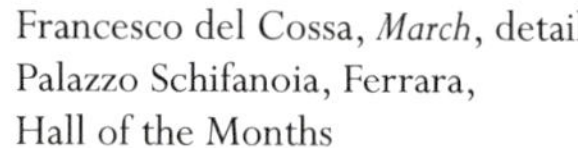

Francesco del Cossa, *March*, detail. Palazzo Schifanoia, Ferrara, Hall of the Months

actions viewed in individual places and containers.[57] The composition holds together the most varied registers: the dignified register of court scenes or the comic one of popular scenes, such as the famous episode of the Palio di San Giorgio in *April*, while his multi-material technique[58] becomes a very sharp instrument for probing all the ways of letting reality enter the work as much as possible. Francesco's description of nature achieves lyrical tones in his portrayal of the animal world and his figures are endowed with accents of reality that are never pompous or pretentious: an extreme focus on precise details in the depiction of gestures and faces really captures character, isolating it within the often obsessive repetition of the same formal motif (fig. 14). In such complex poetics, Cossa's citations of Tura's life-filled snapshots, of Mantegna's *ab imo*[59] (fig. 15), and even recollections of Jan van Eyck[60] reveal the artist's creative efforts and appear in his works as homages to models established by these celebrated masters: demonstrations of his skill and proof of "ongoing study" rather than triggerers of style.

The work at Schifanoia was the occasion of the meeting between the older master and young Ercole de' Roberti, who would eventually follow Cossa to Bologna, glimpsing the possibility of greater opportunities. Critics have diverged on Ercole's identity when he met Cossa ever since Roberto Longhi suggested that he should be acknowledged as

57 Particularly felicitous in this regard are Lugli's evocative references (1990, p. 72) to the "*mansiones* of the medieval sacred theater, the memory of which persisted in the Flemish imagination, in part through tapestry, for a particularly long time."
58 See Gheroldi 1997, p. 153.
59 Both already assigned value by Venturi (1901–40, VII/3, 1914, pp. 630, 638).
60 Volpe 1977 ed. 1988, p. 17: in the upper register of *May*, in the upper right-hand corner, he identifies similarities between the "source of the Muses" and the source in Jan van Eyck's *Mystical Lamb* polyptych in Ghent.

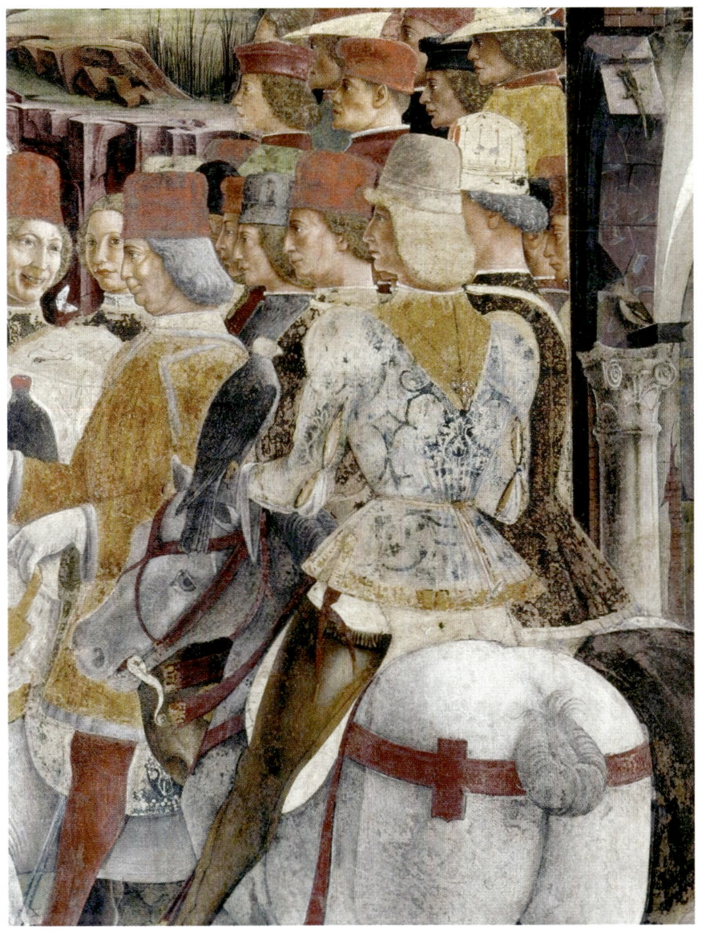

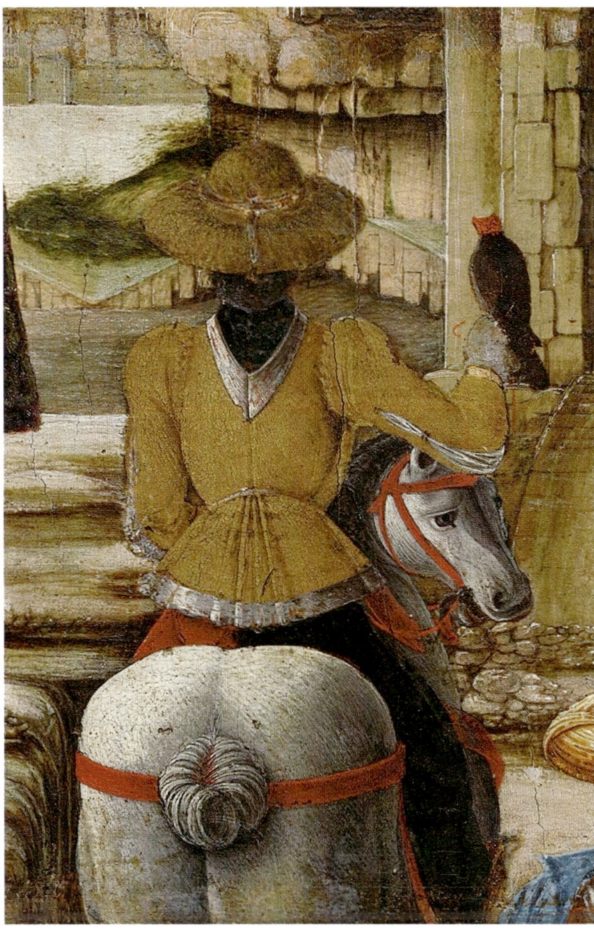

16

Francesco del Cossa, *March*, detail. Palazzo Schifanoia, Ferrara, Hall of the Months

17

Ercole de' Roberti, *Miracles of Saint Vincent Ferrer*, detail. Vatican Museums, Vatican City

the author of the month of *September*[61] (fig. 18). Born around 1450–55, Ercole was still a teenager[62] who, two years earlier, that is in 1467 (we know for sure), had received payments from the Este court as an apprentice to Gherardo di Andrea da Vicenza for work carried out at the villa in Portomaggiore.[63] It's difficult to outline Gherardo's artistic personality from official documents: in 1458 (that is, after Giacomo Sagramoro's death), he became the main decoration painter at court, but unfortunately we do not know of any of his works with certainty.[64] Among the various critical hypotheses that have been

61 Longhi 1934 ed. 1956, pp. 37–42; not in agreement are Ruhmer (1959, p. 32); Lippincott (1989, pp. 117–18, who believes Ercole de' Roberti possibly assisted Cossa on the east wall, for example in the scene of the San Giorgio Palio, as previously stated by Bargellesi 1934, pp. 8–9); Manca (1992, pp. 169–71); Syson (2002, pp. 58–61). In accordance with the full autography: Bacchi (1985, pp. 175–78); Molteni (1995, pp. 107–11, nos. 1–3); G. Sassu (in *Cosmè Tura e Francesco del Cossa* 2007, p. 448, no. 140).

62 In a letter dated March 19, 1491 addressed to the Duke, Ercole claims to be in the middle of his years (Franceschini 1995, doc. 799). Debate has continued over the correct date of birth (1450 or 1455–56) one may infer from this statement. Those who tend toward the latter period rule out, on account of him being too young, that the artist could have been hired to independently execute an entire wall (Syson 1999, p. VI note 26; Varese 2004, pp. 106–7; but see M. Toffanello in Settis and Cupperi 2007, p. 296). The young man's talent, the complex collective nature of the undertaking, and the pressure he was subjected to in view of a swift conclusion of the work meant that the artist's tender years were not necessarily an impediment to using him for large figurative portions of the cycle.

63 Syson 2002, p. 69 note 97, as pointed out by Charles Rosenberg.

64 For a balanced overview of the situation, Toffanello 2010, pp. 207–15, who puts forward, and this may be shared, doubts about the same artist executing, among others, the so-called *Mantegna Tarot* advanced by Syson (2002, pp. 55–65) and supported by Sassu (2007, pp. 420–23) through other additions to the catalogue; regarding the possible author of these engravings, Gnaccolini (2018, pp. 135-161) now brings back a proposal advanced by Longhi (1934 ed. 1956, pp. 97–98 note 59) in favour of Lazzaro Bastiani, around 1465–67.

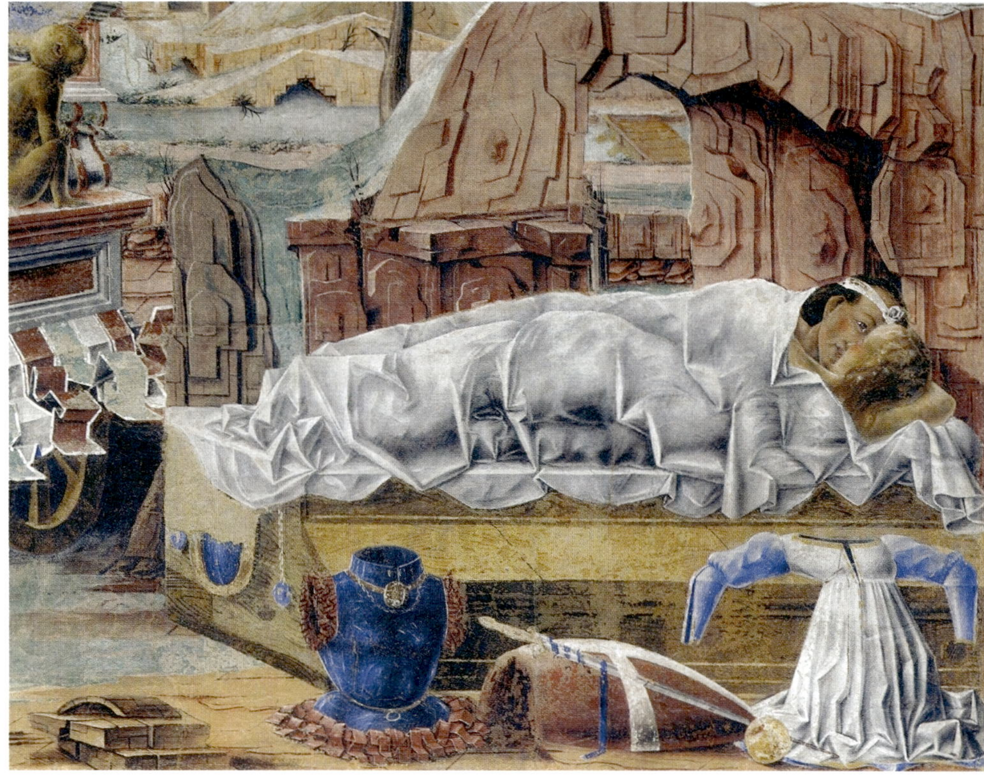

18

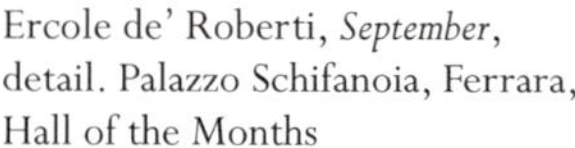
Ercole de' Roberti, *September*, detail. Palazzo Schifanoia, Ferrara, Hall of the Months

put forward, the most accredited obliges us to return to the walls of Palazzo Schifanoia, where Ercole was said to be active, playing an important role in the general design of the frescoes and directly executing the ones on the north wall.[65] Building on this, some critics have developed one of Carlo Volpe's insights, giving it shape.[66] In agreement with Longhi, the scholar considered Ercole to be the author of the month of *September*, speculating that the young artist was brought to the site by one master who was in charge of the month of *August*: given that in 1467 Ercole was in Gherardo's pay, this would make Gherardo the author of *August*, entailing for Ercole an apprenticeship at the Este court in a fully Tura-like spirit.[67]

The young man who followed Cossa to Bologna and contributed to the creation of the Griffoni Polyptych between 1470 and 1473 was undoubtedly an artist endowed with a stylistic cipher that distinguished him from his older master and the other assistants. Beyond the somewhat mechanical data drawn from style and documentary information, and beyond the fact that those who believe *September* should not be attributed to a single hand are probably right, there is no doubt that the minute, nervous line that splinters and crystallizes the volumes in *Vulcan's Forge* and the formal modules exaggerated to the point of deformation, yet always elegant and elongated, that return in the most convincing parts of the courtly register, very much resemble the peculiar features of a physiognomy that, as his relationship with Cossa became closer, would always make Bologna-period Ercole so recognizable (figs. 18–19). To reconcile the pungent style and impudent dynamism of the *September* scenes with the vibrant delicacy of the frail figures that make up the Griffoni

---

65 Syson 2002, pp. 55–61.
66 Volpe 1977 ed. 1988, pp. 20–21.
67 Toffanello 2004–5, pp. 95–96, 221; Buganza 2006, p. 35 note 33; Sassu 2007, pp. 421–22.

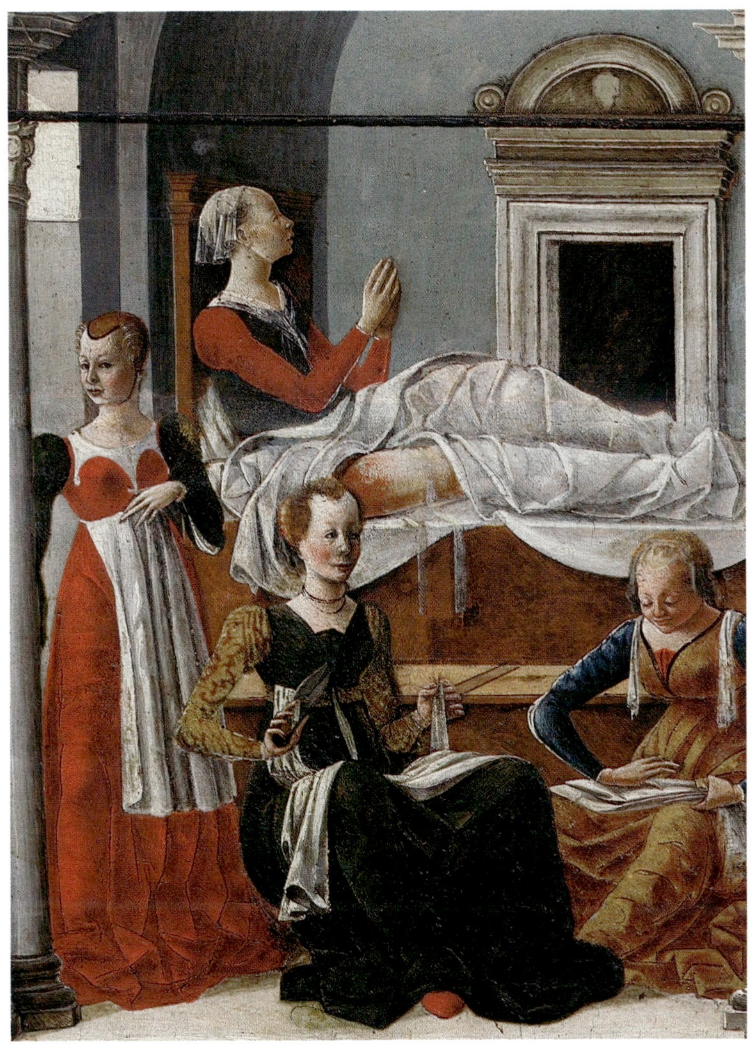

19

Ercole de' Roberti, *Miracles of Saint Vincent Ferrer*, detail. Vatican Museums, Vatican City

predella's groups is, however, neither obvious nor predictable. Intuiting this, Longhi tried until the last to place the altarpiece of San Lazzaro between the two works—an undocumented commission that, thanks to external data, we are able to date to around 1474–75[68] (fig. 22).

In his work for the Griffoni family, Cossa once again played the role of main designer: he conceived the whole scene, made the more detailed drawings—the quality of which is visible in the *Page figure* in the British Museum, London—and in this case in all likelihood handled relations with the carpenter.[69] Ercole leveraged his colleague's great graphic talent: using it with extreme intelligence, he cleverly carved out his own space for authentic expressive autonomy in this team job. The younger artist's stylistic adaptations naturally went to the roots of Cossa's interest in the art of Tura, as expressed at Schifanoia, but he was also able to grasp Mantegna's pauses and contrasts[70] (figs. 15, 17) and combine them with an acknowledged interest in Zoppo's stylistic approach.[71]

Vasari tells of Ercole being affectionately deferent toward Cossa. The two artists continued to work together in the following years, in an arrangement that offered mutual benefits and allowed de' Roberti to find an adequate sphere of action to develop the vision that would soon allow him incomparable achievements.

The turning point came with the commission that certified Cossa as a Bentivoglio artist: the Baraccano fresco[72] (fig. 20). A frescoed mural painting with broad areas of dry finishing, its communicative effectiveness is somewhat weakened by the poor state of conservation, but it nevertheless contributed in an essential way to codifying the Bentivoglio court's expressive register. Francesco worked on it for some

68 See note 73 below.

69 A few months after completing payments to Agostino de' Marchi for construction of the *capsa* that was to enclose the frame of the polyptych, the San Petronio *fabbricieri* paid Cossa for drawings—a *Saint Petronius* and a *Saint Ambrose*—to inlay the stalls of the major choir that Augustine himself worked on; see Filippini and Zucchini 1968, p. 55: September 27 and December 15, 1473.

70 Venturi 1901–40, VII/3, 1914, p. 630.

71 These were mostly iconographic forays (see the entry in this catalogue); this interest derives from a common inclination toward expressive and gestural accentuations that does not seem to substantiate the artist's formal research. Of a different opinion: Syson 1999, p. VII, who in support again refers to the hand of Ercole (Longhi 1940 ed. 1956, p. 131) a drawing with figures derived from the Griffoni predella, published, at Carlo Volpe's suggestion, by Daniele Benati as by the Cento-born artist (1984, p. 191 note, p. 193 note 33); see *Disegni del Rinascimento* 2001, pp. 94–98, no. 5. Previously, Manca insisted on Marco Zoppo's importance for Ercole de' Roberti. This interpretation was based on Armstrong's reading of the style Zoppo developed in Bologna (1976).

72 Bacchi 1991, p. 76; Cavalca 2013, pp. 38, 160–61, 336–37, no. 20.

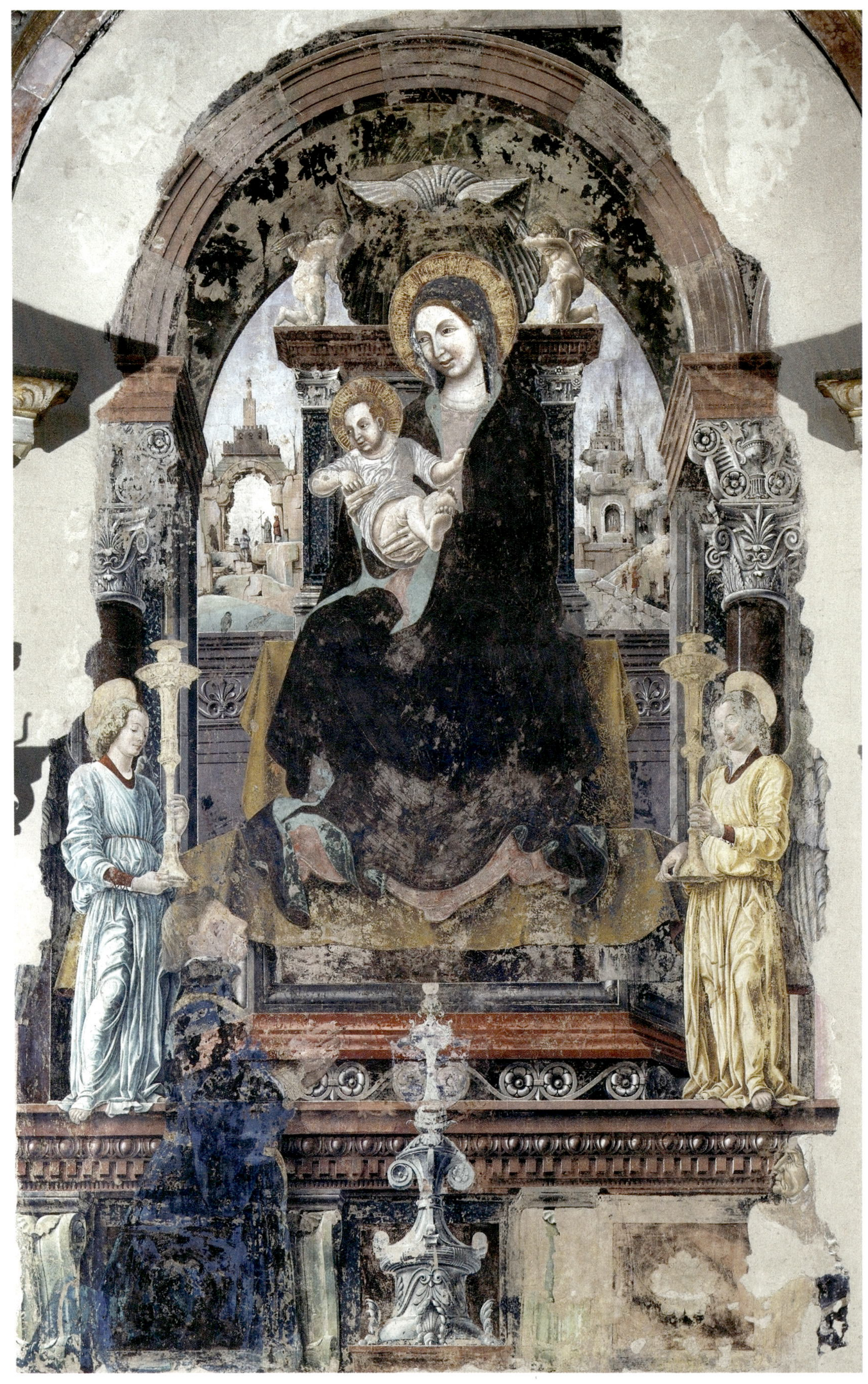

20

Francesco del Cossa, *Madonna del Baraccano*. Sanctuary of Santa Maria del Baraccano, Bologna

21

Francesco del Cossa, "Pala dei Mercanti." Pinacoteca Nazionale, Bologna

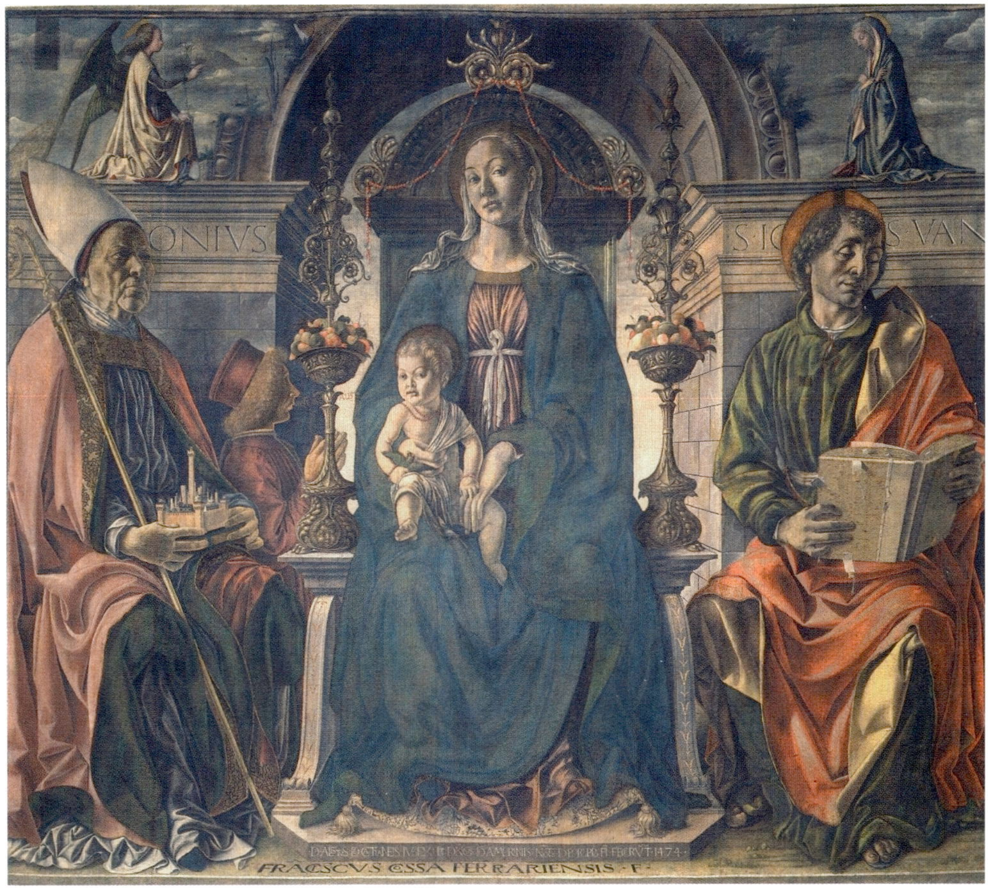

four months, beginning in January 1472, the length of time it took to renew and create a suitable frame around a fourteenth-century icon venerated by the people, a *Madonna and Child* that, having begun to work miracles, had supported the dominant family throughout the fifteenth century. The Renaissance artist approached the old painting with a control of execution that, in the restitution of the draperies, reaches mimetic reverence, with a new layout ready to draw on widely-circulated models while offering a highly individual interpretation. Probably at the client's request, the architectural structure of a barrel vault on free-standing columns alludes clearly to the superb old-fashioned Medicean aediculas made to enhance medieval images associated with cults of origins, while the core of the invention—the figure of Giovanni I Bentivoglio, a forebear of Giovanni II and responsible, in 1401–2, of the family takeover, who responds here to the manifestation of the Divine—recalls (in its profile and volumetric fullness, perceptible in a larval state) the famous Piero della Francesca work at the Malatesta Temple in Rimini (1451). The techniques Cossa used to create distance for the eye through an interlocking of narrative planes—indicated by the candelabra, the angels holding up the candelabra, and the landscape teeming with fragments of reality—nevertheless imbued the figuration with an unexpected and almost unsettling vitality when combined with the imperturbable impression of Piero's figurations. This original creative choice, based on the artist's study of perspective while at the same time ensuring a thread of continuity with local Gothic traditions, must have been highly appreciated by the Bentivoglio family, and most certainly exerted a major influence on the surrounding cultural environment, about

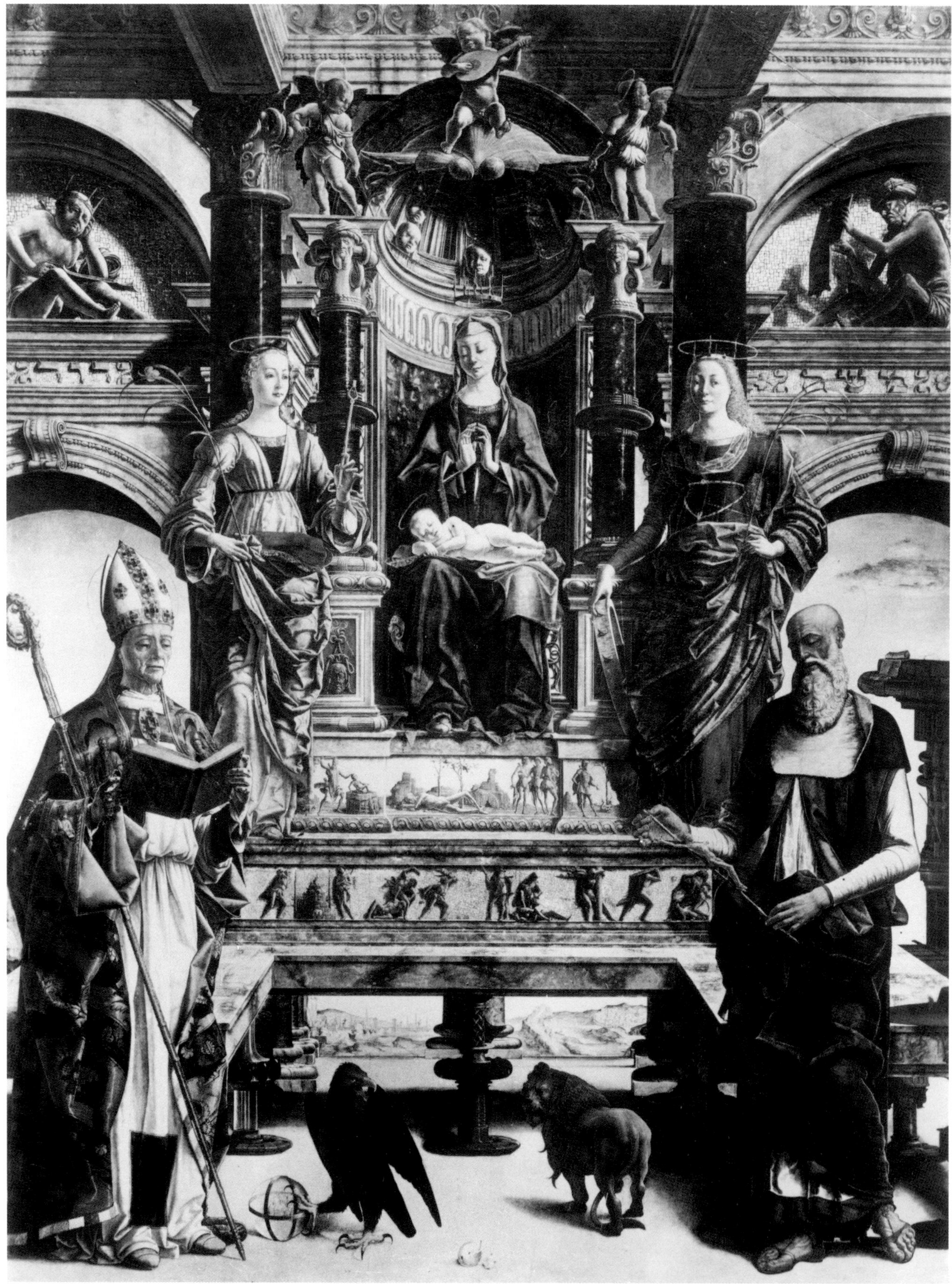

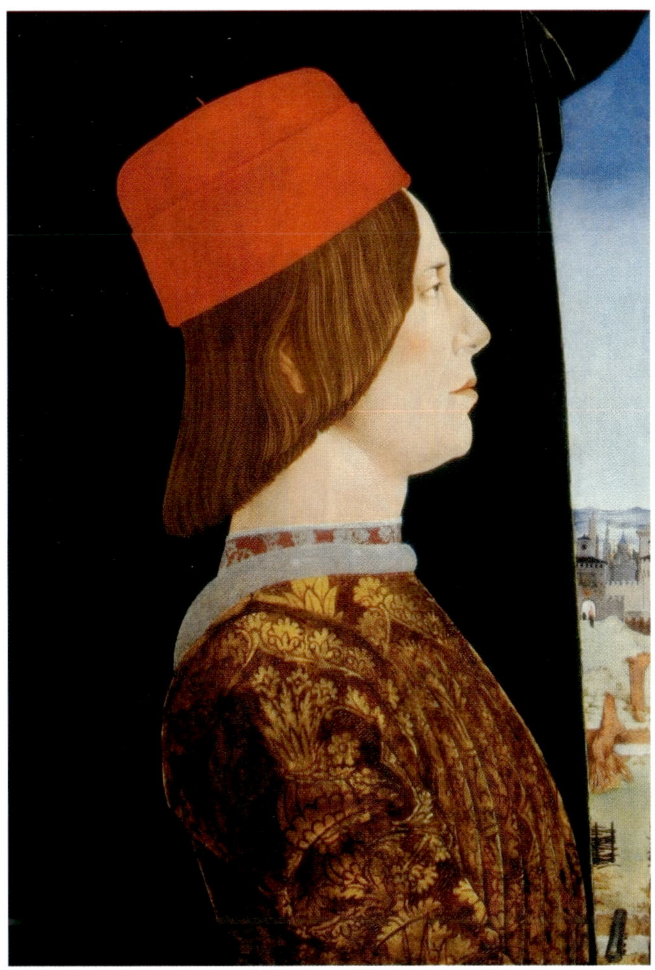

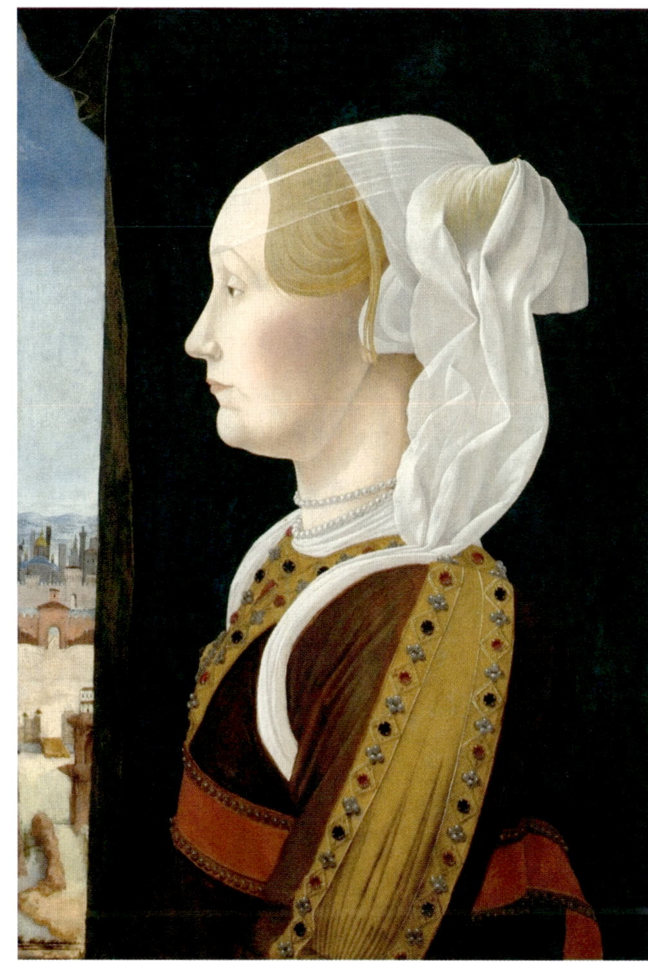

22

Ercole de' Roberti, San Lazzaro altarpiece. Formerly Kaiser Friedrich Museum, Berlin

23

Ercole de' Roberti, *Portrait of Giovanni II Bentivoglio*. National Gallery of Art, Washington, DC

24

Ercole de' Roberti, *Portrait of Ginevra Bentivoglio*. National Gallery of Art, Washington, DC

the way artists thought about representing the Madonna enthroned within a unified space, and about portraiture itself.

Cossa took this further two years later with the "Pala dei Mercanti,"[73] a superb work on canvas that depicts the Madonna enthroned with Child between Saints Petronius and John the Evangelist and the client, Alberto Cattani, to decorate the upper part of the Audience Hall at the Court of Merchants, as a warning and protection of their activities (fig. 21). He refined his technical rigor to achieve the right contextualization: the pictorial layout is millimetric, the chiaroscuro texture perfect, its line reminding us how fundamental Flemish influence always remained for Cossa. This great expertise in imposing a precise feeling onto the three-dimensional shapes of the figures was his truest point of contact with the output not just of Ercole but also of Niccolò dell'Arca and Guido Mazzoni, as Adalgisa Lugli has explained.[74]

Based on the example of the Madonna del Baraccano, Ercole de' Roberti began to lay the foundation for work on the altarpiece for the main altar at the church of San Lazzaro in Ferrara (fig. 22), officiated by the regular Lateran canons. This was an important commission, which the younger Ferrarese probably obtained through his brother's mediation. Despite patent references to Cossa's compositional approaches and inventions,

73 Bacchi 1991, p. 92; F. Fiori in *Pinacoteca Nazionale* 2004, pp. 257–60, no. 99; Cavalca 2013, p. 337, no. 21.
74 Lugli 1990.

so much so that many continued to see his presence here, Francesco managed the job in full autonomy.[75] An intimate understanding of what his master had perfected in the Bentivoglio votive fresco underpins the variations Ercole made to Piero della Francesca's prototype when, immediately after the Lateran altarpiece, he executed the Bentivoglio diptych (c. 1475)[76] (figs. 23–24) with which, before Lorenzo Costa's arrival in Bologna, he fixed the official image of those who enjoyed the greatest social prestige in the city. The decision to place a conspicuous visual screen between the profiles of the two characters and the background landscape evoking the peaceful nature of the city they ruled presents a surprising analogy with the alignment sought between the figures and the landscape at the Baraccano, marking out the deepening of space, plane by plane. As a drape of honor and as curtains that slighly part to reveal what's behind, this sort of gap Ercole imagined accentuates the role of salvatory intermediation the Bentivoglio were playing for the collectivity, while at the same time being a compositional expedient that activates the space, increasing the intensity of the two full-profile, classically-inspired portraits.

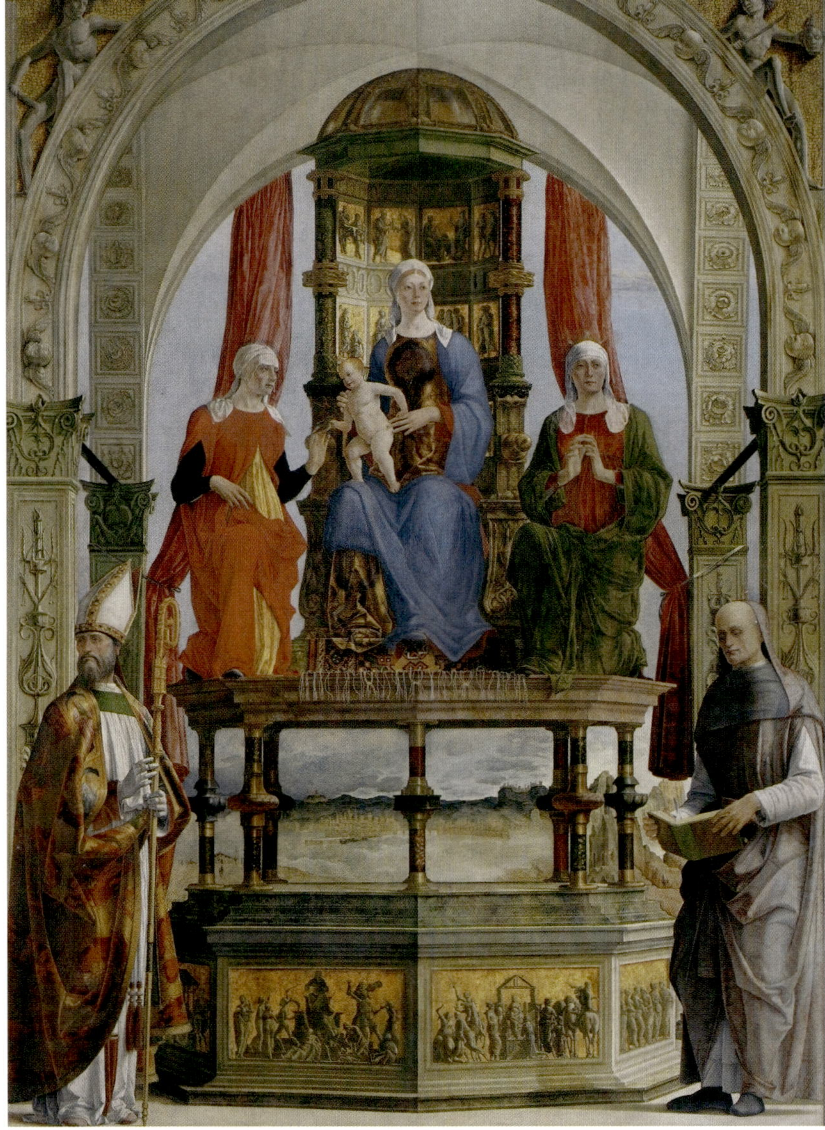

25

Ercole de' Roberti, Portuense altarpiece. Pinacoteca di Brera, Milan

Cossa died in 1478, but de' Roberti, who never lost sight of the Ferrara work horizons, continued to concentrate his activity in Bologna. In all likelihood, it was in Bentivoglio's city that the artist conceived the altarpiece for Santa Maria in Porto Fuori in Ravenna (fig. 25; Pinacoteca di Brera, Milan), which he worked on commuting back and forth between the two cities: we know that, since 1479, master wood craftsman Bernardino Rugeri had been working in Ferrara, perhaps based on a drawing by the artist himself, while Ercole received payments, in

75 For the role played by his brother, Giorgio de' Roberti, see Turrill 1995, pp. 125–26; on the work, Zeri 1965, p. 73 (who promotes full authorship, c. 1475); Molteni 1995, pp. 48–49, 125–26, no. 13 maintains that the compositional invention descends from Tura's Roverella altarpiece, which is on the contrary, as we now know, a considerably later work, for which we must now come to terms with a contemporary chronicle according to which it was set up on the altar in 1487 (Peverada 2009; M. Natale in *Palazzo Colonna* 2019, pp. 346–50; c. 1480–87). Syson 1999, pp. VII–VIII, already insisted on the relationship between the Baraccano fresco and the Portuense work. The commission for the altarpiece is connected with the 1474 transfer of the canons to the church of San Lazzaro that year, and Ercole's chronicled presence in Ferrara that same year (Tuohy 1982, p. 329).

76 See Molteni 1995, p. 128, no. 15; J. Manca in *Italian Paintings* 2003, pp. 602–6.

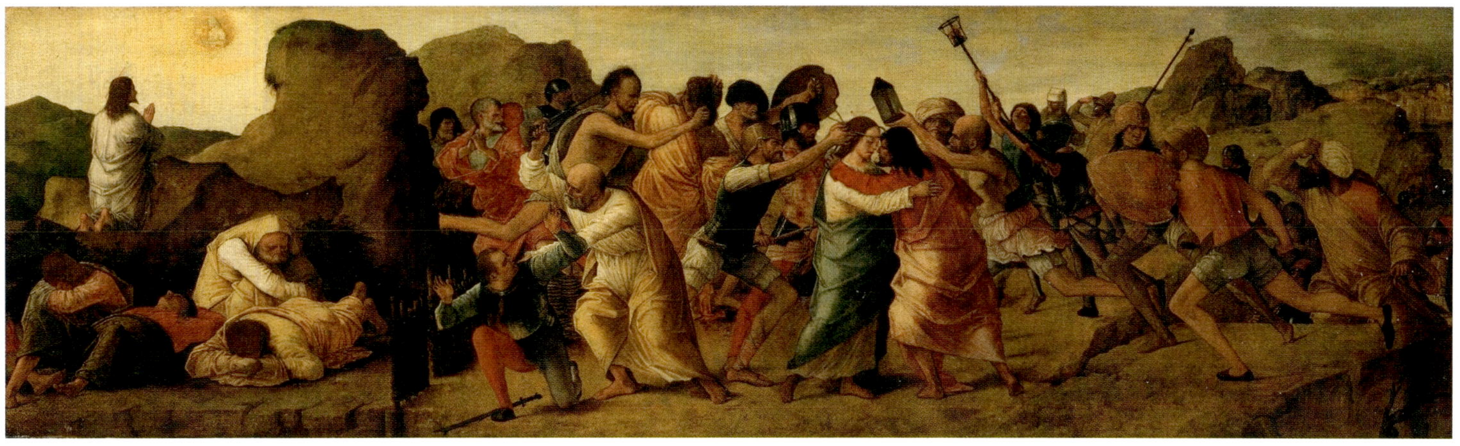

26

Ercole de' Roberti, *The Prayer in the Garden and the Capture of Christ*. Gemäldegalerie Alte Meister, Dresden

March 1481 from both Ferrara and Bologna.[77] In the same period and the years immediately afterwards he painted the predella with the *Stories of the Passion of Christ* for the church of San Giovanni in Monte (*The Prayer in the Garden and the Capture of Christ*, fig. 26; *The Road to Calvary*, Gemäldegalerie Alte Meister, Dresden; *Pietà*, Walker Art Gallery, Liverpool) and a new portrait of Giovanni II Bentivoglio (fig. 29; Museo di Palazzo Poggi, Bologna, c. 1485).[78]

The Portuense altarpiece was not only a unified altarpiece that earned de' Roberti the renown of being an outstanding Northern Italian developer of the Sacred Conversation in a classically-inspired interior, but it was also a significant palimpsest of the changes ushered in by the complex poetics of his master, as well as a response to Giovanni Bellini's paintings. Around this time, Ercole took Cossa's compositions further through new and more extensive treatments. The antique vibrates under the skin of modern forms with exquisite delicacy, reducing the subtle distance between that which is alive and that which, albeit inanimate, is brought to life through painting. The two worlds deflagrate on the horizon, within a broad space of unreal beauty in which Cossa's landscapes fade away into impalpable touches of color, absorbed by a very powerful light, indefinable in its temporal individuation. The very same light marks the visual guidelines of the Passion stories in the narrow, elongated space of the Dresden predella. Diagonal cuts, as in the Griffoni corbel, guide the eye to the infinite concatenation of expressions and gestures compressed between the foreground and a far distance commensurable only by identifying the volume of the individual bodies, because what's interesting is how the figures interrelate. The anachronistic yet sophisticatedly reworked citation from Mantegna's *Prayer in the Garden* scene in London[79]—an invention that could have been part of the workshop repertoire, given that Cossa was still alive—shows which direction the competition was taking. It has been ventured that the winner was Emilia, given that the magnetic force of Ercole's Bolognese painting surprised even the celebrated master

77 Ricci 1904, p. 12; see Manca 1992, doc. 4. On Bernardino Rugeri di Giovanni da Venezia, see Markham Schulz 2011, pp. 90–91, no. 139.

78 Manca 1992, pp. 126–30, nos. 14a–c; p. 132, no. 16; Molteni 1995, pp. 143–49, nos. 22–24.

79 The figure of Christ and the relationship between the figures and the landscape seem to depend on this version of the subject, datable to 1455–56, intended perhaps for Ferrara (K. Christiansen in *Mantegna* 1992, p. 41); nevertheless, the counterpoint built on the contrast between the crouching and lying down apostles does not exclude knowledge of a section with the same subject in the altarpiece at San Zeno in Verona (pointed out by Syson 1999, p. IX); the relationship with Bellini's version (The National Gallery, London), recalled by Molteni 1995, p. 74, would seem more tenuous. For the three versions of *The Prayer in the Garden*, see C. Campbell in *Mantegna & Bellini* 2018, pp. 135–37.

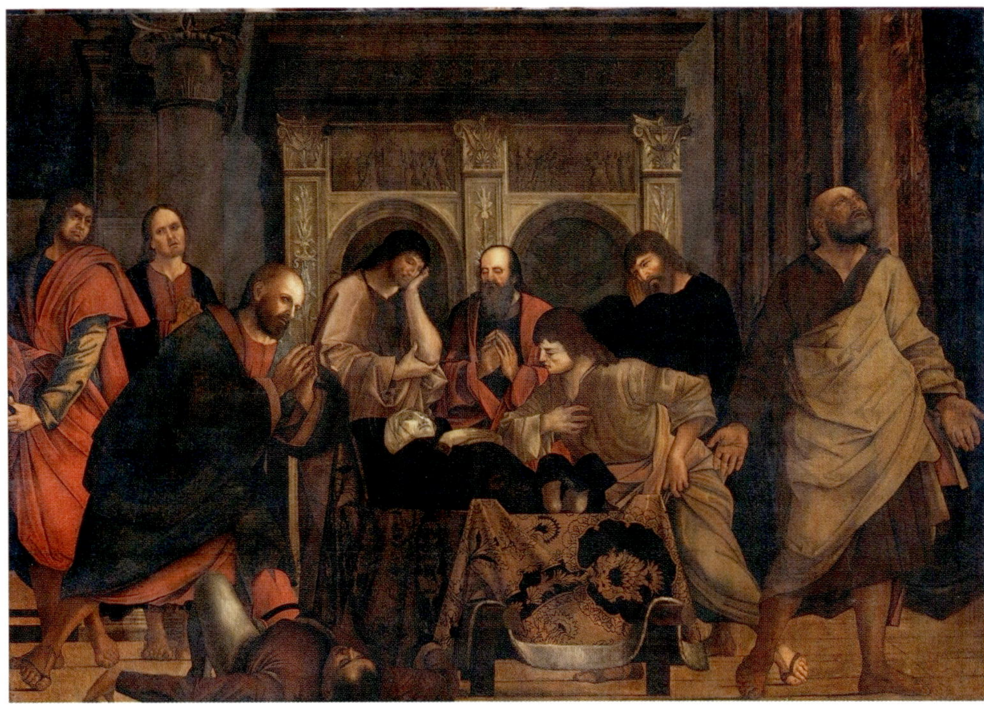

27

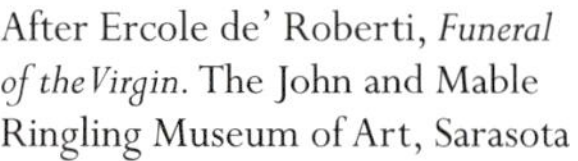

After Ercole de' Roberti, *Funeral of the Virgin*. The John and Mable Ringling Museum of Art, Sarasota

from Isola di Carturo, so much so that he preserved memory of it:[80] a hypothesis that is probably not too far-fetched given the presence in town, from the 1470s onwards, of Cardinal Francesco Gonzaga (1444–83), first as legate and then as bishop.

As we know, after Cossa's death de' Roberti stayed on in Bologna to finish the frescoes at the Garganelli Chapel. Old friends of his master's, who died in the midst of the work, they became his friends as well. Giorgio Vasari tells us that on inheriting the commission, Ercole made it a matter of gratitude and honor, committing twelve years to finishing it off (seven years for the fresco painting and five for the dry finishing),[81] but the lengthy execution was almost certainly due to the fact that the artist was engaged in other commissions, even if we cannot know exactly which.

The most beautiful description of those frescoes, all lost except a single fragment depicting the head of *Mary Magdalene weeping* (Pinacoteca Nazionale, Bologna) and some seventeenth-century copies (figs. 27–28), is that of Vasari: step by step, the writer from Arezzo delved into the scene of the *Crucifixion* that occupied the right wall and the *Funeral of the Virgin* facing it on the left. His words give us a taste of the strength and variety of expression, allow us to see the sharpened profile of the "meagre horse"[82] ridden by Longinus in the act of piercing Christ's side, or the flag puffed up by a gust of wind that almost throws the knight from his mount, twisting his legs toward the spectator; they allow us to intuit the brutal ease of the soldiers' gestures as they carelessly play dice for the Son of God's garments, not to mention the highly-defined morphology of the bystanders at the Virgin's bedside: "six figures, which are the portraits of persons, declared, by those acquainted with them, to be the most animated likeness,"[83] writes

80 Romano 1981, pp. 20–21.
81 Vasari 1568 ed. 1878–81, III, p. 145 (Vasari 1898, vol. 2, p. 154).
82 Ibid., III, p. 144 (translation from Vasari 1898, vol. 2, p. 153).
83 Ibid., III, pp. 143–45, quote on p. 145 (translation from Vasari 1898, vol. 2, p. 154).

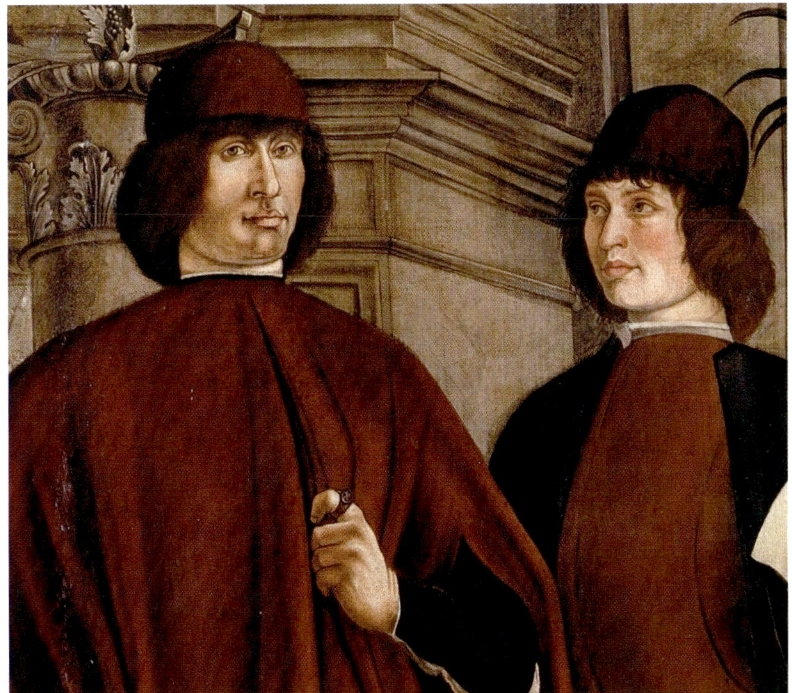

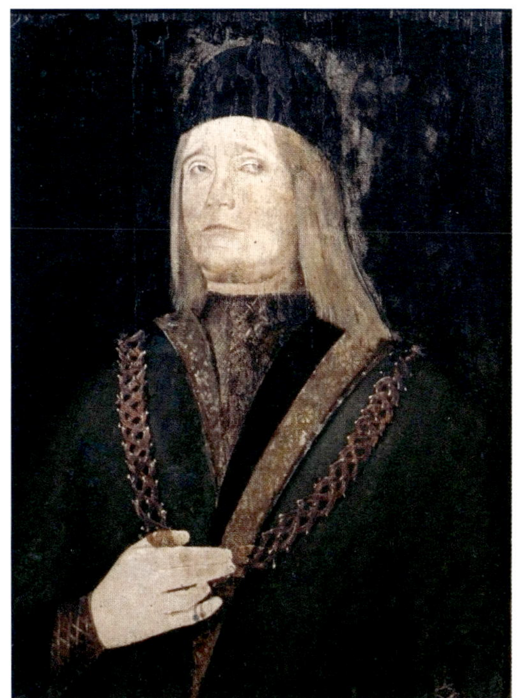

28

After Ercole de' Roberti, *Bartolomeo Garganelli and other figures*, detail. Musée du Louvre, Paris

29

Ercole de' Roberti, *Portrait of Giovanni II Bentivoglio*. Museo di Palazzo Poggi, Bologna

Vasari. As if he were closing the circle of what had been started in Bologna, in terms of naturalism in portraits, in the mid-century by Galasso of Ferrara.

That there was no equal of this in all of the city is borne out in Pietro Lamo's city guide (1560), with its singular appreciation and citation of an opinion expressed by young Michelangelo, one that became proverbial ("this Chapel you have here is as good as half a Rome," "*questa Cappella che avete qua è una meza Roma de bontà*"[84]) and catapulted this Bolognese decoration into the national limelight. We must make the intellectual effort to ideally recompose the whole by fixing the point of style between the Portuense altarpiece and the *Portrait of Giovanni II Bentivoglio* of the University Collections in Bologna (fig. 29), supposing that over the course of the long and highly-refined processing of those complex subjects, in Ercole's hands the pictorial material thinned until it reached the impalpable degree of purity expressed in the double-sided *Annibale Bentivoglio* portrait that formerly belonged to the gallery of Julius Böhler in Munich (now private collection, Milan).[85]

It should, however, never be forgotten that the fame of the renowned decorative installation began with Cossa. Before dying of the plague, the artist had managed to paint about twenty figures within eight partitions on the vault—evangelists, fathers of the Church and prophets—and above the entrance gate an *Annunciation*, reduced in size compared to natural dimensions. We have sufficient information at our disposal to know that Cossa was able to express his greatest *ingegno* in those figures. As we are reminded by the celebratory words of that circle of erudite and humanist friends, an environment with which he has always been associated, his brilliance lay in giving a foundation to painting through drawing ("*Vago pictore et gran mastro al disegno*"), in the quality of his invention

84 Lamo 1560 ed. 1996, p. 90.

85 A. Bacchi in *Le Muse e il principe* 1991, I, pp. 217–19, no. 58; Molteni 1995, pp. 151–52, no. 26; C. Cavalca in *Andrea Mantegna* 2019, p. 141, no. II.13.

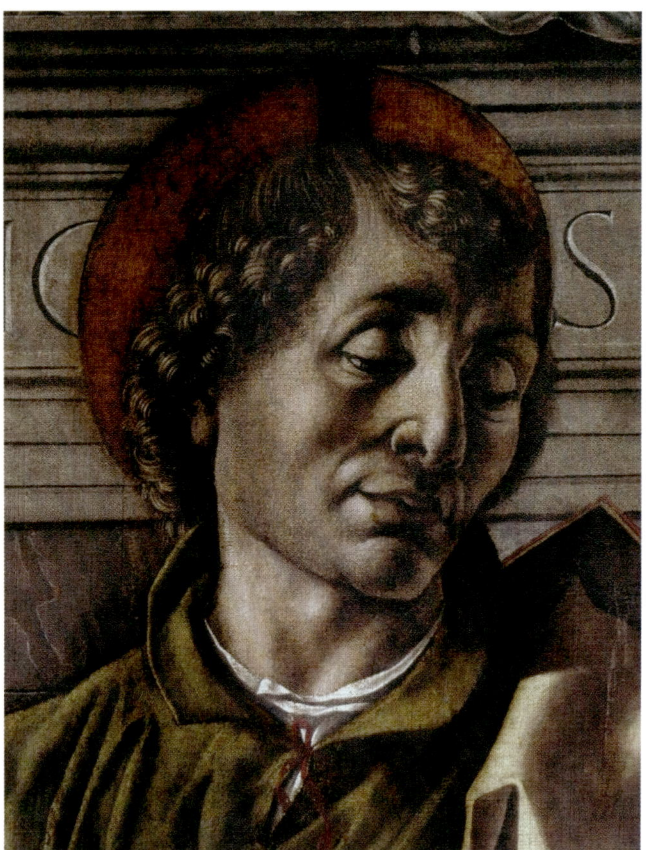

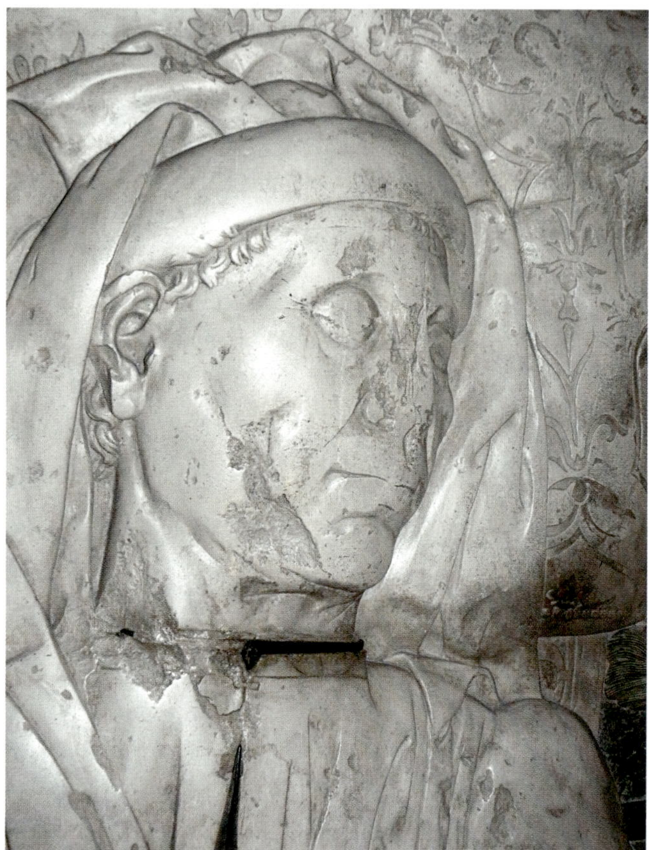

30

Francesco del Cossa, "Pala dei Mercanti," detail. Pinacoteca Nazionale, Bologna

31

Francesco del Cossa, *Tombstone of Domenico Garganelli*, detail. Museo Civico Medievale, Bologna

("*et ultra il saper de l'arte, dava alle sue figure tanta gratia secundo l'offitio loro che l'occhio del ver poco le face differente*") and in his complex perspective views that deceived the eye ("*dove [nella volta] più faticose le cose son finte cum maestrevoli lontani et scurci*").[86] Still other sources suggest the importance of the overall conception and subsequent elaboration and detailing of the graphic design. Ercole started from here, developing independently with the help of all the "cartoons, sketches, and drawings" that would become the subject of Vasari's famous anecdote about them being stolen one night by envious colleagues in Bologna.[87] We cannot rule out the possibility that these included ideas for the beautiful old-style decorations of the marble barrier that closed off access to the chapel.[88]

In the meantime, everything leads us to believe that Francesco del Cossa received payments for conceiving and, perhaps, as Renzo Grandi firmly believed,[89] executing the superb earthen tomb slab, in stone and bronze, bearing an effigy of the deceased in the center of the ground level, commissioned in 1478 by Bartolomeo Garganelli to

86 *Philomathia* [1478]; see Ruhmer 1959, p. 49; once again in Lamo, where the quality of the foreshortenings and inventiveness is always pointed out, the portion frescoed by Cossa is defined as being a very notable work ("*opera molto notabile*"; Lamo 1560 ed. 1996, p. 91).

87 Vasari 1568 ed. 1878–81, III, p. 145 (translation from Vasari 1898, vol. 2, p.154).

88 Ibid., III, p. 146: "Duca Tagliapietra, a sculptor of considerable renown, by whom the beautiful foliage in marble was executed , which decorated the front of the chapel" (translation from Vasari 1898, vol. 2, p.155); Lamo 1560 ed. 1996, p. 91: "*A l'intrar dentro de dita capella, nel basamento è fato di marmoro certi fogliami antichi, dove una foglia maestra che si iudica che sia de valentisimo scultor antico, è de moderno, nominato Duca.*" Duca Tagliapietra, who according to Vasari after executing that work went on to do "all the stone-work of the windows in the palace of the Duke at Ferrara" (translation from Vasari 1898, vol. 2, p. 155) is identified by Adolfo Venturi with Domenico Frisoni (see Franceschini 1995, doc. 366e).

89 Grandi 1989, pp. 33–36; Bacchi 1991, p. 98.

honor the memory of his father Domenico (Museo Civico Medievale, Bologna). The date carved onto the slab coincides with the date of the artist's probable death, but Cossa could have conceived the sculpture and already begun working on it, as we may surmise from a close comparison with the "Pala dei Mercanti" (figs. 30–31); in any case, it was not unheard of for an artist to claim for himself something of which he was not the material author.

The Garganelli worksite proved to be the end of the human and professional relationship between Cossa and de' Roberti and of the endeavors they shared between Ferrara and Bologna. In late 1485, Ercole returned permanently to his hometown, taking over from Cosmè Tura in 1487 as the favorite painter to Duke Ercole d'Este and his son Alfonso, and receiving a regular salary from court.[90] Looking back over his life, among the highly-important commissions that this role earned him at the end of his life, I like to mention his designs for the sculpted decorations of the Addizione Erculea buildings as well as for two facades, internal elevations, and chapels at the Basilica of Santa Maria in Vado (1495–96): what he had learned in Bologna truly remained a viaticum for the rest of his life—in painting and beyond.

---

90 See Farinella 2014, pp. 28–77.

THE GRIFFONI POLYPTYCH

Cecilia Cavalca

The sections

The Griffoni Polyptych is a complex work, an imposing multiple-section structure originally connected through a sumptuously-carved piece of carpentry and dominated by the unitary structure of Francesco del Cossa's and Ercole de' Roberti's figuration, which history thus far has only ever restored to us in fragments.

Giorgio Vasari, the first witness to the artwork, insists on the quality of the predella painting (the lower part of the structure), emphasizing it so highly that the rest of the figuration more or less pales into insignificance; he does not laud its quality, nor leave indications as to the subjects portrayed and form.[1] Vasari's judgment had an immediate and lasting echo. In his *Graticola di Bologna* (1560), Pietro Lamo only recalls the "*peducio*" with "*li miracoli de San Nicola dove sono figure picole ... rarisimi*,"[2] and in the late seventeenth century, in *Bologna perlustrata* (1666), Antonio Masini offers analogous praise, but again reserves it only for the base section.[3] The different perspective introduced by Carlo Cesare Malvasia in his *Pitture di Bologna* (1686)[4] made little difference, given that the attention he paid to the central body with the "Saint Vincent and other Saints" was too general to make up for the previous lack of attention. Indeed, he continued in Vasari's mistake of improperly attributing it to Lorenzo Costa, in an exchange of identity between the two Ferrara-born master artists (Cossa and Costa), which would follow the paintings through that portion of their future history, further helping to conceal their true identity.

The opportunity to understand the appearance of the whole was irreparably lost when the work's fragmentation passed from the conceptual to the physical. This occurred in the 1730s, when the chapel at the Basilica of San Petronio in Bologna—the sixth on the left as you enter—where the altarpiece had been since its creation was given by the last of the Griffoni family, Giovanni Raniero, to Monsignor Pompeo Aldrovandi, who set about renovating its furnishings between 1725 and 1731.[5] At the start of the works, for which

1 Vasari 1568 ed. 1878–81, III, pp. 142–43: "The drawing of Ercole being superior of that of Costa, the former painted certain stories in tempera—the figures of which are small—beneath the painting executed by Lorenzo, for the chapel of San Vincenzo, in the church of San Petronio, and these are so well done, they exhibit a manner so good and so beautiful, that it is not possible to see anything better, nor even imagine the amount of care and labour bestowed by Ercole on that work. The Predella, therefore, is a much better performance than the picture, although both were executed at the same time during the life of Costa" (translation from Vasari 1898, vol. 2, p. 152). Special attention was devoted by Vasari to the predella also in the first edition of his *Lives*: Vasari 1550 ed. 1986, II, p. 428.

2 Lamo 1560 ed. 1996, p. 101.

3 Masini 1666, I, p. 111.

4 Malvasia 1686 ed. 1969, p. 242/16.

5 Torella (1988–89) 1991, p. 41.

Aldrovandi hired two local artists, quadraturist Stefano Orlandi and figurative painter Vittorio Maria Bigari, it was clear that the old decorations would have to be dismantled to make way for a new altarpiece. A letter exchanged on November 21, 1725 between Giuseppe Baraldi, a right-hand man of the Cardinal who was in charge of actualizing his decision, and Aldrovandi himself allows us to get to the heart of the matter, offering an almost direct view of how things proceeded.[6] The frame that embraced the figurative portions was handled roughly, more or less reduced to firewood. Not so the panels, which were recovered with care and transformed into "gallery-sized" paintings: special frames were ordered, craftsmen hired to clean and varnish the pictorial surface in an appropriate way—in Baraldi's opinion, it was in rather poor condition by that time. As far as we are able to judge, Monsignor Aldrovandi chose thirteen in all: all five elements from the main body, the roundel with the *Crucifixion* and the two with the *Annunciation* in the cornice, as well as the predella and four of the fourteen panels of saints that decorated the sides of the altar. The absence of any regard for the polyptych in local guides and a lack of interest in its author—he was not recognized as an "*antico*" Bolognese artist—credibly leads us to believe that those thirteen paintings were earmarked for the prelate's country residence. It's interesting, however, to acknowledge during these crucial circumstances Baraldi's appreciation, again, of the predella: that "*sotto quadro*" (painting base) which the monsignor's trusted man considers "worth more than the others for its antiquity and great number of figures, being the martyrdom of the saint, and for the antiquity of the painter" ("*più de li altri per l'antichità e gran figure, essendo il martirio del Santo e per l'antichità del pitore*").

After this process was completed in 1732, eighteenth-century updates to Malvasia's *Pitture* laconically record the void left by the out-of-fashion work, on which darkness fell for more than a hundred years. The hypocritical frenzy and the contextual precision with which Luigi Crespi denounces the dismantling some twenty years later, while annotating the manuscript of Girolamo Baruffaldi's *Vite* of Ferrara artists,[7] was totally deceiving: indeed, his comments were veined with the ill-concealed irritation of someone who let useful materials for the profitable antiquarian trades slip through his fingers.

Although it is hard to say if it was completely random or not, appreciation of the individual elements of the work, starting with the predella, started to return in the nineteenth century, ultimately leading to a gradual reappraisal of the whole. Ercole de' Roberti's painting began to recoup its renown in around 1829—a time when no one knew who exactly had painted it, what it depicted, or where it had been made for—in the run-up to its sale to the Vatican Museums some ten years later. Renewed interest in the work was not triggered by an appreciation of the quality of the painting by the great Ferrara master, but rather by its fascinating narrative development of the sacred theme. A special Vatican commission interpreted it as the *Prodigies of Saint Hyacinth* and it was advertised in a 1841 pamphlet given to the press with the title "On a painting attributed to Benezzo Gozzoli," also offering the reader a line drawing. Recounted in detail elsewhere in this book,[8] this development significantly hampered any attempts at restoring true identity to an ensemble that Vasari assured us had come from a chapel dedicated to Saint Vincent Ferrer.

---

6 Cavalca 2013, p. 383, doc. XI.24 (transcription by Ilaria Negretti).

7 See Mazza's contribution in this catalogue.

8 See info sheet no. 7 in the catalogue and Mazza's contribution.

1

Gustavo Frizzoni, graphics by Ludovico Pogliaghi, reconstruction of the Griffoni Polyptych (from Frizzoni 1897, p. 224)

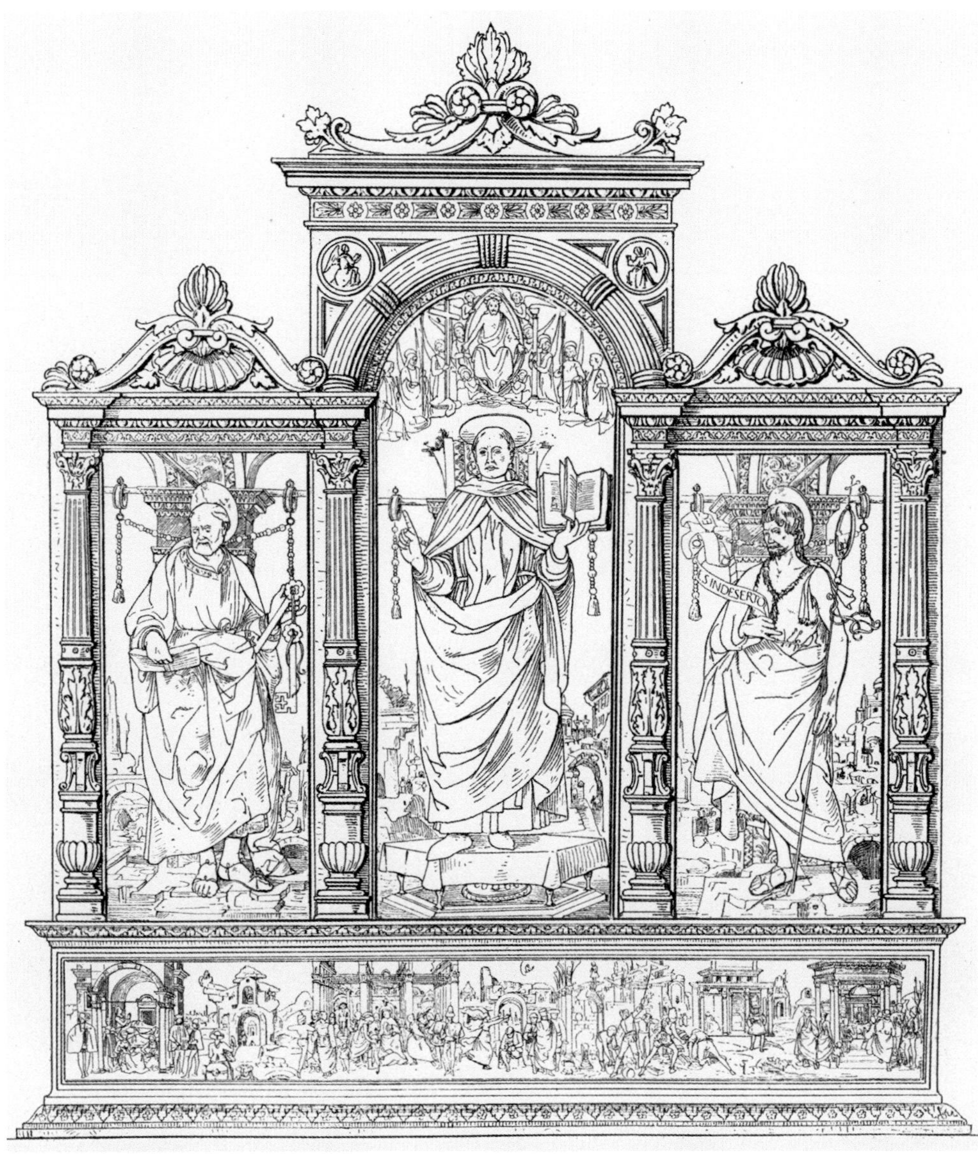

This is the problem Gustavo Frizzoni tackled in 1888, when in the pages of the magazine *Zeitschrift für bildende Kunst* he was the first to attempt to restore the dismembered complex into a whole and to reconnect it with its place of origin.[9] The milieu frequented by this particularly active Bergamo connoisseur was long convinced that the Vatican predella had nothing to do with Benozzo Gozzoli but was a work by an artist from Ferrara whom Giovanni Morelli believed to be close to the manner of Ercole de' Roberti and that same year, Adolfo Venturi identified him as Francesco del Cossa.[10] The opinion already expressed by Giovanni Battista Cavalcaselle was likewise reliable, recognizing the hand of the same painter in the sections with *Saint Peter* and *Saint John the Baptist* (at the time at the Galleria Barbi Cinti in Ferrara) and in the "San Domenico" (which in 1858 had been sold on by the Costabili collection, as a Zoppo, to director Charles Lock Eastlake for the National Gallery in London). But if the London "San Domenico" could,

9 Frizzoni 1888.
10 Venturi 1888.

without too much effort, also be interpreted as a Saint Vincent Ferrer, it was more complex to oppose the wordy iconographic exegesis on the predella compiled "at the papal residence." Frizzoni lined up excellent arguments in support of his thesis, and concluded by inviting his readers to consider the work mentioned in Vasari's *Lives* at San Petronio in Bologna as a triptych, its main body consisting of three elements, "each with a saint in an upright position … connected by an architectural frame with pillars"[11] set over a predella. However, some ten years later, he was forced to retreat, due to prominent scholar Gustave Gruyer's[12] firm opposition to this iconographic interpretation of the Vatican predella. The interest surrounding this debate, which has subsequently been neglected by modern critics, lies not so much in the fact that Frizzoni was left looking for a different destination for his "triptych"—hypothetically identified as a chapel dedicated to Saint Hyacinth in the church of San Domenico in Ferrara, where Cossa may have worked around 1470—but in his defense of the reconstruction hypothesis he had advanced previously, for the first time coming up with a montage of the four fragments enclosed in a neo-Renaissance style frame, executed by Ludovico Pogliaghi (1857–1950) (fig. 1). This invention, one of considerable visual effectiveness, was inspired by the carpentry of Giovanni Bellini's Frari triptych, which was very much in vogue at the time. Frizzoni made it public when he commented on the July 1893 purchase by the Pinacoteca di Brera in Milan, on the advice of his friend Adolfo Venturi, of the two panels with *Saint Peter* and *Saint John the Baptist*, which had formerly belonged to the Barbi Cinti collection.[13] The Frizzoni & Pogliaghi reconstruction of the triptych was published and circulated, accompanied by Frizzoni's avowed hope that "an international agreement will create the conditions to reunite the individual sections, restoring the original altarpiece to the civilized world in its wholeness."[14] As far as we know, the intention was not realized, but records remain of attempts by the Holy See, involving the Secretary of State, Cardinal Mariano Rampolla del Tindaro, who contacted the management at the National Gallery in London.[15]

This internationally-attempted recomposition, which with refined elegance radicalized the relationships between the various elements, resulted in an effect that was as convincing as it turned out to be very distant from the original structure, and had a major impact—over and above misinterpretation of the predella subject—in the diffidence that immediately greeted Roberto Longhi's hypothesis to consider it as a partial restitution of an otherwise articulated altarpiece. With hindsight, it is fascinating to try and reread the exceptional critical feat Longhi achieved in *Officina ferrarese* (1934), which led to the re-assembly of an altarpiece whose complexity nobody had suspected since Giuseppe Baraldi had it broken down into thirteen room-sized paintings.

Longhi's efforts to correctly recombine ("*rincastellare*") the different elements within an ideal original structure went hand in hand with the restoration of the proper stylistic identity of the individual paintings that made up the whole.[16] When it came to

11 Frizzoni 1888, p. 302 (translated from German, also the quotes below).

12 Gruyer 1890. Jacobsen also raised objections to Frizzoni's hypothesis (1896, p. 184).

13 On which Malaguzzi Valeri 1908, pp. 219–21.

14 Frizzoni 1897, p. 226.

15 National Gallery Archive, London (Correspondence, NG.597).

16 Longhi (1934 ed. 1956, p. 33) explains the principle ("*criterio operativo*") adopted in his reconstruction of the Griffoni altar as that of the work's unity ("*unità dell'opera*"), "what I would call a far-reaching, inevitable coherence that binds together the various chapters of a single creative whole, the particular historical set of circumstances circumscribed within each and every work, within a wider personal unity." See also Toffanello's contribution in this catalogue.

2

Roberto Longhi, reconstruction of the Griffoni Polyptych (from Longhi 1934 ed. 1956, fig. 98)

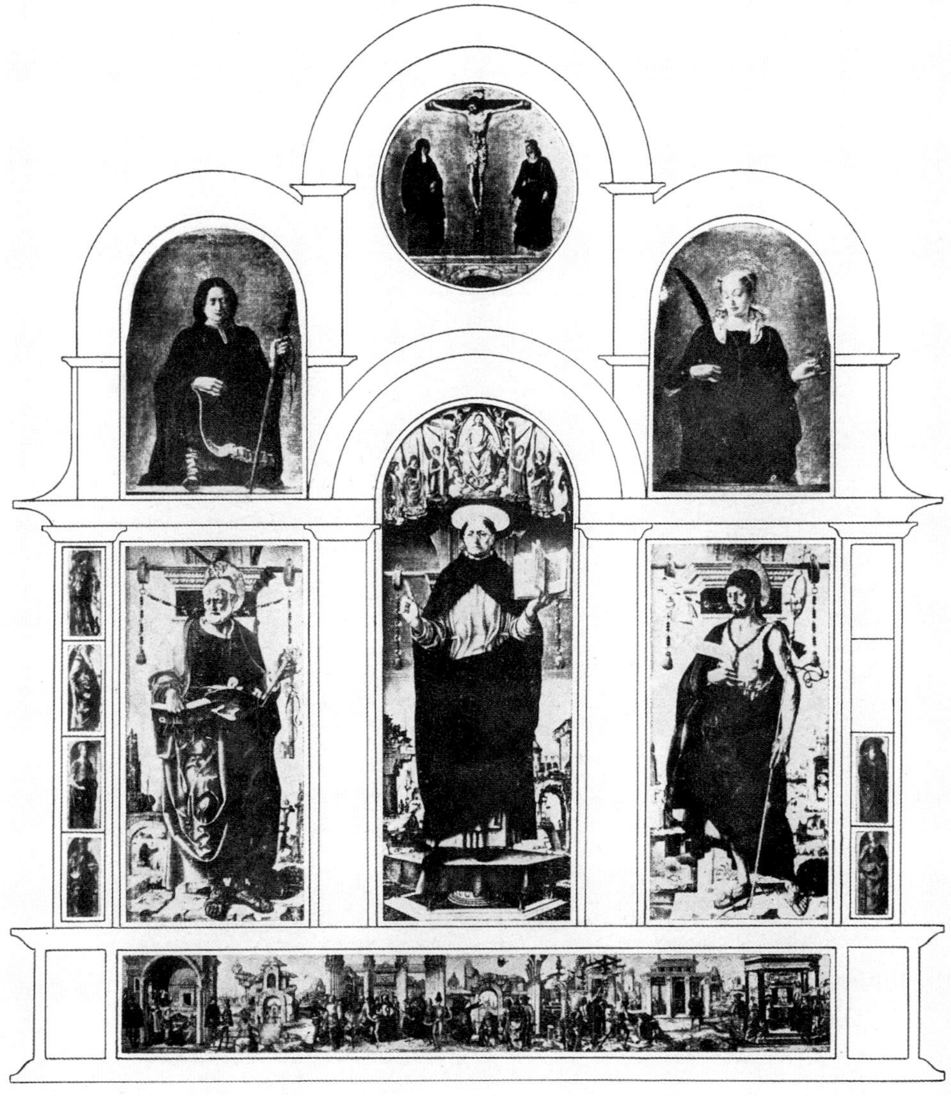

recomposing the Griffoni altar, this way of proceeding was particularly bold, given that the work had a formal originality that obliged the scholar to continuously juggle between what his eye recognized without hesitation as belonging to the hand of the artists who, according to historical sources, were involved in realizing the figurative portions of the work at San Petronio, and the difficulty of recomposing the artifact according to criteria that refer univocally to known, pre-existing instances, so as to effectively add on to Frizzoni's "triptych." Nevertheless, when in his *Ampliamenti nell'Officina ferrarese* (1940) Longhi publicly divulged the most articulate form of the Griffoni Polyptych, he explicitly refused to suggest the possible appearance of the frame. He rejected this practice from the very beginning of his critical effort (equating it with deplorable style-remakes that had been the object of his own vehement reprimands in youth: "I'm not going to draw [the frame] so that no one may infer that I am willing to participate in the competition for the facade of San Petronio"[17]) and became radicalized in his choice of illustrating the final result of his research through a simple proportional juxtaposition of the individual figurative parts against a neutral black background (fig. 3). This approach, however,

17 Longhi 1934 ed. 1956, p. 34.

marked a not insignificant divergence in visual perception of the recomposed work compared with the arrangement presented in *Officina* (1934), where the overall dimensions and the coordinating role played by the carpentry were suggested by an elegant line (fig. 2)[18]— a solution that, instead, will continue to characterize Longhi's reconstruction of two other famous altarpieces: Cosmè Tura's Roverella Polyptych (fig. 6) and the Dresden *Annunciation* altarpiece, another of Cossa's feats.[19]

While Longhi's approach inevitably reduced readers' interest in the frame, the scholar's dense argument based on "structural" comparisons results in a neutral restitution of the altarpiece made for the Griffoni in a very precise form.

As Marcello Toffanello points out in these pages, at the time Longhi was preparing his recomposition of the Griffoni Polyptych to comment on the 1933 Ferrara exhibition, he had already for some time been aware of the majority of the figurative elements necessary to assemble it. Indeed, the Griffoni altar took shape in the *Officina* through a story that progressed in an extremely sophisticated way, by the scholar's own explicit admission adopting a cinematographic narrative (that is, with calculated, progressive visual sequences),[20] that has a very clear starting point, even if never shown (the Frizzoni & Pogliaghi triptych published in 1897),[21] and a surprise ending (dismantling of the late nineteenth-century frame from which the masterpiece emerges, like a cocooned chrysalis, to unfurl in all its magnificence). The black background for the illustration of the final juxtaposition of pictorial elements, "their unity redeemed," is the screen upon which the observers "will, according to their own taste, revive ... the engravings, the candlesticks and the depressed festoons," originally enclosing "with perfect measure" the paintings restored to life once more.[22] Beautiful as it may be, in this refined critical process the frame remains a non-essential element that may be redefined at will. On the other hand, as mentioned above, knowing the woodwork's structural articulation serves as an essential guide to correctly position the figurative portions grouped together through stylistic comparison, offering a counterproof of ultimate success.

On Longhi's pages, the triptych imagined by Frizzoni expands vertically "according to a scheme similar to that of many Venetian polyptychs, including Vivarini's ones from the same period, and even contemporary polyptychs from Master Tura."[23] The three upper figures (*Saint Florian*, the *Crucifixion* and *Saint Lucy*) are on a gold rather than a naturalistic background, but "apart from the examples we have in Venice of similar items (the polyptych by Bartolomeo Vivarini for Conversano and Alvise in Berlin, no. 1143) ... Cossa knows how to make the procedure plausible by modernizing it ... starting from that limit, all of the upper parts are naturally associated through the gold, as though they were on as a supernatural plane."[24] It is not hard to arrange the saints along the sides of the altar according to "the layout of the pillars in the Marco Zoppo

18 Longhi (ibid.) defines it as an "approximate path."

19 Ibid., fig. 94.

20 Ibid, p. 34: "I tried, instead, to back a few more meters away from the secular film that was thus showing the events of the famous polyptych."

21 Regarding Frizzoni's hypothesis (albeit with reference to the article published in 1888), Longhi (1934 ed. 1956, p. 32) writes: "But must one at this point believe that the recomposition is perfect? In the meantime, it is unlikely that around 1470–75 ... it could have already appeared in the form of a triptych so simple that we would only see one completed by Giambellino for the Frari, in 1488."

22 Longhi 1940 ed. 1956, p. 130.

23 Longhi 1934 ed. 1956, p. 32.

24 Ibid., pp. 33–34.

3

Roberto Longhi, reconstruction of the Griffoni Polyptych (photomontage published in *Ampliamenti all'Officina* 1940). Fondazione di Studi di Storia dell'Arte Roberto Longhi, Florence, Photo archive, inv. 087345

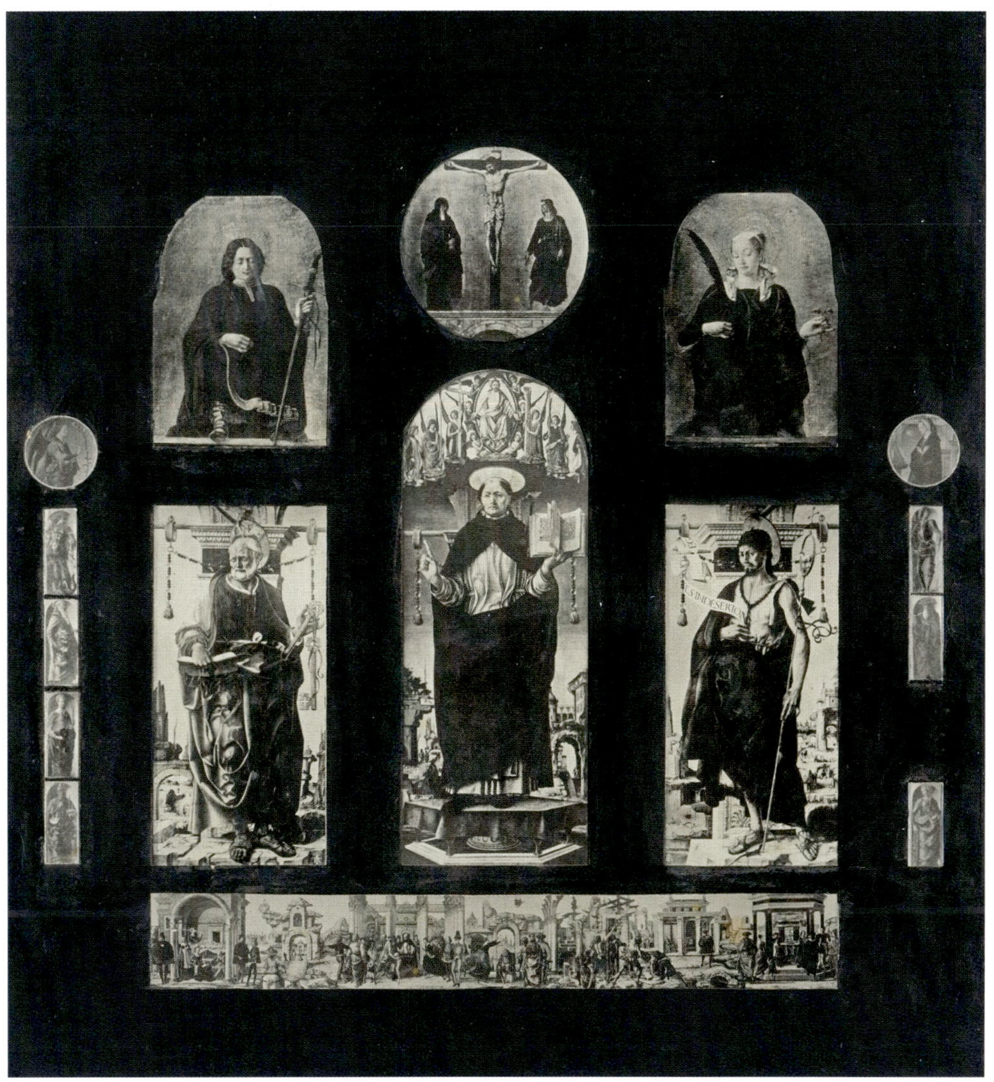

triptych at the College of Spain (c. 1465) or in the Giovanni Bellini Pesaro altarpiece (c. 1475)."[25] The two tondos with the *Annunciation* (now in the Villa Cagnola) throw up some problems when it comes to further defining the grandiose whole. Longhi has no doubt that they belong to the altarpiece—they are acquired knowledge for him, but the absence of the gold background induces him to make a powerful choice: he places them "on the border between the two planes of the painting,"[26] at the head of the series of small saints situated four along each side, albeit without citing examples that justify this unusual configuration. During those years, Igino Supino's[27] discovery of the document mentioning that the altar was enclosed within a *capsa* for which woodcarver Agostino de' Marchi of Crema was paid stimulated him, prior to publication in 1940, to imagine these elements connected to the whole within an exuberant phytomorphic frame, taking an unusual and absolutely eccentric example as his model: "the beautiful remains of the frame of the Pelosio cornice, from the year 1476, at the Pinacoteca of

25 Ibid., p. 35.
26 Longhi 1940 ed. 1956, p. 130.
27 Supino 1938.

Bologna."[28] A pen sketch, presented for the first time at this exhibition, gives this idea material form in a phytomorphic cascade of garlands that "knots" the large roundel of the cornice to the two little tondos ("*rotelle*"), embracing the sides of the altar next to the pillars with figurative panels, until it hugs the sides of the predella; all of this enclosed within Agostino de' Marchi's square encasement (see fig. 10 on p. 159). This "divertissement" (Toffanello) hidden among the famous scholar's worksheets reveals, better than any verbal comment, the rhetorical nature of the refrain, "I do not, however, draw fifteenth-century Bergamo-style frames."[29] Longhi's reconstruction of the polyptych—"an example of honest carpentry"[30]—does not limit itself to define in detail, while at the same time denying, the structure that for the first time brings together all fragments of the Griffoni altarpiece as we know it today, but it also dictates its timing and executive responsibilities. Created during the "1470–75 five-year period,"[31] first Francesco del Cossa was in charge of all of the main sections, and some time later,[32] after being recruited by his older colleague, Ercole de' Roberti joined in. Ercole was commissioned to paint the predella and the other minor figures, the exception being the *Annunciation*, which for Longhi remained the preserve of the head of the workshop. Work proceeded from the lower elements of the structure progressing upwards. As the process went on, the younger artist, who turned out to be endowed with exceptional talent,[33] gained more and more freedom and greater consciousness of the whole, reinterpreting previous design ideas: "Ercole's mind was elegant enough to know to defer to the older artist, ceding on some points to find the convenience not to disturb the unity of the work Cossa undertook," Longhi says.[34] At the end of this narrative, the Griffoni Polyptych is confirmed as a "highly felicitous congress of Cossa and Ercole" at "Bologna's most important church,"[35] as long-since recognized by tradition.

The penetrating and unscrupulous subtlety with which Longhi restores formal identity to the San Petronio altarpiece and the scornful simplicity with which he illustrates the result—an "approximate arrangement of the various members of the polyptych"[36] is how he defines it in the *Ampliamenti*—procure opposing reactions.

The credit earned by the work cited in historical sources and the acknowledgment of its status as the masterpiece of two of Italy's finest Renaissance artists were accompanied by insistent debate on the actual pertinence as part of the whole of the two saints against a gold background, dressed in the fashion of the period, which in Longhi's photomontage arrangement loom frameless from the second register, resulting in an odd out-of-scaleness. Similarly, a close-up and meticulous analysis of the picturework shatters the altar complex into a sequence of figurative panels that for many years were individually studied and researched by scholars, who have been investigating ideational and executional responsibilities without ever coming to a common agreement, at least as far as Ercole's work is concerned.

---

28 Longhi 1940 ed. 1956, p. 130.

29 Ibid.

30 Ibid., p. 129.

31 Ibid., p. 128.

32 Ibid., p. 42: he believes de' Roberti stepped in during Cossa's final years, between 1475 and 1477.

33 Longhi 1934 ed. 1956, p. 41: "In human actions, then, a repertoire so rich in movement, stops, pauses and breaks; so flaming and cruel, overflowing with genius in every direction" (refers to the Vatican predella).

34 Ibid.

35 Ibid., p. 35.

36 Longhi 1940 ed. 1956, p. 130.

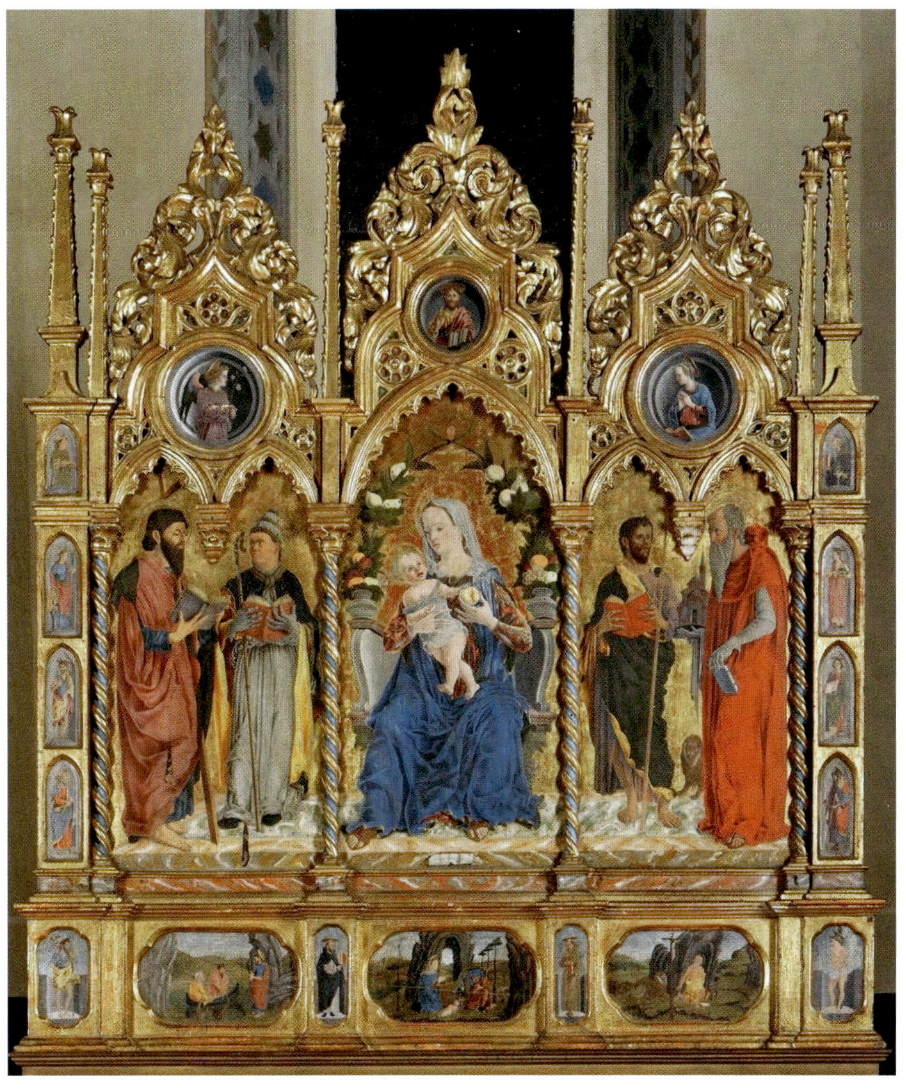

4

Marco Zoppo, Polyptych of San Clemente. The Royal College of Spain, Bologna

Longhi had been dead for fourteen years when in 1984 a fortuitous discovery took place which, in this affair, has had the resonance of a *coup de théâtre*: a sketch by Stefano Orlandi (fig. 7), found in her archive research by Francesca Montefusco Bignozzi, finally revealed the outline of the polyptych before the dismemberment ordered by Monsignor Aldrovandi, confirming in full the famous scholar's hypothetical reconstruction.[37] This proved to be a decisive turning point for knowledge about the work, finally tying down how the pieces were originally assembled, and rendering any future persiflage on the subject vain. The polyptych that adorned the Griffoni Chapel in San Petronio in the fifteenth century was in fact an altarpiece divided into two registers, the main one consisting of three panels, the central of which was arched, on which stood two arched panels and a remarkable central roundel; the work was rounded off by pillars bearing figurative panels, a predella painted along its entire length, and two small roundels set in a high-standing tripartite cornice studded with carvings and pinnacles.

This precious document was discovered during preparation for a major monographic publication on the Basilica of San Petronio, edited, among others, by Carlo Volpe. The discovery offered Daniele Benati an extraordinary chance to illustrate the importance of the new data acquired and put Francesco del Cossa and Ercole de' Roberti's masterpiece back into its original context. The scholar provided a cross-section of figurative facts, still fully relevant today, regarding the time prior to construction of the Griffoni Polyptych: "in that particular strand of fifteenth-century culture, especially in Northern Italy, adapting the new developments of the Renaissance to a natural development of late Gothicism: this is what is defined as … the shadowy Renaissance (*Rinascimento umbratile*)."[38] And indeed, in "the rocaille calligraphy" of Orlandi's drawing, Benati glimpsed the traces left by that

37 See Benati 1984, p. 156, fig. 185. This differed from Longhi's hypothesis regarding the position of the two roundels with the *Annunciation* and the number of saints along the side pillars: twelve, instead of eight, divided over the two registers.
38 Benati 1984, p. 144.

same culture on the now lost carpentry of the Griffoni Polyptych, and, as Longhi had done before him, placed a focus on it. "It stood flamboyant and extraordinarily ornate," wrote the scholar, "a little less fantastical than the one Andrea della Polla carved for the Agnolo and Bartolomeo degli Erri polyptych now at the Pinacoteca Estense in Modena, yet still firm in its architectural construction, following a taste and imagination that would anchor new developments of Renaissance syntax within the fineries of a late Gothic repertoire."[39] Insistence on the example offered by Angelo and Bartolomeo degli Erri's Modena polyptych, accompanying progress in the critical discourse, associated the Griffoni Polyptych's carving work with figurative tendencies previously described by Volpe as belonging to the bedrock of "Leon Battista Alberti's perspective-based" culture that flowed from Piero della Francesca's work in Emilia, and that, as of the 1450s, traveled along the roads linking Modena, Bologna, and Romagna.[40]

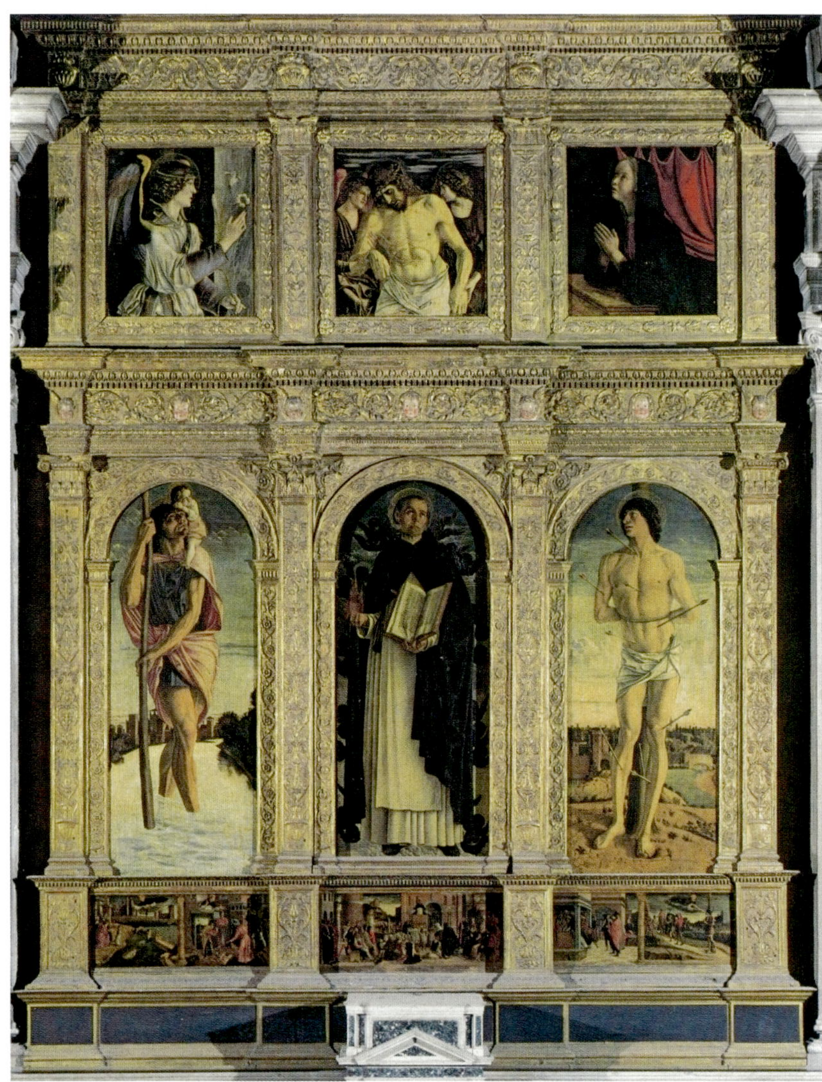

5

Giovanni Bellini, Polyptych of Santi Giovanni e Paolo. Basilica of Santi Giovanni e Paolo, Venice

A rereading of the painted sections moved from similar premises, with the aim of connecting the overall workmanship of the Griffoni altarpiece to the "different cultural climate in Bologna compared with Tura's orthodoxy professed in Ferrara at that time." The methods and chronology of execution suggested previously by Longhi were embraced by Benati, who also made some new advancement in the study of stylistic details that led him to assign the Cagnola *Annunciation* to the younger artist.[41] Confirmation that the group of works associated with the Griffoni commission was in San Petronio spawned research that made it possible to discover the identity of Lucia Battaglia, first wife of the client, Floriano Griffoni, who, alongside him, is evoked in the upper register of the work, and Ludovica Lambertini, his second wife whom he married in 1472.[42] These were soon followed by further historiographical insights that became essential to detailing the commissioning party's circumstances and understanding the work's complex iconography.[43]

39 Ibid., p. 168.

40 Volpe 1958 ed. 1993, pp. 156–57.

41 Benati 1984, p. 170.

42 Benati 1985, p. 174. The evident discordance between the polyptych's depiction of the saint eponymous to his first wife, Lucia, with the marriage between Floriano and Ludovica, means that 1472 is a chronological term *ante quem* for the painted sections.

43 Torella (1985–87) 1988; Torella (1988–89) 1991.

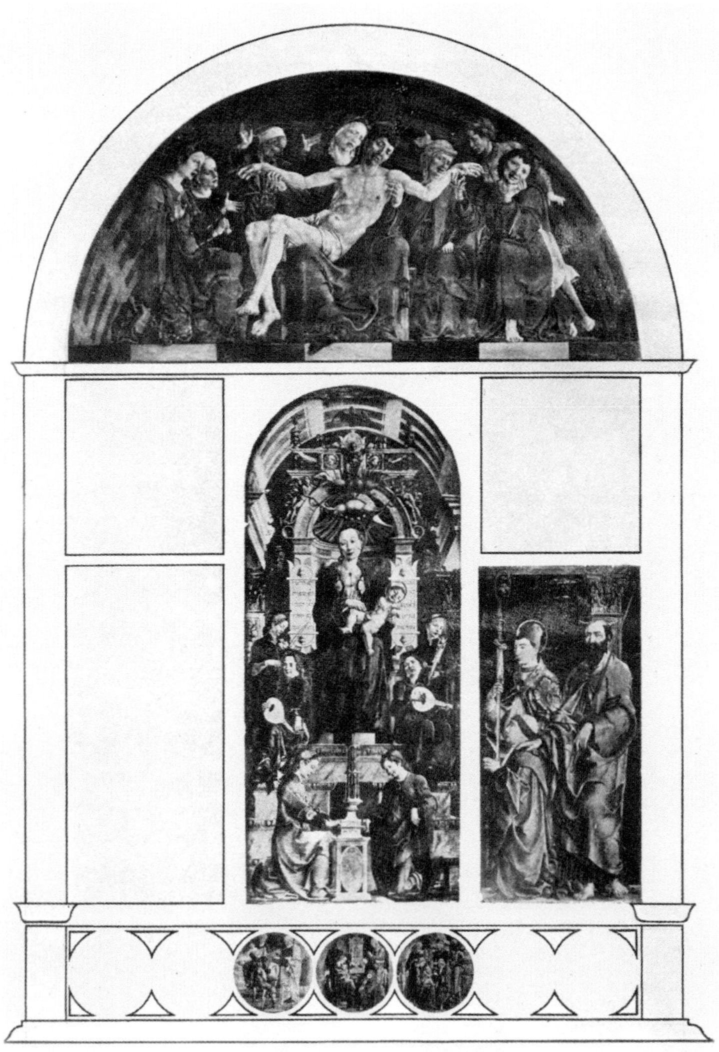

6

Roberto Longhi, reconstruction of the Roverella altarpiece by Cosmè Tura (from Longhi 1934 ed. 1956, fig. 69)

The intelligent opening up toward a closer relationship between the carved and pictorial elements with reference to the dissemination of perspective-related knowledge among Po Valley master woodworkers,[44] however, remained a *de facto* dead letter. In the eighteenth-century "small sketch," the luxuriance of the cornice conceals the value of the structural components that hybridize the polyptych's carpentry, updating it in a modern sense, and discourages comparisons with the monumental layout of the figurative narration Francesco del Cossa and Ercole de' Roberti laid out. Paradoxically, this will seem even more true when we will be sure that the carpenter involved in making the *capsa* for the altarpiece at San Petronio, Agostino de' Marchi, also worked on one of the polyptychs always mentioned in relation to the Griffoni's, Marco Zoppo's altarpiece for San Clemente[45] (fig. 4). A work of rare manual skill and a precedent for understanding events that unfurled at San Petronio some ten years later, it comes in the shape of a triptych divided by twisted columns and developed on a single register with a gold background that, to maintain the assembly's consistency, undoubtedly appears more late-Gothic than Renaissance.

Orlandi's drawing would be published on multiple occasions, more with the intent of confirming the juxtaposition between the various figurative parts envisaged by Longhi—which remained the current illustration of the whole, even when attempts were made to vary the arrangement of the saints along the sides of the altar[46]—than of reflecting on the layout and the correlation between its constituent parts.

The contrast between the clear perspective-based approach and the markedly conservative choice of the eighteenth-century restitution of its format ended up making the Griffoni Polyptych appear as an artistic work of excellent executive quality, albeit typologically backward:[47] a step backwards with respect to the Roverella altarpiece (1480–85) (fig. 6), which Longhi still associated with it, and to a polyptych of similar subject executed a few years earlier by Giovanni Bellini for the church of Santi Giovanni e Paolo in Venice (fig. 5).

44 Benati 1988, pp. 35–68, esp. pp. 38–42, returns to the topic.

45 Biagi Maino 1993.

46 See Lucco 1987, pp. 242, 244, fig. 326; Manca 1992, fig. 21–m; J. Manca in *Italian Paintings* 2003, p. 219; Sgarbi 2003, p. 126.

47 Manca 1992, pp. 27–33.

The sections within the frame

To overturn this point of view, attempts were made to consider the exquisitely hybridized aspect of the artifact as the key to its core essence. The challenge was to understand how far the solution responded to the demands of local tradition, and how reactive the creators had been in adapting it to the forms of the new expressive realism. These evaluations placed the need for adequate assessment of the original shape of the work at the heart of the issue. In order to restore it, the surviving paintings had to be associated with a drawing of the original carpentry[48] (fig. 5).

Such an attempt would have been impractical without Baraldi's attentiveness to preserving the figurative portions in order to turn them into room paintings. Aldrovandi's trusted man ensured in more than one case that the original painting edges were preserved intact, making it possible to precisely fix the frame stops. Put to the test, the carpentry designed in the eighteenth century proved to be decidedly disrespectful of the proportional ratios between the various elements, to the point that the dimension of the area for the central panel was almost twice the size of the real one, with the length of the Vatican predella being disproportionate. These inconsistencies were thrown into even greater relief by some structural annotations that contrasted starkly with the layout of the figuration. This was true of the front of the predella, which in the drawing is interrupted by plinths, but is instead continuous, and the panels depicting *Saint Florian* and *Saint Lucy*, which appear to be very high, even though only three painted panels were aligned on the sides (if the dimensions suggested by the sketch on the pillars of the second register were followed, at least six small saints would fit in, in an inverted and wholly incongruous ratio to the main register's figurative cadence);[49] even the number of the panels on the sides is unrealistic, and has been set at fourteen.[50]

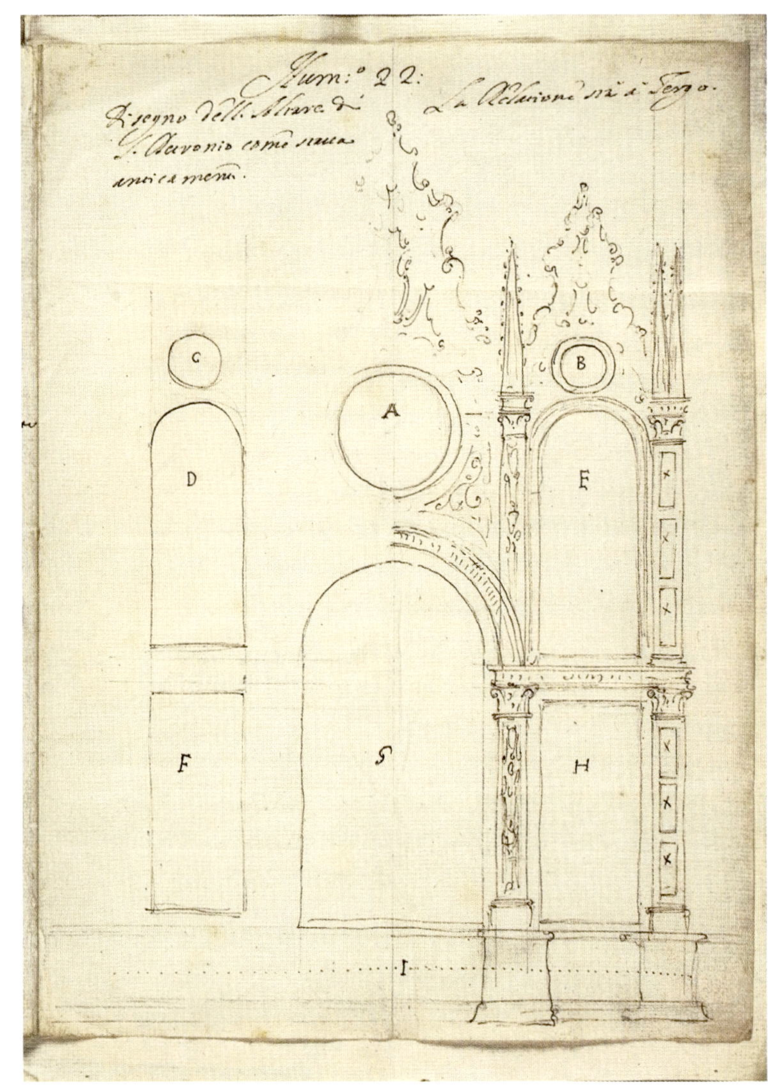

7

Stefano Orlandi, drawing of the Griffoni Polyptych before its dismemberment, 1725. Archivio di Stato di Bologna

Redesigned to take these considerations into account, the shape of the Griffoni Polyptych was restored to its real proportions, turning out to be decidedly more compact and less vertically-imposing than the eighteenth-century sketch would have us believe

48 Cavalca 2013, pp. 136–50, 334–36, no. 19, plate on p. 266.

49 The structural circumstances laid out here are decisive when it comes to doubts posed by the actual height of the Washington panels, which have at their base two non-original end strips (2–2.5 cm). Contrary to what is assumed (Campisi 2018, p. 89), any deviations should therefore be calculated in terms of a few centimeters, which would have no effect on the overall arrangement of the work.

50 For a more detailed examination, see the entry on the work in the catalogue.

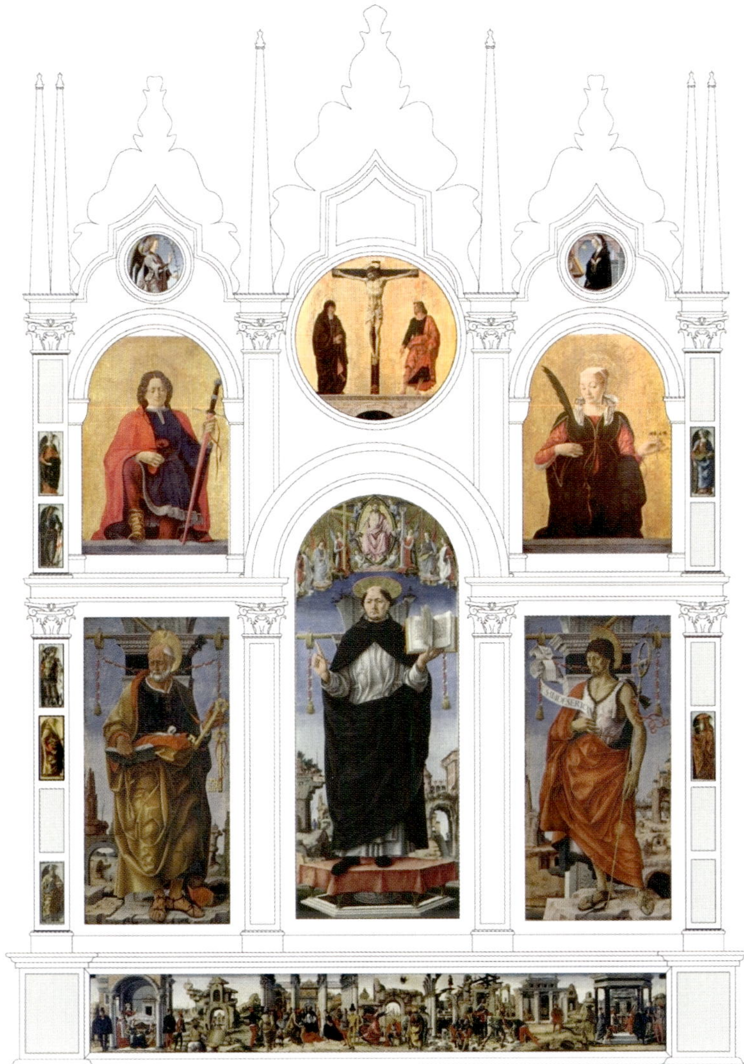

8

Cecilia Cavalca, graphics by Chiara Tarana, reconstruction of the Griffoni Polyptych (from Cavalca 2013, p. 266)

(figs. 7–8 and fig. on p. 163). The rearrangement offered an organic relationship between painting and carving, acquiring clarity in the design of the "*serliana*" structure generated by the junction of the powerful arch that surmounts the central section, centered on the entablature of the side panels and supported by antique-style pilaster strips. Although an essential element for correctly evaluating the work's layout, the structural complexity of the upper order, which had been particularly penalized in previous photographic montages, unsuspectedly re-emerged. An unusual arrangement of great fluency, it harmonizes quadrangular and round forms, its definition highlighting the artist's commitment to showcasing the subject matter in accordance with the new compositional criteria.

As a whole, we are faced with monumental, highly-attractive carpentry that marks a decisive change of gear compared with late-Gothic elevations. Partitions in older multiple-panel structures were in fact regularized and reinterpreted in a courtly key, relying on a syntactic construct of the framed arch drawn from triumphal Roman monuments, a central theme in those years. The place filled by the *Crucifixion* roundel is a sign of the high, fully cognizant quality of this new approach. Boxed in, according to this hypothetical reassembly, between the pilaster and the sloping semi-pillar, with the architectural portion portrayed through painting in perfect harmony with the evident structural grafting point marked by the capitals, it immediately evokes the projectig baldachins in the central section of medieval polyptychs and also brings to mind, since the figuration insists in a numismatic-type partition,[51] the relief roundels above the forms of the classical arches.[52] Based on the eighteenth-century drawing, we may further surmise that the central pilasters were covered in fine phytomorphic carvings (a good example of this may be found in the carpentry of Giovanni Bellini's polyptych of Santi Giovanni e Paolo). Combined with the turgid volutes and the cornice openings made by Agostino de' Marchi, these elegant decorative motifs imbued the gilded surface of the altar complex with a special chiaroscuro effect, capable of exalting in a very effective way, through contrast, the figuration's sharp and luminous orchestration. Sloping in from the left, side lighting illuminates the figures with adamantine clarity, showcasing their gestures while casting deep shadows that lend coherence to the perspective planes defined in the connection between the painted architecture and the lost wooden frame.

51 As maintained in Ortolani 1941, p. 130.

52 See Cavalca 2013, p. 335 (the comparison with the roundels in the ancient arches is from Marco Collareta).

Far from being the fruit of artistic rearguard, if ideally recomposed in its entirety the Griffoni Polyptych is on the contrary a structure that highly intelligently incorporates what Giovanni Bellini foreshadowed in his polyptych of Santi Giovanni e Paolo (fig. 5) and is a prelude to the solution adopted by Cosmè Tura in the Roverella altarpiece (fig. 6) through the exemplary model of Mantegna's altarpiece for San Zeno in Verona (fig. 11).

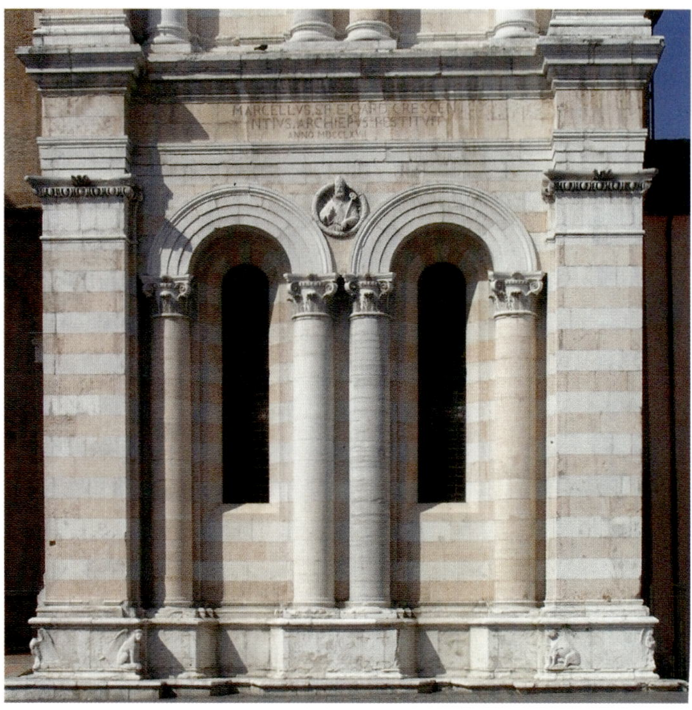

9

Bell tower of the Ferrara Cathedral, first order

Despite the archaic contaminations, for the Emilia region this was an event without precedent. Its conception implies Francesco del Cossa's early, independent dedication to arranging a religious subject within the altarpiece's architectural space. The artist's creative efforts were fully borne out in the design of the Dresden *Annunciation* altarpiece; with surprising consistency, this old-style squared-off altarpiece developed the idea of completing the figuration within a monumental structure that links into it (fig. 10). This model, which existed in Bologna probably as early as 1467–68, strongly affected the Griffoni Polyptych's pictorial organization, helping us to understand how, in the early 1470s, the artist was able to offer his clients a work of art that was destined to make a stir.

A few years before he set to work on the Griffoni Polyptych, we do not know for whom Francesco del Cossa executed the once-unified panel that is today split between Dresden, Barcelona, and Venice. It was, however, certainly a commission of particular importance. Everything leads us to believe that it was associated with the highest circles of Franciscanism, for which, in a completely circumstantial way, I suggest the possible involvement of the Della Rovere family: as a general of the order since 1464 and a future pope under the name Sixtus IV, Francesco was associated with Bologna from early education onwards.[53] The work postulates an architectural frame whose elevation is coherent with the giant order of the extraordinary grooved, rustic-looking column painted in the center of the figuration,[54] and "thanks to its true three-dimensionality, creates the scene of a squared-off pergola (or the quadrilateral segment of a longitudinal space) ... via daring perspective junction points."[55] This new development aimed to break open the limits of the visual field of painting with a force "that in the fifteenth century did not appear elsewhere, if not tempered by the size of the figuration in the altarpiece of San Lazzaro—that is, Ercole de' Roberti at his most Cossa-like."[56] It also helps us to understand what was the effect of the loggia with naturalistic background that, in the Griffoni Polyptych, housed *Saint Vincent Ferrer*, *Saint Peter*, and *Saint John*

53 Cavalca 2013, pp. 159, 174 note 114. I add that Francesco Della Rovere was elected general of the order the same year as Paul II was elected pope. In 1467, Paul II named him cardinal, at the behest of the celebrated Cardinal Bessarione. After his appointment as general of the order, the prelate visited all of the Franciscan See (see Moroni 1840–61, XXV, 1844, pp. 106–7).

54 Cavalca 2005.

55 Ceriana 2014, p. 224.

56 Ibid., p. 225.

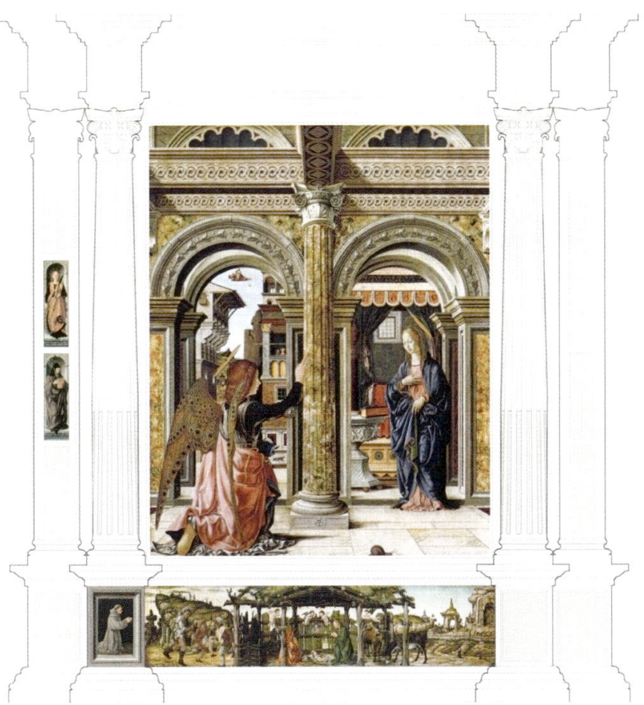

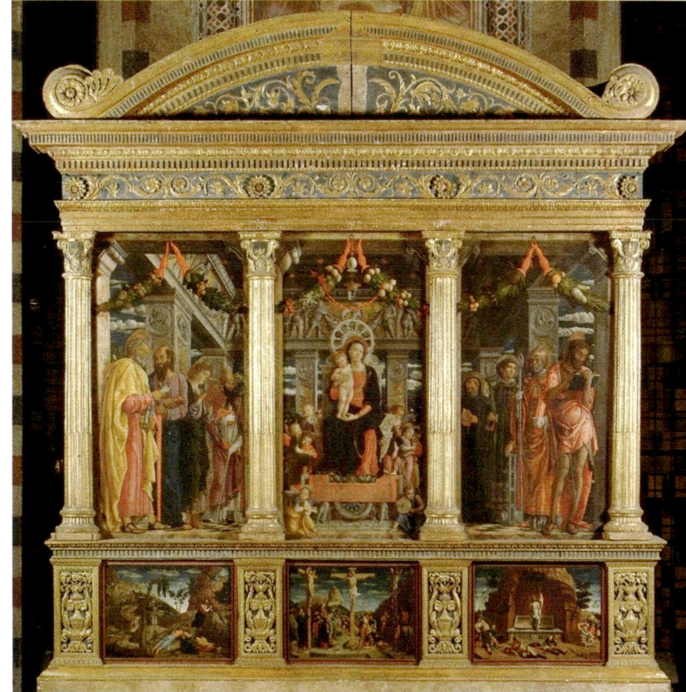

10

Cecilia Cavalca, graphics by Chiara Tarana, reconstruction of the altarpiece with the Dresden *Annunciation* (from Cavalca 2013, p. 264)

11

Andrea Mantegna, Triptych of San Zeno. Basilica of San Zeno, Verona

the Baptist. A geometrical analysis of the central section of the *Annunciation* shows that, in his perspective rendering of painted architecture, Cossa makes use of knowledge that cannot be attributed solely to his practice in the trade but was based on theoretical notions that were not so common at the time.[57] As we have had occasion to note here, these are skills the artist himself claimed, skills that were fully acknowledged by his contemporaries, reflecting a long and complex learning process and fine encounters laid on top of his family's familiarity with building, having been involved in the 1450s on top-tier construction sites (including the first dado of the Cathedral's bell tower; fig. 9),[58] as well as experience gained during a probable reasonably-long stay in Florence around the mid-1460s.

When he agreed to make the polyptych for the Griffoni family chapel at San Petronio, Cossa's qualities set him above other Bolognese painters, not just because he had painted outstanding frescoes to decorate the Hall of the Months at Palazzo Schifanoia in Ferrara, but because he had created one of the most innovative altarpieces of the time, one that stood out in the early 1470s not just in Bologna "but, one may say, throughout Italy."[59] We know that the artist emerged from his previous engagement at the Este court without adequate satisfaction; so a job offer in the city where he presumably had run his own workshop for some years, on a very central building site in full ferment like San Petronio around 1470,[60] must have looked a particularly attractive opportunity. The fact that he was immediately flanked, it would seem, by the best of his assistants, Ercole de' Roberti, is not unimportant at all.

---

57 Last, Incerti 2017, esp. pp. 88–91.

58 Among the meetings mentioned previously, one with architect Meo del Caprina, who after his stay in Ferrara we know worked in Paul II's Rome, and through his father, Prisciano Prisciani (di Pellegrino), who among his many skills boasted knowledge of architectural theories (on these skills, see Incerti 2017, p. 54).

59 Ceriana 2014, p. 224.

60 See Sambin De Norcen's contribution in this catalogue.

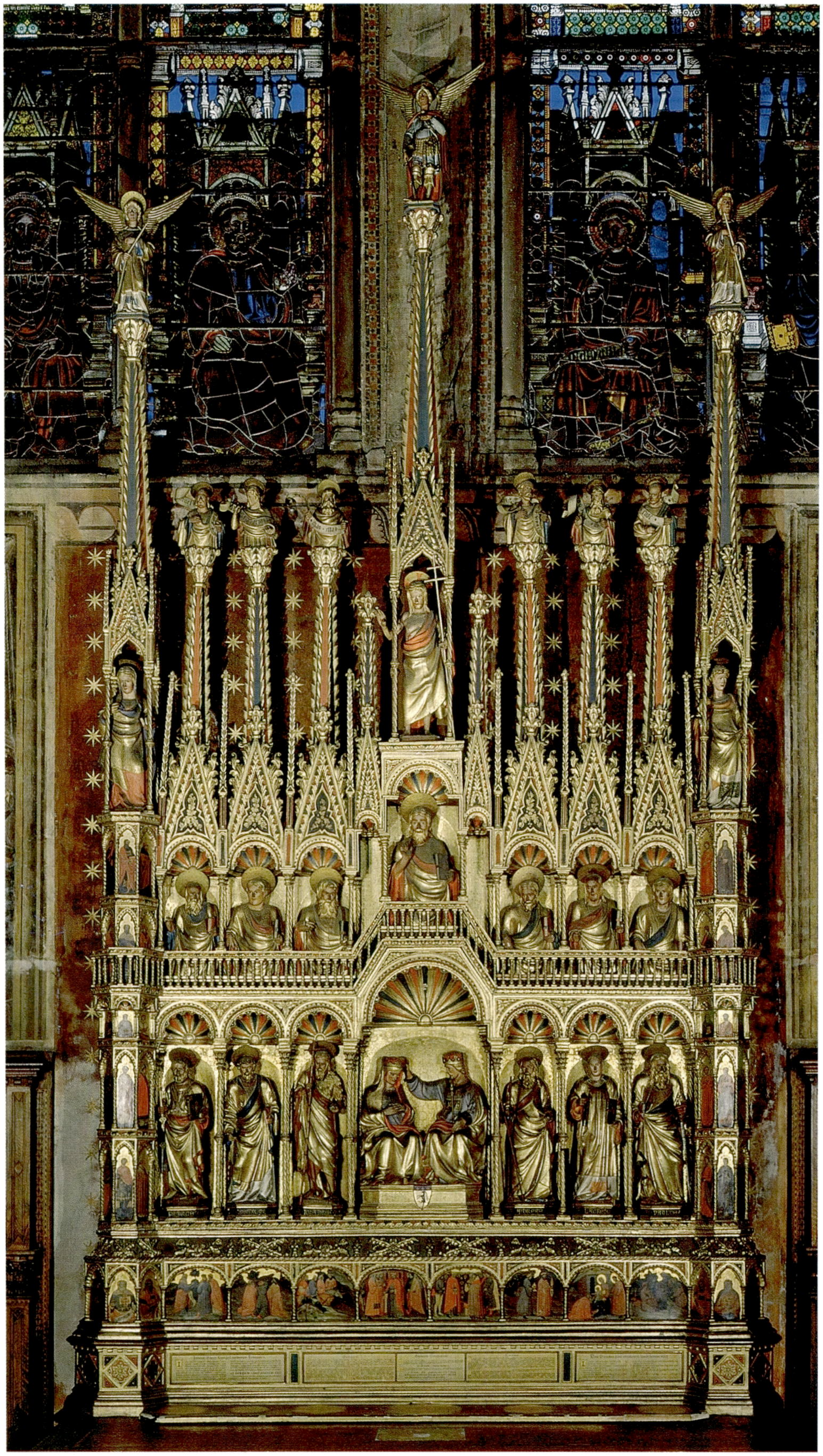

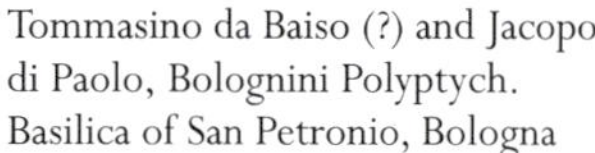

12

Tommasino da Baiso (?) and Jacopo di Paolo, Bolognini Polyptych. Basilica of San Petronio, Bologna

13

Francesco del Cossa, *Saint Florian*, detail. National Gallery of Art, Washington, DC

14

Francesco del Cossa, *Saint John the Baptist*, detail. Pinacoteca di Brera, Milan

The construction of chapels at San Petronio was a major process in the second half of the fifteenth century, one that immediately encouraged competition for patronage by city families ready to seize the opportunity to affirm their social status, and willing to spend considerable sums in pursuit of their intent. Already in the first half of the century, competitive embellishment of the various chapels was heightened by social striving, as testified by the vicissitudes linking the decoration of the Bartolomeo Bolognini Chapel (the fourth on the left entering) and that of the adjoining Foscherari Chapel, which—as we now know—took Bolognini's as its reference. In the same Bolognini Chapel, the majestic late-Gothic altarpiece that still decorates the altar today (fig. 12), a collaboration between painter Jacopo di Paolo and a top master woodworker, perhaps Tommasino da Baiso, credibly referenced two of the most prestigious late-fourteenth-century polyptychs in the city, both Venetian: Lorenzo Veneziano's wooden altarpiece at San Giacomo Maggiore and Jacobello and Pierpaolo dalle Masegne's giant one in marble for San Francesco. The latter work had a complex gestation, overshadowed by protests among the friars; but in time, it was so greatly appreciated that Giovanni II Bentivoglio cited it as a Bologna highlight right into the fifteenth century, as we see in Leandro Alberti's chronicles included in his *Historie* of Bologna.[61]

All of these circumstances taken together confirm that it was the Griffoni family who asked del Cossa to use a model from the recent past when making their altarpiece, while at the same time updating its pomp and monumental nature. It is equally plausible to believe that they turned to this artist because they knew they would obtain artwork suited to emerging devotional needs, capable of guaranteeing the quality necessary to

61 Alberti 1479–1543 ed. 2006, I, pp. 27, 107.

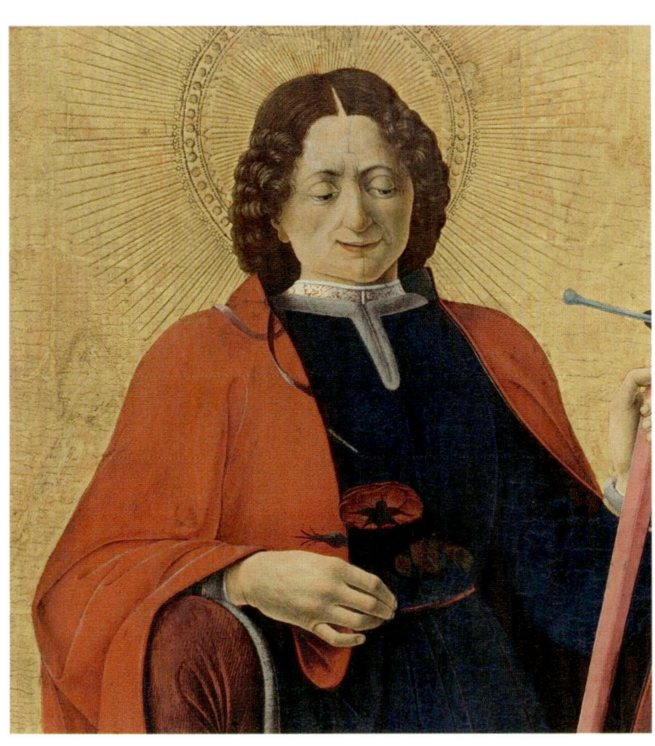

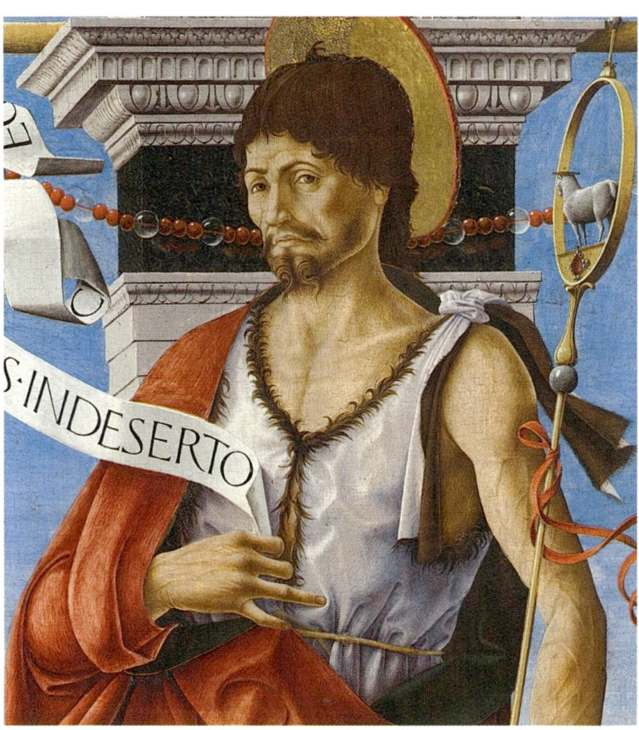

safeguard expression of their magnificence and public munificence.[62]

Indeed, one of the most interesting routes into the work is to examine control over the forgery of the real exercised by Francesco del Cossa and his collaborator Ercole de' Roberti in reshaping the formal envelope burdened by referencing pre-existing work of high symbolic value.

As Longhi so well understood, the polyptych's iconographic layout, which exalts Saint Vincent Ferrer as a preacher on the final destiny of humankind to all peoples and nations, is based, in the vertical development of the figuration, on the contrast between the vibrant brightness of the clear sky in the first register and the upper register's unnatural golden splendor, resolved in the central section where Christ is depicted during the Last Judgment.[63] Equally important, though, is the construction of the foreground, conceived with the frame as a necessary element to join the two orders of reality presented by the artifact: that of the painted figures and that of the observer. It is indeed only the ideal connection between the pilaster strips, the carved entablature, and the fake (painted) construction elements projecting outwards that provides the proscenium on which Saint Vincent Ferrer and Saints Peter and John the Baptist appear, immortalized like actors in a moment of intense and expressive concentration. The same structure is to be found above, where Saints Florian and Lucy bear the features of the clients. These figures stand out impeccably against the golden background, circumscribing the space in the act of genuflecting to witness the sacred representation that is being staged in the register below. Characterized by a fair degree of dynamism, this solution was designed to replicate Floriano Griffoni's and Lucia Battaglia's gesture in front of the altar. This mirror-like interplay, based on the recognizability of the eponymous saints, is what makes the machinery of illusion function. The verism of the two figures is highly controlled (fig. 13), both in the rather abstract definition of their features and in the shape of the garments, which are refined without being sumptuous, and contrasts with a smattering of realistic details throughout the rest of the pictorial narrative, especially in the main register, where they are very much on show, achieving maximum expression in the figure of Saint John the Baptist (fig. 14). If isolated, this expressive motive is likely to be deceiving, raising the issue of possible manufacturing differences between the different parts. For all six panels of the central body, research into the executive technique on the contrary shows an uncommon consistency, based upon a preparatory design attentive to every single detail, suggesting a tightly unitary approach.[64] The extremely high, unblemished quality of the graphic layout led Jill Dunkerton to hypothesize that very detailed cartoons must have been prepared for the main figures, similar to the fragment depicting a foreshortened foot preserved in Stuttgart (fig. 15). Credibly, several other preparatory

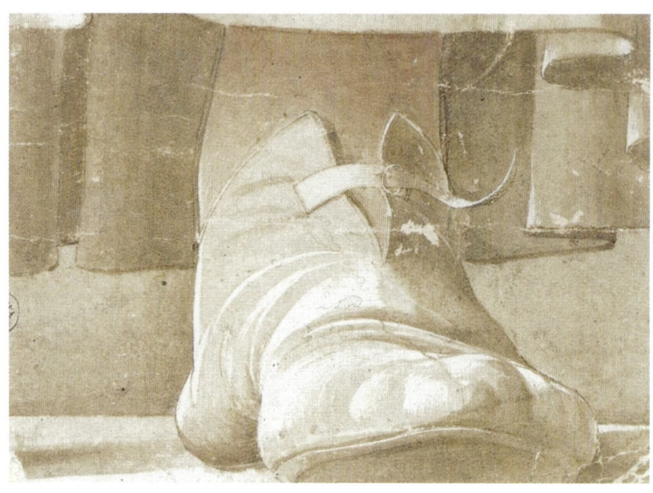

15

Francesco del Cossa, *Study of a foot*. Staatsgalerie, Graphische Sammlung, Stuttgart, Sammlung Schloss Fachsenfeld

62 For more about the commissioning clients, see the catalogue contributions by De Benedictis and Fanti; prior to that, on the representative role played by the commission, with particular reference to the social background of Floriano's wife Lucia, daughter of Andrea Battaglia, Cavalca 2018a.

63 For a more articulated reading of the work's iconography relating to the figuration on the predella, see the catalogue info sheet that I authored and Natale's contribution.

64 See Dunkerton's contribution in this catalogue.

16-17

Ercole de' Roberti, *Miracles of Saint Vincent Ferrer*, details. Vatican Museums, Vatican City

drawings were made, which were of use in studying individual details and assessing the organization of the whole, and would have immediately been made available to Ercole de' Roberti. Indeed, while independently reworking the graphic material necessary to tackle the figuration in the parts of the work assigned to him, Ercole maintained and employed a similar, refined selection of details taken from life for his pictorial narration, using portraiture as the locus of choice for achieving "perfect mimesis" (figs. 16–17). This is visible in the first scene to the left of the predella, where, as noted by Fabrizio Torella, the male figure in crimson red breeches, to the right side of the aedicule, is probably another portrait of Floriano Griffoni, whose recognizability combines the miraculous with specific family events[65] (fig. 16).

The elaborate functioning of the altarpiece was evidently incomprehensible from an analysis of the individual paintings, downplaying the role played by the visual plane created by the frame; a role that was certainly all-important also thanks to the craftsmanship of such as prestigious carver as Agostino de' Marchi. However, notwithstanding the extent to which our knowledge on this topic may be expanded, no circumstantial reconstruction, even the most refined, can ever restore the true scope of these illusionistic artifices in their original context. It is beyond our critical faculties to experience the strong visual impact generated when opening the curtains (or shutters) which, affixed to the protective case for which the frame-maker from Crema was paid in 1473, protected and concealed the virtuoso work of art during ordinary times. Enhanced by the reflections of candles, the unveiling of the pictorial surface must have been to truly spectacular effect. It was this moment—one that is beyond our reach—that really put to the test these two great artists from Ferrara, their design *ingenium* and extraordinary skill at manipulating their materials.

65 Torella (1985–87) 1988, p. 47.

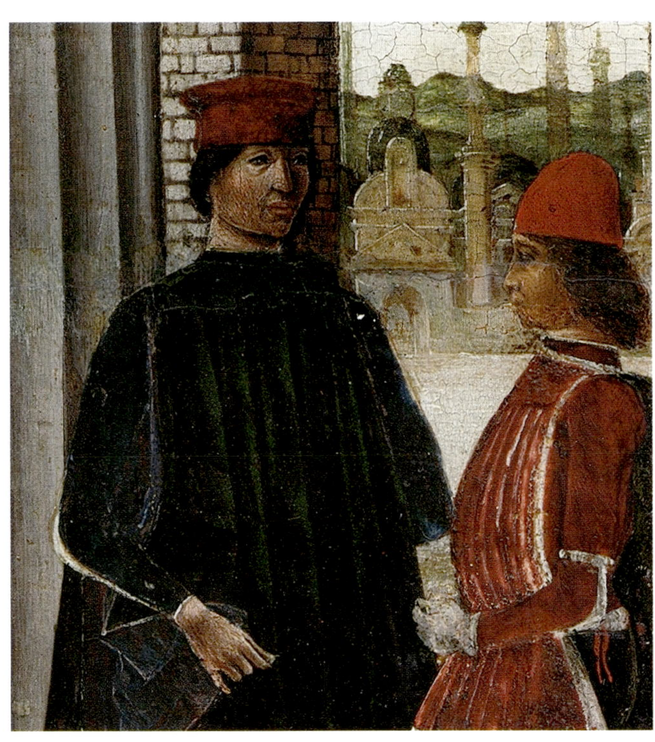

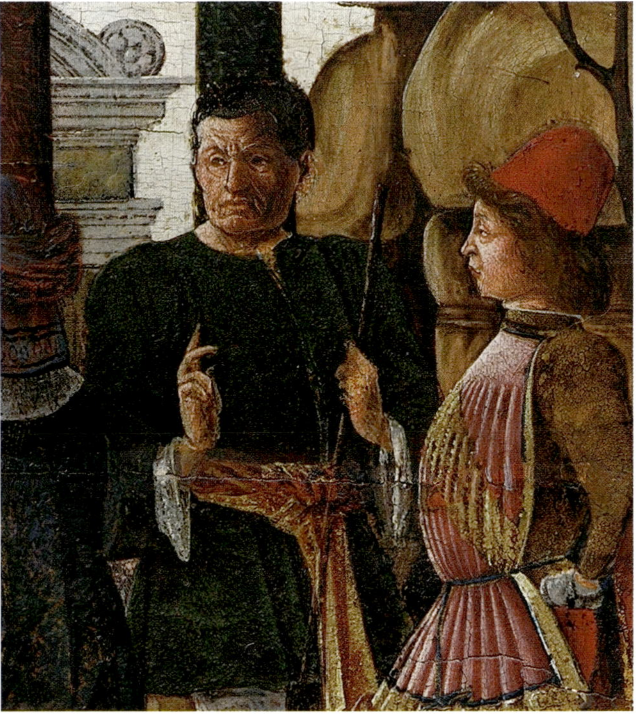

DISMEMBERMENT AND DIASPORA OF THE GRIFFONI POLYPTYCH: ART MARKETS, COLLECTING, AND MUSEUMS

Angelo Mazza

"That could not serve in any way." Monsignor Aldrovandi and the Griffoni Polyptych

When he acquired patronage of the Griffoni Chapel in the Basilica of San Petronio and came into possession of the family's assets, Monsignor Pompeo Aldrovandi (1668–1752) was in the process of rebuilding his reputation. Left in disgrace by the sensational failure of his diplomatic missions as papal nunzio in Spain, he had been relegated to Bologna since 1718.[1] Given the context of the conflict between the Spanish crown and the Holy See, Aldrovandi's alliance with Cardinal Giulio Alberoni and the rather suspicious errors in his failure to execute the directives of Clement XI had led the Pope to lose faith in his nunzio and Philip V to issue an order for his arrest.

Aldrovandi fled to Avignon, compromising relations with Spain and earning the distrust of the Roman Curia, in addition to that of the Pope. It was only with the death of the Albani Pope in 1721 and the subsequent election of Innocent XIII that Aldrovandi's fate took a turn for the better—a recovery further guaranteed by the election of Benedict XIII in 1724. Thereafter, Aldrovandi's career flourished throughout the decade of the papacy of Clement XII, elected in 1730; not only was he awarded the Cardinal's hat in 1734 (fig. 1), but he was nearly elected pope during the 1740 conclave that eventually chose the Bolognese Prospero Lambertini with the name of Benedict XIV.

In these years, after he had come into possession of his paternal inheritance, Pompeo Aldrovandi undertook a series of clever economic and financial operations. In 1723, he acquired a large, 1500-*tornature* agricultural enterprise in Mirabello from Duchess Isabella Ruini Bonelli, which he then combined with the neighboring farms of San Venanzo and Raveda to establish a vast estate. In a show of his astute entrepreneurial gifts, he increased the value still further with land reclamation projects, exploiting his powerful position especially after he was appointed legate of Ravenna.[2] Comprised in the property was the Manzolino estate, which Aldrovandi acquired through a deal with Giovanni Raniero Griffoni, a clergyman and the last descendant of the Griffoni family. By assuming his debt of 17,000 Bolognese liras and assuring him a monthly annuity of twenty *scudi*, the monsignor

---

Thanks to Benedetta Basevi, Mirko Nottoli, Daniela Schiavina, and Matteo Troilo; and especially to Pierangelo Bellettini, Cecilia Cavalca, Giovanni Mazzaferro, and Mauro Natale for reading the text and offering helpful suggestions.

1 See Fasano Guarini 1960; Giacomelli 1994; Troilo 2007; Troilo 2010.

2 Troilo 2010, pp. 85–103. For the palazzo, see Pigozzi 2004, pp. 40–46.

managed to have himself named heir and rightful beneficiary of all Griffoni properties.[3] These included a house adjacent to his own palazzo, which allowed him to carry out his expansion project since, in the meantime, he had acquired still other neighboring lands.[4]

At the end of the second decade and into the next, the enterprising monsignor initiated work on his splendid residence on the Via Galliera, eliminating the traditional portico, evidence of a special exemption. At the same time, he began work on the sumptuous Baroque chapel in the Basilica of San Petronio, bedecked in more marble that any other chapel in the city. With the support of the Lambertini Pope, Aldrovandi obtained the much sought-after head of Saint Petronius for his personal monument, a relic that had previously been conserved in the church of Santo Stefano and whose placement had been sorely contested for years.[5]

Once he was awarded the title of cardinal, Aldrovandi proposed to openly finance the completion of the facade of the Basilica of San Petronio himself, in exchange, however, for a degree of visibility that the civic pride of Bologna could not tolerate.[6] Indeed, he left such burdensome provisions in his will that Pope Benedict XIV intervened with a *motu proprio* in 1753 to mitigate the posthumous effects of the inordinate ambition cultivated by the Cardinal throughout his life.[7] The prelate had had ambitions to establish a public academy of painting, sculpture, and weaving which came into conflict, however, with the Istituto delle Scienze and the Accademia Clementina, sponsored in the beginning of the century by General Luigi Ferdinando Marsili and Giovan Pietro Zanotti and approved by Clement XI Albani. Aldrovandi's overriding desire to leave his mark on the city prompted the sharp-witted Lambertini Pope to write unflattering remarks in a blunt correspondence with the canon Peggi, saying, "The good man was a swindler in life as in death, and in the madness of his Wills and Codicils, nothing can be found to praise except his intention."[8]

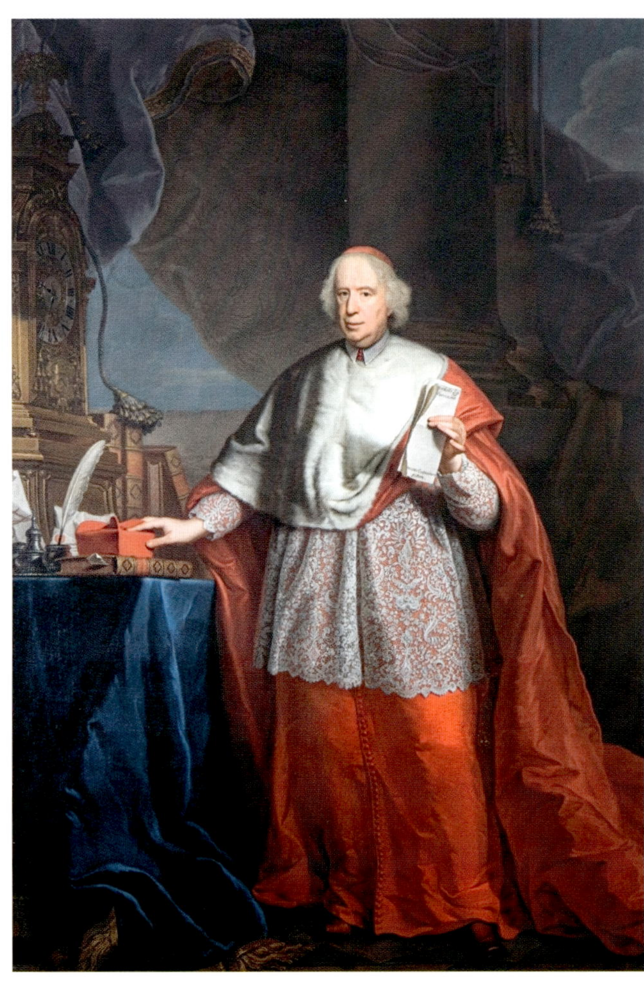

1

Frère Damien Carpentiers, *Portrait of Cardinal Pompeo Aldrovandi*, 1736. Art Collection of Unicredit, Palazzo Magnani, Bologna

Having obtained the patronage of the Griffoni Chapel, dedicated to Saint Vincent Ferrer (sixth on the left in the Basilica of San Petronio), Aldrovandi proceeded to exchange

3 Archivio di Stato di Bologna (hereafter, ASBo), Aldrovandi Marescotti, b. 386; also Troilo 2010, p. 95. For an eighteenth-century printed genealogical tree of the Griffoni family with "*Gio: Raniero vivente*," son of "*Antonio Maria con Vittoria Arrighi*," see ASBo, Aldrovandi Marescotti, b. 386.

4 Troilo 2010, pp. 95 and 260.

5 Giacomelli 1994, p. 104; Troilo 2010, pp. 256–71. On the chapel, see *La cappella di San Petronio* 2002, in particular the essay by Mario Fanti (2002, pp. 18–42). The initiative to endow the chapel with the relic of Saint Petronius, followed personally by the Lambertini Pope, was memorialized in Cardinal Aldrovandi's celebrative medallion, featuring a portrait engraved by Rocco Pozzi after a drawing by Giovanni Domenico Campiglia, as appearing in the two-volume work by Mario Guarnacci with portraits of the cardinals during the papacies of Clement X and Clement XII (Guernacci 1751, II, col. 672).

6 See Lenzi 2001, pp. 45–46; Troilo 2010, p. 104 and note 45; Campisi 2018, p. 92.

7 Troilo 2010, pp. 103–11.

8 *Lettera di papa Benedetto XIV al canonico Pier Francesco Peggi*, October 11, 1752 (*Briefe Benedicts XIV* 1888, p. 91), quoted in Giacomelli 1994, p. 131 note 20; Fanti 2002, p. 49.

it for the Cospi family chapel (second on the left). In the late 1720s, he began the lavish decoration of the chapel with precious marbles, gilded stuccoes, carvings, bronze casts, jewelry, marble sculptures, and frescoes, employing the same artists who were working on restructuring his family residence on Via Galliera, directed by the same architect, Alfonso Torreggiani.[9]

Writing about the chapel of Saint Vincent Ferrer, the 1732 guide took note of the modifications: "Cospi no longer Griffoni. The tempera Saint Vincent Ferrer is by Vittorio Bigari and the decoration of the ceiling by Stefano Orlandi, and both are our Colonna and Mitelli of today." Significantly, there is no reference to the Griffoni Polyptych, although Giorgio Vasari had mentioned it as appearing in this chapel back in 1550.

Indeed, as revealed by the research of Francesca Montefusco Bignozzi and the subsequent work of Cecilia Cavalca, in February 1725, the *quadratura* painter Stefano Orlandi, convinced that "that could serve in no way," warned Aldrovandi of the unlikely coexistence, in fact the virtual incompatibility, of the fifteenth-century polyptych in its late Gothic-style frame with the "modern ornamentation" desired by Monsignor Pompeo Aldrovandi, who intended to commission Orlandi himself and his partner Vittorio Bigari to paint the figures.[10] By November 21, the polyptych had already been dismantled, causing irreparable damage to the antique gilded frame, to the point that it was effectively reduced to firewood ("the rest of the antique and gilded ornamentation, I can say that it fell to pieces and may only be good for burning"). As described specifically in a letter from Giuseppe Baraldi to Aldrovandi, the plan was to place the panels removed from their ornate frames into "simple frames in the shape of the Pistorini frames, and to gild them thereafter."[11]

Going against his contemporaries, who had little interest in works prior to Francesco Francia's gentle proto-classicism, Baraldi considered the panels worthy of appearing in any gallery once they were cleaned, varnished, and had their small gaps filled by the skilled hand of Giuseppe Maria Crespi, Baraldi's choice. A letter of three days later (November 24, 1725) specified recourse to thirteen frames, which were not delivered until May of the following year, however, after restoration by Giuseppe Cesare Mazzoni, a student of Giovan Gioseffo Dal Sole, had provided the panels with an acceptable presentation.[12]

9 Montefusco Bignozzi 1984, pp. 122–34; Fanti 2002, pp. 33–42; Troilo 2010, p. 281. The 1732 edition of *Le pitture di Bologna* reports that the chapel "*presentemente s'adorna, e si compie così di preziosi marmi, come di tutto ciò che più può essere conveniente a una suntuosa cappella, per ordine di Monsignore Aldrovandi*" (*Le pitture di Bologna* 1732, p. 264). The next edition, in 1755, refers to the precious relic of the head of Saint Petronius procured by Lambertini and continues with an analytic description of the chapel that encourages close observation of the painting and sculpture: "*Non poteasi questa cappella con più magnifiche spese compiersi, ed adornare di quelle che fece il Cardinale Pompeo Aldrovandi per renderla vaga, e pomposa*" (*Le pitture di Bologna* 1755, p. 270).

10 Based on a short letter from Stefano Orlandi to Monsignor Pompeo Aldrovandi found in 1984 by Francesca Montefusco Bignozzi (Benati 1984, p. 193 note 26); the transcription is published in Cavalca 2013 (p. 383 doc. XI.23), which offers a critical analysis of the entire matter of the recomposition (ibid., pp. 334–35). On this subject, see also the brilliant discussion by Massimo Campisi (2018, pp. 84–108). For the intervention of Vittorio Bigari in partnership with Stefano Orlandi, see Casali Pedrielli 1991, pp. 86–87, 100–1.

11 The reference is to the frames for the "*pitture comprate in Bologna per Monsig.e Aldrovandi dal dott.e Pistorini per mezzo del Sig. Avv.to Sacchi*" (ASBo, Aldrovandi Marescotti, b. 284).

12 Angelo Fontana wrote to Aldrovandi: "*per l'antichità del Pitore sono di quei quadri che sono assai considerati per poterli ponere in qual si volia Galaria essendo in alcuni luoghi quasi stucato che sarrà spero il Spagnuolo me lo aggiustarà senza spesa come li altri che sono in stato assai cattivo ma proccurarò che siano neti e vernigati che possano comparire assai*" (quoted in Cavalca 2013, p. 383 doc. XI.24). It may have been Crespi's inavailability that caused Aldrovandi's correspondent to turn to Giuseppe Cesare Mazzoni. The story of the material dismemberment of the polyptych and its virtual recomposition by modern criticism is analyzed by Cavalca 2013, pp. 334–35, 383–84 docs. XI.24–XI.27; see also D. Cattoi in *Este* 2004, pp. 288–95. The reference to thirteen frames for a polyptych composed of many more than thirteen panels may seem surprising. However, it should be assumed that the same choices were taken regarding the dismemberment of the Griffoni complex and the dismantling of the polytypch by Simone dei Crocifissi, with even more elements, which once stood in

Their fate is revealed in a follow-up letter of May 18, 1726 in which the correspondent, Angelo Fontana, communicates Aldrovandi's intentions, saying that "they can perfectly well serve for the country house, as he has seen fit to advise me." This provision was confirmed in another letter as well, which makes clear that the choice to use simple, modest frames, "edged in gold and paint" (distinctly less precious than those of the paintings in the city collection, most of which were gilded and adorned with fine carvings), was made in light of their intended destination in the monsignor's country villa.[13]

Although there was no lack of analogous frames in minor rooms of his city residence, Aldrovandi's choice in this case was both intentional and significant, considering that the prelate had begun a serious collection of the highest quality with virtually no antique or even sixteenth-century paintings. Nonetheless, the collection could boast of more than 400 paintings and numerous statues displayed in a sculpture gallery, as recorded in the 1736 inventory and again in that of 1752, the year of Aldrovandi's death. Pompeo had collected the works himself, documenting contemporary trends in Bolognese painting and including numerous paintings from Rome obtained during his long sojourns there. On the contrary, the works in the collection of his elder brother, Filippo Maria, were all inherited from the art collections of their grandfather, also named Filippo Maria, and maternal uncle Riniero Marescotti.[14]

---

the Cospi Chapel in San Petronio, also the property of Monsignor Aldrovandi after the patronage of the two chapels was exchanged. As is documented, the thirty little saints of the Cospi Polyptych were collected into ten frames, each with three panels (see del Monaco 2018, p. 83 note 52). This polyptych is described as "*N. 23 pezzi pitture di diverse grandezze, con cornice gialla, e filetto oro, cavate dall'altare di S. Petronio*" kept "*nella casa, che fu de' SS.i Griffoni*" on two loose pages inserted in *Primo Abozo dell'Inventario di diversi Mobili, Pitture ed altro esistente nell'appartamento dell'E.mo, e Rev.mo Sig.r Card.e Aldrovandi*, a draft of the 1736 inventory. The analytic citations in that draft—for example, "*due figure rappresentante N. S.re che incorona la B.V.*" and another, "*quadro bislongo dipinto in tavola rappresentante diversi misteri della B. V.*"—leave no doubt about the identification (ASBo, Aldrovandi Marescotti, b. 282, *Descrizione delli mobili che si riconoscono nella casa ... annessa alle rimesse*, pp. 9, 11, 15, and 17; also *1736. Inventario delle pitture e statue esistenti nell'Appartamento dell'E.mo, e R.mo Sig.r Card.e Pompeo Aldrovandi*, 1736, pp. 43–44, 46, 47).

13 And again, in a letter sent a few years later, dated December 22, 1731: "*supponendo voglia farli ornare con cornici proprie per campagna*" (Cavalca 2013, p. 384 docs. XI.26 and XI.27). As early as May 1727, Monsignor Aldrovandi had requested Giovanni Galimberti to send thirty-six paintings to Mirabello, some large, some small (ASBo, Aldrovandi Marescotti, b. 282, *Due inventari eguali ... 15 maggio 1727*). For comments on the frames in the city collection, see Bonfait 1987, p. 38. In fact, the panels of the Griffoni Polypytch are registered in the Palazzo Aldrovandi inventories, compiled by the "*perito zavaglio*" Tommaso Rinaldi, first in 1752, at the Cardinal's death, without attribution, and again in 1764, four years after the death of his heir, Senator Riniero Aldrovandi Marescotti (ASBo, Aldrovandi Marescotti, b. 376, *Inventarium bonorum haereditatis clar.mi. e.mi et r.mi D. Cardinalis Pompei Aldrovandi*, notary Gaspare Sacchetti, July 24, 1752; b. 341, *Inventario legale de Beni dell'Eredità della bo. me. Sig.e Co. Sen.e Riniero Aldrovandi Marescotti*, February 28, 1764). Many of the citations are easily identifiable: those of the main panel, then believed to be a *Saint Dominic*, of the side panels with *Saint Peter* and *Saint John the Baptist*, of the predella with the miraculous deeds (attributed to Saint Dominic in the 1752 inventory and to St Vincent Ferrer in that of 1764), of the tondo with the *Crucifixion* and of the two smaller roundels of the *Annunciation*. The generic or imprecise nature of the other citations does not allow for certain identifications. However, between the predella citation and that of the side doors of the first register, displayed in the palace chapel, appears a reference to "*cinque piccoli quadretti rappresentanti Santi dipinti in assa, con cornice gialla et oro*." The assessment of value is rather low considering that the predella is appraised at ten liras, the *Saint Peter* and *Saint John the Baptist* at five liras each, and the *Saint Vincent Ferrer* at six liras. Meanwhile, a "*baldacchino all'antica con sue bandinelle e testiera*" placed over the bed, "*il tutto di brocatone argento falso*," is assessed at twenty liras and a spruce wardrobe "*con due framezzate con sua chiave, e serrature ne sportelli, e sua cima, il tutto dipinto a chiaro e scuro con l'arma di Sua Eminenza*" was likewise valued at twenty liras, actually more than the total of the three panels of the polyptych's main register combined.

14 We know of an inventory drawn up at his death in 1748, in which the paintings were divided into two groups: one with ordinary paintings and the other with higher-quality, more valuable works, which included fifty-five paintings listed by Vittorio Maria Bigari (on the various Aldrovandi collections and their inventories from 1644 to 1811, see targeted studies by Bonfait: Bonfait 1987; Bonfait 2000, *ad indicem*, esp. pp. 350–54; for the economic aspects, see Troilo 2007; Troilo 2010, pp. 271–83). Among the few antique works recorded in the 1736 inventory were compartments, hanging separately in various rooms, of the polyptych by Simone dei Crocifissi removed from the Cospi Chapel in the Basilica of San Petronio. In a ledger with *Varj conti, e memorie di mano del fu E.mo Aldrovandi* (ASBo, Aldrovandi Marescotti, b. 320), Monsignor Pompeo Aldrovandi recorded his expenses upon his return from Spain for luxury items and entertaining

Thus, the relegation of the panels by Francesco del Cossa and Ercole de' Roberti to the Mirabello residence represents a distinct and intentional downgrade. Such devaluations were a consolidated practice: changes in taste, the evolution of styles, the need to update, new devotional requirements, and simply the desire to renovate meant that works on display to the public, rendered outmoded over time, were often substituted and not infrequently sent to the countryside.[15] Such was the fate of many fourteenth-century works even in the time of Carlo Cesare Malvasia who, recalling the appealing combination of "delicacy and grace" in the art of Vitale da Bologna, invited the "seeker of similar antiquities" to frequent "churches in the countryside, where one is more likely to see such antique paintings at times innocently relegated, through no other fault than the pressure of the increasing new luxury, ambitious for that first place which had been given them in the city."[16]

Thus, it is no surprise that Giuseppe Baraldi's appreciation "for the antiquity of the Painter," at least in this case, was not at all shared by Aldrovandi, who consigned the panels to a secondary residence. Actually, in Bologna at the beginning of the eighteenth century, there were any number of curious collectors keen on the so-called Primitives, though perhaps for reasons other than an appreciation of their formal values; there were also those expressing alarm at the dispersion and neglect of these earlier works. Nonetheless, this interest did not rise to the level of the fascination that inspired Marquis Sigismondo Malvezzi in the second half of the century to set up his so-called "antiques chamber," celebrated by Luigi Lanzi.[17] Nor could one have predicted the passion that led Prince Filippo Hercolani, in the 1760s and '70s, to establish the richest collection of fourtenth- and fifteenth-century paintings not only in Bologna but in the entire Emilia area, including a number of altarpieces and other paintings from churches and convents in Bologna and Romagna.[18]

"In these times intent on the destruction of the most beautiful things" (G. P. Zanotti, 1732)

Protest against Aldrovandi's drastic decision did not revolve around his clear disdain for the formal qualities of the polyptych, a Renaissance masterpiece that nonetheless did not correspond to the taste of the epoch. Instead, the grievance focused on its removal from public view, its expulsion from the city church and, most importantly, the extradition from

---

guests as incurred between 1719 and 1721. He had bought carriages which, in 1718, he had decorated by master Gaetano Brunetti, who subsequently worked in England and finally in France; he hired silversmiths, carpenters, embroiderers, and painters and started a painting collection featuring Cittadini, Giovanni Maria Viani, Lorenzo Pasinelli, Antonio Calza, Giacomo Bolognini, Emilio Taruffi, Nunzio Ferraioli, Girolamo Negri known as Il Boccia, Mirandolese, Francesco Monti and, of course, Stefano Orlandi and Vittorio Bigari. He requested works from Donato Creti and commissioned him to restore paintings "*che avevano assai patito*." His relationship with Marcantonio Franceschini is well-documented in the years 1720–22, including the artist's receipts for "*una Maddalena piccola con angeli*," "*una Annunciata grande*" (perhaps the small altarpiece with the Cardinal's coat of arms placed on the altar of the Impresa Chapel in Mirabello), an *Andromeda* and, most importantly, a *Death of Adonis*. For Monsignor Aldrovandi's letter negotiating the price: ASBo, Aldrovandi Marescotti, b. 293, *1723 al 1725. Affari dell'E.mo Aldrovandi, col dott.re Galimberti*.

15 On this subject, see the important discussion by Castelnuovo and Ginzburg 1979, esp. pp. 306–9.

16 "*… qualche chiesa in villa, ove per lo più si vedono innocentemente relegate talora simili anticaglie, non per altra colpa, che del cresciuto lusso, ambizioso di quel primo posto, che dentro la città a quelle diedesi.*" Malvasia 1678 ed. 1841, I, p. 26.

17 Lanzi 1789 ed. 1831, IX, p. 87. A limited sample of small fourteenth- and fifteenth-century panels of unknown provenance were on display, for example, at the Compagnia dei Lombardi immediately after 1717 (Negretti 2019, p. 75).

18 On the fate of the Primitives in eighteenth-century Bolognese collections, see the pivotal essay by Luca Ciancabilla (2012); see also entries by Ciancabilla, by Barbara Ghelfi, and by Valerio Mosso in *La fortuna dei Primitivi* 2014, pp. 181–95; also Negretti 2019. One of the reasons—perhaps the main one at the time of the dismemberment—was the religious value ascribed to those sacred images; over time, recognition of their importance as collectable works grew as well.

the city of a work that, for almost two hundred years, had adorned Bologna's most representative religious building, the church dedicated to its patron saint.

It is perhaps to this and other analogous cases that Giovan Pietro Zanotti alluded in his introduction to the 1732 guide to Bologna, published shortly after the polyptych had been dismantled. He wrote of "the cupidity for novelty" as a sort of mania for change related to the fickleness of fashion, which he blamed for the removal and substitution of paintings in churches, the destruction of frescoes during restoration projects, and the senseless loss of works due to ignorance and neglect. These destructive acts eliminated more and more of the surviving art that had allowed Malvasia, thanks to their verifiable antiquity, to insist on the expressive autonomy of the early Bolognese painters, before and after Giotto, in opposition to the Tuscan-centric vision of Vasari-inspired historiography. Zanotti, who in a mixture of realism and opportunism tolerated sales "out of necessity," condemned the stupidity of those who sacrificed older works on the altar of ephemeral fashion, thereby doubling the damage and bearing the inevitable cost.

He counterbalanced these cases, however, with other virtuous ones, beginning with a decision by the Filippini fathers of the church of Santa Maria di Galliera to bear the cost of cutting away a wall in order to save Ludovico Carracci's large fresco, *Christ presented to the people*, painted under a portico that was to be demolished to make room for a new oratory, in "a rare example in these times intent on the destruction of the most beautiful things."[19] He also cited the Spanish Inquisition priest José Luis de Andujar, who, during the remodeling of the Basilica of San Domenico, took it upon himself to save, at his own expense, part of other frescoes by Carracci in the Lambertini Chapel, which were otherwise slated to be destroyed.[20]

Another inspiring precedent, not mentioned by Zanotti because so much time had passed, was the rescue of frescoes painted by Francesco del Cossa and Ercole de' Roberti. After the partial collapse of the Garganelli Chapel in the Cathedral of San Pietro in 1599, Alessandro Tanari, the papal treasurer in Bologna appointed by Paul V Borghese, took charge personally of their recovery by having the walls cut away. An inventory of his collection drawn up in 1640 by the painter Vincenzo Spisanelli recorded eleven pieces in carved and gilded frames hanging in Tanari's residence on Via Galliera in three adjoining rooms.[21] Indeed, it was probably Tanari himself who had copies made—thereby ensuring that the creations were bequeathed to posterity—by Francesco Carbone, a collaborator of Alessandro Tiarini, and by Giacinto Gilioli, an unexceptional student of Guido Reni. Indeed, it was almost as if Tanari foresaw the inglorious end of the detached frescoes, which were eventually left to deteriorate irretrievably.[22]

---

19 "*... esempio raro in questi tempi intesi alla distruzione delle cose più belle.*" Zanotti 1732, f. 29v (the quotation is on p. 55); on the timely intervention, see Mazza 2001.

20 Zanotti 1732, ff. 29v–30r: "*dovendosi per la fabbrica della nuova chiesa di san Domenico, trarre a terra una cappella dal suddetto Carracci dipinta, egli parte di que' muri fe segare, e trasportare, cioè la bellissima carità, e la figura intera del san Domenico, che ora sono collocati nella santissima Inquisizione.*" A few years later, on the other hand, Zanotti lamented the attacks of fate and men against the frescoes by Nicolò dell'Abate, on both the interiors and exteriors of Bolognese buildings (Mazza 2011).

21 ASBo, Fondo notarile, notary Rinaldi Accursi, 1638–40, *Inventario dei beni mobili e immobili di Alessandro Tanari (Inventario della quadreria del pittore Vincenzo Spisani*, May 1640, ff. 59r–v, 63v–64r), published in Ciammitti 1985, pp. 206–7, 215; Cavalca 2013, pp. 392–93 doc. XXXI.

22 On the entire affair, see Ciammitti 1985; for the copies, also Molteni 1995, pp. 140–42. Not even a fragment remains of the four pieces donated to the Pinacoteca of the Accademia di Belli Arti in the early nineteenth century by the Tanari family. One of these, "*essendo rovinato con generale sconnessione de' mattoni*," was "*buttato altrove come pietrizzi*" in 1843; they were "*distrutti e confusi col rottame*," wrote Michelangelo Gualandi (*Memorie originali* 1840–45, VI, 1845, p. 192). The fate of the others was no better: in 1846, they ended "*in mille pezzi*" as a result of a clumsy effort to move them (Ciammitti 1985, p. 157). Both the frescoes and the copies are recorded in the inventory compiled in 1640 by Vincenzo Spisani,

It is quite possible that Zanotti was actually thinking of Monsignor Aldrovandi when he sadly reported the disappearance of numerous antique paintings in his introduction to the new edition of the guide in 1732. In order to update the pocket guide, which "undeceived and instructed passers-by," the painter, historiographer, and distinguished secretary of the Accademia Clementina needed to traverse the entire city. "In my walks, book in hand, visiting these Churches, and those Palaces, how many worthy ornaments of architecture, and of painting, I found dismembered, and lost, though surely not all of these had been so battered by time as to require such treatment."[23]

In fact, Aldrovandi was responsible not only for the dismemberment and removal of the Griffoni Polyptych, but also for the disappearance of an even older polyptych by Simone dei Crocifissi, which was the original altarpiece in the Cospi Chapel in San Petronio. As was recently verified by Gianluca del Monaco,[24] when Monsignor Aldrovandi acquired the patronage of the Cospi Chapel in exchange for the Griffoni Chapel, he came into possession of "the extremely old gilded panel with compartments, with the *Blessed Virgin crowned* and many lateral Saints," which Malvasia noted bore the inscription "*Symon pinxit hoc opus*."[25] (The only part of the polyptych that can be identified with any certainty is the predella with seven episodes of the life of the Virgin, which entered the Pinacoteca Nazionale di Bologna in 1883 upon the conclusion of a bitter lawsuit over the Zambeccari collection.[26]) That altarpiece had even more sections than the Griffoni Polyptych: as Angelo Fontana explained in a letter to Aldrovandi dated April 16, 1732, "twenty-three small paintings," all properly framed, were obtained when it was dismembered, ten of them containing another three small paintings each.

Years later, after Cardinal Aldrovandi's influence had faded, the polemical canon Luigi Crespi dismissed Zanotti's caution, explicitly condemning the disappearance of the Griffoni Polyptych in a text prepared in vain to be published. In 1751, he received the manuscript of *Vite degl'Artefici delle nobili arti della città di Ferrara scritte già dal fu dottor Girolamo Baruffaldi arciprete dell'insigne collegiata di Cento* from the author shortly before his death, in homage to their friendship.[27] With the intention of publishing the work, Crespi dutifully added concise annotations. In his notes to manuscript B.77 in the Biblioteca Comunale dell'Archiginnasio, at the end of the biography of Lorenzo Costa—widely considered since the time of Vasari as the author of the Griffoni Polyptych, along with Ercole de' Roberti—Crespi deplored the weakness of Zanotti's reproach, even branding the removal of paintings from churches as sacrilege.

The indignant Luigi Crespi vigorously denounced such abuses, supporting his condemnation with statements by the distinguished preacher Jacques Bénigne Bossuet and the Advocate General Dumenil, who argued that "property consecrated to the Church,

---

known as Spisanelli: ASBo, Fondo notarile, notary Rinaldi Accursi, 1638–40, *Inventario dei beni mobili e immobili di Alessandro Tanari* (*Inventario della quadreria del pittore Vincenzo Spisani*, May 1640, ff. 60r–v, 64r), published in Ciammitti 1985, pp. 210, 216. On Giacinto Gilioli and Francesco Carbone, see, respectively, Cellini 1992 and Mazza 2018, pp. 11–12.

23 "*... passeggiere disingannato ed instrutto*," "*Nel girare che ho fatto col libro in mano, visitando queste Chiese, e questi Palagi quanti degni ornamenti di architettura, e di pittura ho io trovati disfatti, e perduti, e non tutti certamente erano stati dal tempo malmenati in guisa, che vi fosse necessità di ciò fare*." Zanotti 1732, f. 28v.

24 del Monaco 2018, pp. 82–86, esp. note 52 on p. 83.

25 Malvasia 1686, p. 243; ed. 1969, p. 164.

26 Massimo Medica (1992) resolved the question of the original destination, identifying the Cospi coat of arms in the last episode on the right (for the Zambeccari provenance, see Cammarota 2000, p. 290 note 38; F. Lollini in *Pinacoteca Nazionale* 2004, pp. 150–52, no. 43). About hypotheses to date of the reconstruction of Simone dei Crocifissi's polyptych, previously in San Petronio, see Negretti 2019, pp. 73–77.

27 On this subject, see Perini Folesani 2019, pp. 76–77; also Novelli 1997, pp. 123–24, 126–27, 132.

whether it be moveable or immoveable, must be considered inviolable and excluded from the use or commerce of men."[28] Further stigmatizing the removal of the polyptych, he wrote, "The Altarpiece of Saint Vincent that was seen painted by Costa on the altar of the Griffoni in San Petronio, with the marvelous corbel painted by Ercole da Ferrara, can no longer be seen, since when the chapel passed into the ownership of others, the panel with the corbel also passed into one of our Galleries, and from there disappeared, and the one, and the other, having been substituted by a panel with Saint Vincent Ferrer painted in tempera by a modern artist. The intact altarpiece could have been placed in one of the two lateral facades of that magnificent chapel, thus conserving within the public eye two singular works by these two talented artists, so named by writers; but no Gentlemen, they were removed, and are now entirely lost."[29]

In truth, the passion of Luigi Crespi's condemnation of the abuses was equaled by the passion of his unscrupulous activities as antiquarian. A champion of incoherence, the combative canon was responsible for the sale of more than a few Bolognese Renaissance paintings, in particular masterpieces by Francesco del Cossa and Ercole de' Roberti that had hung in the city's churches.

In the overall climate of tolerance favoring sales despite the papal ban, Luigi Crespi—along with the abbot Alessandro Branchetta, "gentleman of honor of Cardinal Aldrovandi" who was protected by Lambertini himself, and the painter Carlo Cesare Giovannini, in addition, naturally, to Giovanni Ludovico Bianconi—played a critical role in trade relations with the court of Dresden. August III Elector of Saxony and King of Poland had formed one of the most prestigious galleries in Europe there, thanks to acquisitions on the Venetian market, abetted by Francesco Algarotti, and even more so, in 1745–46, by the successful conclusion of negotiations for one hundred masterpieces from the collection of the Duke of Modena. This immoderate urge to possess art reached its maximum fulfilment in 1753 with Raphael's *Sistine Madonna*, a supreme masterpiece of the High Renaissance, transferred from the church of San Sisto in Piacenza to the court of Dresden to be treated by the painter and restorer Carlo Cesare Giovannini, considered the most authoritative expert on Emilian painting.[30]

Giovannini had been preceded by Luigi Crespi, who had insinuated himself into the routes to Dresden in June 1752, with stopovers in Venice, Trieste, and Vienna. With him, he carried the large painting from the Tanari collection, *Nino and Semiramide*, a much admired Guido Reni work that was anxiously awaited by the court of August III. Sadly, the painting was later destroyed in a bombardment on the night of February 13, 1945. "An astute and

---

28 "*... i beni consacrati alla Chiesa, mobili e immobili, debbono essere riputati inviolabili, e fuor dell'uso, e commercio degli uomini.*" L. Crespi in *Vite degl'Artefici* c. 1770, p. 81; discussed in Perini Folesani 2019, pp. 79–80. The quotations from Jacques Bénigne Bossuet and Advocate General Dusmenil were taken from *Del diritto libero della Chiesa di acquistare, e di possedere beni temporali sì mobili, che stabili*, Book II, Volume II, Part I (Venice, 1769), pp. 70–71.

29 "*L'Ancona del S. Vincenzo che si vedeva dipinta dal Costa all'altare de' Griffoni in S. Petronio, con il mirabile peduccio dipinto da Ercole da Ferrara, più non si vede, dacché passata la capella in dominio d'altri, passò anche la tavola col peduccio in una nostra Galleria, e da questa pure sparì, e l'uno, e l'altro, essendosi in quella vece sostituito un quadro con S. Vincenzo Ferreri dipinto a tempera da un moderno professore. Potevasi collocare tutta l'ancona in una delle due facciate laterali di quella grandiosa capella, e così conservare alla publica vista due opere singolari di questi due valenti professori, tanto da scrittori nominate; ma no Signori, si alienarono, e sonosi affatto smarrite.*" L. Crespi in *Vite degl'Artefici* c. 1770, p. 81. The 1776 guide to Bologna mentions the removal of the polyptych by Cardinal Aldrovandi: "*La tavola del Costa, colle storiette d'Ercole da Ferrara notate dal Vasari furono trasportate in Casa Aldrovandi allorché il Cardinale Pompeo Aldrovandi successore de' Griffoni fece ridurre questa cappella come al presente, prima di cambiarla colla Casa Cospi*" (*Pitture scolture ed architetture* 1776, p. 215).

30 See in particular Roversi 1966; Roversi 1969; Perini 1998, pp. 57–60, 94–95: Giordani 1999, pp. 17–24; Ciancabilla 2012, pp. 79–85; Speranza 2016, with the important letters collected in manuscripts B.153, B.432, and B.943 in the Biblioteca Comunale dell'Archiginnasio; then Perini Folesani 2019.

highly-skilled man," wrote Pietro Minelli, an admirer from Saxony living in Venice,[31] Luigi Crespi also managed to procure for the court a copy of Raphael's *Saint Cecilia* by Denys Calvaert, sold by Senator Bentivoglio, as well as Parmigianino's superb *Madonna of the Rose* belonging to Monsignor Paolo Zani, one of Bologna's most celebrated paintings and universally admired since the time of Vasari.[32]

More significantly here, he procured for the court of Dresden two panels by Ercole de' Roberti from the church of San Giovanni in Monte, portraying the *Capture of Christ* and *The Road to Calvary*. The two panels were in fact elements of the predella, along with the *Pietà* now in the Walker Art Gallery in Liverpool, which Crespi resold to Monsignor Giovanni Maria Riminaldi of Ferrara, later made cardinal,[33] along with the panel of the *Annunciation* by Francesco del Cossa, a masterpiece of the Ferrara Renaissance, the so-called "Pala dell'Osservanza," attributed at the time to Andrea Mantegna. In fact, this altarpiece was already found in Dresden in 1750. The Bolognese canon had given it to Pietro Guarienti,[34] inspector of the picture gallery as of 1746 and former student of Giuseppe Maria Crespi in Bologna, in an unsuccessful bid to accrue credit in the court, and specifically perhaps hoping for a commission. However, the serious conservation problems suffered by Guido Reni's painting during the risky transfer undermined his plans.

Luigi Crespi unquestionably played a major role in the dispersion of the artistic patrimony of fifteenth- and sixteenth-century Bologna. His far-reaching dealings left their mark in the Romagna region as well. One need only consider the events in Imola, where, by ceding his paintings in the church of the Osservanti, Crespi managed to gain possession of an altarpiece by Innocenzo da Imola, signed and dated 1532, now kept in the Hermitage, not to mention a panel with *Christ Child adored by the Virgin and three Franciscan Saints* and its associated lunette with *The Dead Christ with Angels*, painted in 1509 by the brothers Bernardino and Francesco Zaganelli, presently divided between the National Gallery of Ireland in Dublin and Villa Albani in Rome.[35]

These shrewd maneuvers were duly noted by the erudite Marcello Oretti, his antagonist, at least in historiographic research. In 1777, during a tour of Imola, Oretti saw on the high altar of the church of the Osservanti a "Blessed Virgin, Saint Anthony of Padua, Saint Michael the Archangel, Saint Francis of the Canon Crespi, which had a lunette ... paints and a canvas and obtained 400 *scudi*." He went on to say, "The Canon Crespi removed

---

31 "*Uomo assai destro e capace per un maneggio*." Quoted in Liebsch 2017, p. 351.

32 On this subject, see Speranza 2016, pp. 7–15; Liebsch 2017; Perini Folesani 2017b, pp. 34–37; Perini Folesani 2019, esp. pp. 75–84. Of great interest the publication of the correspondence between Luigi Crespi and Prime Minister Heinrich Graf von Brühl over the years 1749–52, for which see Liebsch 2017; Perini Folesani 2017a, pp. 376–79; Perini Folesani 2019, pp. 310–49.

33 It is interesting to note the anonymity behind which Crespi hid his central role in the operation in a text written for the press: "*Furono queste pitture comprate dal Guarienti nel 1751 incettatore di quadri per la Galleria di Dresda ... ed il quadretto di mezzo fu da esso lui rivenduto ad un nostro dilettante, il quale sino all'anno 1769 se l'è tenuto caro, nel quall'anno nel mese di dicembre passò in dominio di Monsignor Riminaldi di Ferrara, che lo collocò nella sua Galleria, d'altri quadri ricca, et adorna*." L. Crespi in *Vite degl'Artefici* c. 1770, p. 94, quoted in Ciancabilla 2012, p. 84 note 21. Statements by Crespi in a letter to Monsignor Giovanni Bottari on August 4, 1752 have a different tone altogether about the two panels: "*due anni sono furono vendute, per opera mia, alla Maestà del re di Polonia*" (Bottari and Ticozzi 1822, IV, p. 380). On the predella, see Molteni 1995, pp. 143–49; Giansante 2016, p. 773; and, of course, the entry by Cecilia Cavalca in this book.

34 See *Estratto dalla Lettera del Sig. Canonico Crespi. Da Bologna li 6 ottobre*: "*Il Canonico non ha parte in quest'acquisto* [the copy of Raphael's *Saint Cecilia* attributed to Denys Calvaert] *ma in quello delle due tavole di Ercole di Ferrara, ed ha regalato al Signor Guarienti la rarissima Annunziazione di Andrea Mantegna*" (published in Perini Folesani 2019, pp. 326–27). For the Ferrarese paintings in the Dresden Gemäldegalerie, see in general the catalogue of the exhibition *Il trionfo di Bacco* 2002, in particular the essay by G. J. M. Weber (pp. 40–48).

35 See Mazza 1988, pp. 43–44.

various antique paintings from these friars and swindled them, as they told me in the convent of Imola on August 18."[36]

Oretti frequently denounced the violations of his day and reported illicit removals of paintings, including, of course, the Griffoni Polyptych ("Griffoni now Aldrovandi, Saint Vincent, and other saints of the said Costa are missing")[37]. Attentive chronicler that he was, he specified, for example, "In the year 1733, on December 16 at 18½ hours I saw leaving the Monastery of San Damiano the junk dealers of the Piazza with their porters who carried an altarpiece with the Most Blessed Holy Virgin enthroned in the style of that by Guido Reni for the Cappuccini in Faenza ... these paintings were sold to the junk dealers ... who were seen for many days in the piazza unable to find buyers."[38]

The contradictory behavior of Luigi Crespi, "a man of the most infuriating cunning," as Pietro Giordani wrote in 1812,[39] becomes even more apparent when seen in contrast to the actions of the Assunteria of the Istituto delle Scienze. In 1785, as a gift from the Foro dei Mercanti, the Assunteria acquired the celebrated painting by Francesco del Cossa, *Madonna and Child enthroned with Saints Petronius and John the Evangelist*, known aptly enough as the "Merchant altarpiece," signed and dated 1474 and now in the Pinacoteca Nazionale of Bologna. Their goal was to unite this work with others received from various distinguished citizens to "enrich the Rooms of this Institute with the already-begun series of Paintings by the oldest and most excellent authors of our Country or of the School of Bologna."[40]

From Palazzo Aldrovandi in Mirabello to Ferrara collections: the beginning of dispersion

In 1835, Gaetano Giordani was received in Ferrara in the palazzo belonging to Giambattista Costabili (fig. 2), on Via Voltapaletto, previously known as Palazzo Bevilacqua Aldobrandini, where he viewed the Ferrara Count's exquisite collection and precious library.[41] With all the passion of a genuine scholar, the young man had followed the affairs of the Pinacoteca Pontificia di Belle Arti of Bologna for many years, having been introduced there by his uncle Giovan Domenico Pancaldi, its caretaker and a former student of Ubaldo Gandolfi. After studying the gallery's holdings since 1818 and obtaining authorization from the faculty

36 "*Il Canonico Crespi portò via varij dipinti antichi a questi frati e li gabò molto come mi dissero in convento d'Imola il giorno 18 agosto.*" Oretti 1777, f. 252v.

37 "*Griffoni ora Aldrovandi, li SS.Vincenzo, ed altri santi del d.° Costa mancano.*" Oretti 1775, p. 37.

38 "*Nell'anno 1733, li 16 decembre in ore 18½ vidi uscire dal Monasterio di San Damiano sud.° li Zavagli della Piazza, con li suoi facchini che avevano una tavola d'altare con la B.Vergine SS.ma in trono sul fare di quello di Guido Reni alli Cappuccini di Faenza... queste pitture furono vendute alli Zavagli... si videro più giorni in piazza sin tanto che ritrovarono compratori.*" Ibid., p. 39 (with a list of the "abuses" suffered by numerous paintings in public places in Bologna, especially those by historic painters, including Simone dei Crocefissi, Antonio da Crevalcore, Cristoforo da Bologna, Bagnacavallo, Ercole de' Roberti, and Ercole Banci. He concludes, "*è troppo abominevole abuso quello del levare dalle chiese le pitture, e venderle agli zavagli di piazza come spesso si vede ai miei giorni*": Oretti 1775, p. 19).

39 "*... uomo alle arti molestissimo.*" See the 1856 Giordani edition, p. 236.

40 ASBo, Assunteria d'Istituto, *Diversorum, Accademia Clementina*, b. 3, no. 9, quoted in Cammarota 1997, p. 12. On the lack of interest, still in the mid-eighteenth century, for works of the so-called Primitives, "easily available on the market at normally low prices because religious orders tended to dispose of them anyway," see the observations by Giovanna Perini Folesani (2019, pp. 74–76), who claims that it is far from certain that the collector's market was so interested in the works of Ercole de' Roberti, despite Crespi's operation in mid-century. Meaningful in this regard was Giovanni Bottari's opinion that Ercole da Ferrara was like "one of the Dossis" (letter from Luigi Crespi to Monsignor Giovanni Bottari, August 4, 1751).

41 On the Costabili collection see, essentially, Padovani 1954, pp. 143–54; Benini 1977; Ugolini 1990; *La leggenda del collezionismo a Ferrara* 1996, pp. 103–18; Mattaliano 1998.

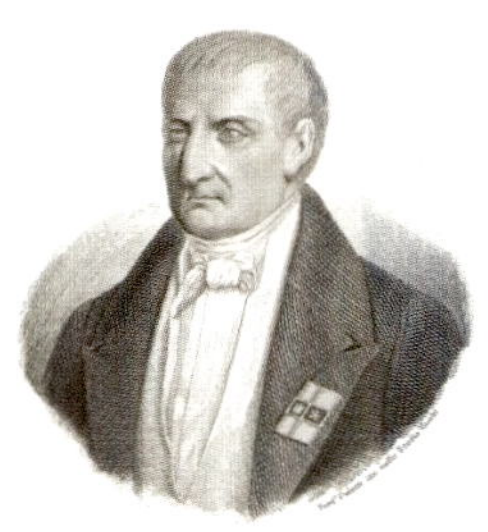

2

Ferdinando Poletti, *Portrait of Marquis Giambattista Costabili Containi*, in G. Petrucci, *Elogio storico del marchese Giambattista Costabili Containi ferrarese* (Novi, 1841)

and the Legation in 1826, Giordani published a catalogue—at his own expense—thereby bringing the Bologna museum into line with those of Milan, Parma, and Florence, all of which had their own helpful catalogues. Identifying almost three hundred paintings, "the precise, most beautiful description, or guide to the Pinacoteca di Bologna, so elegantly written," as Carlo Pepoli described it, was very favorably received, as proven by the multiple editions edited by Giordani himself over the years until 1872 as information grew through fifty years of work and research on that institute.[42]

In 1835, after being admitted into the Ferrara collector's residence near the Cathedral, Giordani edited the fourth edition. His name was surely well-known to Count Costabili, who made a copy of the inventory of his collection for him—luckily for us, as this is the only copy that has survived, providing the first systematic information about it. Significantly, the inventory reports that several compartments of the Griffoni Polyptych had entered the collection, perhaps years earlier, expressly stating that they had come from the Aldrovandi residence in Mirabello. These panels included the central compartment with *Saint Vincent Ferrer*, considered at the time to represent Saint Dominic and attributed to Marco Zoppo (which it still was for many years, even after it was transferred to the National Gallery of London[43]), the tondo with the *Crucifixion, the Virgin and Saint John the Evangelist* in the National Gallery of Washington, DC, two small tondos with *Archangel Gabriel* and the *Annunciation* in the Fondazione Cagnola in Gazzada Schianno and two small panels attributed at the time to Lorenzo Costa with *Saint George*, presently in the Cini Foundation in Venice (fig. 3) and *Saint Anthony the Abbot* in the Museum Boijmans Van Beuningen in Rotterdam, wrongly considered a *Saint Benedict* at the time.

The diaspora had begun.[44] Of twenty-three paintings with a range of different shapes and sizes, encompassed in thirteen frames, only six ended in the Costabili collection, and three others went to the Barbi Cinti collection, also in Ferrara. The misinterpretation of the iconography and mutiplicity of attributions—from Marco Zoppo to Lorenzo Costa, from "in the manner of Lorenzo Costa" to the anonymity of the *Annunciation* tondos—imply that all memory had been lost by this time that the paintings had originally hung in the Bologna chapel of Saint Vincent Ferrer, or that they all belonged to a single complex, despite the fact that their common provenance from Palazzo Aldrovandi in Mirabello was on record.

A few years later, Count Camillo Laderchi repeated these misconceptions substantially unchanged in his *Descrizione della Quadreria Costabili*, where the *Crucifixion* tondo appeared under the name of Lorenzo Costa; the two saints were correctly identified as *Saint George* and *Saint Anthony the Abbot* but described as being "in the manner used by the school of Costa;"[45] the *Saint Vincent Ferrer*, still confused with Saint Dominic, was attributed to Marco Zoppo, and the two *Annunciation* tondos appeared with no comment.[46]

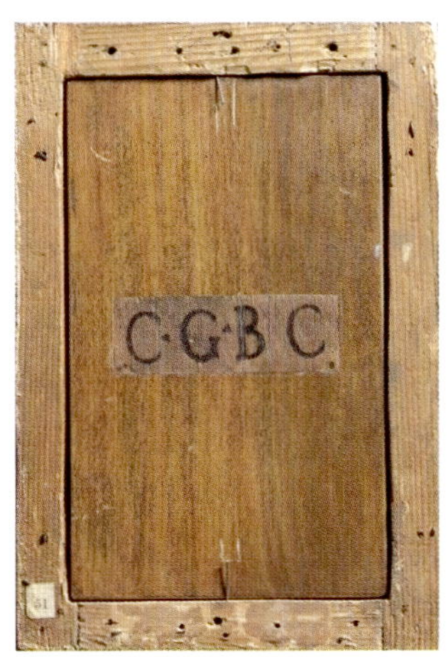

3

Reverse of the panel by Ercole de' Roberti with *Saint George* in the Giorgio Cini Foundation, Venice, marked with the acronym "C. G. B. C." (Count Giovanni Battista Costabili)

42 "*L'esatta, bellissima descrizione, o guida della Pinacoteca di Bologna, scritta assai elegantemente*." Cammarota 2004, pp. 50–52, 53–54 notes 13–17, 55–64. Similarly, in 1834, Amico Ricci wrote words of praise on the verso of a letter received in October 1830: "Gaetano Giordani is one of the most enthusiastic amateurs of our studies that I have ever known … Diligent and erudite is the description he gave of the Bolognese picture gallery" (quoted in Ambrosini Massari 2007, p. 368).

43 Nicholson Wornum 1869, pp. 301–2; Nicholson Wornum 1870, pp. 304–5; *The Abridged Catalogue* 1882, p. 149.

44 For general information on the history of the polyptych with the changes in ownership of each compartment, see Cavalca 2013, pp. 334–36; and now the contribution by the same scholar in this book.

45 "… *maniera usata alla scuola del Costa*." Laderchi 1838, I, pp. 42, 50; Laderchi 1841, pp. 49–50.

46 Camillo Laderchi's observation that "the large plates by Marco Zoppo, like this one, are very rare and valuable, according to Signor Giordani in his description of the Bologna picture gallery" (Laderchi 1841, p. 59), may have been influenced by Gaetano Giordani's visit in 1835. On the initial dispersion of the elements of the Griffoni Polyptych in the

Giambattista Costabili Containi (1756–1841), a member of the landed gentry in the emerging class of bourgeios entrepreneurs, cleverly seized the opportunity of the sale of church assets at the time of the Napoleonic government, in which he participated with influential public positions. He procured substantial advantage from this involvement, only offset by several blows suffered as a result of changing fortunes, as was surely inevitable in those volatile years. Containi had inherited an outstanding collection of about 240 paintings from his uncle Francesco Containi, which he proceeded to increase to 624, as we know from *Descrizione della quadreria Costabili* written by Count Camillo Laderchi in four parts and published between 1838 and 1841.

In addition to the paintings, he cultivated a library "enormously worthy for the beautiful series of editions, both antique and modern, and the splendor and rarity of the codices." At his death, the library held as many as fifteen thousand books.[47] The publication of the catalogue of the picture gallery—comprised predominantly, though not only, of Ferrarese works of the fifteenth and early sixteenth century—confirms that it was Marquis Costabili's intention, as reported in a commemorative biography by Giuseppe Petrucci, to preserve "in Ferrara eminent works of genius, which would otherwise have been lost or removed to foreign countries."[48]

Containi's skillful advisor and agent was the "second-hand dealer" Ubaldo Sgherbi (1788–1872),[49] an expert entrusted by other collectors in Ferrara as well, such as Massimiliano Strozzi and the Mazza Counts. Sgherbi remained quite active even after the death of Marquis Costabili, when the collection was inherited by his great-grandson Giovanni and a slow, inexorable impoverishment began, stretching over several decades until the collection was completely dispersed.

Not a single painting was added after the death of Marquis Giambattista Costabili Containi. Giovanni devoted his energies and fortune exclusively to his social life and the collection suffered the consequences of his expensive passion for horses, though he was also interested in politics and military life.[50] He was easy prey for English collectors, who were the first to recognize the importance of those masterpieces and quickly laid their hands on them. Actually, the collection had been offered in vain to the City of Ferrara in 1856, which lost the precious and unique opportunity to guarantee for themselves a large group of carefully selected paintings with the utmost civic value. In the sale as offered to the city institution, Marquis Giovanni intended to include the library as well, which had been reduced in the meantime to ten thousand books, according to the declaration made at the time.

Vexed by the negative response that came three months later, Giovanni opened negotiations with Anglo-Saxon correspondents.[51] This grave case of indifference and neglect by the representatives of Ferrara recalls the equally dishonorable outcome of an analogous offer, likewise rejected, advanced to the City of Bologna in 1810 by Francesco Sampieri, owner of the city's most important collection. The works were taken immediately thereafter to Milan, where they were divided up, with six famous paintings going to

---

context of Ferrarese collecting, previously revealed by Roberto Longhi (1940 ed. 1956, pp. 128–31), see the relevant observations by Luca Majoli (1998, pp. 20–21).

47 "… *ragguardevolissima per belle serie di edizioni, sì antiche che moderne, e per isplendidezza e rarità di codici*." Petrucci 1841, p. 16; Majoli 1998; Avery-Quash 2011, II, pp. 49–50; Mancini and Penny 2016, pp. 462–66.

48 "… *a Ferrara esimie opere d'ingegno, che smarrite o in estrani paesi sarebbero andate*." Petrucci 1841, p. 16.

49 The "*rigattiere*." Anderson 1993, p. 342; Scardino 1996, pp. 98–99; Majoli 1998, pp. 19–20; Avery-Quash 2011, II, p. 74.

50 Orsi 1998.

51 Ibid., pp. 21–22.

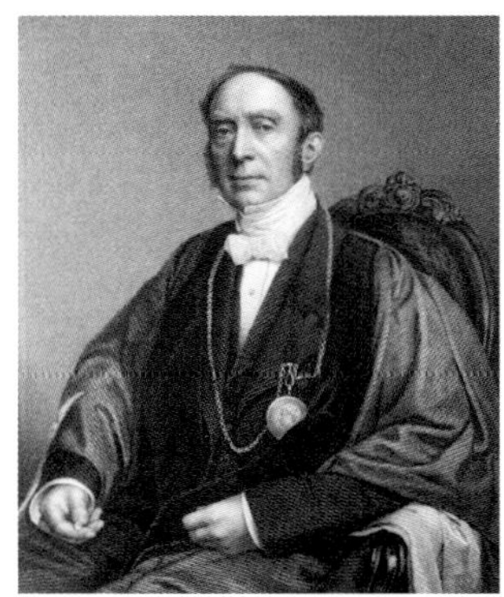

4

D. J. Pound, *Portrait of Sir Charles Lock Eastlake, First Director of the National Gallery of London* (from a photograph by John Watkins)

the Napoleonic Pinacoteca di Brera and 129 works, later dispersed, going to the personal collection of Viceroy Eugène de Beauharnais.[52]

The pre-eminence of the English: travel diaries and sketchbooks

The progressive dissolution of the Costabili collection was the heavy price of the backwardness of art criticism of the time, the rhetoric of the Academies and the widespread ignorance of administrators. These factors explain why a brilliant figure such as Giovanni Battista Cavalcaselle, in political exile since the 1848 uprising, chose to publish in England with the publisher Murray, in collaboration with Joseph Archer Crowe, not only his *Early Flemish Painters* (1856) but also numerous books on Italian Medieval and Renaissance painting between 1864 and 1885. Not to mention that he had been back in Italy for some time without entertaining a dialogue with the dispirited art criticism of the day, whose demeaning rhetoric and unconditioned praise had been denounced in a *Das Kunstblatt* review in 1838.[53]

Like Giovanni Morelli, the other great expert of this time, from whom he was otherwise separated by irreconcilable differences, the majority of Cavalcaselle's relationships were with art historians from Northern Europe and directors of foreign (in particular British) museums. Besides, thanks to its public and even more impressive private collections, Ferrara had become a highly sought-after destination for cultured travelers, often with ulterior motives. Among them were Sir Charles Lock Eastlake (1793–1865), English painter and writer, president of the Royal Academy and, as of 1855, director of the National Gallery of London (fig. 4); Otto Mündler, art historian, art dealer and learned connoisseur, named "Traveling Agent" for the National Gallery of London the same day that Eastlake was named director; Austen Henry Layard, the celebrated archaeologist who rediscovered and excavated the city of Nineveh as well as being a diplomat and collector; and Alexander Barker, *marchant amateur*, who became a collector and member of the Burlington Fine Art Club. Eastlake had spent his summer months in Italy since 1854, traveling alone, with his wife Elizabeth Rigby, or with Mündler, seeking out paintings for the National Gallery and for his own collection. In August 1857, along with Mündler, he traveled to Bergamo, Milan, Genoa, and Rome—cities that had been visited by his collaborator previously—continuing on to Padua.[54] There he met Cavalcaselle, who had returned to Italy and was beginning his never-ending travels to Turin, Castiglione Olona, Lovere, and other places.[55]

Cavalcaselle had met Eastlake in London a number of years earlier and gained his trust and admiration. As we learn from an entry in one of his pocket sketchbooks kept in the Biblioteca Marciana of Venice, Cavalcaselle was in the Pinacoteca in Ferrara on November 5, 1857.[56] He visited the Costabili collection and, as was his custom, drew quick sketches of paintings of particular interest, in this case Francesco Zaganelli's *Saint Sebastian*, signed and dated 1513; *Saint Michael the Archangel*, which later passed into the Cini collection in Venice and is now in private hands and recently associated by critics with the production

52 See Mazza 2014, pp. 33–37; Mazza 2010–17, pp. 281–86.

53 See Venturi 1912, p. 460; Levi 1988, pp. XXI–XXVI; Campisi 2018, p. 105 and note 230.

54 The travel diaries and reports by Otto Mündler and by Charles Lock Eastlake are of utmost interest (Togneri Dowd 1985; Avery-Quash 2011). On their Milanese contacts, see Morandotti 2008, pp. 243–54.

55 Levi 1988, pp. 107–8, 161 note 45.

56 Biblioteca Marciana, Venice, Fondo Cavalcaselle, Manuscripts. It.IV.2036 (=12277), sketchbook V, f. 30r: for drawings from his sojourn in Ferrara, ff. 26v–37r.

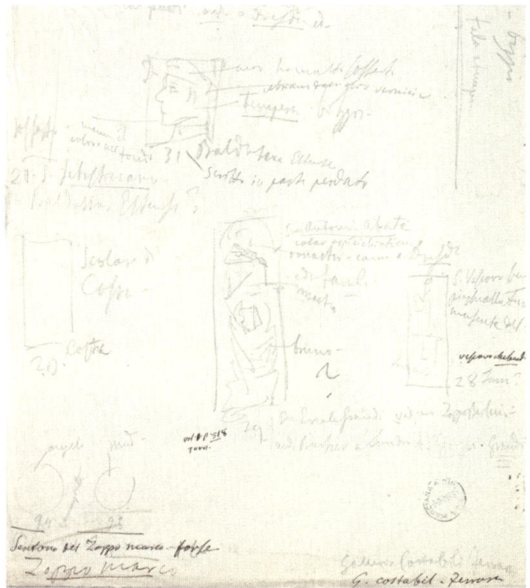

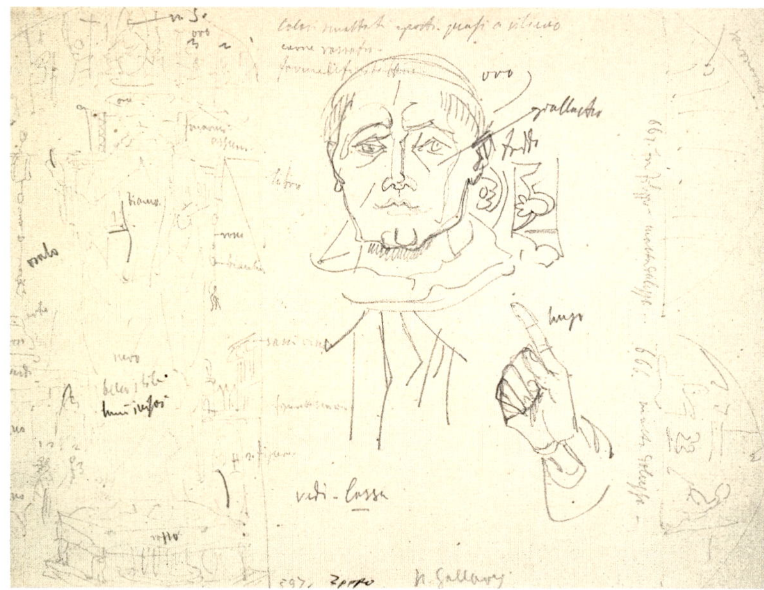

5

Giovanni Battista Cavalcaselle, drawing of paintings in the Costabili collection of Ferrara (*Saint Anthony the Abbot* by Ercole de' Roberti and two small tondos from the Griffoni Polyptych). Biblioteca Marciana, Venice, Fondo Cavalcaselle, It. IV.2030 (=12271), folder VII, f. 25v, detail

6

Giovanni Battista Cavalcaselle, drawing of *Saint Vincent Ferrer* by Francesco del Cossa, the central compartment of the Griffoni Polyptych, now in the National Gallery of London. Biblioteca Marciana, Venice, Fondo Cavalcaselle, It. IV.2033 (=12274), folder XIX, f. 43r

of Ludovico Mazzolino; Giovan Francesco Maineri's altarpiece of *Madonna and Child enthroned with Saint Thomas the Apostle and Saint Nicodemus*, now in the Metropolitan Museum of New York, and still others.[57] Cavalcaselle also devoted attention to elements of the Griffoni Polyptych, specifically the *Archangel Gabriel* and the *Virgin annunciate*, graphically alluded to in the shape of tondos with the notes "Angelo" and "Mad." and the critical observation that they "recall Zoppo Marco perhaps." He made a more recognizable sketch of *Saint Anthony the Abbot* of the Museum Boijmans Van Beuningen of Rotterdam, on which he noted the attributions to Ercole Grandi and Marco Zoppo (fig. 5).[58]

Later, after it had been transfered to the National Gallery in London under the name of Marco Zoppo, Cavalcaselle focused on the central panel with the solemn figure of *Saint Vincent Ferrer*. The scholar had made this attribution in the lower margin of a folio with a rapid pencil sketch of the whole figure of the saint and enlarged, forcefully drawn details of his bust and right hand with pointed index finger. He also jotted down brief notes on the colors in these drawings, along with the precious reference, "see Cossa" (fig. 6).[59]

57 Biblioteca Marciana, Venice, Fondo Cavalcaselle, Manuscripts. It.IV.2030 (=12271), folder VII, ff. 43r–44r, which also includes the *Deposition of Christ in the sepulchre* by a Ferrarese-Paduan painter in the Pinacoteca Nazionale in Ferrara, *Madonna and Child with Bishop Saint and the Patron Pietro de' Lardi* by a Ferrarese painter of c. 1430, now in the Metropolitan Museum of New York, the *Portrait of Lionello d'Este* by Pisanello, now in the Accademia Carrara of Bergamo, *Saint Sebastian* by the young Lorenzo Costa, now in Dresden Gemäldegalerie, *Saint Anthony of Padua*, now in the Galleria Estense in Modena, *The Muse Polymnia* by a Ferrarese painter from the mid-fifteenth century, now in the Staatliche Museum Gemäldegalerie in Berlin, and the probable *Muse Calliope*, a masterpiece by Cosmè Tura now in the National Gallery of London (see Mattaliano 1998, pp. 33–34, nos. 2–3; p. 37, no. 12; pp. 38–39, nos. 15–16; pp. 45–46, no. 43; pp. 48–49, no. 55; pp. 55–56, no. 80; p. 122, no. 406); and also the series of tempera paintings with Biblical stories attributed at the time to Ercole de' Roberti and the *Portrait of the poet Tito Strozzi* by Baldassarre d'Este now in the Cini collection (Biblioteca Marciana, Venice, Fondo Cavalcaselle, Manuscripts. It.IV.2030 (=12271), file VII, ff. 35r–36r; Mattaliano 1998, pp. 53–55, nos. 71–78; for the *Portrait of Baldassarre d'Este*, see L. Siracusano in *La Galleria di palazzo Cini* 2016, pp. 188–91.

58 "*... sentono del Zoppo Marco forse*." Biblioteca Marciana, Venice, Fondo Cavalcaselle, Manuscripts. It.IV.2030 (=12271), file VII, f. 25v, where the *Portrait of the poet Tito Strozzi* by Baldassarre d'Este appears again as a rough sketch. Accompanied by no. 29, this panel was still owned by Marquis Costabili in 1862 and appears, with other paintings, among those requested by Eastlake in the encounter on October 4 in the presence of his wife Elizabeth Rigby and Otto Mündler (Avery-Quash 2011, I, p. 608: "small – 29 – Saint standing in niche – C. Tura or Marco Zoppo").

59 Biblioteca Marciana, Venice, Fondo Cavalcaselle, Manuscripts. It.IV.2033 (=12274), file XIX, f. 43r. See Crowe and Cavalcaselle 1871, I, pp. 527–28 and note 1 on p. 528, combined with the two panels at the time in the Barbi Cinti collection in Ferrara and now in the Brera (it should be noted that Crowe and Cavalcaselle, in a note on p. 350, warn

It was Sir Charles Lock Eastlake, newly-appointed director of the National Gallery, who skillfully orchestrated the acquisition of *Saint Vincent Ferrer* in 1858. He coveted this painting, knowing that its dazzling luminosity would be appreciated by the English public, so receptive to this genre of painting. Two years earlier, writing from Bologna to the publisher John Murray, Austen Henry Layard had declared his admiration for works from the Ferrarese Renaissance of the second half of the fifteenth century, inspired not least by the rediscovery of the Schifanoia frescoes.[60] The letter—enthusiastically praising the paintings of the Primitives in the Costabili collection ("a most interesting series of Ferrarese masters, quite unique") while discrediting the work of the Carracci, which had so enthralled Sir Joshua Reynolds a century before[61]—served as a prelude to the successful sales negotiations begun shortly thereafter.

In 1861, the collector Alexander Barker—who in 1856 had acquired from Ubaldo Sgherbi an altarpiece by Giovanni Battista Benvenuti, known as Ortolano, with *Saints Sebastian, Rocco and Demetrius*, at the time on a panel and presently in the National Gallery in London[62]—came into possession of fourteen paintings. Being primarily of a small format, they were spirited out of the country with a bit of ingenuity. Among these works were Pisanello's *Portrait of Lionello d'Este*, presently in the Accademia Carrara of Bergamo thanks to the mediation of Giovanni Morelli, Cosmè Tura's *Virgin annunciate* now in the National Gallery of London, and Ercole de' Roberti's precious small panel with *Saint George* from the Griffoni Polyptych. This latter painting had a complicated history: after various changes in ownership between London and New York, it reached the gallery of Gualtiero Volterra in Florence, where it was acquired in 1954 by Vittorio Cini, a count originally from Ferrara, acting on the suggestion of Federico Zeri who had taken the place of Nino Barbantini as his advisor (fig. 7).[63]

---

the reader that the works indicated as being in the Costabili collection may have changed hands in the meantime due to ongoing sales). For historical-critical information and on the vicissitudes of the painting, see the detailed entry by Cecilia Cavalca in this book.

60 Laderchi 1841.

61 Quoted in Anderson 1993, p. 539 and note 2, and documents 3–5 on p. 549; Anderson 1985, pp. 192–93. In 1866, after long negotiations, Henry Layard, a friend of Giovanni Morelli's, bought twenty-two paintings from the Costabili collection for his cousin Sir Ivor Guest, later the first Lord Winborne, also keeping some for himself (on the English archaeologist and collector, see *Austen Henry Layard* 1987; on relations with the Milan area of Giovanni Morelli and Giuseppe Molteni, whose workshop not far from the Brera was a meeting place for Eastlake and Mündler, see Mottola Molfino 1991, pp. 228–33). On Sir Joshua Reynolds and his reactions to Bolognese painting during his sojourn in Italy in 1750–52, see Perini 1991.

62 Anderson 1993, p. 542; Mancini and Penny 2016, pp. 383–84.

63 As communicated by Giovanni Mazzaferro (to whom I owe this and other details), Eastlake informed Gualandi, in a letter dated August 2, 1861, that Barker had bought fourteen paintings from the Costabili collection. About the works in the Cini collection, see Bacchi and De Marchi 2016. As has been noted (L. Siracusano in *La Galleria di palazzo Cini* 2016, p. 183), the panel from the Griffoni Polyptych shares a history of ownership with Cosmè Tura's *Saint George*, also in the Cini collection. Both were in the Costabili collection, where they received the acronym "C. G. B. C." on the verso (Bacchi 1990, p. 28, fig. 4a), then passed through the collection of Alexander Barker into that of the Count of Rosebery, who lent them for the 1934 exhibition at Burlington House, where the Griffoni *Saint George* was displayed as the work of Andrea Mantegna. Later the two panels appeared in New York at Kramarski and then returned to Italy, to the Florentine gallery of the antiquarian Gualtiero Volterra. The two other small panels in the Cini collection with *Saint Jerome* and *Saint Catherine of Alexandria* have been unanimously considered part of the Griffoni Polyptych; in this book, however, Cecilia Cavalca maintains that direct comparison with the other analogous panels, beginning with the *Saint George* in the Cini collection, reveals the figures to be visibly larger, out of scale, and therefore incompatible. Their ownership history between the late nineteenth and the twentieth centuries passes from Condover Hall, Reginald Cholmondeley, until c. 1897; Paris, Lord Duveen of Millbank, 1934; Florence, Contini Bonacossi, until 1940; Venice, Vittorio Cini, since 1940 (see Bacchi 1990, pp. 12–29, nos. 22–24; Cavalca 2013, p. 336; G. A. Calogero in *Da Cimabue a Morandi* 2015, pp. 76–79; L. Siracusano in *La Galleria di palazzo Cini* 2016, p. 179). As for the two small panels in the Louvre with *Saint Apollonia* and *Saint Michael the Archangel*, the changes in ownership documented as of 1820 include various transfers between England and France and end in 1889, with the bequest of the Baroness Nathaniel de Rothschild to the French museum (Cavalca 2013, p. 336).

Eastlake documented his various sojourns in Ferrara in a series of travel diaries. The 1855 diary reports that he visited the Mazza, Saroli, Bardi, Strozzi, and Costabili collections and met Marquis Giovanni for the first time.[64] From the 1858 diary we learn that, between August 31 and the first days of September, he concluded the acquisition for the National Gallery of the central panel of the Griffoni Polyptych and a *Saint Francis* now attributed to Botticelli (though at the time to Filippino Lippi), as well as setting the stage to buy for himself the painting by Pisanello, two others assigned to Lorenzo Costa, and one attributed to Cosmè Tura.[65] More diaries record visits between 1860 and 1863.[66]

The intermediary in the sale of the panels by del Cossa and Botticelli was the Bolognese Michelangelo Gualandi along with the "second-hand dealer" Ubaldo Sgherbi, advisor to the Marquis but well-disposed toward the English buyer. Gualandi, a "dealer of paintings" in his own right, had gained public attention with his scholarly studies published in *Memorie originali italiane risguardanti le belle arti* in six series (1840–45, but actually 1846), and in the three-volume *Nuova raccolta di lettere sulla pittura, scultura ed architettura...* (1844–56), which connected to those edited by Giovanni Bottari and Stefano Ticozzi.

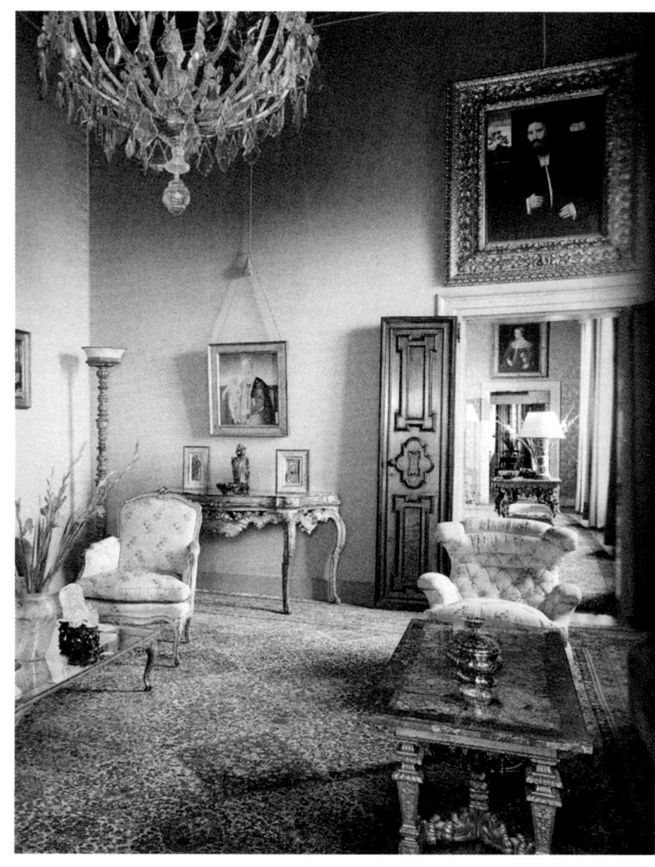

7

Drawing room on the *piano nobile* of Palazzo Cini, Venice (on the console table, the panel with *Saint George* by Ercole de' Roberti from the Griffoni Polyptych)

As we learn from letters preserved in the University of Frankfurt—where part of Gualandi's archive is kept, the rest divided between various sites in Italy, Germany, and the United States, now being studied by Giovanni Mazzaferro[67]—Sir Charles Lock

The early date, before the movements of the predella documented in 1829, could mark the beginning of the dispersion (Campisi 2018, p. 107 and note 235).

64 Avery-Quash 2011, I, pp. 264–65, II, p. 102. The date 1842 of the presumed first encounter between Eastlake and Marquis Costabili, the result of a simple error, was corrected to 1862 by Mancini and Penny 2016, p. 464 and Mazzaferro 2019, https://letteraturaartistica.blogspot.com/2019/11/michelangelo-gualandi.html. For collecting in Ferrara, subject of the laudable documentary research of Lucio Scardino and Antonio P. Torresi, see *La leggenda del collezionismo a Ferrara* 1996; Agostini and Scardino 1997; and in particular Mattaliano 1998.

65 Avery-Quash 2011, I, pp. 417–18 and notes on pp. 422, 423–24 and 437. Eastlake was quite interested in the singular form of the clouds at the base of the almond shape holding the figure of Christ and made a drawing of their stratiform structure (Avery-Quash 2011, II, p. 14, fig. 17.25). Eastlake's letter to Marquis Costabili (Turin, October 26, 1858), with the request for four paintings for his collection, is published in Anderson 1993, p. 549. The successful outcome of negotiations for the central compartment of the Griffoni Polyptych and for the *Saint Francis* attributed to Botticelli that eventually reached the National Gallery is shared in Eastlake's report to the Trustees on November 27, 1858, from which can be sensed his satisfaction at having overcome the obstacles placed by the Marquis, who wanted to sell the collection in one go as a single lot (see Eastlake's report of February 4, 1856 on operations in Italy with Mündler, the preceding autumn; Avery-Quash 2011, II, p. 102). Urged on by necessity, Costabili had capitulated in the hope that the two paintings would make English collectors more aware of the importance of the gallery (for the document, see Avery-Quash 2011, II, pp. 114–17, esp. p. 115).

66 Avery-Quash 2011, I, pp. 567–68 and notes on p. 575 and 608; see also the report by director Eastlake, dated November 19, 1860 recalling the sale in the Costabili house, and another, dated November 1, 1861, which records contacts with Marquis Costabili (Avery-Quash 2011, II, pp. 123, 126).

67 See https://letteraturaartistica.blogspot.com/2019/11/michelangelo-gualandi.html. The role of Michelangelo Gualandi in the sale was already known through his letter dated October 10, 1862 to Marquis Giovanni Costabili, conserved in the Archivio Medri of the Musei Civici of Ferrara, made known by Jaynie Anderson (1993, pp. 548–49, but with the imprecision of the year 1842). Eastlake's letters to Gualandi, identified by Giovanni Mazzaferro in the archive of the University of Frankfurt, concerning the deal (from that of September 9, 1858, sent from Florence, to that of January

Eastlake commissioned Gualandi to oversee the packing and shipping of the "two mediocre paintings" (so described by Eastlake to diminish their importance), urging him to maintain the utmost discretion in the name of the supposed author, known in Bologna for the polyptych in the Royal College of Spain ("one of the paintings is attributed to Marco Zoppo and, whether that denomination be well-founded or not, it is best not to call it that in Bologna"). He also stressed the need for great caution with the payment, which was only to be made after export had been officially authorized or, for even greater security, when the two works had left the Papal State on their way to Livorno, where they were to be shipped out of the country.[68] In the end, the two paintings reached the National Gallery in London in good condition in the first days of January 1859.

Routes of the international antiquarian trade: Washington, Rotterdam, and Paris

Neither the tondo with the *Crucifixion, the Virgin and Saint John the Evangelist*, nor the two other smaller tondos of the *Annunciation* generated enthusiasm among Anglo-Saxon visitors. They also went untouched in the public sales organized by the Costabili family between 1872 and 1874, for which Gaetano Giordani was commissioned to draw up a catalogue of the collection.[69] At that point, the Venetian antiquarian Michelangelo Guggenheim came forward, acquiring thirteeen paintings recommended to him by Giovanni Morelli, while Morelli also chose four for himself.

Only in 1874 did the Ferrara Municipality make a number of acquisitions for the city's picture gallery. Marquis Costabili then commissioned Guilio Sambon's Impresa di vendite, a major national auction house with headquarters in Milan, whose director, the engineer Angelo Genolini, handled the acquisition of a large part of the collection in 1884. The same Genolini also handled the subsequent sale, initially through private negotiations and eventually through an auction in the foyer of the Teatro alla Scala on April 26, 1885. The event was announced in the *Catalogue de tableaux formant la Galerie de M.r le Marquis Costabili de Ferrare*, drawn up by Giulio Carotti, much to the annoyance of the Marquis who had asked in vain that his name not be mentioned.[70]

The catalogue identifies the tondo with the *Crucifixion, the Virgin and Saint John the Evangelist* as the work of an anonymous Bolognese painter; the minute *Saint Anthony the*

10, 1859, written in London), clarify the nature of the operation, confirming the trust placed by the director of the National Gallery in his Bolognese correspondent, with whom he always remained in contact. In fact, in 1862, he visited the Costabili collection with Gualandi again, along with his wife Elizabeth Rigby and Otto Mündler (thanks to Giovanni Mazzaferro for generously making available the copy of the letters about the acquisition of the panel from the Griffoni Polyptych with *Saint Vincent Ferrer*).

68 Letter from Sir Charles Lock Eastlake to Michelangelo Gualandi, Florence, October 2, 1858 (written in Italian): "*Il prezzo stabilito per questi due quadri due cento cinquanta napoleoni (ossia 5000 franchi), la quale somma dev'essere pagata quando l'esportazione dei quadri sarà o effettuata o assicurata … Quando si ricevrà da Lei l'assicurazione che tutto è in ordine, e che i quadri si possono mandare o (meglio ancora) che sono già mandati a Livorno, il pagamento si farà.*" When he finished his travel itinerary, which included Rome, Milan, Genoa, Turin, and Paris, Eastlake wrote from London to Michelangelo Gualandi on January 10, 1859: "I have the pleasure to inform you that the two paintings of the Galleria Costabile you sent from Bologna arrived a few days ago."

69 *Catalogo de' quadri* 1872, pp. 6, 8: no. 35, the *Crucifixion*, is attributed to "Uncertain, perhaps Bolognese, Marco Zoppo's way" ; nos. 79–80, the two tondos with the *Annunciation*, to "Uncertain, Bolognese, perhaps Marco Zoppo or Cosmè from Ferrara."

70 On the sad epilogue of the Costabili collection, see Orsi 1998, pp. 25–27. On the Impresa di vendite Sambon, see M. C. Brunati in Della Peruta and Cantarella 2005, I, pp. 632–33.

Abbot is attributed to "Dürer (School of)" but still identified as Saint Benedict in keeping with previous inventories, and the two *Annunciation* tondos are listed as the work of Cosmè Tura.[71] While the *Saint Anthony the Abbot* entered the Stefan von Auspitz collection in Vienna and ended up in the Museum Boijmans Van Beuningen of Rotterdam, the *Crucifixion* tondo was transported overseas into the prestigious collection of Philip Lehman in New York before 1914, the year when the attribution to Francesco del Cossa was made known, independently, by Joseph Breck and Mason Perkins.[72] It then appeared in the monumental, sumptuous catalogue of the collection printed in 1928, with the explanation "Berenson places this close to Cossa but under the influence of Castagno" whereas "Breck, De Nicola, Offner, Perkins, Van Marle, and Venturi all give it unreservedly to Cossa himself."

Apparently, with the change in attribution—from such a renowned exponent of the illustrious Tuscan school as Andrea del Castagno to a painter from the school of Ferrara deemed by the collector as one of minor importance—Robert Lehman decided to include the *Crucifixion* panel among the fifteen works sold in 1943 to the American magnate Samuel Kress, whose Foundation later turned it over to the National Gallery of Washington, DC.[73] Kress had built an economic empire through his chain of 5-and-10-cent stores, on the profits of which he formed a collection with more than three thousand works of art.

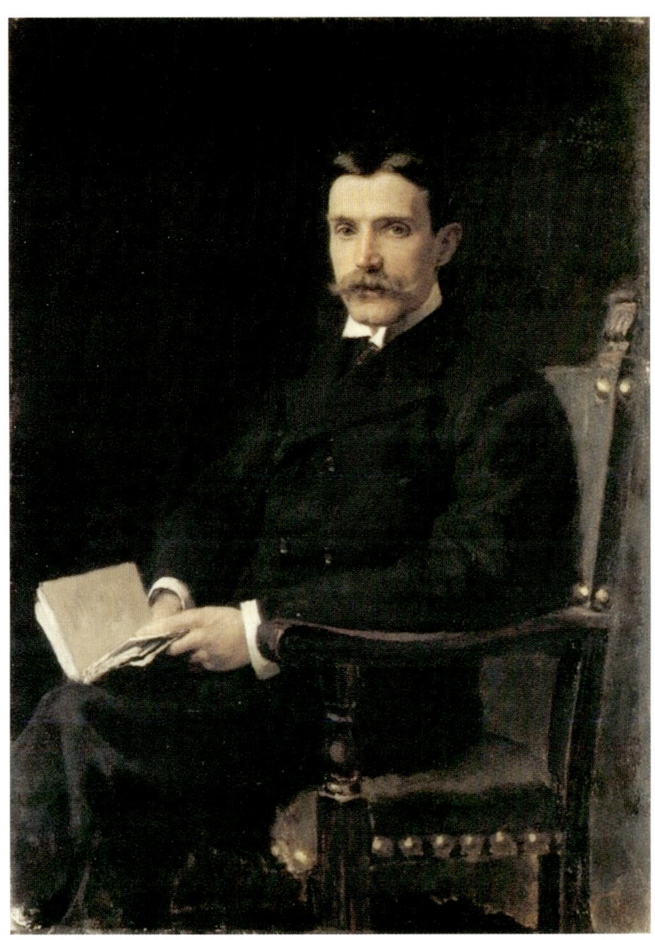

8

Alessandro Vanotti, *Portrait of Guido Cagnola*. Cagnola Art Collection at Villa Cagnola, Gazzada Schianno

It should be recalled here that previously, in May 1936, Kress had acquired the two panels with *Saint Florian* and *Saint Lucy* on a gold background, which, along with the tondo, recomposed the upper register of the Griffoni Polyptych, according to Roberto Longhi's correct reconstruction in *Officina ferrarese* (1934). The history of these two panels with the skillfully foreshortened half-figures of saints has only been partially reconstructed, however. They were seen in the palace of the Beni Counts in Gubbio by Otto Mündler on June 3, 1858, a time when he was about to be removed from his position as "Traveling Agent" of the National Gallery of London and was being attacked in Parliament as well. About two months before, between March 28 and 29, he had seen the compartment with *Saint Vincent Ferrer* in the Costabili collection, attributed to Marco Zoppo, which was acquired by the London museum soon thereafter.

Mündler admired the *Saint Lucy* and *Saint Florian* but did not agree with the attribution to Marco Zoppo ("There is much in them that reminded me of Cosmè").[74] The attribution was still adopted, however, in 1872 by Mariano Guadabassi, who defined the panels at nos. 4 and 5 in the list of works kept in the Palazzo Beni as "Saint Martin by Marco Zoppo"

71 *Impresa di vendite Giulio Sambon* 1885, p. 15, lot 17; p. 18, lot 32; p. 53, lot 203.
72 Breck 1914; Mason Perkins 1914; Lehman 1928, pages not numbered, no. LXXX.
73 Anderson 1993, p. 545. Perhaps Philip Lehman was not as enthusiastic about having added to his collection "another superb masterpiece by one of the great painters of the Italian Renaissance," as Joseph Breck maintained (Breck 1914, p. 317).
74 Togneri Dowd 1985, pp. 246–47.

and "Saint Lucy work of the same author," and also by Oderigi Lucarelli in his book *Memorie e guida storica di Gubbio*, published in Città di Castello in 1888, where he wrote that the "two most beautiful paintings" had been "sold recently in Florence for two thousand liras."[75] Indeed, they had been bought in 1881–82 by the antiquarian Joseph Spiridon of Paris and were later acquired by Duveen Brothers (1929), when Spiridon's collection was dispersed in an auction in Berlin. The president of Duveen Brothers was none other than the Dutch Joel Duveen, later Sir Joseph Joel Duveen and finally Lord Duveen of Millbank, prince of art dealers in the 1920s and '30s during the Berenson-inspired stream of antique paintings from Europe to the United States. In 1936, Duveen sold the two panels to Samuel Kress, who in turn donated them to the National Gallery of Washington, DC.[76]

The two tondos with *Archangel Gabriel* and *Virgin annunciate*, on the other hand, took a different route. First they entered the Levi collection in Milan and thereafter that of the scholar Gustavo Frizzoni of Bergamo, a pupil and friend of Giovanni Morelli. More significantly in this regard, Frizzoni was also the administrator of Morelli's patrimonial and cultural heritage and therefore a leader in private collecting in Lombardy, with an official role in dealings with Milan's Musei Civici, Pinacoteca di Brera, and Pinacoteca Ambrosiana.[77]

Not surprisingly, the two panels then ended up in the collection of the Milanese aristocrat Guido Cagnola (fig. 8), an "orthodox" follower of Morelli and a friend of Frizzoni, who complemented his diplomatic activities in Paris, London, and Constantinople with his lively cultural interests. The collection he acquired from his father Carlo had grown thanks to the advice of Morelli and probably also of Frizzoni, who, in 1888, became the first to propose a simplified reconstruction of the Griffoni Polyptych in the form of a triptych with predella. Receptive to the appeal of Italian purists and pre-Raphaelites, Guido Cagnola (1861–1954) expanded the collection with paintings from the fourteenth and fifteenth centuries. He did not neglect other forms of art, however, especially the decorative arts associated with artistic and finely-crafted furniture, in keeping with the trends in Milanese collecting at the time, clearly expressed in the taste of his friends, the brothers Fausto and Giuseppe Bagatti Valsecchi.[78]

Bound by a close friendship to Bernard Berenson for over fifty years, as he was for years with Francesco Malaguzzi Valeri, Cagnola was one of the founders in 1901 of the magazine *Rassegna d'arte*, and its director for many years. As the first expert to recognize the hand of de' Roberti in the two tondos acquired from Frizzoni,[79] Cagnola was surely able to appreciate their well-rendered volumes, serene luminousness, smooth transparency, and the almost mineral-like depiction of the folds, especially in the angel's sleeve.[80] However, Roberto Longhi still supported the attribution to Francesco del Cossa in a brief exchange of letters with Guido Cagnola, from whom the great critic requested in 1934 a high-quality photograph and information on the dimensions and possible presence of

---

75 "… *due bellissime pitture*" had been "*ultimamente vendute a Firenze per lire duemila*": Lucarelli 1888, p. 597.

76 Also Guardabassi 1872, p. 104; Davies 1951 ed. 1961, p. 152 note 16; Togneri Dowd 1985, pp. 246–47; J. Manca in *The Collections of the National Gallery of Art* 2003, pp. 215, 221 notes 2–5. On Joseph Duveen, "the king of antiquarians," see Behrman 2005.

77 On the personality of Gustavo Frizzoni in relation to Morelli, see Agosti 1994; Fiorio 1994; Kannès 1998.

78 Ciardi 1965, pp. 7–17; Nicora 1991.

79 Ciardi 1965, p. 54 nos. 45–46: "Cagnola was the first to link the two roundels of the *Annunciation* to the Ferrara environment by ascribing them to the school of Ercole da Ferrara."

80 On the tondos in the Cagnola collection, see in particular D. Benati in *La collezione Cagnola* undated [1998], pp. 140–43; C. Cavalca in *Cosmè Tura e Francesco del Cossa* 2007, pp. 470–71, nos. 152–53; G. A. Calogero in *Da Cimabue a Morandi* 2015, pp. 80–81; and of course the entry by Cecilia Cavalca in this book.

gold behind the two figures, as there was in the three Washington panels. With this evidence, he believed the question regarding the placement of the small tondos at the top of the highly-structured polyptych could be resolved.[81]

Entry into Italian museums

After following a completely different route, the predella by Ercole de' Roberti, celebrated by Vasari himself, depicting events from the life of Saint Vincent Ferrer, reached the Vatican Museums in 1839, the first element of the polyptych to find a stable and public home.[82] In the informative panel accompanying the painting in the National Gallery in London,[83] Martin Davies explained the events leading up to the acquisition. Decisive explanations were offered by Cecilia Cavalca and recently by Michele Campisi, who reconstructed the background.[84]

In 1829, the predella was acquired in Bologna by Giovanni Celsi from the lawyer Filicori, who had conserved it among his family's possessions for years. Reports about its provenance from the "Mirabello estate of Aldrovandi's historic property" were almost surely not unfounded, although efforts to document it convincingly failed. A proposal for sale to the Vatican Museums in June 1830 foundered. The dealer Feliciano Brizzi, who was living at the time in Lugo di Romagna and had become co-owner in the meantime, successfully presented the offer again in April 1839, agreeing upon the sum of 2,000 *scudi*.

As to authorship, hypotheses tended toward Mantegna and Melozzo da Forlì, while it was suggested, unsuccessfully, that the episodes represented in the painting referred to the distinguished Dominican, Antoninus of Florence, a fifteenth-century archbishop venerated as a saint.[85] A printed announcement of the panel's arrival in the Pinacoteca Vaticana appeared in 1841 in a pamphlet accompanied by a reproduction of the work in sections, folded into numerous pages, produced by Antonio Mannelli according to the design by Paolo Guglielmi of Rome, who worked in the Calcografia camerale.[86] It was announced again in a brief amendment to the text of an analogous publication in 1843.

Reconsidering the attribution to Benozzo Gozzoli rather than to Filippino Lippi, as advanced by Vincenzo Camuccini, "Inspector of Public Paintings," the author of the pamphlet focused on the individual scenes, incorrectly assuming that they represented episodes from the life and miracles of another friar of the Order of Preachers, Saint Hyacinth of Poland, one of Saint Dominic's first companions.[87] Evidently, all memory had been lost that the predella was part of the polyptych of Saint Vincent Ferrer.

The diaspora of the panels Aldrovandi had kept in his Mirabello residence went on to enrich not only the collection of Giambattista Costabili but also that of Giovanni Barbi (1779–1865), a wealthy landowner who moved to Ferrara from Finale Emilia in 1800. Barbi had made his fortunes acquiring state properties during the confiscations of the

---

81 Letters from Roberto Longhi to Guido Cagnola dated November 4, 15 and 25 and December 13, 1934 (*Lettere a Guido Cagnola* 2012, pp. 296–301).

82 See M. Moschetta in Bentini and Guarino 2002, pp. 350–55; C. Cavalca in *Cosmè Tura and Francesco del Cossa* 2007, pp. 468–69, no. 151; V. Farinella in *Piero della Francesca* 2015, pp. 334–35, no. III.25.

83 Davies 1951 ed. 1961, p. 152 note 11.

84 C. Cavalca in *Cosmè Tura and Francesco del Cossa* 2007, pp. 468–69; Cavalca 2013, p. 335; Campisi 2018, pp. 100–3.

85 Cavalca 2013, p. 393, doc. XXXVI; Campisi 2018, pp. 100–3; see also the detailed entry by Cecilia Cavalca in this book.

86 The information is in Campisi 2018, p. 102 and note 225.

87 *Sopra un dipinto* 1841; *Galleria di quadri al Vaticano* 1843, pp. 83–87.

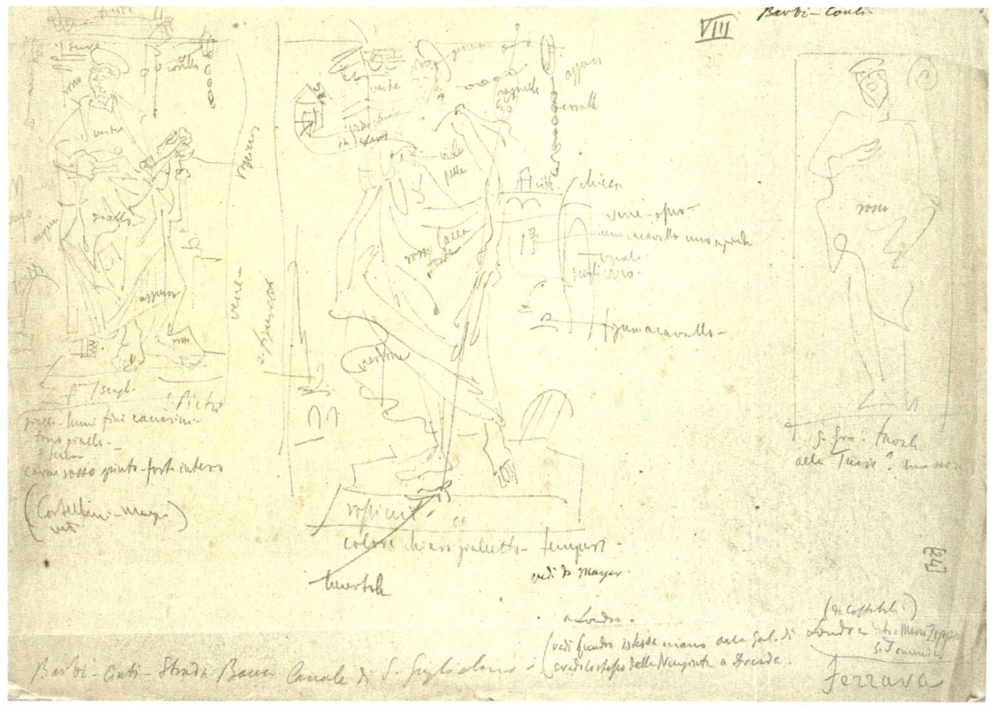

9

Giovanni Battista Cavalcaselle, drawing of paintings in the Barbi Cinti collection in Ferrara (*Saint Peter* and *Saint John the Baptist* by Francesco del Cossa, the lateral compartments of the Griffoni Polyptych's lower register, now in the Pinacoteca di Brera, Milan). Biblioteca Marciana, Venice, Fondo Cavalcaselle, It. IV.2030 (=12271), folder VII, f. 24r

Napoleonic years, and then, in 1812, married Anna Cinti, a woman from a family with solid finances, though not "exceedingly rich" as they had been at one time. His close relationship with Marquis Giambattista Costabili, for whom he worked as attorney and bailiff, is also reflected in his collection. The almost 600 works listed in the 1843 inventory featured many Primitives and were intended to document painting in Ferrara from the fifteenth to the eighteenth century. Many of these paintings came from Ferrara families who had lost their fortunes with the changing circumstances of those years.[88]

Nos. 73 and 74 of the inventory describe the panels with *Saint John the Baptist* and *Saint Peter* that had originally appeared on either side of the *Saint Vincent Ferrer* acquired by Costabili: "Saint Peter and Saint John the Baptist appear whole about two thirds of natural size on oblong panels. Some think it by Marco Zoppo Bolognese who flourished c. 1470 and others by Andrea Mantegna Paduan who flourished c. 1460."[89] These attributions are understandable considering that Marco Zoppo was recognized at the time as the author of the Costabili panel and Andrea Mantegna as the author of Francesco del Cossa's *Annunciation*, which landed in Dresden in the mid-eighteenth century through the efforts of Luigi Crespi.

In the same inventory, no. 177 is described as "Saint Petronius on small oblong panel said to be by Marco Zoppo Bolognese who flourished in 1470 or also by Andrea Mantegna Paduan who flourished around 1460."[90] The item refers to the small panel from the Griffoni Polyptych that came to the Pinocateca Nazionale of Ferrara from the Vendeghini Baldi collection. The identically-worded attribution makes it clear that the owner believed the three compartments belonged to a single complex.

88 On the Barbi Cinti collection, see Padovani 1954, pp. 154–58; Scardino 1996, pp. 95–96; Agostini and Scardino 1997, pp. 13–58, with the 1843 inventory.

89 "*S. Pietro e S. Battista figure intiere circa due terzi della naturale grandezza in tavole oblunghe. Chi le vuole di Marco Zoppo Bolognese che fioriva c.a il 1470 e chi di Andrea Mantegna Padovano che fioriva c.a il 1460.*" Agostini and Scardino 1997, p. 26.

90 "*S. Petronio in tavoletta oblunga dicesi di Marco Zoppo Bolognese che fioriva il 1470 od anche d'Andrea Mantegna Padovano che fioriva circa il 1460.*" Ibid., p. 31.

Giovanni Battista Cavalcaselle focused on the two larger panels of *Saint Peter* and *Saint John the Baptist* during one of his visits to Ferrara, where he was received in Palazzo Barbi Cinti on Via Boccacanale di San Guglielmo, as he noted in the margin of a page with a number of drawings. He made sketches of each of the panels, filling the pages with descriptions of their colors (yellow, blue, dark green, deep red enamel, etc.) and the objects depicted (coral, fruit, horseback rider, one man on a horse and another standing, a lizard, etc.). In particular, after careful analysis, he recorded clear, impeccable associations with distant works: "I saw a painting by the same hand at the London Gallery ascribed to Marco Zoppo" and "I think the same of the *Annunciation* in Dresden,"[91] referring specifically to the *Saint Vincent Ferrer*, of which the two panels before his eyes were the lateral elements, and the so-called "Pala dell'Osservanza," also a work by Francesco del Cossa (fig. 9).

Upon the death of Giovanni Barbi in 1865, the entire collection was inherited by his daughter Maria Giuseppa, who had lived with her father in the house on Via Boccacanale. Only in the 1890s did circumstances require a massive sell-off, which reduced the collection by approximately three hundred paintings, of which about sixty were acquired by another Ferrara collector, Giuseppe Cavalieri. Enea Vendeghini, on the other hand, concentrated his acquisitions on small-format fifteenth-century panels. These deals, however, triggered a scandal that was taken up in the national press, spreading well beyond the Ferrara milieu and setting off an inquiry in Parliament about the involvement in the sale of the liberal Parliamentarian Adolfo Cavalieri, the collector's brother, and subsequent changes in ownership of the two panels by Francesco del Cossa. According to the newspapers of the time, the elderly owner Maria Giuseppa, who suffered from various ailments, had been tricked by Enea Vendeghini into selling the paintings at an exceptionally low price. He then ceded them to Giuseppe Cavalieri, who made an inordinate profit reselling them in 1893 for 25,000 liras to the Italian State.[92] This acquisition was actively encouraged by Adolfo Venturi in the interests of the Pinacoteca di Brera, as the historian himself explained later in his *Memorie autobiografiche*: "Given the impossibility of making acquisitions outside of Italy, I was attentive not to let good opportunities at home escape me. From the Barbi Cinti collection in Ferrara, I bought two paintings by Francesco del Cossa, wings of a triptych that had, in the middle, the *Saint Vincent Ferrer* at the National Gallery of London and, as the predella, the stories of this saint in the Pinacoteca Vaticana."[93]

The collection of Enea Vendeghini (1841–1900) was formed primarily between 1880 and 1885 and comprised, at his death, 180 antique paintings and other miniatures that were then inherited by his daughter Anna, known as Nina. Joining the collection at that time was the panel with *Saint Petronius*, later attributed to Ercole de' Roberti by Adolfo Venturi and included in Longhi's proposal for the reassembling of the Griffoni Polyptych. During his visit to the collection in the palazzo on Corso Giovecca, Longhi also identified a fragment by

---

91 "*... vedi quadro istessa mano alla Gall. di Londra dato a Marco Zoppo ... credo lo stesso della Nunziata a Dresda.*" Biblioteca Marciana, Venice, Fondo Cavalcaselle, Manuscripts. It.IV.2030 (=12271), file VII, f. 24r. The conclusion reached by Cavalcaselle while observing the panels is recorded in full in Crowe and Cavalcaselle 1871, I, pp. 527–28.

92 On the Cavalieri collection, see Padovani 1954, pp. 170–71; Agostini and Scardino 1997, pp. 87–158. The affair is discussed in Mantovani 1996; Agostini and Scardino 1997, pp. 19–21.

93 Venturi 1927 ed. 1991, pp. 42–43, 80 (for the quotation); Agosti 1996, pp. 117 and 247. In 1888, Gustavo Frizzoni made known the publication of the first proposal for the recomposition of the Griffoni Polyptych in the form of a triptych with the Vatican predella, taken up by Adolfo Venturi and illustrated with an imaginative frame in a drawing by Ludovico Pogliaghi in 1897: Frizzoni 1888; Frizzoni 1897, pp. 224, 226 (with thanks to Ludovico Pogliaghi for the graphic vision of the "triptych"); Cavalca 2013, p. 335.

Andrea Mantegna that fit with the *Dormitio Virginis* in the Prado.[94] In 1911, the entire collection was placed under state care through an administrative decree of the superintendency; this arrangement was limited by a new decree in 1940 that only bound thirty-seven works but was then renewed in 1948. Finally, in 1975, thanks to Mario Baldi, grandson of Nina Vendeghini, thirty-five paintings from the collection, including the small *Saint Petronius*, were donated to the Pinacoteca of Ferrara, where they were displayed in a special room.[95]

It is worth noting that, among the numerous compartments of the polyptych present in the Griffoni Chapel in the early 1470s, only the *Saint Peter* and *Saint John the Baptist* by Cossa, today in the Pinacoteca di Brera, actually reached an Italian museum through acquisition by a public institution. Fortunately, joining these two compartments is the aforementioned donation by attorney Mario Baldi in 1975 of *Saint Petronius*, patron of Bologna and titular saint of the Basilica where the multi-faceted altarpiece was destined.[96] Still lacking are quite a few small panels with exquisite figures of saints that had appeared in the lateral strip of the extraordinary polyptych prior to its dismemberment by Monsignor Aldrovandi.

Favored by the backwardness of Italian art criticism, the distractions of the various administrations, and the inadequacy of Italian supervisory authorities in the years after unification,[97] the silent diaspora in the nineteenth and twentieth centuries dispersed the other elements of the altarpiece between London, Washington, DC, Paris, Rotterdam, Vatican City, and, finally, Venice and Gazzada Schianno. In this distribution, the pioneering passion of English collectors and enthusiasts of the Ferrara Renaissance was amply rewarded. In 1894, by private initiative of the Burlington Fine Arts Club, they organized the historic exhibition, curated by Adolfo Venturi, of paintings, drawings, and medallions of the School of Ferrara and Bologna from 1440–1540, supported by 250 photographs taken for the occasion. The bold project might even be called risky considering the theme, place, and years, which "would today be looked upon as dangerously adventurous outside Ferrara itself," as Francis Haskell commented in his *The Ephemeral Museum. Old Master Paintings and the Rise of the Art Exhibition* of 2000 (p. 94). Nonetheless, in an early contribution, the event was hailed by the young Bernard Berenson as "one of the finest retrospective exhibitions that has ever been seen in London."[98]

---

94 On visits to Palazzo Vendeghini by Giorgio Bassani and other students of Longhi, see *Inventari d'arte* 1997, p. 293.

95 On the Vendeghini Baldi collection, see Padovani 1954, pp. 169–70; Scardino 1996, pp. 100–1, also pp. 159–84; *Inventari d'arte* 1997, pp. 287–314.

96 The Griffoni Polyptych can be taken as an emblematic case of the progressive depletion of works from the fifteenth century in Ferrara and, more generally, of the artistic patrimony of Italy, over the course of the nineteenth century, as was succinctly stated by Michele Campisi (2018, p. 104): "The dissolution of Ferrara's heritage in favor of a cynical and unscrupulous ancient art market is the amplified paradigm of what happens in the rest of the Italian states."

97 Worthy of mention is Austen Henry Layard's indignant protest of the deplorable abandonment of antique frescoes in Italy, first expressed in an article in *Quarterly Review* in 1858, the year in which the panel with *Saint Vincent Ferrer* was authorized for export and shipped out from Livorno en route to London: "Talk of London smoke! Why, Italian neglect, indifference, and ignorance have done more to deprive the world of some of its noblest and most precious monuments of art than could be accomplished by the atmospheres of ten Londons! The able and careful editors of the last edition of Vasari's *Lives* have indicated in foot-notes the fate of the works mentioned by the biographer as existing in his day. The extent to which the work of devastation has been carried is amazing. Half, if not more than half, of the great frescoes of the fourteenth and fifteenth centuries are hopelessly and curtly described as '*sono periti*,' '*appena rimane qualche vestigio*,' '*dato di bianco*,' '*la chiesa fu disfatta*'" (Layard 1858, p. 280, quoted in Anderson 1994, pp. 56, 58).

98 On the 1894 London exhibition, see Haskell 2000 (Italian ed. 2008), pp. 127–31. On the decisive contribution of English critics and collectors in the resurgence of interest for the Ferrara Renaissance, see Anderson 1985, pp. 188, 193; Anderson 1993; and not to be forgotten, the attempt to recompose the Griffoni Polyptych according to Gustavo Frizzoni's proposal. The effort failed, however, as the Pinacoteca Vaticana refused to loan the predella in 1930 for the Italian art exhibition at the Royal Academy, curated by Ettore Modigliani, director at the time of the Pinacoteca di Brera, despite the tenacious efforts of Lady Ivy Chamberlain, wife of Sir Austin Chamberlain, Minister of Foreign Affairs in the conservative government, as well as the support of the Italian government (Haskell 2000, Italian ed. 2008, pp. 147–72).

BOLOGNA 1934: ROBERTO LONGHI AND THE *OFFICINA FERRARESE*

Marcello Toffanello

Roberto Longhi arrives in Bologna after winning a university teaching post of Art History at the end of 1934, thus replacing, on one of the oldest chairs of this discipline in Italy (established in 1906), Benvenuto Igino Supino, a prominent representative of the positivist historical method. Nevertheless, the old scholar continues to publish his systematic collections of documents on Bologna's churches and to hold honorary positions in the city's artistic institutions even after retiring, before being sadly put aside by the racial laws in 1938. It was actually Supino who, in 1929, suggested Giuseppe Lipparini for the chair of Art History at the Academy of Fine Arts; Lipparini, a follower of Gabriele d'Annunzio, was a critic and a scholar, the author of a monograph on Francesco Francia in 1913 and a supporter of secessionist painters against the avant-garde.

During the fascist era, the Bolognese culture, mildly touched by the restlessness of the avant-gardes of the beginning of the century, goes through a phase of inertia. The year 1935, when Longhi begins his teaching activity, can be considered a ridge that marks the end of some trends that had distinguished the city's artistic life in the first decades of the twentieth century. The regime's rhetoric presides over the celebrations for the first centenary of the birth of Giosuè Carducci, who had been teacher of many university professors of historical and literary subjects and still represented a model for most of the city's intellectual class. With the sale of the collections of embroidery, drawings, and applied art objects to the Municipality, the floral season of *Aemilia Ars* came to an end; at the same time, the restoration activity of the city monuments promoted by the Committee for Historical and Artistic Bologna, founded in 1899 by architect Alfonso Rubbiani and Count Francesco Cavazza, started to fade. Also in 1935, with the inauguration of the exhibition on eighteenth-century Bolognese art—to which Longhi also contributed—and the subsequent rearrangement of the Municipal Art Collections in Palazzo D'Accursio, the post-unification reorganization of the city museums was concluded. Francesco Malaguzzi Valeri had directed the process toward the rediscovery of seventeenth- and eighteenth-century heritage with the opening of the Museum of Industrial Art and the rearrangement of the halls of the Regia Pinacoteca between 1917 and 1924. A certain continuity is guaranteed by the leading role of Guido Zucchini in these events, and until the post-war period; he was one of Rubbiani's pupils, and therefore a follower of Viollet-le-Duc's restoration principles and a supporter, in Supino's footsteps, of a historical investigation conducted mainly on archive sources.[1]

---

1 On art history and Bologna's cultural context in the first half of the twentieth century: Trento and Riccardi Scassellati 1988; Bazzocchi 2013, pp. 271–317. In particular, on Supino, Bassani Pacht 2006; on Malaguzzi Valeri, *Francesco Malaguzzi Valeri* 2014, esp. the essays Battistini 2014, Cammarota 2014, Pigozzi 2014; on the *Mostra del Settecento*, see *Bologna e le Collezioni* 2011; on Zucchini and restoration in Bologna at the beginning of the twentieth century, Ciancabilla 2004 and 2009.

Longhi's teaching, which lasted until 1949, significantly contributed to impress a change in the Bolognese cultural environment, still so tied to a tradition that was rooted in the nineteenth century: its effects extended from history of art to literature, to the point of influencing the figurative arts and cinema, in an area that was much larger than the one circumscribed by the Petronian walls.

The scholar, born in Alba, Piedmont, in 1890 from Modenese parents, got his chair when he was no longer young, at over forty years of age, without having covered until then any significant positions in the historical-artistic institutions, but actually showing off an anti-academic attitude. When he obtained a university teaching post, winning over about fifteen candidates (among them Achille Bertini Calosso, Umbria superintendent and past director of the Galleria Borghese, Cesare Brandi, who had just been appointed inspector of the Bolognese superintendency, Vittorio Moschini, Stefano Bottari and other younger pupils of Adolfo Venturi's school), Longhi had a long and original critical path behind him that had led him to get involved in some of the most important artistic and critical trends of the twentieth century and to quickly move away from his first teachers, Pietro Toesca and even Venturi.[2]

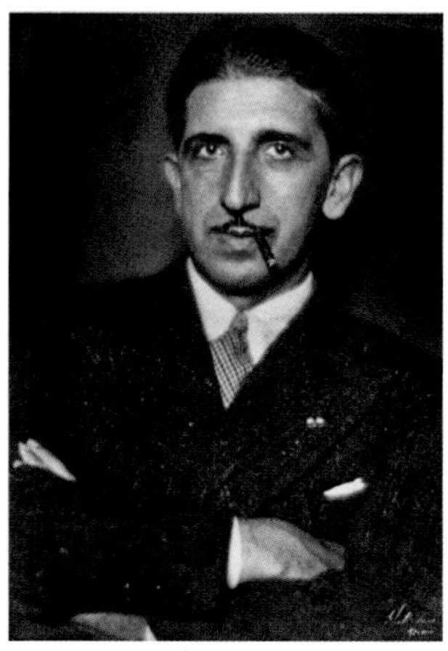

1

Roberto Longhi in 1934 (Photo Ghitta Carell, Fondazione di Studi di Storia dell'Arte Roberto Longhi, Florence)

He began at a very young age by reading the art writings of Charles Baudelaire, Eugène Fromentin, and Walter Pater, as well as Ardengo Soffici's articles on modern painting that appeared in Giuseppe Prezzolini's periodical *La Voce*. Here, in his early twenties, he published his first essays on "pure figurative criticism." With a "purovisibilist" approach he had drawn from the writings of Adolf von Hildebrand and the authors of the Vienna School, in 1914 he published his first book, *La scultura futurista di Boccioni* and the critical study *Piero dei Franceschi e lo sviluppo della pittura veneziana*, to devote himself in the following years to tilling the field of Caravaggesque painting: although almost unexplored until then, it had been the subject of his degree and specialization dissertations. He had also acquired a solid reputation as an expert in the international environment of collectors and antique dealers. This was indeed the context of his enthusiastic approach and subsequent dramatic break with Bernard Berenson, the great American connoisseur and author of the famous volumes on the *Italian Painters of the Renaissance*, which since then became one of Longhi's favorite controversial targets. In 1927, when he became, together with Emilio Cecchi, director of the magazine *Vita artistica*, he signed an editorial in which he distanced himself from the "mystical" interpretation of Croce's idealism offered by Lionello Venturi with his 1926 essay on the "Taste of the Primitives." In that same year, in the midst of a post-avant-garde "return to order" climate, Longhi achieved notoriety by publishing in the magazine *Valori Plastici* his study on Piero della Francesca, which exerted a profound influence on contemporary artists[3].

But it is precisely with the publication in 1934 of the *Officina ferrarese* that Longhi achieves the masterpiece of his maturity, reaching a hitherto untouched summit of historical synthesis and a purely formal reinterpretation of artistic events. His book takes the form of a long comment on the exhibition of Ferrarese painting of the Renaissance held at Palazzo dei Diamanti in 1933–34,[4] but the first reviewers already underline, as we shall see, the author's extraordinary ability to draw a historical synthesis of two centuries

2 On the 1934 competition, see Agosti 1988.

3 For a critical biography of Longhi, see Previtali 1982.

4 On the Ferrara exhibition and Longhi's survey of Ferrarese Renaissance painting carried out in his *Officina*, see Toffanello 2000 and Toffanello 2017.

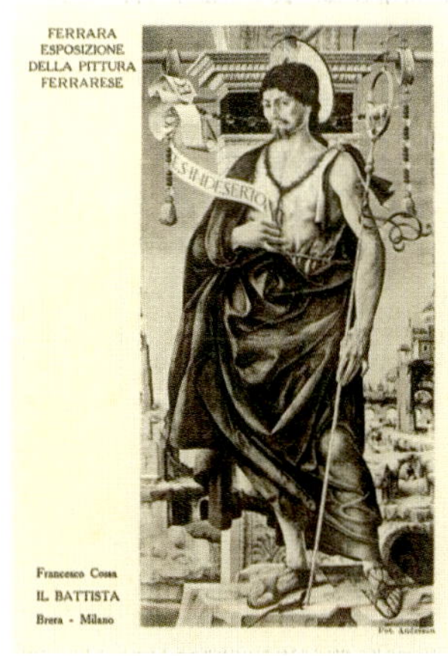

2

Postcard of the 1933 exhibition of Ferrarese Renaissance painting with Francesco del Cossa's *Saint John the Baptist* (Fondazione di Studi di Storia dell'Arte Roberto Longhi, Florence, Photo archive, inv. 0570153)

3

Comparisons between Ercole de' Roberti's saints formerly in the side pillars and details of the predella of the Griffoni Polyptych (from R. Longhi, *Officina ferrarese*, Rome: Edizioni d'Italia, 1934, plate 93)

of Ferrarese painting maintaining a clever balance between a tight narration of the style changes and the extraordinary "synchronic amplifications" he used to retrace a specific local artistic conjuncture and its connections with other territories. In the *Officina*, Longhi's writing reaches one of its heights, not only for its literary quality but for the way the language adapts to the style of the great fifteenth-century Ferrarese painters, managing to reflect the formal characteristics of their works through "verbal equivalences," according to a method whose effectiveness was claimed by the scholar in the "historical critique of figurative arts"[5].

Complementary and equally important to the critical text is the series of images that accompanies it, in which the revealing details of the works are isolated and compared. It is a procedure that Longhi had already used in the book on Piero della Francesca, whose illustrative apparatus, as he recalled fifteen years later, "was also exemplary to many other choices and involuntarily triggered—even too much—the often-careless urge of 'details' and 'details of details.'"[6] However, in the *Officina* the assembly of details is always extremely tight and the comparison never fails to be revealing. As shown by the many clippings still preserved in the photo library of the Longhi Foundation— not all of which were used in the illustrative set of his volume—it is the scholar himself who isolates with a pair of scissors the significant details and orders them in sequence, providing indications to the graphic designer on the back of the photographs.[7] It is the "cinematographic" montage that Pier Paolo Pasolini would see at work in 1942 "in that secluded and hidden room of the University on Via Zamboni," where the slides were projected in sequence as shots, from total framings to details, comparing fragments of similar or opposite formal worlds.[8] Masterful comparisons are conducted in the *Officina* between details of *September* in Palazzo Schifanoia and the Vatican predella, and between the latter and the saints on

5 Previtali 1982, pp. 163–66.

6 *Prefazione alla seconda edizione* (1942), now in Longhi 1963, p. VII.

7 I wish to thank the scientific director of the Roberto Longhi Foundation, Maria Cristina Bandera, and the director of the Photo archive, Paolo Benassai, for allowing me to consult the documentation relating to the Griffoni Polyptych and for facilitating my research.

8 Pasolini's testimony, excerpted from the review of *Roberto Longhi. Da Cimabue a Morandi* (1974), is cited in Trento and Riccardi Scassellati 1988, p. 248.

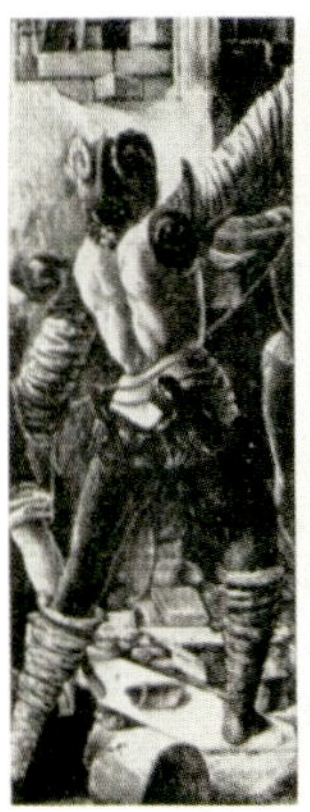
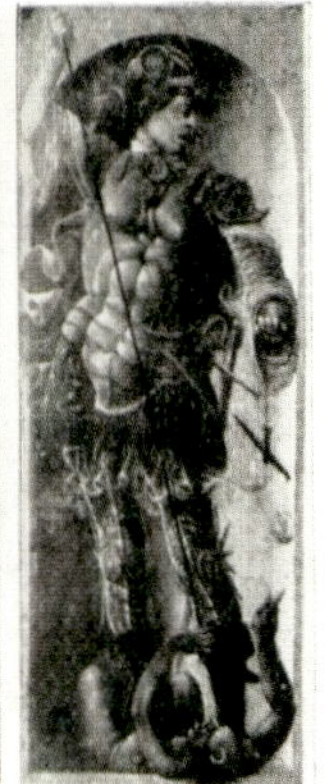
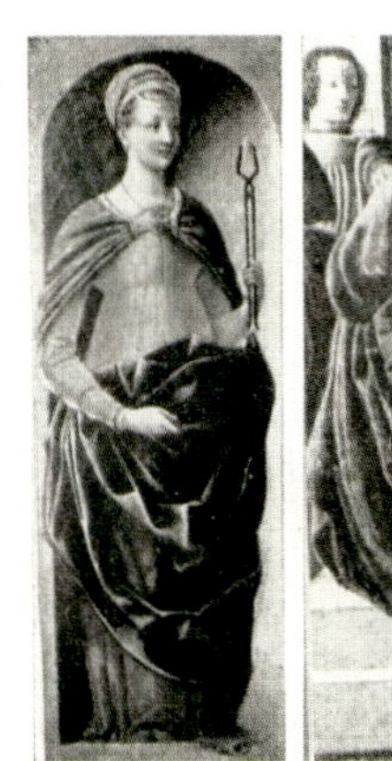
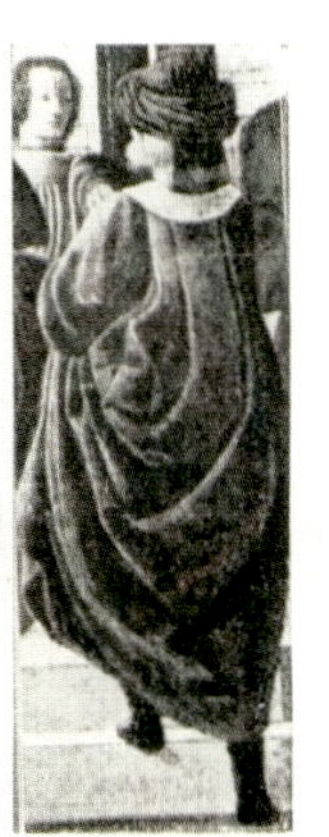
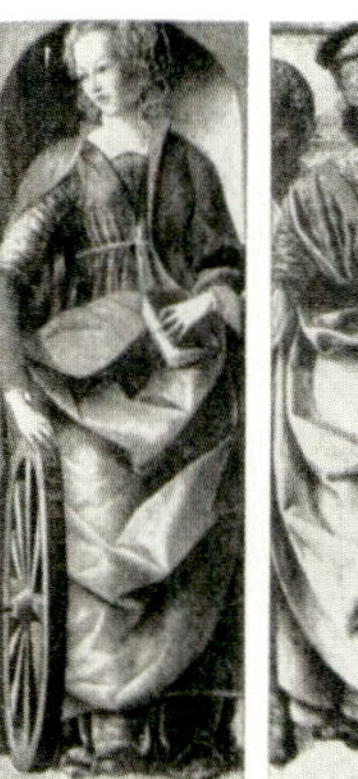
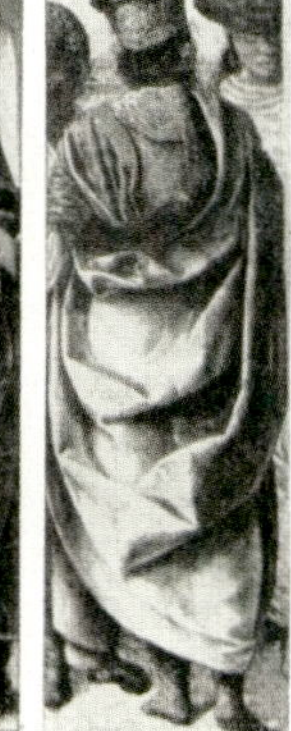

Ercole. *Raffronti tra i pilastri e la predella Griffoni.*

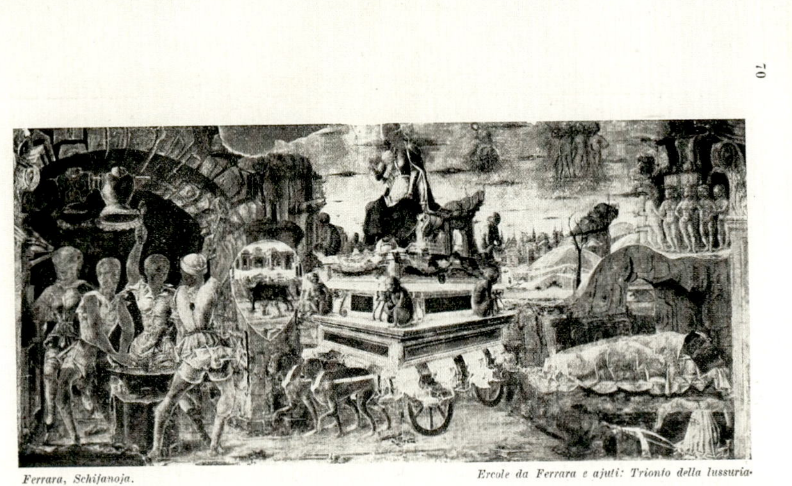

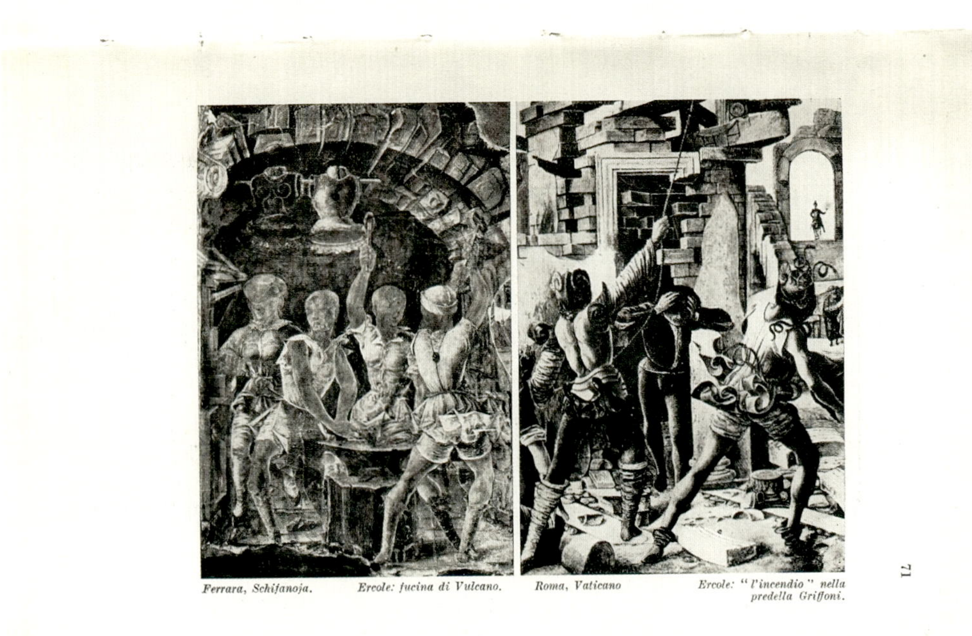

4

The upper register of the month of *September* in Palazzo Schifanoia, Ferrara, attributed to Ercole de' Roberti; comparison between Vulcan's forge in Palazzo Schifanoia and the fire in the Griffoni predella at the Vatican Museums (from R. Longhi, *Officina ferrarese*, Rome: Edizioni d'Italia, 1934, plates 70 and 71)

the pillars of the Griffoni Polyptych: they guide the reader along the artworks and argue their common attribution to Ercole de' Roberti (fig. 3).

The comparison between the images of Vulcan's forge in Palazzo Schifanoia and the extinguishing of the fire in the predella (fig. 4) has been considered as a model for an attribution method strictly based on style, "choosing the parts of figurations where all the conscious activities of the intellect and of the manual mastery interact in unstoppable tension,"[9] as opposed to Giovanni Morelli's "positivist" method founded on the comparison between marginal and repetitive details—which Longhi mocks a few pages before.[10] Together with

9 Gregori 1982, p. 134.

10 Longhi 1934 ed. 1956, p. 33: "Morelli would have bet heavily on the wrinkle formed on the back of the hands, on the folding of the little finger: go also for the wrinkle."

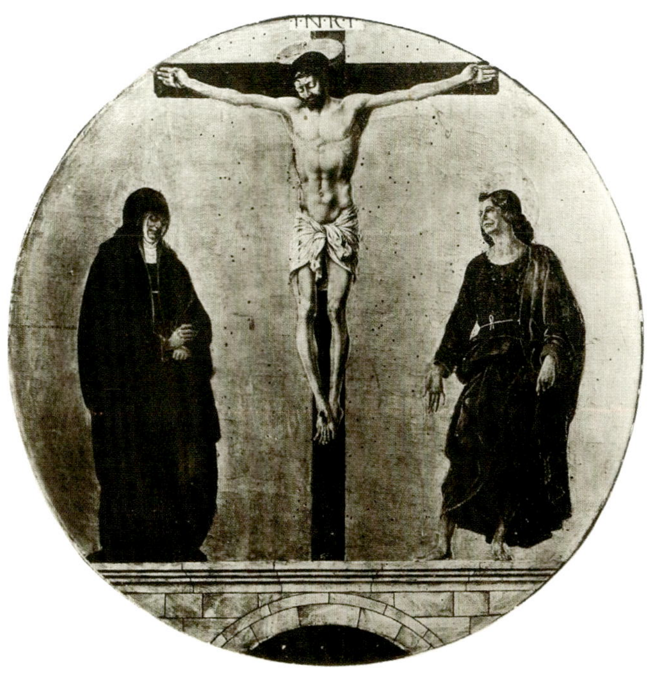

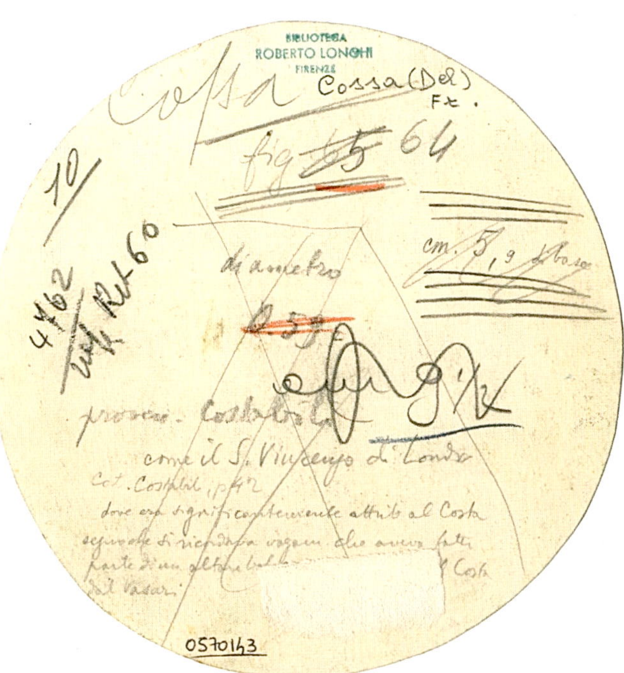

5

Francesco del Cossa, *Crucifixion*, formerly Lehman collection, New York, now at the National Gallery of Art, Washington, DC (Fondazione di Studi di Storia dell'Arte Roberto Longhi, Florence, Photo archive, inv. 0570143)

6

Reverse of previous image with Longhi's handwritten notes

the careful gear of clear albeit small images, contemporary reviewers do not fail to point out among the qualities of the book what for the time was a powerful apparatus of 166 notes "condensed as extracts." André Chastel has compared the "two-storey" structure of the *Officina* and of the other major essays by Longhi to that of an altarpiece: "central painting, all at once, and 'predella,' I dare say with several compartments. Two complementary movements are put together: the patient, integral, meticulous documentary accumulation (controlled state of conservation, verified quotes…) which falls within the 'philology'… and finally the catalogue; it is the register of notes and appendixes."[11] If Longhi composed the general picture of Ferrarese painting in one go, in just a few months on the occasion of the 1933 exhibition, the *Officina* actually contains a wealth of information collected for over a decade, at least. The proof is the quantity of paintings examined—far superior to those exhibited at Palazzo dei Diamanti—which is not even limited to those mentioned in Venturi's *Storia dell'arte italiana* and in Berenson's *Italian Pictures of the Renaissance*.

It is precisely in the reconstruction of the dismembered polyptychs that this long accumulation and sedimentation of photographs in folders becomes especially evident, as the result of his research of museums and private collections and annotations taken from the scrutiny of artistic literature and ancient catalogues. To stay on the subject of this paper, in 1926 Longhi had already hypothesized that the tondo with the *Crucifixion*, then included in the Lehmann collection in New York, might belong to the Griffoni altarpiece, contesting its attribution to Castagno advanced by Giuseppe Fiocco.[12] On that occasion, the scholar had reported on the reverse of the photo—still preserved in the photo library of the Longhi Foundation in Florence—the following notes, part of a circumstantial procedure that accompanied the exercise of *connoisseurship*: "proven. Costabili/ like Saint Vincent in London/ cat. Costabili, p. 42/ where it was significantly attributed to

11 Chastel 1982, p. 57.

12 "Lettera pittorica a Giuseppe Fiocco," in *Vita Artistica*, 1926, pp. 127–39, now in Longhi 1967, I, pp. 77–98, esp. p. 86.

Costa/ proof that it was vaguely remembered that it had been part of an altar [attributed to] Costa/ by Vasari" (figs. 5 and 6).

Other documents preserved at the Longhi Foundation allow to enter the laboratory of this great scholar and to follow the progress he made in the reconstruction of the Griffoni Polyptych. Having learned of the two panels depicting *Saint Florian* and *Saint Lucy*, probably on the occasion of their purchase by Duveen antique dealers in 1929–30,[13] Longhi proceeded to a first rearrangement of the whole by proportionally assembling the images together with the *Crucifixion* tondo and the already known parts of the polyptych (fig. 7).

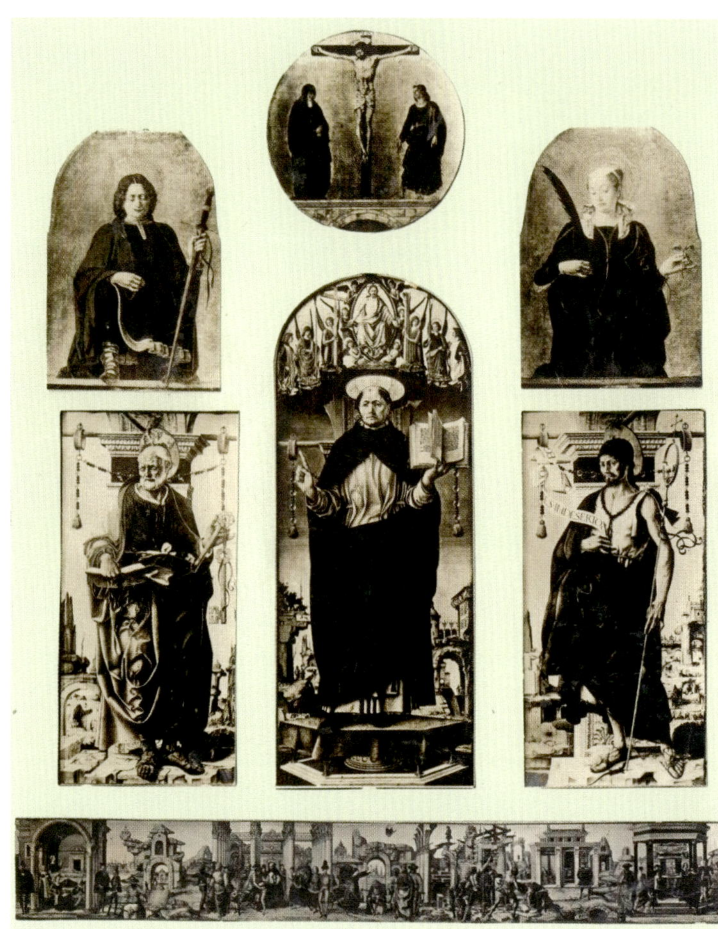

7

Roberto Longhi, first hypothesis of reconstruction of the Roverella altarpiece (c.1930?), photographs pasted on cardboard, 280 × 220 mm (Fondazione di Studi di Storia dell'Arte Roberto Longhi, Florence, Photo archive, inv. 0570130–36)

It is probably only after visiting the Ferrara exhibition in May 1933 that he was definitively convinced that the four panels by Ercole de' Roberti and two others known to him were part of a single series depicting the saints in the pillars of the polyptych.[14] The library of the Longhi Foundation preserves a copy of the first edition of the Ferrara exhibition catalogue, published without images in May 1933 when the exhibition opened. Longhi fixed there his first observations in front of the paintings on display with quick shorthand notes. On page 50, a curly bracket unites the two pairs of Ercole de' Roberti's panels depicting *Saint Apollonia* and *Saint Michael* (at the Louvre) and *Saint Catherine* and *Saint Jerome* (at that time in the Duveen collection in Paris, now the property of the Cini Foundation, Venice) that were kept separate in the catalogue; alongside, under an illegible shorthand note, was the comment: "altarpiece of Saint/ Hyacinth [*sic*]." At the bottom of the page, Longhi added: "another Auspitz [*Saint Anthony the Abbot* now at the Museum Boijmans Van Beuningen in Rotterdam]/ another Vendeghini, Saint Petronius"[15] (fig. 8).

Longhi then proceeded with a reconstruction of a bigger size, which included the saints in the pillars and a sketchy drawing of the frame, published in 1934 as plate 65 in the first edition of the *Officina*. From this reconstruction, currently not available in the photo archive, the Vendeghini *Saint Petronius* is missing (Longhi did not have its photograph at that time), as well as the two tondos depicting the *Archangel Gabriel* and the *Annunciation* in the Cagnola collection, whose images he received too late. They are

13 In the Photo archive there are in fact two images of the paintings (inv. 0570137 and 0570140) without the stamp of the Kress collection, which they entered in 1936, and bearing on the back the measures required to rearrange the whole in scale.

14 Longhi shared his conviction with Francesco Filippini in a letter received on December 21, 1933. By then, he had certainly already reached the conclusion that the Griffoni altar was a two-storey polyptych. About a month earlier he had written to the Bolognese scholar that he was preparing an article on the Ferrara exhibition. The letters are published in Cerasi 2011.

15 The second illustrated edition of the catalogue, printed in May 1933, was instead used on purpose and presents more orderly notes with bibliographic information and other signs that reveal the systematic revision of the information on the artworks while writing the *Officina*.

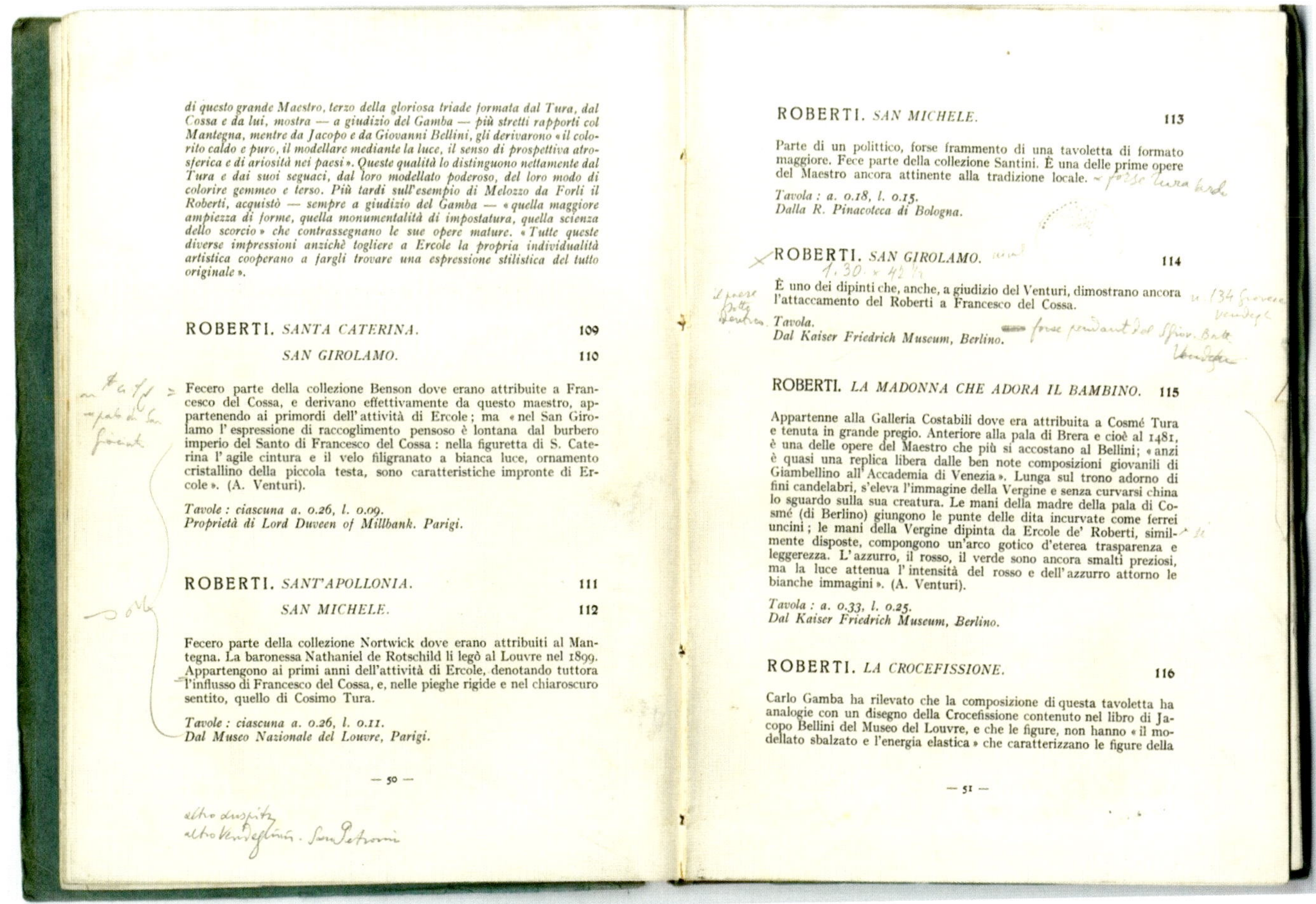

di questo grande Maestro, terzo della gloriosa triade formata dal Tura, dal Cossa e da lui, mostra — a giudizio del Gamba — più stretti rapporti col Mantegna, mentre da Jacopo e da Giovanni Bellini, gli derivarono «il colorito caldo e puro, il modellare mediante la luce, il senso di prospettiva atrosferica e di ariosità nei paesi». Queste qualità lo distinguono nettamente dal Tura e dai suoi seguaci, dal loro modellato poderoso, del loro modo di colorire gemmeo e terso. Più tardi sull'esempio di Melozzo da Forlì il Roberti, acquistò — sempre a giudizio del Gamba — «quella maggiore ampiezza di forme, quella monumentalità di impostatura, quella scienza dello scorcio» che contrassegnano le sue opere mature. «Tutte queste diverse impressioni anzichè togliere a Ercole la propria individualità artistica cooperano a fargli trovare una espressione stilistica del tutto originale».

ROBERTI. *SANTA CATERINA.* 109

SAN GIROLAMO. 110

Fecero parte della collezione Benson dove erano attribuite a Francesco del Cossa, e derivano effettivamente da questo maestro, appartenendo ai primordi dell'attività di Ercole; ma «nel San Girolamo l'espressione di raccoglimento pensoso è lontana dal burbero imperio del Santo di Francesco del Cossa: nella figuretta di S. Caterina l'agile cintura e il velo filigranato a bianca luce, ornamento cristallino della piccola testa, sono caratteristiche impronte di Ercole». (A. Venturi).

Tavole: ciascuna a. 0.26, l. 0.09.
Proprietà di Lord Duveen of Millbank. Parigi.

ROBERTI. *SANT'APOLLONIA.* 111

SAN MICHELE. 112

Fecero parte della collezione Nortwick dove erano attribuiti al Mantegna. La baronessa Nathaniel de Rotschild li legò al Louvre nel 1899. Appartengono ai primi anni dell'attività di Ercole, denotando tuttora l'influsso di Francesco del Cossa, e, nelle pieghe rigide e nel chiaroscuro sentito, quello di Cosimo Tura.

Tavole: ciascuna a. 0.26, l. 0.11.
Dal Museo Nazionale del Louvre, Parigi.

— 50 —

ROBERTI. *SAN MICHELE.* 113

Parte di un polittico, forse frammento di una tavoletta di formato maggiore. Fece parte della collezione Santini. È una delle prime opere del Maestro ancora attinente alla tradizione locale.

Tavola: a. 0.18, l. 0.15.
Dalla R. Pinacoteca di Bologna.

ROBERTI. *SAN GIROLAMO.* 114

È uno dei dipinti che, anche, a giudizio del Venturi, dimostrano ancora l'attaccamento del Roberti a Francesco del Cossa.

Tavola.
Dal Kaiser Friedrich Museum, Berlino.

ROBERTI. *LA MADONNA CHE ADORA IL BAMBINO.* 115

Appartenne alla Galleria Costabili dove era attribuita a Cosmé Tura e tenuta in grande pregio. Anteriore alla pala di Brera e cioè al 1481, è una delle opere del Maestro che più si accostano al Bellini; «anzi è quasi una replica libera dalle ben note composizioni giovanili di Giambellino all'Accademia di Venezia». Lunga sul trono adorno di fini candelabri, s'eleva l'immagine della Vergine e senza curvarsi china lo sguardo sulla sua creatura. Le mani della madre della pala di Cosmé (di Berlino) giungono le punte delle dita incurvate come ferrei uncini; le mani della Vergine dipinta da Ercole de' Roberti, similmente disposte, compongono un'arco gotico d'eterea trasparenza e leggerezza. L'azzurro, il rosso, il verde sono ancora smalti preziosi, ma la luce attenua l'intensità del rosso e dell'azzurro attorno le bianche immagini». (A. Venturi).

Tavola: a. 0.33, l. 0.25.
Dal Kaiser Friedrich Museum, Berlino.

ROBERTI. *LA CROCEFISSIONE.* 116

Carlo Gamba ha rilevato che la composizione di questa tavoletta ha analogie con un disegno della Crocefissione contenuto nel libro di Jacopo Bellini del Museo del Louvre, e che le figure, non hanno «il modellato sbalzato e l'energia elastica» che caratterizzano le figure della

— 51 —

8

Catalogue of the *Esposizione della pittura ferrarese del Rinascimento* (Venice: Ferrari, May 1933), first edition, with Longhi's handwritten notes (Fondazione di Studi di Storia dell'Arte Roberto Longhi, Florence, Library)

therefore mentioned in a note (no. 73) included at the very last minute into the typescript of the *Officina*, which is also preserved in the archive of the Longhi Foundation. The same reconstruction was published in 1956 as plate 89 in the fifth volume of Longhi's complete works with only the addition of *Saint Petronius* (fig. 9).

In January 1937, at the winter exhibition of the Burlington Fine Arts Club in London, a panel depicting *Saint George* and attributed to Andrea Mantegna appeared. Longhi immediately recognized it as belonging to the series of saints painted by Ercole for the Griffoni altar. Probably at that time Francesco Filippini had already informed Longhi of the discovery of a new document that Supino would publish in 1938 in the second volume of his *Arte nelle chiese di Bologna*, certifying the payment on July 19, 1473 to the woodcarver Agostino de' Marchi for the *capsa* (i.e., external case) he made for the altarpiece commissioned by Floriano Griffoni.[16] It is therefore possible to date to these years the sheet (shown and published here for the first time, fig. 10) with the image of *Saint George* taken from the London exhibition catalogue glued on the right half, and on the other half an effective pen drawing by Longhi depicting the frame of the polyptych complete with the case and the two tondos representing the *Annunciation*. It is a pure *divertissement* of the scholar, who imagined it by combining the structures of the altar of San Vincenzo Ferreri and the triptych at the Frari, both by Giovanni Bellini, with the carvings

16 Supino 1938, p. 196. The elderly scholar reproduces on p. 197 the rearrangement of the polyptych made by Longhi, with whom he claims to agree.

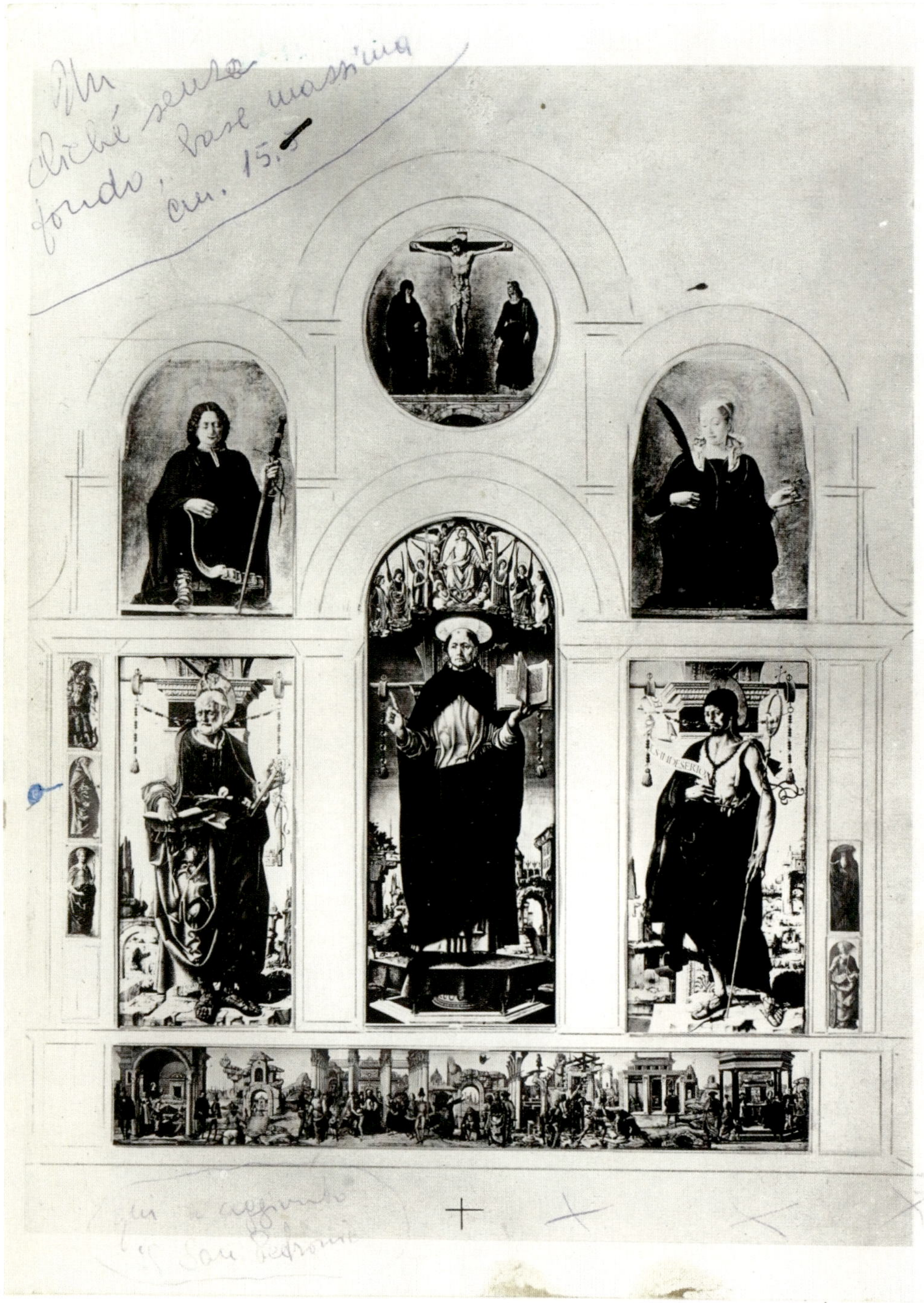

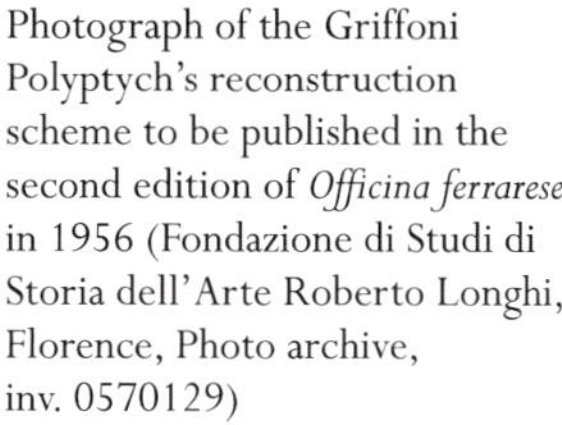

9

Photograph of the Griffoni Polyptych's reconstruction scheme to be published in the second edition of *Officina ferrarese* in 1956 (Fondazione di Studi di Storia dell'Arte Roberto Longhi, Florence, Photo archive, inv. 0570129)

of the upper part of Francesco Pelosio's triptych in the Pinacoteca di Bologna. "However, I do not draw fifteenth-century Crema frames," the distinguished scholar declared when he published, in his *Ampliamenti nell'Officina ferrarese*, a new reconstructive scheme of the polyptych complete with all its known parts, thus limiting himself to "present the approximate disposition of the various parts of the polyptych on a neutral background, which the observer will revive according to his or her taste"[17] (see fig. 3 on p. 107).

17 Longhi 1940 ed. 1956, p. 130 and fig. 309. For an in-depth discussion on Longhi's reconstruction of the polyptych frame, see Cavalca's contribution in this volume.

If indeed around 1930 Longhi had already assembled, at least mentally, Francesco del Cossa's six major panels, it is possible that this is at the origin of the increasing attention that, starting from that year, he showed for tracing the dispersed fragments back to the unity of the original work. In 1928 he had used the rearrangement of a dismembered triptych by Bonifacio Bembo to confirm the attribution of the single panels, which he had advanced when he still did not know that they were part of a single whole. On that occasion, the scholar spoke in terms of a clear pre-eminence of the style analysis over the examination of material facts: "The connection of the three paintings, achieved through that methodical way that we shall call formal, obtained, in the continuation of the investigation, such heavily material confirmations to entice us to feed them promptly to our unbelievers, not as an admission, rather as a large irrefutable morsel about the validity of that primary method"; and then: "that such a belonging [of the three panels to the same painter] had already been discovered through another way, actually long before perceiving that they were materially connected: this does not prove that only the other way was good and effective; to restore, I mean, what is most important—the signs of the painter's personality and spirit?"[18]

Two years later, adding two panels to a Giotto polyptych already partially recomposed by Richard Offner—a master of this kind of assemblages—Longhi adopted a procedure and terminology very similar to those later used for the reconstruction of the polyptychs in the *Officina ferrarese*, associating exquisitely stylistic "internal considerations" with "external" observations concerning the material features of the paintings, quotations from the sources (Ghiberti and Vasari), and iconographic topics.[19] With similar, and even more exhibited, critic tools, in the same months in which he was writing the *Officina*, Longhi achieved the masterful iconographic and perspective reintegration of one of Mantegna's best-known works, *The Death of the Virgin* at the Prado in Madrid, reuniting it with the fragment preserved in the Vendeghini collection in Ferrara, already recognized as such fifteen years earlier.[20]

In the *Officina*, the recomposition of the first dispersed fifteenth-century polyptych, the Roverella altarpiece by Cosmè Tura, is preceded by a short methodological introduction where Longhi regrets that his colleagues do not often exercise that sense which is "indispensable to go beyond the recognition of a generic individual unity [the one leading to the recognition of the author] to achieve the 'unity of work.'"[21] The reconstruction of Tura's polyptych was followed by those of Francesco del Cossa's Griffoni and Osservanza altarpieces and Lorenzo Costa's altarpiece of Santa Maria delle Rondini. These reconstructive exercises, accompanied by graphic renderings of the original whole, were not in fact a current currency at the time, especially outside the Anglo-Saxon scholars' community. Longhi considered the reconstruction of polyptychs, and in particular Cossa's work in San Petronio, one of the main results achieved in the *Officina*, as he declared six years later responding in an extremely piqued way in the *Ampliamenti nell'Officina ferrarese* to Ellis K. Waterhouse's review in the *Burlington Magazine*. Without doubt, the article by the English scholar lacks depth of analysis and its tone seems made on purpose to irritate Longhi from the very beginning, where he states that the two main objectives of his book

18 "La restituzione di un trittico d'arte cremonese circa il 1460 (Bonifacio Bembo)," in *Pinacotheca*, 2 (September–October 1928): 79–87, now in Longhi 1968, pp. 57–66, esp. pp. 57 and 62.
19 "Progressi nella reintegrazione d'un polittico di Giotto," in *Dedalo*, XI (October 1930): 285–91, now in Longhi 1968, pp. 3–6.
20 "Risarcimento di un Mantegna," in *Pan*, II, 3 (March 1934): 504–12, now in Longhi 1968, pp. 67–73.
21 Longhi 1934 ed. 1956, p. 25.

("to establish as rigorous a chronology as possible, and to be as rude to Mr. Berenson as the large vocabulary of the Italian language allows"), to the final advice addressed to the directors of artistic institutions to keep the volume locked because it was "too full of inflammable material for the unfledged mind and too irresponsible in its bright ideas."[22] However, Waterhouse's review shared the main points of the *Officina*, including the drastic revision of the catalogue of works attributed to Ercole de' Roberti by Berenson. Indeed, the objections made to the reconstructions of the Roverella and Griffoni polyptychs—which inaugurated the skeptical and long-lasting attitude of the Anglo-Saxon criticism toward Longhi's reconstructive proposals—provoked a violent reaction in the Italian scholar. Longhi even defined the Englishman as incompetent and Italianized his name in "Casalacqua, for a greater linguistic authority," thus winking in a definitely inelegant way to fascist nationalism, precisely in the year Italy declared war on Great Britain.[23]

The first Italian reviewers, instead, unanimously agreed in considering the re-composition of the fifteenth-century polyptychs among the most remarkable results of the *Officina*. A quick review of Cesare Brandi's judgments in *L'Italia letteraria*, of Stefano Bottari's in *Leonardo*, and Wart Arslan's in *Zeitschrift für Kunstgeschichte* can help assess the impact of the book on the slightly younger generation of scholars, who, by the way, had all participated in the 1934 Bologna competition either as candidates (Brandi and Bottari) or as members of the judging commission (Arslan).

In Brandi's opinion, Longhi's attribution exercise, descending from "Cavalcaselle's great breed philology," is not an "arid target shooting but a radial in-depth research," capable of "tracing an idealistic assessment of personalities and styles."[24] According to Bottari, "the book is pure philology" but nonetheless "supported and enlivened by that very personal Longhi style which, so to say, transforms history into chronicle."[25] Arslan, the only one to focus his comment on the discussion of single attributional issues, concludes by praising the way Longhi, "making use of even the most rigorous philological tools, and not only of them, manages to fully and enviably resurrect the spirit of the artwork. A restless search that fathoms and illuminates the most hidden corners, the most distant intentions: the very springs of the figurative fact."[26]

The passage of the San Lazzaro altarpiece, then in Berlin, from Tura to de' Roberti, the recognition of the young Ercole in the Schifanoia *September*, the reconstruction of Cossa and Costa's first activity, the suppression of Ercole Grandi, and the creation of "Vicino da Ferrara" represent for the three reviewers the turning points through which Longhi proposes a clear and shareable development of the art of the great fifteenth-century masters from Ferrara. And if Brandi regrets that "Piero della Francesca's subtle exegete has almost humbly wanted to force himself into this *dressage* of the most riotous problems, and ... has offered juicy but in the end preliminary and short hints on Tura, Cossa, and Roberti,"[27] Bottari considers Longhi's pages on de' Roberti "the most beautiful monograph written so far on a fifteenth-century great painter; even more than Piero della Francesca, as the critic's sensitivity here is more alert and almost more committed to grasping those active articulations of a language that give the poetic biography a

22 Waterhouse 1936, pp. 150 and 151.
23 Longhi 1940 ed. 1956, pp. 125 and 226; in particular, on the Griffoni Polyptych see pp. 129–31.
24 Brandi 1935, p. 5.
25 Bottari 1935, p. 485.
26 Arslan 1936, p. 183.
27 Brandi 1935, p. 5.

pungent sense of present vitality," while the rest of the book is a "broad preparatory work for future monographs."[28]

Brandi is the only one to question one of the crucial critical issues proposed by Longhi: that "Italianization" of style—the result of the meeting in Venice between Piero della Francesca and Giovanni Bellini on which Longhi had focused his 1914 essay—to which the Ferrarese painting contributed around 1480 with the Santa Maria in Porto altarpiece by de' Roberti. Mentioning the important contribution of Flemish painting in this conjuncture, Brandi shows to be skeptical about the real nature of this national language, which he feared could be "misunderstood, because it seemed based on a criterion of appreciation different from the aesthetic one and, God forbid, raci-" and here the sentence stops abruptly.[29] One would almost think of a clumsy act of censorship, were it not for the fact that the article contains several other typos. Let's then consider it as a *lapsus* of the typographer in making up the magazine, which presents on the front page an excerpt from the famous speech pronounced four days earlier by Mussolini to the Italians, "a people of poets, artists, heroes, etc.," which would have "revealed the qualities of its spirit and the power of its character" invading Ethiopia.

In Bologna, the *Officina ferrarese* was reviewed in the pages of *Archiginnasio* by Guido Zucchini—therefore not by an art historian in the strict sense—who began with a vivid portrait of Longhi: "a tall, thin man with glasses and, behind his glasses, a pair of sharp eyes, with a brown cigarette between his lips, a frugal gesture and a damned desire to ape your voice and gesture while you speak to him."[30] A rather corresponding sketch also from a psychological point of view, considering that, apparently, Longhi had given the engineer from Bologna the nickname "Viollet-le-Zuc."[31]

Zucchini focuses above all on the Bolognese implications of Longhi's essay, expressing his perplexity—just like the reviewers mentioned above—on the attribution to Giovanni da Modena of the frescoes of the Bolognini Chapel in San Petronio while agreeing with him on maintaining the attribution to Cossa of the stained glass windows of San Giovanni in Monte; on the clarification of the relations between Ferrara and Bologna between the fifteenth and sixteenth centuries; and on the re-evaluation of Amico Aspertini. Zucchini believes that the reconstruction of the Griffoni altarpiece is one of the most important topics covered in the book. However, Cossa remains "Bolognese by home in the last years of his life, but Ferrarese by soul and manner and, regrettably, scarcely followed by his contemporary colleagues in Bologna." In the end, Zucchini merely assesses the degree of harmony between Longhi's essay and local history studies (in particular his own) without indicating possible developments in the research, contrary to what Brandi had done. Indeed, Brandi regretted that Longhi had not studied in depth Cossa's legacy in Bologna, removing from the limbo "those two or three not despicable anonymous Emilian painters who worked under the command of the Ferrarese masters before Francia's *vulgata*."[32]

Perhaps we should conclude this report on the first reception of the *Officina ferrarese* with the review penned by Rezio Buscaroli in 1937 in the first issue of the magazine published to commemorate Melozzo da Forlì, not because it is particularly significant

---

28 Bottari 1935, pp. 487 and 489.
29 Brandi 1935, p. 5.
30 Zucchini 1935, p. 319.
31 Ferretti 1999, p. 209.
32 Brandi 1935, p. 5.

from a critical standpoint but because it is indicative of a different conjuncture in studies.[33] In 1931, Buscaroli had published a book titled *Pittura romagnola del Quattrocento* based on his degree dissertation (supervised by Supino in Bologna), and had later reviewed the exhibition of Ferrarese Renaissance in the *Resto del Carlino* paper of May 7, 1933. He recalled in fact how the presence, "appropriate and also inappropriate," of several paintings from Romagna at the Palazzo dei Diamanti exhibition triggered some discussions which were later strengthened by the revision of the attributions conducted by Longhi. Unlike what happened in the Bolognese environment, in Romagna both the Ferrara exhibition and the publication of the *Officina* revived a ferment of studies on the local Renaissance that led to the exhibition on Melozzo and fifteenth-century painting in Romagna held in Forlì in 1938.

If the *Officina ferrarese* proposed a new model of style and critical method to the younger generations of scholars, the inaugural lecture held by Longhi on December 1, 1934 determined the direction of art history studies in Bologna in the decades to come. Longhi's lecture was published with the title "Momenti della pittura bolognese" in the same issue of *Archiginnasio* where Zucchini's review of the *Officina* appeared.[34] In his first Bolognese lesson, Longhi set himself the goal of "bringing some new interpretative light to the darkest areas" of Bolognese artistic history, "implicitly proposing this or that subject as a program for a new and profitable work."[35] In doing so, he followed the usual procedure of overlooking what was already taken for granted to instead dwell on problematic knots: an anti-Vasarian approach that redesigned the geography of art history and preferred minor artists to the acclaimed masters. The controversial targets were therefore identical to those in the *Officina*: "those famous lists of ancient Italian painters" compiled by Berenson (the only one to be explicitly mentioned) "which too many of us consider as gospel truth because of their mental idleness;" Raimond Van Marle's "tourist mishmashes studded with photographs;" some "hasty judgments" by old Adolfo Venturi in the last volumes of his *Storia dell'arte in Italia*, such as the dismissing verdict about Primaticcio. Not to mention the bitter attack on his fellow student Lionello Venturi, the true inspirer of "that very peculiar school of criticism of criticism, which perhaps already regrets having abandoned the history of the artworks for its, in truth modest, contributions to the history of aesthetics, and now demands to come back through the window and even to peek at the paintings—but always with the breviary in its hand."[36] The homage paid to Supino, on the other hand, is purely formal and linked to this particular occasion. Longhi claims to have found in Supino's archival research a "brake on the sometimes-precipitous divinations of attributionism."[37]

For Longhi it was therefore a matter of "bypassing the ... theoretical or, let's say, academic and formalistic impediment ... which demanded to neglect fourteenth-century

33 Buscaroli 1937.

34 Longhi 1935 ed. 1973.

35 Ibid., p. 189.

36 Ibid., p. 198. The attack on Lionello Venturi takes its cue from the contestation of the theses supported by Carlo Ludovico Ragghianti, a pupil of Venturi and Matteo Marangoni, in an essay on "Carracci e la critica d'arte nell'età barocca" published in 1933 in *La Critica* directed by Benedetto Croce. In the same issue of the magazine where Longhi's prolusion is published, Guido Ludovico Luzzatto, a pupil of Adolfo Venturi in Rome and Paolo D'Ancona in Milan, tears to pieces Ragghianti's writing, using arguments similar to those of Longhi in an article dedicated to "Taine e la scuola bolognese" (in *L'Archiginnasio*, XXX, 1–3 [1935]: 135–56, esp. pp. 146–56).

37 The passage was deleted from the text of the conference published by Longhi himself in the sixth volume of his complete works: Agosti 1988, pp. 252–53.

Bolognese painting, considering it little more than a shapeless mass of typos and distortions of the great Tuscan models" and instead recognizing its "supremely memorable, asyntactic, directly expressive, sometimes even 'expressionistic'" attitude. Longhi identifies in Vitale da Bologna "the initiator of those sometimes conflicting senses of lively naturalness, costumed grace, and sudden fabulous lyricism that, from Piedmont to Milan to Verona to Treviso to Udine, make the fourteenth-century Po Valley an aesthetic world certainly incomparable to that of Tuscany—not because it is scarcer, only because it is different." The Middle Ages that comes out of Longhi's pen is very different from the one evoked by Carducci and Rubbiani thanks also to "the still close and present Emilian Romanesque sculptors and their intuitive verism: the dry and sharp wind of the old and highly cultivated Byzantine painting of Venice comes in blowing from the east; from the west the fabulous and perfumed lyrical wind of the royal and papal courts of Paris and Avignon."[38]

Coming to the second crucial point of his speech, Longhi recognizes the same "Lombard motive" at the origin of the Carraccis' work, to which he attributes the great merit of having given life to "a historical novel imagined on the great previous painting" and thus having kept alive the Italian figurative civilization "through the two most dangerous centuries for the national principle."[39] Longhi then rushes through the seventeenth and eighteenth centuries to conclude his lecture with an unexpected tribute to Giorgio Morandi, which causes bewilderment among the audience.

Not only did Longhi proceed to a radical revision of some moments of the Bolognese painting, which thus came out fully transformed, but, in getting into the chair, he managed to contextualize it into the broader context of national events, according to a model of history as the safeguard of civil traditions that Benedetto Croce had taken up from Francesco De Sanctis.[40]

With the final reference to the great Bolognese master who directed his navigation "to the most perilous shoals of modern painting" with "thoughtful slowness" and "affectionate studiousness," Longhi opened a dialogue with that part of the city culture that had hitherto remained at the margins of officialdom. As Riccardo Bacchelli and Giuseppe Raimondi before him, Longhi had found in Morandi's work a parallel of his intellectual and existential path, from his youthful adhesion to Futurism to the construction of a tradition.

Soon a younger generation of intellectuals passionate about Pascoli, Cardarelli, Montale, and Ungaretti's poetry gathered around Longhi. They were more interested in literature than in art history and after the war they became the protagonists of Bologna's—and not only—cultural life. Among them were Attilio Bertolucci, Giorgio Bassani, Lanfranco Caretti, Franco Giovannelli, Augusto Frassineti, Ezio Raimondi, and Pier Paolo Pasolini.[41] Others, such as Francesco Arcangeli and Alberto Graziani, Longhi's first two great pupils, would make art history their main field of interest following their master's example. Graziani died shortly afterwards at the age of twenty-six, leaving illuminating studies on Bartolomeo Cesi and the fourteenth-century masters of Figline and the Osservanza. Arcangeli later oriented his entire critical trajectory on the line of Po Valley naturalism identified by Longhi in his famous speech: from the dissertation on the fourteenth century to the studies on the Carraccis, Bastianino, and Morandi; he even

38 Longhi 1935 ed. 1973, p. 191.
39 Ibid., p. 200.
40 Trento and Riccardi Scassellati 1988, p. 247.
41 On the literary legacy of Longhi's teaching: Lipparini 1992, pp. 65–74; Bazzocchi 2013, pp. 313–35.

ventured beyond the boundaries traced by his master and in the domain of romantic painting and Art Informel.

Longhi dedicated his first three university courses (1934–37, the only years he lived in Bologna) to local painting of the fourteenth and early fifteenth centuries within the context of the figurative culture of the Po Valley. Then he temporarily moved to Rome, where he was commanded to the Directorate General for Antiquities and Fine Arts (1937–39).[42] His interest for this subject, however, had begun in 1930 with the disputed attribution of the famous frescoes of the Camposanto of Pisa to Vitale, had had a first occasional effect on the city in 1932 with the drafting of records on some paintings of the Civic Museum, and later found its crowning expression in the exhibition on fourteenth-century Bolognese painting held in 1950, a sort of farewell to the city when the great scholar had just moved to Florence.[43]

Longhi's innovative directions gave a cue for the Carracci exhibition curated by Cesare Gnudi in 1956, which gave Arcangeli the opportunity to assign to Ludovico instead of Annibale, in disagreement with Longhi, the role of pacesetter in the search for truth of light that belonged also to Caravaggio.[44] If we consider also Longhi's contribution in the catalogue of the 1935 exhibition on eighteenth-century Bolognese art, for which he wrote the artists' biographies, and the curatorship of the 1948 monographic exhibition on Giuseppe Maria Crespi, we will notice that the new address the great critic gave the studies paradoxically confirmed interest in the late Middle Ages and the Baroque era which were already privileged in the city at the time of Supino and Malaguzzi Valeri.

It was necessary to wait for the 1958 essay on the *Tre vetrate ferraresi* by Carlo Volpe, Longhi's last great Bolognese pupil, for a revived attention to the Renaissance in the city, and for identifying its specific physiognomy.[45] Volpe starts from Longhi's belief, confirmed in the *Officina* and in the 1934 speech, that Marco Zoppo was not a follower but a parallel of Tura. Just like him, he was a pupil at Squarcione's school but much more sensitive than Ferrarese painters to the teaching of Piero.[46] He later followed the faint traces of "those brightly Renaissance tendencies that, after the beginning of the Belfiore *studiolo*, led

---

42 The topics of his courses were the following: "Fourteenth-century painting in Northern Italy" (1934–35), "The decline of medieval painting in Northern Italy" (1935–36); "Persistence of medieval currents in fifteenth-century painting" (1936–37). During the last academic year, Longhi also taught the Aesthetics course focused on "Contemporary aesthetic theories in their relationship with figurative art." After the period spent in Rome, and once he moved to Florence in the villa called "Il Tasso," which still houses the Foundation named after him, Longhi taught the following courses: "Caravaggio and the Caravaggesque painters" (1939–40 and 1940–41), "Facts about Masaccio and Masolino" (1941–42, taken from the essay published in 1941), "Late masters of the early fifteenth century in Tuscany" (1942–43). In 1943–45 he was suspended from teaching for not having joined the Italian Social Republic. After the war, his courses focused on Venetian painting: "From the fourteenth century to Giambellino" (1945–46), "From Giambellino to Carpaccio" (1946–47), "Giambellino followers and the beginnings of Lotto" (1947–48). On November 1, 1949 he moved to the University of Florence (Lipparini 1992, pp. 64, 67, 73, and 75).

43 Bolognese painting of the fourteenth century was the central topic of Longhi's studies in the first half of the 1930s. The preface to the catalogue of the 1950 exhibition was republished together with the text of the conference on the frescoes of the Camposanto of Pisa, the 1934 prolusion, and the lecture notes of the first two Bolognese university courses in the first section of the sixth volume of his complete works (Longhi 1973, pp. 3–226). The three short datasheets of the paintings of Barnaba da Modena, Jacopo di Paolo, and Cristoforo Moretti were published by Francesco Filippini in "La collezione dei quadri del Museo civico di Bologna," in *Il Comune di Bologna*, no. 4 (1932): 12–13, 22–25, and 31–32 (later distributed as a separate booklet as well). Filippini recalls when, arranging some small paintings of the fifteenth and sixteenth centuries in the last room of the Bologna Museo Civico, he accidentally met Longhi and received valuable information about the works from him. For the chronology of Longhi's writings when teaching in Bologna: Boschetto 1973, pp. 48–53.

44 For the critical context of the exhibition, see Raimondi 2002.

45 Volpe 1958 ed. 1993.

46 Longhi 1935 ed. 1973, p. 194.

10

Roberto Longhi, sketch of the Griffoni Polyptych's frame and *capsa*, c. 1937–38, ink on paper, 230 × 291 mm; on the right half of the sheet he glued a photograph of Ercole de' Roberti's *Saint George* now at the Cini Foundation, Venice; on the reverse, handwritten: "Coll. Of the Earl of Rosebery/ "St. George – by Andrea Mantegna/ 9 × 3 ½ inch. (22.5 × 8.5)/ Exhib. to the winter Exhib./ at the Burl. F. A. Club, 1937 Jan" (Fondazione di Studi di Storia dell'Arte Roberto Longhi, Florence, Photo archive, inv. 0600109)

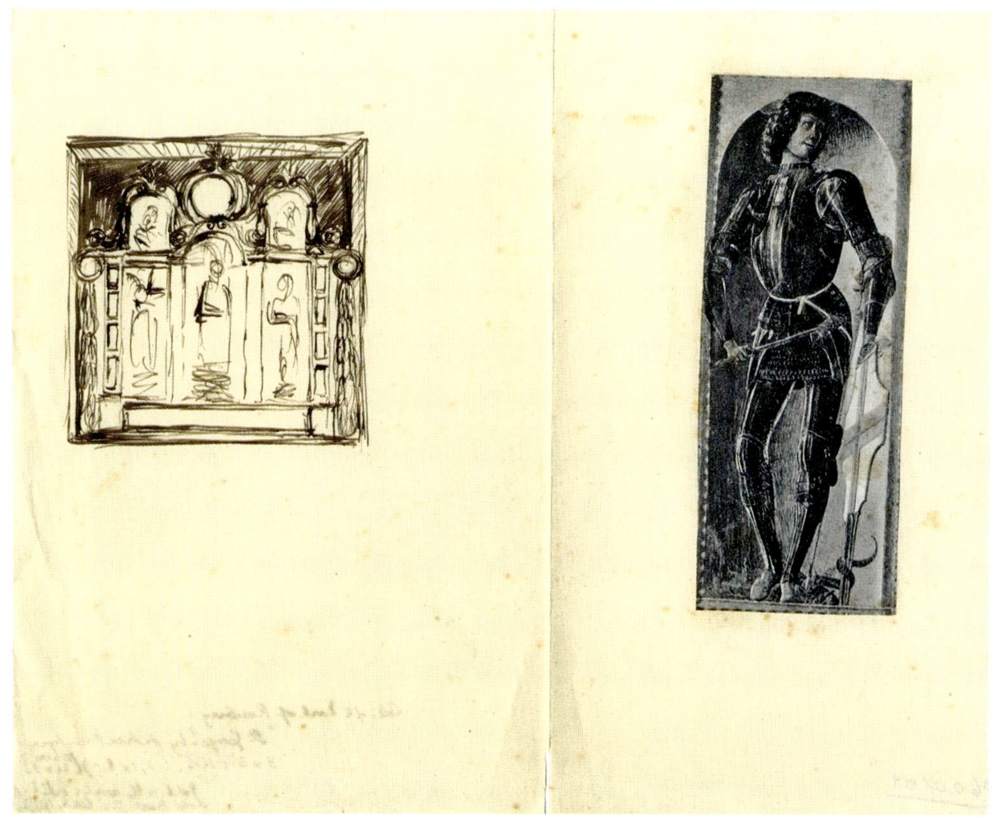

the novelties of Piero and Alberti to fructify elsewhere, between Modena, Bologna, and Romagna, almost banished from Ferrara by Tura's beaked and thorny cart." The scholar therefore identifies the original characters of the Bolognese Renaissance in the superior "dignity of architectural syntax" achieved here by Cossa and de' Roberti, while the grumpy naturalism of the former is read in terms of a distinctive opposition between the "rough peasant lineage of Saints Petronius and John" in the 1474 "Pala dei Mercanti" and "the cultivated and hypocrite humanity of Borso's courtiers" at Palazzo Schifanoia.[47] With the fresco decoration of the Garganelli Chapel in Saint Peter's, the two artists would have produced the very masterpiece—unfortunately lost—of that "culture originated in Ferrara but of Bolognese inclination" that had indeed started with the Griffoni Polyptych.

To conclude, returning to the central topic of this volume, one cannot fail to notice that in Volpe's seminal essay the Griffoni Polyptych, which actually gave rise to the collaboration between the two great Ferrarese painters in the land of the Bentivoglio family, is almost absent, except for a fleeting mention of the Cossa *Crucifixion*. The Bolognese scholar, as Longhi before him, perhaps felt that on both artists—and on the young Ercole in particular—the memory of the common work on the scaffolding at Palazzo Schifanoia was prevailing on the inspiring force of the changed city context.[48] Paraphrasing Volpe himself, we still need to wonder to what extent it is appropriate, as regards the Petronian polyptych, to add the "Bolognese" attribute to the name of Ferrarese art.

47 Volpe 1958 ed. 1993, pp. 156–57. For a reinterpretation of Volpe's essay, see Benati 2012a.

48 See also Volpe 1961 ed. 1993, p. 137, where the formal definition of the polyptych draws on the pages Longhi dedicated to it in his *Officina*.

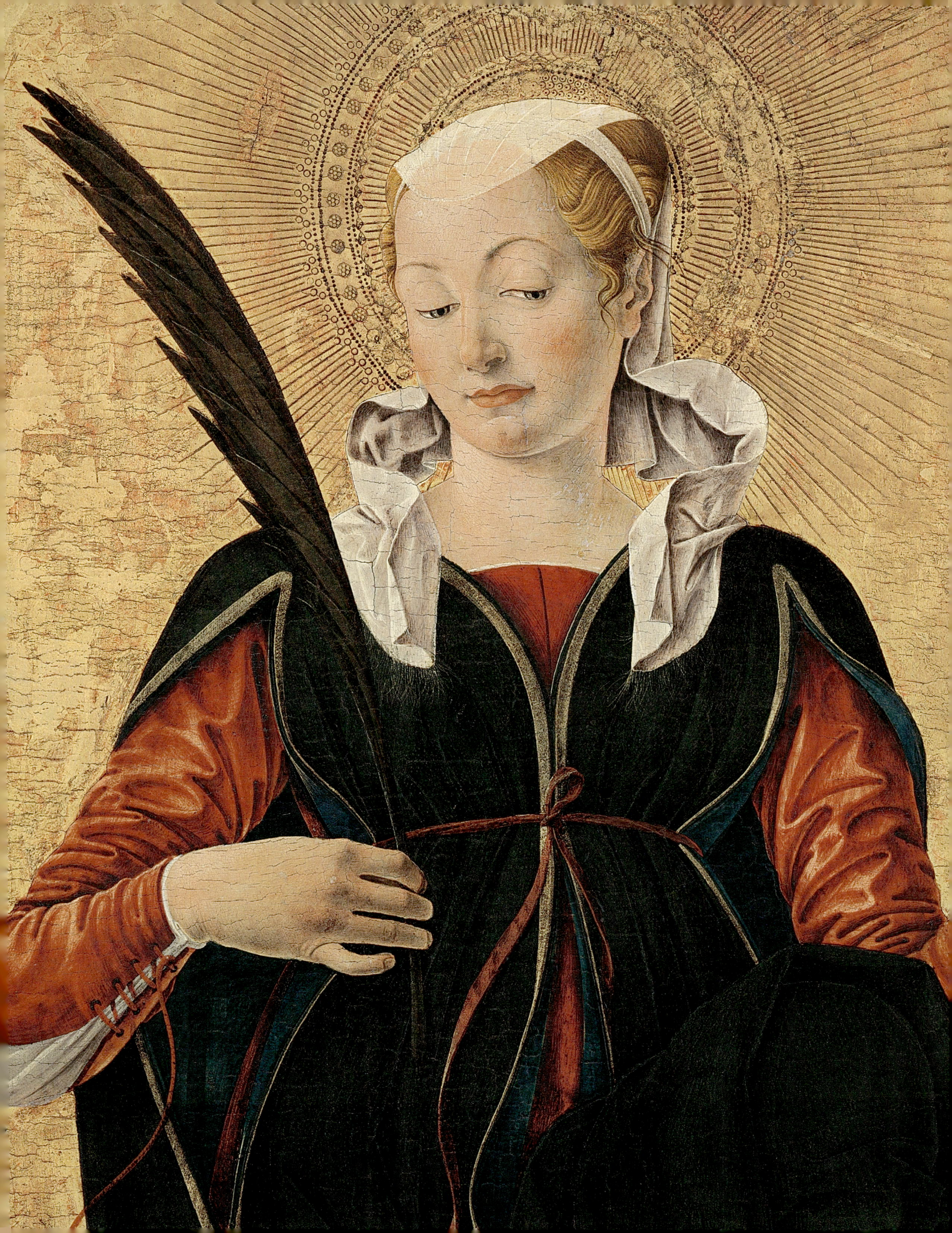

THE GRIFFONI POLYPTYCH

Francesco del Cossa
(Ferrara, c. 1436 – Bologna, 1478)

Ercole de' Roberti
(Ferrara, c. 1450–1496)

The Griffoni Polyptych

1470–1473

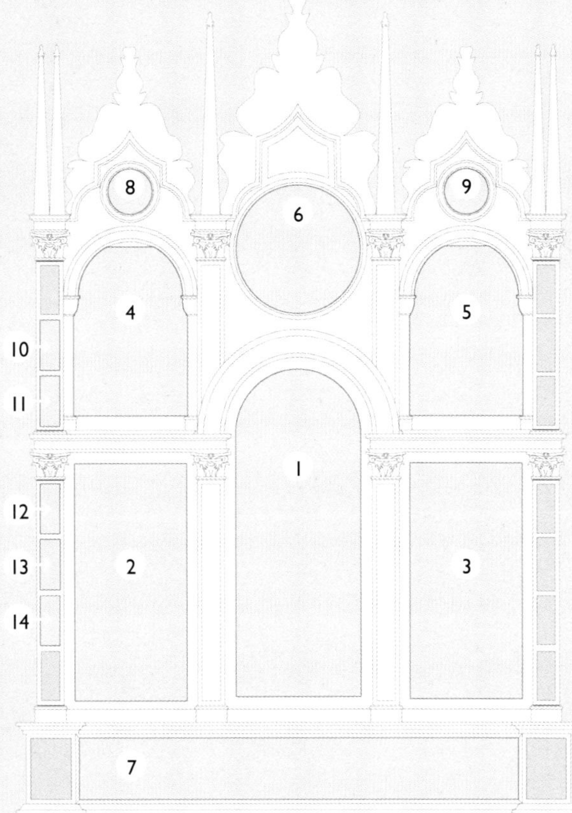

1. *Saint Vincent Ferrer* (Francesco del Cossa). The National Gallery, London
2. *Saint Peter* (Francesco del Cossa). Pinacoteca di Brera, Milan
3. *Saint John the Baptist* (Francesco del Cossa). Pinacoteca di Brera, Milan
4. *Saint Florian* (Francesco del Cossa). National Gallery of Art, Washington, DC
5. *Saint Lucy* (Francesco del Cossa). National Gallery of Art, Washington, DC
6. *Crucifixion* (Francesco del Cossa). National Gallery of Art, Washington, DC
7. *Miracles of Saint Vincent Ferrer* (Ercole de' Roberti). Vatican Museums, Vatican City
8. *Archangel Gabriel* (Ercole de' Roberti). Villa Gagnola, Fondazione Paolo VI, Gazzada (Varese)
9. *Virgin Annunciate* (Ercole de' Roberti). Villa Gagnola, Fondazione Paolo VI, Gazzada (Varese)
10. *Saint Apollonia* (Ercole de' Roberti). Musée du Louvre, Paris
11. *Saint George* (Ercole de' Roberti). Giorgio Cini Foundation, Palazzo Cini Gallery at San Vio, Venice
12. *Archangel Michael* (Ercole de' Roberti). Musée du Louvre, Paris
13. *Saint Anthony the Abbot* (Ercole de' Roberti). Museum Boijmans Van Beuningen, Rotterdam
14. *Saint Petronius* (Ercole de' Roberti). Pinacoteca Nazionale, Ferrara

---

15. *Saint Catherine of Alexandria* (Ercole de' Roberti). Giorgio Cini Foundation, Palazzo Cini Gallery at San Vio, Venice
16. *Saint Jerome* (Ercole de' Roberti). Giorgio Cini Foundation, Palazzo Cini Gallery at San Vio, Venice

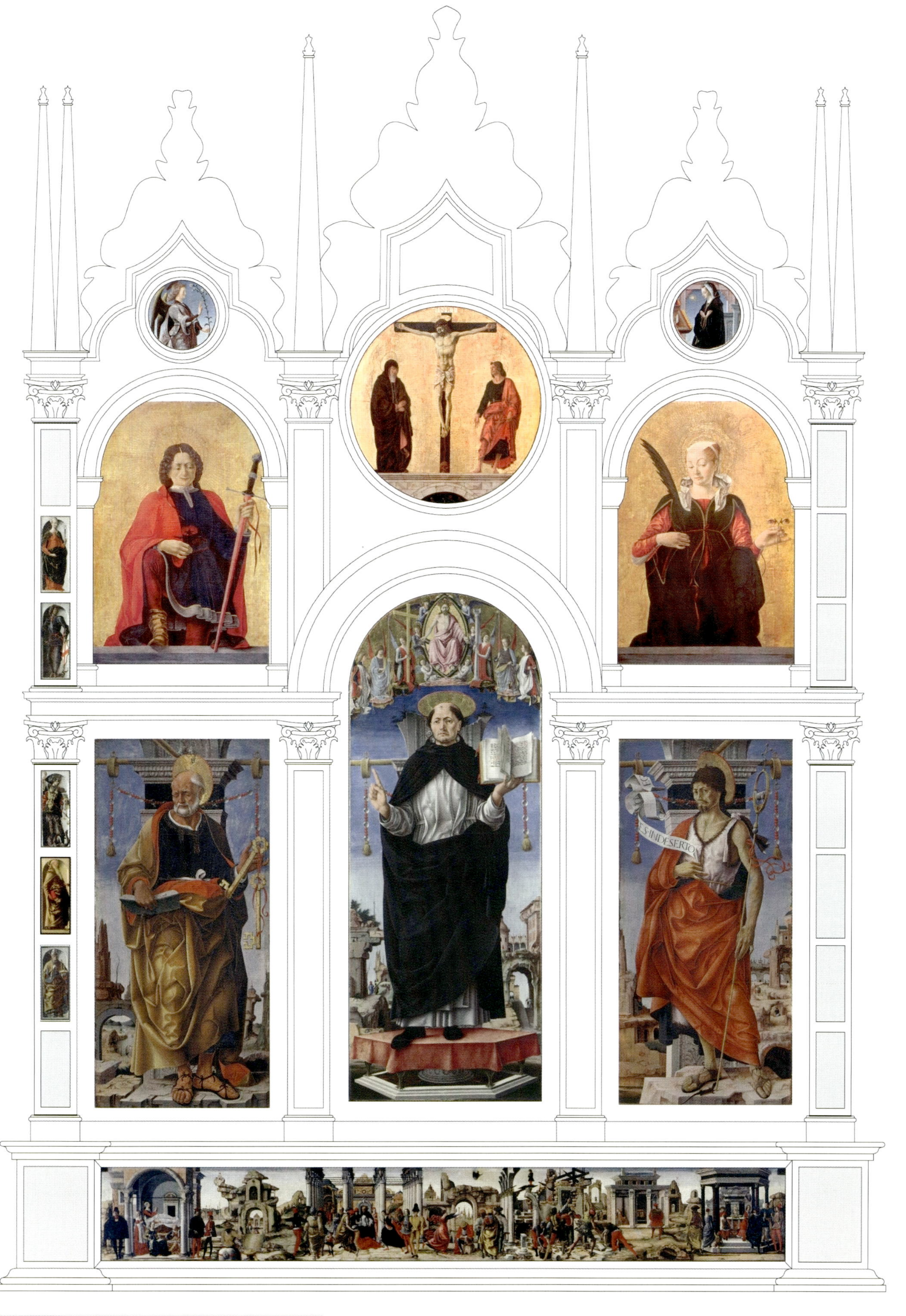
10 20 30 40 50 100

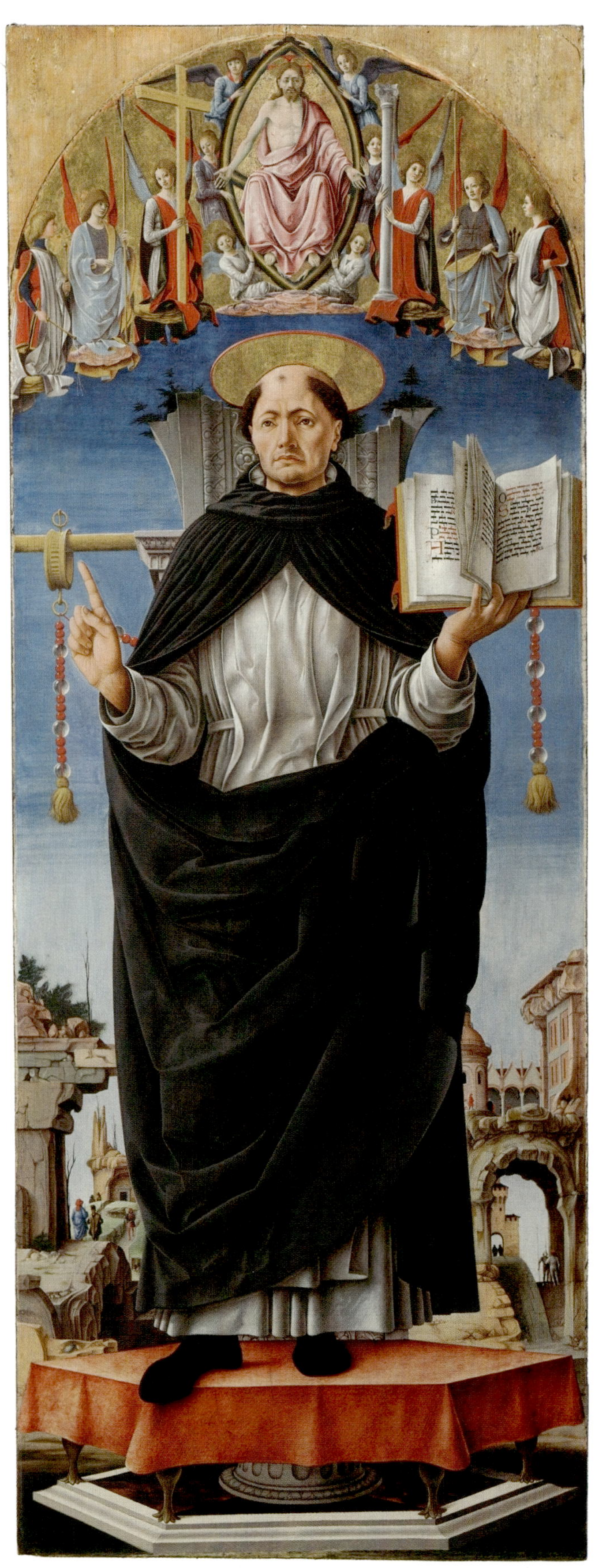

1

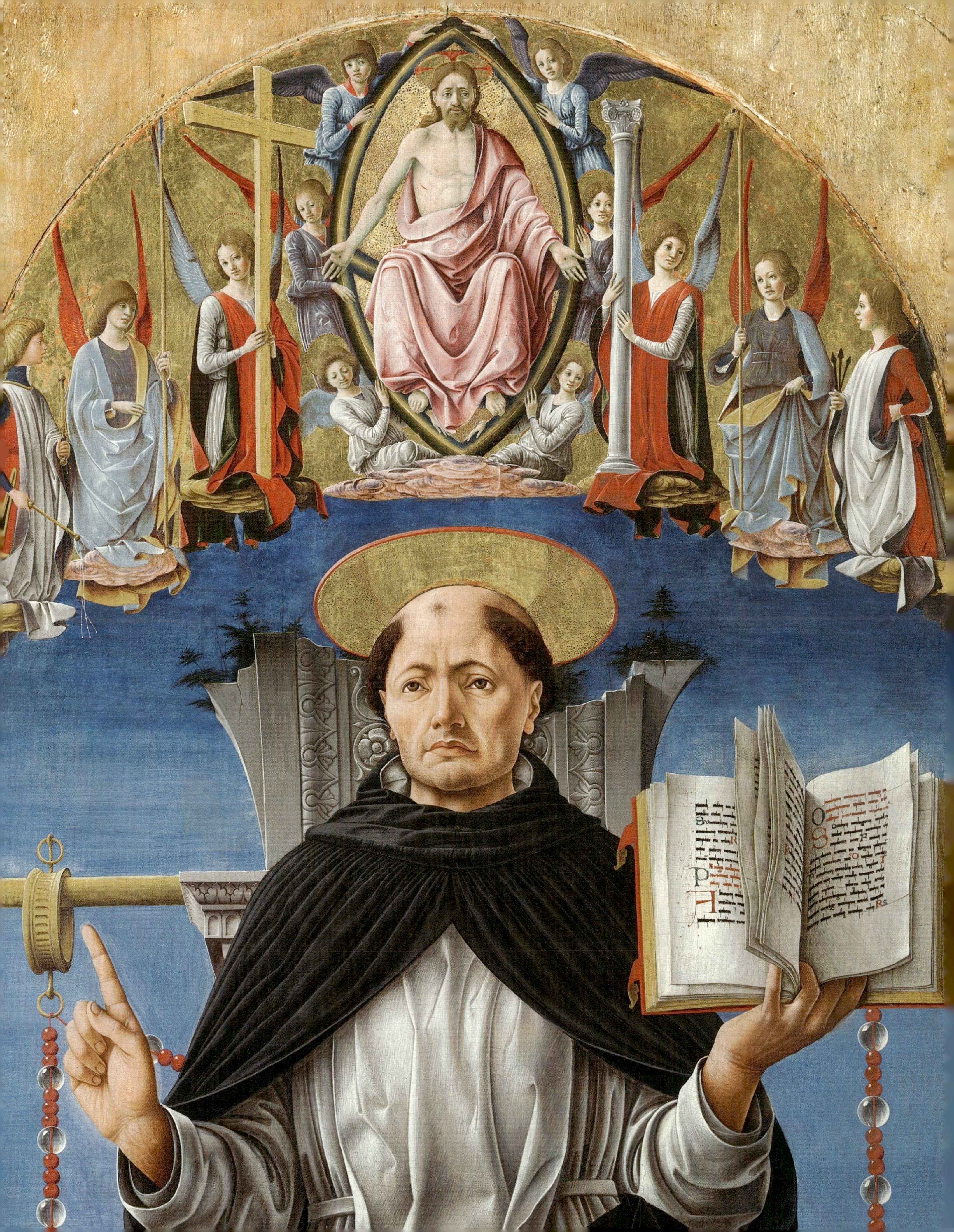

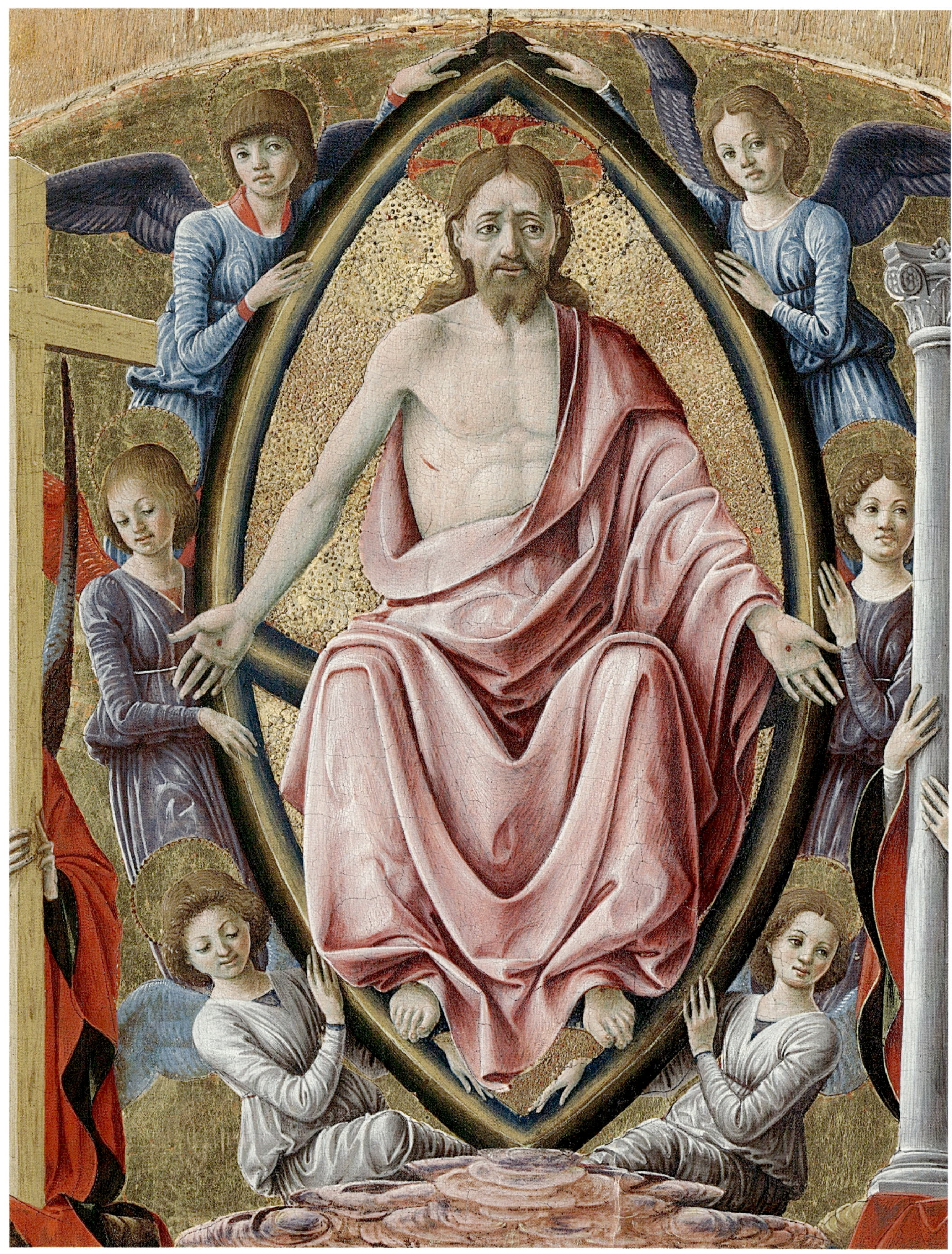

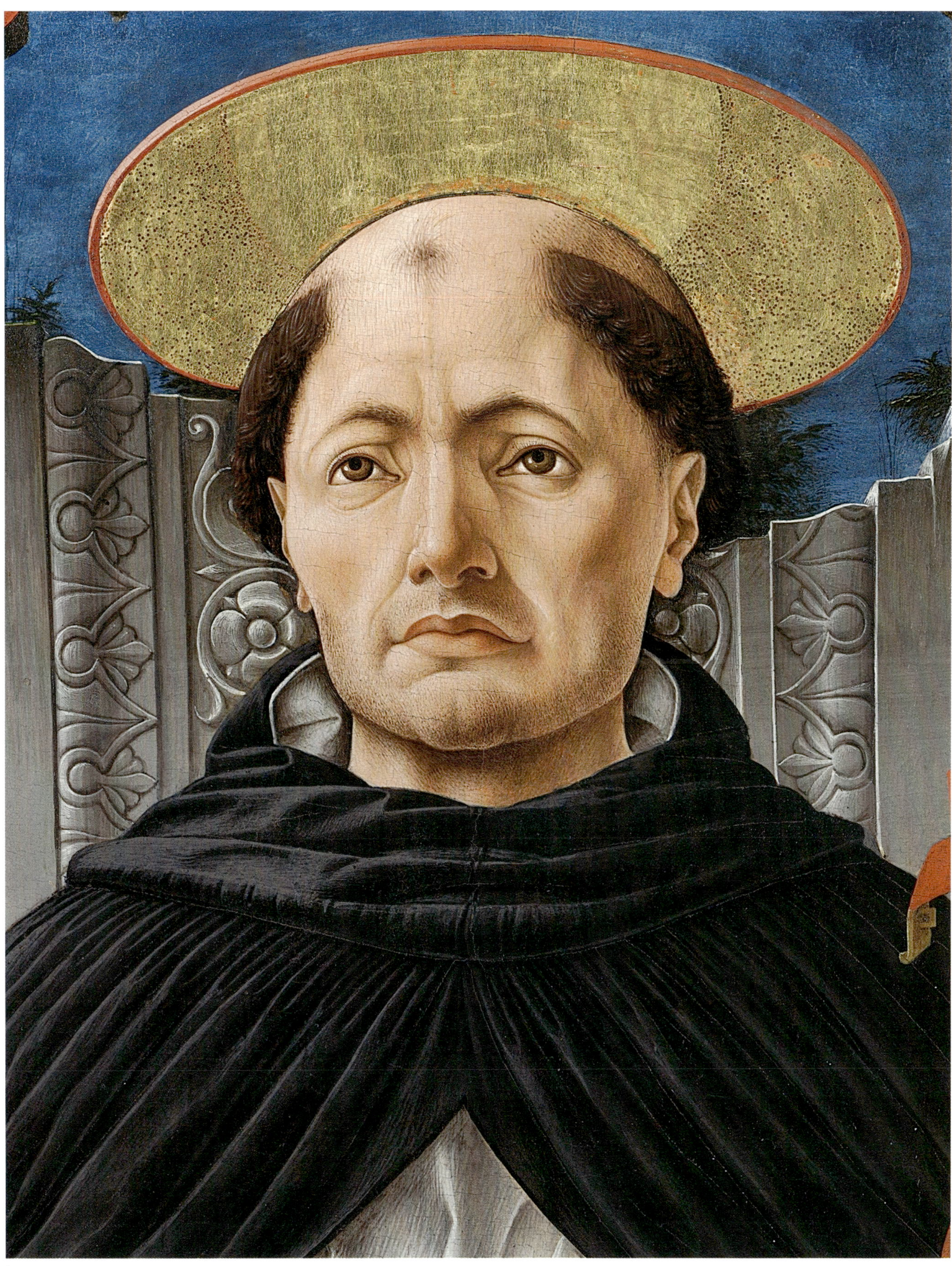

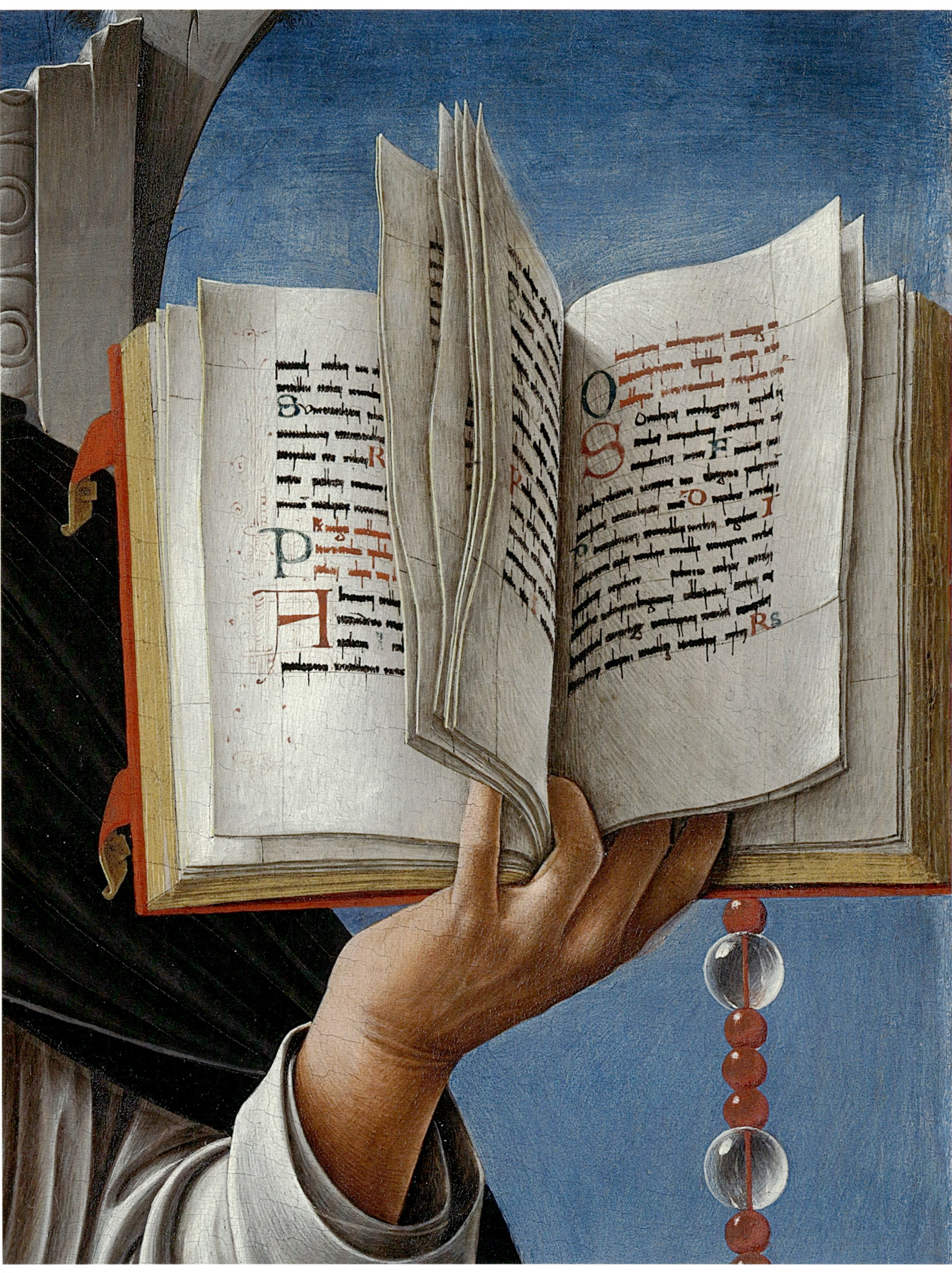

1

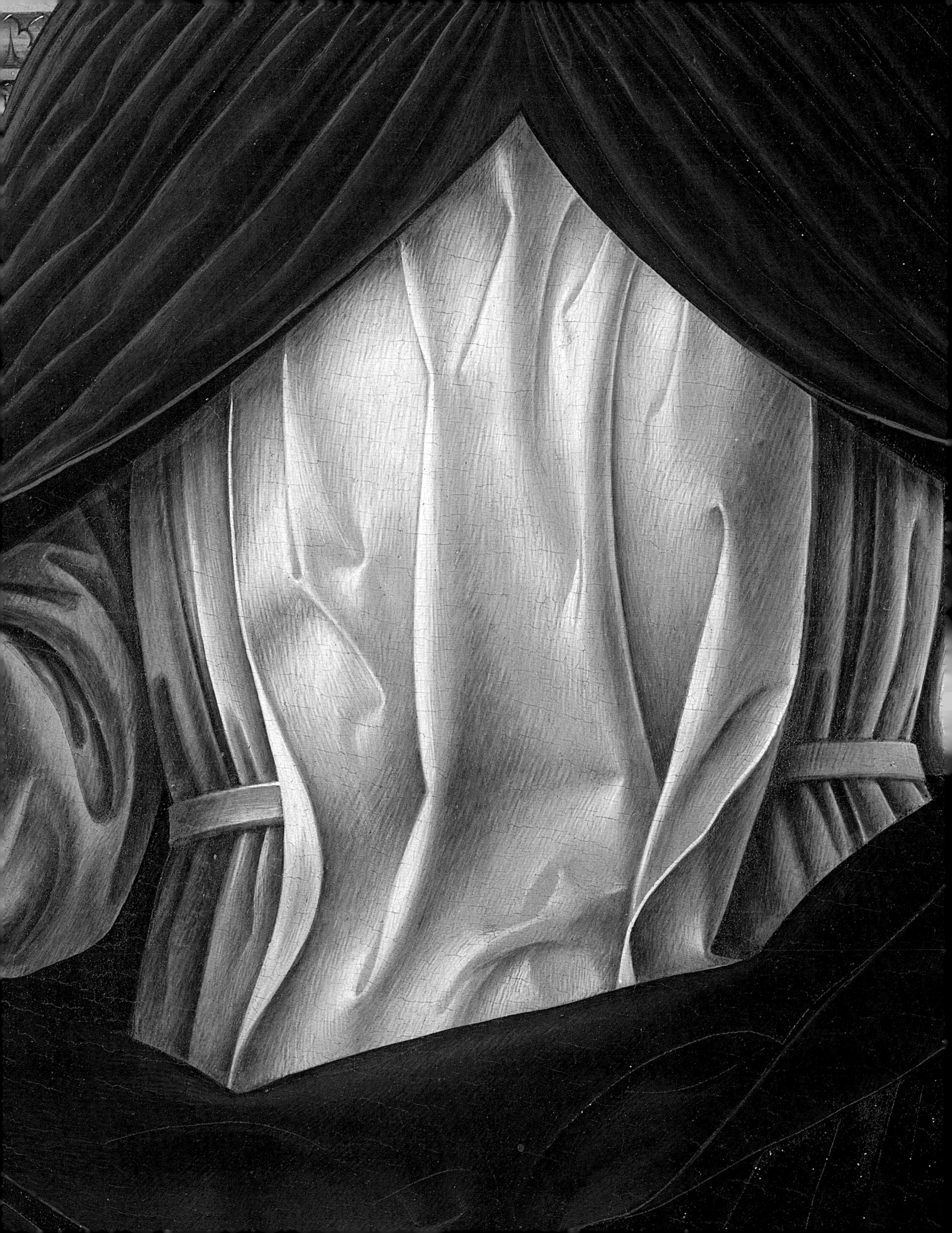

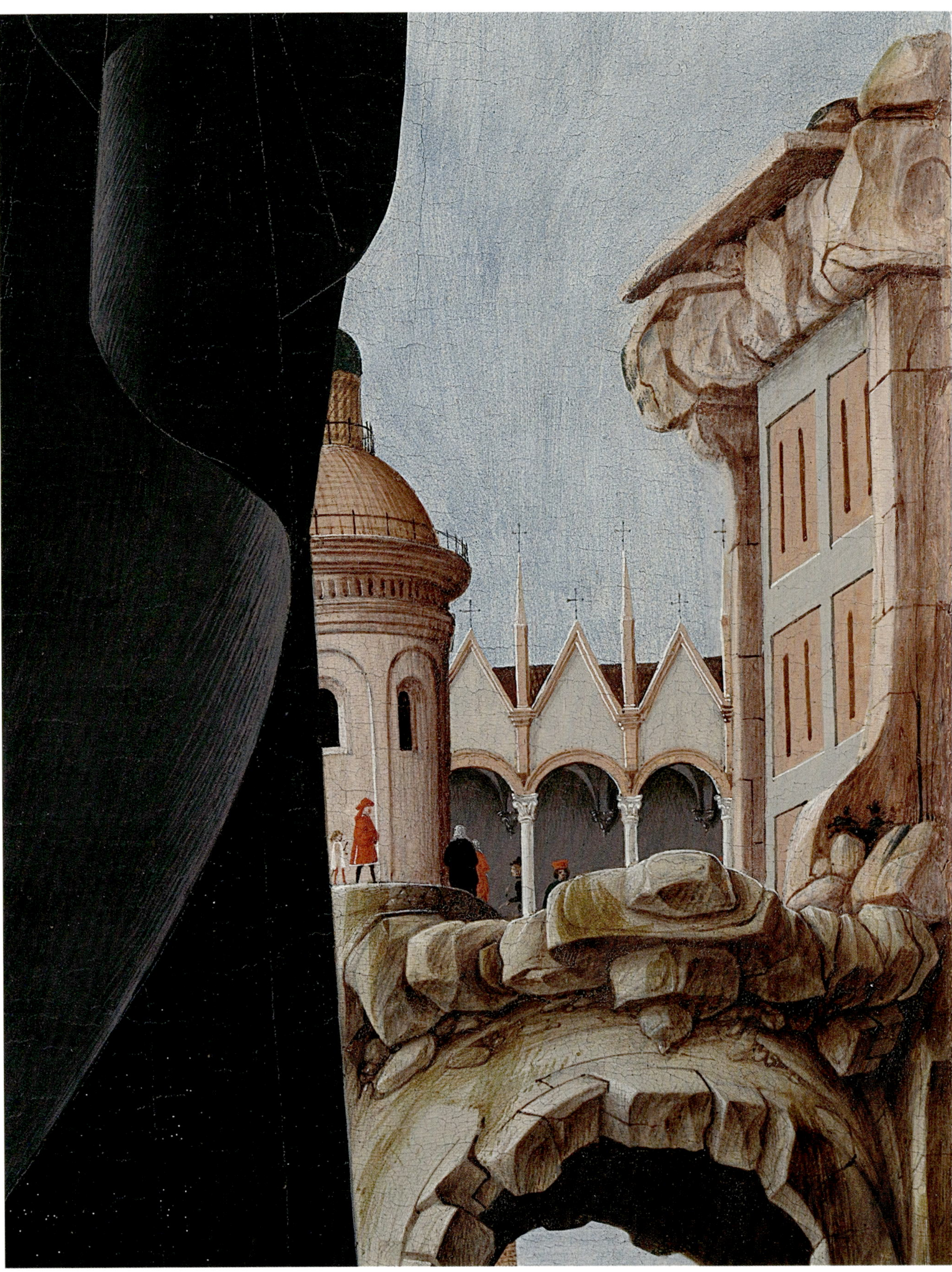

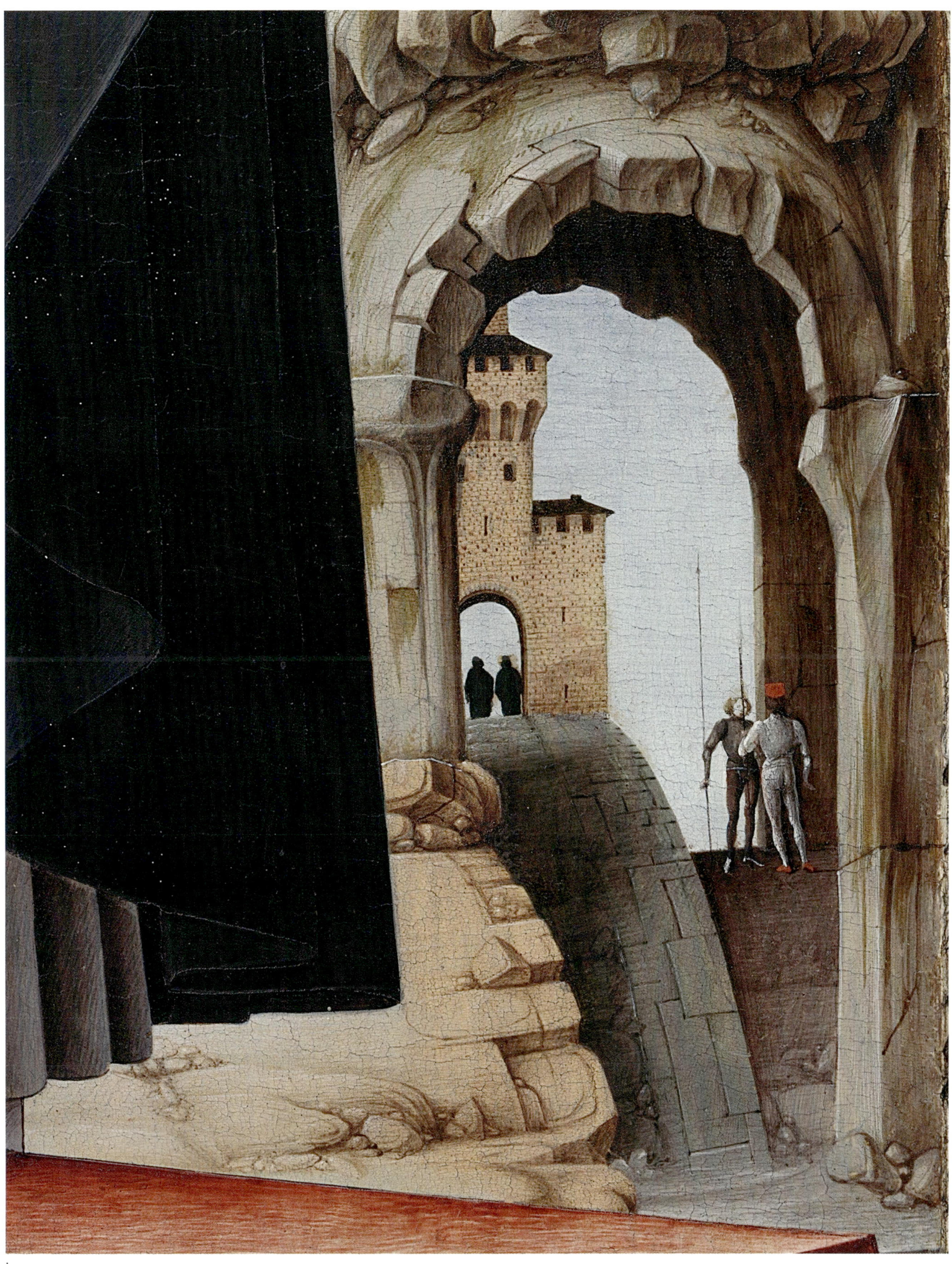

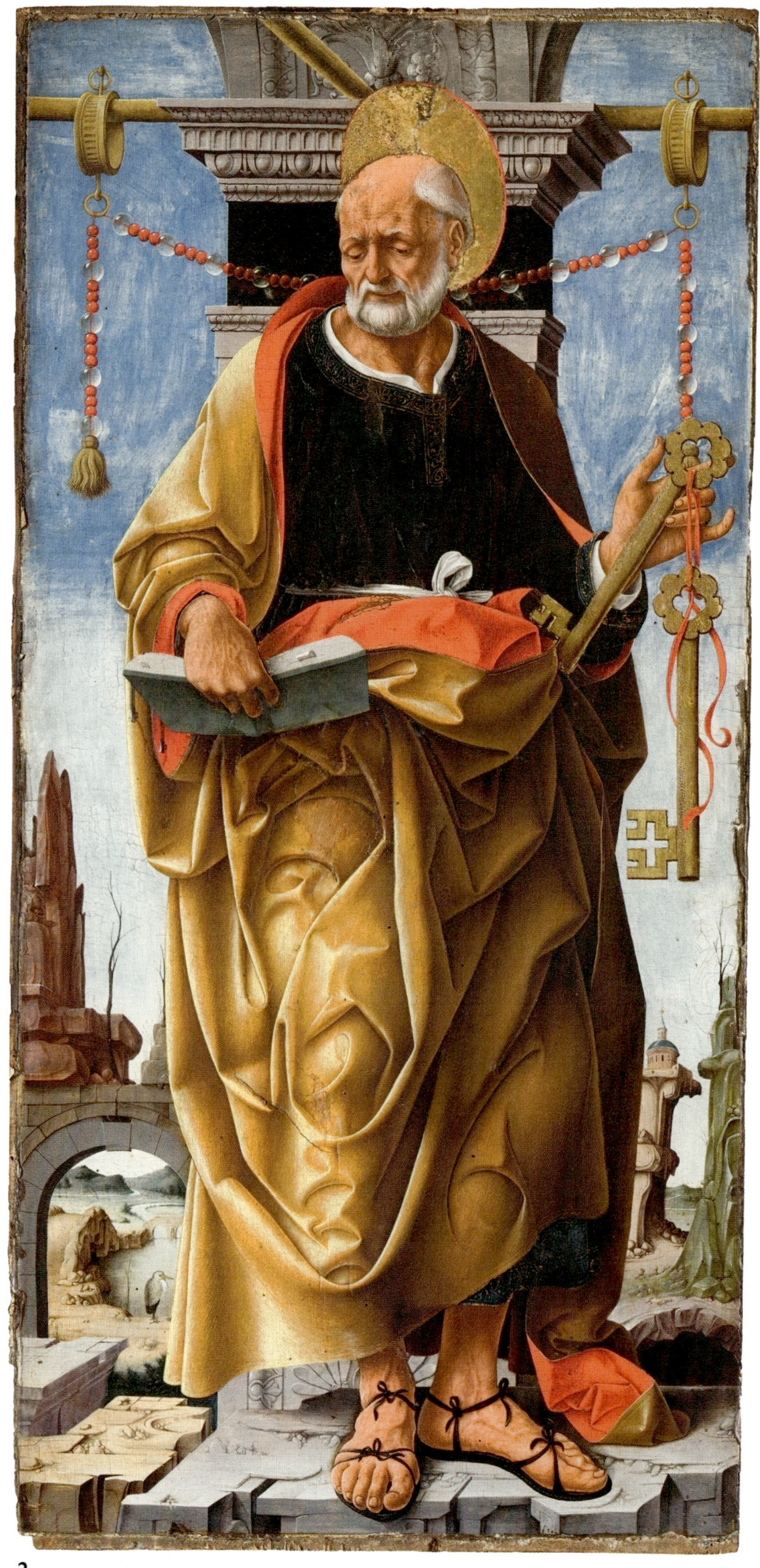

2

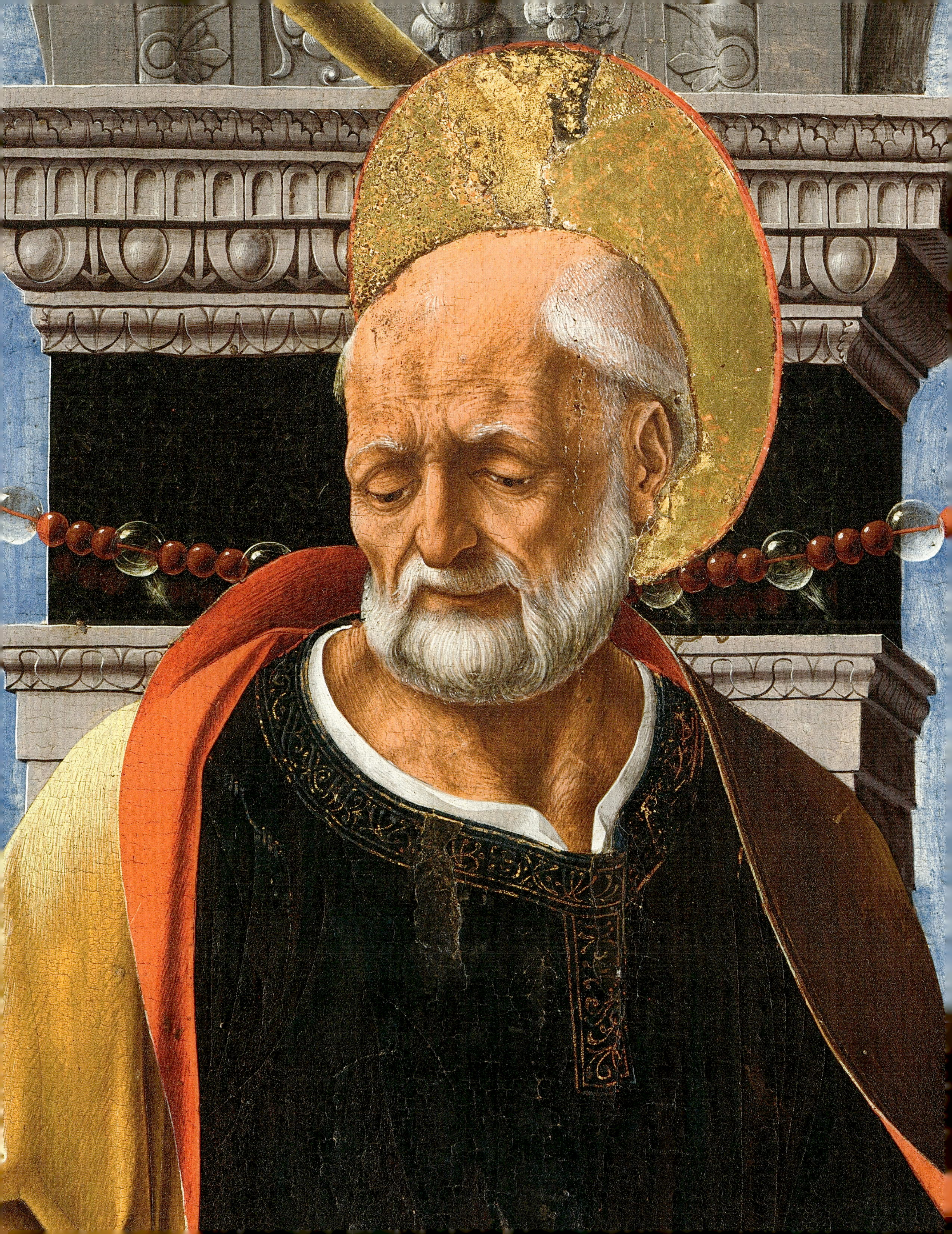

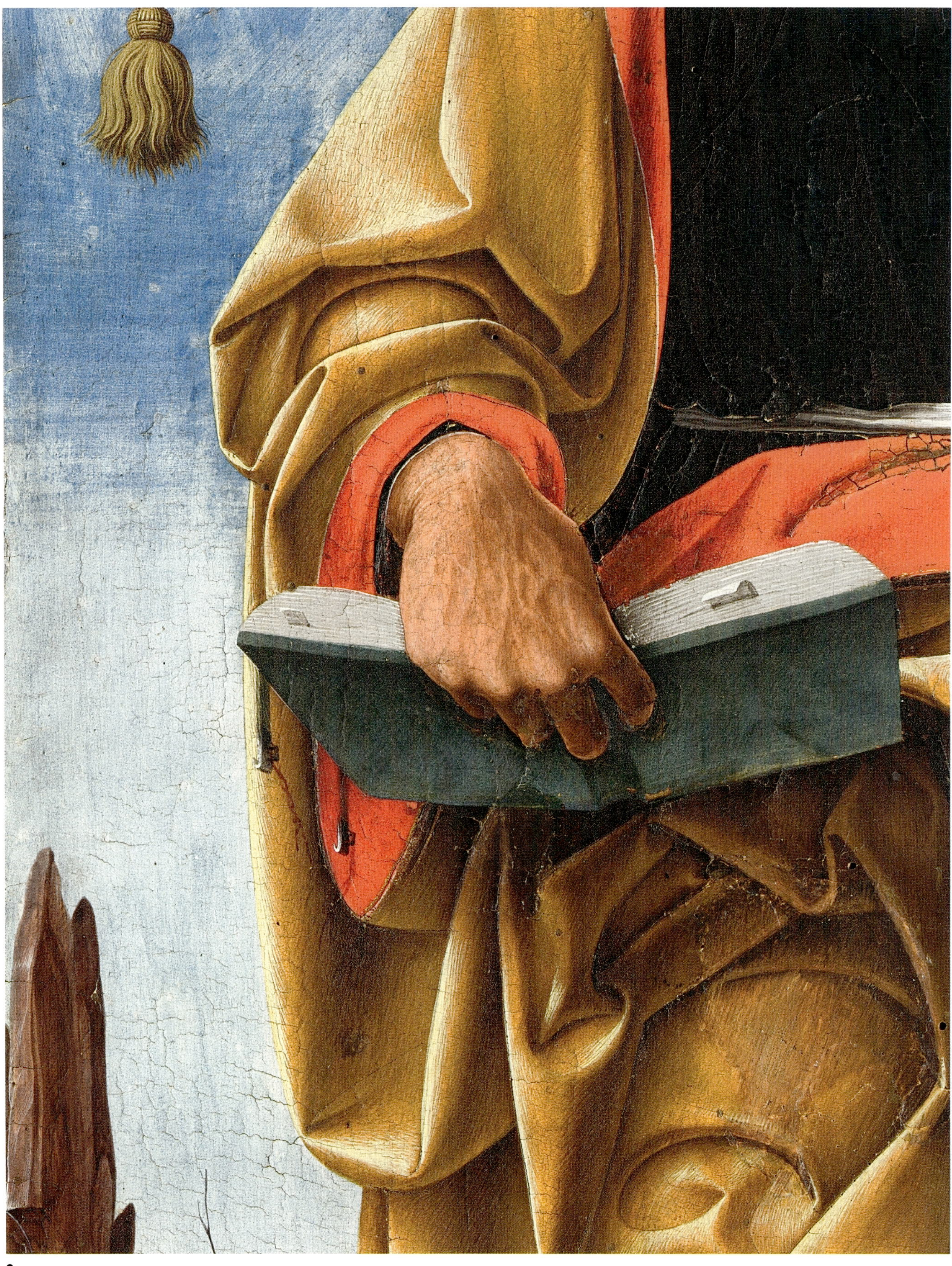

2

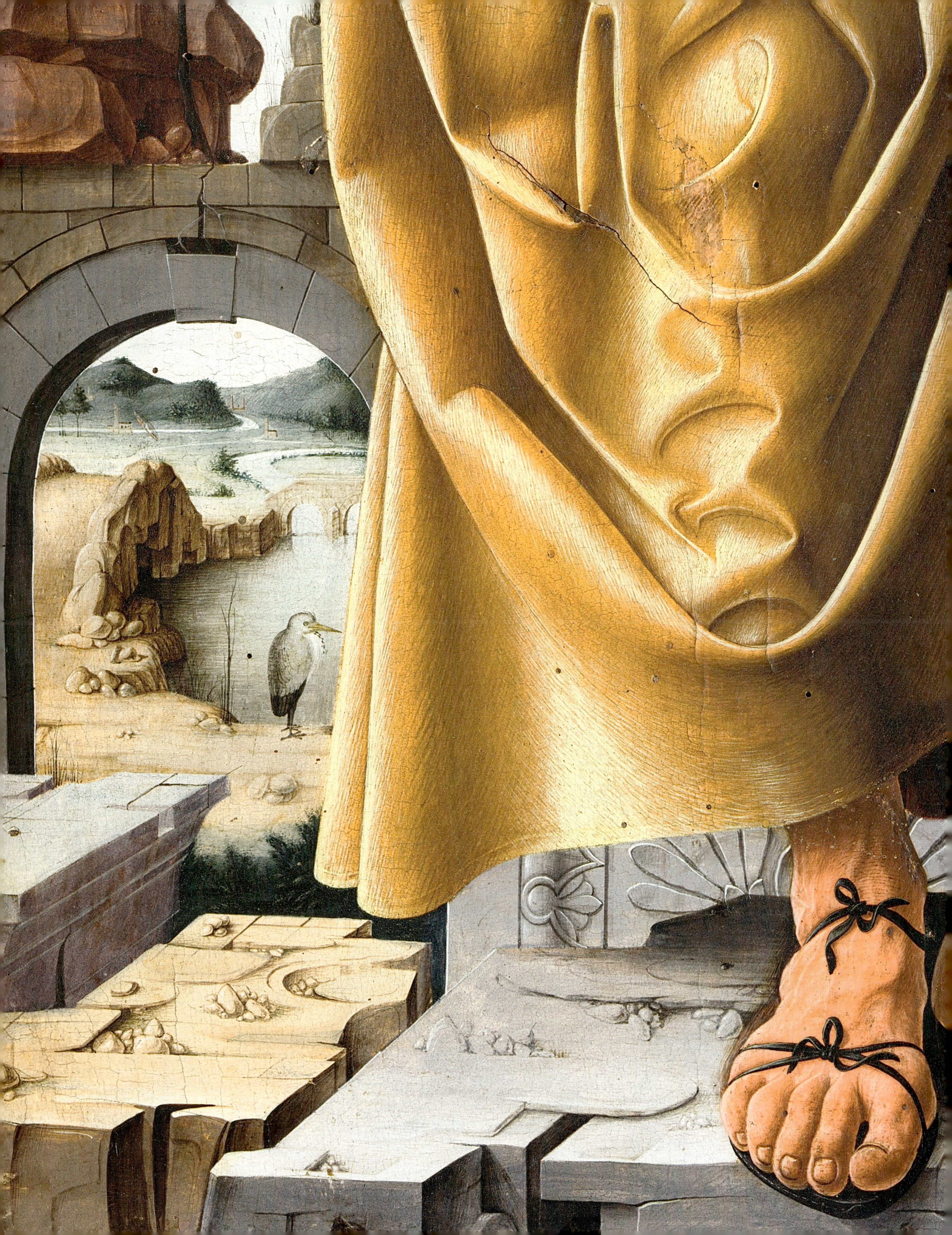

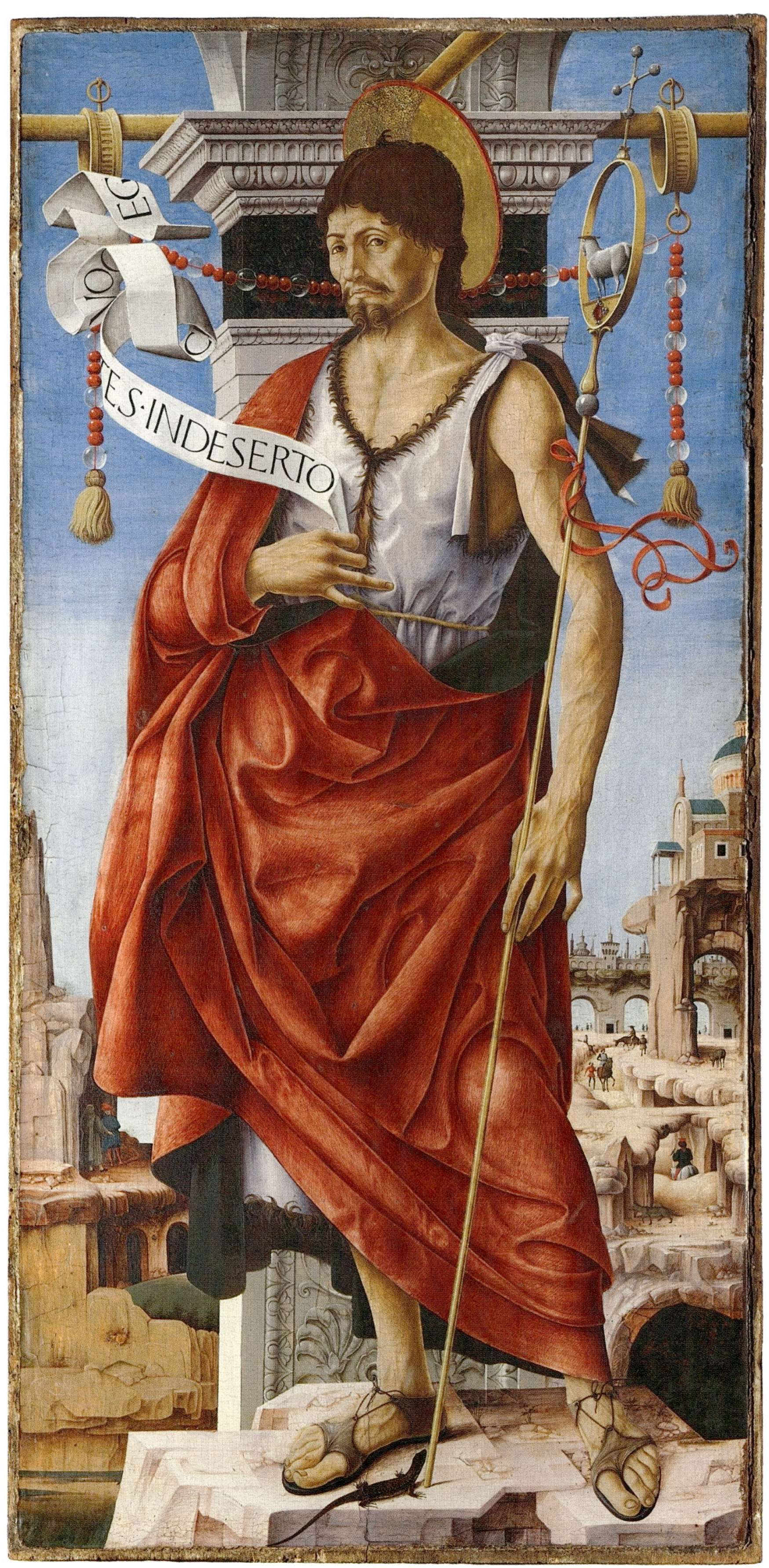

3

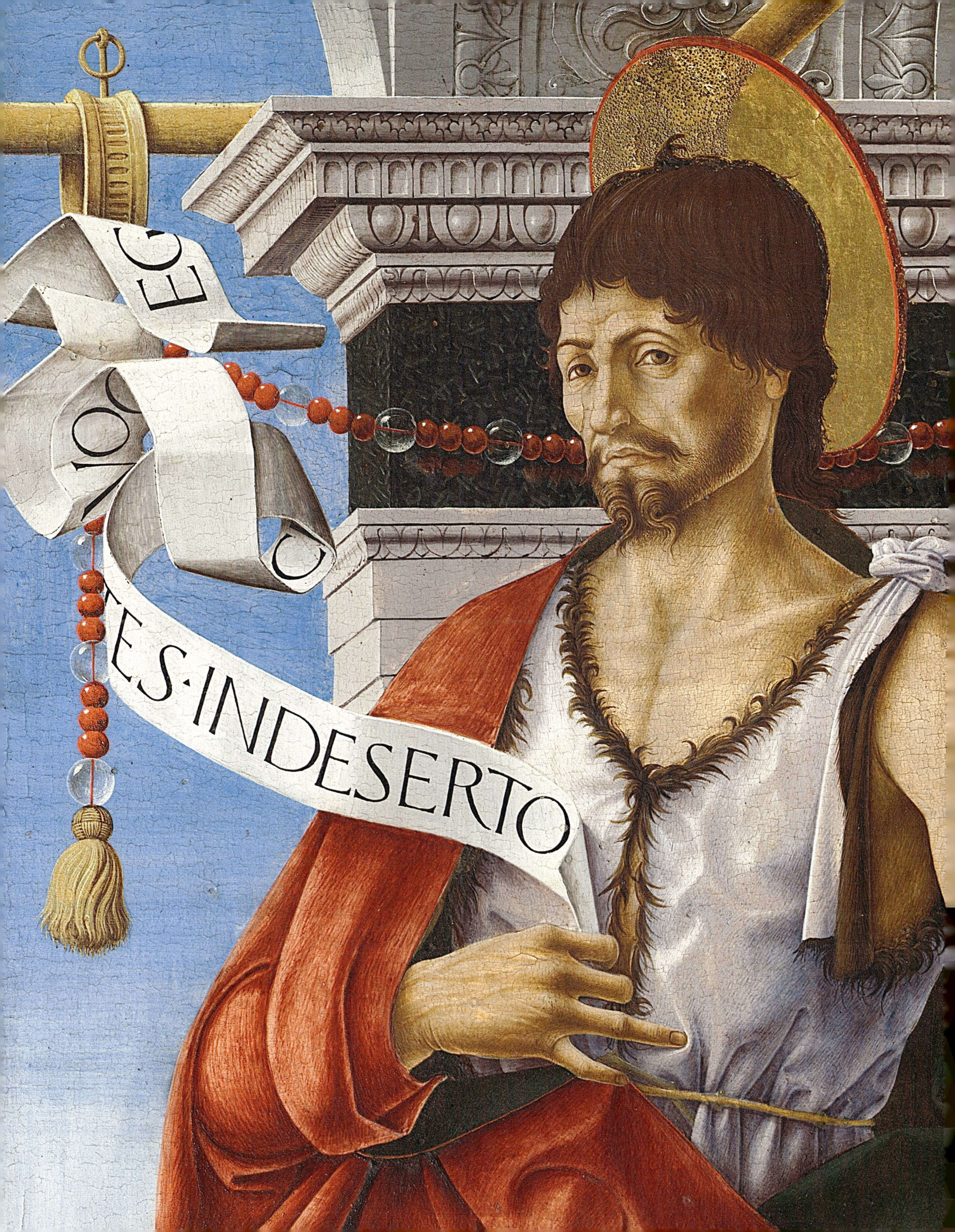
EG
TES·INDESERTO

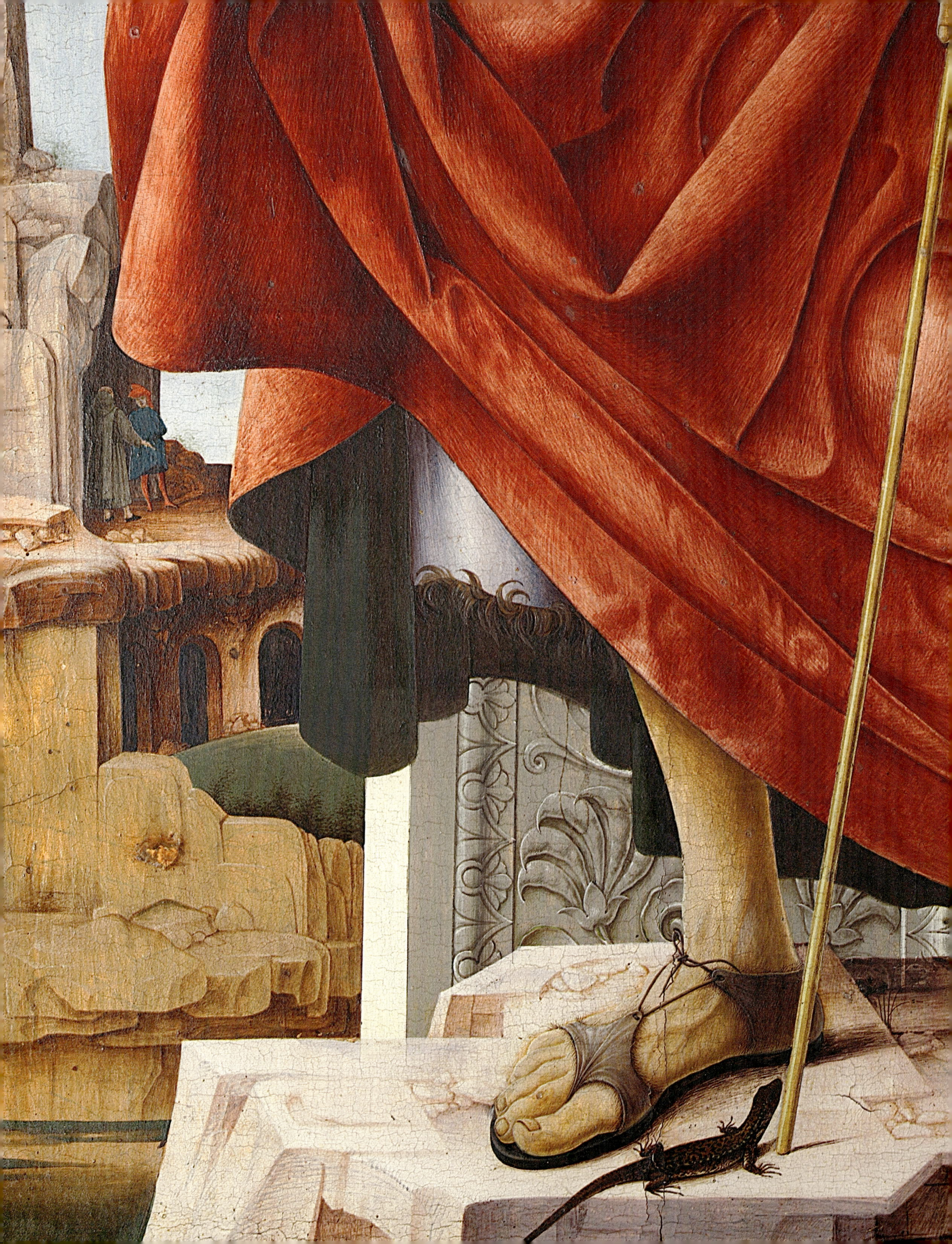

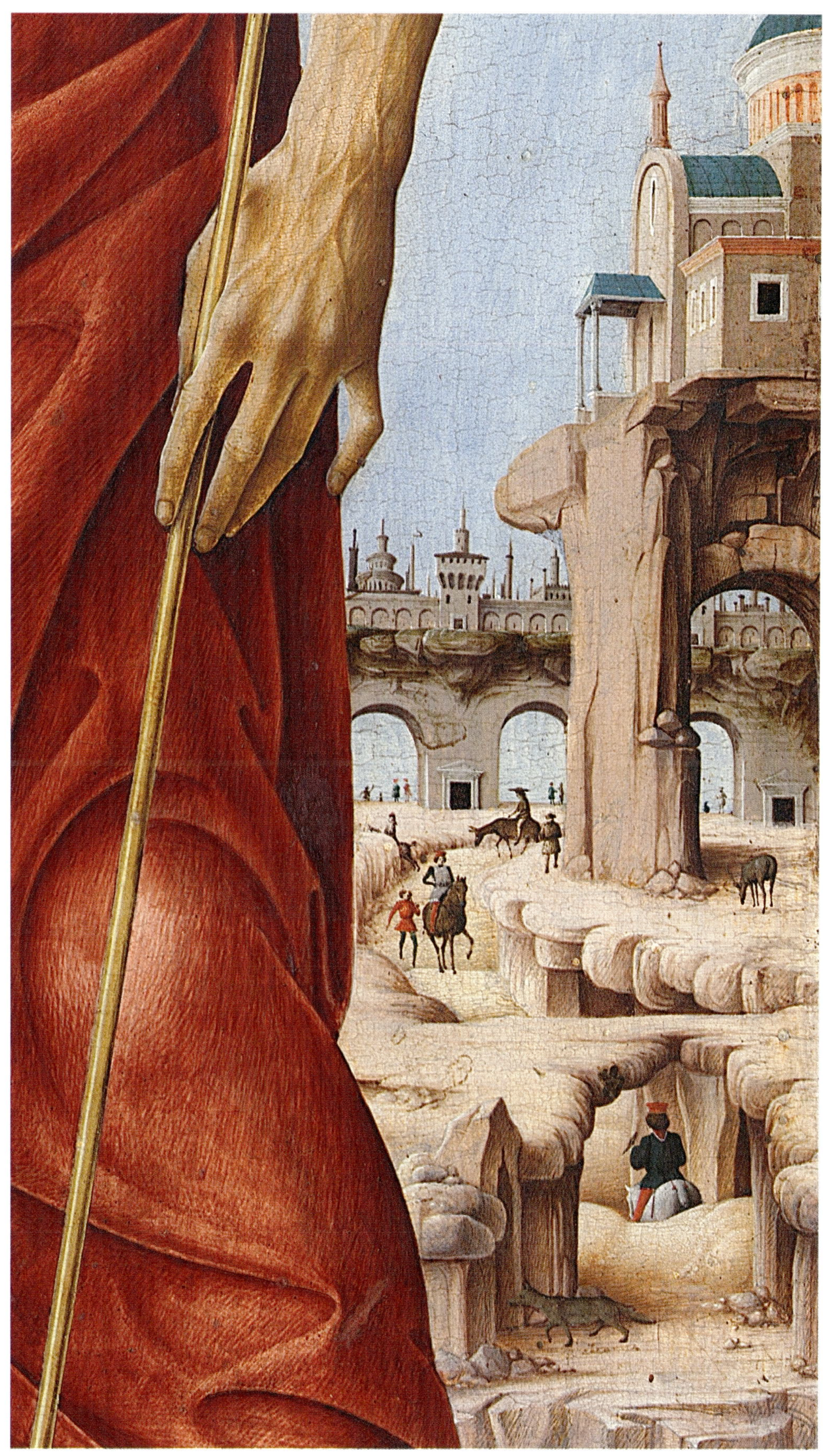

3

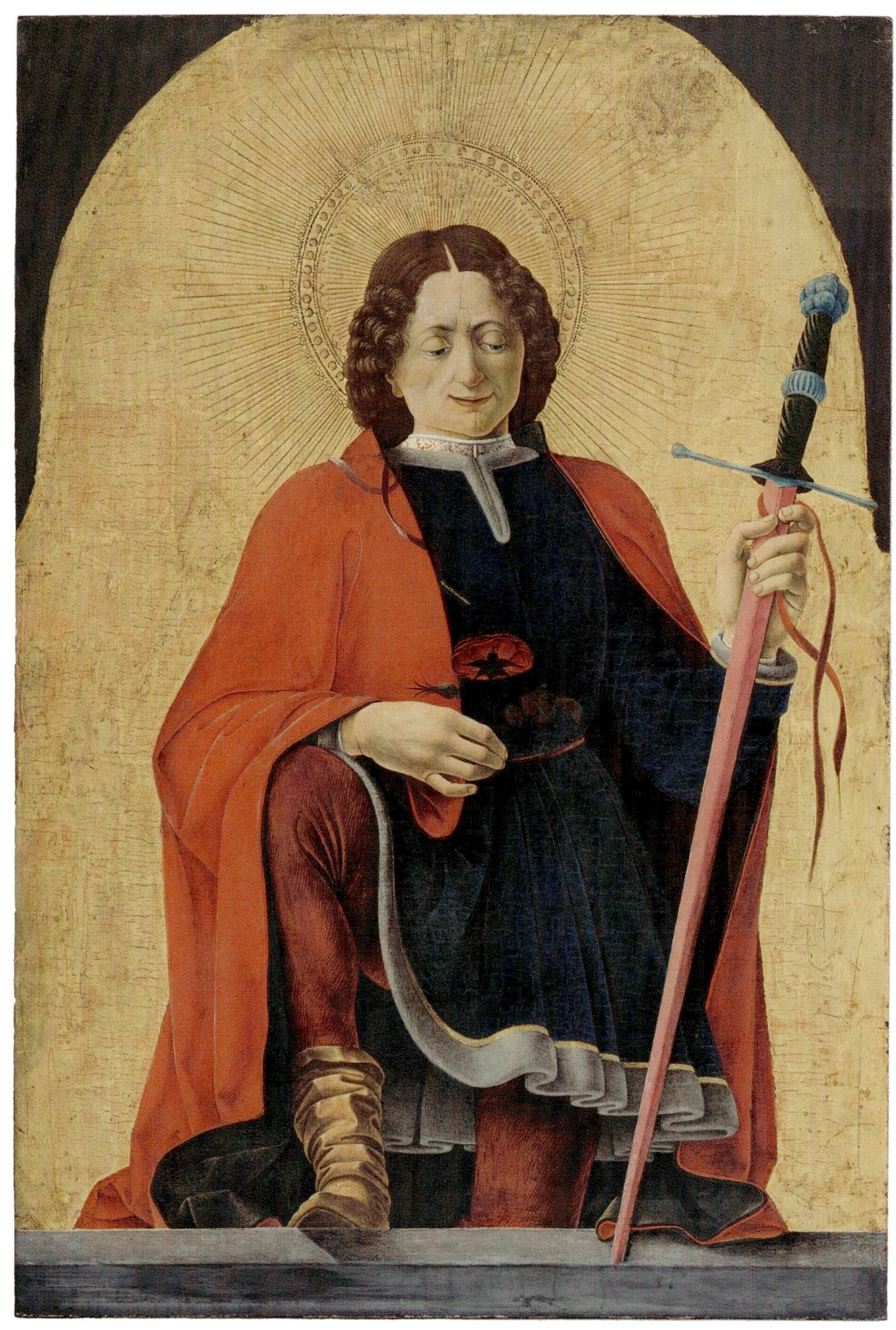

4

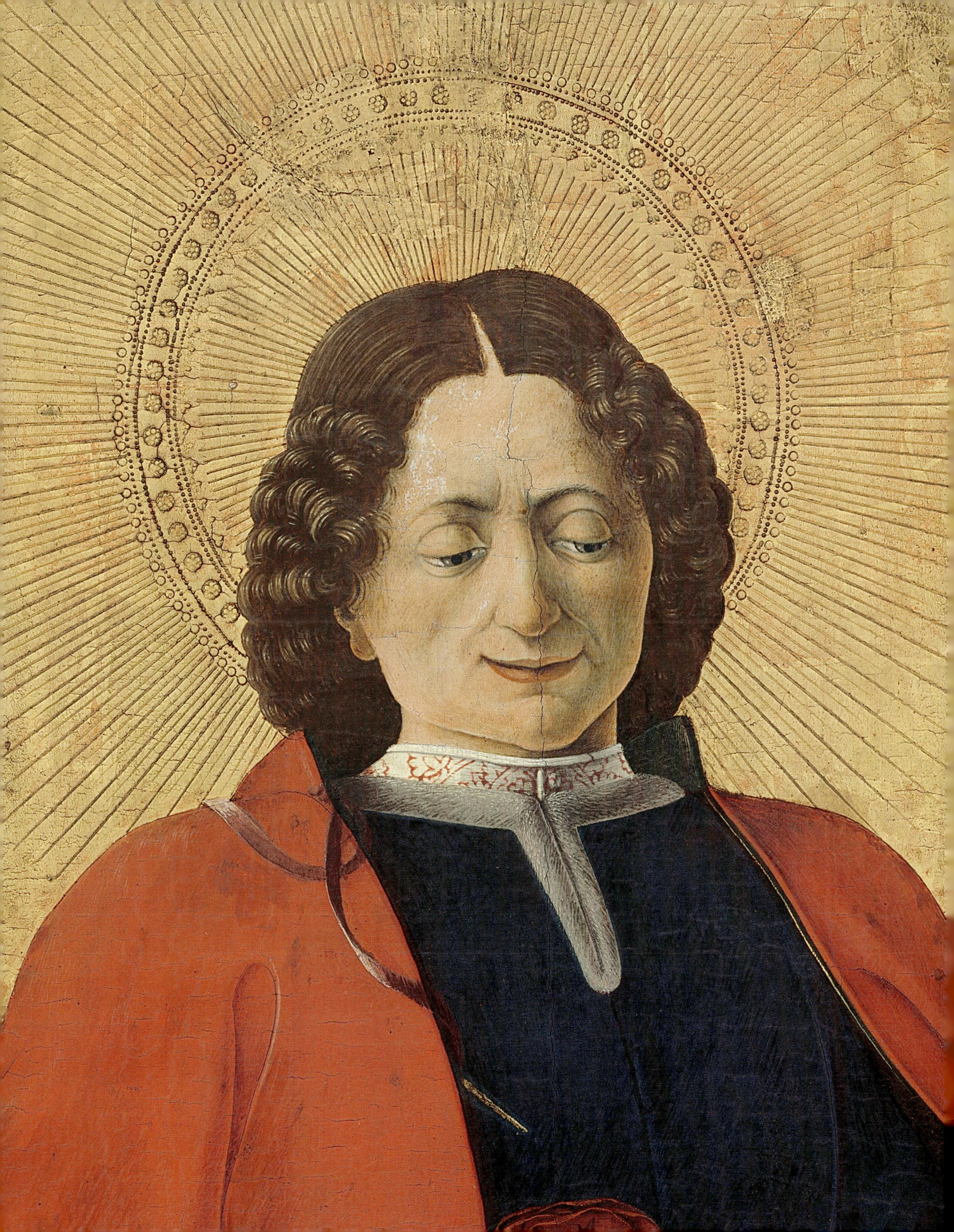

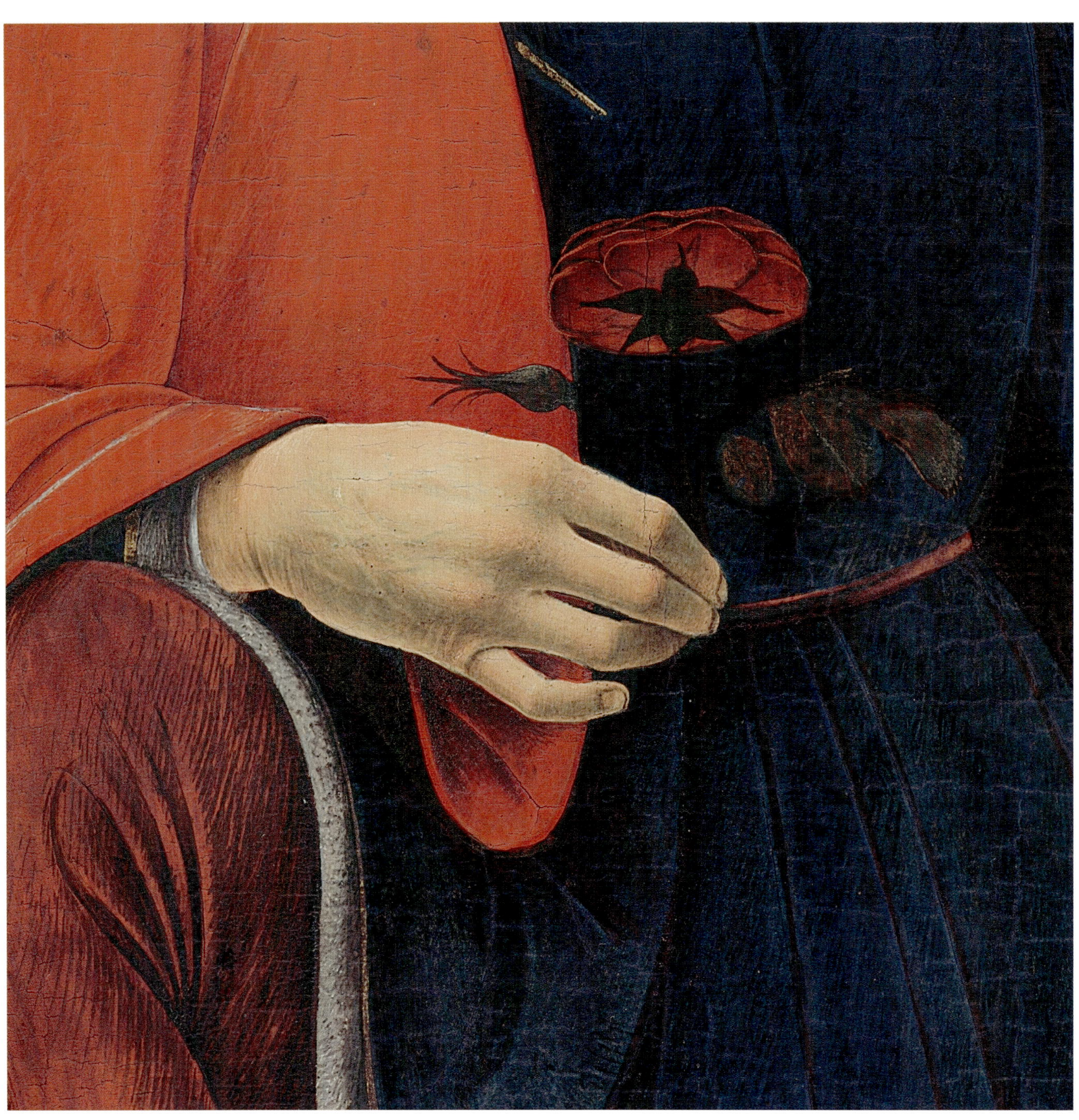

4

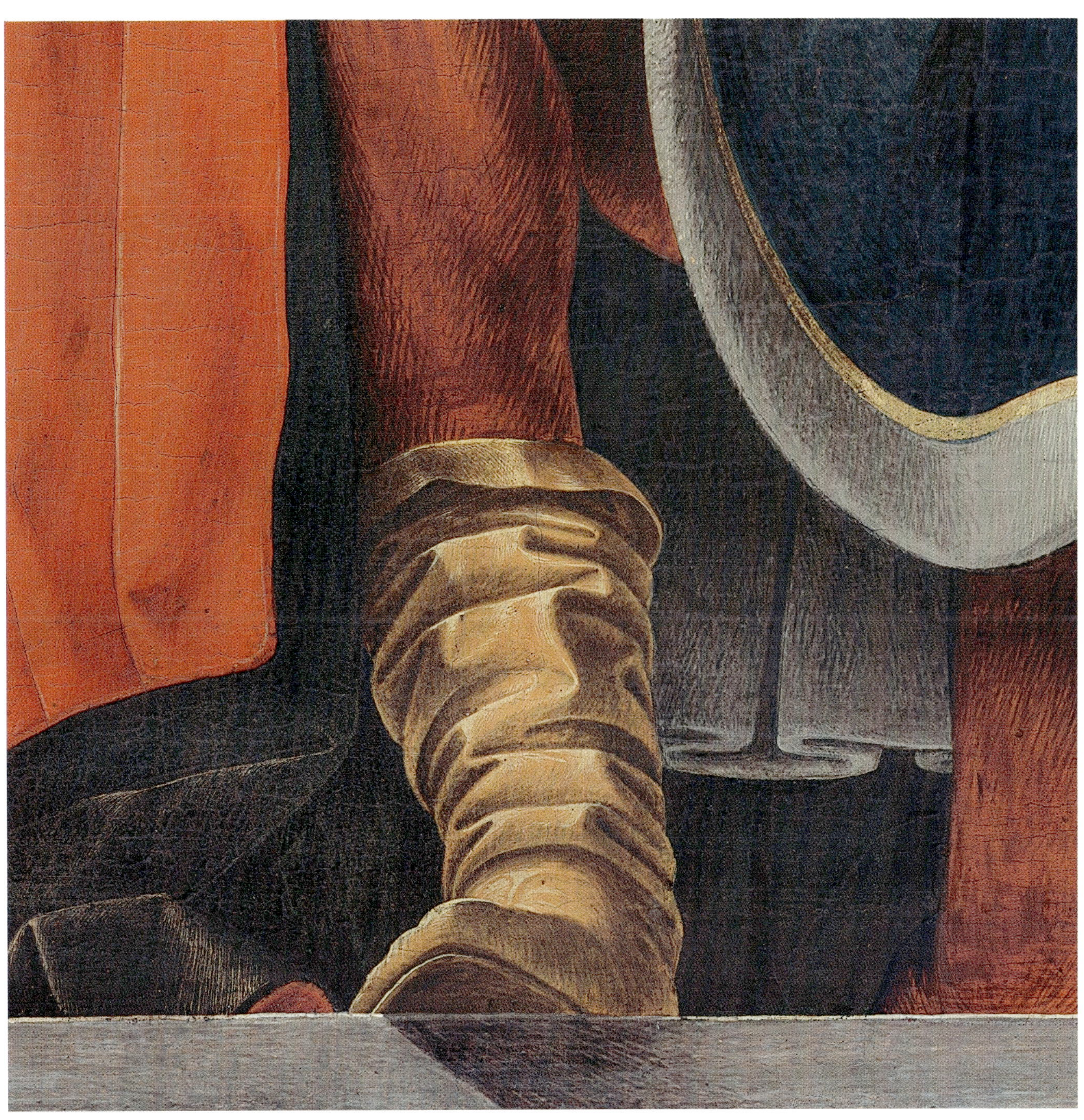

4

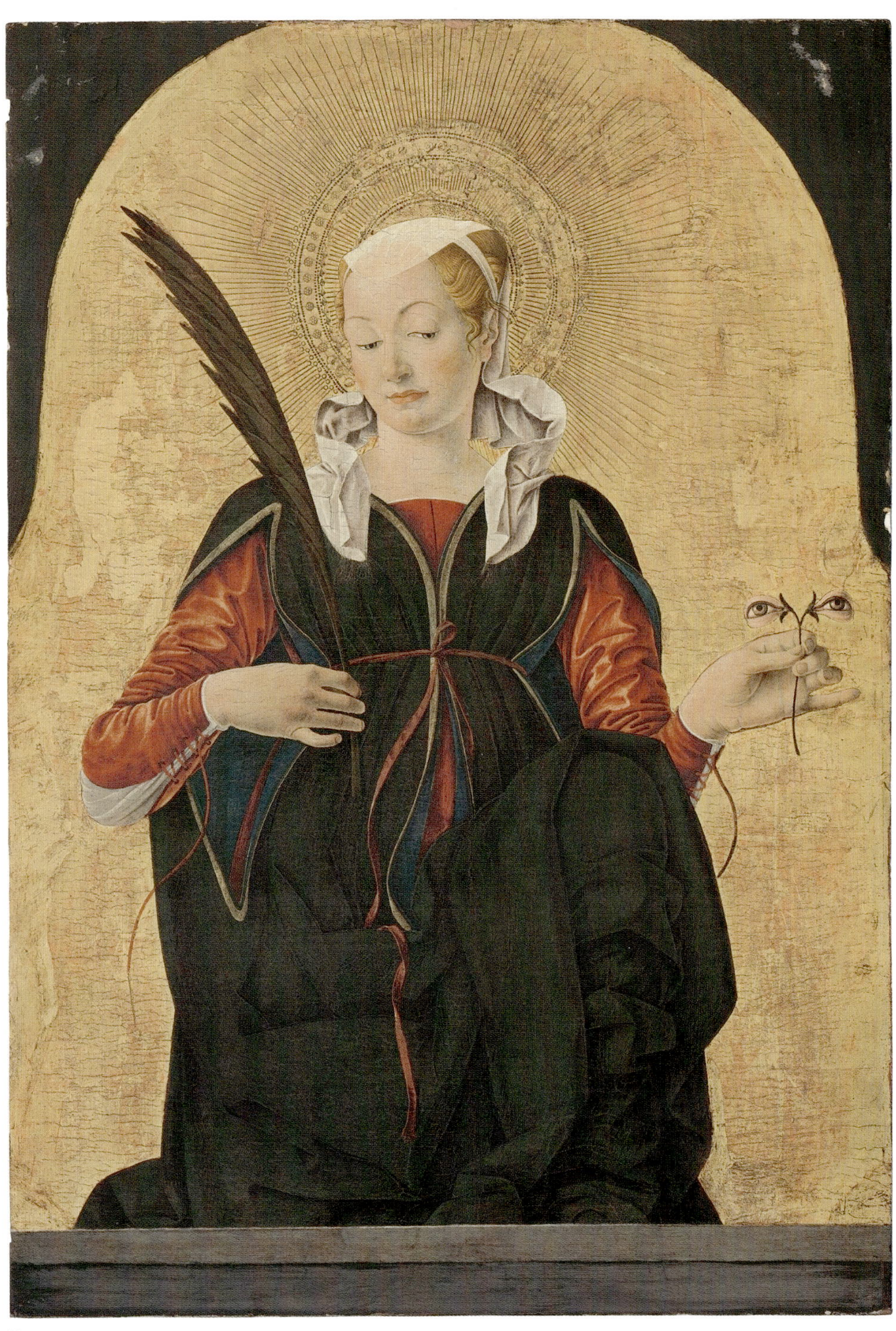

5

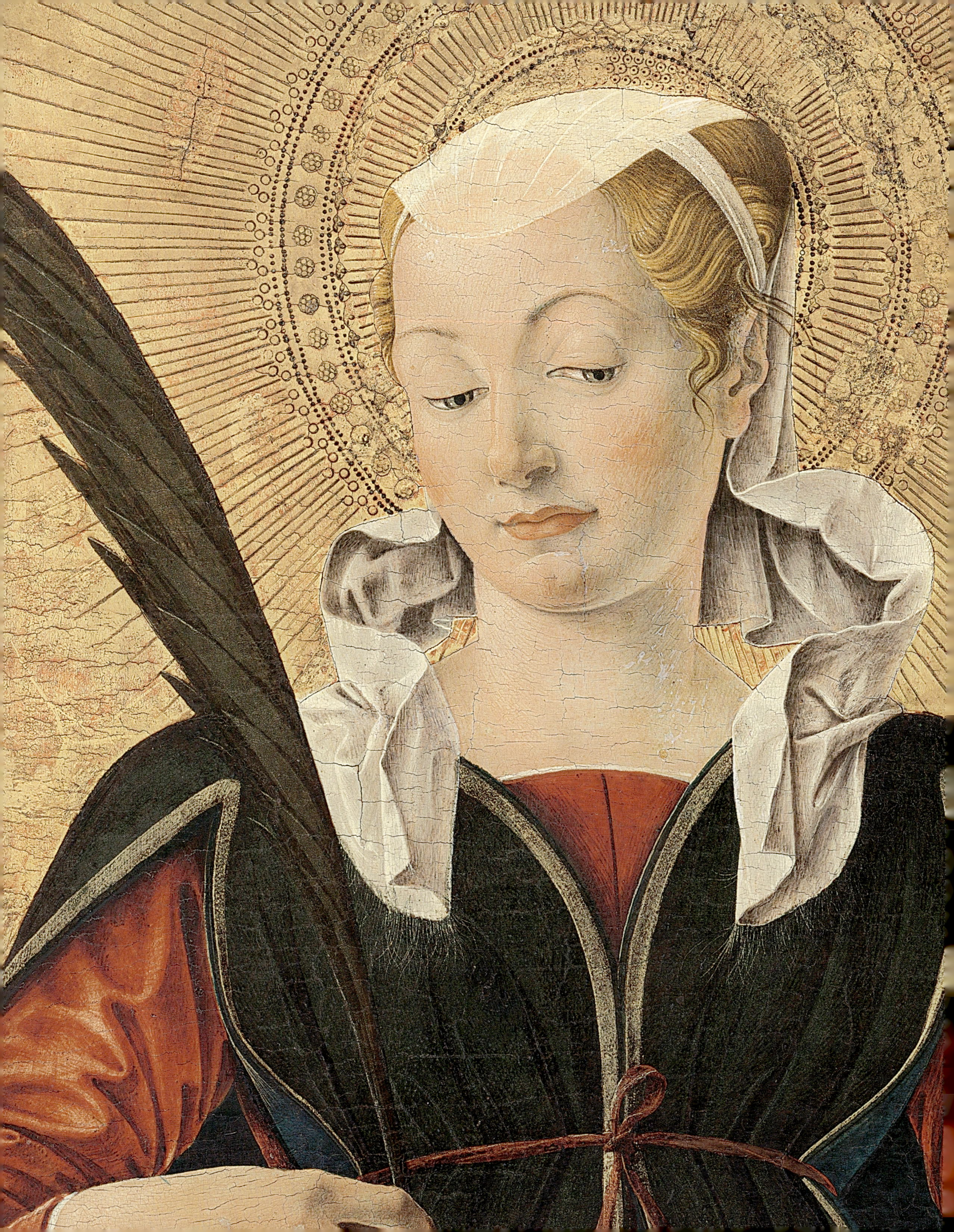

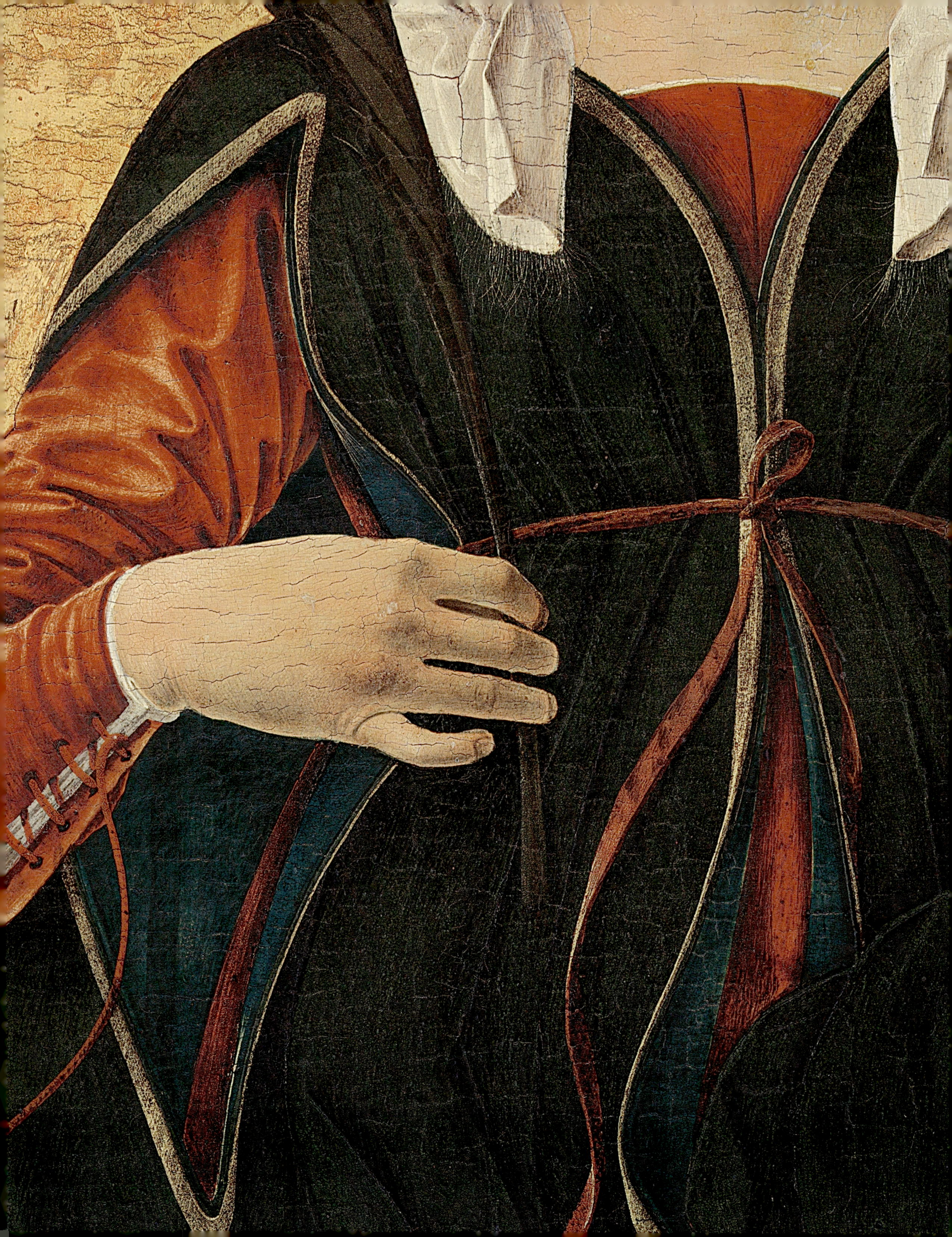

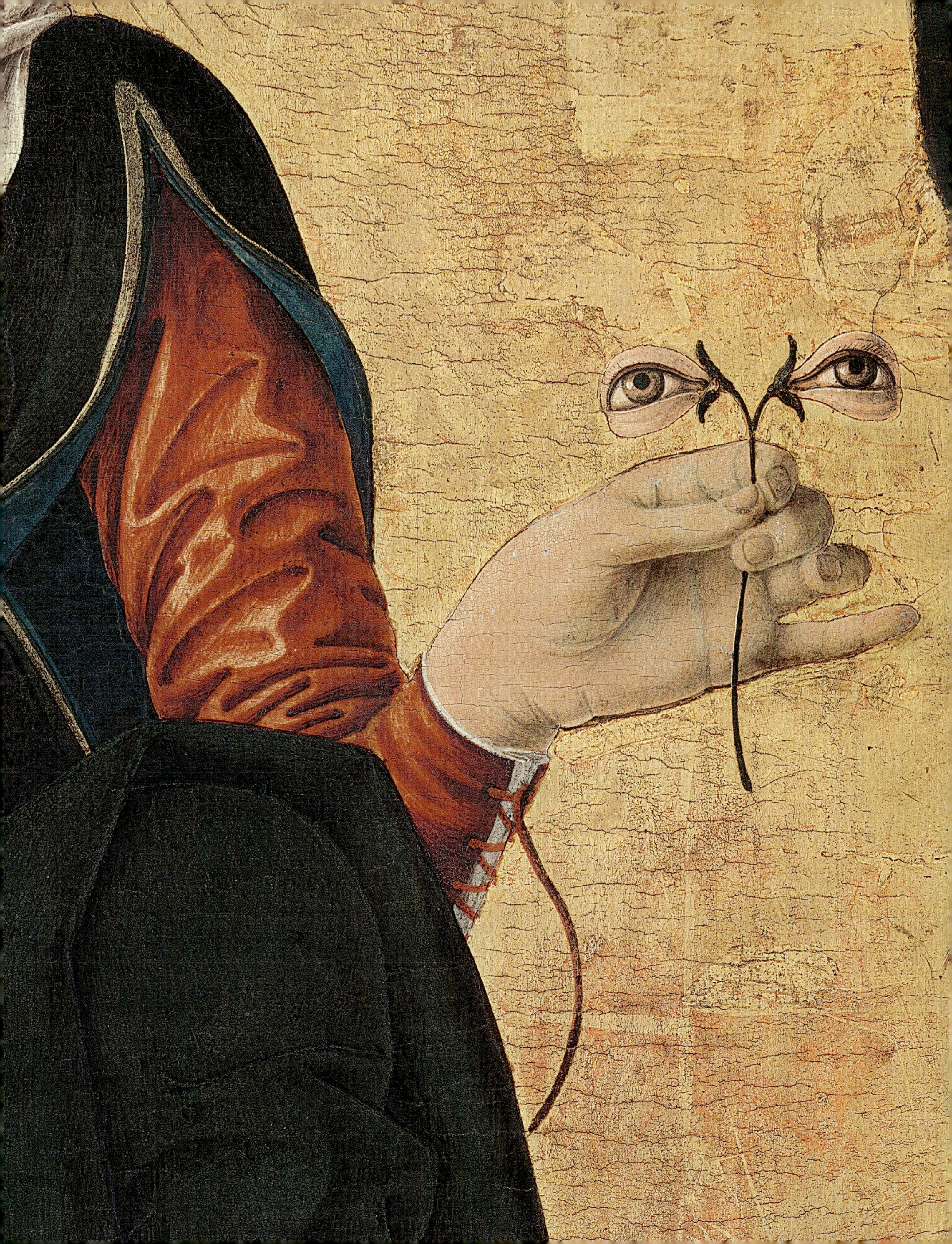

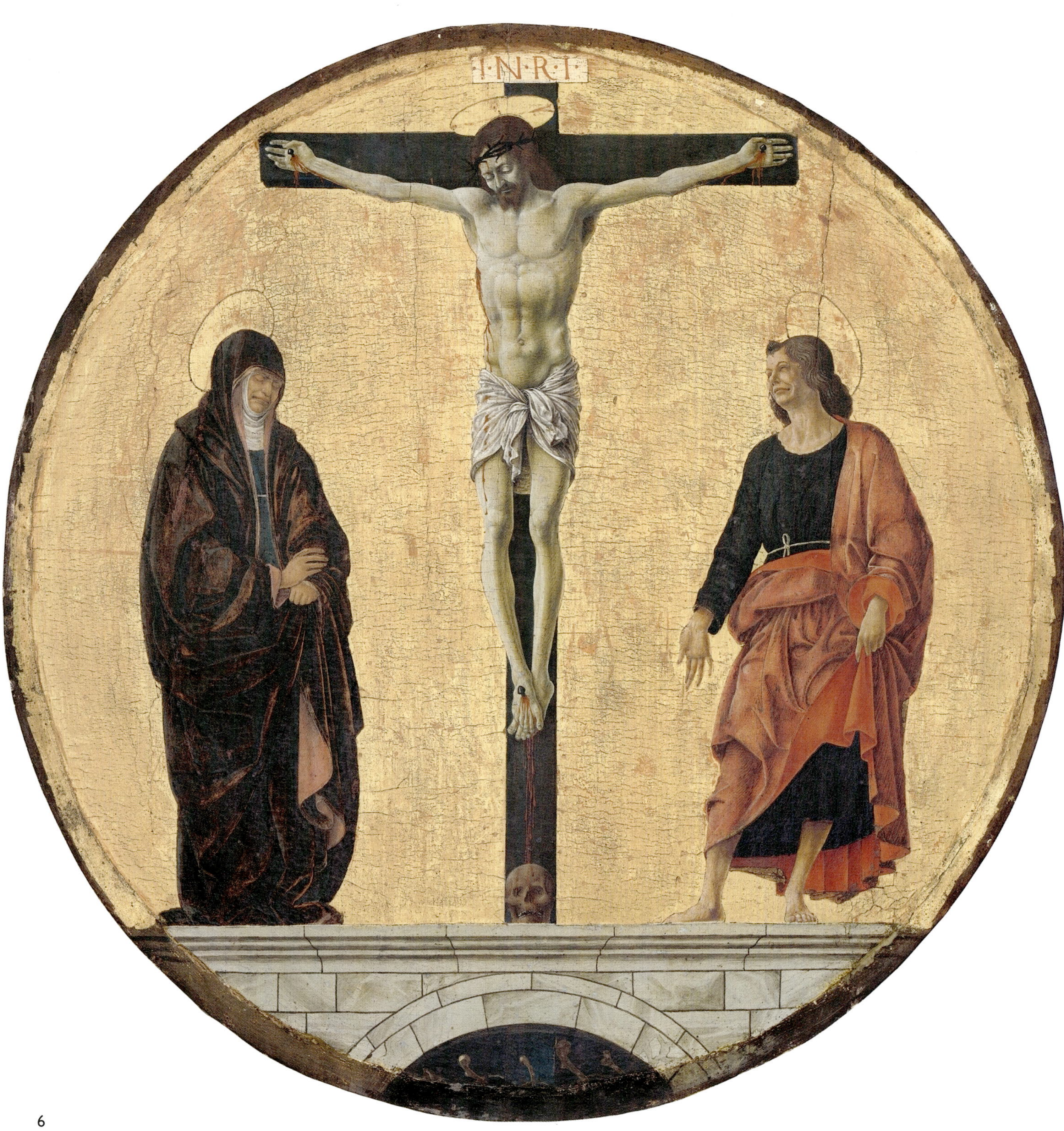

6

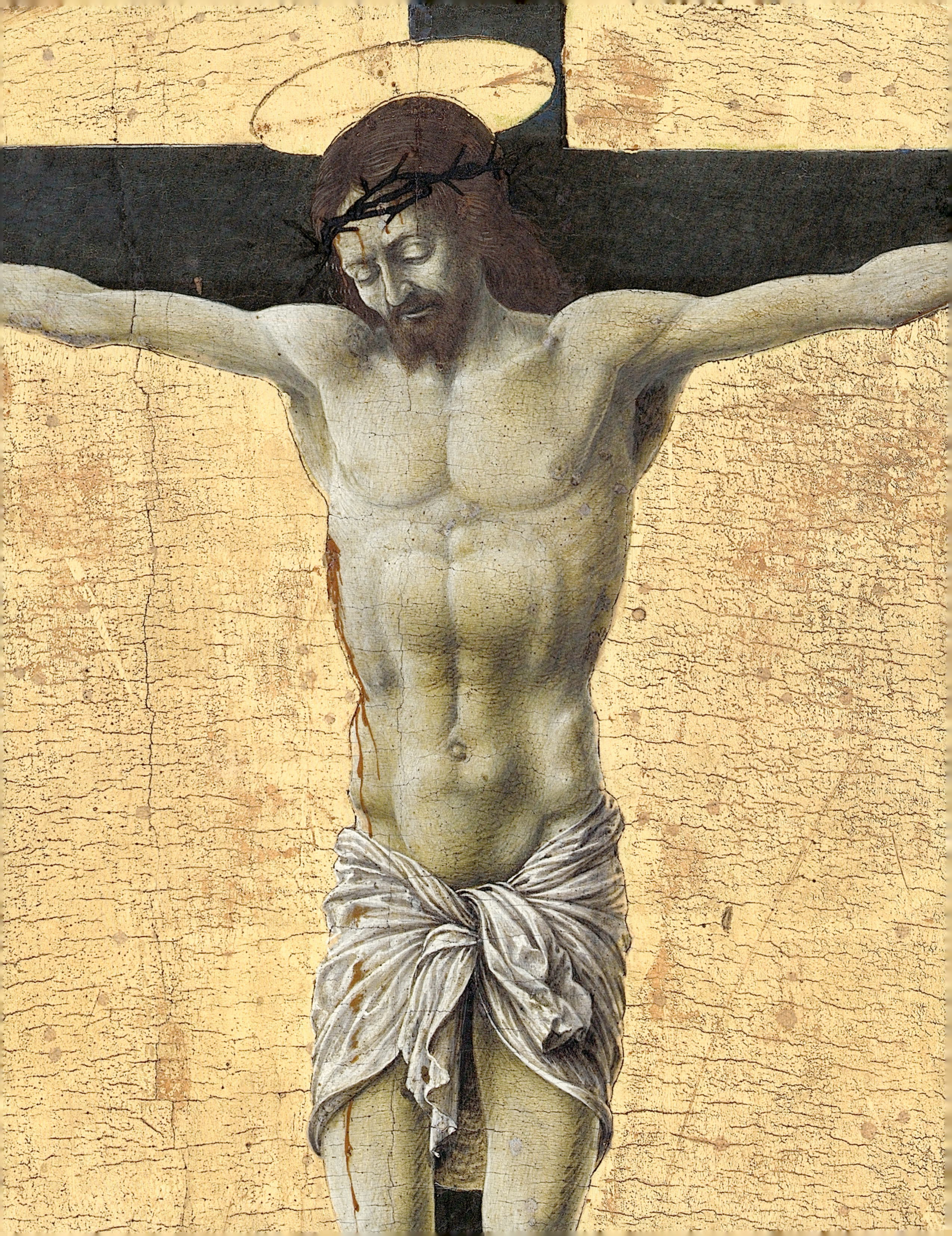

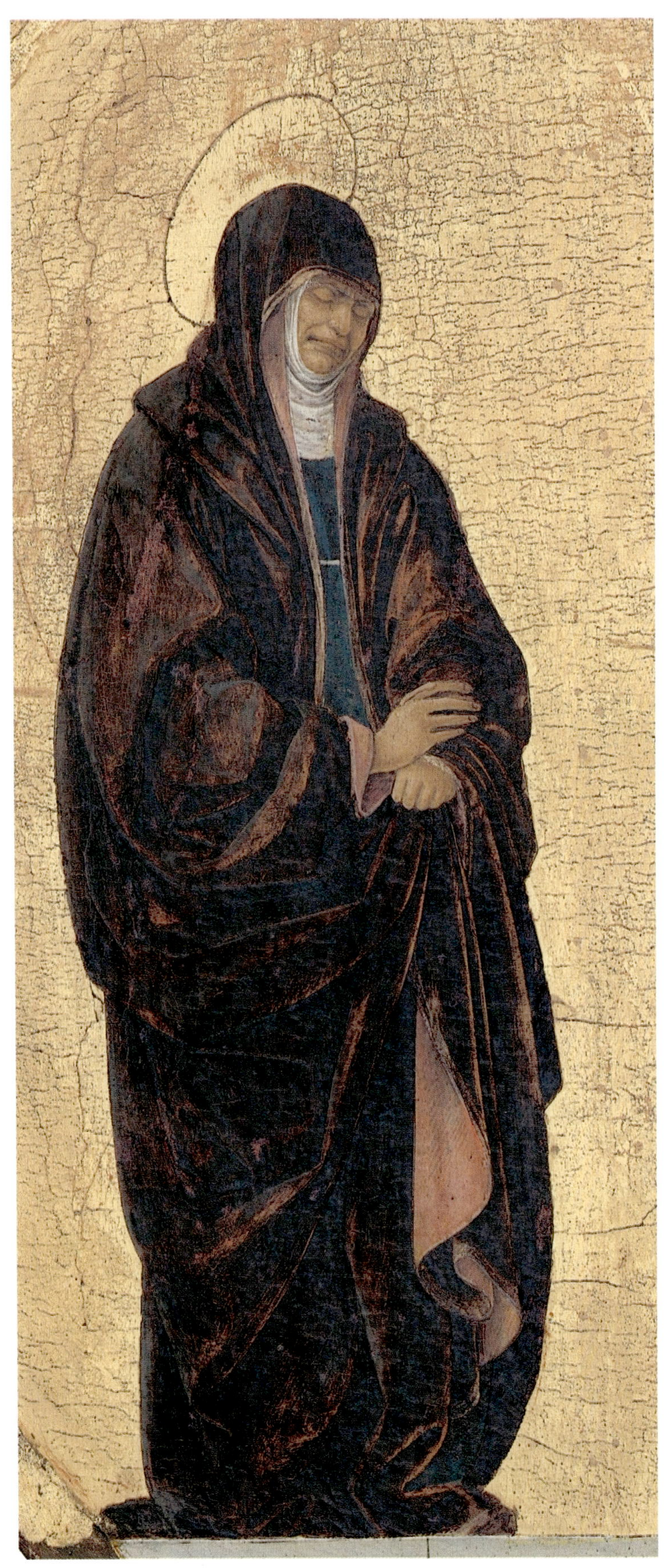

6

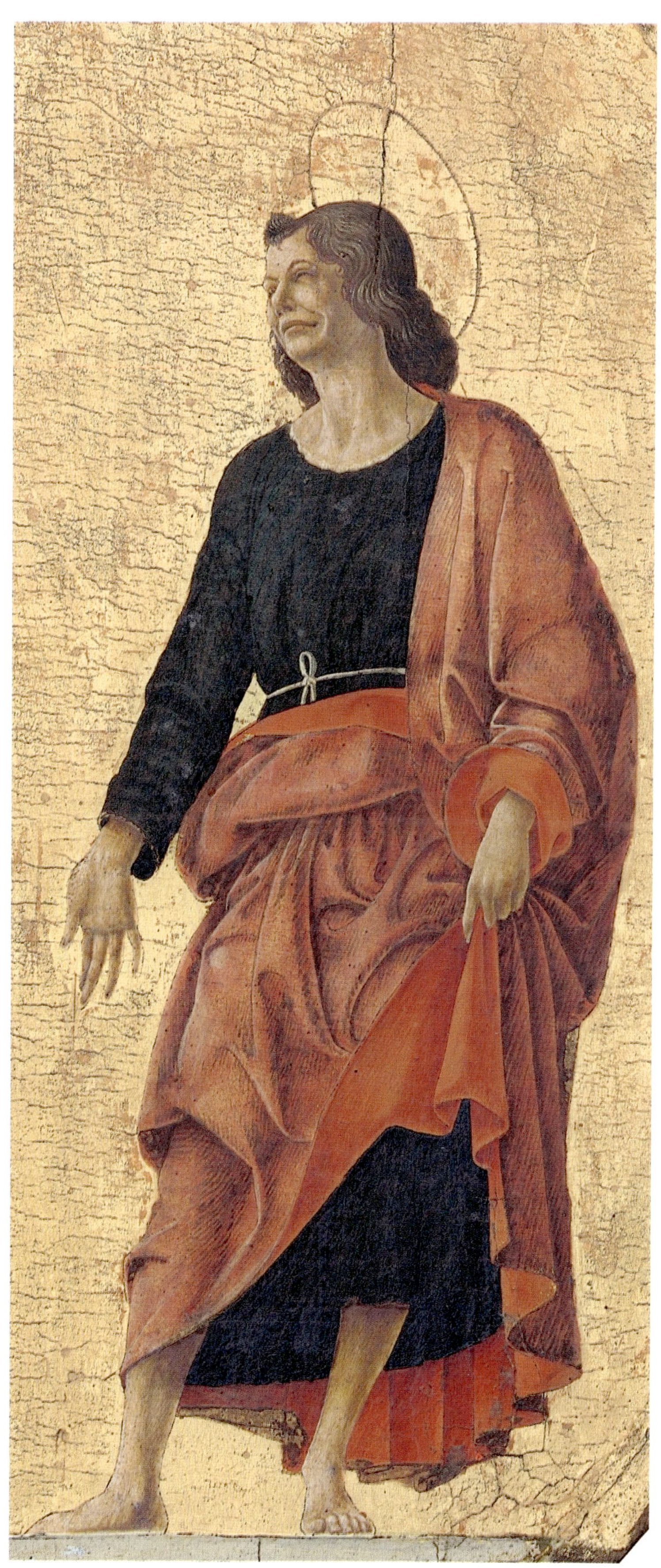

6

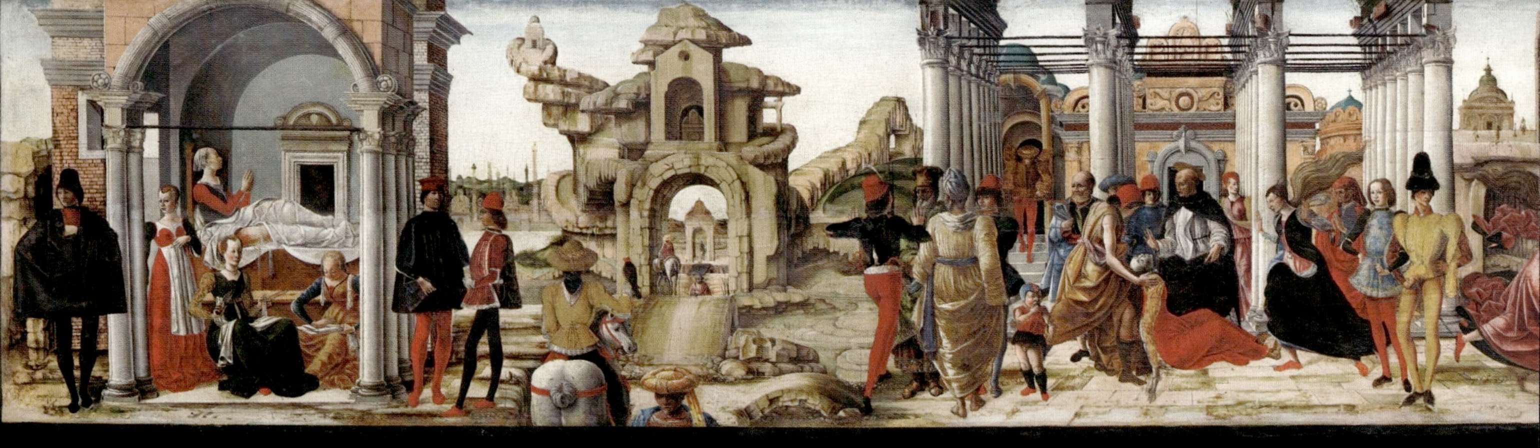

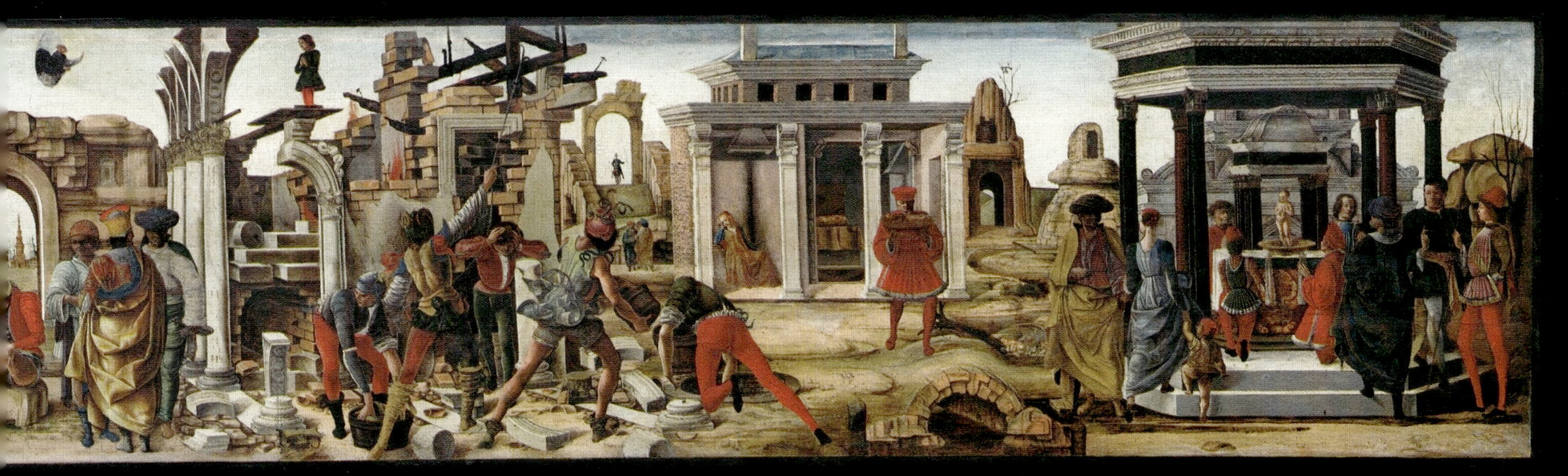

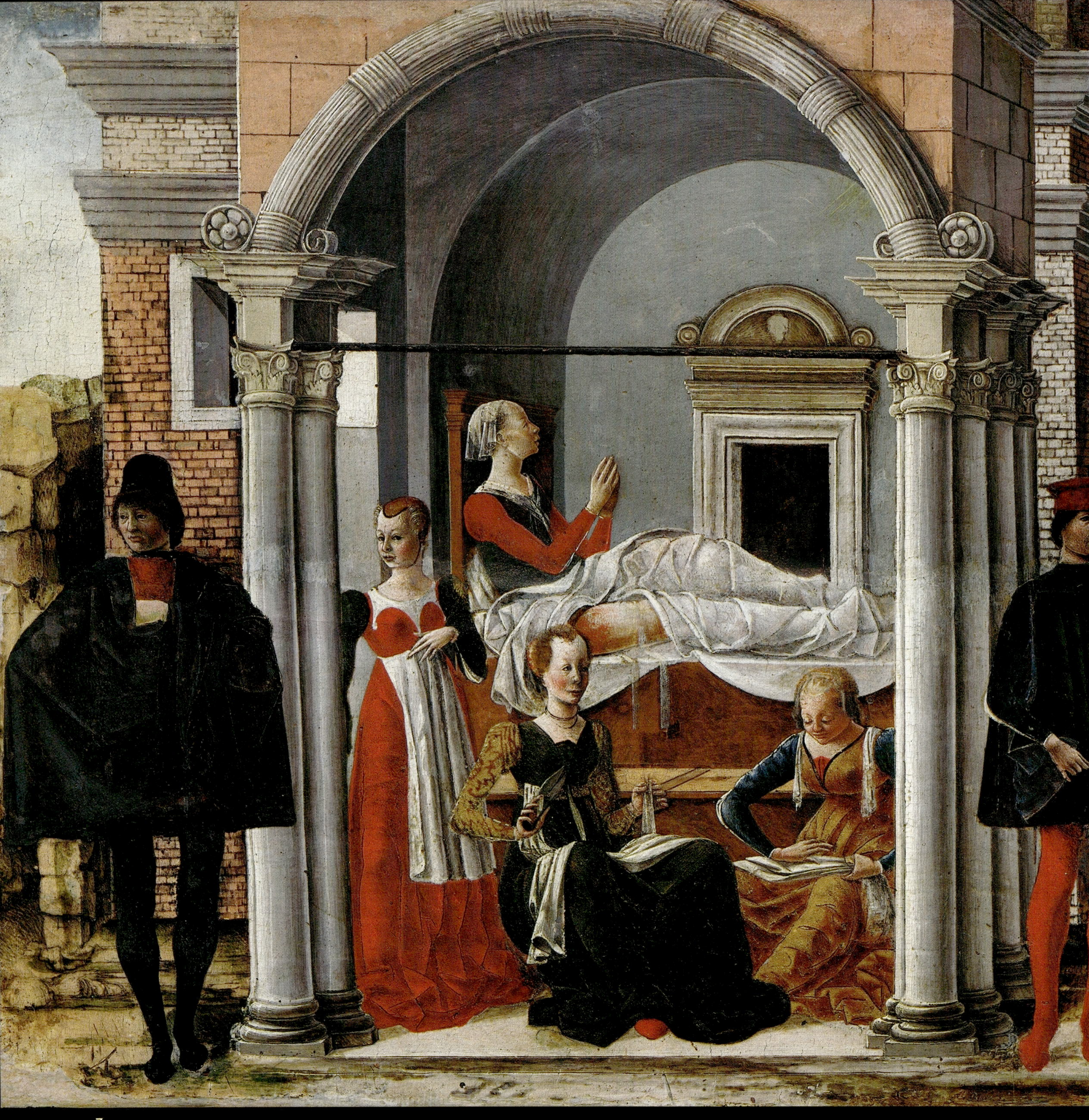

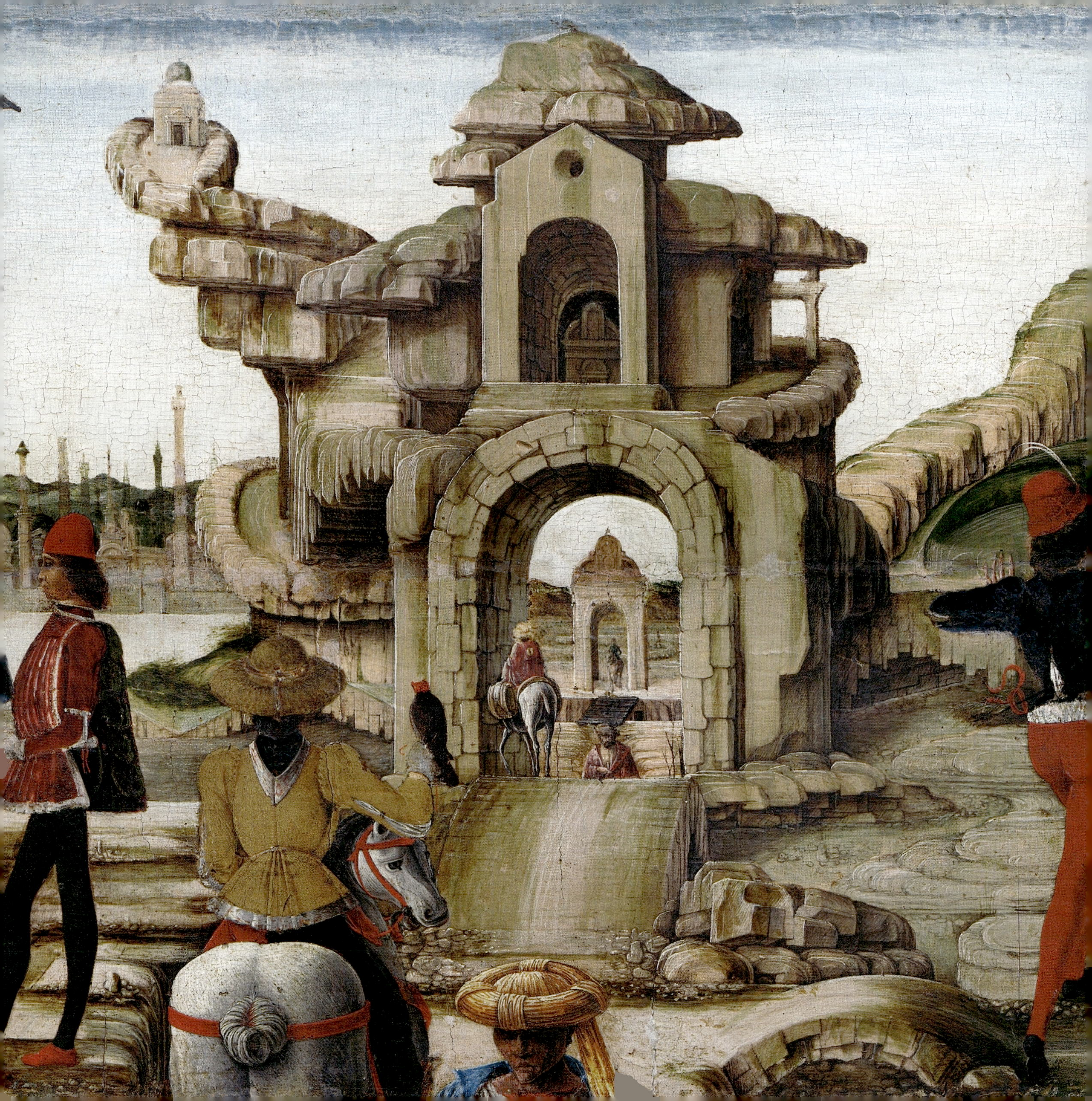

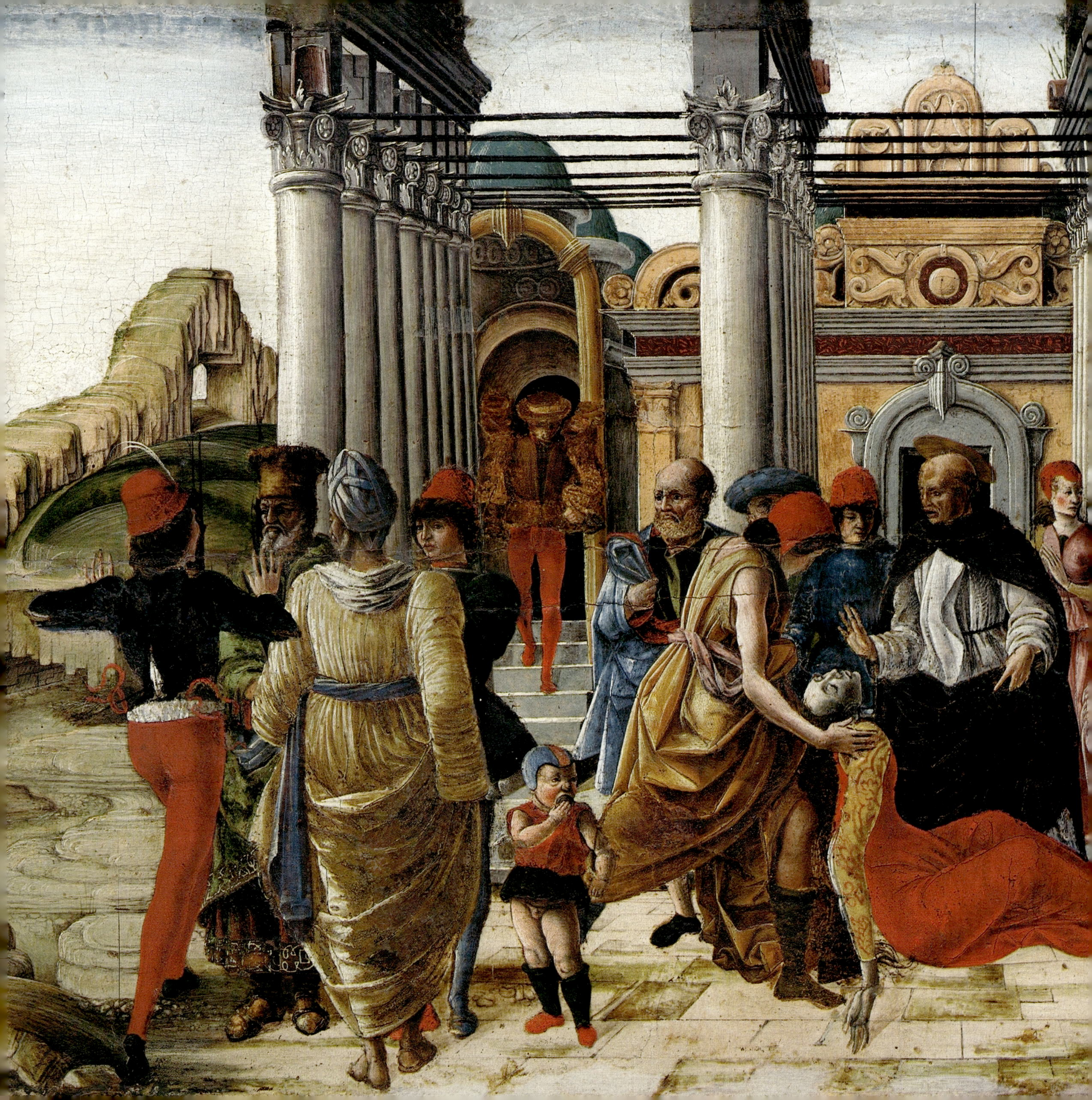

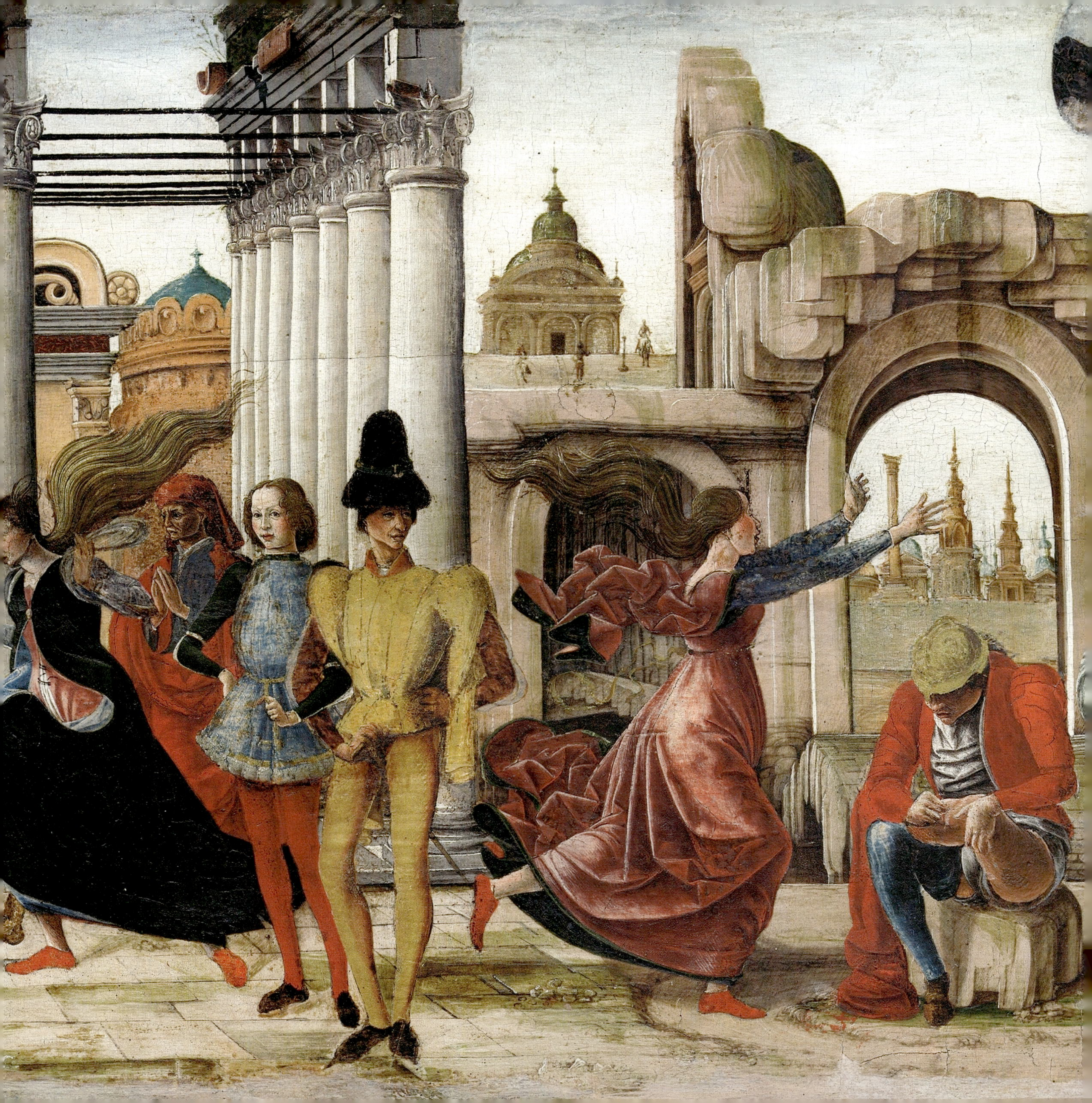

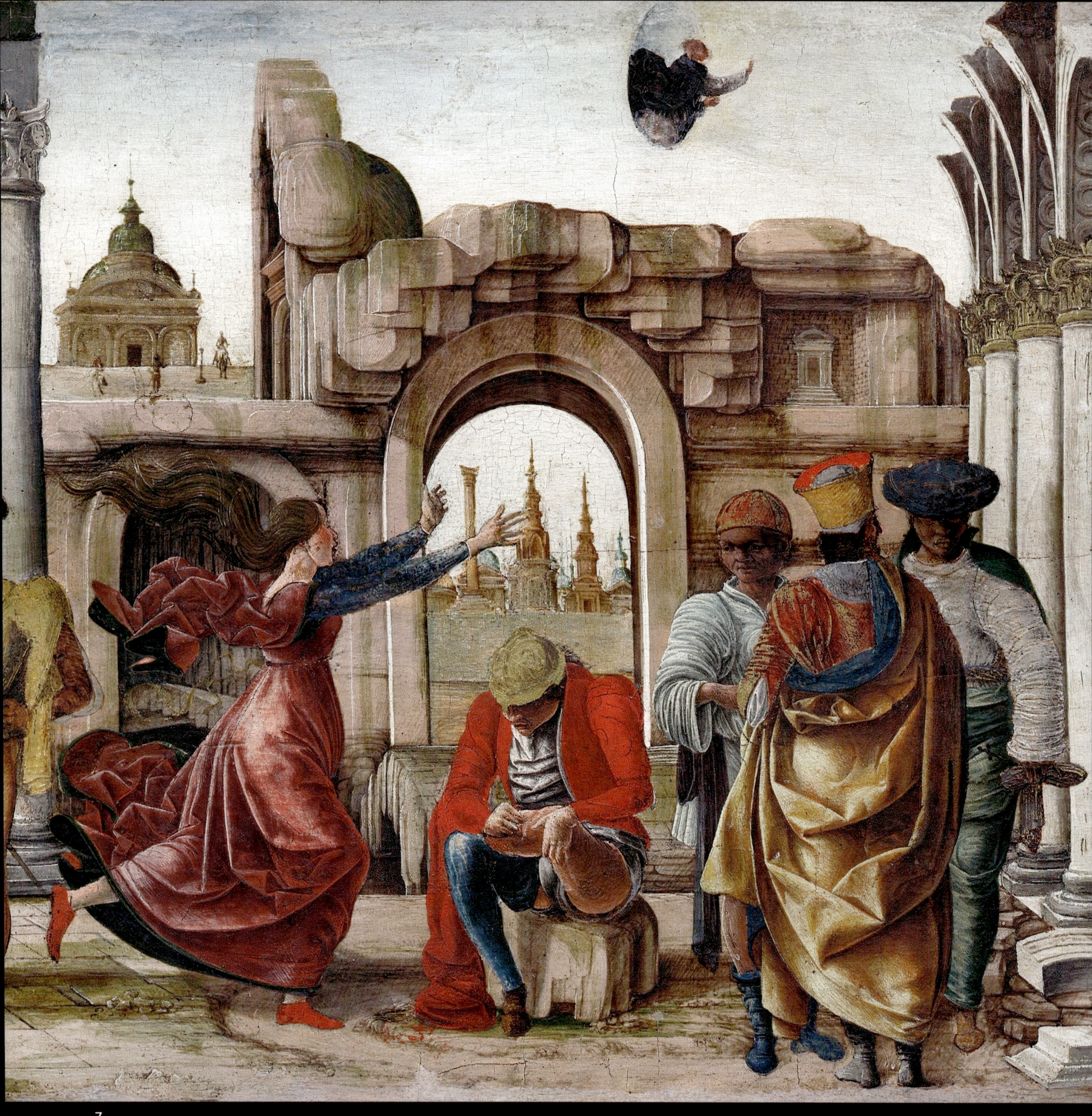

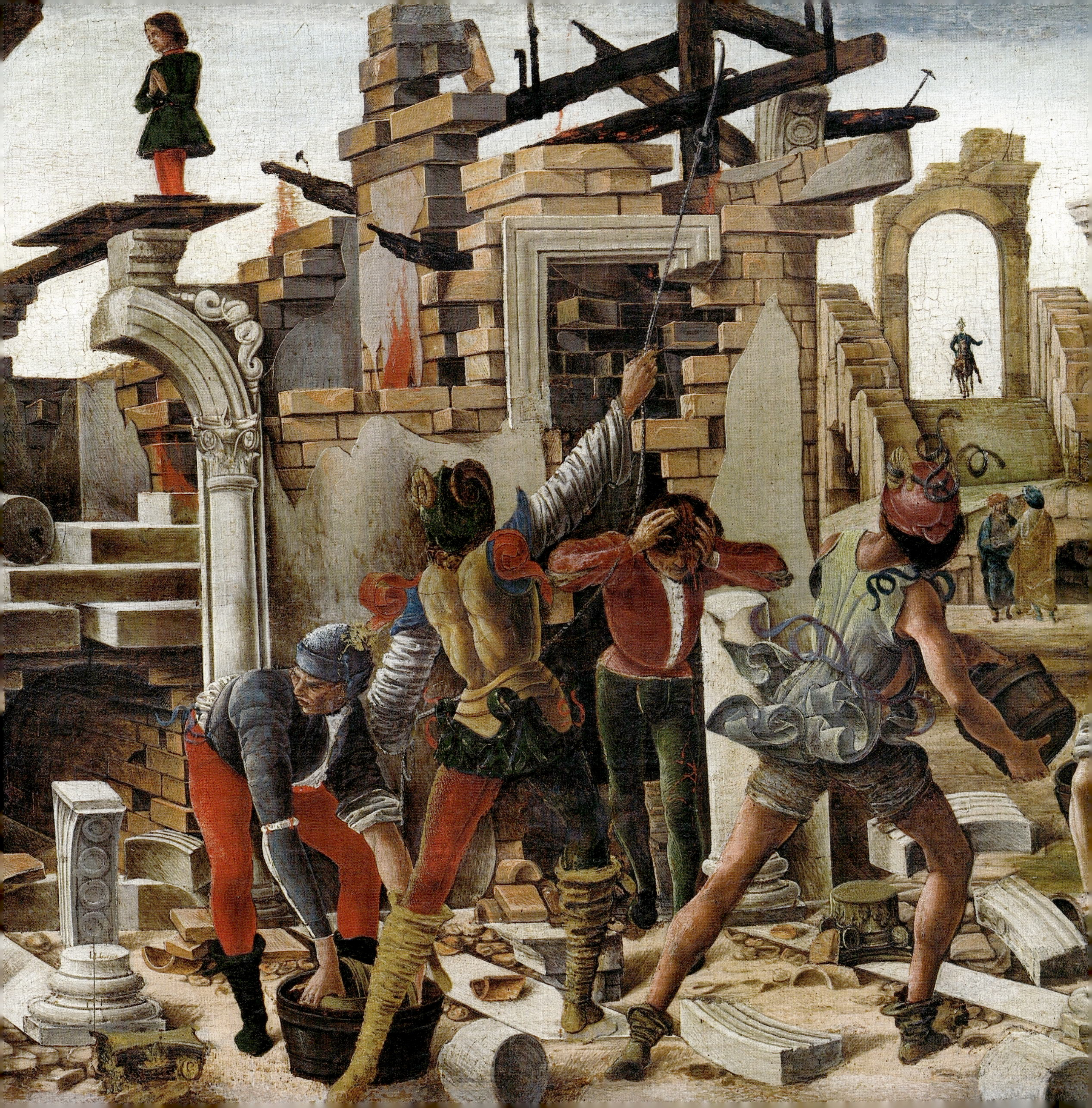

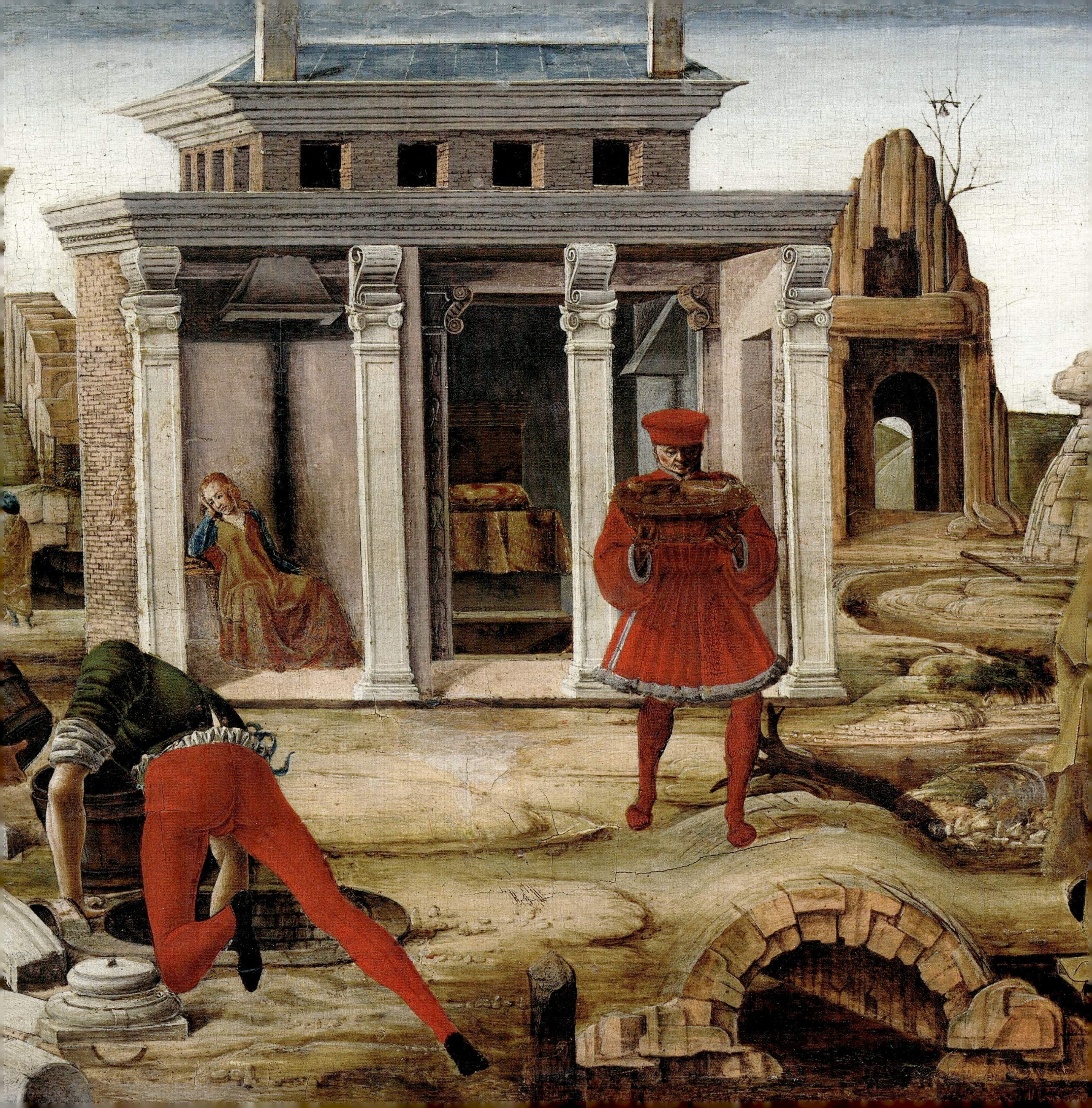

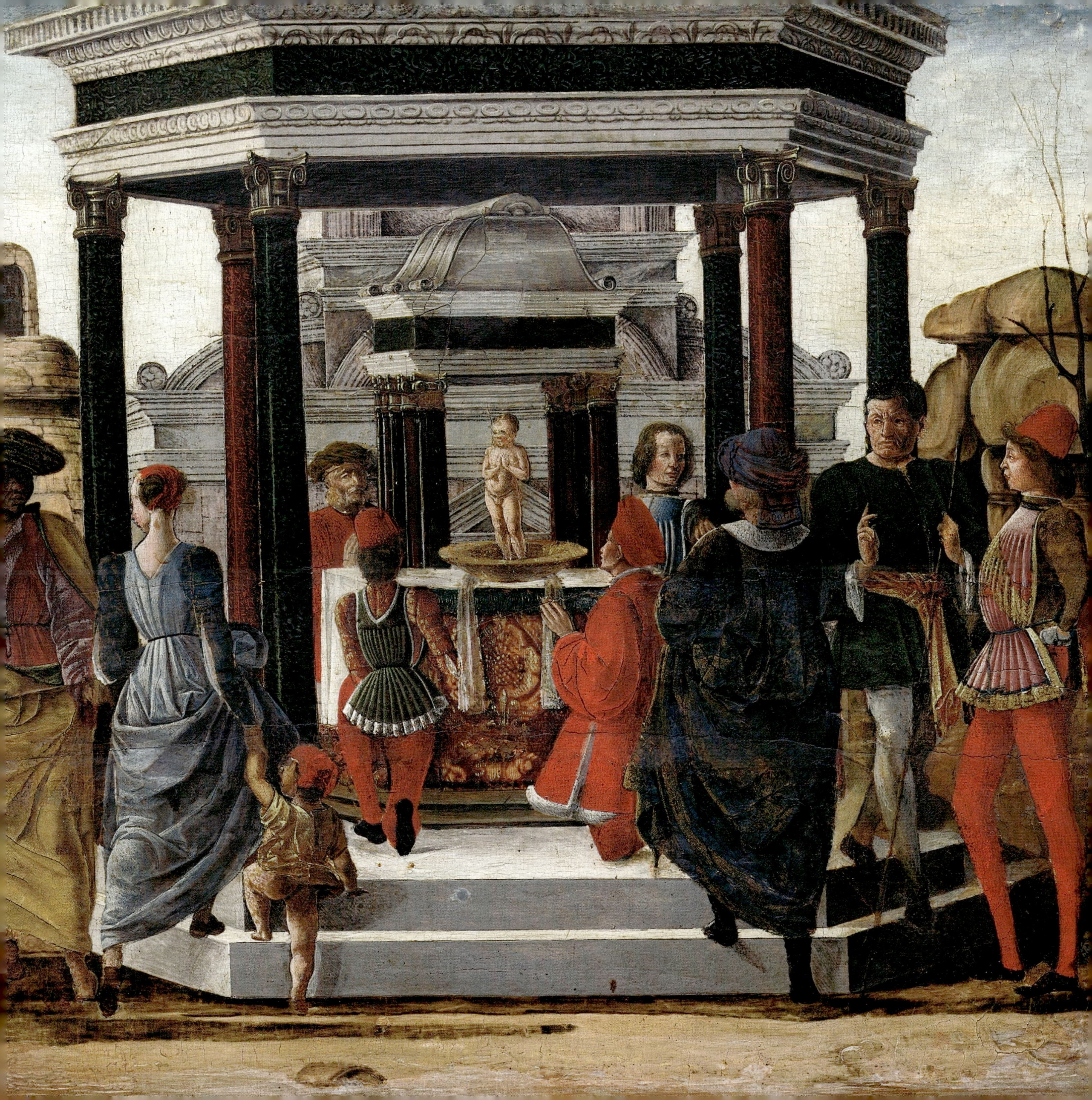

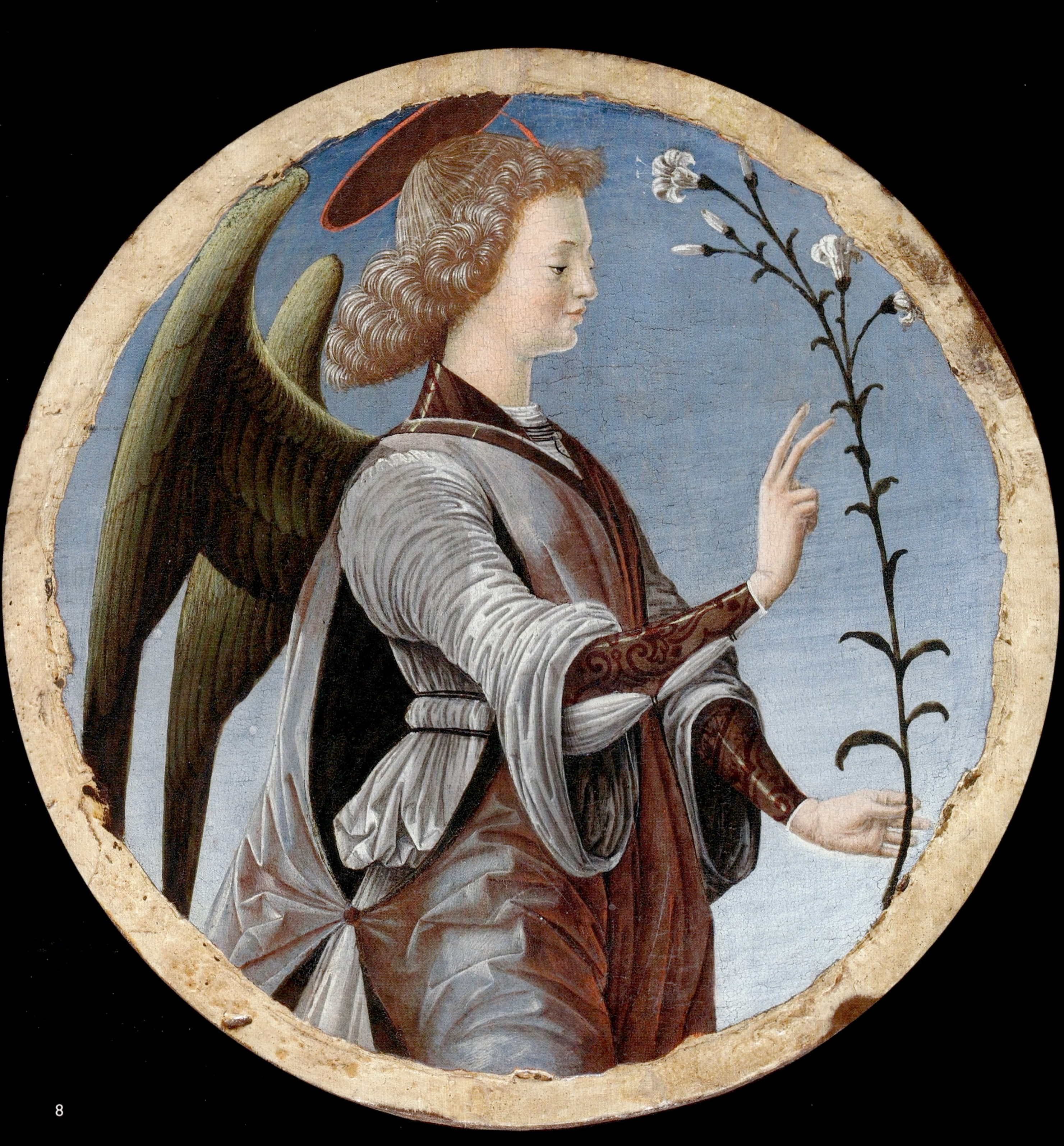

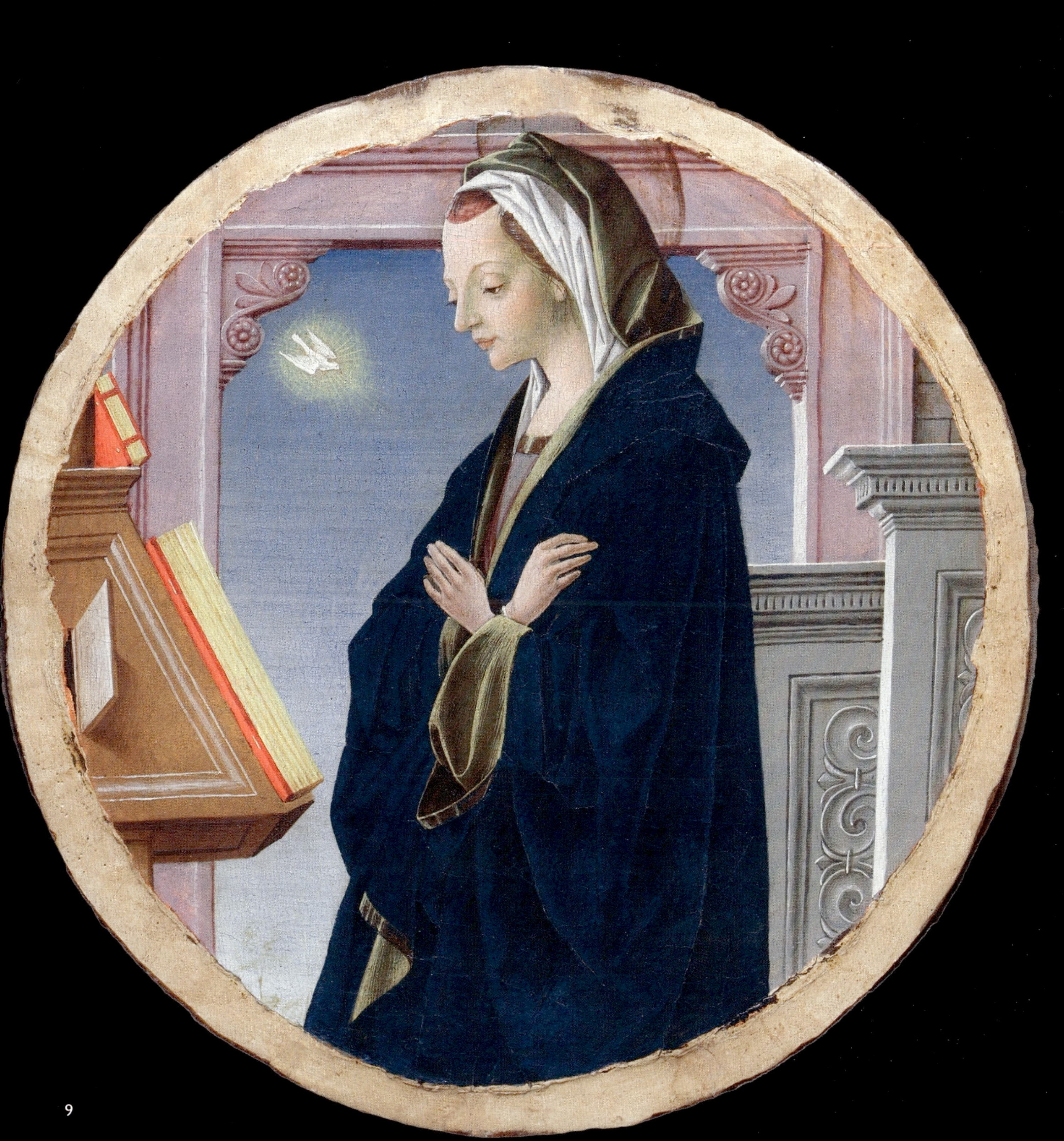

9

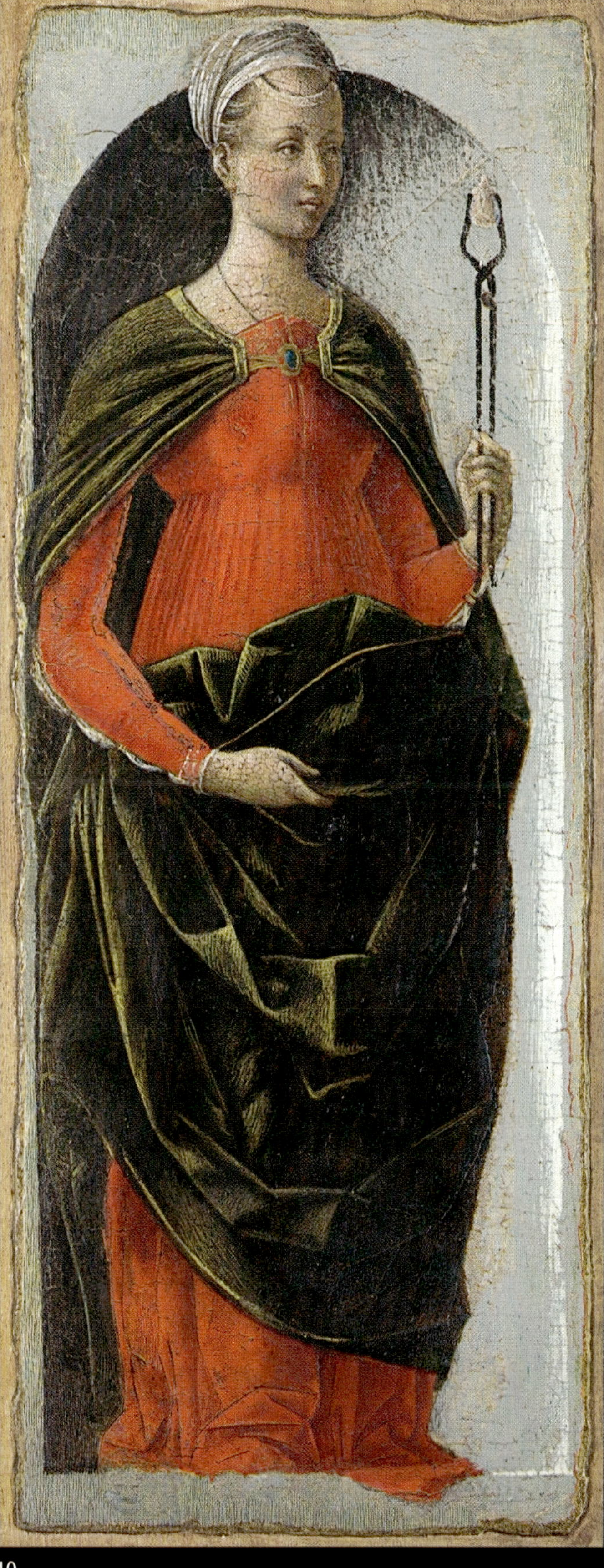

10

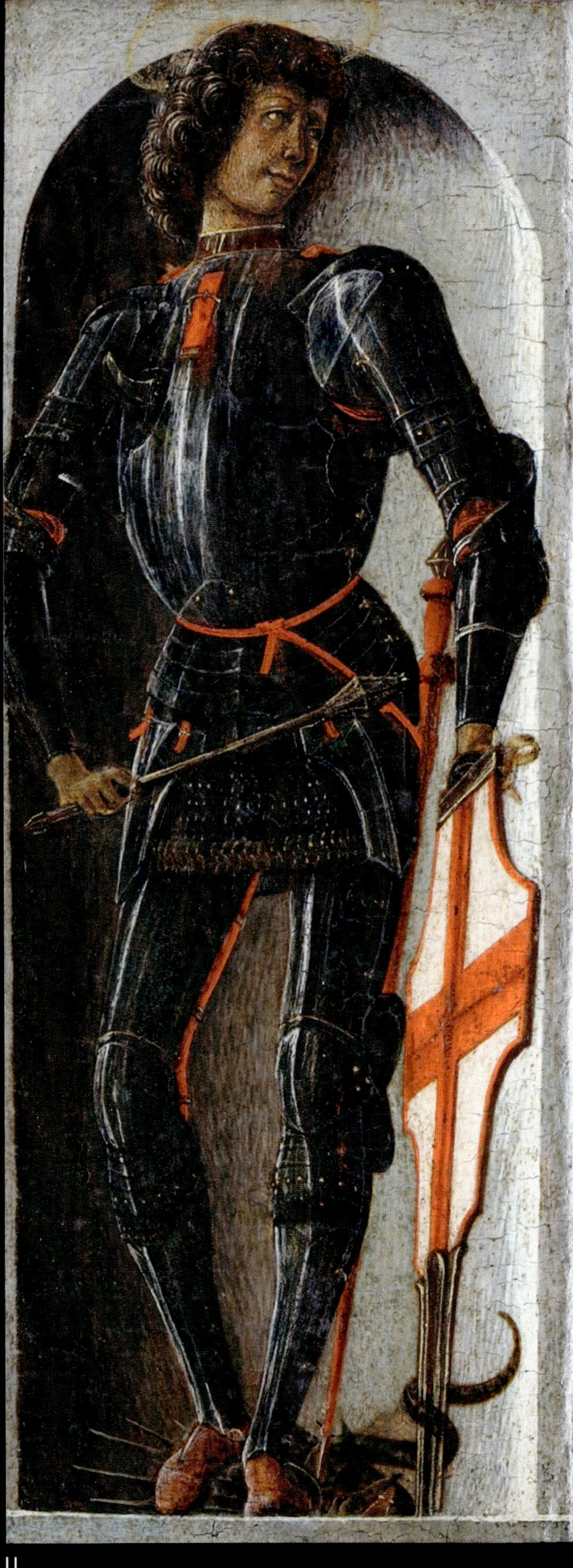

11

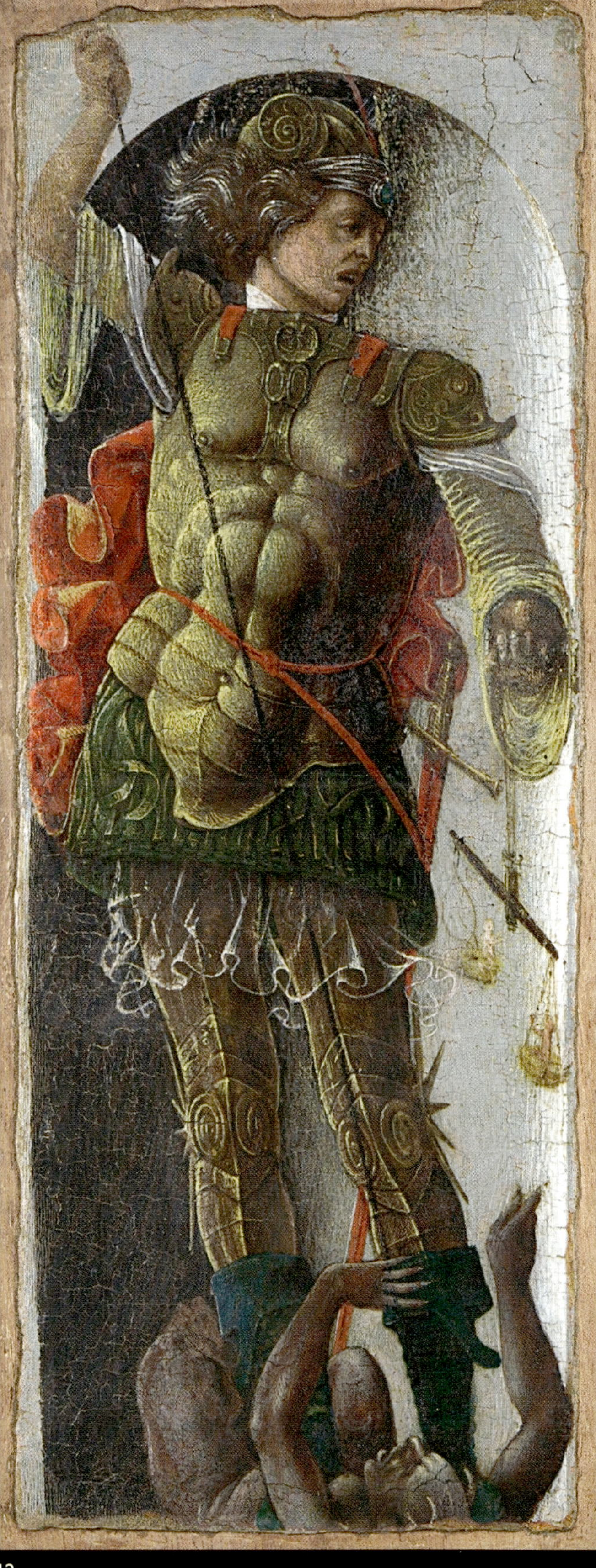

12

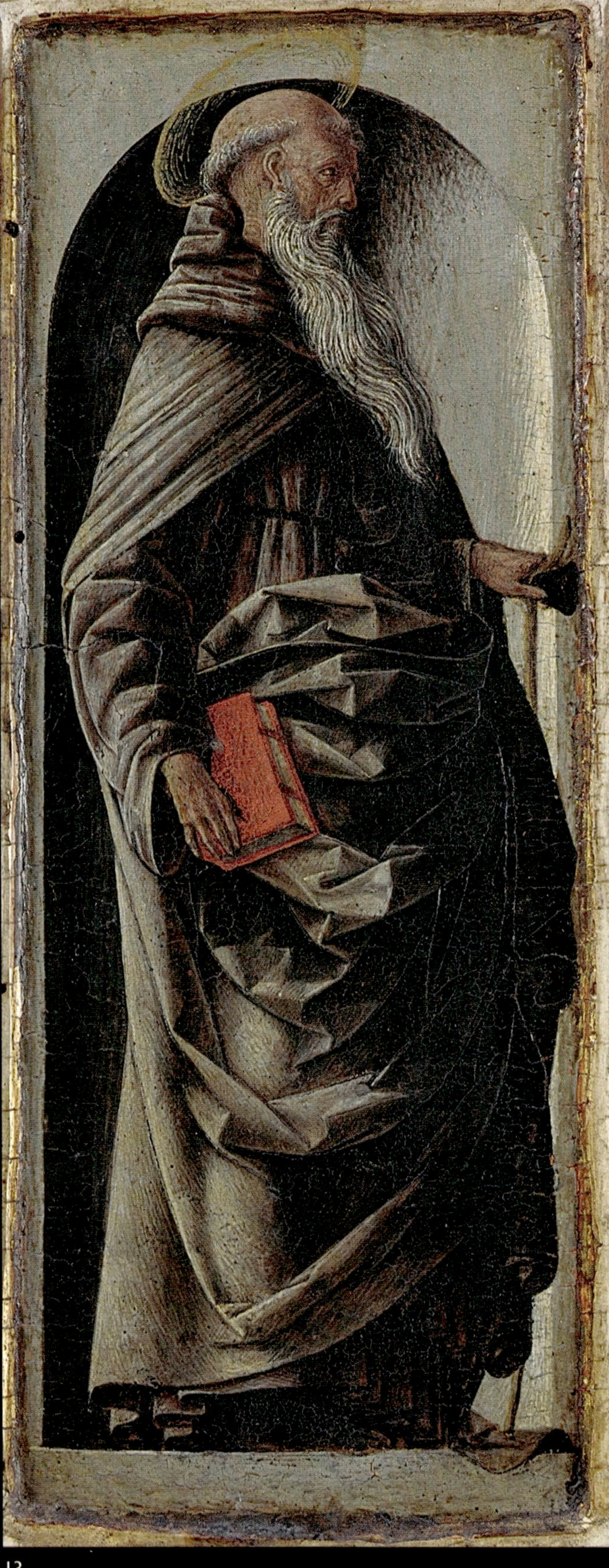

13

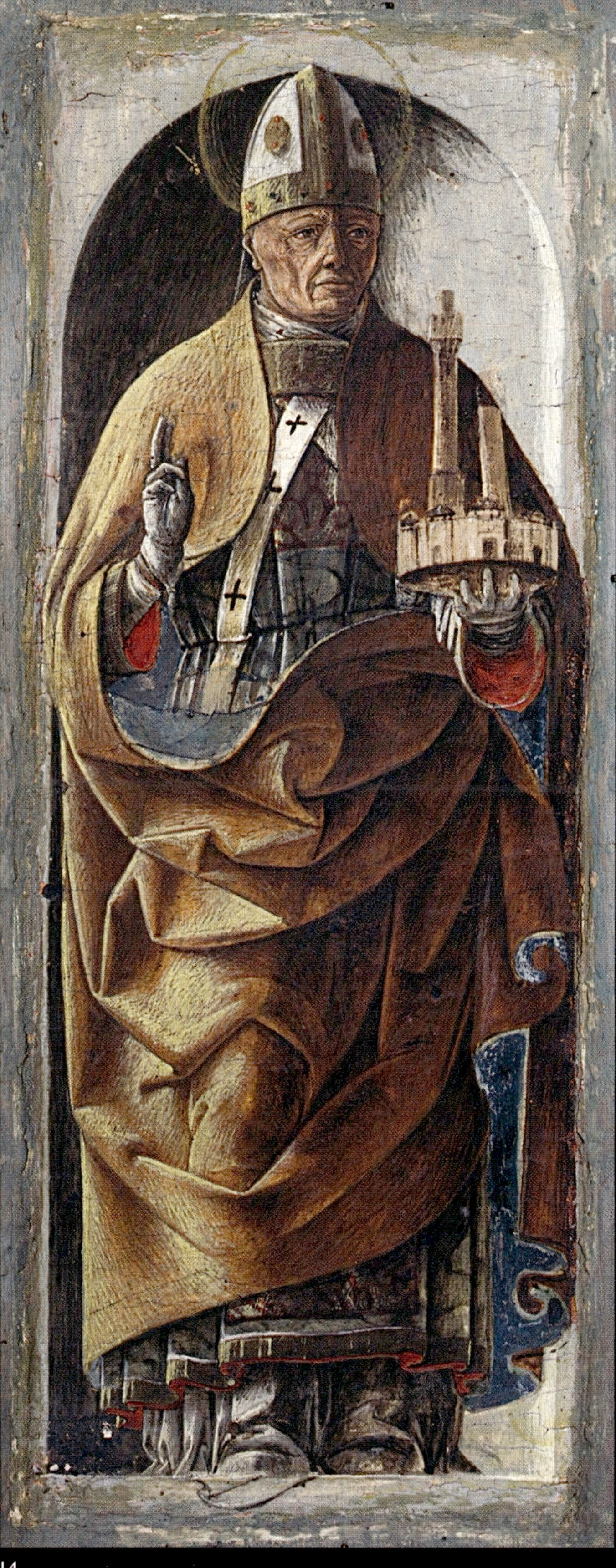

14

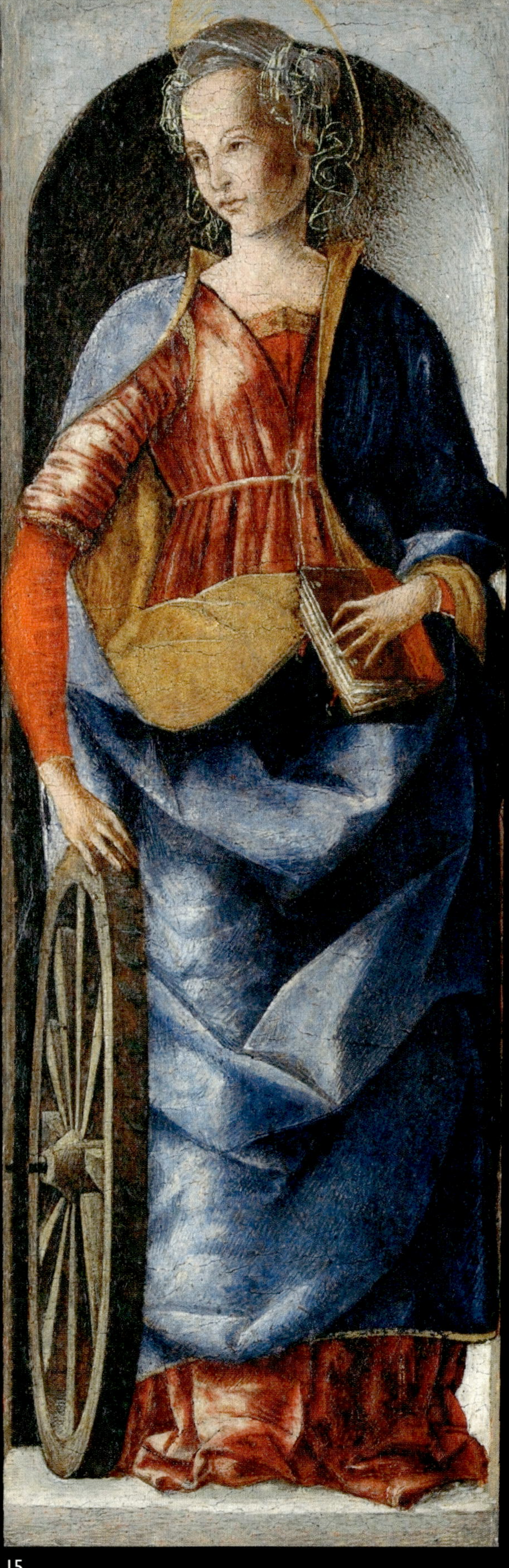
15

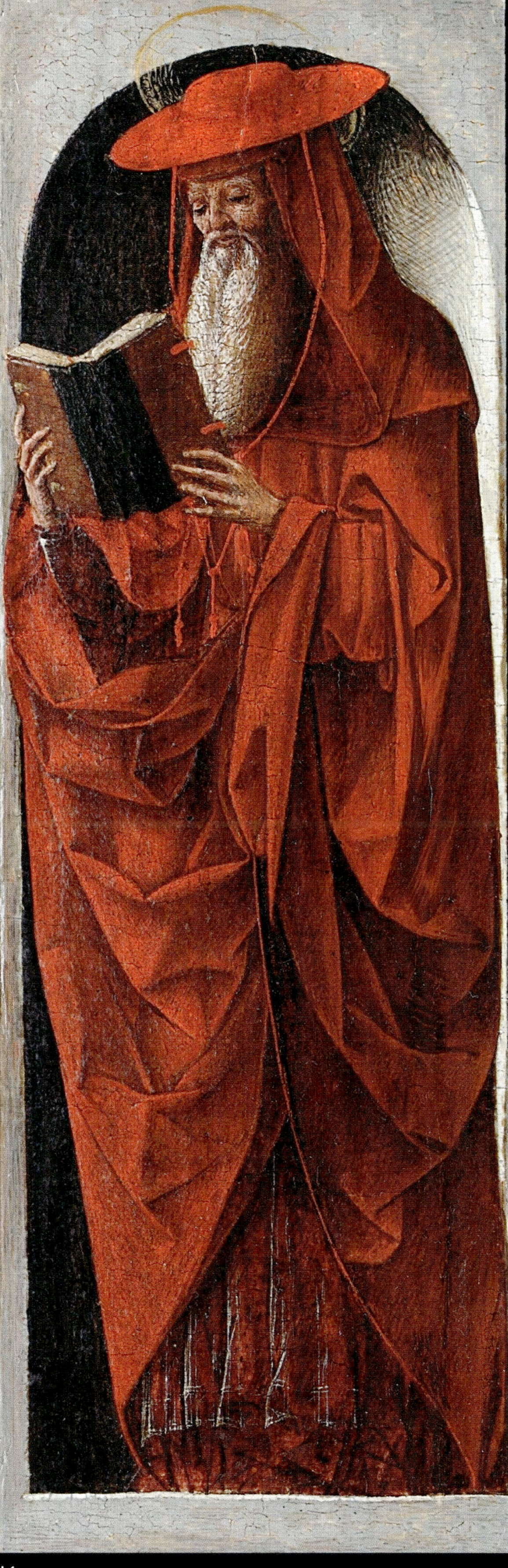

16

Francesco del Cossa

1. Saint Vincent Ferrer

tempera on panel, 153.7 × 59.7 cm
The National Gallery, London, inv. NG 597

The state of conservation of the pictorial surface is fairly good. Before 1931 (?), the support was thinned down and cradled; in 1981, after removing the ancient frame system, it was mounted on a new balsa wood support. On that occasion, it was possible to confirm that the raw wood parts to the sides of the arch, which mark the edges of the frame, are original (see A. Reeve in Smith, Reeve, and Roy 1981, pp. 47–54). Superficial cracks have caused some damage to the face of Christ in the mandorla and other parts of the arch as well as, to a lesser extent, to the saint's clothing, down to his feet (see Davies 1951, p. 115; A. Reeve in Smith, Reeve, and Roy 1981, p. 47). The information gathered and published during the 1980–81 restoration unveiled a confident and accurate planning of the figuration, using thin incisions in profiles and in key points of the drapery, as well as a detailed preparatory drawing, using diagonal strokes in the planes in shadow and for drop shadows. The application of paint reveals a very sophisticated use of egg tempera pigment, which is pushed "to the limits of the optical effects of which it is capable" (A. Roy in Smith, Reeve, and Roy 1981, p. 54). These features of *Saint Vincent Ferrer*'s painting technique are shared by all of the panels in the main body of the polyptych that are attributable to Cossa.

The painting portrays Saint Vincent Ferrer according to the most widespread iconography after his canonization in 1455—that is, with his right hand raised pointing at the vision of Christ on the Day of Judgment, enclosed in a mandorla, and his left hand holding an open book, which usually (but not in this case) contains the announcement of that event: "*Timete Deum et date illi honorem quia venit hora iudicii eius*" (Revelation, 14:7). This arrangement emphasizes the role of the Dominican friar in preaching the last destiny of humankind and of the world to all peoples and nations, according to his exceptional virtues described in the canonization decree and official biography by Pietro Ranzano. As recently noted (Ackerman Smoller 2014, esp. pp. 195–97), this figurative model chooses to overlook the unfulfilled predictions in Vincent Ferrer's sermons concerning the arrival of the Antichrist; rather, it more generally calls for repentance in view of the divine tribunal. The model soon became established, probably because it was based on a prototype that had been circulating in the Dominican Order after being disseminated during the famous ceremony that turned the preacher into a saint (see Cobianchi 2006, pp. 53–54; Cobianchi 2007, esp. pp. 209, 211, 213–14, 219; Velasco González 2008, pp. 235–52), which artists could hardly ignore. In the same posture and with negligible variations Saint Vincent Ferrer is depicted in the painting by Giovanni Francesco da Rimini currently at the Galleria dell'Accademia in Florence (inv. 1890, no. 3461; c. 1455–57), and in the central panel of Angelo and Bartolomeo degli Erri's altarpiece, formerly at the church of San Domenico in Modena and currently at the Seminario Arcivescovile in the same city (c. 1480–85). When compared to the above-mentioned examples, Cossa's painting marks a decisive step forward as regards the elaborate landscape in the background, which is filled with people and architectural structures and dominated by an imposing pillar in the classical style, surmounted by an arch in ruins. The saint is sophisticatedly immersed in the landscape—a human being, yet portrayed as if he were an ancient sculpture, seen from the front and standing on a precious hexagonal raised pedestal covered in polychrome marbles and emphasized by a red drape. Furthermore, the portrayal of Jesus as Judge is so remarkable that it is regarded as one of Cossa's best creations. Although it borrows the iconography imposed by the Order of Preachers (an Oriental-like Majestas Domini: see Klein 1992, pp. 163–64; Christe 1992, pp. 237, 251–55; Ackerman Smoller 2014, pp. 196 and 209, fig. 10), the scene fashioned by our Ferrara artist is unmatched as to the plausibility of the evocation of that supranatural event. The group of angels carrying the mandorla that contains Christ is encompassed in a celestial vision, where other angels, holding the symbols of the Passion, acquire distinct personalities. The ensemble shows an uncommon sensitivity for the current times, which translates into the highly natural appearance of Christ and of the angels themselves—as is especially visible in those seen in profile, which close the bottom sides of the golden dome, their hairdos in the style of the time. As Elisa Tosi Brandi pointed out, the angel holding the whips, on the left-hand side, wears a blue doublet with an unusually high collar for the period, a surcoat with long, open sleeves, and a chlamys-like cloak in an equally antique style. His expressive plausibility is further enhanced by the accurate and bold geometric definition of space and by the precision of the desaturated and iridescent tones that capture the reflection of gold, shining upon the clothes and the compact heaps of clouds.

The London panel can undoubtedly be identified with the central part, depicting "San Vincenzo," of the Griffoni Polyptych, which was sketched out by Stefano Orlandi in his letter to Monsignor Aldrovandi dated February 14, 1725 (exhibited on this occasion), before the work was dismembered (ASBo, Aldrovandi Marescotti, 230: F. Montefusco Bignozzi in Benati 1984, p. 156, fig. 185; hereinafter, *Orlandi's Letter 1725*). Reference thereto is also made in the letter sent by Giuseppe Baraldi to Monsignor Aldrovandi on November 21, 1725 (also exhibited) (ASBo, Aldrovandi Marescotti, 230: Cavalca 2013, p. 383 doc.XI.24; transcription by Ilaria Negretti; hereinafter, *Baraldi's Letter 1725*), which records the progress of the works when the ensemble was dismembered into several panels, ready to be framed and used as individual paintings; the size of the fragment, as far as the painted area is concerned, is said to be approximately 4 Bolognese feet (38.0098), that is to say approximately 152 cm—which perfectly matches the current one.

The *Saint Vincent* was intended, just like the other paintings, for the Aldrovandi's country residence in Mirabello, near Ferrara (see letter of May 18, 1726 from Angelo Fontana to Monsignor Aldrovandi: ASBo, Aldrovandi Marescotti and Marescotti, 230, no. 1(2); see Cavalca 2013, p. 384 doc. XI.26; transcription by Ilaria Negretti; hereinafter, *Fontana's Letter 1726*). It arrived there before 1732, when, according to *Pitture di Bologna*, the Griffoni Polyptych was no longer in its chapel at San Petronio. From the Aldrovandi palace in Mirabello, it was acquired before 1835 into Giovanni Battista Costabili's collection in Ferrara, where it was recorded as a *Saint Dominic* painted by Marco Zoppo (see *Pitture* 1835, f. 13v, no. 83; see Mattaliano 1998, p. 125, no. 415). Thanks to the intermediation of the "merchant of paintings" Michelangelo Gualandi (see Mazza's contribution in this catalogue, p. 136), in 1858 it was purchased as such by Charles Eastlake for the National Gallery of London (see Davies 1951, pp. 115–18). Joseph Archer Crowe and Giovanni Battista Cavalcaselle (1871 ed. 1912, II, pp. 237–38) then shifted its attribution to the School of Ferrara ("an artist who follows in the footsteps of Tura and Cossa") and identified for the first time its resemblance with *Saint Peter* and *Saint John the Baptist* at the Pinacoteca di Brera. Finally, in 1888, Frizzoni correctly identified it as the central panel of the Griffoni Polyptych and linked it, as well as to the panels of Brera, to the predella at the Pinacoteca Vaticana, with the same attribution.

Francesco del Cossa

2. Saint Peter

tempera on panel, support 111.4 × 54.5 cm, painted area 109.9 × 54 cm
Pinacoteca di Brera, Milan, inv. 449 (Reg. Cron. 1182)

3. Saint John the Baptist

tempera on panel, support 113.5 × 55.5 cm, painted area 109.8 × 54 cm
Pinacoteca di Brera, Milan, inv. 449bis (Reg. Cron. 1183)
Inscriptions: in the scroll, *EG[O SUM] VOC[ES] C[LAMAN]TES IN DESERTO*

The pictorial surface of both works is in good conditions and along the perimeter one can clearly see the edges of the original frame. The thickness of the support, which has not been thinned down, is between 2.8 and 3 cm, showing traces of pegs and, on the back, of terminal crossbeams at the bottom and on the top of the same sections (Cavalca 2013, p. 144, fig. 114). Some ancient gaps restored with stucco have been detected in Saint Peter's cloak, clothes, and halo (E. Daffra in *Restituzioni* 2016, figs. on pp. 172–73). The analyses carried out in 2007 (Poldi and Villa 2007, pp. 159, 161, figs. 126–27) and in 2016 (by the Photography Laboratory of the Centro Ricerche sul Dipinto di Brera; see E. Daffra in *Restituzioni* 2016, figs. on pp. 173–74) revealed an accurate planning of the figures and architectures, outlined by a thin and steadfast incision. The preparatory drawing was very accurate too and, using diagonal strokes of different thicknesses, it builds the backbone of light and shade for the application of paint. The composition in the background is instead much freer and has no incisions, showing some significant incongruities between the trace of the pencil and the application of paint. On the right-hand side of *Saint John the Baptist*'s panel, for instance, the silhouette of the fragment of a capital and of some architecturals remains are visible to the naked eye, covered up by a rocky cave on which a built-up area stands (ibid., p. 174; see also Lodi's contribution in this catalogue).

Saint Peter and Saint John the Baptist are portrayed in accordance with traditional iconography. The former wears blue clothes and a yellow cloak, showing as his distinctive attributes the key and the book, which he is reading thoughtfully; the latter, with an inscrutable and penitential look, is dressed in animal skins and wrapped in an ample red drape, holding a scroll in his right hand and a cross with the *Agnus Dei* and a lizard next to the base (according to Levi d'Ancona 2001, p. 155, a symbol of the search for Christ) in his left. The following elements are worth noting. As to Saint Peter, the emphasis placed on the white shirt and red lining of the cloak, as possible allusions to the saint's spiritual purity and martyrdom. As to Saint John the Baptist, the words in the scroll, which distance themselves from the text of the Gospel (John 1, 23: "*ego sum vox clamantis in deserto*") and evoke a plurality of "voices" to be understood (Torella [1985–87] 1988, p. 51) as a reference to Pope Sixtus IV's call to arms against the infidels, symbolized by the fox in the background. Both saints stand on a rock and occupy with their monumental presence the entire scene of a space overlooking a seamless landscape, characterized by bizarre rocky outcrops; only a cormorant populates the scene behind Saint Peter, while the landscape behind the Baptist is teeming with life. As it was the case with the London panel, the two imposing ancient pillars behind them convey the depth of the landscape and provide a support for the elements connecting the various figurations and the frame, now lost. The matrix for the sophisticated counterpoise of Saint John the Baptist with respect to the viewer has been identified in the same saint in Maso Finiguerra's niello depicting the *Coronation of the Virgin* at the Museo Nazionale del Bargello in Florence (inv. 330r; see Collareta 2012, p. 46). The comparison is quite illuminating; however, the aristocratic purity with which every detail in Cossa's Baptist is bent to convey the illusionistic effect of that posture goes well beyond the prompt given by that famous Florentine model, thus emphasizing the maturity of the Ferrara artist's reply to an artistic tradition that is not unfamiliar with the figurative culture of origin, from which he most probably had the chance to borrow by direct comparison.

The paintings can undoubtedly be identified, respectively, with the "San Pietro" and the "San Giovanni Batista" recorded in the main register of the Griffoni Polyptych in Stefano Orlandi's drawing, made before it was dismembered (*Orlandi's Letter 1725*). Reference to them is also made in the subsequent letter from Giuseppe Baraldi (*Baraldi's Letter 1725*), which confirms that they were converted into single paintings and reports that their size was 3 Bolognese feet, that is approximately 114 cm—which perfectly matches the current one.

Intended, just like the other figure paintings of the polyptych, for the Aldrovandi's residence in Mirabello near Ferrara (*Fontana's Letter 1726*), they actually reached that location, as per the contemporary sources that unanimously refer to the transportation to the Aldrovandi "house" of all the sections of the work (see Oretti *ante* 1787, p. 215). There are evidences that already in 1843 both paintings, dubitatively attributed to Zoppo or Mantegna, were in Ferrara, in the collection of Giovanni Barbi Cinti, procurator general at the house of Giovanni Battista Costabili, who in turn owned, in the same years, as many as six panels of the polyptych (see Agostini and Scardino 1997, pp. 13–15, nos. 73–74; Mattaliano 1998, pp. 52, 62, 125, 127, nos. 68, 106–7, 415, 420–21). After being sold to Enea Vendeghini together with a selected group of works form the Barbi Cinti collection, in 1893 they were acquired—and not without some controversy (Mantovani 1997; see also Mazza's contribution in this catalogue)—by Giuseppe Cavalieri for the Pinacoteca di Brera at the suggestion of Adolfo Venturi (Malaguzzi Valeri 1908, p. 250). After Joseph Archer Crowe and Giovanni Battista Cavalcaselle linked them to the *Saint Vincent Ferrer* in London (1871 ed. 1912, II, pp. 237–38; see cat. no. 1), they were recognized for the first time as elements of the Griffoni Polyptych by Gustavo Frizzoni (1888), who also linked to the ensemble the predella at the Pinacoteca Vaticana.

Francesco del Cossa

4. Saint Florian

tempera on panel, 79.4 × 55 cm
National Gallery of Art, Washington, DC, inv. NGA 1939.1.227

5. Saint Lucy

tempera on panel, 79.2 × 56 cm
National Gallery of Art, Washington, DC, inv. NGA 1939.1.228

The pictorial surface of both works is in good conditions. The supports, trimmed on the top and bottom parts, have been thinned down, mounted on a new panel and cradled in 1937 by Stephen Picchetto. The arch structures are the original ones albeit partially reworked (see Dunkerton's contribution in this catalogue) and, under the repainted areas to the sides, the raw wood on which the frame rested is still visible. The bases have been leveled out by adding two non-original, repainted wooden slats, 2 cm (*Saint Florian*) and 2.5 cm (*Saint Lucy*) high. Vast areas of the background had to be regilded, especially in *Saint Lucy*; some minor retouches involved the paint, which had to be reinforced especially in shadow areas, on Saint Florian's hair, and Saint Lucy's left cheek. A vertical crack runs across the center of *Saint Florian*'s panel (see J. Manca in *Italian Paintings* 2003, p. 215). The results of the analysis performed on *Saint Lucy* (ibid.) prove that the planning of the figures and the application of paint are very similar to those of the panels in London and Brera (cat. nos. 2–3). Indeed, also in this case, the profiles of the figures are marked by thin incisions and a line drawing is employed to build shadows (see Dunkerton's contribution in this catalogue).

The identity of the two saints, which bear the features of the clients, Floriano Griffoni and his first wife, Lucia Battaglia, has been long misunderstood. When the polyptych was dismembered, they were described as "San Paolo" and "Santa Rosalia" (*Orlandi's Letter 1725*). Saint Florian was later also mistaken for Saint Martin (in the Ugo Beni collection, sale of April–May 1882, lots 4 and 5; see Davies 1951, p. 118 note 16), and was still believed to be Saint Liberalis in Adolfo Venturi's *Storia dell'Arte* (1901–40, VII/3, 1914, p. 599, fig. 448).

Francesco del Cossa portrayed them both wearing contemporary clothing, thus turning them into two superb crypto-portraits. Saint Florian, who is among the patron saints of the city of Bologna (see G. D. Gordini in *Bibliotheca sanctorum* 1964, pp. 934–38), has a sword and a flower—a reference to his name—in his hands, according to the traditional iconography. A direct precedent is found in the Basilica of San Petronio, where the same saint was frescoed by Giovanni da Modena on the walls of the Bolognini Chapel (see J. Manca in *Italian Paintings* 2003, p. 220), wearing equally luxurious clothes, played on the contrast between the blue of the vestment and the red of the cloak, with a fur linen and hem. On the other hand, the depiction of Saint Lucy's attribute of the eyes as two buds on a stem is unprecedented. It has been speculated that this uncommon iconographic choice is a homage to the name of her husband—certainly, it is nonetheless a clever device to highlight a detail that would otherwise be invisible due to the perspective of the work.

The paintings can definitely be identified with those in the top register of the polyptych in Orlandi's sketch, above *Saint Peter* and *Saint John the Baptist*, respectively (*Orlandi's Letter 1725*). As single paintings, they measured 2 Bolognese feet (*Baraldi's Letter 1725*)—i.e. approximately 76 cm, which, with a slight upward deviation, is their current measure. Intended for the Aldrovandi's country residence in Mirabello (*Fontana's Letter 1726*), in 1858 they were in Gubbio as part of the Ugo Beni collection, attributed to Marco Zoppo (see Davies 1951, p. 118 note 16, with reference to a note dated June 3, 1858 in the diaries of Otto Mündler). In 1882 they reached Paris as part of the Joseph Spiridon collection; in the catalogue of the sale, Oskar Fischel recognized them as Cossa's work (Cassirer and Helbing, Berlin, May 31, 1929, nos.

12– 13). With this new Cossa attribution, between 1929 and 1930 they were in New York at the Duveen Brothers (*Duveen Pictures* 1941, no. 65) and in 1936, under the same authorship, they joined the collection of Samuel H. Kress.

After Venturi confirmed the attribution to our Ferrara master (1906, p. 139; 1901–40, III/3, 1914, p. 596), it was Longhi who, not without some controversy, recognized them as part of the original polyptych (1934, pp. 32–35). The inconsistency between the gold background of *Saint Florian* and *Saint Lucy* and the natural background of the group of works to which they were being associated was further emphasized, according to a number of scholars, by some rather significant stylistic differences (Neppi 1958, pp. 24, 26, 28 and Rhumer 1959, p. 85); disparities had also been noted in the size of the figures and in the shape of the halos (Davies 1951, p. 116; see also A. Smith in Smith, Reeve, and Roy 1981, p. 45; Armstrong 1988, p. 470). However, when the sketch made by Stefano Orlandi before the dismemberment of the polyptych was found in 1984, the validity of Longhi's hypothesis could not but be confirmed (see Benati 1984, p. 156, fig. 185).

Francesco del Cossa

6. Crucifixion

tempera on panel, diameter of support 63.2 cm, of painted surface 60 cm
National Gallery of Art, Washington, DC, inv. NGA 1952.5.5
Inscriptions: in the scroll of the Cross, I.N.R.I.

The painted surface is in excellent condition. The support is made out of a single vertical fiber poplar tree panel, thinned and reinforced with a board in 1944 by Stephen Picchetto. Along the perimeter, the edges of the frame are still clearly visible, marked by raised pictorial pigment, placed about two centimeters from the outer edge, which was originally rough on the external portion. Minor retouches were made to the Virgin's left shoulder, corresponding to a crack in the support, and to some areas at the bottom, which were selectively regilded (see J. Manca in *Italian Paintings* 2003, p. 223). Technical notes from recent museum analyses (see ibid.; previously also Allen 1999, p. XVII) show that this painting matches infrared reflectography findings in other portrayals that we may ascribe to Cossa with certainty: the outlines of the figures, the architectural elements and the haloes are marked by thin engravings, reinforced with a draughtsmanship that defines the areas in shadow with oblique strokes, reprised in the tempera hatching visible to the naked eye.

The gilded, circular background that houses the depiction is separated into two perfectly symmetrical halves by the cross of Christ, on either side of which are the figures of the Virgin and Saint John the Evangelist according to a very common motif, which originally had the function of visualizing the passage of the Gospel in which Jesus, before he dies, entrusts his Mother to the apostle (John 19:26–27). In accordance with the artistic conventions of the day, Cossa depicts Christ dead, his head lolling to the right; the two figures at the foot of the cross are captured in a highly realistic way, expressing the utmost pain. This iconography emphasizes the salvational value entrusted to divine sacrifice, with the representation of the skull as an allusion to Golgotha as well as to the burial of Adam, evoked by the superbly foreshortened bones emerging from the hollow of the bridge-like structure on which the cross stands. In order to emphasize the power of redemption immediately attributed to blood, particular importance is given to the blood that flows from the nails stuck into Christ's palms, streaming down his limbs, coming out of his side and, running over his now bruised body, coagulating on his feet in rivulets that run until they break onto the top of the skull.

The painting can certainly be identified as the "crucifix" described by Stefano Orlandi in the center of the upper register of the polyptych, in correspondence with Saint Vincent Ferrer, today in London (*Orlandi's Letter 1725*). Like the other just-dismembered main sections of the work, it was earmarked for the Aldrovandi's country residence (see *Lettera Baraldi 1725* and *Lettera Fontana 1726*); indeed, as coming from Mirabello, in 1835 it was in the Costabili collection in Ferrara and was described as follows: "A Crucifix, the Blessed Virgin and Saint Giò at its feet. A medium-size round panel with a gold background in the manner of Lorenzo Costa" (see *Pitture* 1835, f. 18r, no. 143; Mattaliano 1998, p. 52, no. 68). Five other "Griffoni compartments" were hidden under different, irrelevant names, as part of the same collection (see cat. nos. 1, 8–9, 11, 13). In 1914, the work was in New York, in the collection of Philip Lehman (1861–1947). In June 1943, it passed into the collection of Samuel H. Kress through the intermediation of Robert Lehman (see J. Manca in *Italian Paintings* 2003, p. 225).

Ascribed to Andrea del Castagno by Wilhelm von Bode (in a handwritten opinion: see Shapley 1966, p. 84), Fiocco (1925, p. 157) who later rectified his judgment, and Berenson (1932, p. 137), the *Crucifixion* had been recognized as a certain Cossa work by Perkins and Breck as early as 1914 (pp. 222–23 and pp. 314–17 respectively), Longhi (1926 ed. 1967, p. 86), Venturi (1931, p. 43), and Salmi (1934, p. 136). It was Longhi (1934 ed. 1956, p. 33) who re-associated it with the polyptych to which it belongs, ideally placing it in its correct position on the second register, between Saints Florian and Lucy. "Anyone who extends their observation to all three pieces at once," he wrote in his *Officina*, "may immediately note, thanks to the perspective from below, that not only did they originally belong to a polyptych, but precisely to the upper part of a Cossa polyptych ... It should further be noted that the practice of crowning a polyptych with a Crucifixion scene (rather than with the Pietà, frequently at the top of Venetian polyptychs) could very naturally have reached Cossa via Tuscany (Masaccio's Pisa polyptych, Piero's polyptych at San Sepolcro)."

Ercole de' Roberti

7. Miracles of Saint Vincent Ferrer

The rescue of a pregnant young woman falling from the stairs, whose son is baptized after birth • The healing of a possessed woman • The healing of Giovanni Limon's left leg from podagra • The rescue of a young man who had fallen asleep and was about to fall from a high place to follow a sermon by the saint in the square of Toulouse • The extinction of fire in a house through the intercession of the saint • The resurrection of the two-year-old son of a lunatic pregnant woman from Vannes, who had been cut into pieces and cooked by her

tempera on panel, 29.6 × 214.6 cm
Vatican Museums, Vatican City, inv. 40286

The pictorial surface is overall in good condition. The support has been thinned down to a thickness of about 0.9 cm and reinforced at the beginning of the last century with a fixed frame (consisting of twelve panels defined by thick wooden struts of about 5 cm) treated with an ochre-colored waterproofing material. The restoration carried out in 1950 by Luigi Brandi under the direction of Redig de Campos (1955, pp. 411–14 and ASMV, ALRP, b. 10, fasc. 7; prot. 2957; ASMV, ALRP, DGF) cleared the panel from multiple repaintings and a thick layer of varnish, highlighting along the entire perimeter an irregularly shaped border of about 1 cm, stuccoed and repainted in ancient times, which is supposedly caused by the "levers with which the predella was brutally detached from the frame." The presence of a long horizontal fissure was also detected, running through the wood panel and causing considerable damage, especially to the last two figures at the right end, almost entirely deprived of their legs. Multiple abrasions and micro color fading are also reported. The results of the most recent analyses carried out at the Vatican Laboratories (RGB, RX, and IR shootings, unpublished report by Ulderico Santamaria, October 11, 2009; see Cavalca 2013, pp. 138–50, figs. 130–33) have shown that the predella is not significantly cut neither on the short right side nor on the left side, as it had long been supposed (see Davies 1951, pp. 116, 117 note 13; Benati 1985, pp. 172–74). It was also possible to acknowledge, in a number of figures and the landscape, the presence of a preparatory drawing carried out with energetic oblique strokes in correspondence with shadow areas. There are evident traces of thin lines engraved in the profiles and different areas of the drapery, as well as measuring points for the architectural structures, which had already been recognized in the past (Brandi restoration, 1950; Allen 1999, p. XVII). Although no noticeable reconsiderations are detectable in the final layout, there are several discrepancies between the graphic and the pictorial layouts; for example, in the outermost portion of landscape of the first scene on the left, or in the head of one of the women who intervene, from the right, in the central miracle, as well as in the Eastern man with a turban on the side of the temple where the last miraculous episode takes place: in the final version he no longer holds a book but extends his arm. Variations in volume and other minor details, which were corrected during the painting process with graphic and chromatic overlaps, suggest an accurate evaluation and constant executive freedom while finalizing the work. The stroke of the drawing is consistent with that found in other minor elements of the polyptych, especially in the Gazzada *Annunciation* (cat. nos. 8–9).

The complex iconography of the predella, on which Lamo already was mistaken (1560 ed. 1996, p. 101: "*li miracoli de San Nicola*") has always been the subject of different interpretations. In the negotiation that led to the purchase of the work by the Vatican Museums, the seller Feliciano Brizi described it as an explanation of the miracles of Saint Antoninus, and then of Saint Vincent Ferrer (letters of June 16, 1830 to the chamberlain Cardinal Galeffi, and of April 13, 1839 to the chamberlain Cardinal Giustiniani: see Davies 1951, p. 118 note 14). When purchasing the work, the Vatican commission corrected the subject into *Prodigies of Dominican Saint Hyacinth*, as shown by four memoirs, one of which a print copy (see Cavalca 2013, p. 393, doc. XXXVI; Campisi 2018, pp. 101–2), and an article by Gustave Gruyer published in *Notes d'Art et d'Archéologie* (January 1890), with such an articulate argument that, although not accepted, they still seemed worthy of attention to Davies (1951, p. 118 note 14).

The interpretation of the various scenes as *The Miracles of Saint Vincent Ferrer* emerged with the reunion of the predella with the Petronian polyptych dedicated to the Dominican saint (Frizzoni 1888, p. 300; who, however, after Gruyer's article, retraced his steps regarding the subject and the destination of the whole, thinking of the chapel of Saint Hyacinth in the church of San Domenico in Ferrara; see Frizzoni 1897, p. 226) and then tended to prevail thanks to the accurate digression by Alberto Serafini in the pages of Venturi's *Storia dell'arte* (1901–40, VII/3, 1914, pp. 624–27). Serafini's interpretation is substantially confirmed by Kaftal (1978, cols. 1072–74, 1079, 1084), who raises the doubt that the central scene may depict not *The resurrection of a wealthy Spanish Jewish woman* but *The liberation of a possessed woman who accuses the saint to have tried to seduce her* (ibid., col. 1072, no. 14). According to Gentili (1982, p. 570) and Torella ([1985–87] 1988, p. 47), who discuss again in detail the meaning of the whole composition, this episode would instead depict the miracle of *The healing of a possessed woman*, while the first scene would not refer to the miracle performed on the lame Teodora Suarez but rather to *The rescue of a pregnant young woman falling from the stairs, whose son is baptized after birth*. The issue is not solved in the more recent monographs dedicated to Ercole de' Roberti, where the traditional interpretation of the two most discussed episodes prevails again (Manca 1992, p. 96; Molteni 1995, p. 115). The perpetuation of these different opinions is justified (as Ackerman Smoller now argues: 2014, pp. 195–218, esp. p. 197) considering that, unlike what happens for the image of the new saint (cat. no. 1), during the fifteenth century his miracles have been represented in many different ways, only partially coinciding with the official narration developed in his biography by Pietro Ranzano (c. 1426–1492) at the behest of the Pope and the Dominican order. The overall reconsideration of the Renaissance iconography of Saint Vincent Ferrer carried out by Ackerman Smoller (2014, pp. 209–11) recovers for the Vatican predella the correction proposals put forward by Gentili and Torella, enhancing the healing of the body as a prelude to the salvation of the soul and alluding to baptism based on Ranzano's biography, on Antoninus of Florence and Francesco Castiglione's *Vitae* and, perhaps, also on the investigations related to the process of canonization. In agreement with Torella, the scholar embraces, besides this theological message, the broader political meaning of this representation, revealed by the presence of several exotic figures—Moors, Jews, Turks, and Arabs. It might be an appeal to mobilize for a crusade, invoked after the traumatic fall of Constantinople in 1453 that caused apocalyptic fears echoed in the prophecies attributed to Saint Vincent Ferrer: this was again a topical issue in 1471, with the election of Sixtus IV, after the conquest of Negroponte in 1470.

The predella can be identified with certainty with the "*storia di figure picole che cuopre tutto l'abasamento*" described by Stefano Orlandi before the dismemberment of the Griffoni Polyptych (*Orlandi's Letter 1725*). The predella is also mentioned in the subsequent letter by Giuseppe Baraldi (*Baraldi's Letter 1725*), who attests to its being an autonomous painting and indicates its size: about 6 Bolognese feet in length and 10 ounces in width, which means about 228 x 31 cm, except for a slight excess difference, perfectly corresponding to the current one.

Destined, like all the other illustrated portions of the polyptych, to the country residence of the Aldrovandi family in Mirabello, near Ferrara (*Fontana's Letter 1726*), it is recorded in the inventory of the palace's assets compiled on the death of Cardinal Pompeo Aldrovandi in 1752 (see Mazza's contribution in this catalogue, p. 124 note 13). The hypothesis of its older provenance already circulated at the time of the purchase of the work in Bologna, around 1829, by Giovanni Celsi (then co-owner of the work with Feliciano Brizi) from the lawyer Vincenzo Filicori, who kept it among the assets of his family but had failed to provide certain evidence of its ancient origin (C. Cavalca in *Cosmè Tura e Francesco del Cossa* 2007, p. 468; Cavalca 2013, p. 393, doc. XXXVI). After a negotiation that lasted for about ten years, the work was sold in 1839 for 2,000 *scudi* by Feliciano Brizi, in charge of the registry office in Viterbo, to the Vatican Apostolic Palaces as the work of Benozzo Gozzoli, as determined by a special committee (see Davies 1951, p. 117 note 11; C. Cavalca in *Cosmè Tura e Francesco del Cossa* 2007, p. 468; Cavalca 2013, p. 393, doc. XXXVI). It became part of the ancient Pinacoteca Vaticana in 1909 (inv. 145) and in 1932, it reached the present one (see Manca 1992, p. 93).

The predella was recognized as an element of the Griffoni Polyptych by Frizzoni (1888) and associated with the London and Brera parts as an authentic work by Francesco del Cossa. The attribution to Ercole de' Roberti, proposed by Vasari (1568 ed. 1878–81, III, pp. 133, 142–43) and generally accepted today, was postulated for the first time by Morelli (1886, p. 112). At the beginning of the last century, Filippini's archival research (1914, pp. 414–49; 1917, p. 63) paved the way for an unfinished debate about the extent of de' Roberti stylistic autonomy in relation to Cossa in the making of the painting. The executive freshness of the whole, confirmed by the high quality of the graphic layout detected with infrared reflectography, declares de' Roberti's complete autography of the final layout and painting process. Nevertheless, it should be taken into account that the younger artist worked alongside Cossa and could rely on a detailed project of the polyptych and, very likely, on single drawings from which he could draw compositional and morphological ideas.

Ercole de' Roberti

8. Archangel Gabriel

tempera on panel, diameter of support 24 cm, of painted area 21 cm
Villa Cagnola, Fondazione Paolo VI, Gazzada (Varese), inv. 32

9. Virgin Annunciate

tempera on panel, diameter of support 23.8 cm, of painted area 21.5 cm
Villa Cagnola, Fondazione Paolo VI, Gazzada (Varese), inv. 33

The conservation of the pictorial surface of both tondos is excellent. The supports are comprised of a single, vertical-grain poplar wood panel, thinned down (approximately 0.5 cm) and reinforced by cradling at an unknown time, yet certainly before 1965 (see Ciardi 1965, p. 54). As is the case with the *Crucifixion* tondo in Washington, DC (cat. no. 6), the edges of the frame are still well visible along the perimeter of each panel, approximately two centimeters from the outer border, which was originally raw and now is stuccoed and gilded. Some micro-falls of the pigment, which were stabilized during the 1995 restoration (A. Zanolini; see D. Benati in *La collezione Cagnola* n.d. [1998], p. 140), and slight retouches affect the upper part of the Virgin's head, where there is a crack reaching the farthest end of the support. Gianluca Poldi's 2014 unpublished infrared reflectography uncovered a rather free preparatory drawing, with corrections and second thoughts involving the silhouette of the angel, especially his arms and fingers, and the tilt angle of the Virgin's halo. The silhouette and drapery of her dark cloak are marked by a thin incision on the preparation layer. More or less thick (but not heavy) diagonal strokes mark some portions of chiaroscuro and the area behind the Virgin, where the drawing also featurs some architectural segments. As a whole, the structure of the drawing for the two tondos is consistent with that of the predella at the Pinacoteca Vaticana (see cat. no. 7 and Dunkerton's contribution in this catalogue).

The two tondos were originally located on the top part of the Griffoni Polyptych. Their overall composition was rather common in late-Gothic Emilian painting, both in Bologna and in Ferrara. The Archangel Gabriel and the Virgin Annunciate, the latter portrayed in a niche that accommodates the bookstand, are also the subjects, set inside polylobate tondos, of the pinnacles of Jacopo di Paolo's polyptych of the *Crucifixion*, later dismembered and now kept at the Pinacoteca Nazionale in Bologna (inv. 238, 233, 243, c. 1400–10). On a monumental scale, a similar iconography but with a completely new perspectival focus was later resumed by Marco Zoppo on the top level of the triptych for the church of the Royal College of Spain in Bologna (1458–61) and, with slight variations, again by Francesco del Cossa in his 1474 "Pala dei Mercanti" (Pinacoteca Nazionale, Bologna, inv. 580). More specifically, the morphology of the Archangel Gabriel, with his thin silhouette and slightly agitated gestures, counterbalanced by the voluminous surcoat that is blown up as he enters the scene to give the announcement, had already been used in Ferrara in a juvenile masterpiece by Cosmè Tura, *Madonna and Child in a Garden* (National Gallery of Art, Washington, DC, inv. 1952.5.29, before 1455), also featuring the same type of Virgin, with her petite figure wrapped in a heavy cloak with a hood.

The paintings can undoubtedly be identified with "*l'angiolo e Maria Vergine anontiata*" described by Stefano Orlandi as the top panels of the Griffoni Polyptych, above *Saint Florian* and *Saint Lucy*, respectively, currently in Washington, DC (*Orlandi's Letter 1725*). Intended for the Aldrovandi's country residence in Mirabello, near Ferrara (*Fontana's Letter 1726*), in 1835 they formed part of the Costabili collection in Ferrara, recorded as coming from the palace in Mirabello and described as "The Annunciation divided into two small round paintings on panel" (see *Pitture* 1835, f. 20v, nos. 181–181/2; see Mattaliano 1998, p. 127, nos. 420–21). At that time, the Costabili collection included, under different and wrong names, other four panels of the Griffoni Polyptych (cat. nos. 1, 6, 11, and 13). Still in 1871, the Catalogo

Giordani (nos. 79–80; see Mattaliano 1998, p. 127) attributed the two tondos to an "Unknown Bolognese, perhaps Marco Zoppo, or the Ferrarese Cosmè." They were sold in Milan in 1885 (Sambon, April 27–29, 1885, no. 32) and joined the Levis collection (see Longhi 1940 ed. 1956, p. 129), then the Frizzoni collection in Bergamo, and finally in 1934 reached the house of Guido Gagnola, who recognized the hand of de' Roberti (see Ciardi 1965, p. 54; D. Benati in *La collezione Cagnola* n.d. [1998], p. 140) even though his friend Berenson (1932, p. 186) had just published them with a very vague authorship, "unknown Ferrarese before 1510." In the same years, Longhi (1934 ed. 1956, pp. 98–99 note 72; 1940 ed. 1956, pp. 129–30) managed to reconnect them, gradually yet undoubtedly, to the Griffoni Polyptych and to Francesco del Cossa, thanks to some brilliant intuitions of Crowe and Cavalcaselle (1871 ed. 1912, II, p. 53) and to the detailed historical and material information he had received from Gagnola himself (see D. Benati in *La collezione Cagnola* n.d. [1998], p. 140; C. Cavalca in *Cosmè Tura e Francesco del Cossa* 2007, p. 470). The position hypothesized by the scholar, "between the two levels of the painting," at the head of the series of small saints aligned along each side, would be corrected after Stefano Orlandi's sketch was found in 1984 (*Orlandi's Letter 1725*); still, the credit he owned for recognizing the hand of Cossa—for a long time favored over de' Roberti's, which was dubiously suggested for the first time by Nicolson (1950, p. 20)—would not fade. The two paintings were considered the work of Cossa by Bacchi (1984, p. 299; in 1991, pp. 32–33 he reviewed his opinion, with reservations), Varignana (1985, pp. 73–74), Turrill (1988, p. 274), Manca (1992, pp. 175–76; in *Italian Paintings* 2003, p. 218, although somewhat open to the hypothesis of de' Roberti), Sgarbi (2003, pp. 230–31). At the same time, Benati (1984, p. 170 and in *La collezione Cagnola* n.d. [1998], pp. 140–43), Lucco (1987, p. 242), Molteni (1995, p. 121), D. Cattoi (in *Gli Este a Ferrara* 2004, p. 295), C. Cavalca (in *Cosmè Tura e Francesco del Cossa* 2007, pp. 470–71; Cavalca 2013, pp. 138–41, 334–36, no. 19), and G. Calogero (in *Da Cimabue a Morandi* 2015, p. 80, no. 15) claimed that the author of the two paintings was actually de' Roberti.

Ercole de' Roberti

10. Saint Apollonia

tempera on panel, support 26.5 × 11 cm, painted area 23 × 8.9 cm
Musée du Louvre, Paris, inv. R. F. 1271A

The pictorial surface of the painting is overall in good condition. The support has been transported on wood (see D. Thiébaut in *Catalogue* 2007, p. 47) and the gaps of the original painting along the external perimeter have been compensated. Minor abrasions and retouches affect the figure and are especially evident in the garment.

According to custom, the saint from Alexandria is depicted as a young woman with a pair of pincers holding a tooth, the symbol of her martyrdom. The delicate features, the sophisticated hairstyle and the refined contemporary costume that distinguish her recall very closely the female characters of the Vatican predella (see cat. no. 7), in particular, the sick girl and her handmaids depicted in the first scene on the left. Longhi (1934 ed. 1956, pp. 34, 41–42, fig. 139; 1940 ed. 1956, p. 129) insists on the comparison between the two smaller portions of the polyptych: when linking this work to the whole, he emphasized the analogies between the drapery of the saint's mantle and that of a figure seen from behind in the scene with the *Resurrection of the son of the woman from Vannes*.

We do not know anything about *Saint Apollonia* until its appearance on the London market at Christie's Piazzetta Sale on May 27, 1825 (no. 65). On this occasion, it was coupled with *Archangel Michael* (cat. no. 12) with which it shared the fate and final destination. Throughout the nineteenth century, both works were believed to be by Mantegna; this reference was validated by an inscription on the back of *Archangel Michael* according to which they were removed from an altar in Padua. As such, they passed through Simon McGillivray (his sale at Christie's London, May 6, 1825, nos. 65–66), Mr. Fennel, Samuel Rogers (1763–1855; his sale at Christie's London, April 28, 1856, no. 686); then they are found in Paris in the Evans collection (sale of April 27, 1863, no. 19) and, later, in the collection of Baron Nathaniel de Rothschild (1812–1870) and his wife (1825–1899) (mentioned in the catalogue of the 1866 exhibition, no. 101; see D. Thiebaut in *Catalogue* 2007, p. 47), who in 1899 left them by testamentary legate to the Louvre.

The two paintings were assigned to Ercole de' Roberti by Venturi (1902, pp. 178–79) and with this credit they were displayed at the Ferrara exhibition of 1933, which confirmed this attribution that has remained undisputed since our day (*Esposizione della pittura ferrarese del Rinascimento* 1933, p. 94, nos. 109–10). On that occasion they were considered as parts of a lost polyptych that Barbantini, however, did not identify with the one from which *Saint Catherine of Alexandria* and *Saint Jerome* (also on display in Ferrara and today in the Cini collection in Venice) belonged. This problem was believed to be definitively shelved after Longhi's proposal to reunite these paintings to the Griffoni altar; but, unexpectedly, this exhibition forced to reconsider the issue (see cat. nos. 15–16).

Although the history of *Saint Apollonia* and *Archangel Michael* does not go back beyond the beginning of the nineteenth century, there is no doubt about their origin, being these two works perfectly consistent in size, shape, and style with the only two tiles depicting saints which passed, after 1731, from the Basilica of San Petronio to the country residence of the Aldrovandi family in Mirabello and then into the collection of Giovanni Battista Costabili in Ferrara, keeping track of their ancient provenance—that is to say, *Saint George* and *Saint Anthony the Abbot* (cat. nos. 11 and 13).

Longhi (1934 ed. 1956, p. 35; 1940 ed. 1956, fig. 309) thought that the whole series was divided, on the main order, into four illustrated panels on each side. He had tried to sort them based on their "perspective layout" and "attitude." In his reconstruction, *Saint Apollonia* was placed on the left pillar, as the second from the bottom and without a corresponding figure on the opposite pillar. After the discovery in 1984 of Orlandi's drawing (*Orlandi's Letter 1725*), Lucco (1987, p. 244, fig. 326) proposed, without any comment, a new arrangement of the lateral saints. In this reconstruction, the little saint occupies the third space; on the opposite side, *Archangel Michael* corresponds to her. In the most recent reconstruction (Cavalca 2013, p. 206), which reshapes the polyptych taking into account the size of the frame and brings the number of saints on the sides of the altar to fourteen (four on each side in the first order, three in the second), *Saint Apollonia* would be placed in the upper order in a median position. The new arrangement of this and the other tiles is guided, alongside the formal criteria highlighted by Longhi (the saint's feet are hidden to the view here, while an edge of the robe, sunk by the shadow, rises outward, beyond the threshold), by the study of the light in each representation. Indeed, light is one of the main unifying elements of the complex altarpiece designed for the Griffoni family. The deep shadows in the niches fade on the walls with surprising precision in relation to the diagonal direction of the lighting. Coming from the top left, it runs through the entire pictorial narration. It is also interesting to note de' Roberti's skill in diversifying the arrangement of the heads of the saints and the profile of the ribs of the niches, so that the figures most distant from the observer, leaning over, surpass them. More generally, the link between these small figures with their counterparts in the predella as well as with the major ones at the center of the polyptych should not be overlooked: in more than one case, they actually seem to be their "miniaturized" variants. The monumental and hieratic layout of *Saint Apollonia* reflects, for example, that of the Madonna in the tondo with the *Crucifixion*, while the elegant posture is one with *Saint Lucy*'s.

Ercole de' Roberti

11. Saint George

tempera on panel, support 24.7 × 10.9 cm, painted area 23 × 9 cm
Giorgio Cini Foundation, Palazzo Cini Gallery at San Vio, Venice, inv. VC6268

The pictorial surface is in excellent condition and along the perimeter there are traces of the inner edges of the original frame. Although the support is now fragile due to the several damages caused by woodworms over time, the pigments are exceptionally stable and the last restoration was limited to a slight cleaning (M. Nahabed, 2003; see L. Siracusano in *La Galleria di Palazzo Cini* 2016, p. 179). The diagnostic investigations with infrared reflectography (G. Poldi and G. F. Villa, 2002) have shown few visible traces of drawing, unlike what was found in the other two panels now preserved at the Cini Foundation, equally certainly attributed to de' Roberti, where a dense and oblique hatching in the shadow areas is evident (see cat. nos. 15–16). The hatching in *Saint George* can be detected only in correspondence with the elbow armor protection. As Gianluca Poldi pointed out, the absence of this intense linear texture is justified by the linear structure of the armor and by a volumetric effect directly obtained through the use of white lead on the black base to emphasize the lights.

Saint George defeating the dragon, a symbol of paganism, is here a willowy young man with mocking and haughty features dressed in a mid-fifteenth century armor. The spikes of the wings and the jaws of the beaten monster behind him are barely visible; only a coil of the tail that clings with no more energy to the crusader shield exhibited in the foreground still reminds of its superhuman strength. The dynamic attitude of the holy warrior fills the narrow space of the niche with life. He seems to want to escape from it to accept the praise of the victory, walking with a firm step (it is possible to distinguish the shadow drawn by the tip of the sole of the shoe most extended toward the observer). The complacency of the Ferrarese artist in describing the reflections on the armor creates an extreme contrast between lights and shadows that remains unmatched in his work for the Griffoni altar. Probably, as it has been suggested, de' Roberti drew inspiration from Andrea Mantegna's *Saint George*, preserved at the Gallerie dell'Accademia in Venice (inv. 98; evoked by Volpe 1977 ed. 1988, p. 21 and, with different accents, by Bacchi 1990, p. 26; Molteni 1995, p. 121; Syson 1999, p. IX; L. Siracusano in *La Galleria di Palazzo Cini* 2016, p. 183), a work that features, as if they were a leitmotiv, a captivating play of light on the metal of the contemporary armor and a concentrated attitude. In any case, de' Roberti's saint undoubtedly derives his truest identity from the courtly models found on the walls of Schifanoia, as Longhi had noticed (1940 ed. 1956, p. 128 and fig. 118; see also Salmi 1960, p. 18; Ruhmer 1963, p. 620 concerning the elements derived from Tura). It should be noticed that the painter employed an identical model in the predella to depict the young courtier dressed in yellow with a sword, arm in arm with another man, in the scene with *The healing of the possessed woman* in the right foreground.

The painting is one of the only two illustrated tiles (the other being *Saint Anthony the Abbot*, cat. no. 13) intended for the sides of the altar that can be identified with certainty with the series of four that were framed and meant to be sent to the country residence owned by the Aldrovandi family in Mirabello (see *Baraldi's Letter 1725*). Although we only know the size of these elements—"about 6 ounces high and 3 ounces wide" wrote Baraldi, providing us with a measure (19 x 9 cm) corresponding to that of the panel in question and the others belonging to the series—we know that in 1835 *Saint George* was with *Saint Anthony the Abbot* (believed to be Saint Benedict) in the Costabili collection in Ferrara, coming from Mirabello, together with four other parts of the Griffoni Polyptych (cat. nos. 1, 6, 8–9). The catalogue of the Ferrarese collection at that time describes the works as "two very small standing panels by Lorenzo Costa" (see *Pitture* 1835, c. 21v, nos. 206–7; see Mattaliano 1998, p. 62, nos. 106–7). In 1871 Crowe and Cavalcaselle (1871 ed. 1912, II, pp. 226–27 note 4) saw the panel in

England in the Alexander Barker collection and believed it to be a work by Cosmè Tura. After being acquired into the Rosebery collection in London, the painting was exhibited in January 1937 at the Burlington Fine Arts Club (Borenius 1937, p. 61) as a work by Andrea Mantegna, together with another *Saint George*, really by Tura (Cini Foundation, Venice, inv. VC6269) and coming from the same place. For Longhi (1940 ed. 1956, pp. 126–29) this was an opportunity to retrace their history backwards, starting from Crowe and Cavalcaselle's notes, and restore their true identity (Longhi 1940 ed. 1956, p. 128). The two *Saint Georges* were later reported by Siegfried Kramarsky to be in New York, where they remained until around 1946 before returning to Italy, first in the collection of Gualtiero Volterra in Florence and then, from April 20, 1954, in Vittorio Cini's (1940–1977). In 1989, by the will of his heirs, they were loaned to the Giorgio Cini Foundation.

With the dragon almost swallowed by the perspective cut, Longhi found it easy to place "the new holy picture at the top of the right pillar" of the Griffoni Polyptych, imagining it as the "hagiological" equivalent of the Louvre's *Archangel Michael*, which he had already placed on the opposite side: two early works by Ercole, dating back to around 1470. In the photographic ensemble proposed by Lucco (1987, p. 244), our *Saint George* remains on the right side but its position is lowered to the second space starting from the bottom. In the most recent reconstruction (Cavalca 2013, p. 266), the warrior-saint gains again a high position but on the left side, occupying the first space in the upper section of the pillar, next to *Saint Florian*, from where he can naturally direct his gaze toward the center of the representation, as Siracusano also reckons (in *La Galleria di Palazzo Cini* 2016, p. 182). I deem probable that this figure was initially connected on the opposite pillar with a lost *Saint Sebastian*, and I like to assume that the beautiful, youthful painting by Lorenzo Costa of analogous subject today in Dresden (Gemäldegalerie, inv. 42A) recalls both of them.

Ercole de' Roberti

12. Archangel Michael

tempera on panel, support 26.5 × 11 cm, painted area 23 × 8.7 cm
Musée du Louvre, Paris, inv. R. F. 1271 B

The pictorial surface is overall in good condition. The support has been transported on wood (see D. Thiébaut in *Catalogue* 2007, p. 47), ancient integrations have been eliminated and some gaps of the original painting compensated along the outer perimeter, extending toward the upper left side and affecting most of the lifted arm. Minor abrasions and retouches are present on the entire figure.

The *Archangel Michael* was connected to the Griffoni Polyptych by Longhi (1934 ed. 1956, pp. 34, 42; 1940 ed. 1956, p. 129); as for its origin and critical antecedents, please see the *Saint Apollonia* entry (cat. no. 10).

Archangel Michael, a symbol of the militant Christian, is depicted in the small Griffoni panel in the act of killing Satan—represented at his feet with semi-human features—with a spear and weighing the souls of the dead to establish the right reward. Drawing on these traditional iconographic assumptions, de' Roberti's representation fills up the small space of the fake niche and stands out for the emphasis put on the vigor of the saint's gesture of opposition and annihilation of evil. This is even more evident if compared to images such as the one recognized by Marco Zoppo in Bologna around the second half of the 1450s and known thanks to a drawing of the Uffizi (no. 59 S.), connected to the bronze *Saint George* by Nicolò Baroncelli and Domenico di Paris in the Cathedral of Ferrara (c. 1456) (see Armstrong 1976, pp. 396–97, no. D3; *Disegni del Rinascimento* 2001, pp. 90–94). As noted by J. Helvey (in *Ercole de' Roberti* 1999, p. XXVIII), not only de' Roberti shifts the weight of the saint on his right hip and rotates the torso and shoulders in a daring frontal view (which reminds very closely the *Saint George* painted by Cosmè Tura on the organ doors of the Cathedral: see Molteni 1995, p. 119), but also, having got rid of the wings, he catapults Michael's action to the extreme limits of the fake threshold, making him surmount with both feet the shoulders of the defeated Satan. The subtle highlights that make the helmet, armor, cloak, and transparent coat of the young celestial warrior sparkle had already led Longhi (1934 ed. 1956, p. 42) to establish accurate comparisons with the admirable and ready "firefighter" with a "forked (*biscornuto*) helmet" that livens up one of the central scenes of the predella. The scholar also remarked, although backwards, the style debts with the decorative cycle of Schifanoia, especially with the "forge of the Cyclop" in the month of *September*, which was attributed to the same artist.

Longhi (ibid., p. 35) imagined the *Archangel Michael* to occupy the last space of the left pillar of the main order, corresponding on the opposite side with *Saint George* now at Palazzo Cini, Venice (cat. no. 11). Lucco (1987, p. 244) instead placed the saint on the right pillar, the third space from the bottom, in connection with *Saint Apollonia* (cat. no. 10). Longhi's proposal has been confirmed by the most recent reconstruction, although its association with *Saint George* fails. Placed in perfect correspondence with the premonitory gesture of Saint Vincent Ferrer, *Saint Michael* resumes his central role in the scenes of the Last Judgment.

Ercole de' Roberti

13. Saint Anthony the Abbot

tempera on panel, support 24.7 × 11 cm, painted area 23 × 9 cm
Museum Boijmans Van Beuningen, Rotterdam, inv. 2561

The state of conservation of the painting is overall very good and, as in the case of *Saint George* (cat. no. 11), along the perimeter there are still traces of the inner edges of the original frame.

Following the recurring iconography, Saint Anthony the Abbot is depicted as an elderly monk with a long white beard, holding a crutch-shaped stick with a tau handle and a bell. Starting from these usual motifs and having at hand a recent precedent such as the *Saint Anthony the Abbot* painted by Zoppo on the pillars of the altar of San Clemente, de' Roberti develops a resolute composition with a remarkably experimental character, and distinguished, once again, by an unconditioned attitude toward the major examples of Cossa. Undoubtedly, the hermit saint is heavily indebted with the *Saint John the Baptist* placed in the main order of the polyptych for his admirable three-quarter perspective and his emotional intensity. The most interesting aspect of this depiction, and its truest stylistic code, as Longhi had already noticed, is the enveloping mantle, crystallized in wide and pointy folds and capable of creating a mass that dilates the space of the architectural niche outward. The saint's small head, inclined in a slightly elusive perspective, his fixed gaze, and the gesture aimed at stopping the tinkling of the bell give the whole an air of solemn concentration. The rendering of light decisively amplifies this lively atmosphere, captured at its expressive peak (the hermit touched by the voice of the Dominican preacher). This is a recurring motif in the figures painted by de' Roberti for the Griffoni Polyptych, but in a few other examples the concentration reaches such high effects—perhaps only in the *Archangel Gabriel* and *Saint George*.

This painting is one of the only two tiles (the other being the *Saint George* of the Cini Foundation cat. no. 11) that can be identified with certainty with the series of four that were framed and meant to be sent to the country residence owned by the Aldrovandi family in Mirabello (see *Baraldi's Letter 1725*). In 1835, with its companion *Saint George* and with the incorrect authorship of Lorenzo Costa, it was in the Costabili collection in Ferrara and indicated as coming from that residence (see *Pitture* 1835, f. 21, nos. 206, 207; see Mattaliano 1998, p. 62, no. 107). Its traces were lost until Venturi, in 1927 (p. 163), published it with the correct reference to de' Roberti among the works of the Auspitz collection in Vienna. Once again on the market, after also gaining Berenson's attributional endorsement (1932, p. 6), in 1934 it passed into the collection of Daniël George van Beuningen (1877–1955) and in 1958 arrived at the Museum.

Longhi is the first who connected *Saint Anthony the Abbot* to the Griffoni Polyptych (1940 ed. 1956, pp. 34–35; 1940 ed. 1956, pp. 128–30). He associated it with *Saint Petronius*, at that time in the Vendeghini Baldi collection in Ferrara (cat. no. 14), tracing Cossa's common, marked, influence. This judgment urged both Ortolani (1941, p. 158) and Nicolson (1950, p. 20) to believe that the small painting was executed by de' Roberti on a drawing prepared by the older Ferrarese artist.

According to Longhi, the tile with *Saint Anthony* occupied the third space from the bottom of the left pillar, on the main order, in association with *Saint Jerome* (cat. no. 16) on the opposite side. The photographic recomposition proposed by Lucco (1987, p. 244) gives the hermit saint a higher position, in the fourth space of the left pillar. In the latest reconstruction (Cavalca 2013, p. 266), in line with what has just been described, *Saint Anthony the Abbot* regains the position already suggested by Longhi.

Ercole de' Roberti

14. Saint Petronius

tempera on panel, support 26.7 × 13 cm, painted area c. 22 × 8.5 cm
Pinacoteca Nazionale, Ferrara, inv. 335

Despite various minor damages and extensive retouching of the pictorial surface, particularly evident in correspondence with the lapels of the cope, the painting is in fair condition.

Saint Petronius was the bishop of Bologna, patron of the city and dedicatee of the Basilica where the polyptych decorated by this small panel was exposed. In this work, he wears luxurious vestments: a white brocade satin robe with crimson and gold silk inserts, a mitre embroidered with precious stones, and a large yellow silk cope. The usual blessing act serves as a counterpoint for showing the scale model of the city, which identifies the saint; de' Roberti imagines it to have a harmonious circular shape, firmly within its walls. In this effective interpretation of one of the most widespread iconographies in the city, the resolute gestures, the absorbed expression and, above all, the enveloping lapel of the cope refer explicitly, as it has been noted (see Manca 1992, p. 102), to *Saint Vincent Ferrer* depicted by Cossa and placed in the center of the main order. As in the other depictions of saints made by de' Roberti for the Griffoni Polyptych, the comparison with the larger scale models of his older colleague creates a solid basis for compositions that could easily have been translated into sculptures. Nonetheless, *Saint Petronius* stands out from the other examples for a more solid interpretation and a more rigid control of the compositional scheme; these qualities make the saint occupy the niche in the most proper sense of the word, almost sealing its space. Cossa's influence is very evident here, to the point that a number of scholars doubted that de' Roberti was the actual author of the panel. The first who thought of it as a work by de' Roberti soon returned to his steps (Venturi 1908, p. 424; Venturi 1901–40, VII/3, 1914, p. 632); Roberto Longhi (1940 ed. 1956, p. 129) believed it to be an inseparable mixture of the two manners; Ortolani (1941, p. 157) and Nicolson (1950, p. 14) imagined it to have been completed based on a drawing by Cossa. The decisive factors for crediting this work to de' Roberti are the minute and contracted realism of the face and the enhancement of the swollen and rippled folds of the drapery through dense and deep highlights. In the complex game of formal and conceptual references that characterizes the Griffoni Polyptych, it is worth comparing this *Saint Petronius* also with Saint Vincent Ferrer healing the possessed woman in the predella.

It's highly probable that *Saint Petronius*, along with *Saint George* of the Cini Foundation and *Saint Anthony the Abbot* of the Museum Boijmans Van Beuningen (cat. nos. 11 and 13), is one of the tiles intended for the sides of the altar, which can be identified with certainty with the series of four that were framed and meant to be sent to the country residence owned by the Aldrovandi family in Mirabello (see *Baraldi's Letter 1725*). From a tag placed on the back, we learn that in the early decades of the nineteenth century it was together with Cossa's *Saint Peter* and *Saint John the Baptist* (cat. nos. 2–3) in Ferrara in the collection of Giovanni Barbi Cinti (see Agostini and Scardino 1997, p. 26), procurator general of the house of Giovanni Battista Costabili. The latter was in turn the owner of the just mentioned Cini and Van Beuningen panels, as well as other four elements of the Griffoni Polyptych from Mirabello (cat. nos. 1, 6, 8–9). From the Barbi Cinti collection, *Saint Petronius* passed to that of Enea Vendeghini (1841–1990), where it is registered as a work by Ercole de' Roberti (inv. 1940, no. 6; see G. Agostini in *La leggenda* 1996, p. 172, no. 63). In 1973, after the death of Mario Baldi, Maria Vendeghini Baldi's son, it reached the Pinacoteca Nazionale of Ferrara (see G. Agostini in *La Pinacoteca Nazionale* 1992, pp. 71–72, no. 77).

When Longhi (1934 ed. 1956, pp. 34–35; 1940 ed. 1956, pp. 129–30) connected *Saint Petronius* (the property of Vendeghini at that time) to the Griffoni Polyptych, he placed it in the first figured space from the bottom of the left pillar, at the base of the main panel depicting *Saint Peter* and in correspondence with the *Saint Catherine of Alexandria* of the Cini Foundation on the opposite side (cat. no. 15; see Longhi 1940 ed. 1956, fig. 309). Due to its frontal perspective, Salmi (1960, p. 19) supposed instead that it flanked the Vatican predella. In a more recent photographic assembly, Lucco (1987, p. 244), on the contrary, makes *Saint Petronius* gain an apical position: the fourth space of the left pillar, faced by *Saint Jerome* now at Palazzo Cini (cat. no. 16). In the last reconstruction (Cavalca 2013, p. 266), the Ferrara tile once again finds its place at the base of the left pillar but is not associated, to the opposite side, with any other saint among those known to us. The direct comparison between the different fragments made possible for the first time by this exhibition allows envisioning an alternative solution, namely moving the painting upwards by one position. This choice is fully respectful of the arrangement of the lights that governs the pictorial complex, but it also offers the advantage of ideally leaving room, in the lower space, for a figure set in a niche with an observation point more consistent with the one of the main order. In both cases, it is easy to assume that *Saint Petronius* was initially associated with Saint Dominic: just like the Bolognese saint and bishop, he was among the four patrons of the city and founder of the order to which Saint Vincent Ferrer, the dedicatee of the Griffoni altar, belonged.

Ercole de' Roberti

15. Saint Catherine of Alexandria

tempera on panel, painted area 26.1 × 8.6 cm (with immovable box-frame 31 × 13.7 cm)
Giorgio Cini Foundation, Palazzo Cini Gallery at San Vio, Venice, inv. VC4053

The painting is in good condition. In unspecified times, the support has been inserted into an immovable frame, welded to the edges with stucco (see Bacchi 1990, p. 12). The pictorial surface, retouched in correspondence with the neck and on the edge of the niche, has suffered from slight upliftings compensated during the most recent restoration (M. Nahabed, 2003; see L. Siracusano in *La Galleria di Palazzo Cini* 2016, p. 179). The diagnostic investigations (IR reflectography) revealed in 2007 (see Poldi and Villa 2007, p. 172, figs. 155–56) have shown a very accurate underlying drawing, a thick oblique hatching identical to that found in the *Saint Jerome* today also in the Cini Foundation (cat. no. 16).

Saint Catherine of Alexandria is distinguishable by her characteristic attribute, the wheel with spikes. Erudite and, according to legend, of royal blood, she is depicted by de' Roberti with a book in her hand and sumptuous contemporary clothes. Among them stands out a large deep blue silk cape, made iridescent by contrasting touches and embellished by a golden-yellow lining that wraps the young figure, giving her a hieratic appearance. The saint has a strong debt to a homolog designed by Francesco del Cossa for a tablet that was originally on the sides of the altarpiece with the *Annunciation* of Dresden (Gemäldegalerie), today in the Thyssen-Bornemisza collection (Museu Nacional d'Art de Catalunya, Barcelona, inv. 104), which we know in another, perhaps slightly previous version, with a similar head orientation to the one in question, used as a model of an embroidery (Archconfraternity of the Christian Doctrine, San Francesco dei Vanchetoni, Florence; see Cavalca 2005; Cavalca 2013, figs. 138–39). With this original transposition of Cossa's model, de' Roberti aims to emphasize the symbol of martyrdom, which is all outside the architectural hollow and is offered to the view in a daring and sloping perspective that forces the spokes of the wheel into an oval. This painting shares the fate of the companion panel depicting *Saint Jerome* (cat. no. 16): until the end of the nineteenth century (around 1897) it was at Condover Hall (Shropshire) as part of Reginald Cholmondeley's collection; then it passed into Robert and Evelyn Benson's collection in London (1907). It was believed to be an original de' Roberti work by Berenson (1907, p. 425) and Venturi (1908, p. 425; later, however, he assigned it to Cossa: Venturi 1901–40, VII/3, 1914, p. 597) and with this attribution it was displayed at the 1933 Ferrara exhibition (at the time it was in Paris, owned by Lord Duveen of Millbank). On this occasion it was again paired with *Saint Jerome* and the two panels were considered parts of the same dismembered complex (see *Esposizione della pittura ferrarese del Rinascimento* 1933, pp. 95–96, nos. 111–12), though not the same one from which the Louvre saints *Apollonia* and *Michael* (also displayed as early works by young de' Roberti) were believed to derive. Since then, this attribution has known no significant opposition and accompanied the two paintings to Florence, at Contini Bonacossi's (until 1940: see Bacchi 1990, p. 18) and then to Venice, at Vittorio Cini's (1940–1977); in 1989, by the will of his heirs, it was loaned to the Giorgio Cini Foundation.

Longhi (1934 ed. 1956, pp. 35, 41–42) was the first to connect *Saint Catherine* and *Saint Jerome* to the decoration of the external pillars of the polyptych commissioned by Floriano Griffoni. The scholar imagined the holy martyr in the lower space of the right pillar, being in correspondence with *Saint Petronius* (cat. no. 4) on the opposite side, eluding the differences between the laying plans of the two figures. Lucco (1987, p. 244) assumed instead that the panel was placed on the left side, maintained its low alignment at the base of the main order, and eliminated the connection with *Saint Petronius*. In the most recent reconstruction, the author (Cavalca 2013, p. 266) places *Saint Catherine* in an apical position, in the right middle space of the upper order, next to *Saint Lucy*, matching her with the

Louvre's *Saint Apollonia* (cat. no. 10). Siracusano did not accept this solution (in *La Galleria di Palazzo Cini* 2016, p. 180) and cautiously returned to Longhi's hypothesis, believing that the perspective chosen for the base does not entirely fit a high position.

As in other early works, we may notice that creating and denying artificially forced architectural spaces is one of the sources of the artist's dynamic illusionism. However, this exhibition and the observations that it has stimulated have suggested reconsidering the delicate question at the root. It is therefore plausible to hypothesize, as it had been implicitly done in the 1933 Ferrara exhibition, that both *Saint Catherine of Alexandra* and *Saint Jerome* are not parts of the Griffoni Polyptych. The compositional expedients used by Ercole de' Roberti in the two paintings—the niches, the articulation of the figures inside them and the treatment of light—allow a precise parallel with the other tiles of the Petronian complex; except some tiny difference in the color gradient, also the execution and the emotional intensity do not differ from the vibrant tone that marks the intervention of the painter on that altar. Nevertheless, the comparative evaluation of these panels with the remaining compartments of the polyptych—made possible for the first time thanks to the facsimiles produced by Factum Arte—highlighted the problem of the significant scale difference that distinguishes the two works from the other paintings meant to decorate the sides of the altar, which, conversely, are perfectly coherent with each other and with the whole. The extension of the pictorial surface differs by around 3 cm in height; if it's true that an adequate analysis of the paintings must take into account that the sides have probably been slightly cut, it is impossible to say to what extent, due to the immovability of the frames.

Although the obvious similarities between *Saint Apollonia*, *Saint Jerome*, and other paintings by de' Roberti understandably led to keep the material datum under the radar, this anomaly does not allow the two figures to be satisfactorily integrated into the right pillars, according to what their postures suggest, and not even into the opposite ones. It is equally difficult to associate the paintings with the predella, since the pictorial surfaces do not seem to be large enough to decorate the base of the pillars. The placement of the two panels, therefore, is still an open issue, waiting for the direct and comparative examination of the originals to boost a new research track.

Ercole de' Roberti

16. Saint Jerome

tempera on panel, painted area 26.1 × 8.9 cm (with immovable box-frame 31 × 13.7 cm)
Giorgio Cini Foundation, Palazzo Cini Gallery at San Vio, Venice, inv. VC4054

The painting is in excellent condition. In unspecified times, the support has been inserted into an immovable frame, welded on the edges with stucco (see Bacchi 1990, p. 12). The pictorial surface, suffering from slight upliftings mainly concentrated along a vertical fissure that runs along the saint's left shoulder, has been compensated in the most recent restoration (M. Nahabed, 2003; see L. Siracusano in *La Galleria di Palazzo Cini* 2016, p. 179). The diagnostic investigations (IR reflectography) revealed in 2007 (Poldi and Villa 2007) have shown a very accurate underlying drawing consisting of oblique lines similar in all to the one found in *Saint Catherine of Alexandria*, also preserved today at the Cini Foundation. For the origin and subsequent critical events of *Saint Jerome*, please refer to this latter work (cat. no. 15).

Saint Jerome is depicted as a Doctor of the Church: dressed as a cardinal, his face is framed by a long white beard and he is immersed in the reading of a text that alludes to his supreme effort as a translator of the Old and New Testament into Latin. Ercole de' Roberti elaborated on this intense and fortunate representation (see Bacchi 1990, p. 23, figs. 2–3g) starting from a very similar prototype, disseminated by the workshop of Giovanni d'Alemagna and the Vivarinis (it can be seen in the *Triptych of Saint Sabina* in the church of San Zaccaria in Venice and, again, in the *Triptych of Charity* in the Gallerie dell'Accademia in Venice). In Bologna, Marco Zoppo had offered a recent version of this figure, with significant variations, in the polyptych at the Royal College of Spain.

In *Saint Jerome*, the young artist from Ferrara used the drapery to emphasize the volume of the figure, which he depicted as obstinately slim and nervous. Masses of color excessively inflated by deep, spectacular shadows and touches of light make the pictorial surface vibrate and reveal precious details, such as the fine transparent chain-mail that caresses the sober cardinal's dress under the mantle.

When Longhi connected the painting to the Griffoni Polyptych (see 1934 ed. 1956, pp. 34–35, 42; 1940 ed. 1956, fig. 309) he imagined it positioned in the third space of the right pillar, in the main order, in correspondence with the *Saint Anthony the Abbot* of the Museum Boijmans Van Beuningen (cat. no. 13). This position differs from that envisioned by Lucco (1987, p. 244), who instead placed the saint in the last space of the same pillar, making him dialogue with the *Saint Petronius* (cat. no. 14) on the opposite side. The most recent reconstruction confirms Longhi's proposal (see Cavalca 2013, p. 266).

The comparisons made possible by this exhibition and the observations emerged have nevertheless suggested that we should carefully reconsider the actual pertinence of this figured panel and its Cini companion *Saint Catherine of Alexandria* to the group of surviving paintings certainly part of the dismantled polyptych (see cat. no. 15).

REFERENCE LITERATURE

Vasari 1550 ed. 1991, p. 428
Lamo c. 1560 ed. 1996, p. 101
Vasari 1568 ed. 1878–81, III, pp. 133, 142–43
Cavazzoni 1603 ed. 1999, p. 19
Masini 1666, I, p. 111
Malvasia 1686 ed. 1969, p. 242/16
Crowe and Cavalcaselle 1871 ed. 1912, II, pp. 237–38, 243, 265
Frizzoni 1888, pp. 299–303
Frizzoni 1897, pp. 223–27
Venturi 1901–40, VII/3, 1914, pp. 616–32
Malaguzzi Valeri 1908, pp. 249–51, no. 449
Longhi 1934 ed. 1956, pp. 32–35
Longhi 1940 ed. 1956, pp. 128–31
Ortolani 1941, pp. 127–32
Nicolson 1950, pp. 13, 19
Davies 1951, pp. 115–18
Berenson 1907 ed. 1952, pp. 161–62
Neppi 1958, pp. 24–30
Ruhmer 1959, pp. 78–79, nos. 62–64, 68–71
Rusk Shapley 1966, pp. 83-85
A. Emiliani in Malvasia 1686 ed. 1969, [pp. 164–65], note 242/16
Smith, Reeve, and Roy 1981, pp. 44–57
Benati 1984, pp. 156–74
D. Benati in *Da Borso a Cesare d'Este* 1985, pp. 172–74
Torella (1985–87) 1988, pp. 43–59
Torella (1988–89) 1991, pp. 39–50
Bacchi 1990, pp. 12–29 nos. 2–4
Bacchi 1991, pp. 78–89, no. 8a–f
A. Bacchi in *Pinacoteca di Brera* 1991, pp. 60–72, nos. 22–23
Manca 1992, pp. 29–32, 93–102, 175, nos. 2a–h, R15
Molteni 1995, pp. 114–24, nos. 4–12
D. Benati in *La collezione Cagnola* n.d. [1998], pp. 140–43, nos. 32–33
J. Helvey in *Ercole de' Roberti* 1999, pp. XXVII–XVIII, nos. I–II
Syson 1999, pp. V–VII
J. Manca in *Italian Paintings* 2003, pp. 214–25
Sgarbi 2003, pp. 136–68
G. Sassu in Sgarbi 2003, pp. 229–31, nos. 16–24
D. Cattoi in *Gli Este a Ferrara* 2004, pp. 288–95, nos. 72–81
C. Cavalca in *Cosmè Tura e Francesco del Cossa* 2007, pp. 466–71, nos. 150–53
Cavalca 2013, pp. 136–50, 334–36, no. 19
G. Calogero in *Da Cimabue a Morandi* 2015, pp. 76–80, nos. 14–15
Degler 2015, pp. 138–59
V. Farinella in *Piero della Francesca* 2015, pp. 334–35, no. III.25
D. Benati in *Piero della Francesca* 2016, pp. 142–45, nos. 38–39
E. Daffra in *Restituzioni* 2016, pp. 169–74, no. 21
L. Siracusano in *La Galleria di Palazzo Cini* 2016, pp. 179–86, nos. 36–38

PERFECTION THROUGH STUDY: THE PAINTING TECHNIQUE OF THE GRIFFONI POLYPTYCH

Jill Dunkerton

In his famous letter addressed to Borso d'Este in 1470 in which he complained about his wages for the execution of the decoration of Schifanoia, Francesco del Cossa emphasized how much he had studied the art of painting and that he continued to do so ("*Et che lo mio avere studiato et continuamente studio*"). That his studies extended to the perfection of his technique is implied by his claims in the letter for the superiority of his fresco technique as recognized by his fellow masters ("*chè io ho lavorato quaxi el tuto a frescho che e lavoro avantazato e bono e questo e noto a tuti li maistri de larte*").[1] It will be demonstrated that the same could be said of his panel painting technique, as exemplified by the panels that formed the Griffoni Polyptych.[2]

As with so much about Cossa's early career, nothing certain is known of where he laid the foundations of that technique. As will be demonstrated, however, the exceptional control of both materials and design that is such a feature of his works indicates that his technical mastery almost certainly derives directly or indirectly from the traditions of the Squarcione workshop in Padua.[3] In common with painters such as Marco Zoppo and Carlo Crivelli, Cossa continued to work within the disciplines of tempera painting, choosing mostly panel supports and often incorporating gilded backgrounds as in parts of the Griffoni Polyptych. Cosmè Tura, on the other hand, while probably starting in the same Paduan circles, soon developed his technique in a different direction, adopting oil paint in imitation of examples of early Netherlandish paintings to be seen in Ferrara.[4] Other differences of approach between Tura and Cossa suggest that he was unlikely to have been the latter's master.

The dismantling of the Griffoni Polyptych and the subsequent conservation history of the individual panels, many of which have been thinned and fitted with

---

I would like to thank David Alan Brown and Gretchen Hirschauer at the National Gallery of Art, Washington, DC for initiating the examination of their panels by Cossa and Elizabeth Walmsley for showing me all the previous technical information held on file. I am especially grateful to John Delaney and Kathryn Dooley for their generosity in sharing with me the results of their examination of the Saint Florian panel using the new techniques of hyperspectral infrared imaging and XRF mapping and allowing me to publish some of the results. At the National Gallery I owe my usual debt of gratitude to Marika Spring, both for re-examining and photographing the paint samples first published in 1981 and for reading and commenting on this text, and also Rachel Billinge and Catherine Higgitt for various forms of assistance.

1 The letter is quoted in full in Bacchi 1991, p. 10.

2 Although many of the panels from the dismembered polyptych have been x-rayed, the most informative technique of examination has been infrared reflectography. In addition, the *Saint Florian* in the National Gallery of Art, Washington, DC has been examined using hyperspectral imaging and macro x-ray fluorescence scanning. The central panel of *Saint Vincent Ferrer* in the National Gallery, London, underwent a detailed scientific examination in 1980, the results of which were published by Ashok Roy in Reeve, Roy, and Smith 1981, pp. 44–57.

3 For a summary of artistic activity in Padua in the 1450s, when Cossa may well have been present, or at least have been a regular visitor, see *Padua in the 1450s* 1998.

4 For Tura and oil painting see Dunkerton 2002, pp. 107–51, esp. 111–22.

cradles, means that few clues survive as to their original construction. There is no reason, however, to think that the polyptych differed radically from other such assemblages from the second half of the fifteenth century. The main panels would all have been constructed and painted and gilded independently and then inserted into the frame, while the predella and the small panels that decorated the pilasters were part of the structure of that frame. The panels were all prepared with a substantial layer of gesso, based on a raw unburnt gypsum.[5] In paint cross-sections the ground is notably white and the careful preparation of the panels for painting is likely to have contributed to their generally good state of preservation.[6] Where a panel had an arched top, as in the central panel of *Saint Vincent Ferrer*, the gesso is likely to have extended roughly into the areas of the spandrels, exactly as in the panels of polyptchs by Carlo Crivelli, for example, since these were to be covered by the frame. In the case of the London panel, the gesso has subsequently been scraped away from the spandrels, while the arch tops of the two Washington saints have been cut at the top and possibly slightly reshaped. These panels have also probably been cut at the lower edges, reducing the depth of the parapets. The false-color hyperspectral infrared image of *Saint Florian* (fig. 1) confirms that the band of paint along the lower edge differs from the rest of the parapet and is not original. The end of the saint's sword has been truncated. Logically the position of these upper tier saints means that the parapet should fall away vertically, with the sword point hanging over the edge. The areas of regilding and the repairs to the gilded background of the *Saint Florian* panel are also easily identified in the false color infrared image.

A likely training in Padua meant that Cossa's painting methods, whether on walls or moveable supports, were based on detailed preparation through drawing. As a result of the paucity of surviving drawings on paper attributed to Cossa, his drawing practice can be only partially reconstructed. The beautiful study of a young man ascending steps, seen from behind, in the British Museum is usually

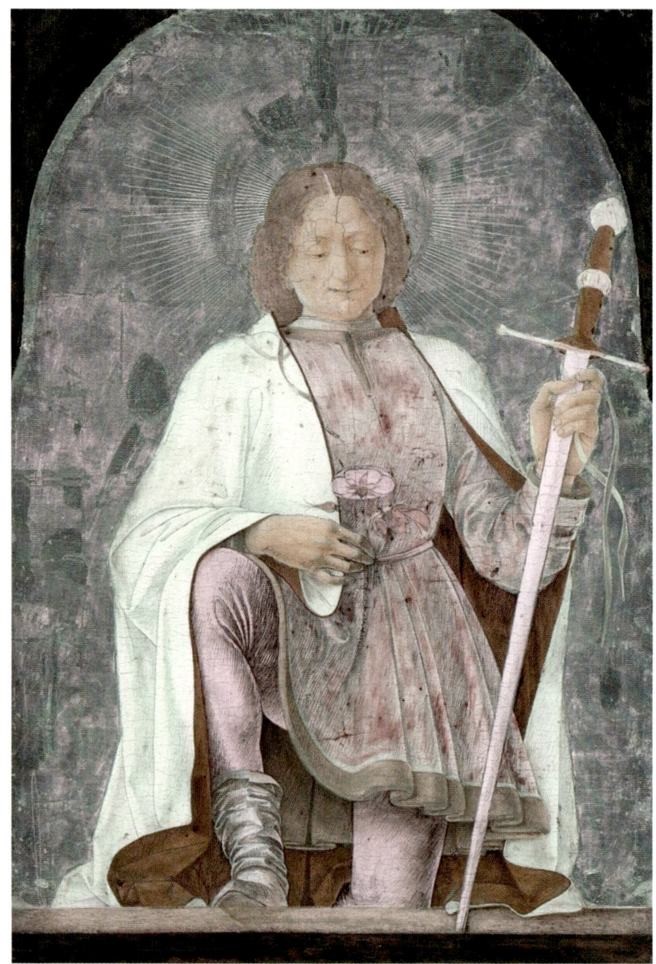

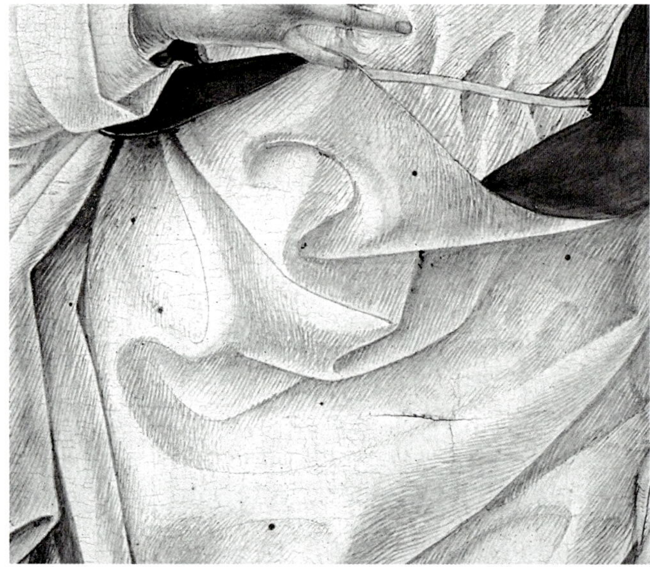

1

False-color hyperspectral infrared image of *Saint Florian*, whole (Red = 1650 nm, Green = 1450 nm, Blue = 1300 nm)

2

Infrared reflectogram of *Saint John the Baptist*, detail

5 Reeve, Roy, and Smith 1981, pp. 54–55.

6 For the condition of *Saint Vincent Ferrer* following cleaning in 1980, see ibid., p. 52. The other panels from the main part of the altarpiece show evidence of localized damage and old repairs, and some feature slightly discolored varnish layers, but in general the paint surfaces are in excellent condition. Judging by the infrared reflectograms, the predella has suffered from surface abrasion in some areas.

3

Infrared reflectogram from the central panel of Cosmè Tura's Roverella altarpiece, detail (The National Gallery, London)

4

Infrared reflectogram of *Saint Peter*, detail

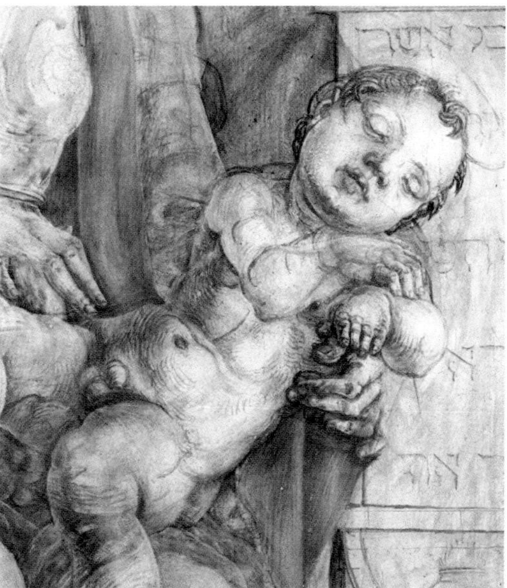

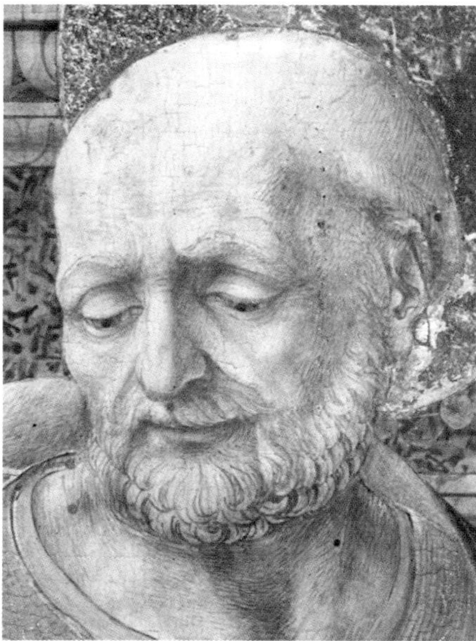

associated with the Schifanoia decorations but it may also have been intended for wider and more general purposes. Cossa perhaps assembled studies in much the same way as Marco Zoppo, for instance.[7] There is nothing improvisatory or searching in the outlines of the figure. Every contour and detail was clearly fixed by the firmly drawn outlines in pen and ink, while the parallel hatched shading varies in density and spacing in order to suggest the structure and fall of light on the drapery folds and the boy's limbs, as well as to set the figure against the background. In a few places, notably the figure's proper right arm, the lines of hatching curve slightly in order to suggest the roundness of the forms.

Comparison of drawings on paper with underdrawings on painted panels as revealed by infrared methods of examination can be misleading, both because of differences of scale and drawing medium and the fact that infrared images are digitally generated. In addition, the appearance of the lines of drawing is inevitably affected by the superimposed paint layers. Nevertheless, the similarities between the British Museum study and the underdrawings found in Cossa's panels from the Griffoni Polyptych are so striking that they seem to confirm the attribution of the study to Cossa. The underdrawing across the six panels is remarkably consistent, although the different imaging techniques employed reveal it to varying extents. Therefore, more of the underdrawing of the dark green areas containing malachite can be seen in the hyperspectral infrared image of *Saint Florian* (fig. 1) than in similar green areas in those panels examined with infrared reflectography alone (fig. 2). Of course, the large amount of carbon black in the habit of Saint Vincent Ferrer in the central panel means that all infrared light is absorbed and no shading can be seen, although it is almost certainly present.

The infrared images demonstrate the exceptional attention that Cossa gave to the systematic establishment of every aspect of his design at the underdrawing stage. It is easy to imagine that the designs were drawn on all the panels, and perhaps shown to the patron, before any color was applied. The lines were evidently drawn with a brush and a liquid medium, either an ink or a diluted black paint. It should be pointed out that some of the lines of hatched shading visible in the infrared images, particularly in areas

7 For these see *Padua in the 1450s* 1998.

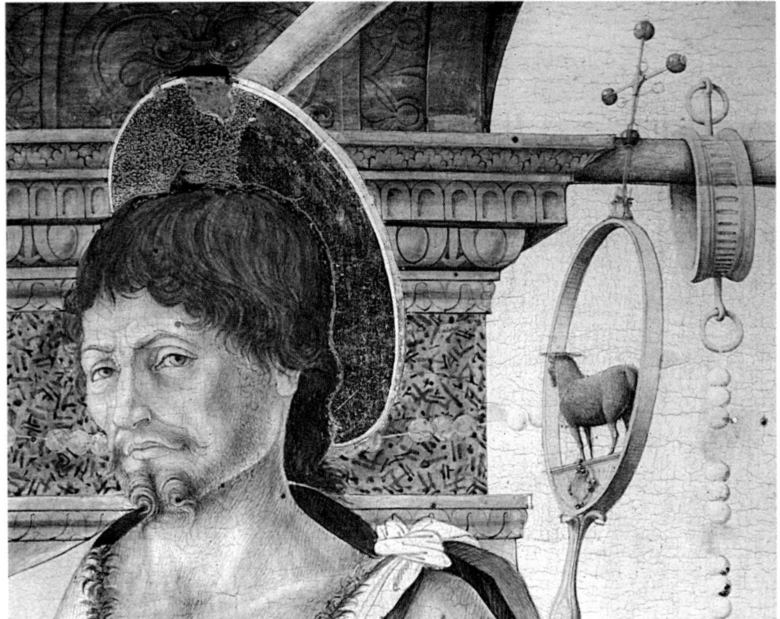
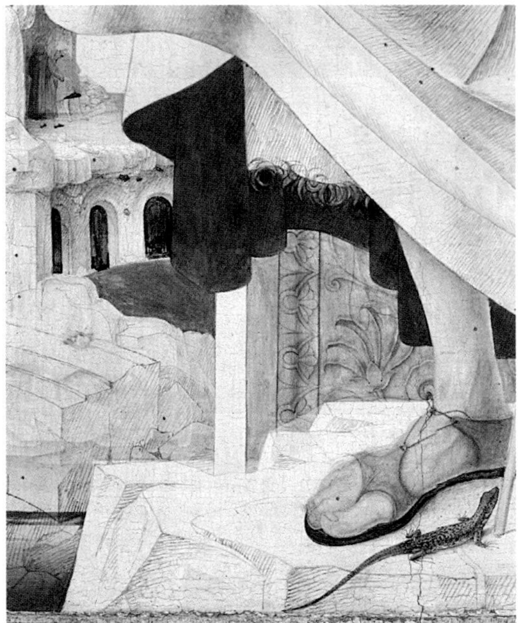

5–6

Infrared reflectograms of *Saint John the Baptist*, details

of dark green, red, and blue, are not always related to the underdrawing. Instead they consist of final strokes of black paint applied to reinforce the deepest folds and shadows. The contours and principal elements of the underdrawing are remarkably precise, with no sign of corrections. In this respect, Cossa's underdrawing differs from that of Cosmè Tura, which, although equally extensive, appears more freely drawn, and in places almost improvised, as though he were still working out important parts of the design while setting it out on the panel. The pose of the Christ Child in the center panel of the Roverella altarpiece (fig. 3), for example, was clearly revised at the underdrawing stage and Tura's outlines and hatched shading are notably broader and more loosely applied than those of the less flamboyant Cossa. In its detail and precision, Cossa's underdrawing is closer to that seen in many panels by Carlo Crivelli, for instance.

This raises the question of whether Cossa's meticulous planning might have extended to the preparation of cartoons for the principal figures, the outlines of which could have been transferred to the prepared panels. Certainly, the making of full-scale cartoons was a significant element of Cossa's production. It has been suggested that the drawing for a foot in Stockholm which is often attributed to him is in fact a fragment of such a cartoon. The cartoons that he supplied for stained glass and also for the *intarsie* in the choir of San Petronio must have been highly detailed, since the final products are easily recognizable as deriving from his designs. Indeed the refinement of the depiction of areas of flesh in some of the windows has led to the suggestion that Cossa might have worked directly with the glass painters in their production.[8] The schematic rendering in the underdrawing of the features of Saint Peter (fig. 4), especially his brow and beard, is so like equivalent features in the *intarsia* of Saint Ambrose as to suggest that the cartoon supplied must have looked very similar, and that it was reproduced with remarkable faithfulness.

The shading of Saint Peter's neck, with short curved strokes that follow round the form, more in the manner of Tura's drawing technique, is one of the few areas where Cossa departs from his regular diagonal hatched shading. In the draperies of the Griffoni

8 Bacchi 1991a, p. 52

panels, especially those of the main tier, the angle of the hatching shifts in order to describe the forms, sometimes intersecting to become cross hatching. In the bulkier draperies, for example Saint John the Baptist's red cloak (fig. 2), this shading seems to be superimposed over a system of curved and looped lines used to indicate the bunched folds of fabric. These often have a schematic, almost abbreviated quality that suggests the possibility that they were transferred from a full-size cartoon by means of tracing. The simplification of some of the features of the three principal saints, especially the drawing of their eyebrows as solid shapes, might also be related to the employment of cartoons, but this can only be speculation. Such elaborate preparation for the drawing of the figures would be in keeping with the considerable care lavished by Cossa on the execution of the polyptych.

He seems to have given equal attention to small details and to the setting of the figures of the lower tier. Saint John the Baptist's twisting scroll and even the fine detail of his staff with its fluttering red ribbon were established in the underdrawing and shaded with hatched strokes where appropriate (fig. 5). A small alteration made during painting was the enlargement of the cross that surmounts the staff—the smaller underdrawn version is clearly visible in the infrared reflectogram. The only significant details that appear to have been an afterthought, added when the painting was almost complete, are the metal rings along the pole that traverses all three panels, from which the strings of rosary beads looped behind each saint are suspended, with their tasselled ends hanging down on either side of them.

The only other departures from the underdrawing appear in the landscapes behind the saints, where the rock structures and architectural features were all drawn and shaded with the same attention as that given to the features. Some changes are minor, for instance the elimination of a projecting rock on the right side of the Saint Peter panel, but the foreground of Saint John the Baptist was entirely reconsidered so that a stretch of deep blue water replaced a curved architectural structure in the lower left corner (fig. 6), while on the right a feature—possibly a cave—was painted over a large stone block, perhaps originally part of the rocky platform on which the saint stands.

The incidental figures and animals that populate the landscapes are mostly very small and were added over the painted rocks and buildings, but infrared reflectography shows that the important figures of Christ in glory and the angels with instruments of the Passion that crown the central saint were drawn with the same detail as the rest of the panel. The folds of the angels' draperies were extensively shaded with the usual parallel hatched strokes (fig. 7). Similarly, the underdrawing of the figures in the *Crucifixion* tondo that surmounted the altarpiece is every bit as detailed as that of the lower panels, but with the breadth of the line and the fineness of the shading reduced to an appropriate scale. Much of this underdrawing can be seen with the naked eye as a result of changes in the transparency of the superimposed paint.

It is widely accepted that Ercole de' Roberti trained with Cossa and that he was still working in a subsidiary role when he was assigned the painting of the predella and pilaster panels of the Griffoni Polyptych. Nevertheless, his artistic identity was already well established, even within the constraints of producing designs that had to be integrated with the main part of the altarpiece. Infrared reflectography confirms that these were his own designs and that they were every bit as carefully planned as those of his probable master. He outlined his figures and the structure of drapery folds in a similar way, drawing fine lines with the point of the brush, but in a manner that is arguably not as solid and emphatic as that of Cossa. Much less hatched shading is evident. In the pilaster panel showing *Saint Catherine*

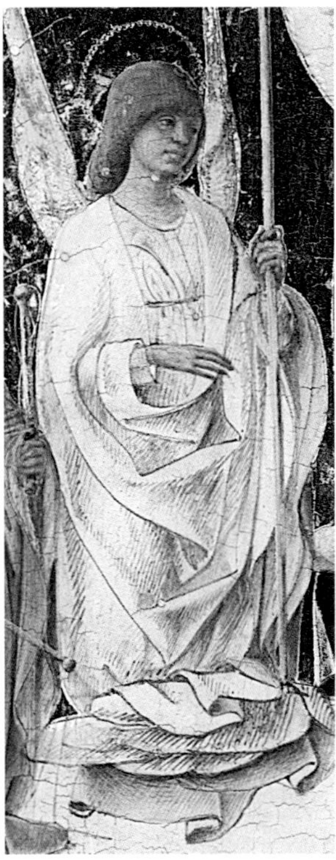

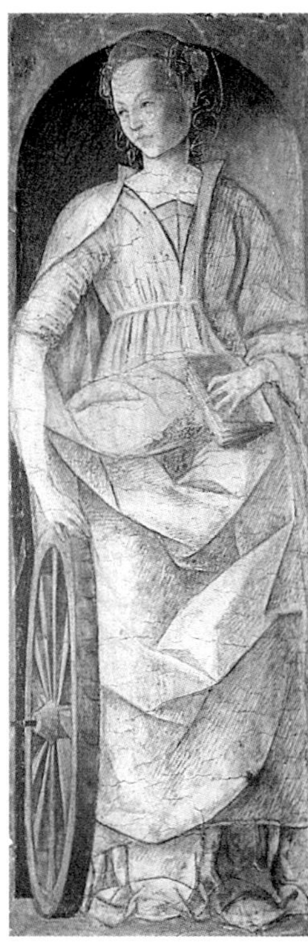

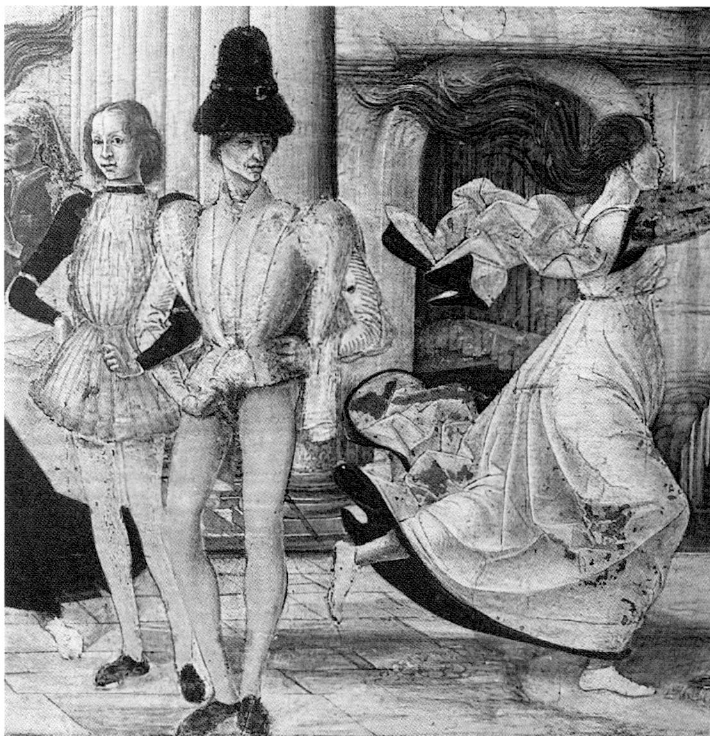

(fig. 8) the shading of her cloak seems more to indicate the lighting of the figure than to describe the modeling of her draperies. Many of the figures on the Vatican predella appear to have been drawn with line alone. Only the occasional area of shading can be detected, for example across the shadowed front of the torso of the fleeing woman toward the center of the predella, otherwise drawn with line alone, and on the sleeves of the elegantly dressed gentleman to her left (fig. 9). This pattern of underdrawing with fine outlines (often difficult to distinguish from the superimposed paint) combined with sporadic use of delicate hatched shading was to continue in Ercole's small-scale paintings.[9]

7

Infrared reflectogram of *Saint Vincent Ferrer*, detail

8

Infrared reflectogram of *Saint Catherine*, detail

9

Infrared reflectogram of *Scenes from the life of Saint Vincent Ferrer*, detail

Both painters made use of incision into the gesso for ruling the straight lines of their architecture, which was normal practice in Italy at the time. So too was the incising of contours of those figures that were to be set against gold, as in the upper parts of the altarpiece. The transition to this highly unusual division of the altarpiece into zones of landscape below and gilded settings above was carefully managed by the introduction of the celestial realm, with its gold background, into the uppermost part of the *Saint Vincent Ferrer* panel. In the gilded parts the gold leaf was laid over the usual orange-red bole, with Cossa—or his gilder—working with great precision so that the pieces of leaf seldom encroach far into the areas to be painted (fig. 10). Segments of the haloes of the three main-tier saints were stippled with a punch to give the discs different reflective properties, which must have increased their impact in the candle-lit gloom of the chapel in San Petronio. The background to Christ's mandorla in the central panel was also stippled, while the haloes of the little angels, and also those of the Crucifixion figures in the tondo,

9 For Ercole's underdrawing and painting technique on small-scale panels see Allen 1999, pp. I–XL. The infrared reflectogram detail of *Saint Jerome in the Wilderness*—an early work—illustrated on p. XVII shows underdrawing very like some of that on the Vatican predella. In addition, John Delaney kindly showed me a hyperspectral image of *The Wife of Hasdrubal* in Washington, DC, which is on a larger scale, but also has a delicate linear underdrawing with occasional areas of fine hatched shading.

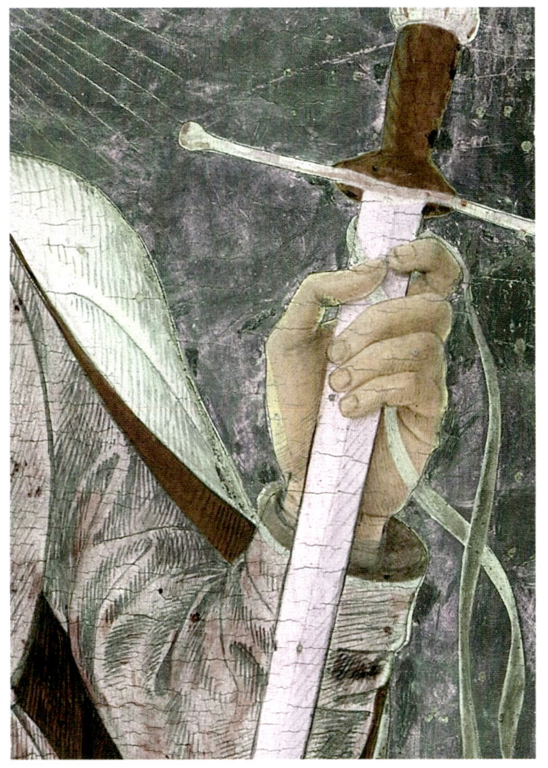

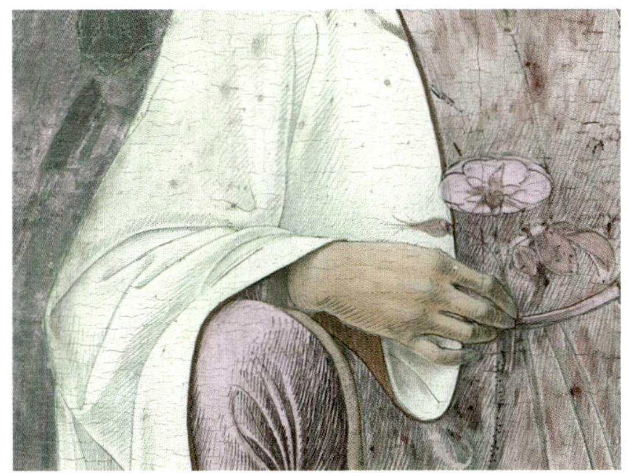

10–11

False-color reflectance spectroscopic image of *Saint Florian*, detail

were indicated with a single row of punched indentations. Saints Florian and Lucy, however, were assigned more complex haloes consisting of concentric rings tooled with motif punches, radiating incised lines extending well beyond the tooled circles. Moreover, Saint Lucy has an additional inner ring of tooled decoration close to her head. It was becoming old-fashioned by the 1470s to decorate gilding with motif punches, which here include a rosette and a small tri-lobate punch, as well as a simple circle and the stippling tools seen elsewhere on the altarpiece. This elaborate ornament may have been at the request of the patron in order to honor his titular saint and that of his first wife, or perhaps it was a deliberate choice, and almost archaizing, made by the artist in acknowledgment of the hybrid nature of the whole altarpiece.

Further incised lines are evident in several of the draperies (fig. 11). These were scored into the gesso after the execution of the underdrawing, following the schematic lines and curves that form the underlying structure of the folds of fabric. Their purpose was to ensure that the information about the folds that had been established in the drawing was not immediately covered by the application of dark or particularly thick and opaque paint layers. Similar incisions are often seen in Italian panel paintings on areas of dark blue drapery, for example Virgin's mantles, but in the case of the Griffoni Polyptych the technique was particularly important for Saint Vincent Ferrer's black habit. This was painted in two layers: the first dark gray underpainting, which defined the structure of the drapery, contains lead white and carbon black, a mixture that would have soon covered any underdrawing. The second upper layer consists of carbon black alone, combined with a high proportion of egg medium in order to achieve a saturated depth of tone, more commonly achieved when using an oil-based binder. That Cossa achieved this effect with egg tempera alone has been confirmed by analysis of a sample at the National Gallery.[10]

More incisions occur in the deep blue and green areas of drapery that are distributed across the polyptych. This was necessary because the pigments used, azurite and malachite respectively, need to be coarse and granular in order to retain their intensity of hue. When combined with a medium they make a thick, dense paint so that Saint Lucy's thinly painted proper right hand seems almost embedded in the deep green and blue paints that make up her outer garment. In this instance, the modeling of the folds was achieved entirely by shading with hatched strokes of black paint over the green. The effect of this is now reduced by discoloration and darkening of the green paint. It is often thought that colors such as this must have been painted with some oil but, again, a sample of dark green from the *Saint Vincent Ferrer* panel was found to contain only egg.[11] In order

10 Reeve, Roy, and Smith 1981, p. 56.

11 Ibid. When the addition of oil has been reported in samples of similar malachite-based greens in Italian tempera paintings it is sometimes possible that it is present as a result of contamination by varnishes that contained oil. The rough surface texture of these paints means that traces of old and possibly original varnishes may be retained.

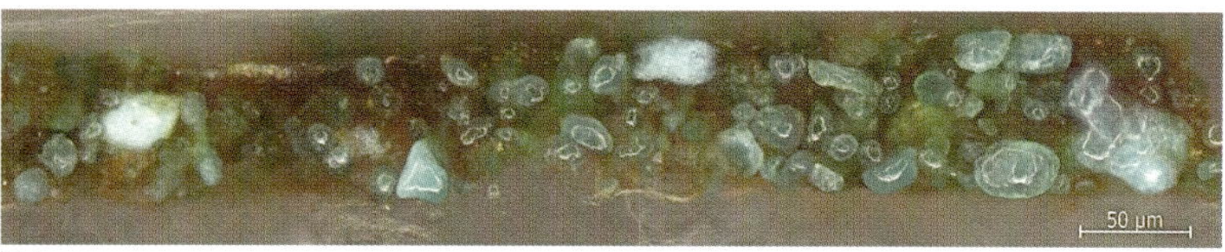

12A

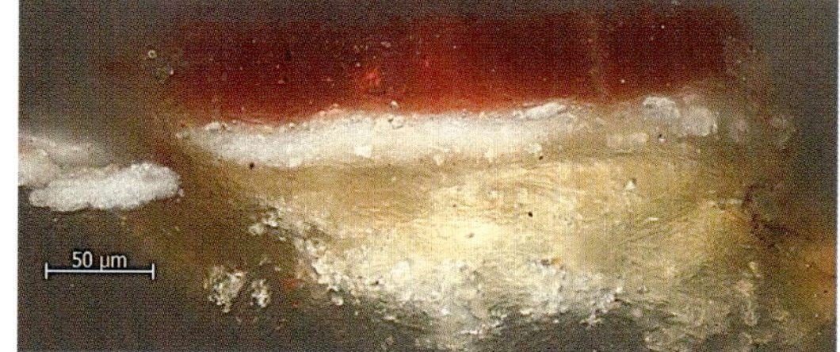

12B

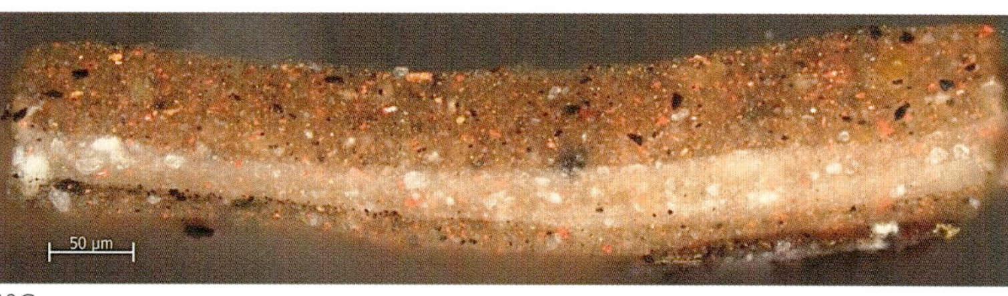

12C

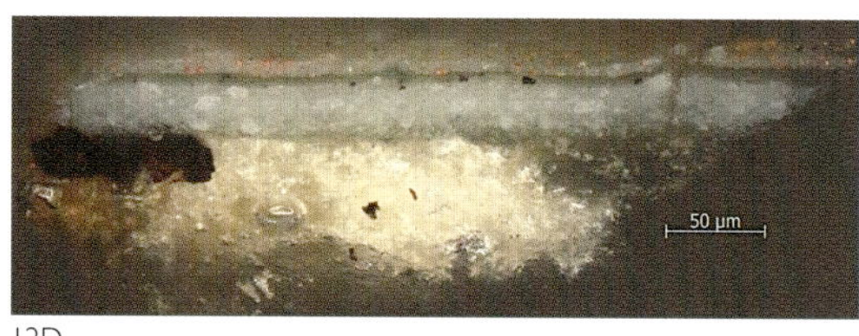

12D

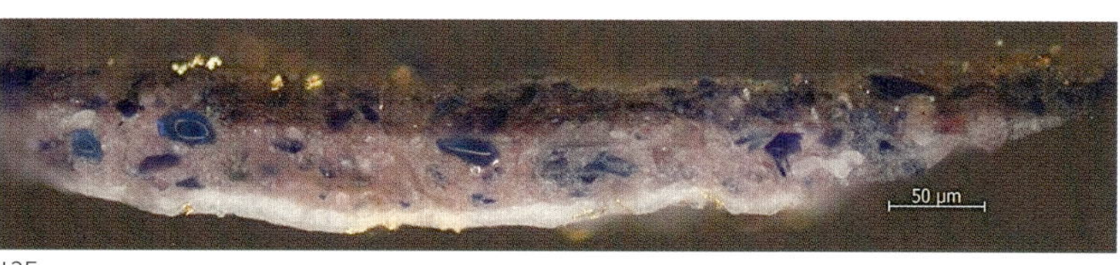

12E

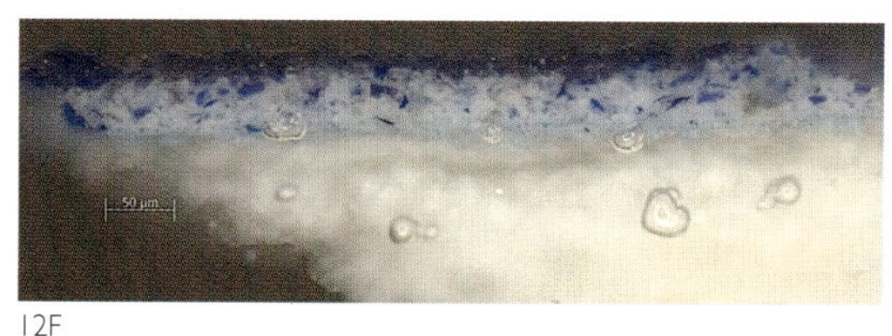

12F

to bind the coarse pigment, a great deal of medium was necessary and it can be seen in the grass sample (fig. 12A) how this has become brown and discolored, thereby darkening the paint layer. The malachite pigment, however, is still bright green, with distinctive rounded particles that were related to the production of the natural pigment.[12]

Cossa also employed the technique of modeling over an unmodulated base color for golden yellow and bright red draperies, and therefore he again took the precaution of first incising the principal folds as established in the underdrawing. For areas of yellow such as Saint Peter's mantle and Saint Florian's boots, a yellow earth pigment was laid in, which was then shaded with brown and perhaps black, and highlighted with a pale-yellow mixture of lead white and yellow earth.[13] Areas of bright red were blocked in with vermilion and then shaded with red lake. Fading of the red lake has almost certainly reduced the contrast in modeling, and so these areas can appear rather flat.

Other areas were painted with red lake alone, for example Saint Vincent's pedestal and, most probably, Saint John the Baptist's red cloak. Here the semi-translucent pigment was used pure and unmixed with lead white, the modeling achieved entirely by varying the density of the hatched modeling of the folds of fabric. In the sample from the London panel (fig. 12B) a layer of lead white occurs between the gesso ground and the paint layers. This does not feature in most of the other cross sections. Therefore, it does not represent an overall *imprimitura* as seen on many fifteenth-century Italian paintings in oil. Instead, its purpose is likely to have been to suppress to some extent the dark lines of underdrawing that would be difficult to cover with a paint based on red lake alone. With time, a further increase in transparency of the paint, and also some fading of the lake dyestuff, means that the hatched application has become somewhat uneven and streaky, but

12

A
Paint cross-section from the dark green grass in the lower left corner of *Saint Vincent Ferrer*

B
Paint cross-section from the deep red fabric over the dais in *Saint Vincent Ferrer*

C
Paint cross-section from the shaded part of the saint's proper left hand in *Saint Vincent Ferrer*

D
Paint cross-section from the neck of the angel (second from the left) in *Saint Vincent Ferrer*

E
Paint cross-section from the wing of the angel on the left who supports the mandorla in *Saint Vincent Ferrer*

F
Paint cross-section from the deep blue sky at the left edge in *Saint Vincent Ferrer*

12 When the samples from the Cossa panel were first published (see Reeve, Roy, and Smith 1981, p. 55), the spherulitic particles were thought to be an indicator that the malachite was of an artificial, manufactured form; but more recent studies have shown that this was not the case (see Heydenreich, Spring, Stillhammerova, and Pina 2005).

13 The highlights on Saint Florian's boots must consist of yellow earth and lead white since there is no sign in the XRF map for tin of any tin, which would indicate lead-tin yellow.

the underdrawing is still barely visible. Since the same applies to the Baptist's red cloak, it can be assumed that it was similarly underpainted with lead white. In the case of the deep, plum color of Saint Florian's hose, however, the underdrawing is now more evident. The appearance of this area in the XRF map for lead suggests the absence of a lead white underlayer. Nevertheless, it is unlikely that the drawing was ever supposed to be visible. A different color was intended and indeed many of the hatched strokes that show in infrared are actually on top of the red lake, since Cossa shaded the folds with black in order to make them darker.

The appearance of these rich colors shows Cossa aspiring to the depth of tone seen in oil paintings by his contemporaries, and perhaps especially those by Tura, yet analysis of samples from the National Gallery panel has shown the use of egg tempera in all the colors examined. The hatched application associated with the quick-drying egg medium is also everywhere apparent, which emphasizes the close association between Cossa's painted brushstrokes and those of his virtuosic graphic style, whether on paper or on the gesso of a panel. This is not to say that Cossa was unaware of how to work in oil. Although his now much darkened Merchants' altarpiece of 1474 (Pinacoteca Nazionale, Bologna) is usually described as being a work in tempera, the large scale of the painting and its canvas support means that it may well have been painted using an oil technique similar to Tura's surviving canvases, notably his very early Ajaccio altarpiece and the organ shutters for the Duomo at Ferrara.[14]

Indeed, a conscious referral to older traditions in the execution of the Griffoni Polyptych is suggested by an unusual feature of the flesh painting in the central panel. The head and hands of Saint Vincent himself are strongly modeled with naturalistic flesh tints based on earth pigments and lead white.[15] The paint sample, from the shadowed part of his proper left hand, shows how the hand was shaped up with short interlaced strokes of tempera paint (fig. 12C). The substantial layers suggest a paint containing mainly pigment and egg yolk, with little added water. Remarkably, however, the flesh tints of Christ in his mandorla and the angels with the instruments of the Passion were thinly painted in shades of pink and white over an underlayer of a cool bluish green earth that was allowed to remain visible in the shadowed areas (fig. 12D). While the underpainting of areas of flesh with green earth was still common among Florentine tempera painters in the 1470s, it had generally ceased to be part of the practice of North Italian artists, and especially those from Cossa's generation such as Mantegna, Giovanni Bellini, and Tura. There is nothing to suggest that these figures are by another painter. Rather, it seems that Cossa was deliberately using the technique to emphasize the visionary aspect of this part of the altarpiece, creating a separation from the solidly sculptural and very present saints below. In addition, the colors of Christ's robe and the angels' draperies are mostly less brilliant than elsewhere, consisting of desaturated shades of pink, gray, pale blue, and lilac (fig. 12E). Conversely, the robes and wings painted with vermilion make a connection with the palette for the rest of the altarpiece.

That the Griffoni Polyptych was a conspicuously expensive commission is confirmed by the use of lavish amounts of high-quality ultramarine for the sky in the three

---

14 For Tura's use of oil on canvas and also references to an association between oil painting and textile supports in Florence see Dunkerton 2002, pp. 135–37.

15 The absence of the opaque red pigment from the flesh tints of male figures, at least, is confirmed by the XRF maps of *Saint Florian* where only lead white and earth pigments register.

main tier panels (fig. 12F). It was applied over an underlayer of indigo, which was quite commonly used for this purpose by North Italian painters, among them Mantegna, Tura, Crivelli, Bellini, and eventually by Titian in the first part of his career.[16] The ultramarine graduates from a pale blue, mixed with white at the horizon, to an intense deep blue, containing large particles of intensely colored mineral, at the top of the *Saint Vincent Ferrer* panel.

Another sophisticated choice of material was that of mosaic gold instead of mordant gilding or shell gold for the rail and rings supporting the chains of rosary beads across the three main tier panels (figs. 13 and 14), and also for picking out details such as Christ's mandorla, the edges of Saint Vincent's book and the feet of his dais.[17] In addition, its dull, slightly metallic lustre appears in the ribbon trim that edges the openings on Saint Lucy's over-garment and along the hem and cuffs of Saint Florian's blue tunic (fig. 15), just above the fur lining, where its presence has been confirmed by XRF mapping.[18] That Cossa used mosaic gold for its particular surface properties rather than as a cheap substitute for real gold is confirmed by the way in which he highlighted it with lead-tin yellow, an opaque and unreflective pigment. Although several recipes for mosaic gold are known, and although it was mentioned—rather disparagingly—by Cennino Cennini, it has most often been found in manuscript illuminations. It may be significant that the few reported occurrences on easel paintings have been mostly on works by painters who, like Cossa, embraced different media, often producing designs for other craftsmen. Moreover, to date mosaic gold has reported only on paintings that were evidently costly luxury products, including works by the likes of Tura and Ercole de' Roberti, working for the Este court,[19] and, in Florence, by Andrea del Verrocchio.[20]

It is not surprising that Ercole is one of those artists found to have used mosaic gold in panel painting, since his technique evidently originated in that of Cossa, and in terms of paint application his execution of the predella and pilaster saints of the Griffoni Polyptych closely follows that of the main panels. Nevertheless, his stylistic characteristics remain distinctive. He also seems to have been able to edit his master's brilliant

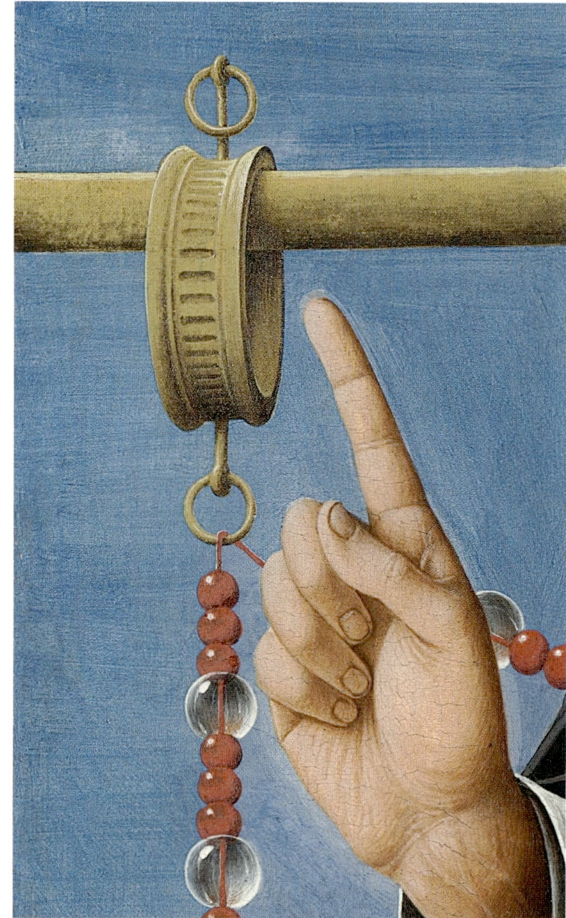

13

Detail of *Saint Vincent Ferrer*

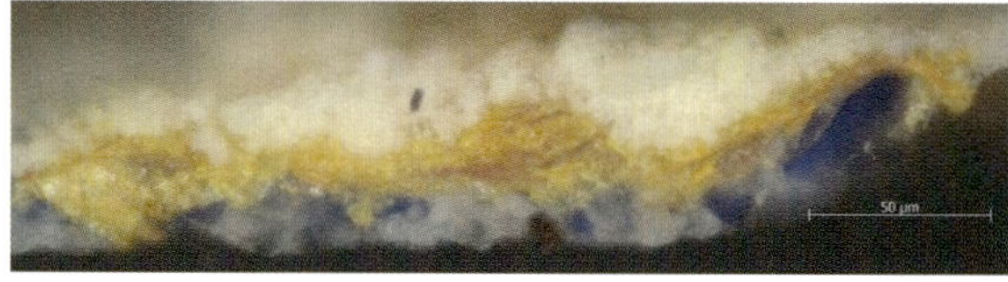

14

Paint cross-section from the pole at the left edge, overlapping the blue sky in *Saint Vincent Ferrer*

16 When the indigo was first reported in Reeve, Roy, and Smith 1981, p. 55, it was considered to be rather unusual. Subsequently many examples of its use in underpainting more expensive blue pigments have been observed.

17 When the identification of mosaic gold was published in Reeve, Roy, and Smith 1981, pp. 55–56, this was the first known occurrence on a panel painting.

18 This was carried out by Kathryn Dooley, who was able to confirm the correlation between the tin and sulphur maps, indicating mosaic gold, while the lead and tin counts along the decorative band indicated highlighting with lead-tin yellow, just as in the London painting.

19 Mosaic gold has been found on Tura's exquisite *Pietà* (Museo Correr, Venice); see *Carpaccio, Bellini, Tura, Antonello* 1993, p. 151; *Ercole de' Roberti. The Renaissance in Ferrara* 1999, p. XXVIII. For the use of mosaic gold on Ercole's *Saint Jerome in the Wilderness* (J. Paul Getty Museum, Los Angeles) and also most probably on the *Wife of Hasdrubal* (National Gallery of Art, Washington, DC), see again *Ercole de' Roberti. The Renaissance in Ferrara* 1999, pp. XXVIII and VVI.

20 For the use of mosaic gold in Verrocchio's very grand *Virgin and Child with Two Angels* in the National Gallery, London, see Dunkerton and Syson 2010, pp. 4–41, esp. 17–19. Mosaic gold has subsequently also been identified in a *Virgin and Child* from his workshop (often attributed to the young Domenico Ghirlandaio) in the National Gallery of Art, Washington, DC: see *Verrocchio* 2019, pp. 220–22, cat. no. 29.

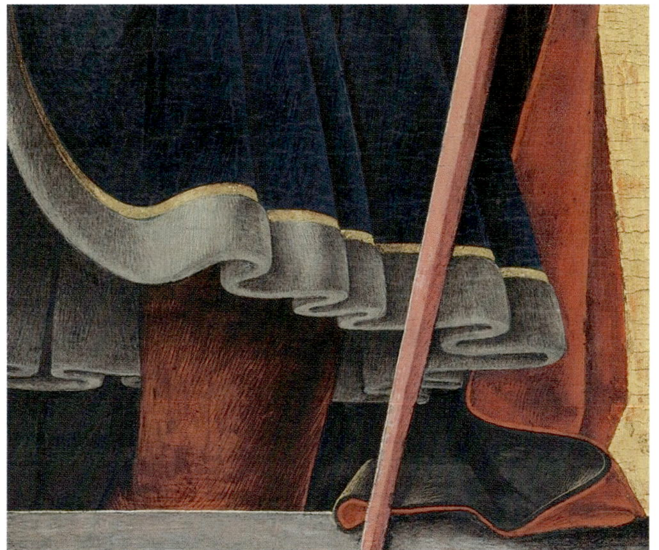

15

Detail of *Saint Florian*

palette to suit his own more subdued taste. Areas of blue and green painted with azurite and malachite have inevitably darkened, but he often seems to have chosen muted and desaturated hues of yellow ochre and mixed shades of gray and violet for his draperies.[21] The landscape and architecture, although still fantastic, are depicted with more natural colors than Cossa's artificial blocks of pink and gray stone. Only the touches of bright vermilion on draperies and details such as hats and stockings serve to connect his panels to the altarpiece as a whole. Ercole continued essentially as a tempera painter when working on a small scale on panel,[22] and even in late works he used techniques that can be seen on Cossa's panels, for example the shading of red draperies with fine hatched strokes of black.[23]

With his fine brushwork, Ercole achieved effects of extraordinary delicacy, whether modeling one of his animated figures or creating a mysterious landscape, full of atmosphere and aerial perspective. In this he differs from Cossa, with his robust clarity, yet for both their painting techniques were inseparable from their practices as draughtsmen. Ercole represented, together with Mantegna, Crivelli, and certain Florentines, above all Domenico Ghirlandaio and—briefly—his young pupil, Michelangelo, the last flourish of this tradition before the spread of oil painting across Italy radically transformed the relationship between the processes of drawing and painting.

21 Ercole's preference for paler and less pure and intense colors than those favored by Cossa has also become evident following the recent cleaning of *The Garden of Gethsemene* and *The Way to Calvary* (Gemäldegalerie Alte Meister, Dresden).
22 His great Portuense altarpiece (Pinacoteca di Brera, Milan) of 1479–81 was painted on canvas and appears to have been executed in oil.
23 For the shading of draperies with black, which makes it difficult to distinguish possible lines of underdrawing, see Dunkerton and Smith 1986, pp. 33–38, esp. 33–34.

SAINT JOHN THE BAPTIST AND SAINT PETER: NOTES ON THE RESTORATIONS AND TECHNIQUE

Letizia Lodi

Thanks to studies in recent decades,[1] to exhibitions such as the one dedicated to *Cosmè Tura e Francesco del Cossa*,[2] and to the precise reconstruction of the Griffoni Polyptych by Cecilia Cavalca, we know a great deal about Francesco del Cossa's two paintings with *Saint Peter* and *Saint John the Baptist*, who stand majestically on broad, contoured stones before pilasters with classical capitals. Cavalca's reconstruction is now the object of this rare and important exhibition, which, for the first time since the dismemberment of the altarpiece, reunites its various painted compartments, otherwise split between nine different museums. We will not discuss here, however, the critical responses and debates of the second half of the nineteenth century, already well articulated by curators in this catalogue and earlier literature.

Following the removal and dismemberment of the polyptych at the behest of Pompeo Aldrovandi in 1725–31,[3] the two paintings were documented as being in Ferrara at the beginning of the nineteenth century in the Barbi Cinti collection, which had formed in parallel with the collection of Marquis Giovanni Battista Costabili, for whom Giovanni Cinti served as attorney. After the heirs sold off the collection, the Brera panels passed first to the painter and collector Enea Vendeghini and then to the industrialist Giuseppe Cavalieri. Cavalieri, in turn, sold them to the Pinacoteca di Brera on July 12, 1893 for 25,000 liras,[4] after negotiations with the Minister of Education Fiorilli and the director of the Pinacoteca Giuseppe Bertini. As has been noted, this purchase was promoted by Adolfo Venturi, who singled out the two paintings in Cavalieri's collection to Bertini and who was among the first to support the attribution to Francesco del Cossa, according to the Pinacoteca's archival documentation.[5]

The acquisition of the two paintings was fundamental for the Pinacoteca, as it allowed the beginning of a new arrangement, exhibiting the works of the Ferrara School

---

I especially thank Barbara Ferriani, who carried out the restoration, Vincenzo Gheroldi, Andrea Carini, Emanuela Daffra, Gianluca Poldi, Anna Lucchini, and, last but surely not least, the exhibition curators Mauro Natale and Cecilia Cavalca for their helpful contributions and exchange of opinions. A more complete version of this text will be available on the website of the Pinacoteca di Brera and on Accademia.edu.

1 Benati 1984, pp. 143–94, esp. 172–74; A. Bacchi in *Pinacoteca di Brera* 1991, pp. 60–72, nos. 22–23; Cavalca 2013, pp. 136–51, 334–36. For complete technical information on *Saint Peter* and *Saint John the Baptist* (tempera on board, 1470–73), please see cat. nos. 2 and 3.

2 *Cosmè Tura e Francesco del Cossa* 2007.

3 Cavalca 2013, pp. 335–36 and documentary appendix; E. Daffra in *Restituzioni* 2016, p. 169.

4 Emiliani 1996a, pp.15–50; Scardino 1996, p. 95.

5 Venturi 1888. Historical Documentary Archive of the Pinacoteca di Brera (former SBSAE, Milan), part I, box 3, file 20 (purchase of paintings by Francesco del Cossa). Of special interest is Gustavo Frizzoni's report on the importance of Cossa's paintings for the Pinacoteca di Brera, sent to Minister of Education Fiorilli, and the attached photographs produced in July–August 1893 by the studio of Giovanni Brogi, which give evidence of the state of preservation at that point.

"according to a rational, scientific plan," placing the *Saint John the Baptist* and *Saint Peter*, which entered the Brera correctly attributed to Cossa, beside Ercole de' Roberti's Portuense altarpiece, Lorenzo Costa's *Adoration of the Magi*, and Dosso Dossi's *Saint Sebastian*.[6] During the whole month of July 1893, the two paintings were exhibited in the Raphael Room, "protected by a pane of glass to safeguard them," as testified to in a letter from Bertini to Minister Fiorilli dated August 5, 1893,[7] and subsequently in Rooms XX and XXI, dedicated to the Ferrara School. They are still displayed today in the re-modeled Room XX.

Beginning with the early insight of Gustavo Frizzoni (1888), it has been recognized that the two Brera paintings belong to the Griffoni Polyptych, where they appeared on either side of the central panel with *Saint Vincent Ferrer*. In 1858 the latter painting was acquired from the Costabili collection by the National Gallery of London, while Ercole de' Roberti's predella with the *Miracles of Saint Vincent Ferrer* has been in the Pinacoteca Vaticana since the same year.

The good condition of the two panels, recorded in the *Registro cronologico* upon their entry into the Pinacoteca in July 1893, was confirmed in the museum's guides and catalogues of the early 1900s: in the 1907 edition, recalling the importance of Guiseppe Bertini's acquisitions, Corrado Ricci praised "those two marvels of vigor and conservation that are the Saints Peter and John the Baptist by Francesco del Cossa."[8] The Historical Photo Archive of the Pinacoteca has a number of reproductions of the altarpiece elements, including a series taken by Giovanni Brogi in July 1893, which were attached to Frizzoni's report (fig. 1), others by Anderson, also from July 1893, and still others by Riccardi and Alinari from the early twentieth century (fig. 2). Careful observation of these photographs reveals visible gaps due to loss of paint in the mantle, the red fabric near the book in *Saint Peter*, and on the upper part of the gold halo and neck of the saint. However, in photographs published several years later in Corrado Ricci's 1907 catalogue and in Francesco Malaguzzi Valeri's in 1908, these spaces have been filled in.[9]

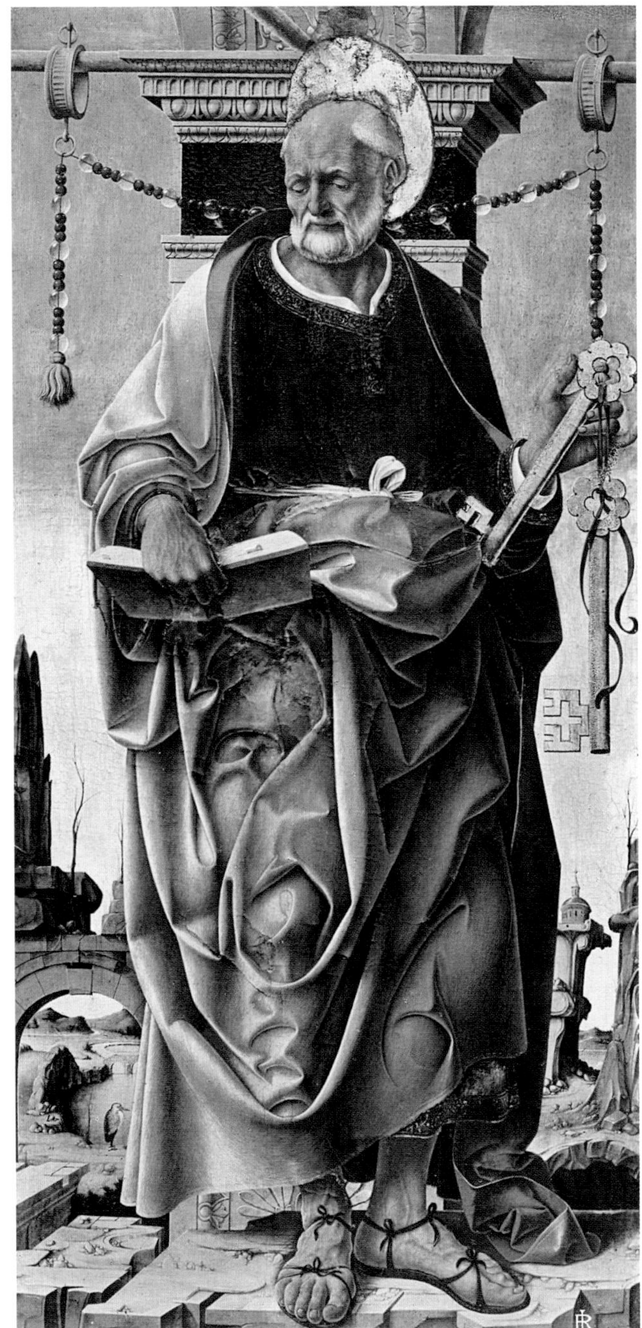

1

Giovanni Brogi, *Saint Peter*, July 1893, photo attached to Frizzoni's report of August 5, 1893 (Pinacoteca di Brera, Photo Archive)

Valeri's catalogue dedicated ample space to a precise, enthusiastic description of the two saints, also commenting on their state of conservation: "... and finally, what is so

6 Carotti 1894.

7 Historical Documentary Archive of the Pinacoteca di Brera (former SBSAE, Milan), part I, box 3, file 20 (purchase of paintings by Francesco del Cossa).

8 Ricci 1907, pp. 230–31 ("... *quei due prodigi di vigoria e di conservazione che sono i Santi Pietro e Giovanni Battista di Francesco del Cossa*") .

9 Malaguzzi Valeri 1908, pp. 250–51. Late nineteenth- and early twentieth-century photographs can also be seen on the website of the Photo Archive of Fondazione Federico Zeri at Bologna University.

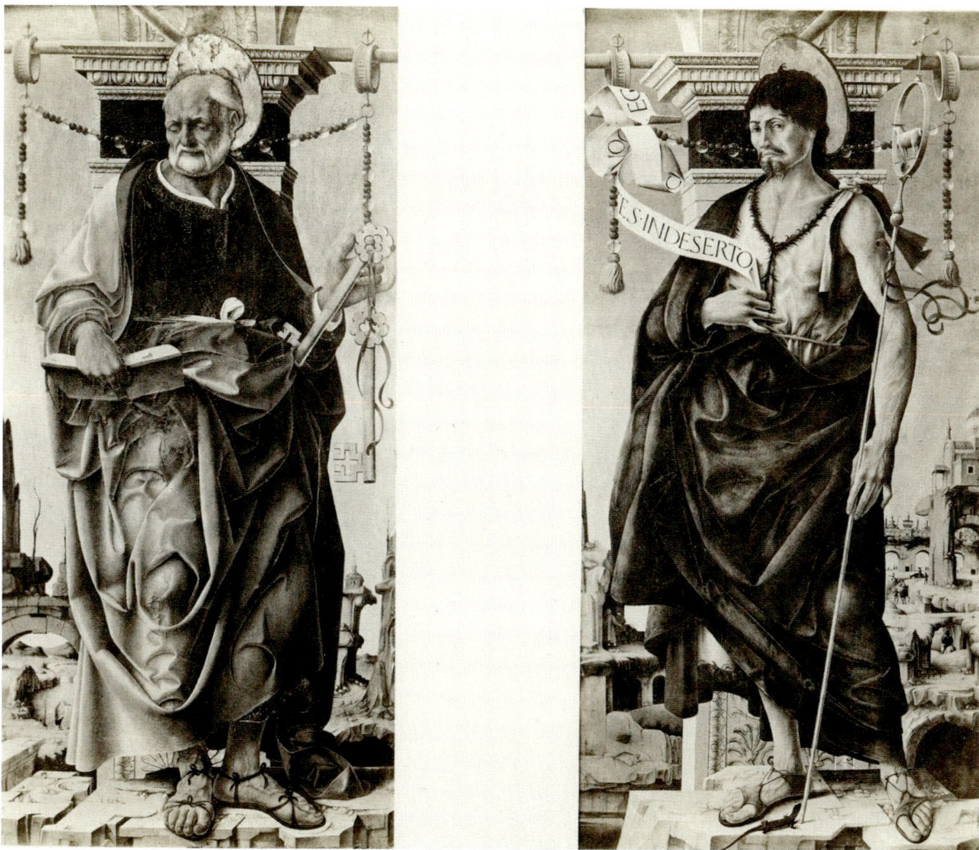

2

Foto Alinari, *Saint Peter and Saint John the Baptist*, early twentieth century (Fondazione Federico Zeri, Photo Archive)

marvelous ... is the clarity and power of the color, which except for some small parts, has been preserved intact through four centuries, serving as a testimony to painters of the quality of the antique system of painting with tempera without needing to resort to superimposing layers of paint. Thanks to its transparency and limpidity, the color creates effects not unlike that of paintings on glass..." Malaguzzi also reprised comments by Frizzoni, who had noted the precision of the body details, where "the web of the veins, the drapery, the hair, the beards are executed with extraordinary precision." Thanks to his careful direct observation, he was able to anticipate the results of later x-ray and reflectographic studies.

Thus, the interventions to conserve the panels and fill in their lacunae can be dated to between 1893 and the first years of the twentieth century, although there is no record of who actually performed these operations. Documents in the Historical Archive (part I, 57) do indicate that in those years, between 1893 and 1907–8, Luigi Cavenaghi, mentioned also by Corrado Ricci, a student and protegee of Giuseppe Bertini, worked in the Pinacoteca on various preservation jobs, though he is not named in connection with the Cossa panels. It is not unlikely that these jobs went unmentioned in the lists of the most important restorations because they were only minor operations to fill in the lacunae.

In addition to the intervention from before 1907–8, it is possible that another one was carried out before the re-opening of the Pinacoteca in 1920 (after damage to the works suffered in World War I) and the redesign of the displays by Ettore Modigliani. Although no direct mention of an intervention on the two paintings has been found, recently-discovered documents in Ettore Modigliani's archive refer to maintenance procedures performed by Pelliccioli on the panels and frames of many works and indeed of almost all those in the Ferrarese and Emilian painting collections.[10]

Next came the preservation efforts of Giovanna Turinetti in 1984. The report on the restoration of *Saint Peter* described the painting's support as in good condition though slightly curved, with a large knot splitting the wood toward the bottom. The layer of paint was found to be relatively well-preserved, with the exception of several raised areas, and the tempera used quite thin. The restorer added that a linen canvas was—and still is—inserted between the support and the gesso preparation, a common practice in sixteenth-century paintings from the Ferrara and Veneto areas, as also noted by Andrea Bacchi.[11]

In fact, the edges had tended to chip off, as evidenced in the photographic documentation seen here (fig. 3), and some of the paint had detached. The report goes on to describe a long vertical line in the center of the painting with distinct and extensive signs of retouching, and that the halo too had been mostly repainted, as seen in the photographs. The restorer made the interesting, novel observation that the saint's blue mantle, with its edges gilded *a missione*, had been abraded by an overly-enthusiastic cleaning in the past.

In general, the intervention was predominantly one of maintenance, fixing the edges that had detached from the linen canvas and paint layer as well as sealing and retouching in various places. The first x-rays were taken on this occasion, which then joined the ample photographic documentation. The images revealed numerous distinct incisions outlining the figures, architectural decoration, rocks, classical capitals, and many folds of the mantle and fabrics. New x-ray studies have been performed recently on both paintings

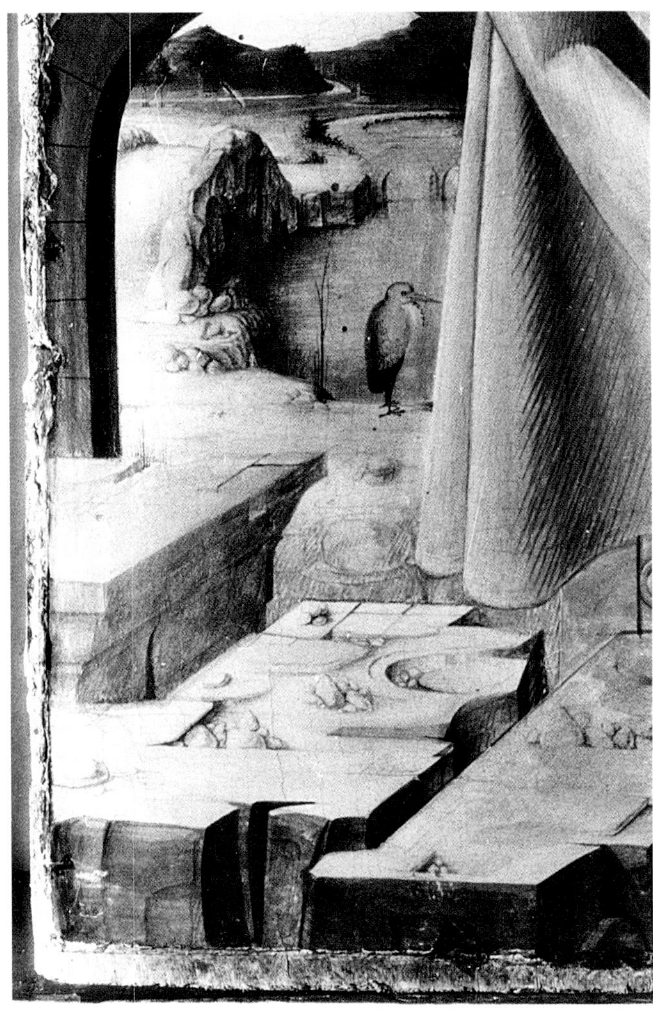

3

Detail of the linen canvas between support and gesso preparation of *Saint Peter*, Turinetti's restoration, 1984

10 Historical Archive of the Pinacoteca di Brera, Fondo Modigliani (under reorganization), documents acquired in September 2019 concerning 1920 *(Il rinnovamento della Pinacoteca)*.
11 A. Bacchi in *Pinacoteca di Brera* 1991, pp. 60–72, nos. 22–23.

by the Photography laboratory of the Brera.[12] The most recent, excellent restoration was carried out in 2016 by Barbara Ferriani under the direction of Emanuela Daffra.[13]

Many details of the structure of the Griffoni Polyptych, such as the marks of wooden crosspieces visible in the Brera x-rays, were already partially noted in Cecilia Cavalca's reconstruction. Similarly, studies of the pigments used by Cossa in the central panel with *Saint Vincent Ferrer* in the National Gallery in London were published after its restoration in 1981.[14]

The most recent restoration freed the paint layer of smudges, later additions, and oxidized paint, allowing a clearer perception of the quality of the light, the lustre of the white edging, and the grays in the shadows. It also revealed new information; in fact, from Ferriani's notes on the state of conservation of the two panels, we learn that they were painted on poplar panels with a vertical grain and that the supports on the back, prepared with an adze, feature imperfections, knots, and deviations in the grain.[15]

Evidence of historical interventions on the figure of *Saint Peter* was revealed both in direct analysis and in ultra-violet fluorescence, which showed signs of substantial restorations, performed repeatedly over the years using diverse impastos.[16]

Ferriani's report theorizes that Cossa used egg tempera as a binder—as is also suggested by a London research on the panel with *Saint Vincent Ferrer*—and that the artist masterfully exploited the expressive potential of this medium, obtaining transparent layers as well as impastos *a corpo*, quite similar to the results with resinous mediums. In this way, he was able to convey the material and tactile consistency of the different surfaces, demonstrating his profound knowledge of the techniques of Flemish painting, which were well-represented in the collections of Borso d'Este's court.[17]

---

12 At the beginning of the 2000s, Duilio Bertani conducted reflectographies with a scanner in an IRR (Infrared Reflectography) project analyzing Lombard and Emilian works from the fifteenth and sixteenth centuries, coordinated by the present author representing the Photography laboratory. Observation of the two panels with oblique light clearly reveals that the artist outlined the silhouettes of the figures and the architecture, the profiles of the pilasters and capitals, Saint Peter's keys and the cartouche held by Saint John the Baptist with deep, detailed incisions, and without *ripensamenti*. These incisions are even more visible in the x-rays. Many also appear in the dense folds of the drapery of the mantles and fabrics. Infra-red reflectography also confirms the use of these thin, meticulous lines. Considering their precision and the total absence of smudges in the outlines, it can be presumed with a high degree of certainty that Cossa used cartoons for the figures and also to draw the architecture, pilasters and capitals. Indeed, the use of cartoons for direct incisions has already been acknowleged as a practice used by Cossa for all his wall paintings, both fresco and *a secco*, in the Hall of the Months in Palazzo Schifanoia, completed in 1470. This is testified to by Gheroldi, who noted that "this cartoon activity is largely described in the Ferrara documents compiled at the time of the Schifanoia project, which often mention the realization of *patroni*, executed by painters for the tapestry makers, goldsmiths, and inlayers." There is evidence that he used cartoons not only in wall paintings but also in panel paintings, as Giovanni Sassu observed in the entry on the refined drawing *Page seen from behind* in the British Museum, a figure seen also in one of the *Months* in Schifanoia and again in a figure descending stairs in Ercole de' Roberti's predella of the Griffoni Polyptych. See Gheroldi 2007, pp. 148–49 and G. Sassu in *Cosmè Tura e Francesco del Cossa* 2007, pp. 406–7.

13 E. Daffra in *Restituzioni* 2016, pp. 169–74.

14 Smith, Reeve, and Roy 1981, pp. 45–57.

15 For reasons of space, we will not discuss here the various observations generated by the restoration, and refer readers to the original version of the text on the Pinacoteca di Brera website (News-eventi). Although there were no crosspieces, there are several indications that in fact two had been applied in the beginning, one on the upper and one on the lower margin, in order to join the supports to the original complex architectural frame of the polyptych. Indeed, the marks of the wood dowel are clearly visible in the x-rays. Also visible along all the edges are traces of a brown/black paint that must have been applied when the polyptych was dismantled—between 1725 and 1731—and the individual panels were placed in new wood frames.

16 Furthermore, the presence of grooves created by wood-eating insects along the lateral thicknesses shows that the two panels were cut down slightly in size at the moment of the dismemberment of the polyptych. Over time, lacking a containing structure, they began to curve and a long crack formed in the lower central part of the *Saint John the Baptist*.

17 See also Dunkerton's contribution in this catalogue.

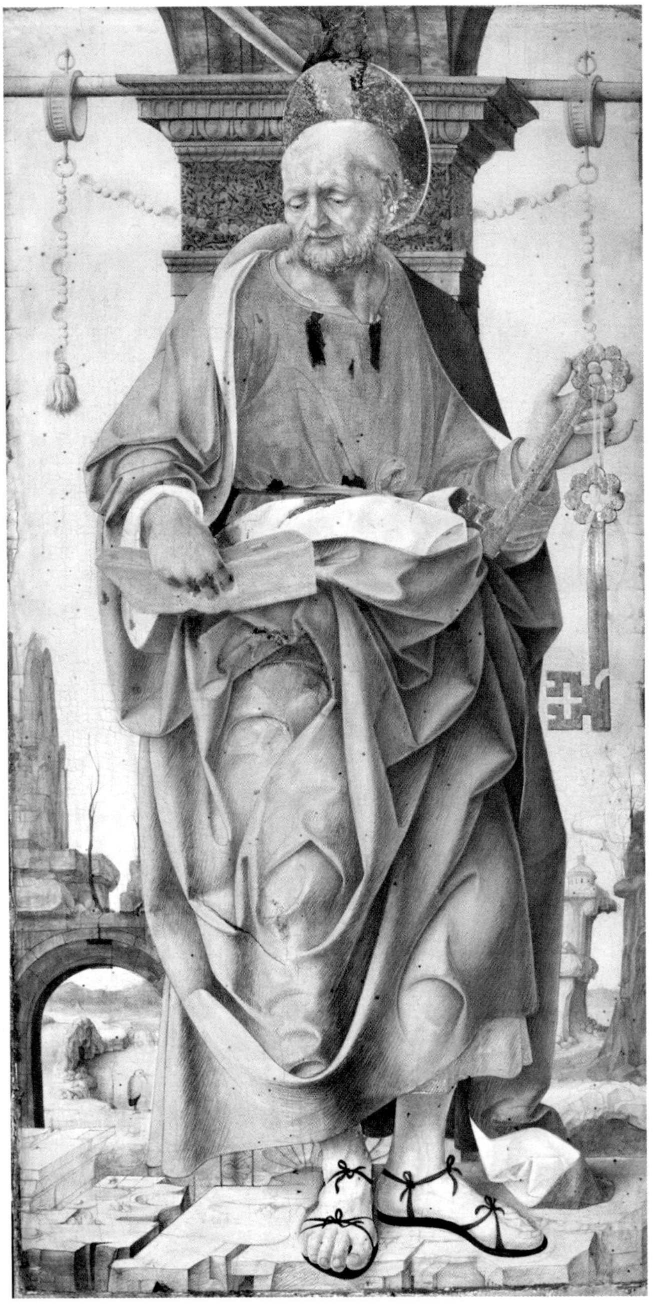

4

Infrared reflectogram of *Saint Peter* performed by the Photography laboratory of Pinacoteca di Brera, 2002

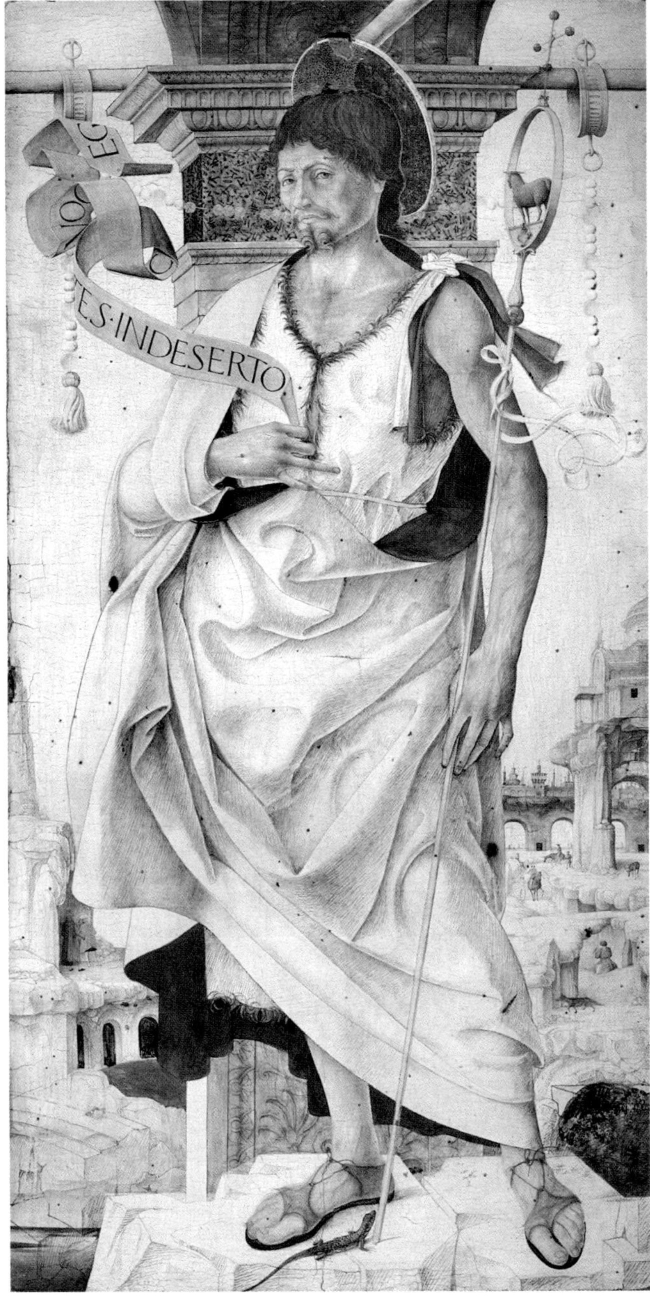

5

Infrared reflectogram of *Saint John the Baptist* performed by the Photography laboratory of Pinacoteca di Brera, 2002

To gild the halos, especially that of Saint Peter and his keys, Cossa used gold leaf applied onto a traditional bole preparation. He intensified their optical effect not only by punching but also by adding tin powder—often used in manuscript production at the Este court—and highlights of tin-lead yellow, as confirmed by the XRF (x-ray fluorescence) analyses performed in the Centro Studio Palladio sul Dipinto in Vicenza.[18] The artist executed a sort of graining of the gold by making tiny perforations with a gentle punching action. He provided the objects with depth, to great effect, by defining the shadows and alternation of glossy and opaque areas, while also differentiating the radiance of the gold.[19] As Gheroldi pointed out, Francesco del Cossa sought effects of *light* and *lustre* in both wall paintings and panel paintings.[20]

Indeed, all the marvelous details of the two panels give evidence of the artist's extraordinary draughtsmanship, confirmed by the reflectographic images (figs. 4 and 5), which is perfectly complemented by his application of the colors, just as del Cossa claimed in his famous, oft-cited letter to Duke Borso d'Este in 1470.[21]

---

18 *Osservazioni sulle indagini XRF*, Centro Ricerche sul Dipinto CSG Palladio, Thierry Radelet 2015/2016, Report, pp. 34–40

19 The XRF analysis found that the pigments in the two panels were the traditional ones used in the second half of the fifteenth century, especially in the Po Valley area: white lead, various earthen ochres, lead-tin yellow, vermilion, cupric pigments such as azurite, verdegris and malachite, mixed with ceruse, carbon black, and layers of red lacquer, clearly visible in the Baptist's mantle. In the sky backgrounding the two saints, beneath azurite and ultramarine glazes, the analyses found a preparatory ground of a vegetable indaco dye, which has lost its original color over time due to its unstable character. According to findings by Gianluca Poldi and Giovanni Villa, indaco was also used along with yellow to render the particular tone of green of the book held by Saint Peter. On this topic see Poldi and Villa 2007, pp. 160–61. Thus, the deterioration of the layers in the sky is not the result of drastic cleanings in the past but rather of the fading of the tones in this preparatory layer, which must originally have been quite intense, and of a natural increase in the transparency of the final applications. The use of indaco has also been found in works by Cosmè Tura, Andrea Mantegna, and Giovanni Bellini. For Cennino Cennini's instructions for graining gold, see Cennini ed. 1975, pp. 109–10, Ch. CXL. For the discussion of "*granare in su l'oro*," see also Lodi 1983, pp. 9–199.

20 Gheroldi 2007, pp. 148–49. The scholar also recalled that Cossa sought effects of light and lustre through "juxtapositions of differently reflecting materials: for instance, in the Saint Vincent Ferrer of the Griffoni Polyptych, the highlighted parts had been differentiated with the use of leaf gilding, purple and light yellow."

21 In addition to the incisions defining the figures and architecture, the IRR of the Brera paintings clearly reveal an elaborate preparatory underdrawing, which brushes over the outlines of the figures, hands, and attributes with dark diluted ink. The drawing extends out with diagonal strokes of varying thicknesses interwoven in various ways, especially in the folds of the saints' garments but also in the details of the rocks and in the arms of *Saint John the Baptist*, to indicate the chiaroscuro, which are taken up later in the application of the paints, creating a remarkable luminousness and endowing the figures with a sculptural quality. Besides the simpler incisions and shortened and diagonal ones in the folds of the mantles, traces of many minute holes made by the *spolvero* technique can be seen in some points, such as the cuff of the red garment at the wrist in *Saint Peter* and the cuff to the right near the *craquelure*. It seems to us that traces of such pouncing are also found in the arch of the eyebrows of *Saint John the Baptist* and in the folds near the waist of his garments. The visionary landscape in the background has no incisions; apparently it was less well-defined in the planning, although the IRR clearly reveal the underdrawing that defines the outlines of the rocks, architecture, and the mountains in the distance. There are, however, some changes between the drawing and the actual painting. For example, where a fragment of a capital and remains of other architectural elements were drawn on the right near the Baptist's foot, there is instead a deep grotto in the final painting. In the lower left corner of *Saint John the Baptist*, a series of lines defining a square block and sketchy indications of rocks that seem to continue those of the saint's pedestal are clearly visible in the underdrawing, whereas they are replaced in the painting by the blue water of a deep well. In the architectural background to the saint's right, painted in remarkable detail, the turret in the center is an explicit reference to the Este Castle built by Bartolino di Novara and the arcade recalls the one that opened from Piazza Castello toward Piazza del Duomo in Ferrara.

REFERENCE LITERATURE

Manuscripts

Oretti 1767
M. Oretti, *Le Pitture nelle Chiese della Città di Bologna descritte … nell'anno 1767*, Biblioteca Comunale dell'Archiginnasio, Bologna, ms. B.30.

Oretti c. 1760–80
M. Oretti, *Notizie de' Professori del Disegno cioè Pittori, Scultori ed Architetti Bolognesi e de' Forestieri di sua Scuola*, c. 1760–80, Biblioteca Comunale dell'Archiginnasio, Bologna, ms. B.123.

Oretti 1775
M. Oretti, *Le chiese nella città di Bologna nel suo stato antico e delle mutazioni di tante pitture e di varij abusi sopra alle s.e immagini di Dio, e della s.a Vergine, e santi levati dalle chiese*, 1775, Biblioteca Comunale dell'Archiginnasio, Bologna, ms. B.30 (part 2).

Oretti 1777
M. Oretti, "Le pitture della città d'Imola descritte da Marcello Oretti nell'anno 1777," in *Pitture di Napoli e dello Stato ecclesiastico*, 1777, Biblioteca Comunale dell'Archiginnasio, Bologna, ms. B.165 bis.

Oretti *ante* 1787
M. Oretti, *Le Pitture che si ammirano nelli Palagi, e Case de' Nobili della Città di Bologna, e di altri edificij in detta Città*, *ante* 1787, Biblioteca Comunale dell'Archiginnasio, Bologna, ms. B.104.

Philomathia [1478]
Philomathia MCCCCLXXVII [1478], Bologna, Biblioteca Universitaria, ms. 1614.

Pitture 1885
Pitture della Raccolta del Co.te Gio Batta Costabili di Ferrara, 1835, Bologna, Biblioteca dell'Archiginnasio, ms. A.1324.

Vite degl'Artefici c. 1770
Vite degl'Artefici delle nobili arti della città di Ferrara scritte dal fu dottor Girolamo Baruffaldi arciprete dell'insigne collegiata di Cento edizione postuma di note arrichita accresciuta, compita, et in due parti divisa, Parte prima, c. 1770, Bologna, Biblioteca Comunale dell'Archiginnasio, ms. B.77.

Printed sources

Acidini Luchinat 1993
C. Acidini Luchinat, "La Cappella dei Magi," in *Benozzo Gozzoli. La Cappella dei Magi*, ed. C. Acidini Luchinat (Milan, 1993), pp. 7–24.

Ackerman Smoller 2014
L. Ackerman Smoller, *The Saint and the Chopped-Up Baby. The Cult of Vincent Ferrer in Medieval and Early Modern Europe* (Ithaca and London, 2014).

Agosti 1988
G. Agosti, "Una postilla su Roberto Longhi al concorso bolognese del 1934," in *L'Accademia di Bologna. Figure del Novecento*, eds. A. Baccilieri and S. Evangelisti, exh. cat., Accademia di Belle Arti, Bologna, 1988 (Bologna, 1988), pp. 251–53.

Agosti 1994
G. Agosti, "Materiali su Gustavo Frizzoni e prime riflessioni sui suoi ambienti di lavoro," in *Giovanni Morelli collezionista di disegni. La donazione al Castello Sforzesco*, ed. G. Bora, exh. cat., Civiche Raccolte d'Arte, Castello Sforzesco, Sale Viscontee, Milan, 1994–95 (Cinisello Balsamo, 1994), pp. 41–51.

Agosti 1996
G. Agosti, *La nascita della storia dell'arte in Italia. Adolfo Venturi: dal museo all'università 1880–1940* (Venice, 1996).

Agosti 2013
B. Agosti, *Giorgio Vasari. Luoghi e tempi delle Vite* (Milan, 2013).

Agostini and Scardino 1997
Inventari d'arte. Documenti su 10 quadrerie ferraresi del XIX secolo, eds. G. Agostini and L. Scardino (Ferrara, 1997).

Ahl 1996
D. C. Ahl, *Benozzo Gozzoli* (New Haven and London, 1996).

Alberti 1479–1543 ed. 2006
L. Alberti, *Historie di Bologna* (1479–1543), eds. A. Antonelli and M. R. Musti, 3 vols. (Bologna, 2006).

Allen 1999
D. Allen, "Some observations on Ercole de' Roberti as painter-draughtsman," in *Ercole de' Roberti. The Renaissance in Ferrara*, eds. D. Allen, L. Syson, et al., exh. cat., The J. Paul Getty Museum, Los Angeles, 1999 (London, 1999), pp. XV–XXIV (also as supplement to *The Burlington Magazine*, vol. CXLI, no. 1153, April 1999: I–XI).

Ambrosini Massari 2007
"Dotti amici". Amico Ricci e la nascita della storia dell'arte nelle Marche, ed. A. M. Ambrosini Massari (Ancona, 2007).

Anderson 1985
J. Anderson, "Una mostra della pittura ferrarese alla Galleria Matthiesen," in *Da Borso a Cesare d'Este: la Scuola di Ferrara. 1450–1628*, ed. E. Mattaliano, enlarged Italian edition of the catalogue for the exhibition staged in London to support The Courtauld Institute of Art Trust Appeal, Matthiesen Fine Art, 1984 (Ferrara, 1985), pp. 188–93.

Anderson 1993
J. Anderson, "The rediscovery of Ferrarese Renaissance painting in the Risorgimento," in *The Burlington Magazine*, vol. CXXXV, no. 1085, August 1993, pp. 539–49.

Anderson 1994
J. Anderson, "Salvare gli affreschi del Rinascimento italiano: la missione di Henry Layard," in A. H. Layard, *Giovanni Santi e l'affresco di Cagli*, ed. R. Varese (Florence, 1994), pp. 51–61.

Andrea Mantegna 2019
Andrea Mantegna. Rivivere l'Antico e costruire il Moderno, eds. S. Bandera, H. Burns, and V. Farinella, exh. cat., Palazzo Madama, Turin, 2019–20 (Venice, 2019).

Angiolini 2002a
E. Angiolini, "Griffoni, Giovanni," in *Dizionario Biografico degli Italiani*, vol. LIX (Rome, 2002).

Angiolini 2002b
E. Angiolini, "Griffoni, Giacomo," in *Dizionario Biografico degli Italiani*, vol. LIX (Rome, 2002).

Angiolini 2002c
E. Angiolini, "Griffoni, Floriano," in *Dizionario Biografico degli Italiani*, vol. LIX (Rome, 2002).

Annali della Fabbrica del duomo 1877
Annali della Fabbrica del duomo di Milano dall'origine fino al presente, vol. I (Milan, 1877).

Anselmi and Scioli 2018
G. M. Anselmi and S. Scioli, "Literary Culture in Bologna from the Duecento to the Cinquecento," in *A Companion to Medieval and Renaissance Bologna*, ed. S. Rubin Blanshei (Leiden and Boston, 2018), pp. 499–529.

Arienti ed. 1888
Giovanni Sabbadino degli Arienti, *Il torneo fatto in Bologna il 4 ottobre 1470*, ed. Antonio Zambiagi (Parma, 1888).

Arienti ed. 1983–84
Sabadino degli Arienti, *De civica salute*, Biblioteca Comunale dell'Archiginnasio, Bologna, ms. B.1444, transcribed by D. Volta in *La Civica salute, di Giovanni Sabadino degli Arienti: edizione interpretativa*, degree thesis in Italian Philology, supervisor C. Mazzotta, Università degli Studi di Bologna, Faculty of Letters and Philosophy, academic year 1983–84.

Armstrong 1976
L. Armstrong, *The Paintings and Drawings of Marco Zoppo* (New York and London 1976).

Armstrong 1988
L. Armstrong, "Del Cossa, Francesco,"

in *Dizionario Biografico degli Italiani*, vol. XXXVI (Rome, 1988), pp. 467–71.

Arslan 1936
W. Arslan, "Roberto Longhi, Officina Ferrarese," in *Zeitschrift für Kunstgeschichte*, year V, no. 2–3, 1936, pp. 174–83.

Ascani 1991
V. Ascani, "I disegni architettonici attribuiti ad Antonio di Vincenzo: caratteristiche tecniche e ruolo degli 'appunti grafici' nella prassi progettuale tardogotica," in *Arte medievale*, series II, V, no. 1, 1991, pp. 105–15.

Austen Henry Layard 1987
Austen Henry Layard tra l'Oriente e Venezia, eds. F. M. Fales and B. J. Hickey, conference papers, Venice, 1983 (Rome, 1987).

Avery-Quash 2011
S. Avery-Quash, *The Travel Notebooks of Sir Charles Eastlake*, 2 vols., Walpole Society 73 (London, 2011).

Bacchi 1984
A. Bacchi, "Vicende della pittura nell'età di Giovanni II Bentivoglio," in *Bentivolorum Magnificentia. Principe e cultura a Bologna nel Rinascimento*, ed. B. Basile (Rome, 1984), pp. 285–335.

Bacchi 1985
A. Bacchi, "Problemi aperti a Schifanoia: il giovane Ercole de' Roberti," in *Da Borso a Cesare d'Este: la Scuola di Ferrara. 1450–1628*, ed. E. Mattaliano, enlarged Italian edition of the catalogue for the exhibition staged in London to support The Courtauld Institute of Art Trust Appeal, Matthiesen Fine Art, 1984 (Ferrara, 1985), pp. 175–78.

Bacchi 1990
A. Bacchi, *Dipinti ferraresi dalla collezione Vittorio Cini* (Vicenza, 1990).

Bacchi 1991
A. Bacchi, *Francesco del Cossa* (Soncino, 1991).

Bacchi della Lega 1892–93
A. Bacchi della Lega, "Bibliografia petroniana," in *Atti e Memorie della Deputazione di storia patria per le province di Romagna*, series III, vol. X, 1892, pp. 324–51; vol. XI, 1893, pp. 159–82.

Bacchi and De Marchi 2016
A. Bacchi and A. De Marchi, "Vittorio Cini collezionista di pittura antica. Una splendida avventura, dal Castello di Monselice alla dimora veneziana, da Nino Barbantini a Federico Zeri," in *La Galleria di Palazzo Cini. Dipinti, sculture, oggetti d'arte*, eds. A. Bacchi and A. De Marchi (Venice, 2016), pp. 389–453.

Bagatin 2004
P. L. Bagatin, *Le pitture lignee di Lorenzo e Cristoforo da Lendinara* (Treviso, 2004).

Basile 1984
"Bentivolorum Magnificentia". Principe e cultura nella Bologna del Rinascimento, ed. B. Basile (Rome, 1984).

Bassani 1816
P. Bassani, *Guida agli amatori delle Belle Arti. Architettura, pittura e scultura per la città di Bologna, suoi sobborghi, e circondario* (Bologna, 1816).

Bassani Pacht 2006
Igino Benvenuto Supino 1858–1940. Omaggio a un padre fondatore, ed. P. Bassani Pacht (Florence, 2006).

Battistini 2014
S. Battistini, "Francesco Malaguzzi Valeri e il Museo Davia Bargellini," in *Francesco Malaguzzi Valeri (1867–1928). Tra storiografia artistica, museo e tutela*, eds. A. Rovetta and G. C. Sciolla, conference papers, Milan and Bologna, 2011 (Milan, 2014), pp. 351–59.

Bazzocchi 2013
M. A. Bazzocchi, "Letterati e intellettuali (1914–1970)," in *Storia di Bologna*, ed. R. Zangheri, vol. IV., t. 2: *Bologna in età contemporanea 1915–2000*, ed. A. Varni (Bologna, 2013), pp. 271–392.

Beck 1970
J. H. Beck, *Jacopo della Quercia e il portale di San Petronio a Bologna: ricerche storiche, documentarie e iconografiche*, Bologna 1970.

Beck 1991
J. H. Beck, *Jacopo della Quercia* (New York, 1991).

Behrman 2005
S. N. Behrman, *Duveen. Il re degli antiquari* (Palermo, 2005).

Belli Barsali 1960
I. Belli Barsali, "Agostino di Duccio," in *Dizionario Biografico degli Italiani*, vol. I (Rome, 1960).

Bellosi 1983
L. Bellosi, "La 'porta magna' di Jacopo della Quercia," in *La basilica di San Petronio in Bologna*, vol. I (Bologna, 1983), pp. 163–212.

Bellosi 1990
L. Bellosi, "Giovanni di Francesco e l'arte fiorentina di metà Quattrocento," in *Pittura di luce. Giovanni di Francesco e l'arte fiorentina di metà Quattrocento*, ed. L. Bellosi, exh. cat., Casa Buonarroti, Florence (Florence, 1990), pp. 11–46.

Bellosi 1992
L. Bellosi, "Sulla formazione fiorentina di Piero della Francesca," in *Una scuola per Piero. Luce, colore e prospettiva nella formazione fiorentina di Piero della Francesca*, ed. L. Bellosi, exh. cat., Gallerie degli Uffizi, Florence, 1992–93 (Florence, 1992), pp. 17–54.

Benati 1982
D. Benati, "Per il problema di 'Vicino da Ferrara' (alias Baldassarre d'Este)," in *Paragone*, year XXXIII, no. 393, 1982, pp. 3–26.

Benati 1984
D. Benati, "La pittura rinascimentale," in *La Basilica di San Petronio in Bologna*, ed. M. Fanti, G. Lorenzoni, A. M. Matteucci, R. Roli, and C. Volpe, coordinated by D. Benati and L. Peruzzi, vol. II (Cinisello Balsamo, 1984), pp. 143–94.

Benati 1985
D. Benati, "Per la ricomposizione del polittico Griffoni," in *Da Borso a Cesare d'Este: la Scuola di Ferrara. 1450–1628*, ed. E. Mattaliano, enlarged Italian edition of the catalogue for the exhibition staged in London to support The Courtauld Institute of Art Trust Appeal, Matthiesen Fine Art, 1984 (Ferrara, 1985), pp. 172–74.

Benati 1987
D. Benati, "La pittura a Ferrara e nei domini estensi nel secondo Quattrocento. Parma e Piacenza," in *La pittura in Italia. Il Quattrocento*, ed. F. Zeri (Milan, 1987), pp. 256–71.

Benati 1988
D. Benati, *La bottega degli Erri e la pittura del Rinascimento a Modena* (Modena, 1988).

Benati 1993
D. Benati, "Carlo Volpe e Francesco del Cossa. Conferme per un'attribuzione," in *Arte a Bologna. Bollettino dei Musei Civici d'Arte Antica*, no. 3, 1993, pp. 26–34.

Benati 2008
D. Benati, "Un modello di Francesco del Cossa da Ferrara a Bologna," in *Storie di artisti, storie di libri. L'editore che inseguiva la Bellezza. Scritti in onore di Franco Cosimo Panini* (Modena and Rome, 2008), pp. 119–23.

Benati 2012a
D. Benati, "Oltre l' 'Officina ferrarese,' la riscoperta del Rinascimento a Bologna," in *Paragone*, year LXII, no. 101–2 (743–45), 2012, pp. 38–55.

Benati 2012b
D. Benati, "Un Rinascimento rustico e fiero. Il Quattrocento a Bologna," in *Da Bononia a Bologna, 189 a.C.–2011. Percorsi d'eccellenza nell'arte bolognese*, ed. G. Pellinghelli del Monticello (Turin, 2012), pp. 77–89.

Benini 1977
L. Benini, "Descrizione della Quadreria Costabili," in *Musei Ferraresi*, no. 7, 1977, pp. 79–96.

Bentini and Guarino 2002
Il museo senza confini. Dipinti ferraresi del Rinascimento nelle raccolte romane, eds. J. Bentini and S. Guarino (Ferrara, 2002).

Berenson 1907 ed. 1952
B. Berenson, *The Italian Painters of the Renaissance* (London, 1907, recommended ed. London, 1952).

Berenson 1909
B. Berenson, *North Italian Painters of the Renaissance* (New York and London 1909).

Berenson 1932
B. Berenson, *Italian Pictures of the Renaissance. A list of the Principal Artist and Their Works With an Index of Places* (Oxford, 1932).

Berenson 1936
B. Berenson, *Pitture italiane del Rinascimento* (Milan, 1936).

Berenson 1968
B. Berenson, *Italian Pictures of the Renaissance: a list of the principal artists and their works with an index of places. Central Italian and North Italian Schools*, vol. III, part 1 (London, 1968).

Bertelli 2007
C. Bertelli, "Piero da Perugia a Roma," in *Piero della Francesca e le corti italiane*, eds. C. Bertelli and A. Paolucci, exh. cat., Museo Statale d'Arte Medievale e Moderna, Arezzo, 2007 (Milan, 2007), pp. 29–45.

Betti, Frosinini, and Refice 2010
Ripensando Piero della Francesca. Il Polittico della Misericordia di Sansepolcro. Storia, studi e indagini tecnico-scientifiche, eds. M. Betti, C. Frosinini, and P. Refice (Florence, 2010).

Biagi Maino 1993
D. Biagi Maino, "Il retablo del Collegio di Spagna," in *Marco Zoppo. Cento 1433–1478 Venezia*, ed. B. Giovannucci Vigi, conference papers, Cento, 1993 (Bologna, 1993), pp. 61–70.

Biagi Maino 2007
D. Biagi Maino, "Marco Zoppo a Bologna," in *La Croce dipinta di Marco Zoppo e la cultura pierfrancescana a Bologna*, eds. D. Biagi Maino and M. Medica, exh. cat., Museo Civico Medievale, Bologna, 2007–8 (Bologna, 2007), pp. 23–37.

Bianconi 1763 ed. 1998
G. L. Bianconi, *Lettere al marchese Filippo Hercolani ciambellano della MM. LL. II. RR. ed AP. sopra alcune particolarità della Baviera ed altri paesi della Germania* (Lucca, 1763), published in G. L. Bianconi, *Scritti tedeschi*, ed. G. Perini (Bologna, 1998), pp. 143–221.

Bibliotheca sanctorum 1964
Bibliotheca sanctorum, Istituto Giovanni XXIII at the Pontificia Università Lateranense, vol. V (Rome, 1964).

Bologna e l'umanesimo 1988
Bologna e l'umanesimo 1490–1510, eds. M. Faietti and K. Oberhuber, exh. cat., Pinacoteca Nazionale, Bologna and Graphische Sammlung Albertina, Vienna, 1988 (Bologna, 1988).

Bologna e le Collezioni 2011
Bologna e le Collezioni comunali d'arte. Dalla Mostra del Settecento bolognese alla nascita del museo (1935–1936), ed. C. Bernardini, conference papers, Bologna, 2010 (Cinisello Balsamo, 2011).

Bologna. Cultural Crossroads 2013
Bologna. Cultural Crossroads from the Medieval to the Baroque: Recent Anglo-American Scholarship, eds. G. M. Anselmi, A. De Benedictis, and N. Terpstra, conference papers, Bologna, 2011 (Bologna, 2013).

Bonfait 1987
O. Bonfait, "Le collezioni Aldrovandi a Bologna in età moderna," in *Il Carrobbio*, year XIII, 1987, pp. 25–50.

Bonfait 2000
O. Bonfait, *Les tableaux et les pinceaux. La naissance de l'École bolonaise (1680–1780)* (Rome, 2000).

Borenius 1937
T. Borenius, "London. Die Burlington Fine Arts Club Ausstellung," in *Pantheon*, year XIX, 1937, pp. 61–62.

Borselli ed. 1912–29
G. de' Borselli (Hyeronimo de Bursellis), *Cronica gestorum ac factorum memorabilium civitatis Bononie (ab urbe condita ad a. 1497)*, with continuation by V. Spargiati (1498–1584), ed. V. Sorbelli, in *Rerum Italicarum Scriptores, raccolta degli storici italiani dal Cinquecento al Millecinquecento*, arranged by L. A. Muratori, new revised and expanded edition, eds. G. Carducci and V. Fiorini, t. XXIII, part II (Città di Castello and Bologna, 1912–29).

Boschetto 1973
Bibliografia di Roberto Longhi, ed. A. Boschetto (Florence, 1973).

Boskovits 1978
M. Boskovits, "Ferrarese Painting about 1450: Some New Arguments," in *The Burlington Magazine*, vol. CXX, no. 903, June 1978, pp. 370–85.

Bottari 1935
S. Bottari, "'Officina Ferrarese' di Roberto Longhi," in *Leonardo. Rassegna bibliografica mensile*, year VI, no. 12, 1935, pp. 485–89.

Bottari and Ticozzi 1822
G. Bottari and S. Ticozzi, *Raccolta di lettere sulla pittura, scultura ed architettura scritte da' più celebri personaggi dei secoli XV, XVI e XVII*, 8 vols. (Milan, 1822–25), vol. IV, 1822.

Branchesi 1992
P. M. Branchesi, "La chiesa e il convento di Santa Maria dei Servi in Bologna prima del 1583," in *Il convento di Santa Maria dei Servi in Bologna: sede della Regione Carabinieri Emilia-Romagna*, ed. L. Nobili (Bologna, 1992), pp. 17–61.

Brandi 1935
C. Brandi, "Officina ferrarese," in *L'Italia letteraria*, year XI, no. 40, October 4, 1935, pp. 1, 5.

Breck 1914
J. Breck, "A Crucifixion by Francesco del Cossa," in *Art in America*, vol. II, 1914, pp. 314–17.

Briefe Benedicts 1888
Briefe Benedicts XIV an den Canonicus Pier Francesco Peggi in Bologna (1729–1758) nebst Benedicts diarium des Conclaves von 1740, ed. F. X. Kraus (Freiburg, 1888).

Buganza 2006
S. Buganza, "Intorno a Baldassarre d'Este e al suo soggiorno lombardo," in *Solchi*, year IX, no. 1–3, 2006, pp. 3–69.

Burckhardt 1855 ed. 1952
J. Burckhardt, *Il Cicerone. Guida al godimento delle opere d'arte in Italia* (1855), eds. P. Mingazzini and F. Pfister, 2 vols. (Florence, 1952, recommended ed. 1992).

Buscaroli 1937
R. Buscaroli, "Roberto Longhi, Officina Ferrarese," in *Melozzo da Forlì. Rassegna d'arte romagnola*, no. 1, October 1937, pp. 49–50.

Caglioti 2000
F. Caglioti, *Donatello e i Medici. Storia del David e della Giuditta* (Florence, 2000).

Calogero 2012
G. A. Calogero, "Tommaso Garelli nel Rinascimento bolognese," in *Nuovi studi. Rivista di arte antica e moderna*, year XVII, no. 18, 2012, pp. 83–99.

Calogero (2016) 2018
G. A. Calogero, "Il polittico di San Clemente di Agostino De Marchi e Marco Zoppo: documenti, cronologia e stile," in *Prospettiva*, nos. 163–64, (2016) 2018, pp. 28-49.

Calogero 2019
G. A. Calogero, "La tela della Compagnia dei Lombardi e la cultura artistica di Tommaso Garelli nel 1466," in *L'antica Compagnia dei Lombardi in Bologna. Un passato presente*, eds. M. Medica and S. Battistini, exh. cat., Collezioni Comunali d'Arte, Bologna, 2019–20 (Cinisello Balsamo, 2019), pp. 57–71.

Cammarota 1997
G. P. Cammarota, *Le origini della Pinacoteca Nazionale di Bologna. Una raccolta di fonti. Volume primo: 1797–1815* (Bologna, 1997).

Cammarota 2000
G. P. Cammarota, *Le origini della Pinacoteca Nazionale di Bologna. Una raccolta di fonti*, III: *La collezione Zambeccari* (Bologna, 2000).

Cammarota 2002
G. P. Cammarota, "Le alterne fortune della pittura quattro-cinquecentesca a Bologna nel secolo di Francesco Zambeccari: una cronaca," in *Il Cinquecento a Bologna. Disegni dal Louvre e dipinti a confronto*, eds. M. Faietti and D. Cordellier, exh. cat., Pinacoteca Nazionale, Bologna, 2002 (Milan, 2002), pp. 25–33.

Cammarota 2004
G. P. Cammarota, *Le origini della Pinacoteca Nazionale di Bologna. Una raccolta di fonti. Dalla Rifondazione all'autonomia (1815–1907)* (Bologna, 2004).

Cammarota 2014
G. P. Cammarota, "Francesco Malaguzzi Valeri direttore e soprintendente," in *Francesco Malaguzzi Valeri (1867–1928). Tra storiografia artistica, museo e tutela*, eds. A. Rovetta and G. C. Sciolla, conference papers, Milano and Bologna, 2011(Milan, 2014), pp. 293–317.

Campisi 2018
M. Campisi, *L'impresentabile storia. Misfatti, delitti e cronache su monumenti, collezioni e antichità* (Rome, 2018).

Carotti 1894
G. Carotti, "La R. Galleria di Brera in Milano," in *Le Gallerie Nazionali Italiane. Notizie e documenti*, year I, 1894, pp. 3–13.

Carpaccio, Bellini, Tura, Antonello 1993
Carpaccio, Bellini, Tura, Antonello e altri restauri quattrocenteschi della Pinacoteca del Museo Correr, ed. A. Dorigato, exh. cat., Museo Correr, Venice (Milan, 1993).

Casali Pedrielli 1991
C. Casali Pedrielli, *Vittorio Maria Bigari. Affreschi dipinti disegni* (Bologna, 1991).

Castelnuovo and Ginzburg 1979
E. Castelnuovo, C. Ginzburg, "Centro e periferia," in *Storia dell'arte italiana*, part I, *Materiali e problemi*, vol. I: *Questioni e metodi* (Turin, 1979), pp. 283–352.

Catalogo de' quadri 1872
Catalogo de' quadri di varie scuole pittoriche della Galleria Costabili in Ferrara (Ferrara, 1872).

Catalogue des peintures italiennes 2007
Catalogue des peintures italiennes du musée du Louvre. Catalogue sommaire, eds. J. Habert, S. Loire, C. Scailliérez, and D. Thiébaut (Paris, 2007).

Cavalca 2004
C. Cavalca, "Pittori ferraresi a Bologna nella seconda metà del Quattrocento," in *Gli Este a Ferrara. Una corte nel Rinascimento*, ed. J. Bentini, exh. cat., Castello Estense, Ferrara, 2004 (Cinisello Balsamo, 2004), pp. 123–29.

Cavalca (2004–5) 2005
C. Cavalca, "Francesco Del Cossa e Firenze: tre ricami e la pala con l'Annunciazione di Dresda," in *Nuovi Studi*, no. 11, (2004–5) 2005, pp. 39–67.

Cavalca 2007
C. Cavalca, "Francesco del Cossa tra Ferrara, Firenze e Bologna," in *Cosmè Tura e Francesco del Cossa. L'arte a Ferrara nell'età di Borso d'Este*, ed. M. Natale, exh. cat., Palazzo dei Diamanti and Palazzo Schifanoia, Ferrara, 2007–8 (Ferrara, 2007), pp. 367–73.

Cavalca 2013
C. Cavalca, *La pala d'altare a Bologna nel Rinascimento. Opere, artisti e città 1450–1500* (Cinisello Balsamo, 2013).

Cavalca 2018a
C. Cavalca, "Dentro e fuori il Palazzo. Ricchezza privata e magnificenza pubblica a Bologna: alcuni esempi attorno e oltre i Bentivoglio," in *The Taste of Virtuosi. Collezionismo e mecenatismo in Italia 1400–1900*, ed. A. Leonardi (Florence, 2018), pp. 17–34.

Cavalca 2018b
C. Cavalca, "Luis de Fuente Encalada e il polittico firmato da Marco Zoppo nel Real Collegio di Spagna: un committente castigliano a Bologna, a metà Quattrocento," in *Domus Hispanica. El Real Colegio de España y el*

cardenal Gil de Albornoz en la Historia del Arte, ed. M. Parada López de Corselas (Bologna, 2018), pp. 319–43.

Cavalca and Negretti 2018
C. Cavalca and I. Negretti, "Dentro il Rinascimento italiano: le scelte di Andrea Battaglia (Bologna ante 1431 –1455)," in *Ars & Renovatio* [journal of the Centro de Estudios de Arte del Renacimiento, University of Saragoza], no. 6, 2018, pp. 3–30.

Cavazza 1905
F. Cavazza, "Finestroni e cappelle in San Petronio di Bologna: restauri recenti e documenti antichi," in *Rassegna d'Arte*, year V. no. 11, 1905, pp. 161–66.

Cavazzoni 1603 ed. 1999
F. Cavazzoni, "Pitture e sculture et altre cose notabile che sono in Bologna e dove si trovano, Anno Domini MDCIII," ed. M. Pigozzi, in *Francesco Cavazzoni, Scritti d'arte* (Bologna, 1999), pp. 12–83.

Ceccarelli 2009
F. Ceccarelli, "La fabbrica del campanile della Cattedrale. Maestri e committenti a Ferrara nell'età di Borso d'Este," in *Leon Battista Alberti. Architetture e committenti*, eds. A. Calzona, J. Connors, F. P. Fiore, and C. Vasoli, conference papers, Florence, Rimini, and Mantua, 2004 (Florence, 2009), pp. 305–47.

Ceccarelli, Marchesi, and Sambin De Norcen 2019
F. Ceccarelli, A. Marchesi, and M. T. Sambin De Norcen, *Biagio Rossetti 1444–1516. Architettura e documenti* (Bologna, 2019).

Cellini 1992
M. Cellini, "Giacinto Gilioli (Bologna, 1594–1665)," in *La Scuola di Guido Reni*, eds. M. Pirondini and E. Negro (Modena, 1992), pp. 271–74.

Cennini ed. 1975
C. Cennini, *Il Libro dell'arte o Trattato della Pittura*, ed. F. Tempesti (Milan, 1975).

Cerasi 2011
L. Cerasi, "Alcune lettere di Roberto Longhi a Francesco Filippini. Su Longhi, l'ambiente bolognese, il Quattrocento ferrarese," in *Bologna e le Collezioni comunali d'arte. Dalla Mostra del Settecento bolognese alla nascita del museo (1935–1936)*, ed. C. Bernardini, conference papers, Bologna, 2010 (Cinisello Balsamo, 2011), pp. 83–86.

Ceriana 2014
M. Ceriana, "Rubriche per la carriera artistica di Bramante," in *Modernamente antichi. Modelli, identità, tradizione nella Lombardia del Tre e Quattrocento*, eds. P. N. Pagliarea and S. Romano (Rome, 2014), pp. 217–55.

Ceriani Sebregondi, Gritti, Repishti, and Schofield 2019
G. Ceriani Sebregondi, J. Gritti, F. Repishti, and R. Schofield, *Ad triangulum. Il duomo di Milano e il suo tiburio da Stornaloco a Bramante, Leonardo e Giovanni Antonio Amadeo* (Padua, 2019).

Ceriani Sebregondi and Schofield 2016
G. Ceriani Sebregondi and R. Schofield, "First Principles: Gabriele Stornaloco and Milan Cathedral," in *Architectural History*, vol. 59, 2016, pp. 53–122.

Chastel 1982
A. Chastel, "Roberto Longhi: il genio dell'*ekphrasis*," in *L'arte di scrivere sull'arte. Roberto Longhi nella cultura del nostro tempo*, ed. G. Previtali, conference papers, Florence, 1980 (Rome, 1982), pp. 56–65.

Chiappini 1955
L. Chiappini, "Appunti sul pittore Francesco del Cossa e la sua famiglia (da documenti inediti)," in *Atti della Deputazione provinciale ferrarese di storia patria*, vol. XIV, 1955, pp. 107–20.

Chiappini 1982
A. Chiappini, "Il campanile della Cattedrale di Ferrara: cronistoria da una serie di note inedite," in *La Cattedrale di Ferrara*, conference papers, Ferrara, 1979 (Ferrara, 1982).

Christe 1992
Y. Christe, "The Apocalypse in Monumental Art," in *The Apocalypse in Middle Ages*, eds. R. K. Emmerson and B. McGinn (Ithaca, 1992), pp. 234–58.

Christiansen 1992
K. Christiansen, "Prime opere: Padova," in *Mantegna*, ed. J. Martineau, exh. cat., Royal Academy of Arts, London and The Metropolitan Museum of Art, New York, 1992 (Milan, 1992), pp. 93–113.

Chronicon Estense ed. 1937
Chronicon Estense, cum additamentis usque ad annum 1478, eds. G. Bertoni and E. P. Vicini, in *Rerum Italicarum Scriptores*, XV, III (Bologna, 1937).

Ciammitti 1985
L. Ciammitti, "Ercole Roberti. La cappella Garganelli in San Pietro," in *Tre artisti nella Bologna dei Bentivoglio*, eds. G. Agostini, L. Ciammitti, and F. Varignana, exh. cat., Pinacoteca Nazionale, Bologna, 1985 (Bologna, 1985), pp. 119–223.

Ciammitti 1995
L. Ciammitti, "Un collezionista marchigiano del Settecento: Filippo Acqua," in *Disegni emiliani dei secoli XVII–XVIII della Pinacoteca di Brera*, ed. D. Pescarmona, exh. cat., San Giorgio in Poggiale, Bologna, 1995 (Milan, 1995), pp. 31–48.

Ciammitti 2007
L. Ciammitti, "'Un non so che di particolare e di nuovo.' Cenni sulla storiografia della scuola ferrarese," in *Cosmè Tura e Francesco del Cossa. L'arte a Ferrara nell'età di Borso d'Este*, ed. M. Natale, exh. cat., Palazzo dei Diamanti and Palazzo Schifanoia, Ferrara, 2007–8 (Ferrara, 2007), pp. 91–109.

Ciancabilla 2004
L. Ciancabilla, "La cultura della conservazione a Bologna tra ripristini e mostre d'arte nei primi decenni del Novecento," in *Proporzioni. Annali della Fondazione Roberto Longhi*, no. V, 2004, pp. 147–83.

Ciancabilla 2009
L. Ciancabilla, "Guido Zucchini, una biografia," in *Annali di Critica d'Arte*, year V, 2009, pp. 205–27.

Ciancabilla 2010
L. Ciancabilla, "Il Settecento di Guido Zucchini nella Bologna di Francesco Malaguzzi Valeri e Roberto Longhi," in *Bologna e le Collezioni comunali d'arte. Dalla Mostra del Settecento bolognese alla nascita del museo (1935–1936)*, ed. C. Bernardini, conference papers, Bologna, 2010 (Cinisello Balsamo, 2011), pp. 101–23.

Ciancabilla 2012
L. Ciancabilla, *La fortuna dei Primitivi a Bologna nel secolo dei lumi. Il Medioevo del Settecento fra erudizione, collezionismo e conservazione* (Bologna, 2012).

Ciardi 1965
R. P. Ciardi, *La raccolta Cagnola. Dipinti e sculture* (Milan, 1965).

Cieco of Florence 1470
Francesco Cieco da Firenze, *Torneamento fatto in Bologna il 4 ottobre 1470 per ordine di Giovanni Bentivoglio* (Bologna, after October 4, 1470), Biblioteca Nazionale Centrale, Florence, Landau Finaly inc. 75, https://archive.org/details/ita-bnc-in1-00000295-001

Ciranna 2008
S. Ciranna, "Matteo di Giovannello, detto Gattapone," in *Dizionario Biografico degli Italiani*, vol. LVII (Rome, 2008).

Cittadella 1864
L. N. Cittadella, *Notizie patrie per la maggiore parte inedite da documenti e illustrate* (Ferrara, 1864).

Cittadella 1868
L. N. Cittadella, *Notizie amministrative, storiche, artistiche relative a Ferrara* (Ferrara, 1868).

Cobianchi 2006
R. Cobianchi, "The Use of Woodcuts in Fifteenth-Century Italy," in *Print Quarterly*, vol. XXIII, no. 1, 2006, pp. 47–54.

Cobianchi 2007
R. Cobianchi, "Raphael, Ceremonial Banners and Devotional Prints," in *Art and the Augustinan Order in Early Renaissance Italy*, eds. L. Bourdua and A. Dunlop (Ashgate, 2007).

Colección Cambó 1990
Colección Cambó, eds. J. Sureda i Pons and A. E. Pérez Sánchez, exh. cat., Sala Sant Jaume, Barcelona, 1990 (Barcelona, 1990).

Collareta 2012
M. Collareta, "I nielli di Maso Finiguerra e l'arte lombarda del Rinascimento," in *L'utilizzo dei modelli seriali nella produzione figurativa lombarda nell'età di Mantegna*, eds. M. Collareta and F. Tasso, conference papers, Castello Sforzesco, Raccolta delle Stampe "A. Bertarelli," Milan, 2008, in *Rassegna di Studi e di Notizie*, year XXXIX, vol. XXXV, 2012, pp. 45–50.

Concina 2003
E. Concina, *Storia dell'architettura di Venezia dal VII al XX secolo* (Milan, 2003).

Cosmè Tura e Francesco del Cossa 2007
Cosmè Tura e Francesco del Cossa. L'arte a Ferrara nell'età di Borso d'Este, ed. M. Natale, exh. cat., Palazzo dei Diamanti and Palazzo Schifanoia, Ferrara, 2007–8 (Ferrara, 2007).

Crespi 1769
L. Crespi, *Felsina Pittrice. Vite de' pittori bolognesi*, vol. III (Rome, 1769).

Crocevia e capitale 2010
Crocevia e capitale della migrazione artistica: forestieri a Bologna e bolognesi nel mondo (secoli XV–XVI), ed. S. Frommel, conference papers, Bologna, 2009 (Bologna, 2010).

Crowe and Cavalcaselle 1871
J. A. Crowe and G. B. Cavalcaselle, *A History of Painting in North Italy: Venice, Padua, Vicenza, Verona, Ferrara, Milan, Friuli, Brescia, from the Fourteenth to the Sixteenth Century*, ed. T. Borenius, 2 vols. (London, 1871).

Crowe and Cavalcaselle 1871 ed. 1912
J. A. Crowe and G. B. Cavalcaselle, *A History of Painting in North Italy* (1871), second ed., ed. T. Borenius, 3 vols. (London, 1912).

Cucini 2018
S. Cucini, "'Contra ribaldos proditores:' From Factional Conflicts to Political Crime in Renaissance Bologna," in *Violence and Justice in Bologna 1250–1700*, ed. S. Rubin Blanshei (Lanham, Boulder, New York, and London, 2018), pp. 125–43.

D'Amico 1990
Sesto centenario di fondazione della basilica di San Petronio: 1390–1990. Documenti per una storia, ed. R. D'Amico (Bologna, 1990).

Da Borso a Cesare d'Este 1985
Da Borso a Cesare d'Este: la Scuola di Ferrara. 1450–1628, ed. E. Mattaliano, enlarged Italian edition of the catalogue for the exhibition staged in London to support The Courtauld Institute of Art Trust Appeal, Matthiesen Fine Art, 1984 (Ferrara, 1985).

Da Cimabue a Morandi 2015
Da Cimabue a Morandi. Felsina Pittrice, ed. V. Sgarbi, exh. cat., Palazzo Fava, Bologna, 2015 (Bologna, 2015).

dalla Tuata ed. 2005
Fileno dalla Tuata, *Istoria di Bologna origini – 1521*, ed. B. Fortunato (Bologna, 2005).

Davies 1951
M. Davies, *National Gallery Catalogues. The Earlier Italian Schools* (London, 1951).

Davies 1951 ed. 1961
M. Davies, *National Gallery Catalogues. The Earlier Italian Schools* (London, 1951, ed. 1961).

De Benedictis 2004
A. De Benedictis, *Una guerra d'Italia, una resistenza di popolo. Bologna 1506* (Bologna, 2004).

De Benedictis 2007
A. Benedictis, "Lo 'stato popolare di libertà:' pratica di governo e cultura di governo (1376–1506)," in *Bologna nel Medioevo*, ed. O. Capitani (Bologna, 2007), pp. 899–950 (*Storia di Bologna*, vol. II).

De Benedictis 2009
A. De Benedictis, "Il papa 'desiderava de havere Bologna libera:' libero dominio papale e libertà cittadina tra Martino V e Niccolò V," in *Lorenzo Valla e l'Umanesimo bolognese*, eds. G. M. Anselmi and M. Guerra, conference papers, Bologna, 2008 (Bologna, 2009), pp. 185–99.

De Benedictis 2018
A. De Benedictis, "Popular Government, Government of the Ottimati, and the Language of Politics: Concord and Discord (1377–1559)," in *A Companion to Medieval and Renaissance Bologna*, ed. S. Rubin Blanshei (Leiden and Boston, 2018), pp. 289–309.

De Silva 2013
J. M. De Silva, "Ecclesiastical Dinasticism in Early Modern Bologna: The Canonical Chapters of San Pietro and San Petronio," in *Bologna Cultural Crossroad from the Medieval to the Baroque. Recent Anglo-American Scholarship*, eds. G. M. Anselmi, A. De Benedictis, and N. Terpstra, conference papers, Bologna, 2011 (Bologna, 2013), pp. 173–91.

de Blaauw 2006
S. de Blaauw, "Innovazioni nello spazio di culto fra basso Medioevo e Cinquecento: la perdita dell'orientamento liturgico e la liberazione della navata," in *Lo spazio e il culto. Relazioni tra edificio ecclesiale e uso liturgico dal XV al XVI secolo*, ed. J. Stabenow, conference papers, Florence, 2003 (Venice, 2006), pp. 43–49.

De Marchi 2012
A. De Marchi, *La pala d'altare. Dal polittico alla pala quadra* (class notes, academic year 2011–12), with the assistance of M. Mazzalupi (Florence, 2012).

De Marchi 2018
A. De Marchi, "Vedere il Quattrocento con occhi nuovi: Georg Puidelko (1905–1972) tra gli studi a Firenze e la Parigi dei surrealisti – II," in *I conoscitori tedeschi tra Otto e Novecento*, eds. F. Caglioti, A. De Marchi, and A. Nova (Milan, 2018), pp. 431–42.

Degler 2015
A. Degler, *Parergon, Attribut, Material und Fragment in der Bildästhetik des Quattrocento* (Paderborn, 2015).

del Monaco 2018
G. del Monaco, *Simone di Filippo detto "dei crocifissi". Pittura e devozione nel secondo Trecento bolognese* (Padua, 2018).
Della Peruta and Cantarella 2005
Bibliografia dei periodici economici lombardi 1815–1914, eds. F. Della Peruta and E. Cantarella, 2 vols. (Milan, 2005).

Dellwing 2010
H. Dellwing, "L'architettura gotica nel Veneto," in *Storia dell'architettura nel Veneto. Il Gotico* (Venice, 2010), pp. 50–187.

Disegni del Rinascimento 2001
Disegni del Rinascimento in Valpadana, ed. G. Agosti, exh. cat., Gabinetto Disegni e Stampe degli Uffizi, Florence, 2001 (Florence, 2001).

Dolfi 1670
P. S. Dolfi, *Cronologia della famiglie nobili di Bologna* (Bologna, 1670).

Drogin 2018
D. J. Drogin, "Art and Patronage in Bologna's 'Long' Quattrocento," in *A Companion to Medieval and Renaissance Bologna*, ed. S. Rubin Blanshei (Leiden and Boston, 2018), pp. 559–600.

Dunkerton 2002
J. Dunkerton, "Cosmè Tura's Painting Technique," in S. J. Campbell, *Cosmè Tura: Painting and Design in Renaissance Ferrara*, exh. cat., Isabella Stewart Gardner Museum, Boston, 2002 (Boston and Milan, 2002), pp. 107–51.

Dunkerton and Smith 1986
J. Dunkerton and A. Smith, "'L'ultima cena' di Ercole de' Roberti," in *National Gallery Technical Bulletin*, vol. 10, 1986, pp. 33–38.

Dunkerton and Syson 2010
J. Dunkerton and L. Syson, "In Search of Verrocchio the Painter: The Cleaning and Examination of 'The Virgin and Child with Two Angels,'" in *National Gallery Technical Bulletin*, vol. 31, 2010, pp. 4–41.

Duranti 2007
Il carteggio di Gerardo Cerruti, oratore sforzesco a Bologna, 1470–1474, ed. T. Duranti (Bologna, 2007).

Duranti 2009
T. Duranti, *Diplomazia e autogoverno a Bologna nel Quattrocento (1392–1466). Fonti per la storia delle istituzioni* (Bologna, 2009).

Duranti 2018
T. Duranti, "Libertas, Oligarchy, Papacy: Government in the Quattrocento," in *A Companion to Medieval and Renaissance Bologna*, ed. S. Rubin Blanshei (Leiden and Boston, 2018), pp. 260–88.

Duveen Pictures 1941
Duveen Pictures in Public Collections of America (New York, 1941).

Emiliani 1981
Jacopo della Quercia e la facciata di San Petronio a Bologna: contributi allo studio della decorazione e notizie sul restauro, ed. A. Emiliani (Bologna, 1981).

Emiliani 1996a
A. Emiliani, "Il collezionismo ferrarese tra leggenda e realtà," in *La leggenda del collezionismo a Ferrara. Le quadrerie storiche ferraresi*, eds. G. Agostini, J. Bentini, and A. Emiliani, exh. cat., Pinacoteca Nazionale Palazzo dei Diamanti, Ferrara, 1996 (Ferrara, 1996), pp. 15–50.

Emiliani 1996b
A. Emiliani, *Leggi, bandi e provvedimenti per la tutela dei beni artistici e culturali negli antichi stati italiani 1571–1860* (Bologna, 1996).

Erasmus of Rotterdam ed. 2014
Erasmo da Rotterdam, *Giulio*, ed. S. Seidel Menchi (Turin, 2014).

"Ercole de' Roberti" 1999
"Ercole de' Roberti: The Making of a court artist," in *Ercole de' Roberti. The Renaissance in Ferrara*, eds. D. Allen, L. Syson, et al., exh. cat., The J. Paul Getty Museum, Los Angeles, 1999 (London, 1999, also as supplement to *The Burlington Magazine*, vol. CXLI, no. 1153, April 1999).

Esposizione della pittura ferrarese del Rinascimento 1933
Esposizione della pittura ferrarese del Rinascimento, ed. N. Barbantini, exh. cat., Palazzo dei Diamanti, Ferrara, 1933 (Venice, 1933).

Fanti 1980
M. Fanti, *La Fabbrica di S. Petronio in Bologna dal XIV al XX secolo: storia di una istituzione* (Rome, 1980) (*Italia Sacra*, 32).

Fanti 1983
M. Fanti, "La Basilica di S. Petronio nella storia religiosa e civile della città. Genesi, vita e significato del monumento," in *La Basilica di San Petronio in Bologna*, eds. M. Fanti, G. Lorenzoni, A. M. Matteucci, R. Roli, and C. Volpe, coordinated by D. Benati and L. Peruzzi, vol. I (Cinisello Balsamo, 1983), pp. 9–40.

Fanti 2002
M. Fanti, "Una magnifica sede per le reliquie del Santo Patrono di Bologna," in *La cappella di San Petronio (cappella Aldrovandi) e il suo restauro* (Bologna, 2002), pp. 11–62.

Fanti 2003
Il museo di San Petronio in Bologna, ed. M. Fanti (Bologna, 2003).

Fanti 2008
M. Fanti, "Sull'incoronazione di Carlo V in San Petronio nel 1530: una precisazione topografica e iconografica," in *Strenna storica bolognese*, year LVIII, 2008, pp. 244–56.

Fanti and Degli Esposti 1986
M. Fanti and C. Degli Esposti, *La basilica di San Petronio in Bologna: guida a vedere e a comprendere* (Cinisello Balsamo, 1986).

Fanti, Lorenzoni, Matteucci, Roli, and Volpe 1983–84
La Basilica di San Petronio in Bologna, eds. M. Fanti, G. Lorenzoni, A. M.

Matteucci, R. Roli, and C. Volpe, coordinated by D. Benati and L. Peruzzi, 2 vols. (Cinisello Balsamo, 1983–84).

Farinella 2007
V. Farinella, "I pittori, gli umanisti, il committente: problemi di ruolo a Schifanoia," in *Il Palazzo Schifanoia a Ferrara*, eds. S. Settis and W. Cupperi (Modena, 2007), I, pp. 83–141.

Farinella 2014
V. Farinella, *Alfonso I d'Este. Le immagini e il potere: da Ercole de' Roberti a Michelangelo* (Milano, 2014).

Fasano Guarini 1960
E. Fasano Guarini, "Aldrovandi, Pompeo," in *Dizionario Biografico degli Italiani*, vol. II (Rome, 1960), pp. 115–18.

Ferretti 1982
M. Ferretti, "I Maestri della prospettiva," in *Storia dell'arte italiana*, vol. XI: *Forme e modelli* (Turin, 1982), pp. 457–585.

Ferretti 1999
M. Ferretti, "Progetto per la riapertura delle Collezioni Comunali d'Arte" [1993], in *Arte a Bologna*, no. 5, 1999, pp. 208–12.

Ferretti 2011
M. Ferretti, "Francesco del Cossa e l'immagine dipinta del Baraccano," in *La fede degli italiani. Per Adriano Prosperi*, eds. G. Dall'Olio, A. Malena, and P. Scaranella, vol. I (Pisa, 2011), pp. 279–91.

Filippini 1913
F. Filippini, "Francesco del Cossa scultore," in *Bollettino d'Arte*, year VII, IX, 1913, pp. 315–19.

Filippini 1914
F. Filippini, "Ercole Grandi da Ferrara, pittore ed architetto del '400," in *Atti e Memorie della Deputazione di storia patria per le provincie di Romagna*, series IV, vol. IV, 1914, pp. 414–49.

Filippini 1917
F. Filippini, "Ercole da Ferrara ed Ercole da Bologna," in *Bollettino d'Arte*, year XI, 1917, pp. 49–63.

Filippini 1922
F. Filippini, "Matteo Gattaponi da Gubbio architetto del collegio di Spagna in Bologna," in *Bollettino d'arte del Ministero della Pubblica istruzione*, series II, year II, 1922, 2, pp. 77–93.

Filippini and Zucchini 1968
F. Filippini and G. Zucchini, *Miniatori e pittori a Bologna. Documenti del secolo XV* (Rome, 1968) (*Fonti e documenti inediti per la storia dell'arte*, III).

Fiocco 1925
G. Fiocco, "Andrea del Castagno nel Veneto," in *Belvedere*, no. 7, 1925, pp. 157–60.

Fiorio 1994
M. T. Fiorio, "Morelli, Frizzoni e i Musei civici," in *Giovanni Morelli collezionista di disegni. La donazione al Castello Sforzesco*, ed. G. Bora, exh. cat., Civiche Raccolte d'Arte, Castello Sforzesco, Sale Viscontee, Milan, 1994–95 (Cinisello Balsamo, 1994), pp. 15–23.

Franceschini 1993
A. Franceschini, *Artisti a Ferrara in età umanistica e rinascimentale. Testimonianze archivistiche. Parte I, dal 1341 al 1471* (Ferrara and Rome, 1993).

Franceschini 1995
A. Franceschini, *Artisti a Ferrara in età umanistica e rinascimentale. Testimonianze archivistiche. Parte II, Tomo I, dal 1472 al 1492* (Ferrara and Rome, 1995).

Francesco Malaguzzi Valeri 2014
Francesco Malaguzzi Valeri (1867–1928). Tra storiografia artistica, museo e tutela, eds. A. Rovetta and G. C. Sciolla, conference papers, Milan and Bologna, 2011 (Milan, 2014).

Frati 1900
L. Frati, "La morte di Francesco del Cossa," in *L'Arte*, year III, 1900, pp. 301–2.

Frati 1917
L. Frati, "Per la storia della musica in Bologna dal XV al XVI secolo: nuovi documenti," in *Rivista musicale italiana*, year XXIV, 3–4, 1917.

Frizzoni 1888
G. Frizzoni, "Zur Wiederherstellung eines altferraresischen Altarwerkes," in *Zeitschrift für bildende Kunst*, vol. XXIII, 1888, pp. 299–303.

Frizzoni 1897
G. Frizzoni, "Die Museen Italiens und Ihre Neuen Errungenschaften," in *Zeitschrift für bildende Kunst*, vol. XXXII, 1897, pp. 223–31.

Frizzoni 1899
G. Frizzoni, "Rassegna di insigni artisti italiani a ricordo dell'incremento dato ai Musei di Milano da Giuseppe Bertini," in *L'arte*, year II, 1899, pp. 147–58, 316–24.

Frommel 1997
C. L. Frommel, "Il San Pietro di Nicolò V," in *L'architettura della Basilica di San Pietro. Storia e costruzione*, ed. G. Spagnesi, conference papers, Rome, 1995 (Rome, 1997), pp. 103–10 (*Quaderni dell'Istituto di Storia dell'Architettura*, 25–30, 1995–97).

Galleria di quadri al Vaticano 1843
Galleria di quadri al Vaticano (Rome, 1843).

Gamberini and Lazzarini 2014
Lo Stato del Rinascimento in Italia, 1350–1520, eds. A. Gamberini and I. Lazzarini (Rome, 2014).

Garboli 1993
C. Garboli, "Prefazione," in *Bernard Berenson–Roberto Longhi, Lettere e scartafacci 1912–1957*, eds. C. Garboli and C. Montagnani, with an essay by G. Agosti (Milan, 1993), pp. 11–63.

Gardi 2018
A. Gardi, "Making of an Oligarchy: The Ruling Classes of Bologna," in *A Companion to Medieval and Renaissance Bologna*, ed. S. Rubin Blanshei (Leiden and Boston, 2018), pp. 310–34.

Garzelli 1973
A. Garzelli, *Il ricamo nell'attività artistica di Pollaiolo, Botticelli, Bartolomeo di Giovanni* (Florence, 1973).

Garzoni ed. 2010
G. Garzoni, *Historiae Bononienses*, ed. A. Mantovani (Bologna, 2010).

Gatti 1887
A. Gatti, *La basilica di S. Petronio ed il concorso per la sua facciata: rassegna critica con illustrazioni dell'autore* (Bologna, 1887).

Gatti 1889
A. Gatti, *La fabbrica di S. Petronio: indagini storiche* (Bologna, 1889).

Gatti 1890
A. Gatti, "La cappella maggiore di San Petronio," in *Atti e Memorie della Deputazione di storia patria per le province di Romagna*, series III, vol. IX, 1890, pp. 350–61.

Gatti 1891
A. Gatti, "Maestro Antonio de Vincenzo architetto bolognese," in *Archivio storico dell'arte*, year IV, 1891, pp. 172–79, 194–201.

Gatti 1913
A. Gatti, *La basilica Petroniana* (Bologna, 1913).

Gatti 1914
A. Gatti, *L'ultima parola sul concetto architettonico di San Petronio: 408 documenti connessi cronologicamente con note e una tavola riassuntiva* (Bologna, 1944).

Gentili 1982
A. Gentili, "Mito cristiano e storia ferrarese nel Polittico Griffoni," in *La corte e lo spazio: Ferrara estense*, eds. G. Papagno and A. Quondam (Rome, 1982), pp. 563–76.

Gheroldi 2007
V. Gheroldi, "Un conflitto sulla qualità tecnica della pittura murale a Ferrara al tempo di Borso d'Este," in *Cosmè Tura e Francesco del Cossa. L'arte a Ferrara nell'età di Borso d'Este*, ed. M. Natale, exh. cat., Palazzo dei Diamanti and Palazzo Schifanoia, Ferrara, 2007–8 (Ferrara, 2007), pp. 143–57.

Ghidiglia Quintavalle 1961
A. Ghidiglia Quintavalle, "Antonio di Vincenzo," in *Dizionario Biografico degli Italiani*, vol. III (Rome, 1961), pp. 581–83.

Ghirardacci ed. 1933
C. Ghirardacci, *Della Historia di Bologna*, III: *1426–1509*, ed. A. Sorbelli, in *Rerum Italicarum Scriptores*, XXXIII 1 (Bologna, 1933).

Giacomelli 1994
A. Giacomelli, "Corporazioni d'arte e famiglie cittadine in relazione con la basilica di San Petronio (secoli XVI–XVIII)," in *Una basilica per una città: sei secoli in San Petronio*, eds. M. Fanti and D. Lenzi, conference papers, Bologna, 1990 (Bologna, 1994), pp. 101–35.

Giansante 2016
M. Giansante, "Roberti (de' Roberti), Ercole," in *Dizionario Biografico degli Italiani*, vol. LXXXVII (Rome, 2016), pp. 771–76.

Ginzburg 1994
C. Ginzburg, *Indagini su Piero. Il Battesimo. Il ciclo di Arezzo. La flagellazione di Urbino. Con l'aggiunta di quattro appendici* (Turin, 1994).

Giordani 1856
P. Giordani, "Sulle pitture di Innocenzo Francucci da Imola. Discorsi tre all'Accademia di Belle Arti in Bologna nell'estate del 1812," in *Scritti editi e postumi*, vol. II (Milan, 1856), pp. 170–264.

Giordani 1999
N. Giordani, *Il restauro dei dipinti a Bologna nella seconda metà del '700. Problemi, metodi, idee, al tempo dell'Accademia Clementina* (Ferrara, 1999).

Giornate di studio 2015
Giornate di studio su Alfonso Rubbiani, ed. P. Monari, conference papers, Bologna, 2013 (Bologna, 2015).

Giovannoni 1933
G. Giovannoni, "Considerazioni architettoniche su S. Petronio di Bologna," in *Miscellanea di storia dell'arte in onore di Igino Benvenuto Supino* (Florence, 1933), pp. 165–82.

Giusberti and Roversi-Monaco 2018
F. Giusberti and F. Roversi-Monaco, "Economy and Demography," in

A Companion to Medieval and Renaissance Bologna, ed. S. Rubin Blanshei (Leiden and Boston, 2018), pp. 154–84.

Gli Este a Ferrara 2004
Gli Este a Ferrara. Una corte nel Rinascimento, ed. J. Bentini, exh. cat., Castello Estense, Ferrara, 2004 (Cinisello Balsamo, 2004).

Gnaccolini 2018
L. P. Gnaccolini, *L'Uomo Divino. Ludovico Lazzarelli tra il mazzo Sola Busca e i "Tarocchi del Mantegna," con una proposta per Lazzaro Bastiani* (Milan, 2018).

Grandi 1981
R. Grandi, "Progetto e maestranze del basamento petroniano," in *Jacopo della Quercia e la facciata di San Petronio a Bologna: contributi allo studio della decorazione e notizie sul restauro*, ed. A. Emiliani (Bologna, 1981), pp. 177–217.

Grandi 1983
R. Grandi, "Cantiere e maestranze agli inizi della scultura petroniana," in *La Basilica di San Petronio in Bologna*, eds. M. Fanti, G. Lorenzoni, A. M. Matteucci, R. Roli, and C. Volpe, coordinated by D. Benati and L. Peruzzi, vol. I (Cinisello Balsamo, 1983), pp. 125–62.

Grandi 1984
R. Grandi, "Sculture del secondo Quattrocento," in *La Basilica di San Petronio in Bologna*, eds. M. Fanti, G. Lorenzoni, A. M. Matteucci, R. Roli, and C. Volpe, coordinated by D. Benati and L. Peruzzi, vol. II (Cinisello Balsamo, 1984), pp. 43–60.

Grandi 1989
R. Grandi, "La scultura a Bologna nell'età di Niccolò," in *Niccolò dell'Arca: seminario di studi*, eds. G. Agostini and L. Ciammitti, introduction by A. Emiliani, conference papers, Bologna, 1987 (Bologna, 1989), pp. 25–57 (*Rapporti della Soprintendenza per i Beni Artisti e Storici per le Province di Bologna, Ferrara, Forlì e Ravenna*, 63).

Gregori 1982
M. Gregori, "Il metodo di Roberto Longhi," in *L'arte di scrivere sull'arte. Roberto Longhi nella cultura del nostro tempo*, ed. G. Previtali, conference papers, Florence, 1980 (Rome, 1982), pp. 126–40.

Gregori 2011
M. Gregori, "Qualche riflessione su Longhi nell'ambiente bolognese," in *Bologna e le Collezioni comunali d'arte. Dalla Mostra del Settecento bolognese alla nascita del museo (1935–1936)*, ed. C. Bernardini, conference papers, Bologna, 2010 (Cinisello Balsamo, 2011), pp. 25–29.

Groja 2017
N. Groja, "La 'Philomathia' di Angelo Michele Salimbeni e Sebastiano Aldrovandi," PhD dissertation, Università Ca' Foscari, Venice, 2017 (open-access institutional archive).

Gruyer 1890
G. Gruyer, "Francesco del Cossa," in *Notes d'art e d'archéologie*, 1890, 11/12, pp. 29 ff.

Guardabassi 1872
M. Guardabassi, *Indice-guida dei monumenti pagani e cristiani riguardanti l'istoria e l'arte esistenti nella provincia dell'Umbria* (Perugia, 1872).

Guarino 1990
S. Guarino, "De Marchi," in *Dizionario Biografico degli Italiani*, vol. XXXVIII (Rome, 1990).

Guarnacci 1751
M. Guarnacci, *Vitae et res gestae Pontificum romanorum et S. R. E. Cardinalium a Clemente X usque ad Clementem XII*, 2 vols. (Rome, 1751).

Guasti 1857
C. Guasti, *La cupola di Santa Maria del Fiore* (Florence, 1857).

Guidicini 1870
G. Guidicini, *Cose notabili della città di Bologna ossia storia cronologica dei suoi stabili pubblici e privati*, vol. II (Bologna, 1870).

Guidicini 1872
G. Guidicini, *Cose notabili della città di Bologna ossia storia cronologica dei suoi stabili pubblici e privati*, vol. IV (Bologna, 1872).

Guido Reni 1988
Guido Reni 1575–1642, exh. cat., Pinacoteca Nazionale, Bologna, 1988 (Bologna, 1988).

Harck 1884 (Italian ed. 1886)
F. Harck, "Die Fresken in Palazzo Schifanoia in Ferrara," in *Jahrbuch der Preussischen Kunstsammlungen*, year V, 1884, pp. 97–127; *Gli affreschi del Palazzo di Schifanoia in Ferrara: studio*, Italian transl. A. Venturi (Ferrara, 1886).

Haskell 2000 (Italian ed. 2008)
F. Haskell, *The Ephemeral Museum Old Master Paintings and the Rise of the Art Exhibition* (New Haven and London 2000); *La nascita delle mostre. I dipinti degli antichi maestri e l'origine delle esposizioni d'arte* (Milan, 2008).

Heydenreich, Spring, Stillhammerova, and Pina 2005
G. Heydenreich, M. Spring, M. Stillhammerova, and C. M. Pina, "Malachite pigment of spherical particle form," in *ICOM Committee for Conservation, 14th Triennial Meeting, The Hague*, vol. I, 2005, pp. 480–89.

Humfrey 1993
P. Humfrey, *The Altarpiece in Renaissance Venice* (New Haven and London 1993).

Il tramonto del Medioevo 1987
Il tramonto del Medioevo a Bologna. Il cantiere di San Petronio (Bologna, 1987).

Il Trecento riminese 1995
Il Trecento riminese. Maestri e botteghe tra Romagna e Marche, ed. D. Benati, exh. cat., Museo della Città, Rimini, 1995–96 (Milan, 1995).

Il trionfo di Bacco 2002
Il trionfo di Bacco. Capolavori della scuola ferrarese a Dresda 1480–1620, ed. G. J. M. Weber, exh. cat., Castello Estense, Ferrara, 2002–3 and Residenzschloss, Dresden, 2003 (Turin, 2002).

Impresa di vendita Giulio Sambon 1885
Impresa di vendita Giulio Sambon. Catalogue de tableaux formant la Galerie de M.r le Maquis Costabili de Ferrare (Milan, 1885).

Incerti 2017
M. Incerti, "Proporzioni numeriche nelle prospettive di Francesco del Cossa (1469–1472)," in *Diminuzioni e accrescimenti, le misure dei maestri di prospettiva*, eds. M. T. Bartoli and M. Lusoli (Florence, 2017), pp. 51–99.

Italian Paintings 2003
Italian Paintings of the Fifteenth Century. The Collections of the National Gallery of Art, Washington, eds. M. Boskovits and D. A. Brown (New York and Oxford 2003) (*The Collections of the National Gallery of Art: systematic catalogue*).

Jacobsen 1896
E. Jacobsen, "Die Neuesten Erwerbungen der Mailänder Galerien," in *Zeitschrift für bildende Kunst*, vol. XXXI, 1896, pp. 183–86.

Juttle 1994
R. J. Tuttle, "La basilica di San Petronio a Bologna," in *Rinascimento da Brunelleschi a Michelangelo. La rappresentazione dell'architettura*, eds. H. Millon and V. Magnago Lampugnani, exh. cat., Palazzo Grassi, Venice, 1994 (Milan, 1994), pp. 522–27.

Kaftal 1978
G. Kaftal, *Iconography of the Saints in the Painting of North East Italy* (Florence, 1978) (*Saints in Italian Art*, 3).

Kannès 1998
G. Kannès, "Case museo ed ateliers di artisti: il problema museografico, dall'Ottocento ad oggi," in *Ateliers e case d'artisti nell'Ottocento*, eds. A. Scotti and L. Giachero (Voghera, 1998), pp. 93–104.

Klein 1992
P. K. Klein, "Introduction: The Apocalypse in Medieval Art," in *The Apocalypse in Middle Ages*, eds. R. K. Emmerson and B. McGinn (Ithaca, 1992), pp. 159–99.

Kloten 1987
I. Kloten, "Il polittico Bolognini nel suo ambiente," in *Il tramonto del Medioevo a Bologna. Il cantiere di San Petronio* (Bologna, 1987), pp. 261–78.

L'antica Compagnia dei Lombardi 2019
L'antica Compagnia dei Lombardi in Bologna. Un passato presente, eds. M. Medica and S. Battistini, exh. cat., Collezioni Comunali d'Arte, Bologna, 2019–20 (Cinisello Balsamo, 2019).

L'architettura a Bologna 2002
L'architettura a Bologna nel Rinascimento (1460–1550): centro o periferia?, ed. M. Ricci, conference papers, Bologna, 2001 (San Giorgio di Piano, 2001).

La cappella di San Petronio 2002
La cappella di San Petronio (cappella Aldrovandi) e il suo restauro (Bologna, 2002).

La Cattedrale di Santa Maria del Fiore 1994–95
La Cattedrale di Santa Maria del Fiore a Firenze, 2 vols. (Florence, 1994–95).

La città come spettacolo in press
La città come spettacolo. Pellegrino Prisciani, filosofo delle arti, e Biagio Rossetti, architetto, nella Ferrara degli Estensi. Atti della XXI Settimana di Alti Studi Rinascimentali, Ferrara, October 11–13, 2018, in *Schifanoia*, nos. 58–59, in press.

La collezione Cagnola n.d. [1998]
La collezione Cagnola, I: *I dipinti dal XII al XIX secolo*, eds. M. Boskovits and G. Fossaluzza (Busto Arsizio, n.d. [1998]).

La fortuna dei Primitivi 2014
La fortuna dei Primitivi. Tesori d'arte dalle collezioni italiane fra Sette e Ottocento, eds. A. Tartuferi and G. Tormen, exh. cat., Galleria dell'Accademia, Florence, 2014 (Florence, 2014).

La Galleria di Palazzo Cini 2016
La Galleria di Palazzo Cini. Dipinti, sculture, oggetti d'arte, eds. A. Bacchi and A. De Marchi (Venice, 2016).

La leggenda del collezionismo a Ferrara 1996
La leggenda del collezionismo a Ferrara. Le quadrerie storiche ferraresi, eds.

G. Agostini, J. Bentini, and A. Emiliani, exh. cat., Pinacoteca Nazionale Palazzo dei Diamanti, Ferrara, 1996 (Ferrara, 1996).

La Pinacoteca Ala Ponzone 2004
La Pinacoteca Ala Ponzone. Dal Duecento al Quattrocento, ed. M. Marubbi (Cinisello Balsamo, 2004).

La Pinacoteca Nazionale 1992
La Pinacoteca Nazionale di Ferrara. Catalogo generale, ed. J. Bentini (Bologna, 1992).

Laderchi 1838
C. Laderchi, *Descrizione della Quadreria Costabili. Parte prima. L'antica Scuola ferrarese* (Ferrara, 1838).

Laderchi 1841
C. Laderchi, *Descrizione della Quadreria Costabili. Parte terza. La scuola ferrarese nei secoli XVII e XVIII. Parte quarta. Pittori d'altre scuole* (Ferrara, 1841).

Lamo 1560 ed. 1844
P. Lamo, *Graticola di Bologna ossia descrizione delle pitture, sculture e architetture della detta città fatta l'anno 1560 del pittore Pietro Lamo ora per la prima volta data in luce* (Bologna, 1844).

Lamo 1560 ed. 1996
P. Lamo, *Graticola di Bologna, ossia descrizione delle pitture, sculture e architetture di detta città fatta l'anno 1560* (Bologna, Biblioteca Comunale dell'Archiginnasio, ms. B.3198), ed. M. Pigozzi, in *Pietro Lamo, Graticola di Bologna* (Bologna, 1996), pp. 51–121.

Lantschner 2012
P. Lantschner, "'The Nourisher of Seditions:' Insurgent Coalitions and the Political Volatility of the Late Medieval Bologna, in *The Culture of Violence in Renaissance Italy*, eds. S. Kline Cohn, Jr. and F. Ricciardelli, conference papers, Fiesole, 2010 (Florence, 2012), pp. 167–89.

Lantschner 2014
P. Lantschner, "Revolts and the Political Order of Cities in the Late Middle Ages," in *Past and Present*, no. 225, 2014, pp. 3–46.

Lanzi 1789 ed. 1831
L. Lanzi, *Storia pittorica dell'Italia dal risorgimento delle belle arti fin presso al fine del XVIII secolo*, 12 vols. (Milan, 1831).

Lanzi 1795–96 ed. 1974
L. Lanzi, *Storia pittorica della Italia. Dal Risorgimento delle Belle Arti fin presso al fine del XVII secolo* (1795–96), ed. M. Capucci (Florence, 1974).

Layard 1858
A. H. Layard, "Fresco-Painting," in *The Quarterly Review*, vol. 104, July–October 1858, pp. 277–325.

Lazzarini 1908 ed. 1974
V. Lazzarini, "Documenti relativi alla pittura padovana del secolo XV," in *Nuovo Archivio Veneto*, XV, 1908, pp. 83–130; enlarged anastatic reprint, with essays and introduction by M. Muraro (Sala Bolognese, 1974).

Le Muse e il principe 1991
Le Muse e il principe. Arte di corte nel Rinascimento padano, 2 vols., eds. A. Di Lorenzo, A. Mottola Molfino, M. Natale, and A. Zanni, exh. cat., Museo Poldi Pezzoli. Milan, 1991, (Milan, 1991).

Le pitture di Bologna 1706
Le pitture di Bologna (Bologna, 1706).

Le pitture di Bologna 1732
Le pitture di Bologna (Bologna, 1732).

Le pitture di Bologna 1755
Le pitture di Bologna (Bologna, 1755).

Lehman 1928
R. Lehman, *The Philip Lehman Collection New York. Paintings* (Paris, 1928).

Lenzi 2001
D. Lenzi, "Da Girolamo Rainaldi a Mauro Tesi: i progetti del Seicento e del Settecento," in *La Basilica incompiuta. Progetti antichi per la facciata di San Petronio*, eds. M. Faietti and M. Medica, exh. cat., Museo Civico Medievale, Bologna, 2001–2 (Ferrara, 2001), pp. 45–57.

Leon Battista Alberti 2006
Leon Battista Alberti e l'architettura, eds. M. Bulgarelli, A. Calzona, M. Ceriana, and F. P. Fiore, exh. cat., Casa del Mantegna, Mantua, 2006–7 (Cinisello Balsamo, 2006).

Lettere a Guido Cagnola 2012
Lettere a Guido Cagnola dal 1892 al 1954, eds. S. Bruzzese and W. Rotelli (Brescia, 2012).

Levi 1988
D. Levi, *Cavalcaselle. Il pioniere della conservazione dell'arte italiana* (Turin, 1988).

Liebsch 2017
T. Liebsch, "Heinrich Graf von Brühl e il commercio di quadri a Bologna. L'epistolario di Luigi Crespi," in *Heinrich Graf von Brühl (1700–1763). Ein sächsischer Mäzen in Europa*, eds. U. C. Koch and C. Ruggero, conference papers, Dresden and Rome, 2014 (Dresden, 2017), pp. 350–67.

Lines 2018
D. A. Lines, "The University and the City: Cultural Interactions," in *A Companion to Medieval and Renaissance Bologna*, ed. S. Rubin Blanshei (Leiden and Boston, 2018), pp. 436–73.

Lipparini 1992
M. Lipparini, "L'insegnamento di Roberto Longhi a Bologna," in *Aspetti della cultura emiliano-romagnola nel ventennio fascista*, ed. A. Battistini (Milan, 1992), pp. 61–80.

Lippincott 1989
K. Lippincott, "Gli affreschi del Salone dei Mesi e il problema dell'attribuzione," in *Atlante di Schifanoia*, ed. R. Varese (Modena, 1989), pp. 111–40.

Lodi 1983
L. Lodi, "Note sulla decorazione punzonata di dipinti su tavola di area emiliana dalla metà alla fine del Trecento," in *Musei Ferraresi*, no. 11, (1981) 1983, pp. 9–208.

Longhi 1926 ed. 1967
R. Longhi, "Lettere pittoriche: Roberto Longhi Giuseppe Fiocco," in *Vita artistica*, I, 1926, pp. 127–39, 147–48 (ed. *Saggi e ricerche, 1925/1928*, in *Opere complete*, II, Florence, 1967).

Longhi 1934 ed. 1956
R. Longhi, *Officina ferrarese* (Rome, 1934), now in *Officina ferrarese 1934, seguita dagli Ampliamenti 1940 e dai Nuovi ampliamenti 1940–55* (Florence, 1956), pp. 5–121 (*Edizione delle opere complete di Roberto Longhi*, V).

Longhi 1934 ed. 1980
R. Longhi, *Officina ferrarese* (Rome, 1934, ed. Florence, 1980).

Longhi 1935 ed. 1973
R. Longhi, "Momenti della pittura bolognese" [Prolusion to university classes of academic year 1934–35], in *L'Archiginnasio*, year XXX, no. 1–3, 1935, pp. 111–35, now in *Lavori in Valpadana dal Trecento al primo Cinquecento 1934–1964* (Florence, 1973), pp. 189–205 (*Edizione delle opere complete di Roberto Longhi*, VI).

Longhi 1940 ed. 1956
R. Longhi, *Ampliamenti nell'Officina ferrarese*, supplement to *La Critica d'Arte*, year IV, 1940, now in *Officina ferrarese 1934, seguita dagli Ampliamenti 1940 e dai Nuovi ampliamenti 1940–55* (Florence, 1956), pp. 123–95 (*Edizione delle opere complete di Roberto Longhi*, V).

Longhi 1963
R. Longhi, *Piero della Francesca, 1927, con aggiunte fino al 1962* (Florence, 1963) (*Edizione delle opere complete di Roberto Longhi*, III).

Longhi 1967
R. Longhi, *Saggi e ricerche, 1925–1928*, 2 vols. (Florence, 1967) (*Edizione delle opere complete di Roberto Longhi*, II).

Longhi 1968
R. Longhi, *"Me Pinxit" e Quesiti caravaggeschi* (Florence, 1968) (*Edizione delle opere complete di Roberto Longhi*, IV).

Longhi 1973
R. Longhi, *Lavori in Valpadana dal Trecento al primo Cinquecento 1934-1964* (Florence, 1973) (*Edizione delle opere complete di Roberto Longhi*, VI).

Lorenzo Valla 2009
Lorenzo Valla e l'Umanesimo bolognese, eds. G. M. Anselmi and M. Guerra, conference papers, Bologna, 2008 (Bologna, 2009).

Lorenzoni 1983
G. Lorenzoni, "L'architettura," in *La basilica di San Petronio in Bologna*, vol. I (Bologna, 1983), pp. 53–124.

Lorenzoni 1983
G. Lorenzoni, "L'architettura," in *La Basilica di San Petronio in Bologna*, eds. M. Fanti, G. Lorenzoni, A. M. Matteucci, R. Roli, and C. Volpe, coordinated by D. Benati and L. Peruzzi (Cinisello Balsamo, 1983), vol. I, pp. 53–124.

Lucarelli 1888
O. Lucarelli, *Memorie e guida storica di Gubbio* (Città di Castello, 1888).

Lucco 1987
M. Lucco, "La pittura a Bologna e in Romagna nel secondo Quattrocento," in *La pittura in Italia. Il Quattrocento*, ed. F. Zeri (Milan, 1987), vol. I, pp. 240–55.

Lugli 1990
A. Lugli, *Guido Mazzoni e la rinascita della terracotta nel '400* (Turin, 1990).

Majoli 1998
L. Majoli, "La collezione Costabili. Formazione, vendita e dispersione," in E. Mattaliano, *La collezione Costabili*, ed. G. Agostini (Venice, 1998), pp. 17–21.

Malaguzzi Valeri 1899
F. Malaguzzi Valeri, *L'architettura a Bologna nel Rinascimento* (Rocca San Casciano, 1899).

Malaguzzi Valeri 1908
F. Malaguzzi Valeri, *Catalogo della R. Pinacoteca di Brera*, historical background by C. Ricci (Bergamo, 1908).

Malvasia 1678 ed. 1841
C. C. Malvasia, *Felsina pittrice. Vite de' pittori bolognesi*, 2 vols. (Bologna, 1678, ed. Bologna, 1841).

Malvasia 1686 ed.1969
C. C. Malvasia, *Le Pitture di Bologna che nella pretesa, e rimostrata sin hora da*

altri maggiore antichità, & impareggiabile eccellenza nella Pittura, con manifesta evidenza di fatto, rendono il Passeggiere Disingannato ed Instrutto dell'Ascoso Academico Gelato (Bologna, 1686; anastatic reprint, ed. A. Emiliani, Bologna, 1969).

[Malvasia] 1782
[C. C. Malvasia], *Pitture, Scolture ed Architetture delle Chiese, Luoghi pubblici, Palazzi, e case della città di Bologna e suoi sobborghi* . . ., addenda by M. Oretti, F. M. Longhi, and A. Giusti (Bologna, 1782).

Manca 1992
J. Manca, *The Art of Ercole de' Roberti* (Cambridge, 1992).

Mancini and Penny 2016
G. Mancini and N. Penny, *National Gallery Catalogues. The Sixteenth Century Italian paintings, III, Bologna and Ferrara* (London, 2016).

Mantegna 1992
Mantegna, ed. J. Martineau, exh. cat., Royal Academy of Arts, London and The Metropolitan Museum of Art, New York, 1992 (Milan, 1992).

Mantegna 2008
Mantegna 1431–1506, eds. G. Agosti and D. Thiébaut, exh. cat., Musée du Louvre, Paris, 2008–9 (Milan, 2008).

Mantegna & Bellini 2018
Mantegna & Bellini, eds. C. Campbell, D. Korbacher, N. Rowley, and S. Vowles, exh. cat., The National Gallery, London, 2018–9 (London, 2018).

Mantovani 1997
D. Mantovani, "Lo scandalo della Galleria Barbi Cinti," in *Ferrara Storia*, no. 6–7, January–April 1997.

Mantovani 2012
A. Mantovani, "History as civic vocation. Historiae Bononienses by Giovanni Garzoni," in "Libertas and Republicanism in Renaissance Bologna," ed. A. De Benedictis, in *Storicamente*, VIII, 2012, art. no. 21, DOI: 10.1473/stor423.

Marani 1960
E. Marani, "Nuovi documenti su Jacobello e Pietropaolo dalle Masegne," in *Atti e memorie dell'Accademia Virgiliana di Mantova*, XXXII, 1960, pp. 71–90.

Marchini 1983
G. Marchini, "Le vetrate (I)," in *La Basilica di San Petronio in Bologna*, eds. M. Fanti, G. Lorenzoni, A. M. Matteucci, R. Roli, and C. Volpe, coordinated by D. Benati and L. Peruzzi (Cinisello Balsamo, 1983), vol. I, pp. 295–308.

Marchini 1984
G. Marchini, "Le vetrate (II)," in *La Basilica di San Petronio in Bologna*, eds. M. Fanti, G. Lorenzoni, A. M. Matteucci, R. Roli, and C. Volpe, coordinated by D. Benati and L. Peruzzi (Cinisello Balsamo, 1984), vol. II, pp. 287–98.

Markham Schulz 2011
A. Markham Schulz, *Woodcarving and Woodcarvers in Venice 1350–1550* (Florence, 2011).

Martini 1883
A. Martini, *Manuale di metrologia, ossia misure, pesi e monete in uso attualmente e anticamente presso tutti i popoli* (Turin, 1883).

Masini 1666
A. Masini, *Bologna perlustrata, terza impressione notabilmente accresciuta, in cui si fa mentione ogni giorno in perpetuo delle fontioni sacre, e profane di tutto l'anno* . . ., 2 vols. (Bologna, 1666).

Mason Perkins 1914
F. Mason Perkins, "La Crocefissione di Francesco del Cossa," in *L'Arte*, year XVII, 1914, pp. 222–23.

Mattaliano 1998
E. Mattaliano, *La collezione Costabili*, ed. G. Agostini (Venice, 1998).

Matteo Griffoni 2004
Matteo Griffoni nello scenario politico-culturale della città (secoli XIV–XV) (Bologna, 2004) (*Deputazione di storia patria per le province di Romagna, Documenti e studi*, XXXIII).

Matteucci 1966
A. M. Matteucci, *La porta magna di San Petronio in Bologna* (Bologna, 1966).

Matteucci 1987
A. M. Matteucci, "Il gotico cittadino di Antonio di Vincenzo," in *Il tramonto del Medioevo a Bologna. Il cantiere di San Petronio* (Bologna, 1987), pp. 27–54.

Matteucci 1994
A. M. Matteucci, "San Petronio: 1463," in *Una basilica per una città. Sei secoli in San Petronio*, eds. M. Fanti and D. Lenzi, conference papers, Bologna, 1990 (Bologna, 1994), pp. 205–14.

Matteucci Armandi 2008
A. M. Matteucci Armandi, *Originalità dell'architettura bolognese ed emiliana* (Bologna, 2008).

Matthaei de Griffonibus Memoriale 1902
Matthaei de Griffonibus Memoriale Historicum de rebus Bononiensium, eds. L. Frati and A. Sorbelli (Città di Castello, 1902).

Mazza 1988
A. Mazza, "Cultura figurativa a Imola tra dispersione e tutela (secoli XVIII-XIX)," in *La Pinacoteca di Imola*, ed. C. Pedrini (Bologna, 1988), pp. 36–71.

Mazza 2001
A. Mazza, "Un esemplare intervento di tutela a Bologna nel primo Settecento: l'affresco di Ludovico Carracci nell'oratorio dei Filippini e l''aggiunta' di Donato Creti," in *L'intelligenza della passione. Scritti per Andrea Emiliani*, eds. M. Scolaro and F. P. Di Teodoro (Bologna, 2001), pp. 275–92.

Mazza 2011
A. Mazza, "La non mai a bastanza lodata Natività del Signore di Nicolò dell'Abate," in *Libri a palazzo. Una sede storica per la biblioteca dell'IBC*, eds. E. Landi and G. Tonet (Bologna, 2011), pp. 65–81.

Mazza 2014
A. Mazza, "Sulle tracce del 'Ballo degli amorini' di Francesco Albani. Vicende settecentesche della Galleria Sampieri, 'superbissimo Museo,'" in *Brera mai vista. La Danza degli amorini (1623–1625) di Francesco Albani: una favola mitologica come dono nuziale*, exh. cat., Pinacoteca di Brera, Milan, 2014–5 (Milan, 2014), pp. 33–43.

Mazza (2010–17) 2018
A. Mazza, "La Galleria Sampieri 'superbissimo Museo,' da Bologna a Milano. Sulle tracce del 'Ballo degli amorini' di Francesco Albani," in *L'Archiginnasio*, year CV-CXII, (2010–17) 2018, pp. 281–327.

Mazza 2018
A. Mazza, "L''oro del Reno.' Il patrimonio artistico di una valle appenninica," in S. Semenzato, *Tra Cinquecento e Settecento. Capolavori svelati nelle chiese di Capugnano e Castelluccio* (Capugnano-Castelluccio, 2018), pp. 7–22.

Mazzaferro 2018
G. Mazzaferro, *La donna che amava i colori. Mary P. Merrifield. Lettere dall'Italia 1845–1846* (Milan, 2018).

Medica 1992
M. Medica, "Quattro tavole di Simone dei Crocifissi alla Compagnia dei Lombardi: un'ipotesi per la loro provenienza," in *La Compagnia dei Lombardi. Contributi per una storia di otto secoli* (Bologna, 1992), pp. 71–76.

Medica 1998
M. Medica, "Il Trecento e il Quattrocento," in *La Certosa di Bologna. Immortalità della memoria*, ed. G. Pesci (Bologna, 1998), pp. 37–45.

Medica 2004
M. Medica, "Su alcune vetrate rinascimentali del Museo civico medievale di Bologna," in *Arti a confronto. Studi in onore di Anna Maria Matteucci*, ed. D. Lenzi (Bologna, 2004), pp. 57–65.

Medica 2007
M. Medica, "L'ombra di Piero a Bologna. La pittura e la miniatura tra sesto e settimo decennio del Quattrocento," in *La croce dipinta di Marco Zoppo e la cultura pierfrancescana a Bologna*, eds. D. Biagi Maino and M. Medica, exh. cat., Museo Civico Medievale, Bologna, 2007–8 (Bologna, 2007), pp. 3–21.

Memorie originali 1840–45
Memorie originali risguardanti le Belle Arti, 6 vols. (Bologna, 1840–45).

Milani 2018
G. Milani, "From One Conflict to Another (13th–14th Centuries)," in *A Companion to Medieval and Renaissance Bologna*, ed. S. Rubin Blanshei (Leiden and Boston, 2018), pp. 239–59.

Millon 1994
H. Millon, "I modelli architettonici nel Rinascimento," in *Rinascimento da Brunelleschi a Michelangelo. La rappresentazione dell'architettura*, eds. H. Millon and V. Magnago Lampugnani (Milan, 1994), pp. 19–73.

Mischiati and Tagliavini 1984
O. Mischiati and L. F. Tagliavini, "Gli organi," in *La Basilica di San Petronio in Bologna*, eds. M. Fanti, G. Lorenzoni, A.M. Matteucci, R. Roli, and C. Volpe, coordinated by D. Benati and L. Peruzzi (Cinisello Balsamo, 1984), vol. II, pp. 313–22.

Molteni 1995
M. Molteni, *Ercole de' Roberti* (Cinisello Balsamo, 1995).

Montefusco Bignozzi 1984
F. Montefusco Bignozzi, "Opere plastiche dal barocco al neoclassico," in *La Basilica di San Petronio in Bologna*, eds. M. Fanti, G. Lorenzoni, A.M. Matteucci, R. Roli, and C. Volpe, coordinated by D. Benati and L. Peruzzi (Cinisello Balsamo, 1984) vol. II, pp. 117–42.

Morandotti 2008
A. Morandotti, *Il collezionismo in Lombardia. Studi e ricerche tra '600 e '800* (Milan, 2008).

Morelli 1886
G. Morelli [J. Lermolieff], *Le opere dei Maestri Italiani nelle Gallerie di Monaco, Dresda e Berlino* (Bologna, 1886).

Moroni 1840–61
G. Moroni, *Dizionario di erudizione storico-ecclestiatica da S. Pietro ai nostri giorni*, 103 vols. (Venice, 1840–61).

Mottola Molfino 1991
A. Mottola Molfino, "Le Muse dello studiolo: la diaspora, il collezionismo, il mercato, i restauri," in *Le Muse e il principe. Arte di corte nel Rinascimento padano*, eds. A. Di Lorenzo, A. Mottola Molfino, M. Natale, and A. Zanni, exh. cat., Museo Poldi Pezzoli, Milan, 1991 (Modena, 1991), vol. I, pp. 223–33.

Natale 1991
M. Natale, "Lo studiolo di Belfiore: un cantiere ancora aperto," in *Le Muse e il principe. Arte di corte nel Rinascimento padano*, eds. A. Di Lorenzo, A. Mottola Molfino, M. Natale, and A. Zanni, exh. cat., Museo Poldi Pezzoli, Milan, 1991 (Modena, 1991), vol. I, pp. 17-44.

Negretti 2019
I. Negretti, "La fortuna dei Primitivi nel Settecento bolognese: le tavole della Compagnia dei Lombardi," in *L'antica Compagnia dei Lombardi in Bologna. Un passato presente*, eds. M. Medica and S. Battistini, exh. cat., Collezioni Comunali d'Arte, Bologna, 2019–20 (Cinisello Balsamo, 2019), pp. 73–83.

Negro and Roio 2001
E. Negro and N. Roio, *Lorenzo Costa. 1460–1535* (Modena, 2001).

Neppi 1958
A. Neppi, *Francesco del Cossa* (Milano, 1958).

Nicholson Wornum 1869
R. Nicholson Wornum, *Descriptive and Historical Catalogue of the Pictures in the National Gallery. Foreign Schools* (London, 1869).

Nicholson Wornum 1870
R. Nicholson Wornum, *Descriptive and Historical Catalogue of the Pictures in the National Gallery. Foreign Schools* (London 1870).

Nicolson 1950
B. Nicolson, *The Painters of Ferrara, Cosmè Tura, Francesco del Cossa, Ercole de' Roberti and others* (London, 1950).

Nicora 1991
C. Nicora, *Guido Cagnola (1861–1954). Collezionista e conoscitore d'arte* (Brescia, 1991).

Novelli 1997
M. A. Novelli, *Storia delle "Vite de' pittori e scultori ferraresi" di Girolamo Baruffaldi. Una vicenda editoriale e culturale del Settecento* (San Giovanni in Persiceto, 1997).

Orioli 1892
G. Orioli, "Il foro dei Mercanti di Bologna," in *Archivio storico dell'arte*, year V, 6, 1892, pp. 387–98.

Orsi 1998
O. Orsi, "La vendita e la dispersione," in E. Mattaliano, *La collezione Costabili*, ed. G. Agostini (Venice, 1998), pp. 21–29.

Ortolani 1941
S. Ortolani, *Cosmè Tura, Francesco del Cossa, Ercole de' Roberti* (Milano, 1941).

Pacioli 1509
L. Pacioli, *De Divina Proportione* (Venice, 1509).

Padovani 1954
C. Padovani, *La critica d'arte e la pittura ferrarese* (Rovigo, 1954).

Padua in the 1450s 1998
Padua in the 1450s. Marco Zoppo and his Contemporaries, ed. H. Chapman, exh. cat., The British Museum, London, 1998 (London, 1998).

Palazzo Colonna 2019
Palazzo Colonna. Appartamento Principessa Isabelle. Catalogo dei dipinti, ed. M. Natale, with the assitsance of P. Piergiovanni (Roma, 2019).

Pasquali Alidosi 1670
G. N. Pasquali Alidosi, *I Signori Anziani Consoli e Gonfalonieri di Giustizia della città di Bologna dall'anno 1456 accresciuti al 1620* (Bologna, 1670).

Pepper 1988
S. Pepper, *Guido Reni, l'opera completa* (Novara, 1988).

Perini 1991
G. Perini, "Sir Joshua Reynolds a Bologna (1752). Considerazioni preliminari ad un'edizione critica dei taccuini di viaggio basate sul taccuino conservato al Sir John Soane's Museum di Londra," in *Storia dell'arte*, no. 73, 1991, pp. 361–412.

Perini 1998
G. Perini, "Giovanni Ludovico Bianconi: un bolognese in Germania," in G. L. Bianconi, *Scritti tedeschi*, ed. G. Perini (Bologna, 1998), pp. 7–140.

Perini Folesani 2017a
G. Perini Folesani, "Giovanni Lodovico Bianconi e la corte di Dresda," in *Heinrich Graf von Brühl (1700–1763). Ein sächsischer Mäzen in Europa*, eds. U. C. Koch and C. Ruggero, conference papers, Dresden and Rome, 2014 (Dresden, 2017), pp. 368–95.

Perini Folesani 2017b
G. Perini Folesani, "Luigi Crespi storiografo, mercante e artista: profilo critico di un avventuriero poco fortunato," in *Luigi Crespi ritrattista nell'età di papa Lambertini*, eds. M. G. D'Apuzzo and I. Graziani, exh. cat., Musei Civici d'Arte Antica, Bologna, 2017 (Cinisello Balsamo, 2017), pp. 27–47.

Perini Folesani 2019
G. Perini Folesani, *Luigi Crespi storiografo, mercante e artista attraverso l'epistolario* (Florence, 2019).

Perkins 1914
F. M. Perkins, "La Crocifissione di Francesco del Cossa," in *L'Arte*, year XVII, 1914, pp. 222–23.

Pesci 1998
La Certosa di Bologna. Immortalità della memoria, ed. G. Pesci (Bologna, 1998).

Petronio e Bologna 2001
Petronio e Bologna. Il volto di una storia: arte, storia e culto del santo patrono, eds. B. Buscaroli and R. Sernicola, exh. cat., Palazzo di Re Enzo e del Podestà, Bologna, 2001–2 (Ferrara, 2001).

Petrucci 1841
G. Petrucci, *Elogio storico del marchese Giambattista Costabili Containi ferrarese* (Novi, 1841).

Peverada 2009
E. Peverada, "Vernissage del 'polittico Roverella' nella chiesa olivetana di San Giorgio (agosto 1487)," in *Analecta Pomposiana*, vol. 34, 2009, pp. 369–83.

Pezzarossa 1984
F. Pezzarossa, "'Ad honore et laude del nome Bentivoglio.' La letteratura della festa nel secondo Quattrocento," in *"Bentivolorum Magnificentia". Principe e cultura nella Bologna del Rinascimento*, ed. B. Basile (Rome, 1984), pp. 35–113.

Piconi 1994
S. Piconi, "Il restauro del paramento murario e della copertura del fianco occidentale di San Petronio," in *Una basilica per una città: sei secoli in San Petronio*, eds. M. Fanti and D. Lenzi, conference papers, Bologna, 1990 (Bologna, 1994), pp. 327–38.

Piero della Francesca 2015
Piero della Francesca. Il disegno tra arte e scienza, eds. F. Camerota, F. P. Di Teodoro, and L. Gasselli, exh. cat., Palazzo Magnani, Reggio Emilia, 2015 (Milan, 2015).

Piero della Francesca 2016
Piero della Francesca. Indagine su un mito, eds. A. Paolucci, D. Benati, et al., exh. cat., Musei San Domenico, Forlì, 2016 (Cinisello Balsamo, 2016).

Pietro di Mattiolo ed. 1885
Pietro di Mattiolo, *Cronaca bolognese*, ed. C. Ricci (Bologna, 1885).

Pigozzi 2004
M. Pigozzi, "I luoghi dell'abitare della classe senatoria bolognese fra Seicento e Settecento. I Marescotti e gli Aldrovandi," in *Arte Lombarda*, 51, 2004/2, pp. 35–46.

Pigozzi 2014
M. Pigozzi, "Francesco Malaguzzi Valeri e Igino Benvenuto Supino, legami e dissonanze," in *Francesco Malaguzzi Valeri (1867–1928). Tra storiografia artistica, museo e tutela*, eds. A. Rovetta and G. C. Sciolla, conference papers, Milan and Bologna, 2011 (Milan, 2014), pp. 319–25.

Pinacoteca di Brera 1991
Pinacoteca di Brera. Scuola emiliana (Milan, 1991).

Pinacoteca Nazionale 2004
Pinacoteca Nazionale di Bologna. Catalogo generale. 1. Dal Duecento a Francesco Francia, eds. J. Bentini, G. P. Cammarota, and D. Scaglietti Kelescian (Venice, 2004).

Pini 1969
A. I. Pini, "Bolognini, Bartolomeo," in *Dizionario Biografico degli Italiani*, vol. XI (Rome, 1969).

Pini 1994
A. I. Pini, "Tra orgoglio civico e 'status symbol:' corporazioni d'arte e famiglie aristocratiche in San Petronio nel XIV e XIV secolo," in *Una basilica per una città. Sei secoli in San Petronio*, eds. M. Fanti and D. Lenzi, conference papers, Bologna, 1990 (Bologna, 1994), pp. 87–100.

Pini 2007
R. Pini, "Ascesa, trionfo e oblio di un patrono cittadino. San Floriano di Bologna nella storia e nell'iconografia," in *Atti e Memorie della Deputazione di storia patria per le province di Romagna*, new series, year LVIII, 2007, pp. 213–33.

Pio 2018
B. Pio, *Giovanni da Legnano. Un intellettuale nell'Europa del Trecento* (Bologna, 2018).

Pitture scolture ed architetture 1776
Pitture scolture ed architetture delle chiese, luoghi pubblici, palazzi, e case della città di Bologna, e suoi sobborghi (Bologna, 1776).

Poldi and Villa 2007
G. Poldi and G. C. F. Villa, "Il morello e il segno. Spigolature per un atlante iconografico," in *Cosmè Tura e Francesco del Cossa. L'arte a Ferrara nell'età di Borso d'Este*, ed. M. Natale, exh. cat., Palazzo dei Diamanti and Palazzo Schifanoia, Ferrara, 2007 (Ferrara, 2007), pp. 159–79.

Previtali 1982
G. Previtali, "Roberto Longhi, profilo biografico," in *L'arte di scrivere sull'arte. Roberto Longhi nella cultura del nostro tempo*, ed. G. Previtali, conference

papers, Florence, 1980 (Rome, 1982), pp. 141–70.

Prodi 1982
P. Prodi, *Il sovrano pontefice. Un corpo e due anime: la monarchia papale nella prima età moderna* (Bologna, 1982).

Prodi 1994
P. Prodi, "Papato, Impero e pace nel teatro politico di San Petronio: l'incoronazione di Carlo V," in *Una basilica per una città. Sei secoli in San Petronio*, eds. M. Fanti and D. Lenzi, conference papers, Bologna, 1990 (Bologna, 1994), pp. 149–58.

Quaquarelli 1993
Censimento delle cronache bolognesi del Medioevo e del Rinascimento, ed. L. Quaquarelli (Bologna, 1993).

Quaquarelli 2004
L. Quaquarelli, "Clara gente e camere pinte: Giovanni Sabadino degli Arienti voce della Bologna cortese," in *Schede Umanistiche. Rivista semestrale dell'Archivio Umanistico Rinascimentale Bolognese*, new series, year XVIII, no. 2, 2004, pp. 9–27.

Raimondi 2002
E. Raimondi, "Filologia e passione," in *Una gloriosa gara nelle pagine di Francesco Arcangeli. L'Oratorio di San Colombano* (San Giorgio di Piano 2002), pp. 11–25.

Raimondi 2010
E. Raimondi, *Ombre e figure. Longhi, Arcangeli e la critica d'arte*, eds. G. Fenocchio and G. Zanetti (Bologna, 2010).

Rebecchini 1998
G. Rebecchini, "Galasso," in *Dizionario Biografico degli Italiani*, vol. LI (Rome, 1998).

Redig de Campos 1955
D. Redig de Campos, "Quadri da cavalletto," in *Atti della Pontificia Accademia Romana di Archeologia (serie III): Rendiconti*, vol. XXVII, III–IV (academic years 1952–53 and 1953–54), 1955, pp. 411–14 (*Restauro predella di Cossa*).

Reeve, Roy, and Smith 1981
A. Reeve, A. Roy, and A. Smith, "Francesco del Cossa's 'San Vincenzo Ferrer,'" in *National Gallery Technical Bulletin*, vol. 5, 1981, pp. 44–57.

Repishti 2018
F. Repishti, *Cristoforo Solari architetto. La sintassi ritrovata* (n.p., 2018).

Restituzioni 2016
Restituzioni 2016. Tesori d'arte restaurati: diciassettesima edizione, eds. C. Bertelli and G. Bonsanti, exh. cat., Gallerie d'Italia, Milan, 2016 (Venice, 2016).

Ricci 1904
C. Ricci, "La Pala Portuense di Ercole de' Roberti," in *Rassegna d'Arte*, year IV, 1904, pp. 11–12.

Ricci 1907
C. Ricci, *La Pinacoteca di Brera* (Bergamo, 1907).

Rinascimento visto da Sud 2019
Rinascimento visto da Sud. Matera, l'Italia meridionale e il Mediterraneo tra '400 e '500, eds. D. Catalano, M. Ceriana, P. Leone de Castris, and M. Ragozzino, exh. cat., Palazzo Lanfranchi, Matera, 2019 (Naples, 2019).

Robertson 2002
I. Robertson, *Tyranny under the Mantle of St Peter. Pope Paul II and Bologna* (Turnhout, 2002).

Romanini 1964
A. M. Romanini, *L'architettura gotica in Lombardia* (Milan, 1964).

Romano 1981
G. Romano, "Verso la maniera moderna: da Mantegna a Raffaello," in *Storia dell'arte italiana*, ed. F. Zeri, I, t. 6: *Dal Cinquecento all'Ottocento. Cinquecento e Seicento* (Turin, 1981), pp. 5–85.

Romano 1984
G. Romano, "Agostino de Marchi e il coro della cappella maggiore," in G. Romano and M. Ferretti, "Opere di tarsia," in *La Basilica di San Petronio in Bologna*, eds. M. Fanti, G. Lorenzoni, A. M. Matteucci, R. Roli, and C. Volpe, coordinated by D. Benati and L. Peruzzi (Cinisello Balsamo, 1984), vol. II, pp. 269–76.

Romano and Ferretti 1984
G. Romano and M. Ferretti, "Opere di tarsia," in *La Basilica di San Petronio in Bologna*, eds. M. Fanti, G. Lorenzoni, A. M. Matteucci, R. Roli, and C. Volpe, coordinated by D. Benati and L. Peruzzi (Cinisello Balsamo, 1984), vol. II, pp. 269–86.

Rosenberg 1975–76
C. M. Rosenberg, "Francesco del Cossa's Letter Reconsidered," in *Musei Ferraresi*, no. 5–8, 1975–76, pp. 11–15.

Roversi 1966
G. Roversi, *Il commercio dei quadri a Bologna nel Settecento* (Bologna, 1966).

Roversi 1969
G. Roversi, "I trafficanti d'arte bolognesi del sec. XVIII e la vendita della Madonna Sistina di Raffaello (parte I)," in *Culta Bononia*, year I, vol. I, 1969, pp. 65–98.

Rubin Blanshei 2018a
A Companion to Medieval and Renaissance Bologna, ed. S. Rubin Blanshei (Leiden and Boston, 2018).

Rubin Blanshei 2018b
S. Rubin Blanshei, "History and Historiography of Bologna," in *A Companion to Medieval and Renaissance Bologna*, ed. S. Rubin Blanshei (Leiden and Boston, 2018), pp. 1–25.

Rubin Blanshei and Cucini 2018
S. Rubin Blanshei and S. Cucini, "Criminal Justice and Conflict Resolution," in *A Companion to Medieval and Renaissance Bologna*, ed. S. Rubin Blanshei (Leiden and Boston, 2018), pp. 335–60.

Ruhmer 1959
E. Ruhmer, *Francesco del Cossa* (Munich, 1959).

Ruhmer 1963
E. Ruhmer, "Ercole de' Roberti," in *Enciclopedia Universale dell'Arte*, vol. XI (Venice and Rome, 1963), pp. 615–22.

Ruhmer 1966
E. Ruhmer, *Marco Zoppo* (Vicenza, 1966).

Rusk Shapley 1966
F. Rusk Shapley, *Complete Catalogue of the Samuel H. Kress Collection. Italian Paintings XIII–XV Century* (London, 1966).

Salmi [1934]
M. Salmi, *Paolo Uccello, Andrea del Castagno, Domenico Veneziano* (Rome, [1934]).

Salmi 1958
M. Salmi, "Francesco del Cossa," in *Enciclopedia Universale dell'Arte*, vol. IV (Venice and Rome, 1958), pp. 1–7.

Salmi 1960
M. Salmi, *Ercole de' Roberti* (Milan, 1960).

Sambin De Norcen (2015) 2017
M. T. Sambin De Norcen, "'Marmoreum scrineum.' Osservazioni sul campanile del duomo di Ferrara e Leon Battista Alberti," in *Palladio*, year LVI, (2015) 2017, pp. 5–26.

Sambin De Norcen 2018
M. T. Sambin De Norcen, "Alla ricerca del linguaggio di Biagio. L'architettura sacra," in *Biagio Rossetti e il suo tempo*, ed. A. Ippoliti, conference papers, Ferrara, 2016 (Rome, 2018), pp. 49–60.

Sambin De Norcen and Schofield 2018
M. T. Sambin De Norcen and R. Schofield, *Palazzo Bentivoglio a Bologna. Studi su un'architettura scomparsa* (Bologna, 2018).

Sapere e/è potere 1990
Sapere e/è potere. Discipline, dispute e professioni nell'università medievale e moderna. Il caso bolognese a confronto, eds. L. Avellini, A. Cristiani, and A. De Benedictis, conference papers, Bologna, 1989, 3 vols. (Bologna, 1990).

Sassu 2007
G. Sassu, "Verso e oltre Schifanoia," in *Cosmè Tura e Francesco del Cossa. L'arte a Ferrara nell'età di Borso d'Este*, ed. M. Natale, exh. cat., Palazzo dei Diamanti and Palazzo Schifanoia, Ferrara, 2007–8 (Ferrara, 2007), pp. 415–25.

Scardino 1996
L. Scardino, "Alcuni collezionisti: un repertorio biografico," in *La leggenda del collezionismo a Ferrara. Le quadrerie storiche ferraresi*, eds. G. Agostini, J. Bentini, and A. Emiliani, exh. cat., Pinacoteca Nazionale Palazzo dei Diamanti, Ferrara, 1996 (Ferrara, 1996), pp. 95–102.

Schofield 2015
R. Schofield with G. Ceriani Sebregondi, "Pianta e sezione del Duomo di Milano, dettaglio della parete orientale della sacrestia nord," 2015, in *Corpus dei disegni di architettura duomo di Milano*, http://www.disegniduomomilano.it/disegni/detail/280/

Settis and Cupperi 2007
Il Palazzo Schifanoia a Ferrara, eds. S. Settis and W. Cupperi, 2 vols. (Modena, 2007).

Severi 2015
A. Severi, *Filippo Beroaldo il Vecchio un maestro per l'Europa* (Bologna, 2015).

Sgarbi 2003
V. Sgarbi, *Francesco del Cossa* (Milan, 2003).

Shaw 2006
C. Shaw, *Popular Government and Oligarchy in Renaissance Italy* (Leiden and Boston, 2006).

Sighinolfi 1913–15
L. Sighinolfi, "Maestro Antonio di Vincenzo e Arduino Arriguzzi architetti di S. Petronio," in *Atti e Memorie della Deputazione di storia patria per le province di Romagna*, series IV, vol. VI, 1913–15, pp. 491–509.

Smith, Reeve, and Roy 1981
A. Smith, A. Reeve, and A. Roy, "Francesco del Cossa's 'S. Vincent Ferrer,'" in *National Gallery Technical Bulletin*, vol. 5, 1981, pp. 45–57.

Sopra un dipinto 1841
Sopra un dipinto attribuito a Benozzo Gozzoli (n.p., 1841).

Sorbelli ed. 2003
A. Sorbelli, *Storia della stampa in Bologna*, ed. M. G. Tavoni (Sala Bolognese, 2003, facsimile repr. 1929).

Speranza 2016
F. Speranza, *Da Bologna a Dresda. Carlo Cesare Giovannini agente per la Gemäldegalerie (1754–1756)* (Rome, 2016).

Supino 1909
I. B. Supino, *L'architettura sacra in Bologna nei secoli XIII e XIV* (Bologna, 1909).

Supino 1910
I. B. Supino, *La scultura in Bologna nel secolo XV. Ricerche e studi* (Bologna, 1910).

Supino 1913
I. B. Supino, "Le fasi costruttive della basilica di San Petronio," in *L'Archiginnasio*, year VIII, 1913, pp. 125–36.

Supino 1914a
I. B. Supino, "La basilica di San Petronio," in *L'Archiginnasio*, year IX, 1914, pp. 296–315.

Supino 1914b
I. B. Supino, *Le sculture delle porte di S. Petronio in Bologna* (Florence, 1914).

Supino 1932
I. B. Supino, *L'arte nelle chiese di Bologna. Secoli VIII–XIV* (Bologna, 1932).

Supino 1938
I. B. Supino, *L'arte nelle chiese di Bologna. Secoli XV–XVI* (Bologna, 1938).

Syson 1999
L. Syson, "Ercole de' Roberti: The Making of Court Artist," in *Ercole de' Roberti. The Renaissance in Ferrara*, eds. D. Allen, L. Syson, et al., exh. cat., The J. Paul Getty Museum, Los Angeles, 1999 (London, 1999, also as supplement to *The Burlington Magazine*, vol. CXLI, no. 1153, April 1999, pp. V–XIV).

Syson 2002
L. Syson, "Tura and the 'Minor Arts': The School of Ferrara," in *Cosmè Tura. Painting and Design in Renaissance Ferrara*, ed. S. J. Campbell, exh. cat., Isabella Stewart Gardner Museum, Boston, 2002 (Boston and Milan, 2002).

Tamba 2018
G. Tamba, "Civic Institutions (12th–early 15th Centuries)," in *A Companion to Medieval and Renaissance Bologna*, ed. S. Rubin Blanshei (Leiden and Boston, 2018), pp. 211–38.

Tambini 2004
A. Tambini, "Jacopo di Paolo," in *Dizionario Biografico degli Italiani*, vol. LXII (Rome, 2004).

Terpstra 1999
Civic Fashioning in Renaissance Bologna, ed. N. Terpstra, special issue of *Renaissance Studies*, vol. 13, no. 4, December 1999.

Terpstra 2013
N. Terpstra, "Republicanism, Public Welfare, and Civil Society in Early Modern Bologna," in *Bologna. Cultural Crossroads from the Medieval to the Baroque: Recent Anglo-American Scholarship*, eds. G. M. Anselmi, A. De Benedictis, and N. Terpstra, conference papers, Bologna, 2011 (Bologna, 2013), pp. 205–16.

Terpstra 2018
N. Terpstra, "Confraternities and Civil Society," in *A Companion to Medieval and Renaissance Bologna*, ed. S. Rubin Blanshei (Leiden and Boston, 2018), pp. 386–410.

The Abridged Catalogue 1882
The Abridged Catalogue of the Pictures in the National Gallery. Foreign Schools (London, 1882).

The Collections of the National Gallery of Art 2003
The Collections of the National Gallery of Art. Italian Paintings of the Fifteenth Century, eds. M. Boskovits and E. A. Brown (Washington, DC, 2003).

Toffanello 2000
M. Toffanello, "La mostra di Barbantini tra Venturi e Longhi," in *L'indimenticabile mostra del '33*, eds. S. Onofri and C. Tracchi (Ferrara, 2000), pp. 17–64.

Toffanello 2002
M. Toffanello, "Tura's Drawing and Its Pictorial Complement," in S. J. Campbell, *Cosmè Tura: Painting and Design in Renaissance Ferrara*, exh. cat., Isabella Stewart Gardner Museum, Boston, 2002 (Boston and Milan, 2002), pp. 152–72.

Toffanello 2004–5
M. Toffanello, *Artisti a Ferrara nel Quattrocento. La corte, le botteghe, i cantieri*, PhD dissertation, Università "G. d'Annunzio," Chieti–Pescara, academic year 2004–5.

Toffanello 2010
M. Toffanello, *Le arti a Ferrara nel Quattrocento. Gli artisti e la corte* (Ferrara, 2010).

Toffanello 2017
M. Toffanello, "L'Esposizione della pittura ferrarese del Rinascimento (1933)," in *All'origine delle grandi mostre in Italia (1933–40). Storia dell'arte e storiografia tra divulgazione di massa e propaganda*, ed. M. Toffanello (Mantua, 2017), pp. 29–51.

Togneri Dowd 1985
The Travel Diaries of Otto Mündler 1855–1858, ed. C. Togneri Dowd (London, 1985) (*Walpole Society*, 51).

Torella (1985–87) 1988
F. Torella, "L'ombra della mezzaluna sull'arte italiana. Il polittico Griffoni," in *Musei Ferraresi*, no. 15, (1985–87) 1988, pp. 43–60.

Torella (1988–89) 1991
F. Torella, "Ancora sul polittico Griffoni. Smembramenti. Ricostruzione. Fortuna (e sfortuna)," in *Musei Ferraresi*, no. 16, (1988–89) 1991, pp. 39–50.

Trento and Riccardi Scassellati 1988
D. Trento and V. Riccardi Scassellati, "Gli storici dell'arte e l'Accademia," in *L'Accademia di Bologna. Figure del Novecento*, eds. A. Baccilieri and S. Evangelisti, exh. cat., Bologna, 1988 (Bologna, 1988), pp. 245–50.

Troilo 2007
M. Troilo, "Tra capolavori e falsi. Considerazioni economiche sul mercato dell'arte nella Bologna del Settecento," in *Strenna storica bolognese*, year LVII, 2007, pp. 407–22.

Troilo 2010
M. Troilo, *Un'economia di famiglia. Strategie patrimoniali e di prestigio sociale degli Aldrovandi di Bologna (secoli XVII–XVIII)* (Bologna, 2010).

Trombetti Budriesi 1994
A. L. Trombetti Budriesi, "I primi anni del cantiere di San Petronio (1390–1397)," in *Una basilica per una città. Sei secoli in San Petronio*, eds. M. Fanti and D. Lenzi, conference papers, Bologna, 1990 (Bologna, 1994).

Tumidei 1991
S. Tumidei, "Terrecotte bolognesi di Sei e Settecento: collezionismo, produzione artistica, consumo devozionale," in *Presepi e terrecotte nei musei civici di Bologna*, ed. R. Grandi, exh. cat., Lapidario del Museo Civico Medievale, Bologna, 1991–92 (Bologna, 1991), pp. 21–51.

Tuohy 1982
T. Tuohy, "Struttura e sistema di contabilità della Camera Estense nel Quattrocento," in *Atti e Memorie della Deputazione di storia patria per le antiche province modenesi*, series XI, vol. IV, 1982, pp. 115–39.

Turrill 1988
C. Turrill, *Ercole de' Roberti's Altarpieces for the Lateran Canons*, PhD dissertation, University of Delaware, 1986 (Ann Arbor, 1988).

Turrill 1995
C. Turrill, "Ercole de' Roberti's San Lazzaro altarpiece," in *Jahrbuch der Berliner Museen*, vol. XXXVII, 1995, pp. 121–41.

Tuttle 1998
R. J. Tuttle, "Bologna," in *Storia dell'architettura italiana. Il Quattrocento*, ed. F. P. Fiore (Milan, 1998), pp. 256–71.

Uginet 2001
F. C. Uginet, "Giovanni XXIII, antipapa," in *Dizionario Biografico degli Italiani*, vol. LV (Rome, 2001).

Ugolini 1990
A. Ugolini, "Rivedendo la collezione Costabili di Ferrara," in *Paragone*, year XLI, no. 489, November 1990, pp. 50–76.

Una basilica per una città 1994
Una basilica per una città. Sei secoli in San Petronio, eds. M. Fanti and D. Lenzi, conference papers, Bologna, 1990 (Bologna, 1994).

Valla ed. 2001
L. Valla, *La falsa donazione di Costantino*, prefaced, translated, and annotated by O. Pugliese, with parallel Latin text (Milan, 2001).

Varese 1989a
R. Varese, *Metodo di lavoro: progetto e repliche*, in *Atlante di Schifanoia*, ed. R. Varese (Modena, 1989), pp. 173–88.

Varese 1989b
Atlante di Schifanoia, ed. R. Varese (Modena, 1989).

Varese 2004
R. Varese, "Gli affreschi di Palazzo Schifanoia," in *Gli Este a Ferrara. Una corte nel Rinascimento*, ed. J. Bentini, exh. cat., Castello Estense, Ferrara, 2004 (Cinisello Balsamo, 2004), pp. 104–7.

Varignana 1985
F. Varignana, "Francesco del Cossa. Le vetrate di San Giovanni in Monte," in *Tre artisti nella Bologna dei Bentivoglio*, eds. G. Agostini, L. Ciammitti, and F. Varignana, exh. cat., Pinacoteca Nazionale, Bologna, 1985 (Bologna, 1985), pp. 6–113.

Vasari 1550 ed. 1986
G. Vasari, *Le Vite de' più eccellenti architetti, pittori, et scultori italiani, da Cimabue, insino a' tempi nostri* (Florence, 1550), eds. L. Bellosi and A. Rossi, 2 vols. (Turin, 1986, recommended ed. Turin, 1991).

Vasari 1550, 1568 ed. 1971
G. Vasari, *Le vite de' più eccellenti pittori, scultori e architettori* (1550T, 1568 G), eds. R. Bettarini and P. Barocchi, III/1 (Florence, 1971).

Vasari 1568 ed. 1878–81
G. Vasari, *Le Vite de' più eccellenti pittori, scultori et architettori, scritte e di nuovo ampliate da M. Giorgio Vasari* (Florence, 1568), ed. G. Milanesi, 8 vols. (Florence, 1878–81).

Vasari 1568 ed. 1967
G. Vasari, *Le vite de' più eccellenti pittori scultori e architettori* (Florence, 1568), eds. P. Della Pergola, L. Grassi, and G. Previtali, 9 vols. (Novara, 1967).

Vasari 1898
G. Vasari, *Lives of the Most Eminent Painters, Sculptors, and Architects*, vol. 2, transl. J. Foster and Henry G. Bohn (London, 1898).

Velasco González 2008
A. Velasco González, "Dos arquetips iconogràfics i dos models de difusió en la iconografia primerenca de sant Vicent Ferrer," in *Hagiografia peninsular en els segles medievals*, eds. F. Español and F. Fité (Lleida, 2008), pp. 235–64.

Venturi 1885
A. Venturi, "Ein Brief von Francesco del Cossa," in *Der Kunstfreund*, 9, 1, May 1885, pp. 129–34.

Venturi 1888
A. Venturi, "Les arts à la cour de Francesco de Ferrare, Francesco del Cossa," in *L'Art*, year XIV, no. 1, 1888, pp. 74–80; no. 2, pp. 96–101.

Venturi 1901–40
A. Venturi, *Storia dell'Arte Italiana*, 25 vols. (Milan, 1901–40).

Venturi 1902
A. Venturi, "Due nuovi quadri di Ercole de' Roberti nel Museo del Louvre", in *L'Arte*, year V, 1902, pp. 178–79.

Venturi 1906
A. Venturi, "Due dipinti di Francesco del Cossa nella raccolta Spiridon a Parigi", in *L'Arte*, year IX, 1906, pp. 139–40.

Venturi 1908
A. Venturi, "Le opere dei pittori ferraresi del '400 secondo il catalogo di B. Berenson," in *L'Arte*, year XI, 1908, pp. 419–32.

Venturi 1912
A. Venturi, "La formazione della Galleria Layard a Venezia," in *L'Arte*, year XV, 6, 1912, pp. 449–62.

Venturi 1927
A. Venturi, *Studi dal vero attraverso le raccolte artistiche d'Europa* (Milan, 1927).

Venturi 1927 ed. 1991
A. Venturi, *Memorie autobiografiche* (Milan, 1927, ed. Turin, 1991).

Venturi 1930
A. Venturi, "Eine Madonna von Francesco del Cossa," in *Pantheon*, V, 1930, pp. 249–50.

Venturi 1931
A. Venturi, *North Italian Painting of the Quattrocento* (Florence and Paris, 1931).

Verrocchio 2019
Verrocchio. Sculptor and Painter of the Renaissance Florence, ed. A. Butterfield, exh. cat., National Gallery of Art, Washington, DC, 2019–20 (Princeton, 2019).

Volpe 1958 ed. 1993
C. Volpe, "Tre vetrate ferraresi e il Rinascimento a Bologna," in *Arte Antica e Moderna*, no. 1, 1958, pp. 23–37; now in C. Volpe, *La pittura nell'Emilia e nella Romagna. Raccolta di scritti sul Trecento e Quattrocento*, eds. D. Benati and L. Peruzzi (Modena, 1993), pp. 152–68.

Volpe 1961 ed. 1993
C. Volpe, "La grande officina ferrarese," in *Tutt'Italia. Emilia Romagna* (Novara, 1961), II, pp. 472–88; now partially in C. Volpe, *La pittura nell'Emilia e nella Romagna. Raccolta di scritti sul Trecento e Quattrocento*, eds. D. Benati and L. Peruzzi (Modena, 1993), pp. 129–40.

Volpe 1977 ed. 1988
C. Volpe, *Palazzo Schifanoia. Gli affreschi* (1977), ed. R. Varese, in *Musei Ferraresi*, no. 15, (1985–87) 1988, pp. 9–28.

Volpe 1979 ed. 1993
C. Volpe, "Il polittico di San Clemente di Marco Zoppo. Un esercizio di lettura iconografica," in *El Cardenal Albornoz y el collegio de Espana*, V, Studia Albornotiana, XXXVI (Bologna and Zaragoza, 1979), pp. 61–75; now in C. Volpe, *La pittura nell'Emilia e nella Romagna. Raccolta di scritti sul Trecento e Quattrocento*, eds. D. Benati and L. Peruzzi (Modena, 1993), pp. 141–51.

Volpe 1980
C. Volpe, "Paolo Uccello a Bologna," in *Paragone*, 365, 1980, pp. 3–28; now in C. Volpe, *La pittura nell'Emilia e nella Romagna. Raccolta di scritti sul Trecento e Quattrocento*, eds. D. Benati and L. Peruzzi (Modena, 1993), pp. 102–23.

Volpe 1983
C. Volpe, "La pittura gotica. Da Lippo di Dalmasio a Giovanni da Modena," in *La Basilica di San Petronio in Bologna*, eds. M. Fanti, G. Lorenzoni, A.M. Matteucci, R. Roli, and C. Volpe, coordinated by D. Benati and L. Peruzzi (Cinisello Balsamo, 1983), vol. I, pp. 213–94.

Volpe 1993
C. Volpe, *La pittura nell'Emilia e nella Romagna. Raccolta di scritti sul Trecento e Quattrocento*, eds. D. Benati and L. Peruzzi (Modena, 1993).

Waterhouse 1936
E. K. Waterhouse, "Officina Ferrarese. By Roberto Longhi," in *The Burlington Magazine for Connoisseurs*, vol. LXVIII, no. 396, March 1936, pp. 150–51.

Weber 2002
G. J. M. Weber, "La collezione di pittura ferrarese a Dresda," in *Il trionfo di Bacco. Capolavori della scuola ferrarese a Dresda 1480–1620*, ed. G. J. M. Weber, exh. cat., Castello Estense, Ferrara, 2002–3 and Residenzschloss, Dresden, 2003 (Turin, 2002), pp. 37–48.

Winkelmann 1987
J. Winkelmann, "'Un certo naturale e facilità carraccesca' per le prime opere di Guido Reni," in *Accademia Clementina, Atti e Memorie*, new series, no. 20–21, 1987.

Zabbia 2002
M. Zabbia, "Griffoni, Matteo," in *Dizionario Biografico degli Italiani*, vol. LIX (Rome, 2002).

Zanotti 1732
G. Zanotti, "Allo Stampatore," in *Le pitture di Bologna* (Bologna, 1732), ff. 25r–31r.

Zarri 2018
G. Zarri, "The Church, Civic Religion and Civic Identity," in *A Companion to Medieval and Renaissance Bologna*, ed. S. Rubin Blanshei (Leiden and Boston, 2018), pp. 361–85.

Zeri 1958
F. Zeri, "Una 'Deposizione' di scuola riminese," in *Paragone*, year IX, no. 99, March 1958, pp. 46–54.

Zeri 1965
F. Zeri, "Appunti per Ercole de' Roberti," in *Bollettino d'Arte*, series V, year L, I–II, 1965, pp. 72–79; now in F. Zeri, *Giorno per giorno nella pittura. Scritti sull'arte dell'Italia settentrionale dal Trecento al primo Cinquecento* (Turin, 1988), pp. 199–207.

Zucchini 1917
G. Zucchini, "Le vetrate di San Giovanni in Monte di Bologna," in *Bollettino d'arte del Ministero della Pubblica Istruzione*, year XI, 1917, pp. 82–90.

Zucchini 1925
G. Zucchini, *Guida della basilica di San Petronio* (Bologna, 1925).

Zucchini 1935
G. Zucchini, "'Officina Ferrarese' di Roberto Longhi," in *L'Archiginnasio*, year XXX, no. 1–3, 1935, pp. 319–27.

Zucchini 1942
G. Zucchini, "Disegni inediti per San Petronio a Bologna," in *Palladio*, year VI, 1942, pp. 153–66.

Zucchini 1947
G. Zucchini, *Artigiani a Bologna nei secoli XIV, XV e XVI* (Bologna. 1947).

Zucchini 1953
G. Zucchini, "Saggio di bibliografia artistica per la basilica di San Petronio in Bologna," in *L'Archiginnasio*, year XLVIII, 1953, pp. 112–22.

Zucchini 1959
G. Zucchini, *La verità sui restauri bolognesi* (Bologna, 1959).

Cover
Francesco del Cossa, *Saint Lucy*, detail.
National Gallery of Art, Washington, DC

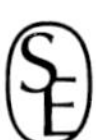

Silvana Editoriale

Direction
Dario Cimorelli

Art Director
Giacomo Merli

Editorial Coordinator
Sergio Di Stefano

Copy Editor
Emanuela Di Lallo

Layout
Daniela Meda, Donatella Ascorti

Translations
Scriptum Srl, Rome
InEdita servizi editoriali, Milan
Paolo Comolli

Production Coordinator
Antonio Micelli

Editorial Assistant
Giulia Mercanti

Photo Editors
Alessandra Olivari, Silvia Sala

Press Office
Lidia Masolini, press@silvanaeditoriale.it

Available through ARTBOOK | D.A.P.
155 Sixth Avenue, 2nd Floor, New York, N.Y. 10013
Tel: (212) 627-1999 Fax: (212) 627-9484

Silvana Editoriale S.p.A.
via dei Lavoratori, 78
20092 Cinisello Balsamo, Milan
tel. 02 453 951 01
fax 02 453 951 51
www.silvanaeditoriale.it

Color separation, printing, and binding were made in Italy
Printed by Grafiche Lang S.r.l., Genoa
Printed in July 2020

Photo credits
© Alamy
© Archivi Alinari
Archivio di Stato di Bologna
Archivio fotografico Direzione Musei Emilia-Romagna
Archivio Fotografico Storico Soprintendenza Archeologica Belle Arti e Paesaggio per la Città Metropolitana di Bologna e le Province di Modena, Reggio Emilia e Ferrara
© 2020 Cameraphoto/Scala, Florence
Collezione Cagnola, Gazzada (Varese)
Collezioni d'Arte e di Storia della Fondazione Cassa di Risparmio in Bologna
Courtesy Ministero per i Beni e le Attività Culturali e per il Turismo – Archivio fotografico delle Gallerie Estensi
Courtesy Ministero dei Beni e delle Attività Culturali e del Turismo – Biblioteca Nazionale Marciana, Dipartimento manoscritti e rari. Unauthorized reproduction prohibited
© A. Dagli Orti/De Agostini Picture Library/Bridgeman Images
© 2020 A. Dagli Orti/Scala, Florence
© De Agostini Picture Library/S. Montanari/Bridgeman Images
© 2020 De Agostini Picture Library/Scala, Florence
© Fondazione di Studi di Storia dell'Arte Roberto Longhi, Florence
© Fondazione Giorgio Cini onlus, Venice
© 2020 Foto Scala, Florence
© 2020 Foto Scala, Florence/bpk, Bildagentur für Kunst, Kultur und Geschichte, Berlin
© 2020 Foto Scala, Florence / Luciano Romano
© 2020 Foto Scala, Florence. Courtesy Ministero Beni e Attività Culturali
© Meridiana Immagini /Archivi Alinari
Museo di San Petronio, Bologna
Museum Boijmans Van Beuningen, Rotterdam
Courtesy National Gallery of Art, Washington, DC
© Nicolò Orsi Battaglini / Bridgeman Images
Photo Factum Foundation
© Pinacoteca di Brera, Milan
Reale Collegio di Spagna, Bologna
© RMN–Grand Palais (musée du Louvre) / Thierry Le Mage
© RMN–Grand Palais (musée du Louvre) / Hervé Lewandowski-rmn distr. Alinari
© The National Gallery, London
© Universal History Archive / UIG / Bridgeman Images
Vatican Museums, Vatican City
© 2020 Voltecupolesoffitti/Scala, Florence

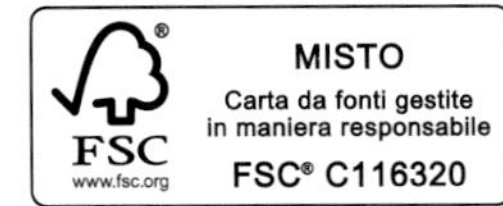